China's Emerging Financial Markets

Challenges and Global Impact

Editors-in-Chief

Zhu Min

Cai Jinqing

Martha Avery

WILEY

John Wiley & Sons (Asia) Pte Ltd

Published in 2009 by John Wiley & Sons (Asia) Pte. Ltd.
2 Clementi Loop, #02-01, Singapore 129809

Other Wiley Editorial Offices
John Wiley & Sons, Inc., 111 River Street, Hoboken, NJ 07030, USA
John Wiley & Sons, Ltd., The Atrium, Southern Gate, Chichester, West Sussex P019 8SQ, UK
John Wiley & Sons (Canada), Ltd., 5353 Dundas Street West, Suite 400, Toronto, Ontario M9B 6H8, Canada
John Wiley & Sons Australia Ltd., 42 McDougall Street, Milton, Queensland 4064, Australia
Wiley-VCH, Boschstrasse 12, D-69469 Weinheim, Germany

Library of Congress Cataloging-in-Publication Data
ISBN: 978-0470-82249-4

Typeset in 10.5/13pt Sabon by Aptara Inc., New Delhi, India
Printed in Singapore by International Press Softcom Limited.
10 9 8 7 6 5 4 3 2 1

CONTENTS

ACKNOWLEDGMENTS

First and foremost, the editors thank the 36 authors who came forward when they were called upon. They recognized the importance of and need for a comprehensive treatment of the subject.

China's emerging financial systems are already a vital part of global systems. Little understood, they nonetheless will play a large role in the future. The financial debacle in the Western world in recent times has made obsolete the references to certain Western banks in this book. It has not changed the fundamental situation in China, however, and that situation is reflected in these chapters. The authors have provided a benchmark that shows where China stands today, 30 years after the start of the national policy to reform and open the country. They have also provided a baseline for the next era. Their words represent the concentrated intelligence of the most senior and far-sighted people in the field. We express our deep appreciation for their contributions.

Secondly, we thank the Ford Foundation for extending the grant that made this volume possible.

Finally, our publisher, John Wiley & Sons, has remained steadfast through the long and trying process. The Wiley team deserves grateful recognition for seeing this volume through to completion.

Zhu Min
Cai Jinqing
Martha Avery

There could not have been in all of history so rapid a development in a functional financial system, and in particular of banking institutions, as in China over recent decades. The old framework was a dominant state-owned and state-run "bank" providing funds for state-owned enterprises (SOEs) in accord with state-directed priorities. It was not, in fact, a banking system at all, which implies a variety of institutions free to respond to the needs of individuals and businesses.

An enormous effort has been required to achieve the needed transition. There was the huge financial cost implicit in dealing with the unpaid and unpayable obligations assumed under the old system by many SOEs that burdened bank balance sheets.

There was the broad political challenge of accepting and supporting a more decentralized, market-responsive financial system as a part of economic reform. Not least, there has been the intellectual and educational need to adapt to the methods and requirements of a more open and competitive economic environment.

Today, the state still has majority ownership of a small group of very large banks and insurance companies, but those institutions have private stockholders, in some cases with foreign participation. They have been joined by a growing number of smaller institutions established with private capital, and by a few affiliates of foreign banks and insurance companies.

A basic framework of supervision and regulation is in place, and a central bank has been provided with the essential tools for conducting monetary policy. International accounting standards are being introduced, along with growing attention to credit analysis, risk management, and the need to operate efficiently with a reasonable margin of profit.

Now there is room to compete in responding to business and individual needs; indeed, there is a necessity to do so. Success is dependent upon the ability to cover expenses, with a margin of profit. As a result, attention needs to be paid to efficiency, to developing a "credit culture" to protect against weak loans, and to provide the variety of financial services required for a modern economy.

Plainly, that process is incomplete. Virtually every chapter in this new volume is replete not just with reports of progress, but of unfinished business. Some of the analysis is technical and detailed, but the basic theme is quite clear.

Chinese banking has become part—a growing part—of the world of finance, supporting the rapid economic growth of China. The basic trend seems to me well-established—more sensitivity to market forces, growing flexibility in pricing, greater reliance on private capital, and, over time, more participation in foreign markets by Chinese banks and by foreign financial institutions in China.

In a country with more than a billion citizens, with massive needs for capital on the one hand, but an equally strong capacity to generate savings on the other, efficient financial intermediation is not an option. It has become an essential ingredient in the effort to sustain rapid growth within China, and a part of its increasing trade with other countries.

The Chinese system is still dominated by institutions, and particularly by very large institutions, with majority government ownership. But the driving force is more and more market-oriented, with a variety of services developing for individuals and with sources of credit for businesses. Lending to SOEs, while still substantial, is receding in relative importance, lending practices are more disciplined, and the provision of credit is increasingly responsive to the needs of business firms rather than to official direction.

No doubt, much remains to be done in terms of technology, in staff training, and in management, to meet the needs of the growing economy. My sense is that foreign participation is assisting in that process, and is capable of still greater contribution.

At the same time, those guiding and participating in the development of the Chinese financial market will want to be alert to important lessons of Western experience, the need to guard against speculative excesses, to maintain adequate capital and effective supervision, and, most importantly, to keep reasonable monetary stability. These lessons are necessary for all nations that want to benefit from a growing, productive economy able to compete effectively in the world.

Paul A. Volcker

Zhou Xiaochuan
Governor, People's Bank of China

One overarching conclusion can be made in reviewing the progress of financial reforms in China and in looking to the future: only firm adherence to Reform and Opening will allow us to make further progress and assure China's financial and economic stability.

PRINCIPALS UNDERLYING FINANCIAL REFORMS

Improvements in China's financial system and its ongoing alignment with market forces in recent years are due primarily to the process of Reform and Opening. Only by creating sound financial institutions can we participate in markets, take advantage of business opportunities, support growth in China's as well as the world's economy, and, finally, preserve stability.

The government has made it clear in recent years that it has firmly decided to achieve financial reform. At the same time, this cannot be accomplished in one fell swoop—it is a long process. Some actions can achieve fast-paced results, while others require the extended accumulation of experience. The next stages will take ongoing determination. They will involve strengthening reforms in both economic and financial systems.

Reform is an exercise in systems engineering. The various parts of the process require integration and a high degree of popular participation. Reform of this sort is not a kind of guerrilla operation with dispersed forces; it requires a full-scale frontal attack.

Institutional reform is the foundation of financial stability. All new developments in financial markets present new challenges to financial stability. We can recognize the importance of preserving stability when we look at the subprime mortgage crisis in the US and related market volatility. Financial stability is closely related to the health of economic and financial institutions. The Chinese government has tried to maintain a balance among three key policy goals: reform, growth, and stability. One of the implications of the phrase "scientific approach to economic development" is that these three must preserve an appropriate balance. Balance must also be maintained in the relationship between government-directed macroeconomic measures and the self-adjusting mechanisms of microeconomic forces.

Progress in reforms to date gives us confidence that the next steps in Reform and Opening will succeed. It also allows China to put increasing weight on Reform and Opening in furthering economic growth by allowing reformed mechanisms to work. We have more experience now in this regard, and hence more confidence.

CHINA'S FINANCIAL SYSTEM
A DECADE AGO

In looking at China's financial reforms in the past few years, it is useful to remember the condition of our finances during the Asian Financial Crisis some 10 years ago. My personal summary of the situation back then includes the following observations.

The percentage of nonperforming loans (NPLs) in commercial banks was high. At the time of the crisis, the reported rate of NPLs was 25%, but due to problems in accounting standards, methods of classifying loans, and overall financial discipline, the market evaluation put the rate at more like 35–40%.

This high rate was brought on to a large degree by the intertwined nature of commercial loans and loans made in response to policy objectives. It was also related to the prevailing "credit culture" at the time. A common saying was that bank loans in China were mainly "relationship loans"; that is, essentially a function of one's relationships.

Commercial banks were not operated as "enterprises" to an adequate degree 10 years ago. There was no clear mandate to run a bank with profit as the key objective; instead, banks were operating under the directives of government institutions. The process of enterprise reform had already begun in China at the time of the Asian Financial Crisis, but there had not yet been great progress. The concept of corporate governance had not even been broached in preliminary fashion. Government and regulatory organizations gave no guidance in appropriate governance measures—institutions generally proceeded with their own understanding of how to do things. In general, financial institutions at the time, like all government institutions, lacked business objectives and lacked both motivating and restraining mechanisms for accomplishing those objectives.

There was a sizable gap between international and Chinese laws, regulations, and rules. The gap between Chinese accounting standards and world standards was particularly large. China's standard loan classification at the time mainly related to the term of the loan and was not, as it is now, divided into a five-tiered structure.

Standards for information disclosure of listed companies were woefully inadequate, so insider trading and share price manipulation were common. Financial reports were not significant since they relied on inadequate accounting standards. Key laws such as the Corporate Law, Securities Law, and Bankruptcy Law were incomplete at the time.

Capital markets in China were still in a rudimentary stage 10 years ago. With immature markets, price determination mechanisms were poor, investment rationale was not developed, and problems abounded.

Regulatory systems at the time of the Asian Financial Crisis were highly unsatisfactory. Throughout the crisis, China debated how best to set up more effective systems. In addition to regulatory systems, an improved overall environment required the setting up of a whole series of rules and regulations. Training of regulators was necessary to raise the level of professionalism and define regulatory goals— all of these had been absent and were now imperative. Setting up systems, organizations, rules, and procedures has been a key task in the intervening years.

Mechanisms for restraining certain behavior and for evaluating performance were insufficient. Indeed, it was unclear exactly what kind of mechanisms should be used with regard to financial institutions. During the crisis, the key criterion used by the Chinese government in judging a financial institution was the percentage of NPLs in its portfolio. It was difficult, however, to know which loans among those NPLs were policy-related loans and which were of a commercial nature. It was hard to differentiate the causes for NPLs, allocate responsibilities, and know how to balance provision for NPLs. In fact, focusing on NPLs was not an easy way to apply restraints on behavior or to evaluate the soundness of a bank. Using the Basel I capital adequacy ratios and core regulatory principles in restraining and evaluating financial institutions became an urgent task. At the same time, this was not an easy thing to accomplish since many commercial banks had negative capital adequacy ratios at the time.

Relatively severe financial pressures existed 10 years ago in the overall economy, and financial services and capacity to innovate in meeting challenges were inadequate. Since financial institutions were unhealthy, and since regulation was insufficient, there were strong financial pressures pulling in the opposite direction to reform. Basically, we could not encourage financial markets to develop and financial products to be developed out of fear that worse problems would appear, and indeed many problems did appear. Some financial institutions wanted to issue new products and some exchanges wanted to trade in new derivative products, but at the time, any application had little chance of being approved within a four- to five-year timeframe. The reason was that institutions were unhealthy, the risk was overly concentrated, and many felt that the new products would run into trouble. One important issue was that China knew it had to encourage the growth of institutional investors, since complex new products could not be sold to retail buyers. At that time, however, the number of Chinese institutional investors was extremely small and financial pressures made it hard for them to grow.

Confidence in the RMB sank at the time of the Asian Financial Crisis. Although China's balance of trade had moved into a positive position by the 1990s, and foreign businessmen were investing in China, an examination of the international balance of payments in the 1990s shows mostly negative numbers, and at times the capital outflow was extreme. This showed a lack of confidence in the RMB with a strong trend toward capital flight. Under these conditions, currency controls were relatively stringent. Opportunities for Chinese businessmen to seize opportunities and participate in international markets were slim.

Administrative interference in banking operations was still prevalent at that time. From 1993, China began to encourage a division of state or government and business or enterprise, and to discourage government interference in policies relating to commercial-type loans of commercial banks. The central government did indeed begin to operate in this direction. There were substantial differences in the way regional governments responded, however.

During the Asian Financial Crisis, one of the main tasks of reform therefore was to insist that regional governments obey the demands of the central government in not applying administrative pressure to loan-making decisions.

THE PACE OF CHINA'S
FINANCIAL REFORMS

From the previous section on the starting point of China's financial reforms—at the time of the Asian Financial Crisis—we can see that taking action was an urgent necessity. Many international authorities described China's situation back then in grave terms. Three basic evaluations surfaced: (1) that China's financial system was a large time-bomb that could go off at any time; (2) that China's commercial banks were technically insolvent; and (3) that China's financial system would be a drag on its economic growth, making it impossible for the system to service the economy and support development.

Given this situation, the Chinese government was determined to carry out reforms. The ailments were multifaceted, but a unified, systematic, overall approach was necessary. It had to be carefully designed, organized, and executed in sequential stages. The Asian Financial Crisis was a tremendous shock to many Asian countries and China was no exception. Many outsiders thought that its effect on China was limited, but China too saw many institutions go bankrupt or close down at the time, and a large number of businesses faced serious losses. Consumer confidence eroded, the economy entered a deflationary period, and in fact the influence on China was extreme. From another angle, however, one could say that the experience hastened the recognition that reform was an urgent necessity.

Pressures were great at the time decisions were being made, but distinctions were made between fast-paced reforms and those that would require a more deliberate approach. The latter, according to the Chinese phrase, recognized that you cannot tug on growing shoots to make a plant grow faster, since you will simply pull up the roots. Longer term reforms included a change to the culture of credit, the development of institutional investors, investor education in rational decision-making, improvement of corporate governance structures, and so on. These were all going to take a long time. At that time, human resources that could enable corporate governance structures were generally not available. Independent directors or outside directors on Boards had to be put through special classes at local universities, in order to learn what was involved, to understand the responsibilities of Boards of Directors, to learn how to conduct proper meetings, and so on. Ten years ago, very few people had much experience in evaluating balance sheets and financial reports.

Other aspects of reform were more pressing. They required not only fast action, but the need to see fast results. One such matter was the need to stop the co-mingling of policy-type loans, made in furtherance of government policies, and commercial loans. Commercial banking had to be forced to enter the path of real commerce, in a way that met the requirements of business enterprises.

A second task was to clean up the balance sheets of financial institutions in a decisive way. Both the Asian Financial Crisis and the Japanese experience had shown that dilatory action was counterproductive. Action had to be decisive or problems would stay unresolved for years. Balance sheet problems would then affect the ability of the financial system to provide the necessary support for overall economic growth. In times of crisis, financial institutions focused on their own pressing problems and had no ability to contribute to building the economy.

A third matter was to establish modern standards of all kinds, including those relating to laws and regulations, accounting standards, disclosure requirements, loan classifications, and provisions and tax codes, and at the same time to set up guidelines for corporate governance. China actually did address these things quite briskly, but it is one thing to be quick in setting up standards and another to implement methods to enforce the standards.

A fourth task was to strengthen regulation. It was necessary to recognize the lessons of past experience and to change the organizational structure of financial regulation, while requiring that institutions themselves develop the human resources to meet regulatory requirements.

The fifth matter was to establish restraining mechanisms in requiring compliance with capital adequacy ratios. This included strengthening compliance with the Basel Accord in the banking system, and with comparable mechanisms in the securities and insurance industries. Without these, any improvement in financial institutions would be slow.

MAIN ASPECTS OF CHINESE FINANCIAL REFORM

Given the above considerations, the main components of China's financial reform include the following issues.

1. Cleaning up and restructuring banks, and improving macroeconomic measures that allow the preconditions for their reform, then implementing a financial reorganization of state-owned commercial banks. The first banks to go through this process were the

Bank of Communications, the Bank of China, the China Construction Bank, and later the Industrial and Commercial Bank of China. The process is ongoing and the next bank to undergo financial restructuring will be the Agricultural Bank of China.

2. Requiring that reconfigured financial institutions, including securities firms and insurance companies, become shareholder companies to the extent that is possible. This includes listing on exchanges, implementing control mechanisms, and setting up adequate corporate governance structures. Without a shareholder system and listing on exchanges, it is hard for corporate governance to take hold, given traditional influences. It is also hard to accomplish serious external oversight and regulation. At the same time, many measures related to opening to the outside have been beneficial in promoting the establishment and stability of corporate governance structures.

3. Truly changing all kinds of standards and rules. After the Asian Financial Crisis, China revised its accounting standards a number of times and these revisions greatly improved China's standards, allowing them to approach international standards. In terms of classification of loans, China began to require strict adherence to a five-tiered classification system, to require capital adequacy ratios as in the Basel Accord, and it required a clear timetable for achieving results. Currently, most banks can comply with Basel I standards; Basel II is to be implemented in large banks within two to three years. In addition, progress has been made in information disclosure requirements and in corporate governance regulations.

4. Strengthening regulation—in 2003, China set up a Banking Regulatory Commission and strengthened the organizational structure of regulation. At the same time, it clarified regulatory principles.

5. Emphasizing the guidance mechanisms of currency policy. Macroeconomic measures must be in alignment with the soundness of financial institutions. Institutions must approach the market in accord with government policy guidance with regard to currencies.

6. Doing away with outdated and excessive administrative controls. When financial institutions exhibit healthy operations, then they should be encouraged to become more involved in international markets, to compete with international institutions in their own lines of business, and to engage in product and organizational innovation. Circumstances have changed in China: we cannot always be requiring administrative review and approval for every new step. This includes entry into the market, initiating new

products, and foreign exchange controls. All of these have to move forward in a new direction and become aligned with market forces.

7. Improving the "financial ecosystem"—in the past, administrative interference was concentrated more in certain financial affairs and certain regions. Regional governmental protection was extended in some cases relating to debts; inadequate enforcement in some cases meant that nationally based financial institutions were being taken advantage of on a regional basis. Local and regional-level governments used to feel this was fine, but a conceptual change is gradually penetrating the system in this regard. It is recognized that only with adequate enforcement and credibility will more financial resources be committed to regional development. Only if the regional financial ecosystem is well-managed, administrative interference is minimized, enforcement is adequate, and credibility is emphasized, will there be more resources in the future. Only then will the region's economy move forward. This change has marked an extremely important conceptual shift since the time of the Asian Financial Crisis.

A SYSTEMIC APPROACH TO CHINA'S FINANCIAL REFORMS

Looking back at the content and the context of China's financial reforms since the Asian Financial Crisis, we see that the Chinese government has proceeded in a sequential manner. One reform has been linked to the next, guided by careful research and design, and implemented in an organized fashion with sets of coordinated actions. Naturally, many unexpected things have happened in the course of economic and financial development. Generally speaking, though, the positive experience of systemic reform has guided the process.

Putting Chinese financial institutions on a healthy track has given them a basis on which to participate in international markets. We must maintain a high degree of vigilance, however, with regard to problems of risk and financial stability. The recent extreme perturbations in international financial markets remind us that markets are often not stable. Macroeconomic government policies and the ability of institutions themselves to moderate risk and maintain soundness are both extremely important aspects of financial security.

We will continue to press forward with ongoing financial reform and financial opening in China. In January 2007, a meeting of the Working Group on National Finance was held in Beijing. It laid out arrangements for the next stages, including the further development of capital markets, building up the insurance industry, reforming the State Development Bank, establishing depository insurance, and so on. Certain future steps can be foreseen, but the world economy continues to present us with new challenges and new circumstances. As we encounter obstacles, we will be making appropriate adjustments, and constantly moving forward with financial Reform and Opening.

China's Emerging Financial Industries and Implications

Zhu Min

Group Executive Vice-President, Bank of China

China's economic growth since reform policies started in 1978 is broadly recognized. For 30 years, the economy has maintained an astounding average annual growth rate of 9.6%. GDP reached US$4 trillion in 2008, making China the world's third-largest economy after the United States (nearly US$14 trillion) and Japan (around US$4.3 trillion). Systemic reform over this period has brought fundamental changes, most importantly a parting of the ways with the old planned economy system. Production of state-owned enterprises (SOEs) was only 9.7% of GDP in 2008, down from 89.1% in 1978. The structure of China's economy has also changed profoundly. If one divides economic production into three main areas of agricultural, industrial, and services, China's GDP in 1978 was 28.2% agricultural, 47.9% in manufacturing, and 23.9% in services. By 2007, these percentages had changed to 11.3%, 48.6%, and 40.1%.

Urbanization has proceeded at a phenomenal pace. Eighteen percent of China's population lived in cities in 1978; in 2007, almost half, or 44.9% of the population lived in cities. China's "opening" policies have caused international trade to increase at an average of 23.6% per year over the course of 30 years. Total trade too has risen from 9.7% of GDP in 1978 to 66.4% of GDP in 2007. At the same time, China has maintained stable macroeconomic policies with financial deficits that are, on average, less than 1.1% of GDP. Inflation has been kept at a fairly low level. Incomes have shown constant increase:

per capita GDP of US$280 in 1978 had risen to US$3,180 in 2008. Three hundred million people have been lifted out of poverty, and life expectancy in China has gone from 68 years in 1978 to 73 years in 2007.

These are extraordinary figures. China's financial industries, however, have seen even more momentous change. In 1978, there was only one People's Bank of China (PBC) responsible for the functions of a central bank, commercial banks, and everything to do with finance. China now has a banking structure that includes a variety of institutions: an independent central bank, policy banks responsible for funding state policy initiatives, large commercial banks, medium-sized commercial banks owned by shareholders, small municipal banks, and rural credit cooperatives. Assets in the banking industry as a whole have gone from RMB115.5 billion in 1978 to RMB52 trillion in 2007. This 500-fold increase has been achieved by growth with an average of nearly 20% per year. Savings deposits of Chinese citizens have gone from RMB21.1 billion in 1978 to RMB17.25 trillion in 2007, an 800-fold increase, with average annual growth of 25%. China's stock markets began from a base of zero in late 1990, when the Shanghai Stock Exchange was founded. By the end of 2007, there were 1,550 listed companies on this exchange, and more than 132 million investor accounts of Chinese citizens. Market capitalization on the exchange totaled RMB32.7 trillion, equivalent to 140% of China's GDP, making the Shanghai Stock Exchange the fifth-largest stock market in the world. In the 25 years since China declared in 1972 that it had neither domestic nor foreign debt, the country has assumed the responsibility for both. China first reissued government bonds in 1981. Since then, the bond market has gone on to include a fairly complete array of government bonds, corporate bonds, short-term financing, and asset-backed securities (ABS), on the scale of RMB12.3 trillion or some 47% of GDP. This has to be one of the most dramatic turnarounds in the history of finance.

In this overview to the book *China's Emerging Financial Markets*, I will review China's 30 years of reforms in the financial sector, sum up the lessons and look to the future. In Section I, I review China's financial reforms. In Section II, I discuss the opening of China's financial sector to the outside world. In Section III, I summarize new challenges facing the industry. In Section IV, I look to the future of the industry, particularly given the impact of global integration.

SECTION I: GROWTH DURING ONGOING REFORM

Banking

Reforms in the banking sector in China have proceeded over 30 years against a backdrop of radical change in China's economic system. These reforms, orderly and systematic, have enabled catapulting growth in the entire system. Before Reform and Opening began in 1978, China had only one bank, the People's Bank of China (PBC), with multiple functions. Within the structure of the PBC, the Bank of China (BOC) was solely responsible for foreign exchange; the Agricultural Bank of China (ABC) was solely responsible for agriculture and rural areas. Under the Ministry of Finance, the China Construction Bank (CCB) was set up to manage and allocate government funds to fixed capital investment according to the State Economic Plan. In 1979, the ABC was the first entity to be reestablished as a separate bank, incorporating all functions of making loans in rural areas. In 1983, the BOC and the CCB were split off from their respective parents, the PBC and the Ministry of Finance. In 1984, the Industrial and Commercial Bank of China (ICBC) was split off from the PBC to become a separate entity responsible for financing activities that had formerly been under the PBC.

China then had a structure that included four large banks, each with a specialized function and a separate mission: providing liquidity to industry and commerce, providing loans for agriculture and rural areas, providing foreign exchange, and providing resources for basic infrastructure. From 1985 to 1993, these four banks underwent "management" reforms, turning them into enterprises in terms of operating procedures. They transitioned from being state organizations with bureaucratic management to becoming enterprises that were responsible not only for disbursing funds, but for taking on the responsibility for those funds. This involved wholesale managerial reforms.

In 1994, three policy banks were established to implement public policy: the China Development Bank, the State Agricultural Policy Bank, and the Export-Import Bank of China. These took over the policy financing work of the four large specialized banks. The four then gradually evolved to become full-scale comprehensive commercial banks in the period from 1994 to 2002. They began to engage in financing business and commerce. In 2003, the Banking Law was promulgated and, for the first time, confirmed in legal form the rights and duties of China's commercial banks, under a regulatory structure. The Banking Regulatory Commission was established in the same year. In January 2004, the BOC and the CCB became pilot cases in undertaking "Corporatization" reform. The government supplemented the capital of these two banks with US$22.5 billion for each bank, mobilized from foreign exchange reserves. In August and September of 2004, reforms at the BOC and the CCB resulted in the two becoming shareholding entities. In October 2005, June and October 2006 respectively, the CCB, BOC, and the ICBC were listed on exchanges in Hong Kong and Shanghai. These historic actions represented breakthroughs in turning China's state-owned commercial banks into entities owned by shareholders.

In 1987, the CCB was reorganized and reestablished; it was the first state-owned but shareholding commercial bank in China to undertake reform. After this, China International Trust and Investment Corporation (CITIC), Merchants Bank, Shenzhen Development Bank, and some 12 other banks that had started as regional banks but gradually developed a nationwide business were set up as shareholding commercial banks. In 1996, the first private owned bank was established; that is, in which the government did not own shares. The foundation for a banking system was now basically complete, with shareholding commercial banks that had developed from regional bases forming a second layer in China's banking system and breaking the monopoly that the state-owned banks had held under the planned economy system. The third layer of China's banking system includes municipal commercial banks, rural commercial banks, postal savings organizations, and so on.

Municipal credit cooperatives grew rapidly in the mid-1980s in order to finance the boom in private business. Their small size meant that the cost of operations was high, however, and the structure of share ownership was often problematic. Starting in 1995, municipal credit cooperatives were merged and consolidated into municipal cooperative banks, with investment coming from various sources including local enterprises, common people, and local government. These rapidly growing banks are currently striding ahead in reorganizing their balance sheets and listing on the market. The Ningpo Bank, the Nanjing Bank, and the Beijing Bank have already successfully listed, and are actively pursuing cross-regional operating strategies.

In the mid-1980s, after the reform of rural finances had started, various financial institutions in rural areas were formed with the participation of various parts in the region. In 2007, postal savings institutions were merged to become the Postal Savings Bank, and other village-based micro-financial banks began to grow.

By the end of 2007, total assets in China's banking and finance institutions came to RMB52.6 trillion, with loans totaling RMB49.6 trillion and shareholder rights totaling RMB3 trillion. The sector included 8,877 registered legal institutions. Operating networks included 189,921 different locations, and employed 2,696,760 people.

By 2008, China's three large state-owned policy banks held 8.1% of total banking assets. Five large commercial banks constituted 53.3% of the banking industry, with RMB28 trillion in total assets; 55.5% of industry savings deposits, totaling some RMB40.1 trillion; 49.9% of total industry loans totaled RMB27.8 trillion. These five commercial banks included 67,392 sites in their network (representing 35.8% of all banking locations), and employed 1,492,000 people (55.3% of all banking employees). Twelve regionally based commercial banks held 13.8% of all banking assets. In addition, 124 municipal commercial banks held 6.6% of bank assets, and there were 42 municipal credit cooperatives.

By end-2007, financial reform in rural areas was progressing in a measured fashion with the formation of provincial-level management and oversight over rural credit cooperatives. There were 8,348 rural credit cooperatives, 17 rural commercial banks, 113 rural cooperative banks, and 19 town-and-village banks. Rural financial institutions held 10.6% of all banking industry assets. In addition to the above, by end-2007, China's banking industry included four loan companies, eight village finance mutual help cooperatives, 54 trust companies, 73 finance companies in enterprise groups, 10 financial leasing companies, two currency brokerages, nine automobile financing companies, one postal savings bank, four financial asset management companies, and 29 foreign-invested financial institutions. From one solitary bank in 1978, the structure of China's banking industry has certainly made progress.

Securities

China's capital markets started from a base of zero 26 years ago. After a long hiatus, government bonds were first issued again in 1981, and the Shanghai Stock Market was established in December 1990. During this period, the markets have created systems and mechanisms that were able to grow in a more organic fashion around the world over the course of 200 years. China's markets have been developing in the midst of ongoing change, of deepening reforms, turbulent times, a volatile global environment, and occasional mistakes. Government support has spurred on the process, using the market to guide results, starting with pilot cases of select enterprises. It has maintained a dual focus on both domestic issues and "opening" policies. China's capital markets have proceeded with reforms inside China and with concurrent attempts to stay in alignment with the rest of the world.

The development of China's securities and futures markets has been in tandem with a tremendous increase in the demand for financing brought on by economic growth. In July 1981, due to the needs of Reform and Opening, China began to issue government bonds, an action that had stopped more than a decade earlier. In 1981 the government issued a total of RMB14.8 billion in bonds, RMB4.866 billion worth of domestic bonds, and foreign-currency bonds equivalent to RMB9.9 billion that were sold on international markets. In the early period of China's resumption of economic development, state-owned commercial banks needed funding in order to finance national economic growth and, in July 1985, ABC issued RMB1.5 billion in bonds to the public. This was the start of China's modern bond business. Later, since the deposit-taking business of large state-owned commercial banks grew rapidly, they did not need to go to the market for funding. Financial bonds mainly became a tool for the funding of policy banks that did not take in deposits.

In the mid-1980s, China saw tremendous need for financing given the rapid growth in China's economy. In order to supplement inadequate capital for important infrastructure projects in the state plan, in 1987, the government began to issue bonds of large SOEs, including those of the electric power, steel, ferrous metals, and petrochemical industries. Such enterprise bonds totaled RMB4.5 billion in 1987. The CCB served as agent for distribution, and providing backup support. In mid-2005, the PBC began to standardize procedures with regard to these short-term bonds. In August 2007, the China Securities Regulatory Commission (CSRC) promulgated a document called "Pilot-program Methods for Issuing Corporate Bonds." This marked the formal start of issuing corporate bonds in China. Back in 1987, a secondary market in government bonds or treasury bills had been set up and trading had begun in government bonds. In 2002, commercial banks began an over-the-counter (OTC) style trade in government bonds, and in 2005, the inter-bank bond market started long-term trading in debt instruments.

China's securities markets were born during the process of on-going economic reforms and also during a period of strong economic growth. Both of these led to tremendous increases in the demand for corporate financing. In the early 1980s, economic growth was strong, but bank loans were still constrained by the planned economy process and governmental restrictions. As a result, a spontaneous market developed for share investment in enterprises. The government encouraged certain pilot cases among small and medium enterprises. In November 1984, the first company share was issued in China. This was the "Flying Music" tape recording company in Shanghai. In January 1985, the Shanghai Yanzhong Company became the first collectively owned enterprise to issue shares openly to the public. In September 1986, the Jing'an Securities Department of the Shanghai Trust and Investment Company, under the ICBC, declared itself in business. It became the first financial institution authorized to serve as agent in selling shares in China. With the increase in the numbers of companies issuing shares and in OTC trading, the Shanghai Stock Exchange was born in December 1990, in order to standardize the business and facilitate liquidity. In July 1991, it announced it was establishing an index composed of eight different shares. In April 1991, the Shenzhen Stock Exchange was established.

The stock market developed rapidly after the birth of these two exchanges, and the question of regulation was put on the agenda for China. The CSRC was established in October 1992. It was empowered to regulate all national securities and futures business in a unified manner. In 1993, the Shanghai Stock Exchange began publicizing five different share indexes, including industrial, commercial, real estate, public utilities, and one that was comprehensive. The first Securities Law of China began to be implemented in July 1999. In January 2002, the CSRC promulgated the "Security Companies Management Methods," which set forth rules and regulations on many aspects of the business, including application and approval procedures for institutions, business regulations, personnel management, and risk management. In March 2001, the China Securities Depository and Clearing Corporation Limited (CSDCC) was established as per requirements of the Securities Law and the Company Law. It was responsible for registering and clearing listed shares on the exchanges. In October 2002, the CSRC issued two documents that aided the process of mergers and acquisitions (M&As) and also corporate reorganizations in China. In November 2002, two further regulations were put into effect that dealt with trading corporate bonds. These were the

"Rules on Tradable Corporate Bonds Traded on the Shanghai Stock Exchange," and "Rules on Tradable Corporate Bonds Traded on the Shenzhen Stock Exchange." In May 2002, the China Securities Commission promulgated "Work Procedures for Audit Committees Evaluating Major Reorganizations and Share-issuing Companies." In order to strengthen oversight of information disclosure of listed companies, and to set up warning mechanisms for the market, both Shanghai and Shenzhen Stock Exchanges issued a notification on this subject in April 2003. It was called "Notification Regarding Issues to Do With Increasing the Public's Awareness of the Risks Involved in the Possibility of Delisting Shares." The Exchanges also issued "Special Measures Dealing With Risk of Existing Shares Being Delisted." The symbol *ST was placed before such company shares: this was one of the unique features of the Chinese capital markets. In October 2003, the Investment Funds Law of the People's Republic of China was passed. Following the promulgation and implementation of the Securities Law, this was another major milestone in the development of China's capital markets. In May 2004, the Shenzhen Stock Exchange received permission to establish a Small and Medium-sized Enterprise Board for trading such shares.

Due to historical reasons, companies that decided to list on the market in the early period issued only new shares that were then traded on the exchanges. "Old shares" were not put in circulation, as a result of either direct or indirect fiat by these companies. This practice reflected the concern that SOEs would lose control of their shares, or of their favorable position as majority shareholders. Three kinds of shares therefore came into existence: "circulation shares," or those that could be traded on the market, "state-owned shares," or those that were held by the government and that could not be traded on the market, and "legal-person shares," or shares that were held by different kinds of owners, including state-owned, group-owned or privately owned enterprises, and that also could not be traded. Tradable shares accounted for 36% of total shares of listed companies at the end of 2004. State-owned shares accounted for 47%. Legal-person shares accounted for 17%. The government did not explicitly forbid the circulation of state-owned shares, but in fact there were no clear rules to deal with the matter. This basically led to their being "set aside," so that they could not form part of circulated shares and dilute the ownership of control shares. The result was that the absolute majority of state-owned and legal-person shares were de facto, not traded. This distorted the ownership pattern of shares and enabled extreme deficiencies in the corporate governance of listed companies. The percentage of shares of listed companies that could actually be traded was small. This skewed the pricing ability of the market, increased share-price speculation, and allowed for the possibility of manipulation by market-makers. Insider manipulations were also possible because of the existence of a predominance of untraded shares. Since shares for any given company did not enjoy the same rights or powers, the phenomenon of one dominant shareholder became prevalent. The legal rights of small- and medium-sized shareholders of circulating shares were severely trampled.

In the end, the system ran itself down. The problems led to depressed markets from 2001 to 2004, and frequent problematic cases. Refinancing was hard. It was difficult for the government to finance enterprise reform and social security in the face of this situation. In April 2005, China's Securities Regulatory Commission promulgated a "Notification Regarding Issues to Do With Test-Case Reforms of Share Distribution of Listed Companies." It undertook reform of share allocations in certain selected companies. The share allocation reform aimed at eliminating the systemic difference between circulating shares and those that could not be traded. It eliminated "same shares but unequal rights," and "same shares but unequal benefits." It eventually was able to make all shares of a listed company tradable, or put all shares in circulation. A two-track price system of the markets was changed into a unified market price, with the same shares enjoying the same rights, and with small and medium-sized shareholders being protected. This initiated a pricing system that could work in a rational manner. It improved corporate governance structures, and provided a new route to reduction in state-owned shares. The share-allocation reforms used a method of allowing shareholders of untraded shares to compensate tradable shares a certain amount in order to allow their shares to be tradable. Specifics for each company were determined by the shareholders meeting together and the company's board of directors.

The CSRC used this opportunity to further reform China's securities markets. It required that enterprises not conforming to the standards of the share reform undergo full scale reform and reorganization to bring them up to the required status. At the same time, the Commission increased information disclosure requirements, strengthened punishment for illegal behavior, and took other useful measures. By end-2006, a total of 1,269 companies on the Shanghai and Shenzhen exchanges had either completed share-allocation reform or begun the process. The market capitalization of these firms was 97% of the total, meaning that the work of share-allocation reform was basically complete. This then stimulated a tremendous increase in share prices in 2007.

As China's stock exchanges were being established, China's commodity futures markets were also being set up. In October 1990, the Zhengzhou Grain Wholesale market adopted measures for trading in futures and became the first commodity futures market in China, dealing mainly in wheat and soybeans. In February 1993, the Dalian Commodity Exchange was established. In December 1999, three futures exchanges in Shanghai combined to form the Shanghai Futures Exchange and begin formal operations. These three were the Shanghai Metal Exchange (established in May 1992), the Shanghai Cereal and Oils Exchange (established in June 1993), and the Shanghai Commodity Exchange (formed in May 1995). In October 2002, the Shanghai Gold Exchange was formally inaugurated and in September 2006, the China Financial Futures Exchange was established.

China's securities and futures markets currently trade eight types of investments: A-shares (RMB-denominated common shares), B-shares (foreign-exchange-denominated shares listed within the country), government bonds (spot market), government bonds (repo market), corporate bonds, convertible bonds, securities investment funds, commodities, and foreign exchange futures. By end-2007, 1,550 companies were listed on the markets inside China, with a total market capitalization of RMB32.7 trillion, roughly equal to 140% of GDP. China stood third in the world in terms of capital markets, and first in terms of newly established markets. In 2007, initial public offerings (IPOs) took in a total of RMB459.579 billion in China, ranking it first in the world of IPOs. The index for the big board, share capitalization, and annual increase in value of executed trades all ranked first in the world. Trading volume came to an average of RMB109.3 billion per day, making China's one of the most active markets in the world.

In the bond and investment fund markets, by end-2007, government bonds, financing bonds, and corporate bond markets were booming. The volumes of those markets were respectively RMB7.8666 trillion, RMB3.0605 trillion, and RMB801.1 billion. There were 138,870,000 individual accounts of investors in securities. There were 104 securities companies, with total assets approaching RMB1 trillion and operating networks including more than 3,100 locations. Fund management companies totaled 58; already established securities investment funds totaled 363, the net value of fund assets was RMB3.28 trillion.

Paperless distribution and trading is now employed by all share trading and closed-end securities investment funds. All institutions engaging in the securities business adopt unified standards for trading and clearing. In the commodity futures and financial derivatives markets, by end-2007, China had three commodity futures exchanges, 183 commodity futures brokerages, and 12 types of traded products, including soybeans, wheat, and various other agricultural products; and copper, aluminum, and various other metals. In 2007, 728 million trades were made, with accomplished trade valued at RMB40.97 trillion. The inter-bank market for foreign exchange and the China Foreign Exchange Center can now execute spot and forward trades and swaps. In 2007, the daily average volume was already reaching US$9 billion. A financial futures exchange was established in 2006 that at present is doing mock trades preparatory to actual opening. There is one Gold Exchange whose turnover in 2007 came to RMB316.49 billion, with a daily average traded quantity of 7554.3 kilograms of gold.

Insurance

Different from the way in which it handled the banking and securities industries, in 1950 the government of China set up a China People's Insurance Company to handle its insurance business. After 1959, however, the insurance industry within China was dismantled and this company turned to handling only insurance related to the outside world. Inside China, the industry was later resurrected under the impetus of Reform and Opening in 1979.

In 1981, the People's Insurance Company of China was changed from being a governmental department to being a specialized company. It became the only insurance company at the time in China. As the need for insurance grew and reforms in China deepened, regional insurance companies now began to form. In 1988, the first shareholding insurance company in China was set up, which was also a regional company. This was the precursor to the Ping An Insurance Company, and was called the "Shenzhen Ping An Insurance Company" at the time. In 1991, the China Pacific Insurance Company was established, with its headquarters in Shanghai. This became the first nationally based shareholding commercial insurance company in China.

In the latter part of the 1990s, state-owned insurance companies began to undergo reform in the direction of becoming "corporatized" operations. In 1996, the state-owned China People's Insurance Company undertook "corporatization" reform and reorganized itself to become China People's Insurance (Group) Company. Under this were placed the "Zhong-bao" or "China Insurance" Asset Insurance Company, Ltd, the China Insurance Life Insurance Company, Ltd, and the China Insurance Reinsurance Company. In October 1998, China Insurance Group's three subsidiaries became independent companies: China People's Insurance Company, China Life Insurance Company, and China Reinsurance Company. In 2003, the three large state-owned insurance companies proceeded with shareholding reforms. The China People's Insurance Company reorganized itself once more to become the China People's Insurance Holding Company, under which were placed the China People's Property and Casualty Insurance Share Company Ltd, and the China People's Asset Management Company Ltd. The China Life Insurance Company was also reorganized to become China Life Insurance (Group) Company and China Life Insurance Company, Ltd. China Reinsurance Company became the China Reinsurance (Group) Company, under which was the China Property Reinsurance Company Ltd, the China Life Reinsurance Company, Ltd, and the China Property and Casualty Insurance Company Ltd.

At the same time, specialized insurance companies began to develop. In 2000, the Beijing Jiangtai, Shanghai Dongda, and Guangzhou Changcheng insurance brokerages were set up, all operating on a national basis. In 2004, the first health insurance company in China was set up, the China People's Health Insurance Company, Ltd. The first annuity company, the Ping An Annuity Insurance Company, Ltd was also set up.

Reform of insurance companies in recent years has enabled the establishment of a modern commercial system. The main insurance companies have completed "corporatization" reform and have been listed on the market, which has helped in resolving one of the problems of the industry: insufficient payback or compensation ability. The listing has also forced insurance companies to change their way of operating and begin from a new starting point. The regulatory system governing the insurance industry is constantly being upgraded. Standards are getting better and there is now strong cooperation with the international regulatory regime. To at least an initial degree, the insurance industry has set up the three main pillars of baseline regulatory structure: corporate governance, market behavior, and compensation ability. Improvements are continually being made. New actuarial tables, new non-life insurance evaluation systems, better statistical systems, information systems, accounting systems and so forth are being applied to all the various forms of insurance.

China's insurance industry has been through three stages: an initial period, a cessation, and a rebirth. In the process, it has accumulated more than 40 years of experience and helped in stabilizing the security of many aspects of people's lives. It has also been able to provide a multilayered product offering with various investment opportunities for people's savings. In 2007, the insurance industry's premium income reached RMB703.58 billion, of which insurance premiums from property and casualty insurance totaled RMB199.77 billion, and life insurance RMB503.8 billion. The gross assets of the insurance industry continue to increase at a fast clip. From 1980 to 2004, over the course of 24 years, the industry accumulated RMB1 trillion in assets. Since then, the growth from RMB1 trillion to nearly RMB3 trillion in assets has taken only four years—by end-2007, gross assets of the industry had reached RMB2.9 trillion. The number of insurance companies has also continued to rise. In 1980, there was only one company; by end-2007, there were 117, representing all kinds of insurance. For example, there were nine insurance asset management companies, 2,327 companies involved in brokering and agenting, and 139 representative offices of foreign-invested insurance companies. By end-2007, realized profits of the industry in China came up to RMB67.27 billion.

Summary

Overall, after 30 years, China has developed banking and financial systems of respectable size. After reorganization, the country's financial institutions have been able to resolve their historical legacy of nonperforming assets, which continue to decline in number, and the quality of assets continues to improve. Balance sheets are far stronger than they were.

The banking industry overall has seen the nonperforming loan (NPL) rate fall from 17.9% in 2003 to 6.17% in 2007. Among major banks, the NPL rates for ICBC, BOC, and CCB have fallen to lower than 3%. The provisional coverage rate is over 100%. Ability to withstand risk is improved. Capital adequacy ratios are far higher than they were: at the end of 2003, only eight banks in China had capital adequacy ratios of over 8%; by end-2007, the average rate among financial institutions as a whole had risen to 8%, for the first time reaching international regulatory levels. Profit levels have also risen dramatically. From 1997 to 1999, China's banking industry saw all banks making a loss; before-tax profit in 2000 came to only RMB13.31 billion. This rose to before-tax profits of RMB32.28 billion in 2003, and to RMB337.92 billion in 2006. At the end of 2007, China's banking institutions showed an after-tax profit of RMB446.73 billion, return on equity of 16.7%, and return on assets of 0.9%.

As seen from the above figures, China's before-tax profits in the banking industry increased by 32 times between 2000 and 2007. After undergoing "corporatization" reform, taking in institutional investors, and listing on the market both inside and outside China, China's financial institutions are now in the process of diversifying shareholders. They are becoming legitimate share holding corporations in the sense that they are setting up basic corporate governance structures according to the requirements of modern financial institutions. Shareholders meetings, Board of Directors, supervisory committees, and senior management are all gradually fulfilling their respective roles, with mechanisms for effective balancing of interests and structures that harmonize proper results. Information disclosure systems are gradually improving. Transparency is considerably better. Financial institutions that are listed on the market are able to provide operating results in a manner that complies with requirements. They are conscientiously accepting market regulation. Rational management systems that adopt risk management as the basic premise are being established, and the level of risk containment is greatly improved. Even as the financial industries are growing, China has taken initial steps in erecting the legal system and regulations governing those industries that operate according to prudent practices. China has established a separated regulatory system that applies to each of the financial industries, banking, securities, and insurance, and it has laid the foundation for a financial industry that operates according to a legal structure both in terms of operating and regulating. It has provided guarantees for an environment in which the industry can improve risk management, improve competitiveness and innovativeness. Policies regarding market entry are more standardized and transparent by the day, and non-filed inspection has begun to play an important role.

At the same time, cross-border regulatory cooperation and information exchange have been strengthened, and mechanisms for information exchange are being realized. The CRBC issued an Opinion in 2007 called "Guiding Opinion on Compliance of China's Banking Industry With the New Capital Accord," which states that from end-2010, China's banks must all implement the New Capital Accord of 2002 (the BIS II of the Basel Committee on Banking Supervision). Overall, the systemic risk in China's financial industries has already abated, the industries are able to support China's economic growth and, at the same time, through reform, have been able to propel themselves to further growth.

SECTION II: STRENGTHENING BY OPENING TO THE OUTSIDE

The "opening to the outside" of China's financial industries is being done concurrently with domestic reforms. At the beginning of China's economic reforms, in 1980, the government allowed the Japanese Import/Export Bank to establish a representative office in Beijing. In 1981, the Nanyang Bank, which is registered in Hong Kong, was first to establish a branch in Shenzhen, signaling the opening of China's banking market to banks from outside its borders. HSBC, Citibank, and others subsequently established branches inside China and carried on foreign-exchange business in China's special economic zones.

By 2001, when China entered the World Trade Organization (WTO), there were 19 financial institutions registered as foreign-invested banks in China. They held assets of RMB373.9 billion, holding 1.8% of China's total banking assets at that time. In December 2006, at the end of the five-year transition period of entering WTO, China's banking industry opened completely, and, in particular, China completely opened RMB retail business to foreign-invested banks. It did away with such restrictions as regional limits on RMB-denominated business. It adopted same-treatment status as Chinese banks for foreign-invested banks, and foreign-invested banks began to develop rapidly inside China.

By end-2007, 193 banks from 47 countries and regions had established 242 representative offices inside China. There are now 24 solely foreign-invested banks (with 119 branches), two joint venture banks (with five branches and one affiliated institution), and three solely foreign-invested financial-affairs companies. In addition, 71 foreign banks from 23 countries and regions have set up 117 branches inside China. Assets of foreign-invested financial institutions come to

RMB1.25 trillion, representing 2.4% of total assets of China's banking industry. Fifty foreign-invested banking institutions have received permission to do business in financial derivatives.

Reform of internal management mechanisms and the building of systems are daily becoming more important in China's financial institutions. China's financial industries are gradually moving from opening markets to opening participation in share-ownership. Starting in 1998, China began to experiment with bringing foreign direct investment into small-scale Chinese banks. The scope of this experiment was small, and was limited to putting investment of international financial institutions into small banks. That same year, Shanghai Bank took in US$24 million in investment from a multinational financial company. Starting in 2003, with the unfolding of the "corporatization" reform in China's state-owned commercial banks, the "opening" of China's banking industry progressed from allowing foreign-invested banks to open for business in China to allowing foreign-invested banks to invest in the shares of Chinese banks. China then began to allow foreign investors to participate on a much larger scale by putting strategic investment into Chinese banks. By the end of 2007, a total of 25 Chinese commercial banks had brought in 33 foreign institutional investors who had invested a total of US$21.25 billion.

At the same time, China's banks began to be listed on stock markets overseas. By the end of 2007, Chinese banks that had listed as such had taken in US$45.51 billion in IPO proceeds. By the end of 2007, China's banking institutions had collectively absorbed a foreign investment total of US$82.32 billion.

The opening of the Chinese securities markets has also been done concurrently with the process of domestic reform. It has constantly moved forward with the method of "crossing the river by feeling for the stones as you go." In April 1991, when the Shenzhen Stock Exchange had just been established. It opened a market for Chinese stocks that were specifically for foreign investment. These were the so-called B-shares, priced in foreign currencies and specifically targeted at foreign-nationals who wanted to invest in Chinese companies. In October 1991, for the first time, China's shareholding companies began trading B-shares. Ten years later, in February 2001, the Securities Regulatory Commission determined that Chinese residents could also invest in B-shares, and from this point onward, the B-share market became a Chinese internal stock market that was traded and priced in foreign currencies.

Due to the convenient proximity of capital markets in Hong Kong, from 1991, China began to permit domestic companies to list their shares on the Hong Kong market. Since the name Hong Kong starts with an H, these became known as H-shares. In July 1993, Tsingtao Brewery Company Limited listed on the Hong Kong Stock Exchange and became the first Chinese company to list abroad. In July 2002, Bank of China (Hong Kong) Ltd also listed on the Hong Kong Stock Exchange, and became the first state-owned commercial bank to list successfully abroad.

In 1992, the Chinese government began to permit domestic companies to list on the New York Stock Exchange. Since New York begins with an N, these were then called N-shares. In 1993, the Shanghai Jinshan Petrochemical Company listed on the New York Stock Exchange, to become the first domestic Chinese company to list in New York. By December of 2007, a total of 148 domestic companies had listed H-shares in Hong Kong, and 45 companies had listed N-shares in New York. In 2007, the amount garnered from these listings came up to US$9.17 billion. In 2002, China complied with the promises to open the securities industry made at the time of entering the WTO, and permitted foreign investment to invest shares of Chinese fund management and securities companies. By the end of 2007, 11 foreign-invested financial institutions had invested in the shares of Chinese securities companies, including Goldman Sachs, Morgan Stanley, Credit Suisse, UBS, and Daiwa Securities.

The opening of the insurance industry to outside forces was earlier, faster, and also more broadly based than either banking or securities. In September 1992, AIG became the first foreign insurance company to receive a license to operate general and life insurance business in China. AIG General's parent company AIU set up a branch in Shanghai, which marked the formal opening of the Chinese insurance market to foreign participation. In June 1994, China's Ping An Insurance Company successfully took in share investment from Morgan Stanley and Goldman Sachs, becoming the first insurance company in China to allow foreign investment in its share. In November 1996, the Manulife insurance company of Canada and CITIC group of China formed the Zhong Hong Life Insurance Co. Ltd, which became the first joint-venture insurance company in China. This is now called the Manulife Sinochem Insurance Co. Ltd. In June 2000, the China Insurance International Holding Company Ltd registered in Hong Kong, listed on the Hong Kong Stock Exchange. This was the first China-invested insurance enterprise to list outside China's borders. In November

2001, after entering the WTO, China's insurance industry committed to lifting all regional restrictions on foreign companies within three years of entry into the WTO in the markets of reinsurance, asset insurance, group insurance, health insurance, and others. Since joining the WTO in 2002, China has permitted six foreign insurance companies to enter the market and set up operating entities, and has allowed 15 foreign-invested insurance operating institutions to engage in business.

In November 2003, the People's Property Insurance Holding Company of China successfully listed on the Hong Kong Stock Exchange. This then became the first domestic financial institution to list there. In December, China Life Insurance Company Ltd listed on the New York Stock Exchange and on December 18, it also listed on the Hong Kong Stock Exchange, becoming the first domestic financial enterprise to list simultaneously in both the Hong Kong and US markets. This listing took in some US$3.5 billion, setting a global record for financing via stock market listing in 2003. December 11, 2004 marked the conclusion of the transition period for the entry of China's insurance industry into the WTO. China's insurance industry now entered a new period of complete opening to outside participation. Foreign-invested insurance companies no longer have regional or quantitative limitations on setting up new institutions in China, and their scope of operations is not restricted.

China's insurance industry has gradually met the demands of globalization and financial integration. By 2007, foreign-invested insurance companies held 5.97% of China's overall insurance market. Of the total, foreign-invested companies held 8% of China's life insurance business. In casualty insurance, they held 1.16%. The percentage of foreign-invested insurance business in the economically advanced coastal regions far exceeded these national averages. By the end of September 2007, 47 foreign-invested insurance companies from 15 countries and regions were active in China with 135 operating entities, including main offices and branches.

In terms of "striding out into the world," at present China's insurance industry has established 42 operating institutions, and nine representative and liaison offices overseas, effectively furthering the internationalization of China's insurance industry.

Allowing foreign institutions to enter the Chinese financial system has been significant to improvements in the competitiveness of China's own institutions and in the deepening of its financial markets. First, foreign-invested financial institutions provide a greater range of products and a wealth of financial services to China's enterprises and citizens. One of the defects of China's financial markets is its paucity of products: an example is the banking industry, where the main product is still traditional deposits and loans. Non-interest income in the industry was still only 12% of the total income by the end of 2007. Relying on their tremendous experience in international markets and on their global product platforms, foreign-invested financial institutions have rapidly expanded intermediary business and fee-based products in China's banking markets.

Foreign-invested financial institutions have also brought new sales and service concepts into China. The insurance industry provides one example: in November 1992, AIG trained the first group of life insurance agents. Using life insurance agents was a tremendous change in China's way of operating, and the system was swiftly adopted by China's own life insurance industry. The entry of foreign-invested financial institutions also led to an upgrading of market competition in China, by putting competition on the basis of products and services, not just pricing, which had hitherto been the case.

Foreign-invested financial institutions operate on the basis of international regulatory standards, and this has improved the Chinese regulatory environment. It has stimulated the internationalization of China's own regulatory standards. Once China allowed domestic companies to list in Hong Kong, this forced a standardization between the stock markets of China and Hong Kong. Both began competing for the high-quality companies that they wanted to list on their exchanges. This had an extremely beneficial impact on the internationalization of China's domestic stock exchanges and on the improvement of regulatory capacity in those exchanges. It greatly enhanced the degree of transparency of China's domestic exchanges.

The entry of foreign-invested financial institutions into the Chinese market has also heightened the demands on China's basic financial infrastructure, and spurred the development of systems that are in line with international practices. These include payment and clearance systems and other basic infrastructure that now have to comply with the best practices of international models. This has led to breakthrough advances in China's financial infrastructure.

Finally, the entry of foreign-invested financial institutions into China's markets has provided an exemplary model to Chinese firms, and heightened their sense of urgency in improving their own competitiveness. Foreign institutions have provided a strong challenge in the areas of high-end customer services and in innovative products in particular. They have forced the pace of reform in the internal management systems of Chinese financial institutions, especially with respect to human resources, risk management, IT systems, and product innovation.

Bringing foreign capital and foreign share participation into Chinese financial institutions has had a direct and profound effect on improving their core competitiveness and assuring their sustainable healthy growth. First, foreign strategic investment has strengthened the capital base of China's institutions, allowing them to expand more quickly in both scale of operations and lines of business. Since 2003, foreign financial institutions have invested more than US$100 billion in Chinese financial institutions.

Second, foreign strategic investment by overseas financial institutions has changed the monopolistic nature of the shareholding structure of Chinese state-owned institutions. This has enabled more significant reform. The most fundamental problem in state-owned enterprises (SOEs) has been unclear delineation of ownership. The process of bringing in strategic foreign investment has forced China to clarify ownership of its state-owned assets, and has improved the "definition" and the "regularization" of asset ownership.

Third, cooperating with strategic foreign investors has improved the level of corporate governance in Chinese financial institutions, stimulating change in operating concepts and methods. The existence of foreign shareholders has greatly improved the understanding of shareholders' meetings, boards meetings, and governance structures, as well as rules and procedures. It has increased transparency and raised the activist role of performance review mechanisms. Accountability systems have been vastly strengthened.

Fourth, cooperation with strategic investors in actual business has greatly enriched Chinese institutions in terms of their product offerings and service capabilities. It has improved their innovativeness. Fifth, working with strategic investors in risk management, in accounting and human resource management and other such broad areas, has improved the quality of management of Chinese institutions.

Foreign participation in China's financial markets has at the same time put competitive pressure on Chinese financial institutions, increasing their sense of urgency about strengthening their own competitiveness and forcing them to undertake internal reforms. The process has resulted in faster and more broadly based overhauls of internal systems. The lessons have forced China's financial industry to take the path to a stronger industry in all respects, from scale of operations to actual results.

From the outset, China's overall national policies affirmed the desirability of "opening." These guided, encouraged, and propelled China's financial institutions and regulatory agencies to adhere to international standards, to study international best practices, and to conform to international conventions in order to improve competitiveness. The strategic plan for opening China's financial industry has included taking in foreign investment in order to jumpstart the formation of China's financial markets, allowing foreign share ownership in Chinese institutions, and allowing foreign-invested institutions to participate in all kinds of Chinese financial institutions to stimulate improvements in internal mechanisms and raise the competitiveness of China's financial institutions. All of this has been done to internationalize China's financial markets and to enable China to participate in the integration of global economics and finance.

Today, China's financial markets are in a situation that could be described as mutual competition and also mutual cooperation between inside and outside. Virtually every major China-invested financial institution has taken in investment from international financial institutions. Virtually every major international institution has branch operations in China. Virtually every major China-invested financial institution accepts the regulation of both Chinese and international financial regulatory institutions. Under the coexistence of both competition and cooperation, China's financial institutions are rapidly studying best practices of international organizations, constantly improving their core competencies and competitiveness, and constantly improving the quality of both markets and regulation.

At the same time, international financial institutions are delving more deeply into China's financial markets by the day. They have made China-related business and international business related to China a key strategic component of their long-range plans. Finally, the market participation of foreign firms in China's financial markets has already taken on a portion of the financial risk of China's financial markets. It is also beneficial in improving the efficiency with which capital resources are allocated. It has spurred a more efficient allocation of resources with respect to China's overall economy.

The opening of China's financial systems is now irreversible. China's systems are already intimately bound up with global financial markets, and already form a part of the global financial system.

SECTION III: FACING NEW CHALLENGES

Reform of China's financial industry has accomplished tremendous results in the short space of 30 years, but future growth in the industry still faces tremendous challenges. China's financial systems are still in their infancy, and future reforms and growth will have to move the emphasis from "quantity" to "quality;" they will also have to move toward maturity and greater depth.

China's financial enterprises now face the need to raise management capability and improve core competitiveness in order to meet ever more complex domestic competition, as well as ever more fierce international competition. At the company level, the challenge includes five different aspects in terms of corporate management: improving capacities in product innovation and services, raising management capabilities in the areas of risk management and accounting, improving corporate governance mechanisms, shifting organizational structure from a fragmented regional basis to a structure based on product lines, and cultivating the human resources and the risk and service culture.

In terms of macro considerations, China's financial systems are facing tremendous changes in overall market structure. They face the challenge of the marketization of both interest rates and exchange rates. They face the pressures of an increasingly sluggish "financial ecosystem." They face the need to comply with international competition and regulation. All of these will test and measure the future of the country's financial system. As global economics and finance increasingly integrate, China's financial institutions are moving forward on the international stage even as international financial institutions are relying more heavily on Chinese markets. All of this means that China's financial systems are facing at the very least the following 10 major challenges.

The first challenge is that there is still a clear gap between the needs of the market and the level of services and innovative capacity of China's financial system. As the market environment for China's financial industries undergoes rapid change, the needs of customers have shifted from traditional simple business to a need for a comprehensive financial services style of diverse offerings. The main thrust of competition in financial markets today is to provide services and products. Although China's financial markets are able to stand together with competitors on global markets in terms of size, in terms of financial services, they fall far short. The main weakness is insufficient innovative capacity in financial markets, leading to overly uniform products that are not able to meet the needs of a Chinese economy that is experiencing ferocious growth and also ferocious change in economic structure. In a market with identical products, competition can only be based on price cutting. This is detrimental to creating larger and more in-depth financial markets. Taking banking as an example: one indicator of the level of products is non-interest income as a percentage of gross income. China's percentage is only 12%, far lower than banking industries in developed economies, but also lower than the 26% of banking industries in other parts of Asia. China's three largest banks already rank among the ten largest on the globe, but their non-interest income level is only around one-third of banks in the same tier. Weak capacity in this area can be attributed to such underlying causes as low caliber of employees, luck of evaluation mechanisms, an insufficiently innovative culture, and so on. In the final analysis, these are all systemic problems that will take a long time and many further stages of reform to resolve.

The second challenge facing China's financial system is that risk management and financial management are still relatively backwards. Initial steps in setting up risk management systems were made during the restructuring and IPO process. Reforms in risk management were implemented, financial institutions started to train professionals, to consolidate jurisdiction over this aspect, make the process more rational, strengthen evaluation of customers, and so on. Risk management is nonetheless still weak, particularly in market risk management, liquidity risk management, and operating risk management. China's financial enterprises are not yet adequately geared up in terms of overall financial risk management. They must maintain a high degree of awareness in this arena. Ability to price risk and to manage information is another important area. Since China will be expanding capital markets in a major way in the future, including securities markets, debt markets, financial derivative markets and so on, and since at the same time domestic markets will be increasingly internationalized, management of market risk and liquidity risk is critical. In terms of financial management, balance sheets were much improved by removing nonperforming assets in the course of reorganizations and by injecting capital. Most Chinese financial enterprises are already adopting International Financial Reporting Standards (IFRS). After undertaking two major systemic reforms in China's financial accounting in 1993 and 2001, the rules have consistently improved and now are extremely close to international standards. However, setting up enterprise-wide management systems for ensuring clarity and accuracy of reporting, and compliance with international standards, has yet to be instituted. Standardizing of financial budgeting systems needs improvement. The ability to perform sound financial analysis is inadequate. Improving capacities in financial and risk management remain long-term projects.

The third challenge facing China's financial systems is ongoing improvement of corporate governance mechanisms. As a result of "corporatization" reform, taking in institutional investors, listing on domestic and international markets and so on, China's financial institutions have been able to establish basic corporate governance structures. Separate functions adhere to the various roles of shareholders meetings, Board of Directors, and senior management. Effective balance and harmonized action of these different roles has been accomplished to a degree, but more effective corporate governance is still needed. This includes further defining the roles and functions of what in Chinese are called the "three meetings": shareholders meetings, and meetings of Board of Directors and board of supervisors; and includes the responsibilities, rights, and benefits of those three. Performance review and proper incentive schemes are yet to be well-formed and are in their initial stages; effective accountability is not yet in place. Information disclosure systems are coming along, but transparency still needs further improvement. The biggest challenge to China as it improves its corporate governance systems is that reforms mainly occur at the headquarters level of a company, but China is vast and its network of financial institutions is extensive. How to ensure that corporate governance mechanisms reach all components of the system is a long-term and important challenge.

The fourth challenge facing China's financial system is a restructuring of the way regional offices do their business, with a view to allowing management-by-product lines and business rationale rather than by geographic location. China's financial institutions are mainly divided into regions that correspond to China's administrative units. Management is done "piecemeal," divided by province or by a directly administered city. Within provinces, management of any given institution conforms to the administrative districts, cities, and management units of the Chinese bureaucracy. The system is not managed in the way international financial institutions handle their affairs, with financial matters and risk management dealt with in a centralized way, or product lines and business divisions administered in a direct-line fashion. The Chinese management reality, given the way China's local government has been administered for decades, gives considerable managerial control to branch institutions. Given the size of China, the financial and economic scale of one province, or even one city, often surpasses the economic scale of some mid-size countries in the world. Because of this, a financial branch in any one province may operate as an independent financial institution. This applies to everything from products to sales, from finances to risk management, from general affairs to human resources. Transparency is rather opaque in such a system, and the quality of information is poor. Business logistics are not unified; an overall strategic approach is difficult. The situation is not conducive to comprehensive servicing of customers. This model meant China's institutions are far from being able to satisfy the basic operating needs of a market that is already quite sizable, let alone the demands of global competition.

In the course of reforms over the past 10 years, China's financial institutions have made efforts to strengthen policies, management, and systems in the areas of risk and finance. They have tried to centralize policies and they have begun to unify payment clearance and IT systems. Some financial institutions have also gone a step further, within the "piecemeal structure" of China's regional administration, by creating overlapping and strengthened matrix systems in the areas of product, customer, financial and risk control management, and they have linked clearance and IT systems together.

China's financial markets clearly need to move in the direction of how international institutions are structured. They need to move from "piecemeal" to a direct line management structure that is organized along product lines and that has unified operations. However, China's economic development is still based on the governmental administrative unit in terms of how economic objectives are planned and implemented. Local administrations have a very considerable influence on local finances. Traditional thinking is still heavily weighted in the direction of local administrative units. Reform that involves moving from piecemeal to unified systems also involves change in external aspects that are difficult to control by the financial institutions. Among aspects that can be manageable, it involves reform in conceptual approach, in management capacities, human resource training, as well as the more concrete elements of IT systems. Twenty years ago, mainstream financial institutions in Europe and the US transitioned from doing business on a traditional regional model to being structured along product lines and doing business in a unified fashion. It took them more than 10 years to complete the transition. China's financial institutions still have a long road ahead of them in this regard.

The fifth challenge facing China's financial institutions is to internationalize human resources and the culture of the institution, including a culture of enterprise trustworthiness, a culture of risk management, and a culture of service. Financial institutions are in a service industry that relies on high-quality human capital. Since China's financial enterprises are moving toward a market economy from within a state-owned system, they face reform and renovation of corporate culture and human resources systems. The industry as a whole is facing the trends of internationalized operations, diversification of customer needs, greater complexities in product innovation, and daily intensification of market competition. It is facing a rapidly changing domestic environment as well as an "opening" to the outside. To deal with this, it must cultivate high-level talent that is highly conversant with international financial markets; that has management experience in financial operations; and that is fluent in foreign languages and steeped in law, accounting and other professional knowledge. Finance and economics are globally integrating and customer demands are diversifying. In this overall environment, market competition requires that China's corporate culture change to meet the demands.

High-level, qualified professional talent is available in China. The reality is not that China lacks talent, but that the systems in place for using talent in Chinese institutions are inadequate. They lack the flexibility and the attractiveness to take in professional, innovative people. They have not yet formed scientifically sound and effective operating mechanisms in terms of compensation based on performance and motivational management of salary levels. Reforming human resource management systems is highly important right now in China's financial institutions. They have parted ways with the traditional state-owned enterprise (SOE) administration, but the culture of institutions has not yet made the transition. China's institutions now need to set up new corporate cultures that are in line with and guided by market reforms. They need to cultivate employees' sense of identity with the organization and a sense of belonging; to unify the behavior, thinking, emotions, trust, and customs of employees; and to make the entire organization unify in an organic way. They need to stimulate individual initiative and put it to work for the common objectives of the enterprise. China's financial enterprises will be effective and competitive only when their employees are able to manage risk through a comprehensive risk culture, to service customers by holding mutually understood concepts of service, and to forge commonalities through a mutually understood sense of value. This is one of the key challenges facing China's financial industry in the longer term.

The sixth challenge facing China's financial system is the imbalance in the structure of how business is financed in the country. Rapid growth over the past 20 years means that China's financial industry is fairly sizable. As in many transitioning economies, however, that growth has been uneven, unbalanced, and contains structural problems. China's financing system is overly weighted in the direction of indirect financing via banks, as opposed to direct financing via various kinds of securities. At the end of 2007, the assets of China's banking industry were 213% of GDP, while stock market capitalization was 140% of GDP, and the total value of the bond market was 47% of GDP. In 2007, China's stock market developed rapidly; however, the banking industry still provided 79% of the demand for business financing. Financing via the stock market provided 13%. Bond and other forms of debt financing provided 8%. An over reliance on indirect finance, and the lack of long-term and stable financing markets such as bond markets, subjected China's financial system more directly to macroeconomic conditions. This is not beneficial to long-term, stable, financing of both enterprises and financial institutions.

Structural issues in China's financial systems include the lack of specialized services. All institutions are seeking to grow in all ways, all aim to be "large and comprehensive," or at the very least "small but comprehensive." They all do the same kind of business, the same products, duplicating each others' efforts in low-level competition. Banks are all seeking to be full-capacity banks, for example, and to develop securities and other investment banking business outside their normal lines. Insurance companies are trying to develop traditional commercial banking businesses. Together with investment banks, securities companies are developing asset management businesses, and also want to grow private banking, trustee services, and so on. Meanwhile, China's banking system does not have a company specializing in credit cards; it does not have a custody bank specializing in trustee business; it does not have a housing mortgage firm specializing in mortgage lending for homeowners; it does not have a company specializing in corporate loans; or personal consumer finance. Not having specialized financing institutions leads to low efficiency in the financial markets.

A final structural issue is the dual nature of China's economy, which is echoed in a duality in the country's financial system. Financing in China's rural areas—that is, "agricultural" or "rural financing"—is falling far behind financing in cities. Similarly, the middle and western parts of the country get much less financing than the eastern part. Distribution of banking outlets can serve as one example. At the end of 2005, a survey indicated that urban areas in China had 175,000 banking locations, while rural area had only 27,000. In cities, each 10,000 people had on average 1.34 banking locations at their disposal, while in rural areas, the average per 10,000 people was 0.35. Bank coverage in rural areas remains low. Fifty-five percent of China's population lives in rural areas, yet loans and deposit amounts in these areas are 15% of the national total. The eastern part of the country enjoys 61% of total deposits. East China savings deposits make up 55% of the national total, enterprise deposits are 70% of the national total, and foreign-exchange deposits are 83% of the national total. Such an uneven distribution means that credit is mostly concentrated in the east. Loans in the east are 57% of the national total, while the middle, western, and northeastern regions hold only 14.9%, 16.4%, and 7.7% respectively. The percentage of securities and insurance institutions in rural areas and in central and western regions is far lower. Even worse, financial reforms scarcely touch upon rural financial institutions, risk management is weak, nonperforming asset ratios are high, and financing products are not diverse enough to respond to different needs. At present, this gap between urban and rural is continuing to widen. Rural finance and finance in central and western regions has already become a major risk area for China's financial systems, keeping the financial markets from moving forward. In the coming 10 years, China will be putting major efforts into developing agriculture and developing the central and western parts of the country, and this will require both larger amounts and a higher quality of financial services. The institutions that currently exist in these areas are not able to satisfy this demand. The dual structure of China's current financing presents a bottleneck that constrains China's economy overall, as well as skewing balanced and equitable growth.

The seventh challenge facing China's financial system is the less than satisfactory "financial ecosystem," meaning all the elements, like an adequate legal system, that support the business. The survival and growth of financial enterprises require a nurturing ecosystem, including a stable economic environment. Although China has established a series of laws in recent years that are appropriate for a market economy, China's current legal environment for business is still not ideal. Conceptual awareness of property rights and property protection is still fragile, and many parts of the inherited legal systems are inappropriate for realizing a market economy. For example, there is still no individual bankruptcy law, no law determining financial transgressions deemed to be criminal acts, and so on. In terms of upholding the law, various kinds of relationships hamper the ability of judicial entities to enforce laws on the books, including local relationships and personal relationships. Difficulties in enforcing laws are extreme and costs are high.

Second, the social culture of being trustworthy in China needs improvement; especially as credit rating systems are incomplete. An understanding of the value of being trustworthy needs to be cultivated among government departments, enterprises, and the populace in general. Methods of gathering information on creditworthiness and the establishment of intermediary organizations in credit are still in their initial stages. Information on the creditworthiness of institutional investors cannot be accurately ascertained, let alone on the creditworthiness of people at large. It is not effectively gathered, and there generally is no way to record and make public circumstances that relate to the lack of creditworthiness. Financial enterprises cannot make accurate operating decisions based on the true credit circumstances of customers, while mechanisms for punishing those who misrepresent themselves have not been established to an effective degree.

Third, there is still some influence, either direct or indirect, on how loans are made. Faced with the pressure of growing the economy in a given region, local government officials might appeal indirectly to banks, requesting that they provide loans for enterprises in that region.

Fourth, China lacks mechanisms for harmonizing or coordinating financial regulation, and cross-regional regulation. Some cross-regional capital flows are not at this time included in the scope of regulation. Financial information on cross-regional capital flows is not smooth and forthcoming. In brief, the external environment or ecosystem for sustaining and growing China's financial system awaits further improvement.

The eighth challenge facing China's financial system is further marketization of interest rates and exchange rates, even though this will put pressure on the profits of financial institutions and on their risk management. Managed interest rates and exchange rates to a certain degree mean that the achievements of China's financial industry in recent times have been within the context of a closed system, one that is not fully subject to outside market forces. During the planned economy period, China operated under the basis of a rigorously controlled interest rate system. This lasted up to 1986, when reforms finally began to experiment with marketizing rates to a modest degree. The specialized banks were allowed to loan to one another with interest rate and term considerations being decided by mutual discussion between the banks. Only in 1996 were inter-bank loan rates finally allowed to operate on a market basis, on the basis of supply and demand. In 1999, the PBC allowed foreign-exchange loans and large-sum foreign-exchange deposit rates to operate on a market basis—it released or "opened" those rates to market forces. In 2004, the PBC stopped setting the ceiling rates for RMB loan rates in financial institutions and the floor rates for deposits, and the gradual marketization of interest rates began. They were operated on a basis of "managed lower limits on loan rates and managed upper limits on deposits." In January 2007, what is known as "SHIBOR" or the Shanghai inter-bank offering rate, began to operate, and a standardized market-based rate system for China's currency markets began to be established. However, rates on loans charged by financial institutions are still subject to governmental guidelines and are not linked to SHIBOR.

Due to this managed interest rate system, China's banks enjoy higher margins than is common in international institutions. To take a one-year term deposit/loan as an example: at present, the one-year gross spread on such deposits/loan is 306 basis points (bps), which is roughly twice the international level. This is one of the reasons China's banks have enjoyed relatively solid profit levels over the past several years. That margin will erode under pressure of competition once interest rates are fully marketized. At the same time, banks will be required to improve their interest-rate and market-risk management, and the cost of risk containment will rise.

China has a managed float system with regard to currency exchange rates. In 1996, China adopted the eighth proviso of the International Monetary Fund (IMF) and abolished the exchange rate restrictions applying to current accounts. It implemented an exchangeable rate for RMB-denominated current accounts. The RMB exchange rate was basically maintained at a level of US$1 to RMB8.27. On July 21 2005, the PBC went a step further in improving the exchange rate mechanisms and implemented a managed float that took market supply and demand as the basis, with reference to a basket of currencies for adjustment purposes. By June 30 2008, the RMB had appreciated against the US$ by 20.5%, to the level of US$1 per RMB7.3046. Ongoing marketization reforms in the currency exchange rate system have required that financial enterprises greatly increase their management capacity in managing market risk and assuring adequate liquidity.

The ninth challenge facing China's financial system is that of a possible downturn of the macroeconomic situation in general. Over the past few years, China's macroeconomic situation has been excellent and the income of its financial institutions has increased rapidly. The government has supported extensive reforms; the burden of past nonperforming assets has basically been resolved by separating them from the operating entities. Although China's financial enterprises have industriously used this window of opportunity, setting up risk management systems in particular, those systems have not experienced the test of a declining economy. Today, as the global economy experiences a slowdown and as financial markets face violent swings, as China's own economy begins to soften, the risk management systems of China's financial enterprises will face their first true test.

The tenth challenge facing China's financial system is that of global financial risk and global financial regulation. Given an increasingly integrated global economy and financial system, China's institutions are taking on unavoidable global financial risk as they move toward global markets. The Asian Financial Crisis of 10 years ago and today's subprime mortgage crisis in the US remind us of the global scale of financial shocks. They also remind us that the speed and force of these events can be far greater than we previously imagined. Since China's domestic market and financial product structure is relatively simple, since risk management technology and systems are relatively basic, and since employees still lack relevant experience, the risk that global financial shocks can present to China's financial industry is rather large.

At the same time, adopting international regulation is also a challenge for China's existing regulatory systems, for the people involved and the financial institutions themselves. For example, one of the key elements of the New Capital Accord is to set up active incentive mechanisms for capital and risk management, which is precisely one of the major deficits in China's existing financial regulation. Higher information disclosure standards are also a challenge. China's financial institutions are facing the task of transitioning from being business flow driven as their key operating mode mechanism to using risk management as guidance mechanism. To create this entire risk management structure is a challenge.

SECTION IV: GLOBAL INTEGRATION AND WORKING TOGETHER

China's financial industry is an important part of the world's system. As a key component of the financial industry, China's banking industry already forms an important part of the global system. According to the British magazine *The Banker* (in 2008) 31 of China's commercial banks were ranked among the top 1,000 first-tier global banks by capital. The ICBC ranked #7, and the BOC ranked #9. This was the first time Chinese banks had entered the top 10. By market capitalization, at the end of 2007, the ICBC, the CCB, and the BOC became the top five in the world and remained so in 2008.

On June 27, 2008, according to a ranking done by *Asiaweek*, the total net profit of Chinese banks for the first time exceeded that of Japanese banks, thus becoming first in Asia. Among Chinese banks, ICBC became the most profitable bank in Asia with net profits of US$10.6 billion.

China's stock markets too are integrating within the world. With ongoing reforms, China's securities and futures markets have undergone dramatic change, laws and regulations have gradually been put in place, and basic infrastructure has improved resulting in a dramatic increase in the number and quality of investors. The size of the markets has expanded rapidly to the extent that, in 2007, the financing of IPOs in China for the first time took the global lead in terms of listing and financing. China's enterprises are now briskly getting financing from world capital markets. China's capital markets have already become an important component of the global capital market system.

China's Financial Institutions Are Moving Onto the World Stage

Concurrent with the progress inside China, China's banking industry is moving in measured steps onto the world stage. In 2006, that industry began breaking into overseas markets with the "stride out" policy. In December 2006, the ICBC purchased 90% of shares in an Indonesian Bank called Bank Halim. In August 2007, it purchased the Chengxing Bank of Macao and in October, it purchased 20% of the shares of the largest bank in South Africa, the Standard Bank. In August, the China Development Bank purchased 3% of shares of

England's Barclay Bank. In October, the BOC purchased Asia's largest airplane leasing company, the Singapore Leasing Company, for US$965 million. At the same time, the Moscow Branch of ICBC started operations, the CCB opened a representative office in Sydney, and the Bank of Communications set up branches in Frankfurt and in Macao. The Export-Import Bank of China set up a representative office in St. Petersburg. In November 2007, the US's Banking Regulatory Commission authorized the China Merchant Bank to establish a branch in New York, which is the first China-invested bank operation to be authorized in the US, since the US passed a law in 1991 on regulating foreign banks. By the end of 2007, China had established 60 branch and subsidiary organizations in 29 countries and regions, including the US, Japan, England, Germany, Australia, Singapore, Hong Kong, and Macao. Overseas capital in these institutions came to some US$267.4 billion.

China's Capital Is Moving Outside Its Borders

While capital accounts in China are still not "opened" or RMB is nonconvertible, China is gradually relaxing controls on cross-border financial investments, including allowing foreigners to invest in China's A-shares market. International institutions can invest in Chinese RMB stock market, and China's residents can invest in overseas securities markets. In November 2002, the Chinese government launched a Qualified Foreign Institutional Investor (QFII) program to allow foreign investors access to the country's stock markets. It authorized investment in China's RMB-denominated A-shares market. In May 2003, the Swiss investment bank UBS and the Japanese brokerage Nomura Securities both received permission to enter China's Stock Markets, as the first foreign investors to gain a QFII license. By the end of 2007, 53 foreign financial institutions had obtained QFII licenses, and they had invested US$30 billion into Chinese markets. In March 2005, international institutions were authorized to issue RMB-denominated bonds, and in the same year the World Bank, through the International Finance Corporation, issued the first RMB-denominated bonds in China. In July 2007, China began a test program in allowing Qualified Domestic Institutional Investors (QDII) to invest in overseas stock markets, and by the end of the year, there were 50 such authorized institutions with investments that already came up to some US$35.3 billion.

China 2013

China's per capita GDP doubled between the years 1980 and 2000. According to the Chinese government's plan of 2007, from 2000 to 2020, it is expected to double again. By conservative estimates, this goal will be accomplished ahead of time. In fact, in 2006, China's GDP had already reached RMB21.2 trillion, which translates to US$2.65 trillion. Per capital GDP was RMB16,000 or roughly US$2,000. If China's GDP continues to maintain an average of 8.5% growth in the next five years from 2009 to 2013, then by 2013, China will reach a total GDP of RMB40 trillion or around US$7 trillion. GDP per capita will be more than RMB30,000 or roughly US$5,000. A doubling of per capita GDP will be achieved seven years in advance of the stated goal of 2020. By these projections, within five years, China will indisputably become the second-largest economic entity in the world.

The size of China's economy is impressive, but its ongoing structural evolution is perhaps more important. China is moving forward in changing its method of growing the economy, from the current investment and export-driven model to a more balanced model based on a combination of domestic consumption, investment, and exports. Given government policies, growth of service industries will be promoted, and focus on the development of science and technology will allow China to become a more innovative country. China will continue to put major effort into growing its pension systems. China's middle class will continue to expand and to own more financial assets. The larger economy and the evolution of its structure, the focus on service industries, and on innovations are all intended to allow China's enterprises to move into the world on a greater scale. More Chinese companies will be entering the ranks of the *Fortune 500*, and will actively participate in international markets. Chinese companies will "stride out" onto the international stage in terms of seeking technology, markets, brands, and resources, and will more actively participate in overseas M&As. All of this, however, will require the support of the financial industry. Quite different financial structures and innovations in financial products will be required to meet the new changes.

By 2013, China is expected to be number one in terms of foreign exchange reserves in the world. Reserves are expected to grow in stable fashion to a size of around US$3 trillion. Assets in the Chinese banking industry may reach US$15 trillion. Deposits may reach US$5 trillion. The overall size of China's capital markets will continue to expand as the bond market reaches US$10 trillion and the stock markets reach US$10 trillion. Market structure will continue to improve; market mechanisms are expected to function more efficiently, the soundness of listed companies should improve as competition increases among securities companies. Corporate governance inside companies as well as external restraining mechanisms should improve the climate of business. The structure of investors will become more balanced, the legal environment will improve, and institutions should be better placed to implement regulatory requirements.

China's insurance industry is facing the tremendous opportunities for growth, as insurance markets are reaching a size of US$1 trillion. The increase in personal wealth of Chinese citizens is becoming a long-term driver for the insurance industry. The upgrading of the structure of consumption is also driving demand: as people's standard of living improves, expenditures on health, old age, education, housing, and automobiles rise, bringing commensurate demands for insurance in those areas. As middle-income people in particular become a greater percentage of the population, their need for security and guarantees will rise, and insurance demands will become a major part of modern consumption. Pressure to improve the social security system is growing ever greater: a robust insurance industry is needed to satisfy people's pension and medical needs. In the next five years, the insurance industry will continue to maintain rapid growth.

This presents both opportunities and challenges to China's financial institutions. It presents difficult choices for its investors and its regulators. New products and services are needed. New approaches are necessary. China's financial institutions not only need to innovate themselves, but they need to welcome financial products and services from the rest of the world into the country. Along the same lines, China's capital needs to go out to world markets, to find new investment opportunities, to cooperate with and co-invest in international financial institutions.

These steps will propel the growth of China's financial markets. Reforms in the interest rate and exchange rate markets should speed up; stock and bond markets will become the bellwether in market growth. Financial derivative products based on stocks, bonds, interest rates and exchange rates should develop rapidly. Securitization of assets is becoming more common. When China's financial markets completely embrace global financial markets, China unavoidably will enter into global financial risk, meaning that China's financial institutions must take steps to strengthen their risk management and raise the level of their financial regulation.

The internationalization of China's financial system can only hasten the interlocking global nature of all financial systems. The process will and is already redrawing the map of the world financial system. We are entering an age of extraordinary developments, an age in which Chinese finances and those of the rest of the world are surging together. The speed with which China's financial markets are growing presents enormous challenges and opportunities, not just to China but also to the world. Are we prepared for it? By "we," I mean not only Chinese financial institutions, markets, and regulatory agencies, but also financial institutions, markets, and regulatory agencies throughout the world.

EDITORS-IN-CHIEF

Zhu Min

Zhu Min is group executive vice-president of the Bank of China, responsible for group finance, internal control, legal and compliance, strategy and research. He joined the Bank of China in 1996, and led the group restructuring and the US$15 billion initial public offering (IPO) in 2006, and the Bank of China Hong Kong restructuring and IPO in 2002. Prior to joining the Bank of China, Mr Zhu worked as an economist at the World Bank in Washington, DC, for six years, before which he taught economics at Johns Hopkins University and Fudan University. Mr Zhu received a PhD and an MA in economics from Johns Hopkins University, an MPA from the Woodrow Wilson School of Public and International Affairs of Princeton University, and a BA in economics from Fudan University.

Cai Jinqing

Cai Jinqing is a partner of the Brunswick Group, an international financial communication firm. She advises multinational corporations and Chinese companies on strategic communication issues, as well as on cross-border merger and acquisition (M&A) transactions in the region. Between 1993 and 2002, she worked in New York and Hong Kong in management consulting and venture capital, focusing on China investments. Ms Cai graduated from Wellesley College with a BA in 1991, and obtained her Master of Public Affairs from the Woodrow Wilson School of International and Public Affairs of Princeton University in 1993.

Martha Avery

Martha Avery is president, of Avery Press, Inc., which works with Chinese publishers and individuals in bringing Chinese intellectual property to a Western market. She served as General Manager for

John Wiley in China from 1982 to 1990, following four years in the Commerce Department handling China trade in the 1970s, an MBA at the Wharton School, and a period in Warburg Paribas Becker in Wall Street. She established the Publishing Program for the Soros Foundation in Mongolia, and went on to serve in the Budapest offices of OSI. Throughout her career, Ms Avery has continued to translate Chinese fiction and non-fiction, and to author books. She took her BA in Chinese and Japanese language and literature, with college credits derived primarily from institutions in Taiwan, Hong Kong, and Tokyo in the early 1970s.

AUTHORS

Preface, Introduction, and Overview

Paul Volcker

Paul Volcker served as chairman of the Board of Governors of the US Federal Reserve System. He is former chairman of Wolfensohn & Co., Inc., as well as professor emeritus of international economic policy at Princeton University. Educated at Princeton, Harvard, and the London School of Economics, Mr Volcker spent the earlier stages of his career at the Federal Reserve Bank of New York, Chase Manhattan Bank, and the US Treasury Department. He was recently chairman of the Board of Trustees of the International Accounting Standards Committee and of the Independent Inquiry Committee for the United Nations Oil-for-Food Programme. He was former North American chairman of the Trilateral Commission, and is currently chairman of the Group of 30 in Washington DC.

Zhou Xiaochuan

Zhou Xiaochuan is governor of the People's Bank of China (PBC). He served as chairman of the China Securities Regulatory Commission from February 2000 to December 2002, during which time he earned a reputation for pushing the institutionalization of strict supervision requirements over China's nascent stock markets. Beginning in March 2000, Dr Zhou became a member of the PBC Monetary Policy Commission and was named PBC governor in December 2002. He was appointed governor of the China Construction Bank in 1999, and was director of the State Administration of Foreign Exchange until 1998. Dr Zhou graduated from the Beijing Chemical Engineering

Institute in 1975. He later graduated from Tsinghua University in 1985 with a doctorate in systems engineering. Dr Zhou has published more than 10 books and more than 100 academic articles.

Zhu Min

See above.

SECTION 1: MACRO

Guo Shuqing

Guo Shuqing has been chairman of the Board of Directors of China Construction Bank Corporation since March 2005. Prior to the current position, he successively held the posts of deputy director of the State Planning Commission of China, director general and secretary general of the State Commission for Restructuring the Economic Systems, deputy governor of Guizhou Province, deputy governor of the People's Bank of China, administrator of the State Administration of Foreign Exchange and chairman of the board of Central Huijin Investment Ltd. Mr Guo holds a Bachelor's degree in philosophy from Nankai University, and a Master's and Doctorate degree in law from the Chinese Academy of Social Sciences. He was a visiting fellow at the University of Oxford from 1986 to 1987. Since 1980, he has published many academic research papers and 16 books regarding various economic issues.

Stephen S. Roach

Stephen S. Roach is chairman of Morgan Stanley Asia. Prior to his appointment as Asia Chairman, Mr Roach was Morgan Stanley's chief economist. During his 25-year career as an economist at Morgan Stanley, Mr Roach was widely recognized as one of Wall Street's most influential thought leaders. Before joining Morgan Stanley in 1982, Mr Roach was Vice-President for Economic Analysis for the Morgan Guaranty Trust Company. He also served in a senior capacity on the research staff of the Federal Reserve Board in Washington, DC from 1972–79. Prior to that, he was a research fellow at the Brookings Institution in Washington, DC. Mr Roach holds a PhD in economics from New York University and a Bachelor's degree in economics from the University of Wisconsin.

Li Yang

Li Yang is an academy member and director of the Institute of Finance and Banking at the Chinese Academy of Social Sciences. He was also a member of the Monetary Policy Committee at the PBC. He graduated from Fudan University in 1984, and obtained his doctorate degree in economics from Renmin University in 1989. His research field includes monetary policy, banking, finance, and fiscal policy. Dr Li has published 12 books and about 100 academic papers, several of which have won the highest academic achievement awards in China.

Pieter Bottelier

Pieter Bottelier is an economist and China scholar. He is a senior adjunct professor and has been teaching on China's economy at Johns Hopkins School of Advanced International Studies (SAIS) since he retired from the World Bank (1999). He also taught at Harvard (2001–04) and at Georgetown University (2004), and is senior advisor on China to The Conference Board. He is the author of many articles and book chapters on China's economy. During his World Bank career, he held several key positions, including senior advisor to the Vice-President for East Asia (1997–98), Chief of the Bank's Resident Mission in Beijing (1993–97), and directorships for Latin America and North Africa. Before joining the World Bank in 1970, he taught at the University of Amsterdam, served as advisor to the government of Zambia (1965–70), and as consultant to UNCTAD (Geneva) on non-ferrous metal markets. He studied economics at the University of Amsterdam and at Massachusetts Institute of Technology.

SECTION 2: BANKING

Wang Zhaoxing

Wang Zhaoxing is vice chairman of the China Banking Regulatory Commission (CBRC). He also currently serves as the executive director of China Society for Finance and Banking, the deputy chairman of China International Finance Society, and Member of Corporate Internal Control Practice Committee of Ministry of Finance. Mr Wang has had extensive experience in policy research and banking regulations at the PBC and at the CBRC since the 1990s, including leading major projects such as the Core Principles of Effective Banking Supervision, and the implementation of the Basel New Capital Agreement.

Mr Wang is the author of a number of books and papers on financial subjects. He holds a doctorate degree from Shaanxi University of Finance.

Stephen K. Green

Stephen Green is group chairman, HSBC Holdings plc. Mr Green began his career with the British government's Ministry of Overseas Development. In 1977, he joined McKinsey & Co. Inc. He joined The Hongkong and Shanghai Banking Corporation Limited in 1982, with responsibility for corporate planning activities and, in 1985, he was put in charge of the development of the bank's global treasury operations. In 1992, Mr Green became group treasurer, HSBC Holdings plc. In March 1998, he was appointed to the Board of HSBC Holdings plc as Executive Director, Investment Banking and Markets. He assumed additional responsibility for the Group's corporate banking business in May 2002. He became group chief executive on 1 June 2003 and group chairman on 26 May 2006. Mr Green has degrees from Oxford University and Massachusetts Institute of Technology.

Wang Jianxi

Wang Jianxi is executive vice-president and chief risk officer at China Investment Corporation (CIC). Prior to joining CIC, he was vice-chairman of Central Huijin Investment Ltd, and chairman of China International Capital Corporation, a joint venture investment bank established between China Construction Bank and Morgan Stanley. He had previously served as assistant chairman of China Securities Regulatory Commission, president of Bank of China International (UK), chief financial officer and executive vice-president of Bank of China International, and chief accountant and director general of the International Department under China Securities Regulatory Commission. Dr Wang holds a doctorate degree in accounting.

Nicholas Calcina Howson

Nicholas Calcina Howson is an assistant professor at the University of Michigan Law School in Ann Arbor, Michigan, and was previously a partner at the New York-based international law firm of Paul, Weiss, Rifkind, Wharton & Garrison LLP, where he served as a managing partner of the firm's China Practice based in Beijing. Mr Howson writes and lectures widely on Chinese corporate and securities law topics, and has acted as a consultant to foreign foundations and think tanks, and various Chinese ministries and administrative departments. He has taught Chinese law at Columbia Law School, Harvard Law School, and Cornell Law School. Mr Howson earned his JD from Columbia Law School in 1988 and BA from Williams College in 1983. He was also a graduate fellow at Fudan University in Shanghai, China, working in the field of late Qing Dynasty–early modern Chinese literature.

Jamie Dimon

Jamie Dimon is chairman of the board and chief executive officer (CEO) of JPMorgan Chase & Co. He assumed the title of president upon JPMorgan Chase's merger with Bank One Corporation in July 2004. Mr Dimon was named chairman and CEO of Bank One in 2000. Prior to Bank One, he had held various senior executive positions at Citigroup Inc., its subsidiary Salomon Smith Barney, and its predecessor company, Travelers Group, Inc. Mr Dimon is a graduate of Tufts University and received an MBA from Harvard Business School. He serves on the Board of Directors of a number of nonprofit institutions, including the Federal Reserve Bank of New York, Harvard Business School, and the United Negro College Fund.

Chen Xiwen

Chen Xiwen is deputy director, Office of the Central Leadership Group on Financial and Economic Affairs, and director, Office of the Central Leadership Group on Rural Work. He joined the institute of agricultural economics at Chinese Academy of Social Sciences in 1982. He served concurrently as deputy director of the State Rural Study and Survey Group. Mr Chen was later deputy director of the State Rural Study and Survey Center of the State Council and then served as the Center's director. In 1994, he joined the general office of the central financial and economic leadership group at the State Council. He assumed deputy director responsibilities of the Development Research Center of the State Council in 2000. Mr Chen studied in the Agricultural Economics Department at Renmin University of China.

Hans-Paul Buerkner

Hans-Paul Buerkner has been president and chief executive officer of the Boston Consulting Group (BCG) since 2003. He joined the firm in 1981 and was a member of the teams that opened BCG's Düsseldorf (1982) and Frankfurt (1991) offices. Before becoming the firm's first chief executive officer from Europe, he was head of BCG's global Financial Services practice. During his 25 years at BCG, he has counted among his clients many of the world's leading financial institutions. Dr Buerkner studied economics, business administration, and Chinese, receiving a Diploma from the University of Bochum, an MA from Yale University, and a PhD from the University of Oxford.

Ma Weihua

Ma Weihua has been the president and chief executive officer of the China Merchants Bank Co., Ltd since January 1999. He has been chairman of the board of CMB International Capital Corporation Limited, and of CIGNA and CMC Life Insurance Company Ltd, and China Merchants Fund Management Co., Ltd since September 1999, September 2003, and November 2007 respectively. He previously served at the general office and at the Planning and Funding Department of the PBC from 1990–92, and was governor of the PBC, Hainan Branch, and head of the State Administration of Foreign Exchange, Hainan Branch from 1992 to 1998. Dr Ma earned a doctorate degree in economics in 1999.

SECTION 3: CAPITAL MARKETS

Zhou Qinye

Zhou Qinye is executive vice-president of the Shanghai Stock Exchange. He serves as a member of the Accounting Standards Committee of the Ministry of Finance, China Internal Control Standards Committee, the Auditing Standards Committee of the Chinese Institute of Certified Public Accountants (CICPA), and the Internal Control Instruction Committee of CICPA and as a director of CICPA. He is also a standing director of the Shanghai Accounting Institute and a member of the Shanghai Judiciary Expertise Committee. He serves as an adjunct professor at top Chinese universities. He holds a Master's

Degree in Economics from the Shanghai University of Finance and Economics.

Wang Dongming

Wang Dongming is chairman of CITIC Securities Co., Ltd. He is a board director and assistant president of CITIC Group, board director of CITIC Holdings Ltd, board director of CITIC International Financial Holdings Ltd, board director of CITIC Capital Holdings Ltd, and chairman of CITIC Fund Management Co., Ltd. Mr Wang previously held positions as president of Investment Banking Department of China Securities, executive vice-president of China Southern Securities, and he worked at Scotia McLeode Securities of Canada. His career has been dedicated to developing China's investment banking industry and improving corporate governance in securities companies. Mr Wang graduated from Beijing Foreign Studies University, and later from Georgetown University and University of Southern California.

Kevan Watts

Kevan Watts is president, DSP Merrill Lynch Ltd. and former chairman of Merrill Lynch International Inc. Mr Watts joined Merrill Lynch in 1981 and has worked for the firm in New York, London, Hong Kong, and now Mumbai. He has held a number of senior positions at Merrill Lynch, including co-head of global investment banking, head of investment banking in EMEA, chairman of Asia Pacific, chairman of EMEA, and chairman of International. Mr Watts has been actively involved in Merrill Lynch's business throughout Asia since 1997, focusing particularly on China and India. Before joining Merrill Lynch, he was an official at H M Treasury in the UK, which he joined in 1974 from university. He was educated at Oxford where he was awarded a first-class degree in politics, philosophy and economics, and a postgraduate degree in philosophy.

Qi Bin

Qi Bin is director general of the Research Center, the think tank of the China Securities Regulatory Commission (CSRC). Prior to his current position, Dr Qi was a deputy director of the Fund Supervision Department of CSRC for five years, supervising the mutual fund industry and QFII in Chinese capital markets. He was also a member of its Strategy and Planning Committee since joining CSRC in 2000. Prior to that, Dr Qi was a partner of a New York-based venture capital firm, and also worked with Goldman Sachs Asset Management and Paribas Capital Market in New York and London. Dr Qi holds a PhD in economics from Tsinghua University, an MBA from the University of Chicago, and an MS in Biophysics from the University of Rochester, as well as a BS in physics from Tsinghua University.

Lin Yixiang

Lin Yixiang is president of Tianxiang Investment Consulting Company, which he founded in 2001. He was a senior expert and deputy general director of the Research and Information Department, and the head of the Market Surveillance System of the China Securities Regulatory Commission. He joined China Securities Co., Ltd as a vice-president. Mr Lin is president of the Securities Analysts Associations of China, and vice-president of the Securities Associations of China. Mr Lin holds a PhD in economics from the University of Paris (France). He is an adjunct professor of several of China's top universities.

Fan Yonghong

Fan Yonghong is chairman of the board of Huaxia Fund Management Company, vice-chairman of the Securities Association of China, and standing member of China Society for Finance and Banking. Mr Fan has extensive working experience in commercial banks, securities companies, as well as the fund management industry from the beginning of the industry in China in 1998. Mr Fan takes an active interest in the development of the securities industry in China and was, for many years, one of the commissioners on the Stock-Issuing Committee of the China Securities Regulatory Committee (CSRC). He currently works as an advisor on M&A business to the Department of Listed Company Supervision in CSRC.

John S. Wadsworth Jr.

John S. Wadsworth Jr. is Honorary Chairman of Morgan Stanley Asia and Advisory Director of Morgan Stanley globally. In January of 2001, he retired after nearly 40 years in investment banking, including 15 years with First Boston and 25 years with Morgan Stanley. From 1987, Mr Wadsworth was responsible for creating Morgan Stanley's business in Asia beginning with five years in Tokyo and 10 years in Hong Kong. He is currently co-founder and chairman of Ceyuan Ventures, an early stage venture capital partnership based in Beijing focusing primarily on IT. He earned a BA from Williams College in 1961, and an MBA from the University of Chicago, Graduate School of Business in 1963.

Wu Shangzhi

Wu Shangzhi is chairman of CDH Investment. Prior to founding CDH, he was the head of China International Capital Corporation's (CICC) private equity group from its inception in 1995, a managing director since 1998, and a member of CICC's Management Committee from 2000–02. From 1991 to 1993, he was a senior investment officer at the International Finance Corporation. From 1984 to 1991, he was an operation officer at the World Bank. After leaving the International Financial Corporation/World Bank, Dr Wu returned to China to become a founding partner and managing director at Beijing Copia Consulting Company Ltd. Dr Wu received his PhD in mechanical engineering and MS in management of technology from Massachusetts Institute of Technology.

SECTION 4: INSURANCE
Yuan Li

Yuan Li is assistant chairman of the China Insurance Regulatory Commission. Mr Yuan is deputy chairman of China International Finance Society and has been working in the insurance industry in China since 1984. Mr Yuan holds a doctorate degree.

Yang Chao

Yang Chao is chairman and president of China Life Insurance (Group) Company. He is also Chairman of the Board in China Life Property and Casualty Insurance Company. Mr Yang has nearly 30 years of experience in the insurance and banking industries. Between 2000 and 2005, he was the chairman and the president in both China Insurance (Holdings) Company Limited and China Insurance H.K. (Holding) Company Ltd. Between 1996 and 2000, he was the chairman and the president of CIC Holdings (Europe) Ltd. Between 1976 and 1996, Mr Yang was a director and general manager of the operations department of The People's Insurance Company of China. Mr Yang graduated from Shanghai International Studies University and Middlesex University in the United Kingdom with a Master's degree in business administration.

Wu Yan

Wu Yan is chairman of the People's Insurance Company (Group) of China and honorary chairman, China Insurance Industry Association. He was chief editor of the *China Non-Life Insurance Market Research Report*, and author of numerous papers that were published in leading Chinese economic and policy research journals. Mr Wu holds a doctorate degree.

Jacques Kemp

Jacques Kemp is vice-chairman, ING Insurance & Investment Asia/Pacific. Mr Kemp served as general manager of ING Bank International and as its chairman in the 1990s. He started his career in ING Group in 1974 in the risk management department. He was one of the key executives in building ING's prime position in Latin America in the 1980s. After the merger of and integration with Barings, he became a member of the executive committee responsible for the general banking activities and the international network worldwide. In 2000, he took the position of Global Head e-Business, ING Group. Mr Kemp joined EC A/P in July 2002 and served as CEO between 2003 and May 2008. Jacques graduated from the Higher Economic School in Rotterdam. He holds an MBA degree from the University of Chicago.

Gao Xiqing

Gao Xiqing is the vice-chairman, president, and chief investment officer of China Investment Corporation. Prior to this position, he served as vice-chairman of the National Council for the Social Security Fund. He also worked as vice-chairman at the China Securities Regulatory Commission (CSRC). As a co-founder of the Stock Exchange Executive Council, he was instrumental in the establishment of the

Shanghai and Shenzhen Stock Exchanges in 1990. Mr Gao served as General Counsel and Director, Public Offerings, CSRC from 1992 to 1995. From 1997 to July 1999, he was vice-chairman and CEO of BOC International, the investment banking arm of the Bank of China in Hong Kong. Mr Gao received his BA equivalent in 1978 and a Master of Laws in 1981 from the University of International Business and Economics. He obtained his Juris Doctor from Duke University Law School in 1986. From 1986 to 1988, he practiced law in a major Wall Street law firm before returning to China.

SECTION 5: MONETARY POLICY

Wu Xiaoling

Wu Xiaoling, former deputy governor of the People's Bank of China (PBC), is the vice-chairman of the Financial and Economic Committee of the National People's Congress, the executive vice-chairman of the Finance and Banking Society of China, and the chairman of the Financial Accounting Society of China. Ms Wu started her career at the PBC in 1985 at the Research Institute. In 1994, she was appointed as director general of the PBC's Research Bureau. She was promoted to administrator of the State Administration of Foreign Exchange under the PBC in April 1998. In November 1998, she was appointed as president of the PBC's Shanghai branch. She ranked 18 on Forbes's "100 Most Powerful Women 2007," and was included in the "Top 50 Women to Watch," released by the *Wall Street Journal* on November 8, 2004. She graduated from the Graduate School of the PBC in 1984.

Hu Xiaolian

Hu Xiaolian has been deputy governor, PBC, and administrator of State Administration of Foreign Exchange (SAFE) since 2005. She began her career with SAFE, where she served as deputy director general of the Policy and Regulation Department, director general of the Reserve Management Department. In March 2001, she became deputy administrator of SAFE. She was appointed as assistant governor, PBC, in July 2004. Ms Hu holds a Bachelor degree in philosophy and a Master's degree in economics. She has been deeply involved in the evolution of China's exchange rate regime, foreign exchange market, current account and capital account convertibility, and management of foreign exchange reserves.

Xie Duo

Xie Duo is president of the China Foreign Exchange Trade System. He has extensive experience in macroeconomic research and the policymaking process under Chinese government agencies. From 1996 to 2005, he held positions at various departments in the PBC, including deputy director general of the Statistics Department and deputy director general of the Monetary Policy Department. From 1988 to 1996, he worked at the State Commission for Restructuring the Economic Systems. Mr Xie holds Master's degrees in economics from both Oxford University and Peking University.

Zhu Yuchen

Zhu Yuchen is president of the China Financial Futures Exchange. He was president of Dalian Commodity Exchange, chairman of China Futures Association, and headed several branches of China International Futures Co. Ltd (CIFCO) in Shenzhen, Shanghai, and Beijing. He also worked at China National Cereals Trade Corp, which is a subsidiary of COFCO. Mr Zhu is China's leading expert in the field of financial futures. He is also an adjunct professor at the Strategic Management Institute, Wuhan University, and at the China Agricultural University.

Stephen Green

Stephen Green is head, China Research and senior economist at Standard Chartered Bank and is based in Shanghai. Prior to joining Standard Chartered, Mr Green was head of the Asia Programme at Chatham House (The Royal Institute of International Affairs) in London and deputy editor of *The Economist*. Before that, he worked in rural Kenya and Mozambique in food relief. Mr Green has a PhD from the London School of Economics and Political Science, and a first-class Honours degree from Cambridge University. He has been a visiting researcher at Fudan University in Shanghai and at the Shenzhen Stock Exchange. He speaks Mandarin Chinese and has published a number of books on China.

SECTION 6: SERVICES

Wu Zhipan

Wu Zhipan has been vice-president of Peking University from 2002 to the present. He is director, the Financial Law Institute, and professor of Law, Peking University, from 1993 to the present. He was dean of the Law School from 1996–2001. He was an Eisenhower Foundation Fellow (1997) and a visiting scholar at Harvard University School of Law and Hong Kong Shun Yan College. He earned a doctorate degree in 1988 and an LLB in 1982 from Peking University.

Xiao Wei

Xiao Wei is managing partner, Junhe Law Offices. Mr Xiao specializes in foreign investments, securities, M&As, and general corporate practices. From 1985 to 1989, Mr Xiao practiced law first with Beijing No. 7 Law Firm and then with China Legal Affairs Centre. In 1991, he was a visiting attorney in London and Hong Kong under an exchange program jointly sponsored by the Ministry of Justice of the PRC and the British Council. Mr Xiao earned an LLB from Peking University in 1984 and an LLM in International Economic Law from the Graduate School of the Chinese Academy of Social Science in 1987. He also obtained an LLM in American Corporate and Commercial Law from Columbia University School of Law in 1995.

James Turley

James Turley is chairman and CEO of Ernst & Young since 2001. He joined the firm in 1977 and has since held a series of leadership positions. Based in New York and London, Mr Turley serves as senior advisory partner for many of Ernst & Young's largest global clients. He is actively engaged in enhancing the public's trust in professional services firms and in the quality of financial reporting. He has encouraged dialogue between key stakeholders on issues such as the advent of the Sarbanes-Oxley Act in the US, the introduction of International Financial Reporting Standards, and the convergence of global accounting standards and governance. Mr Turley co-chairs, with the Russian prime minister, the Russia Foreign Investment Advisory Council. He is also a member of the Business Roundtable and Transatlantic Business Dialog, and in October 2007 was appointed Chair for the Governing Board of the US Center for Audit Quality.

Mr Turley holds a Master's and a BA in accounting from Rice University in Houston, Texas.

Xu Shanda

Xu Shanda is the former deputy commissioner and member of the Board of Directors of the State Administration of Taxation (SAT). Mr Xu has long been engaged in research in macroeconomics, banking, finance, and taxation theories. He was successively appointed as deputy division chief, Research Division of the State Tax Bureau under the Ministry of Finance, and director, Research Office of the Research Institute of Taxation Sciences of the State Tax Bureau, among other posts. Mr Xu graduated from the Automatic Control Department of Tsinghua University in 1970, earned a Master of Agricultural Economic Administration degree at the Graduate School of the China Academy of Agricultural Sciences in 1984, and a Master of Arts degree in public finance at the University of Bath in the UK in 1990.

SECTION 1

MACRO

CHAPTER 1

Fundamental Issues and Challenges Facing the Chinese Economy

Guo Shuqing

Chairman, China Construction Bank

China's economy has sustained rapid growth for over 30 years now, which is a remarkable record in the history of the world. Globalization and the revolution in new technologies have helped, by giving China, as well as other developing economies, the chance to develop industrial and information societies in tandem. The significance of this is that what had been regarded as "non-economic variables" in the past are now influencing the course of economic modernization, in addition to traditional economic variables. Later-developing countries have also been able to take advantage of lessons and experiences gained elsewhere in dealing with environmental protection issues. Theoretically, China should be able to avoid repeating most of the mistakes of Western countries in this regard. Actual development in different countries presents great variation, however, no single country can be regarded as wholly ideal. Some have imbalances in a certain respect, others in some other respect. It may well be that China's circumstances are most controversial.

BASIC CHANGES IN CHINA'S ECONOMY SINCE REFORM AND OPENING

Since Reform and Opening began in the late 1970s, China has been experiencing growth in a way that neither resembles our own past nor the experience of foreign countries, but that has absorbed and inherited from both. After adopting the overarching policy of "opening to the outside and enlivening the inside," both government and market in China have served as guiding entities in the process. Rural communities and cities have been mobilized, quantitative and qualitative goals have enjoyed equal standing, and China's economy has industrialized in concert with its development as an "information society." The market has played an important role in this process. It has spurred foreign trade and foreign investment. The importing of advanced technology and management that resulted has had a revolutionary impact. At the same time, we can see the influence of development policies that we espoused in the past; for example, loosening ownership rights and allowing profit, mobilizing the efforts of local regions, raising up large, middle and small enterprises at the same time, merging both native Chinese and foreign elements, allowing villages to engage in industry, and so on.

After more than 10 years of Reform and Opening, the machinery set in motion to reform the Chinese economy was producing real change by the end of the 1980s and the beginning of the 1990s. An economy that had specialized in long-term shortages as a defining feature now specialized in warehouses overstocked with consumer goods and indeed overstocked inventories of all kinds. Imports had exceeded exports for many years; this changed as the balance of trade swung in the other direction. Structural imbalances continued to be the main source of price inflation—for example, bottlenecks of grain, resources, and transportation—but these ceased to be a major cause of alarm in terms of supply and demand of goods. The price indicators of interest rates and exchange rates began to play a role in China's economy in the late 1980s. Even though that role was extremely limited at the time, the effectiveness of policy measures in dealing with two periods of inflation in the latter part of the twentieth century exceeded the expectations of most economists, and savings deposits were able to maintain their value through subsidies.

The qualitative changes, or one could say semi-qualitative changes in economic operations, had a significance that was not trivial. First, they indicated that the traditional planned economy or "command economy" of the country had already gone halfway in its transition toward a market economy. This was called at the time a "commodity-oriented planned economy." Although difficulties remain in realizing a fully transitioned economy, it is now not so far in the distance that it is impossible to hope for. Second, the changes indicated that, in terms of managing the economy, we could no longer rely solely on administrative measures, but instead had to shift to indirect measures to influence economic performance. It became impossible not to change the entire formulation and operating mode of macroeconomic policies in China. Third, taking a gradual, step-by-step approach to moving the economic system from one track to another made it apparent that this approach had both benefits and drawbacks. It is now our task to take advantage of practical experience, to enhance the benefits and eliminate the drawbacks and effect a faster and smoother transition to a market economy.

The achievements of economic growth during this transitional period cannot be denied, but the process also incurred negative consequences. Problems became severe in the mid-1990s when economic contradictions began to sharpen. The causes were multifaceted. First, as the level of industrialization rose in China, ordinary manufactured goods were soon in over-supply and competition became fierce. Not just state-owned enterprises (SOEs) but also town-and-village enterprises began to feel the results. Second was the way in which industrialization took place across the landscape with no regard for environmental factors: the ecological situation worsened as dramatically as people's living conditions. The true costs of economic growth soon became something from which people could no longer avert their gaze. Third, as foreign-invested enterprises continued to increase, not only did this lead to greater foreign trade, but it influenced domestic markets and sectors as well. Fourth, nonperforming loans (NPLs) at China's banks became more unsupportable by the day, and it was increasingly hard to rely on massive loans to finance a rapidly growing economy. Fifth, for a long time, agriculture continued to employ small-scale family-farming operations—it was increasingly hard to reconcile these with modernized industry and markets, leading to volatility and duplication of efforts.

When the ninth Five Year Plan was being researched and formulated, we proposed a so-called "two transformations" policy that was aimed at transforming both the economic system and economic growth mode. The eruption of the Asian Financial Crisis increased the urgency of making strategic changes in the economic system in China. Since that time, the economy has performed extremely well, but the transformation of the growth mode has not been as ideal as we might have hoped.

Starting in 1998, China's economy began to experience an overall surplus on the supply side. It became difficult to sell products, there was an excess of labor, investment funds sat idle, and since inventories of grain were now excessive, for a time even land became a non-scarce resource. All of this happened in a Chinese economy that was sustaining a rapid rate of growth. This was not only unprecedented in China's history, but unique in the history of the world.

All of the above problems could correctly be summarized as having insufficient effective demand. They could also, however, be attributed to the irrational structure of production and thus to having insufficient effective supply. The economy was experiencing duplication in productive efforts and excessive competition at the low-end level, but at the same time, scarcity at the high-end level of value-added products. A key issue was that our manufacturing industries were extremely weak in opening up markets, guiding demand, and creating new products. In addition, they needed to import a relatively high percentage of high-tech equipment. While quantities of products were stuck in inventory, many social services in support of citizens and the society at large were in short supply. Indeed, close analysis shows that virtually all service industries were in short supply. Wholesale and retail industries were far below the quality standards of developed countries; in contrast to those countries, counterfeit and shoddy goods were pervasive throughout China. The phenomenon of producers cheating consumers in all ways could be seen everywhere. Meanwhile, financial services provided to individual citizens were substantially below the level that developed countries had achieved decades earlier. Education, culture, science and technology, healthcare and hygiene, law, accounting and auditing, were even more severely stunted. Without doubt, there was a severe imbalance in allocation of resources.

Since entering the twenty-first century, especially with the entry of China into the World Trade Organization (WTO), China's economy has seen a more profound change. On the one hand, China has entered the global economy on a higher level and broader scale, and begun to play an important role in the international division of labor. The country has thereby become an important stimulus in world economic growth. On the other hand, as market reform has proceeded apace inside China, and as the fundamental nature of market mechanisms has taken hold, it has become evident that there is a greater need to employ macroeconomic management and other economic and legal measures to assure the improvement of the socialist market economic structure. Employing these measures will provide the material basis and foundations of a system that ensures relatively fast growth into the future.

CHINA'S UNIQUE ECONOMIC ISSUES

China's macroeconomic policies are fundamentally different from those of the West for the key reason that we cannot afford to attend only to the short-term economic balance, but must keep our attention focused on mid- and long-term change. In evaluating the course of China's economic development in the future, we must keep in mind unique circumstances that pertain to China, even as, equally important, we make reference to the experience of the rest of the world. On the one hand, this requires looking back over the process of industrialization; and on the other, looking forward to future modes of development.

China should not follow the same sequence of development that countries which have already reached post-industrial mode have followed. This is due primarily to the fact that scientific advances have brought on structural changes in economic activity that allows backward countries to enjoy certain "benefits of being later in development." In theory, China should be able to experience the three stages of development concurrently, or one could say pursue policies that turn it into an industrial and information society at the same time.

In reality, this concept encounters severe challenges. The growth rate of China's service industries has neither surpassed the growth rate of industrialization nor remotely reached the rate existing in other countries some decades or even centuries ago. Even at the most favorable estimation, China's secondary industries occupy something approaching one-half of the country's GDP, while tertiary industries occupy only around 40%. The imbalance of this ratio has unfortunate consequences for income distribution, consumption ratios, growth potential, and environmental protection. There are perhaps two fundamental reasons for this. The first is that urbanization has fallen behind industrialization and the overall economic rate of growth; the second is that universal education remains far below its potential.

China has pursued an unusual course of development over the past 50 years, which is a root cause of the country's current structural issues and delayed urbanization. From the 1950s, when People's Communes were established, industrialization began to extend throughout the country's towns and villages. With the failure of the "Great Leap Forward" in 1958, however, in order to adjust the economy, it was imperative to send large numbers of people to the countryside, and a stringent policy of dividing urban and rural residents was enforced so that the country's economic structure was de facto segmented as well. The industrialization of cities was undertaken to service those cities, while villages were permitted to create their own forms of industrialization. "Commune Troop Enterprises" were already forming in the 1970s. After Reform and Opening began, their commercial activity burst through the dikes and began to surge throughout the country in a positive flood.

The appearance of Town-and-Village Enterprises (TVEs) was fundamental in the structural change of the economic system during China's economic transition. Without this new force, China's economic reform would not have had the same rapid and sustained growth and the mechanisms of a market economy would not have steadily achieved irreversible dominance. Urban economic institutions at the same time would not have played the stable and irreversible role of supporting that change. However, since governmental policies and the entire system followed a dual arrangement, TVEs, together with their resources, were forced to operate outside the urban economic system. They were forced to find their own way. The tremendous blooming of such enterprises led to industrial entities being widely dispersed in terms of spatial distribution. In the early 1990s, roughly 87% of TVEs were located in rural communities, and even today only around 30% have entered towns and cities and commercial parks. One consequence is that the market for service industries has lagged behind. This phenomenon of overly dispersed industrialization presents negative consequences for long-term sustained development and for a balanced domestic structure. Such consequences have become more pronounced in the past decade. In addition to ongoing problems over many years of NPLs in the banking sector, and waste of capital investment in recent years, a heavy price has been paid in terms of resources, environment, and people's quality of life.

THE AGRICULTURAL SECTOR

The importance of agriculture in the economy of any country is a given. China's urbanization issues are similar to those long ago encountered by all industrialized countries. These include what are known as the three "agricultural issues" facing all levels of government in China: the agricultural industry itself, people engaged in agriculture and the condition of rural areas in general. In order to manage an appropriate scale of agriculture, turn farming into a profession, guarantee services, and transfer high technology, one vital precondition is the essential mobility of the farming population.

Unfortunately, there are fundamental constraints on this essential mobility in China. We have an extremely complex employment structure. A person engaged in farming is often also a construction worker on a seasonal basis, he or she might also be a part-time salesperson, or work in a restaurant or perhaps in an abattoir. Division of labor in both farming and in towns and villages is an extremely slow process and this situation of multiple extra jobs and mixed-employment will necessarily persist for a long time. It is one reason both agriculture and rural areas stagnated after the 1980s in China. Another complexity arises from the fact that many farming areas with highly developed enterprises have in fact gradually become cities. This has happened even as the farming population of other areas moved into existing cities to work and do business.

People who have moved into cities have not been absorbed by them on a long-term basis, however. They are still labeled with the somewhat pejorative term "peasant workers." Meanwhile, towns and villages that have long since become de facto cities and that are dominated by non-farming commercial activities are still, in policy terms, being administered as "rural areas." The legal status of the inhabitants of these places is different from the status of people in cities; this is seen most clearly in terms of employment, public services, and social benefits. In recent years, recognition of de facto urbanization has been increasing in the policy sphere, but awaits clarification in terms of actual strategy. Appropriate laws and regulations need to be formulated and there is an urgent need to address issues arising from the spontaneous urbanization of China.

INDUSTRIAL STRUCTURE

From the early 1990s, severe structural imbalances were apparent in China's industrial and manufacturing sectors. Basic industries were stagnating behind value-added industries, an imbalance that was gradually addressed after price and tax reforms. By the early twenty-first century, people even began to be concerned about whether or not there had been an excessive shift to making industries more "heavy." A second imbalance related to the slow pace of upgrading value-added industries: the manufacturing chain was too short and overly concentrated on the low-end, with insufficient value-added. A third was that industry was overly concentrated along the coastal areas: the regional distribution that could be seen in other industrialized countries was hard to find in China and in fact the opposite tendency was the rule, the so-called "peacock flies to the south and east" phenomenon. The latter two issues have been tied together in remorseless fashion for a long time. It was only in the past couple of years that we have seen any change for the better.

China's strategy of developing its western regions began to be implemented in 1999. After this came proposals to revitalize the old industries of the northeast, as well as to "lift up" the central regions. The central government hoped to reduce regional disparities, and positive change was in fact made in the course of implementing these proposals, such as improvements in basic infrastructure. Real upgrading of industries fell far short of expectations, however. It became apparent that market forces were going to be insufficient in turning the situation around. The problems were structural as well as policy related. Certain so-called "special treatment policies" effectively distorted the parameters of the market, slowing down marketization. Such special treatment ranged from the way land was priced, to wages, to preferential treatment in taxation and exchange rates.

Recognizing these problems, and resolving them, is fundamental in order to propel economic growth and create a harmonious society. There are many obstacles. Some people fear that industries along the coast will be "hollowed out," others fear that the direct investment of foreign companies will be affected. Even more importantly, many people fear the consequences of loss of jobs. In fact, it is precisely in order to expand employment that we should hasten structural adjustments in industries. China has a vast territory and after upgrading the structure of industries along the coast, new high-tech and new service industries will create new employment opportunities. The central and western regions can grow from new starting points as industries are transferred to those regions; their own employment will improve and there will be an increase in overall employment nationwide. Moreover, as the structure of employment changes in line with market demands, we will see an improvement in regional economic balance. The ongoing movement of population to the south and eastern coastal regions will slow down, and only when that happens will the overloading of certain super-metropolises begin to be alleviated.

LABOR MARKET ISSUES

Long-term segmentation of the labor market has been a fundamental reason for China's irrational economic structure. Many Chinese economists, and even a considerable number of foreign economists, feel that China's economic advantage lies in the stagnation of wage levels and lack of employment security. This is not wholly without reason, but the evidence for the argument is not what it appears to be.

The first argument relates to the so-called primitive accumulation theory. It indiscriminately applies to China a situation that existed during the Industrial Revolution or after the Second World War, when economies took off in certain countries. It emphasizes the extreme scarcity of capital, a situation as different as night and day from today's China, which, for a number of years, has had net capital outflows. The second relates to the so-called theory of unlimited labor supply. This contradicts the most basic principle of economics. All resources are limited, labor resources even more so, with a balance of supply and demand derived from pricing. The third is the so-called theory of elasticity in the labor market. It segments labor into urban and village, local and that which has come in from elsewhere, fixed and temporary. Different compensation for the same labor can only increase friction and business risk, however, and can only lower efficiency. This kind of "elasticity" is absolutely not what is needed to spur economic vitality.

Fourth is the idea that such segmentation is beneficial to fluid mobility between urban and rural areas. In fact, this assumes that municipalities and government bear no responsibility for what happens in economic downturns, when workers who have come in from outside lose their jobs. The assumption is that they voluntarily simply go away again. This idea fails to recognize that urbanization is an irreversible phenomenon of modernization. Fifth is the idea of preserving competitiveness by keeping labor cheap. In fact, modern economic competitiveness relies on advanced technology, product innovation, and increases in productivity. Basing market advantage on cheap labor over a long period will simply lead to a declining economy and failure. Sixth is the concept that one must protect and preserve the farmers, for not doing so will shake the foundations of agriculture in the country. This theory holds that if wages of "peasants" coming into the cities are higher than wages of those who remain at home, the agricultural situation will deteriorate.

There are plenty of other high-sounding theories. We cannot fail to raise a most simple question. China's economy grew by 1.38 times in the decade after 1995, and yet the wages of countless hundreds of millions of farmers did not increase at all. Who was consuming all the newly produced products? Without taking into consideration ethics or social conscience, and temporarily not discussing the purpose and social value of production, looking only at the economic cycle itself, we have to ask: can this situation persist, can it be viewed as normal? One thing worth celebrating is that since 2005, we have finally seen some improvement in the situation.

Intimately tied to the question of the labor market is the question of reform of the social security system—to a large degree, this will determine the stability and sustainability of a new economic system. China faces two challenges in such fundamental social security areas as the elderly, healthcare, and the unemployed. One challenge is similar to that other countries face in financing a system that pays out today with money that is currently being received and that will be hard to sustain into the future. The second is that many hundreds of millions of workers and their families have not been absorbed into any kind of social security system at all in China. China doesn't face the burdens of some countries with already existing high benefit costs, due to fast economic development and the fact that its population is relatively young. Relatively speaking, therefore, China's social security problems are more easily resolved.

What must first be done in China is to set up a way of accumulating savings for a social security plan. We are not able to repeat Europe's system of a "large rice bowl," but at the same time we cannot have freely operating dispersed funds as a partial solution. Second, we must have an open system that incorporates both farmers who have entered cities and those who have not, that does not discriminate between the two. The question immediately arises, "Where is all the money going to come from?" Who will provide the funding needed for all those middle-aged and old people who never saved up for the future, not to mention the farmers? One could entertain the idea of "one stone hits three birds." First, a certain allocation of national resources and the income from state-owned land could be earmarked for a social security fund. An "accumulated-in-advance fund" could thereby begin to function immediately. The amount for each person could be calculated down to the year and the month, without need to set up some kind of transition process for the elderly, middle-aged, and the young. State-owned industries could immediately be turned into entities "with an absentee owner," and market mechanisms could then be allowed to adjust the ownership of their assets in a more stable and convenient manner. The urbanization of agricultural populations could carry on in a stable fashion, avoiding the way in which all levels of government have been diverting land to other uses for income, also avoiding the way in which the existing subsidies to farmers have been squandered.

HUMAN RESOURCES

China has traditionally held education and culture in high regard. For a long time now, however, people have been focused on making a living and have not been very keen to discuss these other things. Indeed, there are currently some strange attitudes with regard to education in our society. Some people appear to feel that economics and technology create value, while education and culture simply consume resources. For example, "Education is in the category called 'consumption.' If we make economic development our core focus, that means we must first put production in order—that is, focus on making money—for only then can we begin to talk about spending money." In fact, as the research of many international organizations and scholars shows, returns from an investment in education are higher than from any other form of investment. This holds whether you are looking at a nation overall or individual households. Another strange thing that people are saying: "The proposed nine years of mandatory education in China is out of touch with reality. It is simply a pipe dream to think that China can afford the expenditure required to reach world standards." In fact, when the main countries in Europe instituted mandatory education, the average income of people at the time was not much higher than it is in China today. When newly industrialized countries in Asia implemented mandatory basic education, their economic level was in general lower than ours was in the 1980s. Relative to its economic level, China's education has in fact long since fallen behind.

The issue with regard to culture has elicited even sharper statements. Ten years ago, raising the subject of the economic significance of "culture" made it hard for some people to sleep at night. After years of promoting a renewal in science and technology, however, we see the term "creative industries" coming into vogue. For some hundreds and even thousands of years, the concept of "culture" embodied value; like science and technology, it determined the value of goods and services. In an age when you had to knot strings to keep track of accounts, and to paint pictures to narrate events, culture and science and technology were in fact inseparable.

STRATEGIC MEASURES

For China's economy to grow in a balanced and harmonious way means that it must comply with the laws of economic society. Measures taken in compliance with such economic laws must help revise the structural imbalances in China's productive industries. The proper adjustment of macroeconomic policies must speed up economic reform and the process of opening to the outside. One can propose five items as strategic starting points in this process.

First, allow the market to play a more complete role in adjusting China's economic structure. Without wavering in our resolve, we must allow the pricing of product inputs to become more rational. That is, we must eliminate distortions in the system that affect interest rates, rents, tax rates, exchange rates, and wages. Based on our policy goals of "unification, opening up, competition, orderliness," we must bring all the defects and inadequacies in each realm out into the open, implement measures to resolve the inadequacies, and make it clear which departments are responsible for doing so. We must put in order relevant policies and regulations, continue to deal with all kinds of corruption and "fees" or bribe-taking, focus on issues that go against principles of fair competition and that allow preferential treatment to interfere with actual costs of production and actual income. We want to punish behavior that adds to the cost of market transactions, and put a stop to administrative pressures that lower factor prices. We must be fully aware of the market characteristics of different kinds of products and different kinds of factors, and formulate and implement appropriate measures. For example, coal and electric power are both products, but the market attributes of these two differ greatly. Adopting a sweeping blanket system to deal with them does not work and we cannot continue to operate as usual, thinking that it does. In terms of service industries, we must pay particular attention to the fact that many have a public interest and a business at the same time. The market for many is often half-market half-public interest or even fully public interest. Education, scientific research, culture, public health, physical fitness, and so on, share this dual nature, although there are distinctions among them. An important but difficult part of allowing market mechanisms to play a greater role in allocating resources will be drawing up and implementing appropriate measures that recognize the unique character of public interest sectors.

Second, have the government fulfill its own responsibilities in the public sector. The function of government has already been clarified as lying in four main areas: making economic adjustments, providing market regulation, social administration, and public welfare. The so-called economic adjustment area, in terms of a market economy, means indirect actions taken with regard to the economy, specifically, macroeconomic measures. Because of this, the function should increasingly be concentrated in the hands of the central government.

Regional governments should retire from this arena, for it is hard to avoid market distortions and administrative interference if they do not. Market regulation involves both central and local responsibilities, and requires that regional governments also play a role. The dynamics of market regulation in particular are sorely in need of strengthening. Further work has to be done with regard to carving out and assigning responsibilities, but the direction of the task is already fairly clear. In contrast, it is quite unclear who is to be made responsible for social administration and public welfare. First of all, an adequate supply of the most basic public goods has not been secured. Mandatory education is one example. There is a great disparity of this public good between cities and local regions. The same applies to public health, public security, the administration of justice, and basic cultural and physical facilities. Second, there are many gaps in what we call social administration. The "work unit" was traditionally the entity for this responsibility in China. It has gradually dissolved but new organizational structures have not evolved to take over its functions. Third, ways in which the government operates cannot be transformed quickly. Government previously relied on an administrative fiat, on red-letter documents, on meetings, and so on to put its decisions into effect; these are increasingly costly and have diminishing results. Autonomous organizations that were to play a greater role in such things, as well as semi-governmental and non-governmental organizations, have in fact not born fruit. Some organizations that existed long ago, such as trade unions and the Women's Association, have become heavily bureaucratized and are facing the formidable task of transforming their own thinking and modes of operation.

Third, allow farmers to move into cities and towns in a stable and orderly fashion. Concentration in cities and towns is a necessary trend in a developing economic society. It can neither be suppressed nor can it be made to leap forward. It is not impossible that we will see the urbanization rate in China rise at an annual average of 2% for quite a while. The critical issues arise as people move into cities and encounter problems. Policies should be adopted that are encouraging to them, that are receptive and that help merge differing populations. People moving into cities need guarantees with regard to education, training, and employment rights, including wages, housing, and social security. All organizations in China should apply equal-treatment policies to workers coming into cities, including schools; factories; the Party; the government; and the Labor, Youth, and Women's organizations. We must stop defining the status of these people as "peasant workers." We must promote policies that create a unified employment market, that provide the underlying conditions for both farmers and non-farmers to find jobs. The labor unions of all institutions and at all levels should take people coming from villages into their organizations, and assure that they have fair and equal treatment in terms of wages, benefits, and citizen's rights. Housing problems should receive particular attention, as well as primary education, and there must be a planned, staged process for incorporating such people into the scope of public policies. We must establish social security for all employees working in cities and towns. Those farmers whose land has been requisitioned and who have therefore moved into urban areas must absolutely, by regulation, be provided with basic pensions and health insurance. We must establish land funds, in order to provide services for farmers in such situations.

Fourth, establish closer ties between the disparate regions of coastal zones and the interior. This is a strategic issue that will in fact determine China's economic future. We must strengthen the relationships and cooperation between regions, using methods that are in accord with market rules and going through market mechanisms. This goal is absolutely achievable if we proceed through orderly markets for financing, land, and labor. Industries in the eastern region must be elevated to a higher level and some basic industries, and those employing high-density labor should be transferred to the interior. Along the coastal region, the most important thing is to make market relationships function on the basis of a real market, to eliminate "low price selling," restrict over-production, and encourage an increase in quality. We must go further in implementing the plan to open up and develop the western regions, as well as to revitalize the northeast and other places with antiquated industrial infrastructure. We must support the ability of the central region to absorb the transfer of production from the east, by forming integrated industrial structures that complement each other and that allow for technology and human talent transfer to the west as well. We should use foreign-investment policies to address the inequality among regions. We must put an end to the fact that investors from eastern parts of the country are able to obtain land, investment, and labor resources at lower-than-market prices. We must deepen the process of land reform, and promote market competition for land that is not going to be used for agricultural purposes. We must deepen the process of fiscal and financial reform in order to improve the funding environment of the western regions.

Fifth, allow China's domestic economy to merge with that of the outside world in a more rational way. Adjusting and resolving imbalances in our national economy will benefit not only China, but also the rest of the world. Given the presumption of mutual benefit, we can only develop in connection with the outside world. In the realms of investment and trade, we must promote policies that treat Chinese citizens in a proper fashion, gradually phasing out the preferential treatment of foreign businesses. In the international market arenas of food, energy resources, raw materials, finished goods, finance, and foreign exchange, we must form stable and cooperative supply-and-demand relationships based on harmonization of interests and mutual trust. We must implement mutual prosperity, with a responsible attitude, looking to long-term benefits for both sides. Fair and reasonable handling of trade frictions requires appropriate handling of economic-benefit contradictions and issues. We must address practical and feasible protection of the rights of investors. We must speed up implementation of the strategy of "going out" into the world, actively participating in bilateral and multilateral investment and trade agreements. We must strengthen relations with international financial institutions, develop multilateral cooperation, and still in all ways protect and preserve our own national economic security.

CHAPTER 2

China's Global Challenge

Stephen S. Roach
Chairman, Morgan Stanley Asia

China has rewritten both the theory and history of economic development. In just 30 years, the world's most populous nation has gone from the brink of economic collapse to the cusp of a newfound prosperity. Driven by the "opening up" of a state-owned system, bold reforms have spawned an increasingly market-based economy. The results are nothing short of extraordinary. Following nearly three decades of 9.5% average growth in real GDP, per capita income in China now exceeds US$2,000—up more than five-fold since the early 1990s. For a vast nation of 1.3 billion citizens, such an explosive increase in aggregate living standards is all the more astonishing.

China owes much of its remarkable success to an outward-looking development model—heavily dependent on foreign trade and on concomitant increases in investments in infrastructure and industrialization that support its all-powerful export platform. Fortunately, for China, its commitment to such an externally led strain of economic growth coincided with the flourishing of a new era of globalization. This serendipitous combination has left China in the enviable position as perhaps the greatest beneficiary of modern-day globalization.

With those benefits, of course, also come risks and responsibilities. China now faces plenty of both as it peers into the immediate future. The export-led growth model needs rebalancing. The Chinese leadership is the first to admit that it now needs greater focus on the development of autonomous support from internal demand—especially private consumption. The export-led growth model also leaves China overly exposed to cyclical developments in the global economy. After riding a wave of nearly five years of the strongest growth in global activity since the early 1970s, there is now good reason for China to worry about a US-led slowing in world GDP growth. China's export-led development model has also put the world's most populous nation in the cross-hairs of a worrisome anti-globalization backlash. As a responsible global citizen, China must now address those concerns head-on. All in all, as the most open development model in modern history, China now faces a daunting global challenge.

CHINA'S OUTWARD TILT

Export-led growth models have long been the mainstay of economic development. Yet China has taken this approach to an entirely new level, as can be seen in Figure 2.1, China's share of world trade has risen nearly eight-fold since its economic take-off in 1982, according to estimates by the International Monetary Fund (IMF). This is well in excess of the norm experienced by other Asian economies over comparable periods of their economic development. Closest to China are the so-called NIEs—Asia's newly industrialized economies of Korea, Taiwan, Hong Kong, and Singapore. For this group as a whole—which includes two tiny city-states—their share of world trade share increased five-fold in the first 25 years after their collective economic take-off. While that's an impressive performance, it pales in comparison to that experienced by China. For the rapidly growing

FIGURE 2.1   Globalization's greatest beneficiary

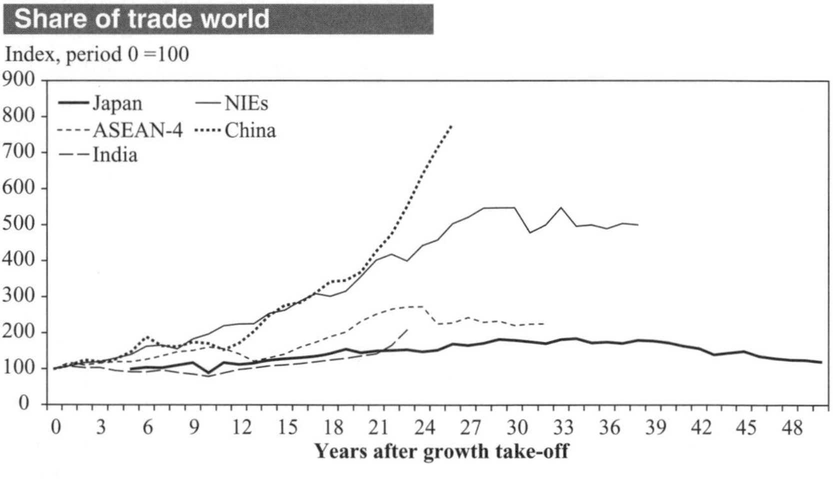

Share of trade world

Index, period 0 =100

Source: IMF.

ASEAN-4—Indonesia, Malaysia, the Philippines, and Thailand—world trade shares were up only a little more than two-fold over a comparable 25-year time period.

The comparison with Japan—Asia's largest and long most dominant economy—is particularly impressive. Dating Japan's post-Second World War take-off in 1955, the Japanese share of world trade rose only 1.7 times in the ensuing 25 years, or only about 20% the gain experienced by China in a comparable quarter century interval after its take-off. Long known for its trading prowess, Japan's external push pales in comparison to that of China. The same is the case with respect to India, whose world trade share has only doubled since its take-off in 1990. Asia has, by far, enjoyed the most outward-looking, trade-oriented strain of development in modern history. Yet China stands out from the rest of Asia by a wide margin.

There has been an especially dramatic increase in China's outward tilt since 2000. China's share of world trade has basically doubled in that relatively short period of time. For China, this accelerated push in its outward focus came at just the right time. It coincided with an especially powerful wave of world GDP growth, with the 5.5% average global growth pace over the 2003–07 period the strongest five-year interval since the early 1970s. For an externally driven Chinese economy, this was the functional equivalent of "manna from heaven"—a sharply increased share of world trade coming at precisely the time when the global growth dynamic was experiencing its most powerful acceleration in a generation. For that reason alone, China could well be the greatest beneficiary of the modern wave of globalization.

UNSTABLE, UNBALANCED, UNCOORDINATED, AND UNSUSTAINABLE

There is nothing wrong with externally led economic growth—provided, of course, that it eventually gives way to support from internal demand. This may well underscore China's greatest macro challenge—the need to realign the composition of its macro structure. That was best stated by Premier Wen Jiabao at the conclusion of the last National People's Congress on March 16, 2007. While extolling the strength of China's overall GDP growth and employment record, Premier Wen was quite emphatic in warning of the problems that were building beneath the surface. In his words, the Chinese economy was increasingly "unstable, unbalanced, uncoordinated, and unsustainable." In my view, Premier Wen's prognosis offers a frank and important assessment of the stresses and strains bearing down on China's macro structure. The resolution of such tensions could well be decisive in shaping the course of the Chinese economy over the next several years.

What did Premier Wen mean when he cited the elements above as key challenges for China? With respect to *imbalances*, I suspect he was referring to a lopsided macro structure, with China currently having nearly 80% of its GDP comprised of exports and fixed investment, and only about 36% of its output directed at private consumption (see Figure 2.2). Of course, this doesn't mean that private consumption isn't growing in China. To the contrary, this segment of the economy has been expanding at nearly a 9% average annual rate in real terms over the past five years. But this rate of growth pales in comparison to the more rapidly expanding export and investment sectors. By our calculations, the combined contribution of exports and investment to overall GDP growth in China is still running at more than four times the magnitude of the private consumption contribution. This speaks of a Chinese economy whose growth dynamic remains predominantly focused on the supply side—with production supported largely by exports and investment in export-oriented activity. As the unusually depressed consumption share indicates, China is very deficient in drawing support from the internal demand side of its macro equation. A continuation of these trends would lead to a massive imbalance between aggregate supply and demand—a deflationary outcome for any economy.

Wen Jiabao's warning of an *unstable* economy pertains especially to China's excess consumption of natural resources and energy. Over the past five to six years, our calculations suggest that China has accounted for around 50% of the cumulative growth in the global consumption of base metals and oil—roughly 10 times its 5.5% share of world GDP. At the same time, China is a very inefficient user of oil. While its oil intensity per unit of GDP has been reduced sharply since the late 1970s, it still has an oil efficiency quotient that is double that for the world as a whole. In the eleventh Five Year Plan, China was explicit in targeting a 20% reduction in its oil-per-unit of GDP ratio. While that goal was not met in 2006, the record in 2007 was much closer to hitting the planned target. The longer China fosters excess demand for natural resources, the higher the prices of these commodities. That boosts production costs and squeezes profit margins—making it exceedingly difficult to fathom how China can afford to stay the course.

FIGURE 2.2 China: beneath the surface

"Unstable, unbalanced, uncoordinated, and unsustainable."
—Premier Wen Jiabao, March 16, 2007

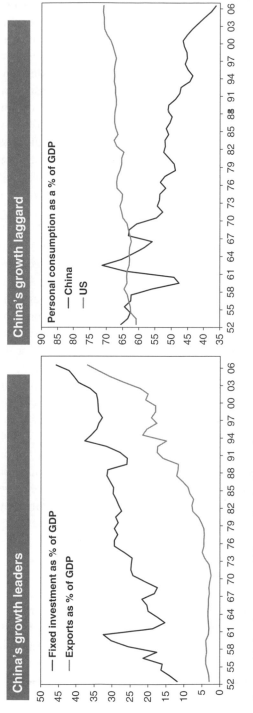

Sources: National sources and Morgan Stanley Research.

Premier Wen also underscored his concerns over an *uncoordinated* system, driven by a regional fragmentation of economic and financial activity that is very difficult to control by central economic policies. One key repercussion of this tendency is the relative inefficient character of Chinese fixed investment. Due to its development imperatives of urbanization, industrialization, and infrastructure, China is certainly justified in running a high-investment economy. But when compared with the Japanese experience of the 1960s—when post-Second World War reconstruction saw Japan with quite similar investment motives—China stands out for its excess investment. During that earlier period, Japanese GDP growth actually exceeded that recorded by China for all but one year. Yet at no point in the 1960s did the Japanese investment share climb above 34%. By contrast, in China, that share is now nearing 50%. Dominated by the credit intermediation of a still highly fragmented banking system, the investment inefficiencies of an uncoordinated Chinese economy risk a serious misallocation of resources.

Finally, Wen Jiabao was particularly emphatic in voicing fears over the potentially lethal and *unsustainable* combination of pollution and environmental degradation (see Figure 2.3). Climate change is obviously a major issue for the world as a whole. Yet there remains sharp disagreement between the developed and developing economies as to how the burden for the remediation of environmental damage should be shared. However, China is now sending a signal that it has now reached the point of moving on this front for its own good, and with good reason. Seven of the 10 most polluted cities in the world are in China, while Chinese water pollution has gapped out well above that elsewhere. Meanwhile, China is on a path to become the world's leading emitter of greenhouse emissions in a relatively short period of time. This is not sustainable for China—or for the planet. By owning up to this problem, Premier Wen is giving a new and important focus to the quality of Chinese economic growth.

The "four uns" should not be viewed as immediate threats of pending disaster. They are, instead, important by-products of China's unique strain of externally oriented economic development. In the parlance of economics, the open-ended investment and industrialization that has been required of China's export-led growth dynamic has now spawned a number of negative "externalities." Equally disconcerting are cyclical pressures of an overheated Chinese economy as manifested in the forms of an accelerating CPI-based inflation (see Figure 2.4 on page 26), as well as by a torrid rate of asset inflation,

FIGURE 2.3 China: unsustainable

Environmental degradation

Air pollution
(SO₂ mcg per cubic meter)

1.	Guiyang, China	**424**
2.	Chongqing, China	**340**
3.	Taiyuan, China	**211**
4.	Tehran, Iran	209
5.	Zibo, China	**198**
6.	Quingdao, China	**190**
7.	Jihan, China	**132**
8.	Rio de Janeiro, Brazil	129
9.	Istanbul, Turkey	120
10.	Anshow, China	**115**

Emissions of organic water pollutants
(kg per day, millions)

1.	China	**6.09**
2.	US	1.81
3.	India	1.52
4.	Russia	1.39
5.	Japan	1.18
6.	Germany	0.97
7.	Indonesia	0.73
8.	France	0.56
9.	Italy	0.49
10.	Ukraine	0.45

Source: World Bank.

Annual CO₂ emissions

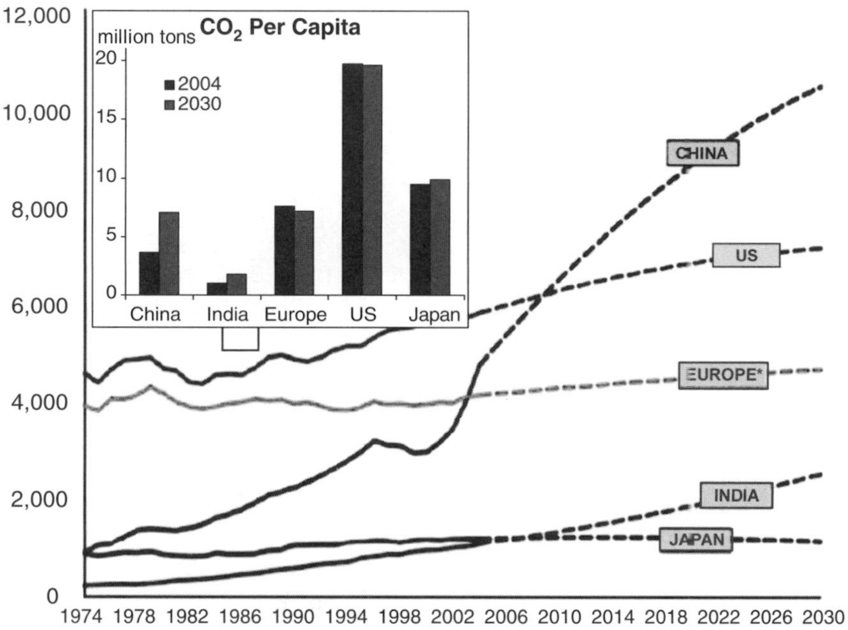

million tons

CHINA
US
EUROPE*
INDIA
JAPAN

12,000
10,000
8,000
6,000
4,000
2,000
0

1974 1978 1982 1986 1990 1994 1998 2002 2006 2010 2014 2018 2022 2026 2030

CO₂ Per Capita

million tons

■ 2004
■ 2030

20
15
10
5
0

China India Europe US Japan

Sources: EIU, IEA, and China Strategic Advisory.

FIGURE 2.4   China: overheating risks

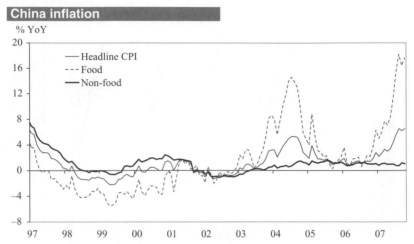

Sources: CEIC and Morgan Stanley Research.

especially equities (see Figure 2.5). Driven predominantly by retail investors, the recent surge in equity prices is especially disconcerting. Should the Chinese stock market plunge—hardly idle conjecture for the Shanghai A-shares, which are still up five-fold from levels prevailing two and a half years ago—the risk of social instability

FIGURE 2.5   China: speculative excesses

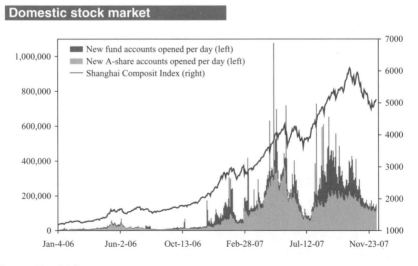

Source: Wind Info.

cannot be minimized. For China, this has long been the deepest worry of all.

All this points to a Chinese economy that can no longer afford to stay the same course of the past 30 years. The good news is that the Chinese leadership is focused on addressing these problems. Coping with the "four uns" is very much a key focus of the eleventh Five Year Plan enacted nearly two years ago. The annual Central Economic Work Conference held in late 2007 left little doubt of an administrative tightening in bank lending policy that was aimed at dealing with the inflationary risks of overheating—both with respect to CPI inflation as well as asset inflation. But the jury is out on whether these policies are sufficient for the tasks at hand. Owning problems are one thing. Having the will and the determination to solve them are different matters altogether.

If I have learned one thing in these 10 years of steadfast bullishness of the Chinese economy, it is never to underestimate the Chinese leadership with respect to the will and determination of their problem-solving initiatives. I remain very much in that camp today. But there are no guarantees that the tasks ahead for Chinese policymakers will be easy. In fact, there is good reason to believe that the challenges for this externally focused economy are going to be especially tough in the years immediately ahead.

POLICY TRACTION IN A BLENDED ECONOMY

Today's Chinese economy is very much a blended system—trapped in the middle ground between state and private ownership. While some 800 state-owned enterprises (SOEs) have had their shares listed in public markets in the past 10 years, the government still maintains majority ownership in most of these newly constituted companies. In China, privatization is more of a "corporatization." At the same time, capital market reforms have lagged, leaving banks as the dominant force in driving overall credit intermediation. Moreover, the banking system, itself, remains highly fragmented, with considerable autonomy exhibited by vast networks of local and regional branches. All this tends to compromise the efficacy of Beijing's central government policymakers. The ancient Chinese proverb puts it best: "The mountains are high and the Emperor is so far away."

Price signals also reflect the blended character of the Chinese economy. Administrative controls limit price fluctuations of energy and utilities. Of course, the currency remains tightly managed as well. While interest rates are set by the central bank, this is not a politically independent organization. While China has all the trappings of traditional macro stabilization policies—monetary, fiscal, and currency—they are far from fully functioning in this blended economy. As a result, the most effective tools of the Chinese policy arsenal remain in the hands of the modern-day equivalent of the old central planners—the National Development and Reform Commission (NDRC). The latest monetary tightening campaign is a case in point. The People's Bank of China (PBC) has boosted interest rates five times and reserve requirements 10 times this year. Yet bank lending and monetary expansion remain excessive by any standards. So the NDRC has now been empowered to slow bank lending growth with administrative constraints on the quantity of credit—a far cry from the time-honored approach of market-based systems that rely mainly on the price mechanism (that is, interest rates) to do the job.

Finally, there is also a strong perception—both inside and outside of China—that the nation's macro policy stance is heavily conditioned by an event-driven mindset. For 2008, that pertains to the Beijing Olympics and the upcoming leadership rotation. For the 2010, there is the Shanghai Expo to consider. Conventional wisdom has it that the Chinese leadership wouldn't dare disturb these events with a policy-induced macro slowdown. The sooner Chinese authorities dispel these antiquated perceptions, the greater the chances that its policymakers achieve the credibility required for macro traction. The recently announced monetary tightening may well be an important development in China's policy credibility campaign—provided the authorities stay the course.

The lack of market-based policy traction makes it exceedingly difficult for the "invisible hand" to foster an efficient allocation of China's resources. That leaves China still very much beholden to the wisdom of its bureaucrats and the guidelines of its five-year plans. This has not been a problem in the nearly 30 years of spectacular development. But that may not be the case going forward—especially if China is to come to grips with the types of problems that Premier Wen Jiabao has highlighted in the form of the "four uns." Yet at some point, China will have to let go and put greater trust in market-based signals. Until that happens, mid-course corrections could well be increasingly difficult to execute. This remains a potential pitfall for a still blended Chinese economy and its "incomplete" financial system—leaving it far more exposed to macro shocks than otherwise might be the case. That may be an especially serious problem as an externally oriented Chinese economy now faces an increasingly challenging global climate.

THE DOUBLE-EDGED SWORD

What globalization giveth, it can also taketh. This is true of the global business cycle. It is also true of the world's collective commitment to the architecture of globalization. No economy has benefited more than China from increasingly unencumbered cross-border flows of trade, capital, information, and labor. And, now, those tailwinds could well turn into headwinds. For China, the double-edged sword of globalization is both its greatest opportunity as well as its most vexing challenge.

The upside of the global business cycle has smiled very kindly on China in recent years. With world GDP growth surging at a 5.5% average pace over the 2003–07 period, China's increasingly powerful export machine couldn't have asked for more. Chinese export growth averaged 30% over that same five-year interval—nearly four times the 8% average gains in world trade for the world as a whole.

But now the smile of the global business cycle is about to turn into a frown. A US-led global downshift is very much in the cards, as the US feels the full force of a bursting of its enormous property bubble. The so-called subprime crisis is but one symptom of this post-bubble shakeout. But it is not the endgame. The biggest risk is the staying power of the US consumer. Courtesy of ever-rising home prices, in conjunction with easy and relatively costless access to home equity borrowing programs, US consumers had turned into asset-dependent spending machines over the past six years. Net equity extraction from residential property holdings rose from 3% to nearly 9% of disposable personal income over the 2000–05 period—more than sufficient to offset a seemingly chronic shortfall of labor income generation.

In an income-short, asset-dependent era, the US's macro support was turned inside out. The income-based personal saving rate plunged and the overall US net domestic saving rate fell to a record low of just 1.4% of national income over the 2003–07 period. Lacking in income-based saving, the US has had to import surplus saving in order to keep growing—and run massive current account and trade deficits in order to attract the foreign capital. Consequently, not only were asset-dependent consumers over-extended when the housing bubble burst, but the US had also gotten itself into a serious and equally unsustainable international financing deficit.

That movie is about to run in reverse. With the income-short US consumer now losing support from the housing bubble—not only being affected by a rare decline in nationwide house prices, but also by a subprime contagion that crimps home equity borrowing—consumption support to the aggregate economy is likely to turn negative. With personal consumption expenditures currently accounting for a record 72% of real GDP, as the housing bubble now bursts, it will be very difficult for a housing-dependent US economy to avoid outright recession in 2008. The silver lining of this outcome is a likely narrowing of the US current account deficit. As consumers prune spending in order to rebuild income-based saving rates in a post-housing bubble climate, the US will be able to reduce its demand for saving from abroad—an important and long-awaited step on the road to global rebalancing.

Alas, the rest of the world, including China, must pay a price for this rebalancing—sharply diminished support from the US consumer and economy. While many are enamored of the possibility of a "global decoupling"—a classic rosy scenario whereby the world is mirac- ulously shielded from a US downshift—such an outcome is highly unlikely in an increasingly globalized world. This is especially the case for an externally led Chinese economy. Lacking in autonomous support from internal demand—with China's domestic private con- sumption only about 36% of GDP in 2006—the external shock of a US recession will most certainly put downward pressure on a tor- rid Chinese growth rate. With exports nearly 40% of Chinese GDP and fully 21% of them going to the US, it is hard to imagine other- wise. For export-led China—the greatest beneficiary of globalization, which draws heavy export support from end-market demand in the US—there can be no decoupling from the US. This is especially likely as its recession now shifts from homebuilding activity—the US's least global sector—to personal consumption, the US's most global sector.

BACKSLIDING ON GLOBALIZATION

Equally disconcerting for an externally oriented Chinese economy are growing signs of a backlash against globalization. That has shown up most acutely in the form of an increasingly protectionist US Congress. Over the past year, at least 18 separate legislative actions have been introduced on Capitol Hill aimed at imposing some type of trade sanc- tions on China. Unlike previous years, two of these measures actually have passed the key Senate Finance and Banking Committees—both by overwhelming bipartisan majorities. The subprime crisis seems to have diverted congressional attention away from this line of attack. That limits the likelihood of imminent action. But if I am right and the US slips into recession in 2008, unemployment will rise—putting even more pressure on the protectionist "remedy" in a highly charged presidential election year.

In the meantime, a weaker dollar has only increased the decibel level of the protectionist drumbeat. Since the onset of the subprime crisis last August, a broad trade-weighted index of the dollar has fallen about 6% in real terms (through November 2007), bringing the cumulative depreciation to 23% since February 2002. With the Chinese currency still tightly aligned with the dollar, Washington politicians haven't exactly gotten the RMB break they were looking for. Moreover, with the dollar's latest downleg especially severe against the euro, European politicians have now jumped on the RMB-appreciation bandwagon. China, the greatest beneficiary of globalization, is now facing an increasingly broad-based assault by US and European politicians alike.

However misplaced, the political backlash against globalization has not occurred in a vacuum. Over the last 10 years, the rich countries of the developed world have experienced a dramatic and disturbing deterioration in their income distribution. For G7-type economies, the labor share of national income is at a record low, whereas the share accruing to the owners of capital in the form of corporate profits is at a record high. This problem is particularly vexing in the US, where more than a decade of surging productivity growth has been accompanied by near stagnation in real hourly compensation for the median worker. This is a sharp contradiction of one of the basic premises of economics—that workers are ultimately paid their just reward in accordance with their marginal productivity contribution.

The resulting middle class angst, in the context of a massive US trade deficit whose largest bilateral piece is with China, has triggered an outbreak of China bashing that might only get worse if the US now slips into recession as I suspect. As I found in testifying three times in front of the US Congress in early 2007, it does little good to argue against this temptation on either theoretical or empirical terms. The politics of scapegoating has taken Washington by storm. The anti-China voices in Europe are now getting louder as well. Unfortunately, China—the greatest beneficiary of globalization—is now bearing the brunt of a major geopolitical backlash.

ONLY A CYCLE

It is important to put these developments in perspective. The world is hardly coming to an end. At work are the time-honored forces of the business cycle. All cycles are different, and it may well be that this one is tougher than the shallow downturns of the recent past—especially since it entails a major round of deleveraging and a rare but significant pullback of the US consumer, long the dominant engine on the demand side of the global economy. But it is still only a cycle—one that eventually finds a bottom and then sets the stage for the recovery that invariably follows.

However painful, cyclical adjustments are also an opportunity. In this case, there are important opportunities for China, the US, and the broader global economy. For China, recent and prospective developments in its external markets underscore the imperative of shifting its growth impetus to private consumption. With the all-important US piece of China's external demand equation about to soften, the need for an offset from internal consumer demand is all the more important. China cannot count on instant gratification on this front. Lacking a safety net—namely, well-developed programs that offer nationwide security of pensions, social security, unemployment insurance, and medical care—Chinese households are likely to remain very focused on "precautionary saving." But to the extent that China's leadership responds to a shortfall in external demand by accelerating the construction of a safety net, the transition to a consumer-led economy could well occur sooner rather than later.

For the US, there is an equally important opportunity to break the vicious and increasingly destabilizing strain of asset-dependent growth. With each successive asset bubble, the daisy chain of leverage and the excesses of asset-led growth have become far too precarious. The US has an opportunity to return to income-based spending and saving—thereby lowering its massive and increasingly destabilizing current account deficit. In doing so, the US can also put a floor under the dollar—tempering one of the most destabilizing forces in world financial markets. As such, this cycle is also an important opportunity for global rebalancing—a reduction of the tensions that have opened up between the world's current account deficit and surplus nations.

No one wants a cyclical downturn. That is especially the case in China, where recessions have long been the ultimate threat for a leadership that is desperate to maintain social stability. The good news is that China has an enormous growth cushion heading into a likely downshift in the global business cycle. Even if its GDP growth rate slows from 11% to around 8% on a worst-case basis in the face of a US demand shock, that would hardly be a disaster. The bad news would be if China—or the US, for that matter—were to dig in its heels and squander the opportunity for rebalancing that arises when the business cycle turns.

I am hopeful that China will seize the moment and stay focused on reforms, especially those that provide support for a long-needed strain of consumer-led growth. Time and again over the past 30 years, China has taken advantage of cyclical downturns to get its macro house in order. I suspect this will be another one of those times. As the world's greatest beneficiary of globalization, an externally oriented Chinese economy now has no choice other than to face its global challenges head-on.

CHAPTER 3

China's High Savings, Investment, and Growth Rates, and Arguments for the Rapid Development of Financial Markets

Li Yang

Director, Institute of Finance and Banking,
Chinese Academy of Sciences

China must develop financial institutions and products that allow for diversified, long-term, sources of funding. Stock markets with greater depth to them, bond markets, pension funds, all are needed to gain direct financing for China's growth, as opposed to indirect financing via banks. This chapter makes the case for urgent action, based on an analysis of economic factors.

Since 1978, the indicator in China's economy that reflects investment has stayed relatively high and maintained a gradually rising trend (see Figure 3.1 on page 36). China's economic growth and fluctuations in growth have been closely linked to the growth and fluctuations in this investment indicator. The GDP growth rate and investment rate were in close step in the 1980s; since the 1990s, they have shown an ever more closely aligned synchronization. Since the end of 2002, when the current economic cycle began, the concurrent rise in investment and growth has been the dominant reason for overheating in parts of the economy. Logical macroeconomic measures ostensibly would involve suppressing investment in certain sectors and certain regions of the country, in order to stabilize economic growth and control price levels.

The situation is not so easy. Although discussions continue to be rampant in theoretical circles about what to do, and many

FIGURE 3.1 China's savings and investment rates

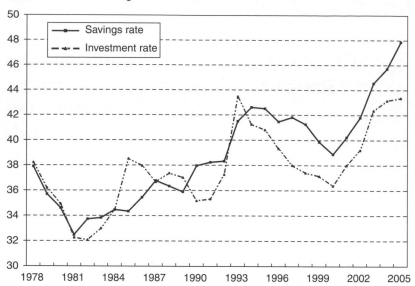

"prescriptions" to deal with sustained high investment have been written, the thorny problem is that investment has shown no fundamental signs of slowing down while the corresponding domestic consumption rate has continued to decline. For a phenomenon to persist for 20 years, and even to become more and more pronounced, indicates some kind of internal rationale. We cannot simply attribute China's high savings and high investment to some kind of short-term irrational factor. It is time to look more closely at the economic mechanisms at play behind the scenes.

THE CHINESE ECONOMY SINCE REFORM AND OPENING

The Chinese economy continues to exhibit a high investment rate and an even higher savings rate. Savings, investment, and the relationship between them form a core part of the functioning of macroeconomics. In analyzing a high investment rate and its overall effect on the national economy, one must look at the other side of the coin as well: the state of savings. The relationship can be clarified by using the basic equation of national income. It is simplest to look first at the situation of a closed economy. In a market economy, where demand determines economic growth, national production [Y] can simply be broken down into the two main components of consumption [C] and investment [I]. $Y = C + I$, which can also be stated as the equivalency of savings and investment, $S = I$.

If investment is greater than savings, a so-called "savings gap" appears, signifying that a portion of investment is not supported by domestic resources and that the economy faces the threat of inflation. If investment is less than savings, a so-called "investment gap" appears in which domestic resources are not fully utilized and the economy comes under the pressure of deflation, or economic contraction.

In an open economy, a domestic savings or investment gap can be balanced by taking in foreign savings or foreign investment; namely, $Y = C + I + (X - M)$. The equivalency expresses the fact that the difference between domestic savings and investment is equal to foreign demand: $S - I = X - M$.

When savings and investment are not equivalent or when imports and exports are not equivalent, either can be seen as an imbalance in a national economy. Internal imbalance indicates domestic savings and investment out of balance; correspondingly, external imbalance indicates long-term imbalance between imports and exports. In an open economy, internal and external imbalances correspond to each other; in other words, the difference between imports and exports is a balancing factor participating in the normal functioning of a country's macro-economy. When a country's savings are greater than its investment, the net sum of exports (accompanied by a net increase in foreign exchange reserves or by capital outflows) can allow a country to have balanced growth without deflation. When investment is greater than savings, the net sum of imports (accompanied by decrease in foreign exchange reserves or capital inflows) allows a country to have balanced growth without inflation.

China's economy has been in a long-term state of both internal and external imbalance. The year 1989 can be regarded as a dividing line in the years since Reform and Opening, in delineating two major periods of internal and external imbalances. The first period lasted from 1978 to 1989. During this time, the prevailing situation was investment greater than savings, except for the years 1982 and 1983. This conformed to the classic model of a developing economy: as a developing country, a lack of resources or "savings gap" was China's main problem. Importing foreign resources, which resulted in trade deficits, was China's route to spurring fast growth. The second period was from 1989 to now. During this time, savings exceeded investment with the exception of the year 1993. In other words, even though the investment rate was unbelievably high, it was not sufficiently high to absorb all domestic savings. It was therefore necessary to take in a portion of external or foreign demand; that is, net exports, in order to supplement or fill in the domestic investment gap. If net exports were not sufficiently large to absorb the overly abundant domestic savings, then the country would still experience deflation. China's economic imbalances in the last fifteen or so years have stemmed from high investment. Their underlying cause, however, can more fully be attributed to the inability of investment to absorb domestic savings. Because of this, long-term high investment not only has not led to inflationary pressures but, on the contrary, the specter of deflation keeps showing its head.

In a globalizing economic situation, the operations of any one country's economy must be placed in context with other economies. Since the global economy is theoretically always in balance, the imbalances of one country or a number of countries will lead to corresponding imbalances among other countries. In light of this, the analysis of one country's economic imbalance requires a new and more complex global perspective. In the second half of 2005, the IMF completed a major research project regarding global economic imbalances. This study concluded that the global economy is in a perilously imbalanced state. Concrete manifestations of this include the following. Among the major economies of the world, the US and Europe continue to exhibit long-term deficits in current accounts, with savings being smaller than investment. Virtually all other countries have long-term situations of savings greater than investment, and hence a long-term positive balance in current accounts. Since the end of the twentieth century, net savings in China, Japan, and other Asian countries have supplemented or filled in insufficient savings in the US, propping up US domestic demand and economic growth. America, the richest nation on earth, has become the world's largest debtor and importer of capital. China, a relatively backward, developing nation, has constantly exported capital and at the same time accumulated large quantities of "creditors' rights;" that is, ownership of US debt.

The so-called global economic imbalance is manifested in an imbalance in current accounts among countries. In a deeper sense, however, it points to an imbalance in savings and investment among the world's countries. The underlying source of imbalance in savings and investment is an overall imbalance in the national economies of countries themselves.

Theoretically, such an imbalance is the natural state of affairs. The world proceeds in balanced growth by each part supplying what the other needs. People are quite alarmed at the current ongoing imbalance, however, and the reason is fairly clear. Developing countries are showing long-term positive trade balances while developed countries are showing trade deficits; as a result, developing countries are "subsidizing" developed countries in material goods, as well as exporting capital to them. The repercussions of this are "unnatural" in terms of a balanced relationship; the rationality has to be questioned and the sustainability is doubtful. The moment the tenuous nature of this cycle is broken, the globe faces the potential for economic crisis.

DEMOGRAPHICS

In China, high investment and concurrent high savings are in large part the result of changes in demographics. Over the short term, the savings rate is mainly a function of money-market rates, and the investment rate is mainly a function of the return on capital. Over the long term, however, the level of savings is determined by demographics, while the investment rate relies on the correlation between return on capital and long-term interest rates.

The phenomenon of concurrent high savings and high investment is intimately tied to what in China is known as the "population bonus." A population bonus results from changes in age structure. In the decades after a baby boom, the percentage of people reaching labor-force age increases while the percentage of children and old people, both of whom must be supported, decreases. If the labor force can be constructively employed in the course of this change, then the total percentage of labor participants goes up. This spurs an increased savings rate for at least two reasons. First, as the percentage of people working rises, overall income rises and this lifts the level of savings. The second is that the relative increase in the number of young people working leads to a declining trend in consumption of the overall population and an increase in the trend of savings. If investment can be increased in corresponding fashion then the result is high-paced economic growth. The three "highs" resulting from demographic changes—high savings, high investment, and high growth—are known as the "population bonus."

Since 1949, China's population experienced two baby booms (see Figures 3.2 and 3.3 on page 40). One was in the 1960s, when the natural increase in population was maintained at a 20% to 30% level. Another was in the 1980s after the start of Reform and Opening, when

FIGURE 3.2   Population: birth and death rates, and natural increase, 1949–2004

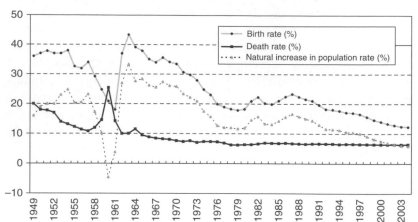

the natural rate of population increase was maintained at around 15%. Baby boomers born in the 1960s are now between the ages of 35 and 45. Not only is this cohort the main component of the "labor force" during the current period of Reform and Opening, but, as work is stable and children grow into adulthood, the consumption rate of this cohort in comparative terms declines, making this population segment the main "savers" of China. By the same reasoning, the baby boomers of the 1980s will be China's main productive force and also main savers in the next 10 to 20 years.

FIGURE 3.3   Change in demographic structure, showing declining percentage in the 15–64 age bracket and increase in the over-65 age bracket

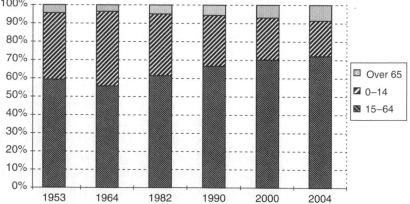

The two baby booms, but particularly that of the 1960s, propelled a change in China's demographics. According to census figures over the years and also the results of the random sampling of 1% of the population done in 2004, we can see that, starting in the 1960s, the number of employable people in the population (aged 15 to 64) rose gradually until, in 2004, employable people constituted 72% of the population.

Age demographics that are making the country overall more youthful are, in China, leading to the population bonus of the three "highs." While the ratio of employable people in the population rises, in China the percentage of people actually employed in this age group has stayed at around 98%. The percentage of participants in the labor force basically matches the changes in China's demographics. When Reform and Opening began in China in 1979, the percentage of people participating in the labor force stood at just 42% of total population. By 2004, that figure had risen to 58% of total population. From the trend lines (see Figure 3.4), we can see that the rates of savings and investment are consistently rising in step with the percentage of participants in the labor force.

According to predictions made by Cai Fang of the *China Population and Development Research Center*, the high percentage of people at an age to be in the labor force in China will persist until the year 2010. After 2020, under the impetus of an overall decline in the absolute number of people in the labor force, the percentage of those in the age range 15 to 64 will begin to go down. In other words, China's high savings rate will continue to be supported by the demographics for

FIGURE 3.4 Percentage of China's population in the labor force 1979–2003, with savings and capital formation rates

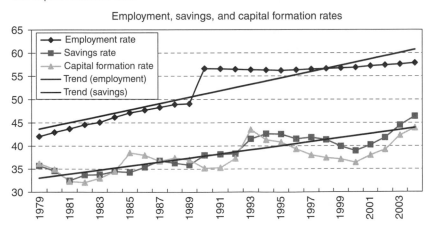

Employment, savings, and capital formation rates

the next five to 15 years, after which it will gradually decline. High savings, high investment, and high growth should continue to coexist in China for five to 15 years. If we cannot maintain high investment during this period to fully utilize the high savings, and thereby promote fast but stable economic growth, we may not have the opportunity after that.

INDUSTRIALIZATION AND URBANIZATION

High investment and concurrent high savings in China are closely related to industrialization and urbanization. Changes in demographics are only one of the preconditions for simultaneously high savings, investment, and economic growth, as seen in the experience of other countries. Another precondition is the employability of the labor force, especially in non-agricultural sectors where the value-added component is higher. Since labor productivity in non-agricultural sectors is higher, work in such sectors leads to marked increase in income, which again draws savings rates upwards. At the same time, as labor transitions from agricultural to non-agricultural industries, in China this reduces the excessive population in the agricultural sector and may result in higher incomes for those who stay in agriculture as well. Increasing income in the overall population must result in an increase in savings. This forms a positive cycle: increase in non-agricultural employment, increase in income, increase in savings, increase in investment, non-agricultural employment goes up yet further, and so on.

In short, the increase in the percentage of those employed in non-agricultural sectors is closely tied to industrialization. If demographic change is the sufficient condition for the population bonus, then industrialization is the necessary condition. This implies that the population bonus relies on the deepening of industrialization.

The increase in the percentage of those employed in non-agricultural sectors is not only closely tied to industrialization, but also manifested in fast growth in urbanization. In fact, the cause and effect of industrialization and urbanization make them inseparable parts of the same phenomenon. One clear feature of the difference between cities and towns is the density of people. The reason people are able to concentrate in cities—a reason that is a propelling force in urbanization—is division of labor and a "deepening" or increase in exchange activity. In both theory and practice, division of labor and exchange are early factors, as well as ongoing factors, spurring economic growth. As compared to the trading centers and feudal cities prior to the Industrial Revolution, cities after industrialization greatly expanded in size and function for two main reasons. First, industrialization allowed factories to develop with the advantage of economies of scale. Second, industrialization enabled the mutual stimulation between one factory and another, one industry and another. In turn, urbanization greatly propelled the development of industrialization as the scope of markets in intermediary goods and consumer goods expanded.

Put simply, high savings and high investment are common in the process of industrialization and accompanying urbanization. And, turned around, high savings and high investment create the necessary conditions for a country's industrialization and urbanization.

INDUSTRIALIZATION, URBANIZATION, AND SYSTEMIC REFORM

As a developing country, China's savings and investment are in sync with its urbanization and industrialization. At the same time, as a country changing from one economic system to another, structural reforms in the economic model have strongly impacted savings and investment. The two cardinal features in China's reforms called "emerging" and "transitional" have determined and will continue to determine the status of savings and investment.

(1) The Influence of Industrialization

China's model for industrialization before Reform and Opening was radically different from the model espoused after those reforms began. Before Reform and Opening, a planned economy system and an impulse to emphasize heavy industry without regard to objective economic laws constrained China's normal industrialization process. After Reform and Opening, a market economy system was gradually established and the process of industrialization began to follow objective laws and move forward with greater ease.

The number of people employed in the non-agricultural sector has gradually risen as a percentage of all those employed (see Figure 3.5 on page 44), which is a clear indicator of industrialization after Reform and Opening. Using non-agricultural employment as an indicator of "industrialization," we can divide China's industrialization after 1978 into three stages. The first was from 1978 to 1990. Under the impetus of economic reforms in rural areas,

FIGURE 3.5 Comparison of China's non-agricultural employment (left axis) and savings and capital formation rates (right axis)

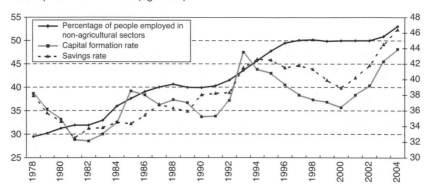

industrialization developed broadly with the main beneficiary being light industry. The second stage was from 1991 to 2000. The main propelling force in this period was the reform of the state-owned economic system, as well as "Opening" to outside investment. Export-oriented processing industries and manufacturing in general developed rapidly as a result. The third period has been since 2001. During these recent years, all of China's policies relating to Reform and Opening have deepened considerably and, in terms of industries, the clear trend has been heavy industrialization. Along with industrialization, the trend in savings and investment rates has been upward overall, in the midst of minor fluctuations.

During the first period from 1978 to 1990, average savings and investments rates were, respectively, 35.26% and 35.69%. In the second period, from 1991 to 2000, those rates were 40.65% and 38.64%. In the third period, after 2001, the rates went even higher to 43.23% and 40.85%.

Even as these rates were going up in tandem with industrialization, they also rose and fell in cyclical fashion with a certain periodicity. Industrialization has a mutual cause and effect relationship with high savings and high investment, so periodic fluctuations in the two rates closely mimic fluctuations of the process of industrialization. Let's turn now to the ratio of the non-agricultural employed, the indicator of "industrialization." Figure 3.6 compares the annual changes in this ratio to annual changes in the savings and investment rates. Periodic fluctuations in the savings and investment rates bear a close resemblance to the periodic fluctuations in non-agricultural employment. Whether it is in absolute levels or in their fluctuations,

FIGURE 3.6   Changes in percentage of non-agricultural labor force (solid line), with savings and capital formation rates, 1979–2004

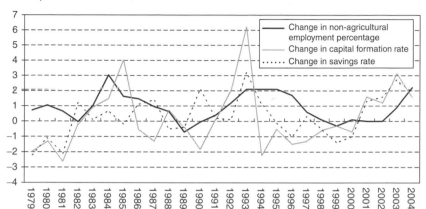

the savings and investment rates bear an intimate relationship to industrialization.

It is clear that China's industrializing will be continuing for quite some time. Savings and investment rates will therefore also be sustained at high levels as well. In 2004, China reached a per capita GDP of a little over US$1,000 (using the exchange rate at that time), and was already entering the so-called "middle period of industrialization." The GDP structure of primary, secondary, and tertiary industries was 15:53:32, which put the economy in a maturing period of industrialization; the employment structure in these industries was 49:22:29—that is, the early period of industrialization. The rate of urbanization including towns was 41.8%, denoting an "early" transitioning to the "middle" period of industrialization. Summarizing the above four indicators, we can generally conclude that China's industrialization is in the middle stage. If this determination is accurate, the conclusion is that industrialization, high savings and high investment will continue for some years.

At different stages of per capita production—that is, at different stages of industrialization—key industries exhibit differences in the course of development, as shown in other developing countries. China is currently in a stage of fast industrialization and the main thrust of its industrial development is in basic industries and construction. China's future economic growth will be led by these sectors, all of which are capital intensive. Their growth clearly requires the support of even higher levels of savings and investment.

(2) The Role of Urbanization

In concert with industrialization, China's degree of urbanization rose swiftly after the start of Reform and Opening. In 1964, the urban-based population constituted less than 20% of the total population. In 1984, it was over 20% and by 1990, it had reached 30%. In 2000, the urban population was approaching 40%. From the change in distribution of non-agricultural employment, we can clearly see the advance of urbanization in China. In 1978, less than 24% of all employed people were employed in cities. In 2004, that figure had risen to 35%. Like the three stages of industrialization noted above, the percentage of urban employed also progressed in stages. The first was from 1978 to 1990, when it took 12 years for the percentage of urban employed to increase by three percentage points. In the 10 years from 1991 to 2000, the percentage of urban employed rose by five percentage points, from 27% of total employed to over 32%. The third stage started in 2001. In the four years from 2001 to 2004, the percentage of urban employed rose another three points, showing a clear acceleration. Forecasting on into the future, the percentage of urban employed will rise to around 43% by the year 2010.

The increase in the urban population and urban employed is a key factor in the increase in savings and investment rates. Urban employed are concentrated in secondary and tertiary sectors that enjoy higher income, and increases in income necessarily lead to increases in savings. Figure 3.7 shows that the trends of urbanization and increasing savings and investment rates are in alignment.

The process of urbanization not only directly pushes savings and investment upwards, but indirectly leads to greater investment by upgrading people's consumption habits. The impact of per capita income in China exceeding US$1,000 is tremendous, for it also signifies a fundamental change in the consumption structure of the Chinese. Despite the undisputed phenomenon of unfair income distribution in China, and the ongoing problem of poverty in the country, more and more urban inhabitants are now able to purchase housing and an automobile, more have leisure time and are able to travel. Starting in the mid-1990s, an expansion of consumer credit became one of the primary thrusts of adjustments in the financial structure. This effectively eliminated budgetary constraints that kept people from buying such major purchases as housing. It enabled people to "smooth out" their lifelong expected income, and pay now for major consumer items with anticipated future earnings.

FIGURE 3.7 Percentage of labor force in urban areas, with high investment and high savings rate trend lines, 1978–2004

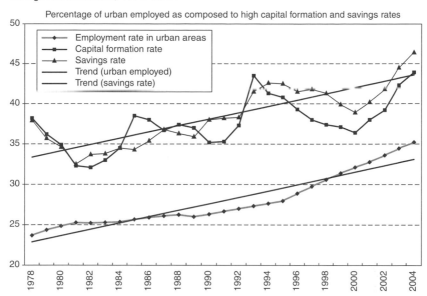

Percentage of urban employed as composed to high capital formation and savings rates

At the end of 2004, the percentage of consumer loans to total new loans of commercial banks exceeded 25% for the first time. Meanwhile, loans for real estate development have constituted more than 10% of all new loans ever since 1998. These statistics indicate significant financial support for the upgrading of consumer demand to a new "third level." Naturally, all the new consumer demand puts greater demands on basic infrastructure, municipal systems, transport and housing, which in turn put extreme pressure on the long-term sustainable supply of such resources as coal, electricity, and gas.

(3) Marketization Reforms

In addition to industrialization and urbanization as major factors in elevating savings and investment, ongoing marketization reforms have played a major role.

Marketization reforms were of course the basis for enabling the process of urbanization and industrialization in China, and so were a prerequisite for high savings and investment rates. A direct result of the reforms was to shift primary investment from state-owned entities to diversified bodies. This shift meant that the mechanisms of a market economy could gradually begin to play a dominant role in the allocation of investment. This not only greatly stimulated increase in investment, but improved the efficiency of investment. A diversification of investment entities was the fundamental systemic factor enabling China's industrialization, urbanization, and even high savings and investment rates.

It is interesting to note, however, that the percentage of people employed in the state sector is far lower than the ongoing investment in this sector. In 2004, the percentage of people employed in the state-owned economy was 9%, whereas the percentage of investment in this sector was 35%. This inconsistency reflects the fact that state-owned investment is mainly concentrated in capital-intensive heavy industries including the chemicals industry.

As marketization reforms proceed, social benefits formerly applied to people in what traditionally were planned economy entities have gradually diminished to the point of being eliminated altogether. Demand for benefits and social services has been marketized. This means that people must save up in order to have the capacity to pay for these services. Under the planned economy system, employment benefits such as housing and social security were all part of one entity; now, marketization reforms are creating heightened uncertainties in the working population about the future. This in turn reinforces the need to save for future contingencies. On the supply side, as planned economy mechanisms were supplanted by market economy mechanisms, this naturally stimulated investment. The rise in factor prices began to reflect the true market price of items that previously had been gratis to people. As reforms proceeded, however, since market mechanisms were still less than perfect, prices were often pumped up even higher, to distorted levels. This has led to tremendous increases in supply-side costs, and to the necessity for commensurate investment.

The impact of these secondary consequences of marketization reforms is being felt in such areas as health costs, education, and social security. It is particularly felt in housing, an issue that is much debated today.

ECONOMIC IMBALANCES

Summarizing the above analysis, we can see that high savings, high investment, and high economic growth rates are necessary consequences of the mutually reinforcing factors of China's demographic changes, industrialization, and urbanization. Since the relatively high percentage of the population participating in the labor force is going to continue for some time, given the age-bracket structure, and since urbanization and industrialization form the foundation for China's economic growth, it is necessary to recognize that the three "highs" (investment, savings, and growth) will persist in China for a long time to come.

One might think that these three "highs," coupled with a relatively low inflation rate, are an ideal state for ongoing growth. Unfortunately, this does not mean that China's economy is perfect. On the contrary, potential problems make it very hard for economists to rest easy. A tremendous amount of research has been done in recent years both inside and outside China with regard to these problems. Some people denounce the high investment rate, others doubt the wisdom of a long-term positive balance of trade, and still others worry about distortions in the economic structure.

We feel that all of these analyses have their merits but don't go far enough. The really difficult problem is that, on a long-term basis, China's savings rate is higher than its investment rate. Numerous problems stem from this, ranging from high investment to high positive balance of trade to related issues. The disparity in these two rates causes China's economy to be imbalanced both internally and externally over a long time frame. Ongoing internal imbalances force us to rely on high investment to support economic growth; external imbalances (positive balance or surplus in current accounts) lead to ever-increasing trade frictions, cross-border capital flows, build-up of large amounts of foreign-exchange reserves, and daily increasing pressures on exchange rate adjustments. The complexity of the problem is exacerbated by the fact that, realistically, there is not much that can be done about it. An overly high savings rate, as noted above, is the result of a combination of intractable problems including demographic structure, industrialization, urbanization, and economic reform. The problems are brought on by both systemic factors and practical economic factors. Moreover, China's domestic economic imbalance is fundamentally an expression of global economic imbalances. Realistically, starting out with adjustments to China's domestic economic structures will not contribute that much to the overall situation.

One urgent thing that must be resolved, however, and that we feel can at least be ameliorated, is the unfortunate consequences of sustained high investment. In a modern market economy, turning savings into investment relies mainly on the intermediary function of the financial system. Economic imbalances brought on by having long-term savings higher than long-term investment are intimately connected to deficiencies in China's financial system. We feel that a financial system that relies primarily on indirect financing by banks is not only a cause of long-term savings being higher than long-term investment, but a main reason for extreme volatility. The great range of volatility, moreover, enhances the recurring problem of nonperforming loans (NPLs) and threatens financial stability.

Two things should be noted in this regard. First, in terms of operations, the total volume of bank loans is naturally cyclical. It exaggerates the economic trend at any given time. When the economy is booming, the strong inducement to invest in real entities that are making money means that loans increase and banking contributes to a general overheating trend. When the economy is contracting, bank loans pull back in the same fashion, overshooting and contributing to an economic decline.

Second, under China's circumstances of "opening to the outside," a system that mainly uses indirect bank financing can lead to currency "mismatch" and thereby influence exchange rate policy and international balance of payments. A currency mismatch means that when an economic entity (an enterprise, inhabitants of the country, a government), engages in international exchange, changes in the exchange rate will influence their balance sheets since assets/liabilities and income/payment use different currencies in reckoning price. Historically, most developing countries' foreign currency assets have been smaller than their foreign currency liabilities, leading to risk exposure of devaluation of their currencies. China's situation is the opposite. Its foreign currency assets are greater than its foreign currency liabilities, so the risk exposure of China's currency mismatch is in an appreciation of the RMB. Appreciation can lead to foreign exchange assets shrinking as figured in our local currency.

Other countries in the world have been working hard since the 1980s to increase the proportion of direct financing via securities in their economies, since they recognize the faults of over-reliance on indirect bank financing. The Asian Financial Crisis accelerated this process. In China, however, even though both government and the public have long been aware of the need to grow direct financing, the country actually has a diminishing percentage of direct financing. This is an indisputable fact, and the consequences are bad loans. The many unfavorable results of tightening policy measures begin to show up on bank balance sheets in the form of accumulating NPLs.

The proper way to deal with the situation is clear. The fundamental way to change China's severe imbalance in risk apportioning mechanisms in investment activity is to develop financial institutions with the capacity to source long-term funding.

Speaking more specifically, in furthering financial reforms we must do all we can to grow the stock markets, the bond market, and fund markets, and provide long-term capital for all kinds of investments. Bond markets should have a special emphasis on growth-company bonds and municipal bonds for urban construction. We must do this in order to provide long-term sourcing of funds for all kinds of investments. Second, we should grow insurance and pension funds and other contract-based financial mechanisms, as well as financial institutions with long-term funding sources like development banks. The aim is to avoid the problems that arise when financial institutions borrow short-term in order to fund long-term ("borrow short use long"). Third, we should promote financial innovation, support securitization (collateralized loan securitization as well as asset securitization), and other methods to resolve the inadequate asset liquidity of financial institutions and particularly of commercial banks. Given the above analysis of underlying economic forces, growing China's financial capacities is becoming quite urgent.

CHAPTER 4

The Evolution of Banking and Finance in China: Domestic and International Aspects

Pieter Bottelier

Senior Adjunct Professor, Johns Hopkins University,
Former Chief of the World Bank Mission in China

In this chapter, I will share some personal thoughts on the evolution of China's financial system and challenges ahead. The story of China's economic reforms is unique, remarkable, and not well-understood in the West. When China started its market reforms under the leadership of Deng Xiaoping in the late 1970s, its financial system consisted of just one institution: the People's Bank of China (PBC). Before Liberation, the PBC successfully substituted the Yuan Renminbi for the Gold Yuan in northwest China after the communists had wrested control of that area from the Nationalist government during the civil war. This currency reform experience served the PBC well after it became the central bank of the People's Republic of China in October 1949 and had to manage currency reform at the national level to fight the inherited hyperinflation. Until the start of financial system reform in 1979, the PBC served as deposit bank, lending bank, payment system, and cash agent for the government. There was no capital market and there were no insurance companies.

Western economists often have trouble understanding China's approach to economic reform since the late 1970s. Its transition from a planned to market economy was managed in ways that did not follow easily recognizable patterns. Many reforms were unorthodox in design, scope, and sequencing. For example, China's state banks—after they had been created—were long used as quasi-fiscal agents to facilitate reform and development of the real economy in accordance with Plan priorities. They helped preserve full employment in urban areas, even if that meant keeping loss-making state-owned enterprises (SOEs) alive. Nobody in China worried much about the accumulation of NPLs on the balance sheet of state banks until the Asian Financial Crisis of 1997–98, which was a wake-up call to China's leadership.

Most banks did not begin to report nonperforming loans (NPLs) systematically until the Bank of China (BOC) applied for the listing of its consolidated Hong Kong subsidiaries on the Hong Kong stock exchange (early 2001), which started a new chapter in banking reform. It marked the beginning of a process that included the gradual adoption of international standards for loan classification, capital adequacy, accounting, auditing, and reporting. China's financial sector reforms slowed developments in the real economy until then. A catching-up process was set in motion in 1998. When China joined the World Trade Organization (WTO) (December 2001), it committed to a significant opening of the financial sector. Financial reforms accelerated and became easier to understand for outside observers.

From a Western perspective, China's financial system seemed until recently backward and inefficient. Corporate governance was poor and a "credit culture" was lacking. SOEs—even loss-making ones—had privileged access to bank credit and share capital for many years after the start of market reforms. In retrospect, one has to wonder whether this system was perhaps better suited to China's needs at the time than foreign observers thought, and also whether China's economy could have performed better if the financial system had been reformed and liberalized sooner. Its "backward" financial system notwithstanding, China achieved high and sustained growth for several decades, while the economy was being opened to foreign trade and investment, and a dynamic non-state economy grew in parallel. All this was accomplished while full employment in urban areas was preserved until the mid-1990s—much longer than otherwise would have been possible. The contrast between China's experience in this regard and Russia's during the first half of the 1990s is striking.

Until the late 1990s, China used its state banks to allocate credit in accordance with Plan priorities and as "dustbins" for NPLs that were not recognized as such in earlier years. However, this unorthodox approach produced superior results and bought China valuable time: time for the real economy to develop, time for people to get used to the realities of a market economy, time for new institutions and policy instruments to be created, and time for government to learn how to use them. The system also allowed the state to allocate resources for the construction of critical infrastructure that would otherwise almost certainly not have been available today. Although one can quarrel about details—for example, stock and bond markets might have been reformed faster and social security reform could have started sooner—I am of the opinion that banking reforms moved about as fast as China's society and political system could handle. From a development perspective (and with the benefit of hindsight) we cannot say that China's banking system of the 1980s and 1990s was "inefficient." Nor can we say that China's unorthodox sequencing of reforms slowed growth.

Now that China is a member of the WTO and has defined its reform objectives and methods more precisely, the main questions are: how fast should China move to complete system reforms and what are the priorities? With regard to the financial sector, the WTO accession agreement sets some time tables for the first five years of membership (2002–06), but important policy areas such as interest rate liberalization, capital account opening, exchange rate management, domestic capital market development, foreign participation in existing financial institutions, and the management of outward investment are not covered by the agreement. Although most foreign observers urge China to reform the financial system faster, I am more concerned that China may try to complete the reform process too fast and lose control. The financial sector is the nerve center of a market economy. China cannot afford to lose control. Its regulatory institutions must stay ahead of system manipulators and innovative swindlers, which is a major challenge. My other worry is that the regulatory institutions may operate in isolation and not in consultation with each other. Effective lateral cooperation between parallel agencies remains a big challenge for China, and not only in the financial sector. Consolidation of regulatory powers in one single agency, such as Britain's Financial Services Authority is an option, but not one I would favor for China, because it would concentrate too much power in one agency.

In the remainder of this chapter, I will focus on (1) reform progress since 1998, (2) immediate challenges posed by asset price inflation, and (3) medium-term challenges related to the need to restore both domestic and international economic imbalances.

PROGRESS SINCE 1998

It is hard not to be impressed by the progress in financial system reform and development that has been made during the past decade. When the Asian Financial Crisis hit South Korea in late November 1997, just after that country had become a member of the OECD, China's leaders were shocked. Suddenly, a keen and broadly shared awareness developed of the risks to which China's own financial system could be exposed. It was then accepted that the state banks had to become real banks, that corporate governance had to be taken seriously, and that the financial system had to be developed in line with international rules and norms to serve the needs of China's globalizing economy. Consequently, the pace of financial sector reform quickened markedly. In 1999, four newly created state-owned asset management companies (AMCs) absorbed an initial RMB1.4 trillion worth of nominal NPLs from five state banks. Reforms intensified in 2001 with the listing of BOC's subsidiary in Hong Kong and the first strategic minority participation by a foreign bank (Hong Kong Shanghai Bank, or HSBC) in a Chinese bank (Bank of Shanghai), and again in 2003 with the establishment of the China Banking Regulatory Commission (CBRC). There had been numerous earlier banking reforms since 1979, but they were mostly administrative in nature and none had the far-reaching impact of post-1998 measures.

Suddenly, the reform and development of China's financial system became an autonomous objective. This involved a significant change in the mindset and attitude of planners, regulators, and bank managers, as well as an enormous amount of staff training. Indeed, of all the changes in China's financial sector during the past decade, the human resource and institutional developments have been the most impressive. From a technical banking perspective the most important development was the successful sequestering (in successive transactions) of most NPLs on the balance sheets of AMCs. This means that the NPL problem ceased to be a threat to the stability of China's banking system, *not* that the cost of an NPL clean-up had been paid. The NPL ratio for major commercial banks (in the aggregate) was gradually reduced from almost 25% in 2002 to 6.2% by the end of September 2007. There were many other important financial sector developments. I draw attention to the following selected examples.

(1) **Close cooperation with international financial agencies, including the Bank for International Settlements (BIS) in Basel Switzerland**

China became a member of the BIS in 1996. It took full advantage of the training and other development opportunities offered by this and other international financial institutions that it had joined earlier, such as the IMF, the World Bank, IFC, and the Asian Development Bank. In parallel, PBC developed close cooperation with the monetary authorities of Hong Kong, Singapore, and several other countries for staff training and system development. It is hard to imagine a developing country central bank that worked harder to understand and adopt international standards and best practice than PBC. China has adopted a full set of international loan classification, bank supervision, accounting, and International Financial Accounting Standards (IFRS). The quality, timeliness, and transparency of central bank monetary reports, annual bank reports, and financial statistics have improved significantly, with one important exception: the accounts of the four state-owned AMCs are not publicly available, and information on their operations is scant.

(2) Establishment of an independent banking regulator/supervisor

The establishment of China Banking Regulatory Commission (CBRC) in March 2003 was a watershed institutional development. It separated critical banking supervisory and regulatory functions from the central bank and allowed PBC to concentrate on increasingly complex monetary policy challenges. CBRC has since grown into a respected and increasingly effective bank supervisor/regulator with some 24,000 staff nationwide. The three main financial sector regulatory agencies, CBRC, China Securities Regulatory Commission (CSRC), and China Insurance Regulatory Commission (CIRC) have agreed on a framework for interagency consultations, but effective collaboration between these three and other key financial government agencies such as PBC and the Ministry of Finance (MOF) remains problematic. A clear example is the embarrassing confusion that arose over a breakthrough announcement on August 20, 2007, by the State Agency for Foreign Exchange (SAFE) that Chinese households would be permitted to invest (unlimited amounts) on the Hong Kong stock exchange through the Tianjin branch of BOC. The announcement was effectively contradicted by Premier Wen Jiabao in November, as will be discussed below . . .

(3) Internal restructuring of almost all major state banks

Details of internal restructuring plans were decided by the banks themselves. These plans were often very drastic. They included the lay-off of large numbers of redundant personnel and the closure of numerous bank branches. For example, BOC required all its managers above a certain level to resign and reapply for jobs in a slimmed down organization that had been restructured with the help of international management consultants. Those who were not successful in securing a new job after three applications were out. BOC and practically all other banks required their staff, including managers to undergo various training programs. Management information and accounting systems were integrated and computerized. This made it possible—often for the first time—for top managers of large banks with numerous branches to have up-to-date and comprehensive information on the organization for which they were responsible. It also facilitated bank supervision by the regulator, which had been extremely difficult before bank accounts were consolidated and computerized. All major banks (except the Agricultural Bank of China, ABC) were incorporated under China's Company Law before they could sell shares to foreign strategic investors and financial investors through initial public offerings (IPOs). The weakest part of China's banking system remains ABC and the rural banking system in general, but even there, progress is being made. A restructuring plan for ABC is likely to be announced soon. The government has already reserved US$40 billion from foreign exchange reserves for its recapitalization.

(4) Strategic participation in almost all major Chinese banks by foreign banks as minority investor (up to 19.9% for individual foreign banks) and board member

Nobody would have predicted in 1998 that China's state banks would become investment targets for major international banks only a few years later. In the late 1990s, the state banking system was (not unrealistically) regarded as a "black box": inefficient and technically insolvent. In 2007, almost all major banks had foreign strategic minority partners (with board representation) and are listed on the Hong Kong and/or Shanghai stock exchange. This has changed the landscape of banking in China. It created significant opportunities and new challenges to modernize and adopt international standards. In my view, China would benefit from a further increase in foreign participation in existing Chinese banks and other parts of the financial system, including financial service companies.

(5) Full recapitalization—often beyond the minimum capital adequacy standard of 8%—of most important state banks

This was the result of direct capital injections by the government from foreign exchange reserves and from the budget, participation by foreign strategic minority investors, IPOs in Hong Kong and/or Shanghai (for a float of up to 30% of the shares), the issue of subordinated bonds by banks, and increased provisioning by the banks themselves from increased operating profits. Restructuring and recapitalization plans were tailored to the specific circumstances of each bank. The use of foreign exchange reserves for bank recapitalization was unorthodox, but innovative and effective. It involved restrictions on the conversion of that capital into local currency and a measure of protection of the recapitalized banks against exchange risk.

(6) Introduction of futures markets, new financial instruments, and new intermediaries

The range of tradable financial instruments has significantly broadened in recent years. Among the more important new products are short-term corporate bills, NPLs and mortgage-backed securities, subordinated bank bonds, US dollar-denominated domestic bonds, RMB-denominated bonds issued by multilateral agencies, and central bank bills of various maturities (to conduct open market operations). Futures markets for various commodities were established. The bond market remains dominated by securities issued by the Ministry of Finance and the China Development Bank (CBD). The corporate bond market has remained small and constrained in its development by government regulations, but there are reasons to expect that even the corporate bond market will take off before long, as will be discussed later. The emergence of venture capital, angel investors, and private equity funds in China (both foreign and domestic) has also contributed to a diversification of corporate funding sources and capital market development.

(7) Adoption of market-based solutions for making non-tradable public shares in listed companies gradually tradable

When the stock exchanges of Shanghai and Shenzhen were established (late 1990 and early 1991 respectively), China sought to reconcile socialist and capitalist development objectives by reserving majority ownership (normally at least 65%) of listed state companies for the state. Those shares were not tradable. The large overhang of non-tradable shares was not a problem for the market until China began to reserve 10% of IPO proceeds for the funding of the National Social Security Fund (2000) and some local governments began to sell non-tradable shares to foreign investors in private deals outside the stock exchanges, at deep discounts, around the same time. The combination of these two developments severely depressed the market value of tradable shares for several years while the economy boomed. New listings slowed and were suspended in 2005 when the government began to experiment with a market-based approach to making non-tradable public shares tradable without spoiling the market for the existing float. The approach rested on giving the owners of tradable shares power to block the conversion of non-tradable shares into tradable shares. This power was used to extract negotiated compensation for consent to make non-tradable shares tradable (gradually, after a lock-up period of several years). In 2006, the successful experiments of 2005 were extended to all listed companies that were majority state-owned (that is, well over 90% of all listed companies) and IPOs were resumed. This led to a return of public confidence in the stock market and a bull run that continued in 2007. While the bubble that developed is potentially dangerous, the solution that was found for the conundrum of China's non-tradable shares was innovative and consistent with market reforms.

(8) Development of a primary mortgage market and consumer credit following the accelerated privatization of urban housing

In 1998, in the wake of the Asian Financial Crisis, the government decided to significantly accelerate the privatization of urban housing. The main objective was to relieve state-owned corporations, most of which were performing poorly at that time, of the obligation to provide housing to their employees, and to promote commercial urban housing markets. Other objectives were to promote private construction industries and to create an important source of domestic demand (for house improvements) to help shield the economy form the negative effects of the regional financial crisis. Since cash wages and salaries were still very low and mortgage loans generally unavailable, most existing urban dwellings were transferred to their occupants at a fraction of market value. For the commercial sale of new housing, however, a mortgage finance industry had to be developed. In less than 10 years, China developed thriving commercial housing markets in most cities, a large mortgage finance industry, and associated commercial insurance. All of this contributed significantly to improved bank asset quality, capital market development, and private wealth accumulation in the cities.

(9) Removal of the cap on lending rates and the floor under deposit rates (2004)

This was one of many measures aimed at promoting the commercialization of state banks and at improving their profitability. The government wanted state banks to become more independent and discriminating in their lending operations, through systematic risk analysis and differential lending rates. Improved profitability would help to make the banks more attractive to potential foreign partners and enable them to contribute more to their own recapitalization through provisioning. The partial liberalization of interest rates, combined with the development of new financial instruments and long-term contractual savings (insurance and mortgage finance) also contributed to the development and commercialization of capital markets. For example, in 2002, yield curves for government bonds and corporate bonds were still almost entirely flat. In other words, there was no link between the maturity and pricing of bonds and therefore no meaningful yield curve to serve as a benchmark for capital markets. This has changed in recent years; yield curves for government bonds now show an upward slope, as is typical under normal circumstances in market economies.

(10)   Transfer of responsibility for the issue of most corporate bonds from the National Development and Reform Commission (NDRC) to CSRC

The decision was taken in January 2007, but remains to be fully implemented at the time of writing. In principle, this is a very important institutional change. It holds the promise that China's small and underdeveloped corporate bond market may finally take off after having languished since the early 1990s. In 1993, the authorization of corporate bonds was shifted from PBC to the State Planning Commission (predecessor of the NDRC) to improve discipline in the issue and underwriting of such bonds. However, NDRC limited new issues to a small group of very large state-owned corporations and required that all new issues be fully guaranteed by a state-owned commercial bank. In 2005, PBC authorized the issue of short-term corporate bills that almost instantly became a large market, because corporate China badly needed additional sources of short-term finance for liquidity management. A large and diversified corporate bond market would supplement already existing bond markets and make life more interesting (and challenging) for the rating agencies.

The cumulative effect of these and other financial sector reforms on corporate governance and credit culture in China, though hard to measure precisely, has undoubtedly been positive. China has built the foundations for what may become a strong, diversified financial system based substantially on market principles. Majority state ownership of major banks and financial service organizations is likely to continue, perhaps indefinitely. But even so, there is considerable room for increased participation by foreign companies and private domestic shareholders that would be beneficial for the maturation of China's financial system. Though interagency coordination leaves much to be desired and is potentially the Achilles heel of financial system stability, it is reassuring that the system is supervised by increasingly professional and effective regulatory agencies.

IMMEDIATE CHALLENGES
The Stock Market Bubble

Asset price inflation, liquidity management, and interagency coordination are some of the most immediate challenges facing China. The successful experimentation with market-based solutions for the conundrum of non-tradable state-owned shares in 2005 and the adoption of those solutions for all majority state-owned listed companies triggered a revival of China's stock markets in 2006. The A-share markets in Shanghai and Shenzhen became runaway bull markets, outperforming all major stock exchanges in the world. At the end of October 2007, the average price-earnings (PE) ratio (on forward earnings) for Shanghai listed A-shares was over 50, compared to about 20 for emerging East Asia (excluding China) and India. The ratio was about 70 in Japan before that bubble burst in 1990. In spite of a substantial market correction in November 2007, the government is understandably concerned about the risk of new bubbles and the consequences of a possible market crash.

There is little doubt that China's stock market, in spite of the November 2007 market correction, remains in bubble territory. This entails both economic and political risks. The latter is important in China, because of the very large number individual households that owns shares—probably over 60 million. The risk that a stock market crash might trigger an economic recession is hard to assess, but is probably lower than in otherwise similar circumstances in developed market economies. Since buying on margin is officially prohibited (and believed to be rare) in China, the situation is different from that in Japan in the late 1980s or in the US in 1929; it entails less risk that a downturn becomes irreversible once it has started. Yet, a sharp downturn could be dangerous for financial system stability if a large proportion of share purchases is financed with borrowed funds.

Information on this is not readily available. Generally, the higher the proportion of "own funds" used to finance share purchases, the lower the systemic risk. It is probably fair to assume that a high percentage of share purchases in China by households, corporations, and public agencies alike is financed from "own funds." A-share purchases by foreign interests are relatively small and strictly regulated under the Qualified Foreign Institutional Investor (QFII) scheme.

The government has been trying to cool the market[1] but, except for the market correction in November 2007, the risk of bubble conditions has not been eliminated. Furthermore, on August 20, 2007, the State Administration of Foreign Exchange (SAFE) announced that Chinese households would be permitted to invest (unlimited amounts) directly on the Hong Kong stock exchange. This announcement was undoubtedly inspired by the desire to reduce pressure on the domestic stock exchanges and slow the accumulation of unwanted foreign exchange reserves. However, in early November, after the Hong Kong market had risen by some 40% following the SAFE announcement, Premier Wen Jiabao indicated that final approval of the scheme would be withheld until a number of conditions had been met, which could take a long time. The episode illustrates the difficulty of managing liquidity in the hands of the public and the embarrassing lack of policy coordination between relevant agencies of the state. A sudden large outflow of private savings from China to Hong Kong could indeed destabilize both domestic and Hong Kong capital markets; liquidity in the hands of the public—total deposits in the banking system at the end of the third quarter of 2007 amounted to some RMB37 trillion (about US$5 trillion equivalent). More than half of that amount was owned by households and increasingly held in liquid form as bank demand deposits.

Although China's central bank is primarily concerned with the management of liquidity in the banking system (narrow liquidity: the margin of loanable funds; that is, deposits minus outstanding loans and reserve requirements), it should in my view also play a role in the control of asset price bubbles driven by excess liquidity in the hands of the public. In spite of several rate increases during the past six months, bank deposit rates have become negative with respect to current CPI inflation. This has not only accelerated to shift from time deposits to more liquid demand deposits and from demand deposits to share purchases, but it has also driven more financial intermediation underground to unregulated informal money and capital markets that reduces the effectiveness of macroeconomic controls. As China knows well from earlier experience, negative real deposit rates can undermine the health of the entire financial system.

Controlling asset price bubbles fueled by excess liquidity in the hand of the public is always much more difficult than controlling bank liquidity and bank lending, but it should not be impossible. To tackle the problem, all relevant government authorities have to cooperate, including PBC, CBRC, CSRC, the state-owned Assets Supervision and Administration Commission (SASAC), and the Ministry of Finance (MOF). MOF could introduce a ban on the use of cash flow surpluses for share purchases by local governments and their agencies. The government could even introduce a ban on share ownership by most public agencies. SASAC could prohibit share speculation by companies under its control. CBRC and CSRC together should try to eliminate the use of bank and brokerage loans for share purchases and guard against the emergence of leveraged share buying. PBC should raise deposit rates. This will not stop bubbles, but it has to be done for other reasons anyway. CSRC should accelerate the listing in Shanghai and Shenzhen of high-quality companies and fully integrate the domestic B- and A-share markets as soon as possible. In addition, share transaction taxes could be further increased, the Qualified Domestic Institutional Investor (QDII) ceiling further lifted and the corporate bond market enlarged.

Urban Real Estate Price Inflation

Since the beginning of this century, urban real estate price inflation has also been high, but there is less concern about the formation of dangerous bubbles. Although information on the magnitude of urban real estate price inflation is conflicting,[2] it too is driven, in part, by excess domestic liquidity in the hands of the public. Unregulated "hot money" inflows from abroad have probably been a more important factor in urban real estate markets than in the domestic stock market. Current real estate price inflation in China is believed to be less dangerous and easier to control than share price inflation for the following reasons:

- According to official information, average urban incomes have risen faster than average urban housing prices, implying that the average "affordability index" has improved.
- Several local governments have succeeded in reducing speculative house buying by raising down-payment requirements

and/or by requiring that the first mortgage is paid off before a second mortgage can be applied for.

- The supply elasticity of urban housing is probably greater than the supply elasticity of domestic A-shares.

It should furthermore be noted that urban real estate price inflation has been associated with the monetization of housing subsidies and the emergence of a large private housing construction and mortgage finance industry. As SOEs were relieved of their traditional responsibility to provide housing for employees, the enforcement of *hukou* restrictions was relaxed in many cities that helped to promote greater labor mobility. These are all very positive developments for China's economy and its financial system. The urban real estate price inflation that China has experienced so far is not a threat to financial system stability; it is a small price to pay for the effective liberalization and privatization of China's urban housing markets.

ECONOMIC IMBALANCES AND FINANCIAL SYSTEM REFORM

Domestic Dimensions

China's economic and social imbalances—over-reliance for GDP growth on investment and net-exports, growing social inequality, and environmental degradation—have become very serious and need to be addressed by all available policy, administrative, and regulatory tools, including further financial sector reform. One of the reasons for over-investment, particularly in manufacturing, is the low ceiling on deposit rates that renders them negative with respect to current CPI inflation. Low deposit rates have tended to increase excess liquidity in the corporate sector and depress the entire interest rate structure. Negative real deposit rates drive financial intermediation from regulated into unregulated—sometimes "underground"—financial markets. Especially for large corporations with ready access to the official financial system, capital tends to be relatively cheap in China and, since deposit rates are unattractive, every available penny is usually invested as quickly as possible.

Other factors that have contributed to "over-investment"[3] by corporate China in recent years include: (1) a sharp improvement in corporate profitability since the beginning of this century, combined with the virtual absence of dividend payments by either state or non-state enterprises, (2) the fact that privatization proceeds have typically accrued to the enterprises being privatized (or their holding companies), thus increasing resources available for investment, and (3) easy access to international markets where prices are often better than in domestic markets. Even in cases where export prices are lower than domestic prices, corporate profitability does not necessarily fall due to scale economies and/or continued high productivity growth. This explains how the combination of low interest rates, high liquidity, high corporate profits, and strong productivity growth has created a kind of manufacturing investment "flywheel" effect that is contributing to growing imbalances in China's economy. Part of the cure for these imbalances therefore lies in an upward adjustment of the entire interest rate structure and other measures that will have the effect of suppressing unregulated financial markets. Faster exchange rate appreciation would also help to redress domestic economic imbalances.

Although short-term money market interest rates and rates on government and corporate bonds are essentially market-driven, China maintains, as mentioned, a ceiling on bank deposit rates and a floor under bank lending rates (mainly to protect gross margins in the state-controlled banking system). Liberalization of the entire interest rate system would promote healthy competition in financial intermediation, which will have adverse consequences for the profitability of relatively inefficient financial institutions, as is normal in a market economy. In the interest of completing market reforms and addressing economic imbalances, China should liberalize all deposit and lending rates as soon as this can be done without risking stability of the financial system.

International Dimensions: China's Dilemma

The international dimensions of domestic financial liberalization are very important. The last thing China needs under current circumstances is additional "hot money" inflows in response to higher domestic deposit rates. To reduce that risk, domestic interest rate liberalization should be combined with the "flexibilization" of exchange rate management and greater capital account opening. However, there are good reasons why China may wish to keep at least some capital controls and to continue managing its exchange rate, though much more flexibly than in the past. The current international financial system is not well-supervised or regulated and inherently unstable, because since the collapse of the Bretton Woods system in 1971, there are no built-in restrictions on international liquidity creation through US current account deficits. In any event, China may wish to protect its economy against unwanted speculative capital inflows (or outflows) and other potentially destabilizing cross-border financial transactions. In light of the very serious international economic imbalances that plague the global economy, the current US dollar-based international financial system may not be sustainable.

Since the beginning of this century, the world has seen an unprecedented worsening of global trade imbalances, reserve accumulation in surplus economies (such as China), and an accumulation of net external liabilities in the US, custodian of the international monetary system since the collapse of Bretton Woods. Most international reserves are invested in US dollar-denominated financial instruments. The US has become the world's largest debtor nation. Unprecedented global economic imbalances have caused much anxiety about the present international monetary system. The declining international value of the US dollar in recent years has reduced its attractiveness as reserve currency and increased pressures for the development of alternative ways to invest reserves and store wealth. In fact, the very foundation of the international monetary system as it has developed since the collapse of Bretton Woods (when the US de-linked the dollar from gold), has been called into question.

If the custodian and greatest beneficiary of the international monetary system—that is, the US—is unable, for whatever reason, to reduce its unsustainable external deficit without forcing major wealth losses on its creditors in the form of a declining dollar, then the system itself is potentially at risk. Under the Bretton Woods system, the massive global trade imbalances and excess liquidity that characterize the present situation could not have arisen, because self-correcting forces would have kicked in much earlier. Since returning to a Bretton Woods-type international financial system (which requires much greater *domestic* policy discipline than the current system) is implausible, the question arises what a large developing country like China can do to protect its economy from the vagaries of the current system without contributing to instability. When its domestic financial system is sufficiently mature some years down the line, China faces a dilemma: join the international system fully and play by its rules, or maintain at least some capital controls and influence over the exchange rate. The first choice risks importing instability; the second risks contributing to instability.

Some have argued that the main source of the current global economic imbalances is the inability or unwillingness of the US to avoid sustained large external deficits through *domestic* policy adjustments. Others emphasize that a large part of the weakness of the current international financial system is precisely the fact that large surplus economies like China do not play by the same rules, but instead link their currencies to the US dollar and avoid market-based exchange rate adjustments through market intervention. As China's example demonstrates, such intervention permits global imbalances to grow larger than otherwise would have been the case. In addition, China's efforts to prevent or slow both nominal *and* real exchange rate appreciation (through domestic sterilization) present huge challenges of domestic monetary management. Since China's trade and current account surpluses have become the largest in the world in absolute terms (2006 and 2007), and are now also among the largest in relative terms, it is hard to avoid the conclusion that China has become a major contributor to global imbalances. However, the solution is not that simple as China is in a "catch-22" situation. Although China's exchange rate is, in my opinion, definitely undervalued and should be allowed to appreciate faster, the question remains: How can countries like China be expected to fully play by current international rules if those rules are (or can be) a source of international financial instability?

It is hard to avoid the conclusion that a new international monetary agreement is needed to replace the anchor-less system that has developed since 1971. The internationally agreed, IMF-led Special Drawing Rights (SDRs) scheme that was introduced in 1969 was by all accounts a system innovation of monumental importance. SDRs are international reserve assets designed to supplement existing official reserves of member countries. This innovation turned the IMF into a kind of global central bank responsible for ensuring adequate international liquidity to finance economic growth and trade. But the SRD scheme was essentially made redundant by the collapse of Bretton Woods and the large-scale international liquidity creation that followed in the form of US external deficits. In the absence of credible Western leadership on global monetary system reform, Asia, including China, may have to take the lead in developing new schemes designed to ensure global economic balance with enough new liquidity to finance growth.

The limited scope of this chapter does not permit a full discussion of this critical issue. China has to complete its domestic financial system reforms in the midst of uncertainty over the future of the international monetary system. It has to make its own assumptions about the merits of the US dollar as reserve currency, invest its mammoth reserves in ways that best serve the country's long-term economic interests, which include global stability and development. A strategic economic dialogue between the US and China on bilateral issues and trade imbalances is important, but not sufficient to solve the conundrum of unsustainable global economic imbalances. China should, in my view, continue to open its financial system to foreign participation, liberalize financial markets, increase its exchange rate management flexibility, and gradually open its capital account. However, it may wish to stop short of fully embracing all aspects of the current international financial system. That should not prevent China from actively participating in international efforts to improve the current international financial system.

ENDNOTES

[1] For example, the Stamp Duty on share transactions was raised in mid-2007, the ceiling on QDII outflows was lifted and large domestic IPOs by state banks and state energy companies were promoted to increase the supply of tradable shares.

[2] Official data on urban housing prices suggest that on average, they have been rising more slowly than disposable urban incomes. This would imply that the "affordability index" for urban housing has improved, which is good for middle class development. However, there is much anecdotal evidence to suggest that in many cities, housing prices have been rising faster than disposable incomes, which would imply the opposite for affordability. A declining affordability index is inimical to the development of a stable middle class. In this chapter, official data are used to guide the discussion.

[3] I am putting over-investment between quotation marks, because under current circumstances in China, we see relatively clear evidence of idle production capacity due to the fact that producers are usually able to increase export sales or substitute for imports, thus adding to the country's ballooning net exports since 2005.

SECTION 2

BANKING

CHAPTER 5

China's Banking Industry: Moving Forward in Accord with Reform and Opening

Wang Zhaoxing

Vice Chairman, China Banking Regulatory Commission

Finance is the core of modern economics. China's long-term fundamental policy is to adhere to the process of Reform and Opening, which is also necessary in realizing a model for economic development that raises the competitiveness of China's banking industry. Since the start of this fundamental national policy, the banking industry has played an extremely important role in economic growth and social development. In recent years, the emphasis that the Chinese government has placed on banking reform has resulted in a number of key measures. These initiated reform in some highly problematic policy areas that had been festering for years. Reform of state-owned banks has made break-through progress, step-by-step reform has been achieved in rural finance, and steady advances have been accomplished with regard to small and medium-sized commercial banks. Since concluding the transition period into full entry in the World Trade Organization (WTO), the Chinese banking industry too has arrived at a new level. By strengthening effective regulation and adhering to Reform and Opening, the industry has been able to achieve historic change. It is now facing both opportunities and unprecedented challenges.

FIGURE 5.1   Number of banks meeting capital adequacy standards, and percentage of assets 2003–06

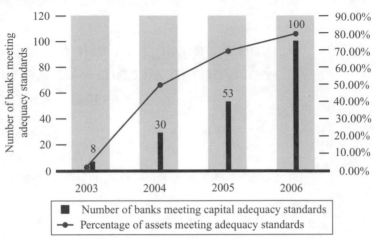

Source: CBRC.

HISTORIC CHANGES IN CHINA'S BANKING INDUSTRY

At the end of 2006, total assets in China's banking and financial institutions came to RMB43.95 trillion. This was an increase of nearly 60% over the figure at the end of 2003. China's various banking and financial institutions included: three "policy-type" banks, five state-owned or state-controlled large commercial banks, 12 joint-stock commercial banks, and 113 municipal commercial banks. By the end of 2006, nine of the commercial banks had listed on stock exchanges either inside or outside China. In addition to these, there were also 78 municipal credit associations, 19,348 rural credit associations, 13 rural-area commercial banks, 80 rural cooperative banks, four financial asset management companies (AMCs), one postal savings bank, 54 trust companies, 70 enterprise group finance companies, six finance leasing companies, one currency management company, seven automobile financing companies, and 14 foreign-invested legal-entity financial institutions. Thus, there were already close to 20,000 registered legal-entity financial institutions in China's banking industry.

Progress in Banking Reform

China's banking industry has traveled a difficult path in the course of emerging from the planned economy period. The industry as a whole has contributed to a number of national policy goals. Over an extended period, these have included stimulating the national economy, supporting reform of state-owned enterprises (SOEs), and preserving both financial and social stability in the country. At the same time, however, the industry has inherited historical burdens as well as accumulated considerable risk. For a long time, China's state-owned commercial banks faced the compounding problems of large amounts of nonperforming loans (NPLs), low capital reserves, poor corporate governance practices, and weak risk management. These reflected contradictions and problems in society at large, but in the banking field their effect was magnified. The problems were exacerbated by organizational roadblocks in the banking industry itself. Risk built up in the banking system. It attracted widespread international attention and the international press and some organizations went so far as to say that China's commercial banking was "technically already bankrupt."

The state has in recent years invested tremendous resources to deal with the accumulation of NPLs in the system. These included the issuance of RMB270 billion worth of special state bonds in 1998 to bolster the capital of the four solely state-owned commercial banks. The state then removed RMB1.3939 trillion worth of NPLs from the balance sheets of these four banks in 1999, handing them over to specially established financial AMCs. Since both the mechanisms and the overall systems of the banking industry were not reformed, however, the old burdens were not totally shucked off while new risk was steadily being added to old risk. Restructuring of state-owned commercial banks was formally initiated in 2003, with strong support from the state. Reform of the entire system and of specific banking mechanisms was carried out while registered capital was strengthened.

By the end of 2006, the overall risk parameters of China's banks showed a historic turn for the better. NPL amounts on balance sheets continued to drop, while NPLs as a percentage of performing loans fell from more than 20% in 2002 to 7.5% in 2006. The level of reserves, or capital adequacy, has increased substantially: the number of banks conforming to adequate reserve standards has gone from eight at the end of 2003 to 100 at the end of 2006. Of total assets in the banking industry, the amount held in banks that meet the required standards has risen to 77.4% from 0.6%. Profitability has seen a marked increase, with pretax profits going from RMB36.4 billion in 2002 to RMB240.9 billion in 2006. The structure of income has also seen positive change; financial sustainability has been substantially improved.

Among the five large state-owned banks, four have undergone financial restructuring and share-reform or "corporatization." They have taken in strategic investors and listed on exchanges either in China or abroad. These four are the Industrial and Commercial Bank of China (ICBC), Bank of China (BOC), China Construction Bank (CCB), and Bank of Communications (BoCom). Having improved operating security, profitability, and competitiveness, these are already large banks with a certain degree of influence on the international stage. Three are among the world's top 10 banks as judged by market capitalization at the end of 2006: ICBC (third), BOC (sixth), and CCB (seventh). Modern corporate governance structures are being instituted in these banks. Such management concepts as "taking the customer as the core" are being implemented and organizational structure and business procedures are being reformulated. A portion of banks have begun to implement total risk management, information systems are being strengthened, risk management capacities are being improved and profit-making and self-accumulation capacities are steadily increasing. Certain banks have adopted such indicators of results as EVA (economic value-added) and RAROC (risk-adjusted return on capital), focusing on operational efficiencies and management quality. At the same time, in order to increase the sensitivity to risk of their own capital, large commercial banks have begun to set up internal evaluation systems. In line with the spirit of the New Basel Accord, these are aimed at meeting international standards and they involve modeling estimates of development capital, improving levels of risk management, and gradually lessening the gap between Chinese and international banking practices.

In the same period, reform of rural cooperative financial systems has been accomplished in successive stages. New property rights modes and organizational forms are being set up, and with both local and central government support, progress has been made in overcoming inherited financial burdens and in lessening risk. Support of the "three agricultures" and improvement in the developmental capacity of county-level economies has been noticeable. Other types of financial organizations in the banking industry have similarly made progress in reforming property rights systems and internal organizational structures.

Opening to the Outside

The common experience of the banking industry in all countries is that "opening" to outside participation must be done in accord with internal realities of a given country. This includes its regulatory capacities, the state of its banking reform, and the developmental stage of its domestic economy. The opening of China's banking industry proceeded from the coast toward the interior, from a regional to a national basis, from foreign exchange to domestic currency business, and from corporate customers to individual customers. This sequential process has been done in alignment with the reform of China's domestic economy and banking industry. It has basically been consistent with the overall process of China's opening to the outside; that is, it has maintained an orderly and stable course.

As a member country of the WTO, throughout the five-year transition process, China has conscientiously met its entry obligations with regard to the factors involving market entry into the financial industry, RMB-customer partners, and regional development. These obligations have included implementing a multilayered, wide-scale, "opening," involving active adoption of measures that allow foreign banks to operate in the central, western, and northeastern parts of China. Upon finishing the transition period, China promulgated "Regulations on Management of Foreign-invested Banks" and got rid of all "non-prudent" restrictions on foreign-invested banks. Trading in RMB was completely opened to foreign-invested banks, by bestowing [on them] "citizenship status" or the same treatment as Chinese legal entities. By the end of December 2006, 14 solely foreign-invested or joint-invested banking institutions were registered as legal persons in China, under which were 19 branches and/or subsidiary organizations. Seventy-four foreign-invested banks from 22 countries and regions had set up 200 subsidiaries and 79 branches in 25 cities in China (as opposed to being legally registered as China legal-persons). One hundred and eighty-six foreign-invested banks from 42 countries and regions had set up 242 representative offices in 24 cities in China. These foreign-invested banks were involved in over 100 types of banking activities, and 115 foreign-invested banking organizations had received permission to transact RMB business. The total foreign capital of foreign-invested banks in China came to US$1.33 billion

TABLE 5.1 Foreign-invested banking operating organizations in China

	2003	2004	2005	2006
Number	192	211	254	312
Assets (hundred million RMB)	4,159	5,823	7,155	9,279
% of total banking assets	1.50%	1.84%	1.91%	2.11%

Source: CBRC 2006 Yearbook.

(or RMB927.9 RMB), approximately 2% of China's total banking industry (see Table 5.1).

At the same time, the Chinese Banking Regulatory Commission (CBRC) has cautiously begun to evaluate and authorize some Chinese financial institutions in the banking industry to accept investment from foreign institutions. The selection emphasizes the strategic nature of contributions the investor can make, and how well cooperation with the Chinese institution can be achieved at various levels of administration. The purpose is to use the attractiveness of investing in China as a way for China's banks to gain systems and knowledge. By the end of 2006, a total of 21 Chinese commercial banks had brought in 29 institutional investors from overseas who had invested a total of US$19 billion. The investment in Chinese shares by foreign-invested financial institutions not only strengthened the capital positions of Chinese banks, but modified the share-ownership structure of these banks that had previously been too uniform. Importantly, it also led to improvement in China's corporate governance in the banking sector, and encouraged management methods and operating concepts that will allow Chinese banks to come into line with international modern practices. The experience has proven that both the overall strategic policy and specific measures with regard to China's banking industry have been effective in promoting further reform of the industry. They have brought in competitive mechanisms—which have helped financial innovation of Chinese banks—they have improved risk-avoidance, and they have strengthened the management capacities of these banks.

While opening to foreign-invested financial institutions, the China Banking Regulatory Commission (CBRC) also actively set up cooperative relations with foreign regulatory bodies. The process has improved our functioning in a number of ways: it has improved capital adequacy ratios, corporate governance, internal controls, and the stability of operations. It has helped prepare the conditions for China's domestic financial enterprises to "stride out" with operating capacity outside China. Such striding out will include setting up subsidiaries and branch organizations overseas and undertaking mergers and acquisitions with foreign banks to further the growth of both parties. At present, China's leading commercial banks have primary branch organizations in 29 different countries and regions, and have acquired or merged with two overseas financial institutions.

Financial Innovations

China's banks now "take the customer as the core, the market as the guiding force." This credo is the foundation of improving the quality of service and the core competitiveness of China's financial institutions. It is also the key to understanding the allocation and effective hedging of risk. The principles have become important components of sustainable growth strategies for China's banks.

In recent years, in accord with guiding-principle regulatory concepts, the CBRC has simplified or done away with requiring administrative licenses on financial products, improved the banking environment for innovation, and actively promoted the practice of financial innovation, all under the preconditions of maintaining measurable costs, controllable risk, and open and adequate disclosure of risk conditions to the public. The Commission issued a "Guide to Financial Innovations in Commercial Banking." It has drawn up regulations relating to commercial banks' subordinated bonds, transactions in financial derivatives, personal wealth management, electronic banking, securitization of assets, and so on. It has drawn up regulatory systems for these, to encourage innovative banking behavior that is in accord with standard rules.

Commercial banks have in recent years begun cash management services for enterprises; issued personal wealth management products with different maturities and in different currencies coupled to interest rates, exchange rates, stock index, and precious metals prices; and both acted as agent and operated on their own account foreign exchange derivative products such as foreign exchange forwards, swaps, and options. They have developed widespread use of mobile phone banking, telephone banking, Internet banking, as well as banking brokerage cooperation, and banking insurance cooperation. They have improved their innovative capacities to quite a respectable degree in both products and services, improved their income and customer base, their balance sheet structure and their profit models.

By the end of 2006, statistics show that almost 70 China- and foreign-invested banks were qualified to trade in derivative transactions in China. Thirty·China- and foreign-invested banks had started business in RMB and foreign-currency wealth management, and the funds being managed reached RMB400 billion. From July 2006, after the first batch of QDII products were listed on the exchange, 11 Chinese banks had put out 14 different QDII products. By the end of 2006, the volume of electronic-banking transactions reached RMB122 trillion, an increase of 101% over 2005, of which Internet banking business transactions rose from 52 trillion in 2005 to 94 trillion in 2006, an increase of 80.8%, while telephone banking rose 51.2%, and mobile phone banking rose 2.7 times. The number of issued bankcards went from 960 million in 2005 to 1.17 billion in 2006, basically the equivalent of one person one card. Bankcard consumption increased from 10% of total consumer goods retail business in 2005 to 17% in 2006. Some banks successfully set up fund management companies and pilot project companies involved in securitized assets.

Financial Services

In evaluating a bank's performance, it is important to look at the adequacy of its financial services in economically undeveloped areas or where coverage is weak, in addition to the normal measures of competitiveness in developed areas. To resolve problems of low coverage of financial institutions in rural areas and often insufficient competition, the CBRC has energetically promoted innovation in rural finance organizations. It has actively encouraged financial institutions to strengthen their services to the "three agricultures;" for example, farmers, farm land, and agricultural industry, in order to improve agricultural production, farmers' income, and rural economic growth. At present, the percentage of total loans related to agriculture among rural credit associations, agricultural banks, and agricultural development banks already amounts to some 20%. Some 31.2% of farming families receive small credit loans and agricultural household loans. Those farming households with a need for loans and who also meet the loan requirements constitute 57.6% of farming households. Approximately 300 million people in towns and villages are currently receiving benefits.

New forms of banking institutions have been established in rural areas such as town and village banks, loan companies, and farmer's financial mutual organizations. Together with the spread into rural areas of an extensive postal savings bank network, support of the banking system for the "three agricultures" has greatly improved. The new capability has strengthened the construction of "new socialist rural areas." At the same time, due to the lack of knowledge about modern finance among most people in rural areas, and due especially to a scant understanding of financial risk, the CBRC is promoting an activity that is meant to take financial knowledge down to the village level. It is trying to disseminate financial risk education through all different forms of media in order to put financial knowledge in the hands of farmers themselves.

Since Reform and Opening, small enterprises have been the most vital and active part of China's economy. An important propulsive force in China's economic growth, they have played an extremely important role in creating new products, in adjusting the structure of production, in stimulating regional economies, resolving employment problems, and helping in the transition of rural labor. The current level of financial services in China cannot, however, begin to satisfy their abundant need for funding as they continue to grow. In order to resolve the difficult problems of funding small enterprises, the CBRC has encouraged financial institutions to improve their services to small businesses and make them of primary importance in their priorities. The Commission has guided banks in recognizing that loans to small enterprises are an opportunity to diversify risk, expand profits, and adjust strategies.

Taking full advantage of the well-established foundation and experience of international banking, the Commission has promulgated a succession of documents on six important banking mechanisms that relate to this shift in priorities. A series of "Guiding Opinions on Bank Loans to Small Enterprises" includes encouraging the banking industry to put its efforts into setting up risk-based pricing, independent accounting, efficient means of evaluation and approval, adequate restraints, professional training, and ways to deal with problems of violations of information disclosure requirements. After years of hard work, most financial institutions in the banking industry have basically completed a full set of systems relating to the different aspects of making loans to small enterprises: authorization, evaluation and approval, accounting, due diligence, auditing, accountability mechanisms, and so on. These have helped considerably in developing banks' business in extending loans to small enterprises.

Banking Regulation

From the beginning of the CBRC, certain principles were set forth describing the Commission's purpose: "regulation of legal entities, regulation of risk, regulation of internal controls and increase in transparency." New regulatory concepts of modern international regulatory regimes were adopted as models to follow, together with the "Four Regulatory Goals," and the "Six Optimum Regulatory Standards." In terms of implementing the new risk regulation concepts, and in line with the general thinking of "raising the accuracy of discriminating among different types of loans—adequate preparation—adoption of realistic interest ratios—capital adequacy rates that meet the standard requirements," the Commission went on to implement prudent regulation that takes risk as the primary consideration in dealing with the banking industry.

The CBRC uses the "Law of the PRC on Banking Regulation and Supervision" as its core basis for establishing rules and regulations for the regulatory system. From this, it has set forth a total of 220 regulations and documents that serve as standards to follow, covering such aspects of the industry as terms under which participants are allowed to participate in the market, risk management, internal controls, capital controls, and so on. The Commission created a preliminary structure for prudent regulatory laws and rules. In the course of establishing these laws and rules, the CBRC paid particular attention to the establishment of procedures relating to transparency. Before setting forth the most important rules, it thoroughly canvassed both the public at large and the banking industry for their input and opinions.

With regard to carrying out regulatory activities, the CBRC has regarded the establishment of an international advisory commission as a very important step, in order to be able to take advantage of recent advances in international banking regulation, and in order to learn the best practices and experience of international regulatory agencies. The intent was to make sure that China's regulatory system was in line with international practices. Taking into account actual practices of the banking industry, the CBRC formulated and put into effect "Mid-range and Long-term Plans for Improving Effective Banking Regulation." Its aim was to increase the capabilities of the regulatory system. At the same time, using the Basel Commission as reference and using its "Core Principles for Effective Banking Supervision," the Banking Regulatory Commission instituted a periodic self-evaluation process. After several years of hard work, the distance between international [Basel] standards and the effectiveness of CBRC has noticeably decreased.

In recent years, the CBRC has relentlessly revised and improved its regulatory ways and means, forcing financial institutions to improve corporate governance and internal controls, getting commercial banks to set up capital control systems. It has comprehensively adopted the five categories of loan-ratings in accord with standard international practices in the industry, as well as capital adequacy ratios, risk evaluation methods, and CAMELS regulatory ratings. [Note: CAMELS = capital, asset quality, management, earnings, liquidity, and sensitivity. This is a private, internal bank rating system of the regulators for 8,000 + FDIC (Federal Deposit Insurance Corporation) insured banks that include operational risks and overall bank ratings. A variation, CAMEL, is a private, internal credit union rating system of the NCUA (National Credit Union Administration) for 8,000 + NCUA insured credit unions.]

In addition, the Commission has implemented a series of prudent regulatory measures relating to such things as large sum credit, and related transactions, while actively employing such investigation methods as loan "degree of deviation," loan "migration" analysis, same-quality-same-type comparisons and other scientific regulatory methods. It has supported work related to full information disclosure, and to improving market restraints. To an appropriate degree, it has furthered a transition from a dictated and rule-driven style of regulation to regulation governed by guiding principles. Under conditions of manageable risk, it has encouraged the loosening of regulatory regimes, and the speeding up of innovation. At the same time, the CBRC has gradually improved its own organizational structure and its processing systems. It has developed new regulatory information systems, implemented targeted on-the-spot investigations focused on special risk circumstances, made its deployment of regulatory resources more scientific, and markedly strengthened the efficacy and the professionalism of banking regulation.

In order to manage risk that is cross-industry and cross-border, the CBRC has cooperated with the China Securities Regulatory Commission (CSRC) and the China Insurance Regulatory Commission (CIRC) in signing a memorandum on financial regulatory cooperation. Three chairmen of the three agencies have been appointed to a "Joint Conference System" that promotes cross-industry regulatory policy coordination, in order to work together in preventing cross-industry and cross-system risk. At the same time, the CBRC has signed memo-randums of cooperation and understanding with regulatory agencies of more than 20 countries and regions, including the US, England, Canada, Germany, Korea, Singapore, Hong Kong, Macao, France, Australia, and Italy. These memorandums set up cooperative regula-tions and mechanisms for communication.

NEW CHALLENGES

After several years of ongoing reform and opening to the outside, China's banking industry is now standing at a new starting point. Both the industry and the regulatory system are facing new opportunities but at the same time huge challenges.

External Shocks to China's Banking System

The financial situation both inside and outside China is currently exhibiting wholly new features. On the international front, in recent years the world's economic and financial situation is far more volatile and complex, price inflation is occurring in all kinds of globally traded commodities, exchange rates of the main foreign currencies are highly volatile, trade protectionism continues unabated, and the transferring of risk on global financial markets has increased greatly in both scale and speed. The US subprime mortgage loan crisis that erupted in the summer of 2007 has led to erratic disturbances in the international financial markets. A number of well-known financial institutions face severe liquidity problems, Western credit markets have shrunk dramatically, and uncertainties have grown with respect to the prospects for continued global economic growth.

Meanwhile, China has continued to open its economic and finan-cial systems to the outside. Along with this process has come the abil-ity of outside risk factors to influence China's macro-environment. Economic integration is prey to multiple risk factors. Seen from the domestic perspective, China's GDP has maintained a positive trend, but in the face of such problems as trade imbalances, overly high investment, an overly fast increase in credit, and dramatic rises in asset prices. Such non-harmonized elements have begun to exert a destabilizing influence. China has passed a whole series of macroeco-nomic policies relating to interest rates and exchange rates—speeding up the marketization of exchange rates and improving exchange rate mechanisms. Along with the difficulties in managing these, changes in the foreign economic and financial environment now mean a commensurate increase in the difficulties of risk management.

The work of the financial industry with regard to risk management is therefore increasing. Higher demands are being placed on the resilience of bank managers, their ability to be flexible, and their ability to withstand pressure.

Further Reform

We recognize that even though the banking industry has accomplished breakthrough progress in recent years, compared to modern systems abroad it still lags behind in corporate governance, strategic positioning, financial innovations, and risk management in particular. Modern corporate governance has not yet reached a stage of "possessing both form and spirit." Internal control and risk-management culture needs to be further cultivated throughout banking organizations. Strategic growth positioning needs to be sharpened, and quality control of product services needs to be strengthened. Furthermore, areas of overly uniform income structures, operations efficiency, risk pricing in financial innovations, and support capability of management information systems all await improvement. Finally, the quality of people engaged in the banking industry needs to be more professional in order to develop the industry and face the challenges of international competition.

Risk Management

The opening to the outside of China's banking industry has entered a new stage, one that is affecting risk parameters. Under new conditions, management of foreign-invested banks is more diversified and risk also becomes more complex. Difficulties are increasing in terms of regulation as well, given the trend for banks with foreign funding to become Chinese legal entities. First, the diversification of foreign-invested banks in China is placing increasing demands on regulatory systems and allocation of resources. In addition to setting up legal entity banks and branches in China, many large foreign-invested banks have now become strategic investors in Chinese banks. New questions are raising new needs, such as how to harmonize the need for adequate financial services in some areas and the need for fair competition, how to prevent conflicts of interest and at the same time prevent market monopolization. Second, the greater complexities in management-related risk in foreign-invested banks are presenting challenges to the regulatory capacity of China's regulatory bodies. At present, China has a regulatory system that is divided by industry, just as management is divided by industry. The large international financial groups, which have jurisdiction over most foreign-invested banks in China, generally employ "integrated management." Inside China, they can apply to different regulatory agencies to get business licenses for doing different things. The issue for Chinese authorities is how to harmonize regulatory agencies and still maintain and increase "opening," and how to avoid the possibility of having regulatory vacuums in some areas. How to accomplish integrated regulation of foreign-invested banks and still create a fair competitive environment is something that requires further study.

Regulatory Capacity

The complexity of bank management is increasing tremendously, given the cross-industry, cross-market, and cross-border nature of financial innovations and financial mergers. Forms of risk are also diversifying. Regulatory bodies have not yet instituted effective, scientifically based systems to deal with the risk that accompanies complex products. Even with simpler products, our regulatory bodies lack practiced methods and mature regulatory experience. If the knowledge levels and professionalism of our personnel are not able to keep up with changes in the market, it will be hard to adopt timely and effective regulatory measures. The effectiveness of regulation and effective control over cross-industry and cross-border risk will be greatly compromised.

New developments in international banking regulations have also made improvement of China's regulatory system an urgent need. The New Basel Capital Accord was formally promulgated in June 2004. It then became the new standard for regulation of capital adequacy ratios. The Group of 10 and other such developed country financial markets, as well as the main new market economy countries, have already announced policy frameworks that put the New Capital Accord into effect. At the same time, in order to meet the changes of international accounting standards, China began to implement a new accounting standards system in 2007 that is in accord with international standards.

Steps are being taken, but in such a short space of time, it is a challenge for China's regulatory capacity to establish rules that are in accord with international standards and that are also appropriate to the unique features of the Chinese banking industry.

BETTER BANKING REGULATION

Faced with these challenges, we must approach the situation with a scientific point of view, as well as a sense of responsibility. We should continue to promote the Reform and Opening of the banking industry in line with similar goals in the financial sector. We should vigorously promote positive change in the system as well as the mechanisms and products of the banking industry, in order to improve the core competitiveness and the overall competitiveness of China's banking industry. We must constantly improve our methods and measures of regulation, in line with ongoing developments and changes in the business risk and macro-environment. We must promote fair competition, protect the rights of depositors, and preserve the safe operating of the banking system by implementing prudent regulation, under Chinese law that uses international standards as our model.

Monitoring External Factors

China's banking industry should fully recognize that the country's finances are increasingly tied to a global economy that has in recent years been in imbalance, seen excessive overall liquidity, and experienced increased volatility in the financial markets. Shocks coming from financial risk factors outside China are now far more direct. We in China must pursue ongoing growth policies, but must recognize that many risks are magnified by our global involvement. These include credit risk, market risk, operating risk, and liquidity risk. We must improve our ability to recognize and differentiate among different kinds of risk, and to monitor, predict, and contain risk. Even as we grow at a fast rate, we must find ways to test external risk and be able to take appropriate action.

Improving Systems, Mechanisms, and Products

The banking industry must continue to deepen corporate governance reform, by setting up and improving a framework of modern corporate governance that is in accord with China's national characteristics. It must further establish internal controls, improve business and management procedures, cultivate and set up a corporate culture that is in accord with regulations. It must improve both the technology and the measures of risk management, and must improve risk management capacity. The industry must create new methods of human resource recruitment, as well as new systems of rewards and restraints. It must set up a scientific system of personnel selection, and actively cultivate a professional team of people in the financial industry that is of the highest quality. It must encourage financial institutions in the banking industry to improve innovative capacity, in order to raise both core and comprehensive competitiveness. With effective regulation as a precondition, it must encourage financial institutions to develop comprehensive financial services, put cross-industry management into effect, and offer intersecting products and services.

Assuring Financial Security

A primary consideration is furthering banking reform for China's own banks while continuing to "open" to the outside and competitive banks. The question for China is how to use this process to spur further reform in its domestic banking system. The emphasis should be placed on increasing the core competitiveness of Chinese banks through this process of reform. Second, how do we achieve the government's macroeconomic goals, and further the harmonious development of the banking industry by utilizing the self-directed quality of "opening" policies in the banking industry? We must further study and test alternative policy measures in resolving the problems of imbalances in the degree of opening among China's geographic regions; we must continue to research the preferential policies extended to such regions as Hong Kong and Macao by CEPA (CEPA is the Closer Economic Partnership Arrangement between the central government of China and its Special Administrative Regions).

At the same time, we must fully utilize cross-border regulatory cooperative mechanisms, and actively promote cooperative relations with more countries and regions. We must thoroughly understand the management and risk situation of foreign-invested banks in their own mother countries, in order to be able to recognize problems or unfavorable trends in a timely manner. We must be able to apply regulatory measures, given timely forewarning mechanisms. Along with the gradual implementation of the New Basel Capital Accord, we must further improve ourselves by strengthening communications and exchange with other regulatory bodies, and by building effective cross-border regulation that is able to maintain financial security.

By participating in the market-entry negotiations and the rules formulation process at the WTO, we want to create the conditions whereby Chinese banks can enter international markets. With the strengthening of reform and restructuring of Chinese commercial banks, such things as capital strength, corporate governance, management standards, and information disclosure are gradually being brought into conformity with rules. The effective regulatory capacity of China's financial regulatory bodies is being greatly improved, so that it will in the future approach or reach entry requirements of target market countries. As we follow WTO rules and comply with obligations, we should actively participate in negotiations, and in a targeted manner ask that member countries go further in opening their markets, enabling those restructured Chinese commercial banks that meet the required conditions to develop their business abroad.

Strengthening Effective Banking Regulation

The basic tenets of China's banking regulation are to "regulate legal persons, regulate risk, regulate internal controls, and raise transparency." Emphasis is put on primary risks of commercial banks and systemic risks of the banking system at large. We oversee and encourage commercial banks to establish adequate risk control systems and strict internal control mechanisms, and we pass mandatory market requirements on information disclosure. At the same time, we are adopting more systematic and in-depth risk control measures, strengthening off-site evaluation and analysis procedures, raising risk evaluation capacity, raising our on-site investigation abilities, and strengthening enforcement measures and punishments. We must now research and develop comprehensive forecasting measures for risk and crisis management systems, set up sequential crisis-management methods according to the degree of risk and the scope involved, and guard against abrupt or unexpected risk as well as systemic risk. In line with the "Core Principles for Effective Banking Regulation" and other such international standards, we must improve regulatory efficiency and transparency, and constantly seek to improve the professionalism and effectiveness of China's banking regulation.

CHAPTER 6

China's Financial Transformation and New Challenges

Stephen K. Green
Group Chairman, HSBC Holdings plc

A new era of Chinese economic development has been ushered in with the full opening of China's financial markets. This marks the culmination of decades of reforms and provides a platform for financial institutions, both domestic and foreign, to promote new entrepreneurial activities, more efficient allocation of capital and greater financial choice for customers.

The impact of this openness has been felt most immediately in the banking sector itself—with foreign banks gaining increased market access and local banks exploiting new technologies, management skills, partnerships and capital—but the benefits reach far beyond financial institutions alone. A more modern and competitive financial system offers the Chinese people better tools for managing their increasing prosperity, China's state-owned enterprises have become more market-oriented, and China's small and medium-sized enterprises enjoy improved access to capital. And with a more competitive financial sector, China's economy has become increasingly robust and resilient to shocks.

There is, of course, still work to be done. But in comparison to the turn of this century, when major state-owned banks were saddled with nonperforming loans and risk assessment mechanisms were significantly less developed, the financial system has undergone a stunning transformation.

That Chinese regulators recognised problems and took effective action to fortify the financial system is of tremendous significance to both China and the world. Indeed, history has demonstrated that economic progress can be delayed or even erased if financial sector reforms are not pursued in conjunction with broader market reforms. Within Asia, major shocks, like the financial crisis of the late 1990s and the bursting of Japan's economic bubble, were exacerbated—if not directly caused—by banking systems that were either structurally weak or insufficiently market-oriented.

It would seem indisputable, then, that the reform of China's financial system is vital to ensuring stability in the global market. China is already the world's fourth-largest economy and the third-largest trading nation, and has the potential to become, within just a few decades, the world's largest economy. The preservation of a healthy and stable economy in China is essential for the maintenance of the global economy.

In this essay, I analyze the implementation of recent reforms, offer an overview of the current market environment, and consider future trends.

THREE DECADES OF REFORM

The ongoing transformation of China's banking system is a particularly impressive achievement, given both the scale and depth of the challenges over the last 30 years, as the country made the rapid transition from a planned economy to a market-oriented one.

The beginning of the transformation of China's banking system largely coincides with the reform process instigated by Deng Xiaoping. From the initial founding of the People's Republic of China in 1949 until Deng's reforms in the late 1970s, all commercial banking was handled by the People's Bank of China (PBC), which encompassed treasury and central banking functions.

The PBC's control over the banking system was orchestrated through its control of three specialised banks: Agricultural Bank of China (ABC), which loaned to the agricultural sector; the China Construction Bank (CCB), which provided infrastructure finance; and the Bank of China (BOC), which managed the country's foreign exchange, including conversion rates, foreign loans and letters of credit. These three units were spun off from the PBC in 1979, effectively marking the start of the reform process.

China's final member of the "Big Four" commercial banks was founded in 1984, when the PBC was restructured with more narrowly defined goals and functions and formally established as the central bank. At the same time, the Industrial and Commercial Bank of China was founded to take over the PBC's commercial banking functions. (As an indicator of the rapid rate and massive scale of change in China's financial sector, it is worth noting that, in the 23 years since its restructuring, the PBC has become one of the world's most influential central banks, while ICBC has become the world's largest bank in terms of market capitalization.)

Still, the drive to transform the Big Four into true commercial operations was difficult, since they retained their role as policy banks. As such, Chinese banks largely approached credit allocation based on the overall development needs of China as a nation. This meant that the lion's share of lending went to finance projects that had been prioritized by planning authorities and regional governments. Few mechanisms existed to assess credit risk according to normal banking standards.

In light of the rapid credit expansion and increased commercialization within China that occurred from the 1980s to the mid-1990s, the decision was taken to move toward a more market-oriented banking system.

In the mid-1990s, a new Commercial Banking Law was established and three policy banks were simultaneously created to finance the infrastructure development to support China's agricultural sector and export industries—the China Development Bank (CDB), the Agricultural Development Bank (ADB) and Export-Import Bank of China (China Exim Bank). This decision freed the Big Four to become more focused on commercial business.

Since then, China has made rapid progress in developing credit-assessment techniques—reducing the proportion of non-performing loans in bank portfolios and aggressively recapitalizing where necessary, both through the creation of asset management companies (AMCs) and through subsequent injection of capital into the biggest banks in preparation for partial share listings in the international market.

Much of this process has taken place since 2000. According to estimates by Ernst & Young, between 2003 and 2005 about RMB608 billion (US$78.2 billion) was injected into the banking sector, while RMB420 billion in bad loans were written off by the 'Big Four' banks. In addition, RMB796 billion in nonperforming loans were sold to newly created AMCs.

As a further aid to the transformation of the sector, strategic investors were introduced to help banks improve their risk management systems. HSBC was a pioneer in this process, with the 2001 agreement to take an eight percent shareholding in Bank of Shanghai, the first ever investment by a foreign bank in a domestic bank. The process accelerated in 2004, when HSBC invested US$1.75 billion for a 19.9 percent stake in Bank of Communications (BoCom), China's fifth-largest bank. At that time, this was the single largest foreign investment in a domestic bank.

Since this process began, more than 30 mainland Chinese institutions have received strategic foreign investments.

The final step in the transformation process was the public offering of shares in China's banks, which brought both increased market review of operations and helped the banks to further strengthen their capital positions. BoCom had a US$1.9 billion Hong Kong offering in June 2005. CCB followed with a US$9.2 billion Hong Kong listing in October 2005. There was a US$9.2 billion BOC Hong Kong listing in May 2006. In October 2006, ICBC listed for US$19.1 billion in both Shanghai and Hong Kong: the first simultaneous, dual Mainland and offshore listing and, at that time, the world's largest ever IPO.

The result of all of these efforts is that today most of all the major Chinese banks have capital adequacy ratios that meet international standards. All the major banks—both the state-owned commercial banks and the joint-stock commercial banks—have actively been developing a much broader range of products, including mortgages, consumer finance and credit cards. There has also been significant progress in developing modern management techniques and structures, as well as disclosure standards, thereby improving overall corporate governance.

FURTHER REFORMS IN PROGRESS

As China's economy expands still further, we anticipate continued strong growth in the financial services sector on both the investment and consumer finance sides. Firstly, China is increasingly liberalizing its financial services sector. Foreign firms gained full market access under the WTO from 2007—with HSBC being one of the first foreign banks to locally incorporate and take advantage of the new operating environment.

Secondly, the Chinese government aims to rebalance its economy away from investment-led growth and toward personal consumption-led growth, so consumers will need credit cards, debit cards and the full range of retail banking services, which are still developing in China. Equally, as China's financial markets and institutions develop, depositors will want access to longer term financial products such as pensions, insurance and asset management products.

This rebalancing is an important objective for Chinese policy makers. The ultimate solution for raising consumption is to further develop both the welfare system and the financial sector. With greater security and better financial planning, both individuals and enterprises are comfortable consuming, rather than just saving; they can invest in a way that better supports productive enterprises. Pension contributions, for example, are being changed to a funded system that more effectively caters to China's aging population.

Rising government spending on education and healthcare would also lower expected future costs for consumers. These are key reasons for Chinese households to save, and such developments will lower the excess household savings rate, further supporting the shift toward consumption in coming years. This can be additionally enhanced through the future development of consumer banking products and also a wider range of saving and investment products that provide better returns on savings to bank customers.

Given these trends, I have no doubt that competition for business will become more and more robust, bringing better deals for customers, a wider product range and a stronger financial system generally.

However, whilst China is moving rapidly toward a modern banking system, much remains to be done.

The Chinese economy still relies heavily on bank finance in comparison to other economies. In order to fully develop its financial system, further steps must be taken to develop a full range of capital market products and techniques. The introduction of futures, repurchase agreements, options and other hedging tools is an important component in managing risk—provided the regulatory framework ensures they are correctly used. Encouraging an institutional investor base will also play a key role in stabilizing market operations and reducing market volatility.

Bank loans, even today, constitute a very high share of total financing. China's government has already recognized the need to diversify capital sources and improve the efficiency with which capital is allocated. In response, there have been a number of ground-breaking reforms to develop China's capital markets, improve the stability of the organisations involved, and broaden the products available.

Significant measures have included the recapitalization and consolidation of securities companies, the development of the domestic debt market (which is progressing rapidly), and the introduction of risk management tools, such as interest rate swaps and foreign exchange forwards. The further development of onshore stock markets—including a proposed bourse for small and medium enterprises—and the opening of China's corporate bond market will further this process.

Already, turnover in the bond, foreign exchange and derivatives markets is increasing and the equity market has stabilized, thanks to the careful and astute management of the state in disposing share holdings in major listed companies. Nevertheless, China's capital markets are currently still in a transitional stage, and further action will be needed to create financial markets which are of a size appropriate to so large an economy growing so rapidly.

At the same time, given the continued importance during this transition of the banks as the major source of finance, China's regulators and the senior management of its banks need to continue to emphasize the importance of a strong risk management culture among branch staff at every level. Key factors, of course, include not only a good understanding of the techniques of credit assessment for both consumer and commercial lending, but also a broader awareness of corporate governance issues such as reputational, market and portfolio risk. It is essential to ensure not only that individual credits are robustly assessed, but also that the overall credit portfolios are balanced and risk is not unduly concentrated. This is particularly important given the buoyancy of the property sector and other vital industries in China today.

At present, China's financial system still gives state-owned enterprises (SOEs) better access to funds than it allocates to more efficient, private companies. However, following China's profound economic reforms, the scope of private ownership has become substantial. The private sector currently accounts for well over half of China's GDP and an overwhelming share of its exports. Private enterprise generates most new jobs and is improving the productivity and profitability of the whole economy.

China's banking reforms support banks' efforts to allocate a larger portion of funding to private companies, thereby raising China's overall productivity. Moreover, equity market reforms will also improve the performance of SOEs and the access of private enterprise to alternative sources of capital. Further opening up of the financial system, greater transparency and a more level playing field will promote better governance, more shareholder oversight and the creation of new, more productive jobs in the private sector.

To achieve these benefits, it is important to examine the way in which risk and reward dynamics work in the financial system, both for bank staff and for customers. For banks in China, there is a need to strengthen banking skills, information systems, auditing procedures and staff reward and appraisal techniques. Loan officers have traditionally faced few consequences for approving bad loans, particularly to state-owned companies, and enjoyed little reward for taking a well-calculated risk in new segments, such as consumer lending or small and medium-sized enterprise (SME) loans. On the customer side, the previous focus on lending to SOEs made retail banking in China less developed, with the exception of bank deposits, although the consumer portion of banks' portfolios has started to increase rapidly in recent years.

Similarly, the very high level of household savings in part reflects the fact that the financial system's current structure has generally left consumers with few investment options outside of low-yield, low-risk bank deposits. Although growing real estate prices and a resurgent stock market have in recent years given Chinese citizens further options, the relative lack of investment choices has created fears of overheating in both equity and property markets. Further avenues for Chinese citizens to manage their savings and the availability of additional investment channels could help mitigate these risks.

A positive response to this is the Qualified Domestic Institutional Investor (QDII) programme, initially launched in mid-2006, which has given institutional and retail investors the ability to invest in overseas markets through approved QDII institutions. Initially, QDII offerings were limited to secure fixed-income investments such as government bonds. These offerings had a relatively muted reception from Chinese investors, who were faced with a surging equity market and expectations of an appreciating currency.

Aware of this, the Chinese government took steps to improve the QDII programme in July 2007, broadening the scheme to include offshore equity investments that were able to provide higher returns. HSBC China was the first foreign bank to offer QDII products under this revamped scheme. Since its launch, we have witnessed an increasingly strong investor appetite for new QDII offerings, with Chinese citizens becoming increasingly receptive to new investment tools and means to diversify risk.

Personal financial services such as consumer lending, mortgages, credit cards and auto loans remain at an early stage of development, although they are quickly growing in popularity. This shift to a more even balance between corporate lending and personal financial services, and between state-owned and private lending within the commercial portfolio, will take time. Most Chinese banks are still developing their internal credit assessment capabilities, and access to external information on the credit history and the financial condition of potential borrowers remains limited. However, this situation should change rapidly as China is also making significant progress in developing a national consumer credit bureau, with the PBC credit check database building an increasingly comprehensive guide to consumer and business credit history, to which other institutions are gaining access.

Still, there is as yet no nationwide standard for collecting and sharing the necessary data. On the corporate side, there remains a pressing need to improve financial disclosure, accounting standards and auditing for private sector companies. This may only occur once companies have increased access to the equities market and pressure from shareholders builds for accurate and regular financial reporting. Such shortfalls in the availability of information and in the transparency of financial statements are causing limits both on consumer and small business lending.

The opening of China's financial sector under the WTO entry agreements has already led to greater competition and enhanced product ranges in the banking sector. At the same time, the legal and regulatory framework has some notable developments in the pipeline, which will further enhance and support the operating environment for banks in China, including a deposit insurance scheme. Further reforms to the interest rate and exchange rate regime will no doubt be introduced at the appropriate time.

LOCAL INCORPORATION OF FOREIGN BANKS

In 2007, China undertook a historic step in transforming its banking sector by allowing foreign banks to locally incorporate so as to have full access to the financial market. In April 2007, HSBC became one of the first four foreign banks to establish a locally incorporated unit; five other banks soon followed. These units operate under the same laws and requirements as China's domestic banks, in an environment that ensures the equal treatment of all foreign and domestic banks. Locally incorporated banks can offer RMB financing and deposit services, with no geographical restrictions on their business.

According to the China Banking Regulatory Commission (CBRC), these nine institutions in 2006 collectively accounted for 34 percent of all foreign bank branches in China, 55 percent of total assets held by foreign banks and 58 percent of profits by foreign banks. The clear indication here is that foreign institutions view local incorporation as essential to building businesses of a significant scale in China.

However, what a foreign bank considers a large scale operation in China must be seen in relative terms, as illustrated by a side-by-side comparison of the largest foreign institution in China with the country's largest domestic institution: HSBC's 61-outlet network (as at end-December 2007) is dwarfed by the more than 20,000 outlets of ICBC. Given this vast chasm, international institutions will not be able to challenge the leading role of China's domestic institutions in the local market.

Therefore, foreign banks that are seeking to run profitable and sustainable operations as locally incorporated entities must have clearly defined and precisely executed business strategies that serve niche rather than diverse customer segments.

For example, HSBC's strategy in mainland China is two-pronged: both the partnership with BoCom and the expansion of our own network—a network that has existed since the establishment of HSBC in Hong Kong and Shanghai in 1865, denoting the special significance of our business in China.

We have chosen to focus on our strength in wealth management for the retail segment, while building our Chinese organic network to better offer products and services to global businesses in China, and to Chinese businesses that have global ambitions and requirements. Although we will remain, by comparison, a small presence, I believe that foreign banks offer significant expertise that will add value to China's overall economic development.

While I have thus far been discussing the opening of China's mainstream commercial banking sector, it should also be noted that in 2007 a second important frontier opened for both international and domestic banks as new regulations on banking in rural areas came into effect. In December 2006, the CBRC dramatically lowered the entry threshold for banks seeking to enter rural areas and eased access conditions to the rural marketplace. These reforms promise to extend the benefits of financial modernization beyond China's bustling cities, thereby supporting the delivery of quality financial services for the country's rural majority and the development of the countryside.

These rules seek to help modernize the rural banking system, address the problems of the relative low coverage of banking outlets, insufficient supply of financial services and the lack of competition in these areas.

In addition, the new policy opens up a market of untapped potential for international banks. While such banks have thus far limited their China operations to large coastal cities and industrialised centres, the attractiveness of China's rural regions is clear for international banks. Although geographically dispersed, the size of the rural market is very large. *The 2006 China Statistical Yearbook* estimated that rural deposits totalled more than RMB2 trillion in 2004, and the rural population is, conservatively, more than 600 million.

HSBC was the first international bank to enter China's rural market with the establishment of Hubei Suzhou Chengdu HSBC Rural Bank Company Limited (HSBC Rural Bank) in December 2007. We plan to open additional rural banks in the coming years. Given the size and the potential of the market it is expected that other international peers will soon set up similar operations, creating competition and bringing further international expertise to the countryside.

THE HSBC EXPERIENCE

Our experience is that China's government has fully acknowledged the importance of international financial institutions to its banking sector. Over the years, foreign banks, including our own, have helped contribute to the changing landscape of China's banking industry through enhanced competition and the introduction of technology and management expertise.

Our partnership with Bank of Communications (BoCom), which commenced in 2004, marked a deepening and strengthening of our historic ties to China and has led to a particularly fruitful cooperation in consumer banking. BoCom has now issued over four million BoCom-HSBC co-branded credit cards with technical and management support from HSBC.

This is a multi faceted relationship that extends much further than collaboration on selected products; BoCom and HSBC have a cooperation framework, sustained by regular meetings between executives and management at many levels, and allows both banks, as partners, to leverage each other's network—thereby extending the ability to serve customers and benefit from the combined domestic and international reach of both banks.

The pairing of HSBC and BoCom is perhaps the largest and most comprehensive partnership between a Chinese and foreign institution. However, it is only one example of the numerous ways that Chinese and international institutions have sought to develop mutually beneficial synergies. Tie-ups vary immensely in both scale and execution: we have seen international investment bank Goldman Sachs link with China's largest bank ICBC, US banking giant Bank of America partner with China Construction Bank (CCB) and have also seen Australia's ANZ collaborate with the municipal Shanghai Rural Commercial Bank.

Thus the Chinese model, which supports cooperation between foreign and Chinese banks, means a win-win situation: sharing best practice, developing new products, improving service to customers.

NEW FRONTIERS FOR CHINESE BANKS

With the full opening of China's financial market to the world in 2007, we are starting to see the reciprocal opening of the world's financial markets to China's banks. In the first half of this decade, the trend was for Chinese financial institutions to welcome international investment as a means of boosting capital, acquiring skills and management systems. Now, with the domestic banking sector heavily capitalized from domestic and international IPOs, we are seeing Chinese institutions looking outward for strategic shareholdings in overseas institutions. International institutions, in turn, are highly receptive to investment from Chinese institutions as a means to attain exposure to the China market and gain from the local knowledge of their Chinese investors.

Deals struck in 2007 include some of China's largest firms and some of the world's oldest and best-known financial institutions. We have seen ICBC's US$5.6 billion purchase of a 20-percent stake in South Africa's Standard Bank and China Development Bank make a €2.2 billion investment in Barclays plc of the UK. At the time of writing, Ping An Insurance (Group) Co has announced a planned €1.8 billion purchase of a 4.2 percent stake in the Belgian-Dutch Fortis N.V.

The offshore earnings generated by these investments will create enormous benefit for China's banks—enhancing the diversification of earnings, and thereby reducing volatility and risk. The increasing interconnectedness of China with the global financial system will further foster trade and investment in other areas—both among international firms seeking opportunities in China and domestic firms seeking investment overseas—thereby helping to ensure continued global growth and economic development.

BANKS AND THE ENVIRONMENT

I have noted the economic benefits arising from the strengthening of China's banking system and from the increasing integration of the national and global financial systems, processes which are developing alongside China's increasing participation in global trade, economics and politics. China is also very aware of the important part that it plays in the global ecosystem—especially in light of the challenges that we collectively face in terms of resource management and climate change.

All banks operating in China must recognize that the country's long-term development is not merely a matter of economics, and that conservation and social development must be given high priority in order to ensure that the tremendous gains made by China are sustainable. This is not a matter of altruism; banks must recognize that actions and policies that damage the environment will undermine economic growth and can result in institutions losing the support of their shareholders and customers.

As a result, HSBC and its banking peers—internationally and within China—are increasingly adopting policies on sustainable banking and building sustainability into their own businesses.

International banks have adopted numerous internal guidelines that help facilitate environmental and socially sustainable economic development. HSBC, for instance, has adopted rigorous internal guidelines that apply across its global operations, with specific sector guidelines governing lending in sensitive sectors such as forest land and forest products; freshwater infrastructure; chemicals; energy; metals and mining.

HSBC was also an early adopter of the Equator Principles, which are a common set of voluntary guidelines, based on best practice, to help financial institutions and their clients address the social and environmental impact of their project financing activities. The Principles, which reference the International Financial Corporation's performance standards, require that risk assessment be conducted on project financing activities of a value of US$10 million or greater.

We have undertaken to ensure that all applicable project finance proposals, including where we advise on the structuring of project finance transactions, fall within the requirements of the Principles.

We will not provide loans directly to projects where the borrower will not, or is not able to, comply with either the Equator Principles or our own internal sector guidelines, whichever carries the higher standard.

Among global financial institutions, there has been a significant increase in the number of banks adopting the Equator Principles. According to the International Financial Corporation (IFC), Equator Principle banks collectively accounted for about 30 percent of project finance in emerging markets when the Equator Principles were established in 2003. In October 2007, the IFC estimated that adopter banks are responsible for about 85 percent of project financing worldwide, indicating that ethical lending has moved from the margins to the mainstream.

While the Equator Principles directly apply only to projects of US$10 million or greater, banks can also facilitate the adoption of sustainable practices among small and medium-sized enterprises. HSBC, for instance, has introduced a scheme under which businesses that deploy equipment in Hong Kong or mainland China are eligible to apply for the Green Equipment Financing scheme, which offers beneficial rates for companies investing in equipment that reduces energy and resource consumption, or reduces waste production. Schemes such as this indicate the banking sector's recognition of the viability of green businesses and acknowledgment that green initiatives can contribute to profitability.

While these polices involve banks restricting negative actions—such as refusing lending to high-polluting and energy inefficient enterprises—banks can also contribute to the environment by taking positive actions within their own core business. We believe that there are significant economic opportunities associated with the development of a lower carbon economy. We have established a Climate Change Centre of Excellence that will help the bank identify economic opportunities associated with a lower carbon economy for the benefit of the Group's clients and for the Group's own businesses.

Meanwhile, in September 2007, we created a family of climate change indices to track and reflect the stock market performance of key companies that we believe are best-placed to profit from the challenges of climate change. These include industries and companies involved in emissions reduction, those concerned with reacting to the effects of climate change, and those focused on adapting to the impact of climate change.

In addition, banks—indeed all enterprises—can work to ensure that their own operations are sustainable. HSBC, the first major bank to become carbon neutral, has in 2007 committed a further US$90 million over five years to reduce the bank's impact on the environment through a series of initiatives, including the introduction of renewable energy technology, water and waste reduction programs and employee engagement. In our experience, initiatives such as these are not only of benefit to the environment, but can also deliver increased cost savings over time that reinforces the sustainability of business growth.

While green initiatives by the financial sector are largely being driven by business interest, government can encourage the adoption of best practices in sustainable banking through education and incentive mechanisms. Sustainable banking practices are gaining particular traction in the Chinese market, with focus on reduced lending to polluting, high-energy and high-resource consuming industries, in line with guidance of regulators and the targets set by the eleventh Five-year Plan.

China's recognition that the banking sector has a key role to play in environmental protection and development can be seen in several new initiatives. These include the environmental credit database developed by the State Environmental Protection Administration and the People's Bank of China (PBC), which should ensure the increased adoption of sustainable banking practices in China. Similarly, the Shanghai bureau of the China Banking Regulatory Commission (CBRC) has issued guidance requiring that financial institutions report on their corporate social responsibility activities.

These moves are in line with China's increased commitment to harmonious and scientific development—which puts an emphasis on energy and resource management, social development and environmental sustainability. With the concept of "the scientific outlook on development" now enshrined in the constitution of China's governing party, the promotion of social and environmental development has become a key consideration for the government and, in turn, for all businesses that operate within China.

CONCLUSIONS

Since China opened its doors to the world in the late 1970s, the nation has made tremendous progress in developing both its broad economy and its financial systems. While regulatory and financial systems in mature markets took centuries to evolve—a process which is still very much ongoing—the transformation of China's systems from a controlled economy to a market-based one has been truly revolutionary in its scale and breadth.

There is still much work ongoing, with new developments continuing apace in nearly every sub-sector of the financial industry, but these will be of great benefit as the Chinese economy continues to mature.

In the new environment, foreign banks will have an increasingly important role to play in ensuring continued economic development and financial system modernization. Still, given the relatively limited size of foreign financial institutions within China, the overall success of China's economic development will continue to be largely driven by domestic banks.

Domestic banks have shown themselves very able in this regard. In mere decades, China's major banks have rapidly developed into world-scale financial institutions and have been quick in their adoption of international standards. The openness of China's institutions has contributed to this process: first with local banks welcoming strategic shareholders and, more recently, with Chinese banks becoming strategic shareholders in overseas institutions. Over the same period, China's regulators have ably led the nation from being a closed, state directed economy to being a global force in world trade and financial markets.

As China seeks to further refine its economic model, there will be greater challenges ahead, particularly in terms of balancing environmental and social development with the need for continued economic growth. While the challenges facing China are indeed tremendous, so too are the opportunities for leadership. Given the nation's remarkable success at transforming its financial system in recent decades, there is every reason to be optimistic about the ability of the Chinese people and government to continue to develop a sustainable economy that benefits both the Chinese people and the world.

Editor's note, January 2009:

Mr. Stephen Green, Group Chairman of HSBC Holdings plc contributed an article for this publication in late 2007. In the months since the submission of his manuscript, world financial markets plunged into deep turmoil, market and macroeconomic conditions deteriorated sharply and several of the financial institutions referred to herein, ceased to exist.

Nevertheless, this article remains a fascinating overview of China's financial reforms from 1978 onward. It is worth noting that HSBC has remained resilient throughout this credit crisis while continuing to grow its business in China.)

CHAPTER 7

Commercial Banking Reform

Wang Jianxi

Former Vice Chairman, Central Huijin Investment Company, Ltd;[1]
Executive Vice-President, Chief Risk Officer,
China Investment Corporation

China's commercial banking reform was the focus of tremendous attention in China as well as abroad in the early part of this century. This reform, on one hand, represented a continuation of reforms undertaken for more than 20 years with regard to state-owned banks, it also represented a systemic change from previous banking reforms. The new reforms brought breakthrough progress in just three years. They had a very considerable impact on Chinese financial history.

BACKGROUND

A Review of China's Earlier State-owned Bank Reforms

During the centralized planned economy period in China, operations of China's entire financial system were highly concentrated in the hands of central authorities. The public finance authority was the guiding force in allocating fund resources while banks were merely cashiers or "big tellers" for the government and for enterprises.

As with other parts of the national economy, banks began to participate in economic reforms and "opening" policies starting in 1978. The first step as the banking industry started along the path to Reform and Opening was to restore state-owned banks that had been dismantled and merged during the Cultural Revolution, and to separate the loan-making and deposit-taking functions of the People's Bank of China (PBC) and put these under the newly established Industrial and Commercial Bank of China (ICBC). By 1984, a situation had emerged in which four state-owned banks, engaging in specific lines of business, were under the authority and the regulatory jurisdiction of the PBC. The four were ICBC, the Agricultural Bank of China (ABC), the Bank of China (BOC), and the China Construction Bank (CCB). The overall direction of bank reform was pursued in line with the path of a socialist market economy. On the one hand, the state now gradually relaxed restrictions on entering the industry by allowing regional governments, state-owned enterprises (SOEs), and private investors to engage in banking, as well as allowing foreign banks to enter China's market to a limited degree. On the other hand, reform of the four state-owned banks continued.

In 1995, China promulgated the Commercial Banking Law and the Law on the People's Bank of China. The laws stipulated that the four big banks were state-owned banks with the responsibilities to operate, take business risks and bear operating results by themselves. The laws also broke down the segregation of business lines for the four specialized banks so that business competition among four banks with overlapping business lines could proceed. The PBC took on the responsibility of being both the lender of the last resort and the "banker's bank." It strengthened its regulatory role over commercial banks. At the same time, China then set up three new "policy" banks specifically to take the policy-type business out of the four state-owned banks. Such banks undertake funding in furtherance of government policies. Policy banks and commercial banks were now separated into different entities.

The intent to marketize in the process of this significant reform was very clear, but putting the intent into practice turned out to be a disappointing process. One of the main reasons was that the reform of SOEs and reform of government functions did not keep pace with ongoing reform of the banks. In this environment, the regulation that the PBC was able to exercise over the commercial banks turned out to be more form than substance. State-owned commercial banks continued to be one of the more important and convenient tools for various priorities at all levels of government while they were exercising their economic control function.

When the Asian Financial Crisis erupted in Asia in 1997, China's banks were able to avoid direct damage hit due to their relative isolation from global banking systems. Capital adequacy ratios of these four large state-owned banks were grossly insufficient, however, and the ratios of nonperforming loans (NPLs) were exceedingly high. Their operational performance were quite poor, and Western observers were known to say that "Technically, [the four] are already bankrupt."

Given the Asian Financial Crisis of 1997, protecting the stability of the banking system became an urgent task. In 1998, in order to eliminate the tremendous latent risk in commercial banks, the central government issued RMB270 billion special treasury bonds to buttress the capital of the state-owned banks and to improve their capital adequacy ratios. In 1999, RMB1.4 trillion worth of NPLs were removed from the accounts of the four large state-owned banks, and four corresponding asset management companies (AMCs) were established. Named Huarong, Changcheng, Dongfang, and Xinda were set up specifically to attend to the task of disposing of the NPLs of the state-owned banks.

The NPLs of the four banks declined tremendously after this reform and capital adequacy ratios, as well as other financial indicators, saw some improvement. The improved conditions did not last, however, as NPLs on the books came back with a vengeance by the end of 2002. Liu Mingkang, the Chairman of China Banking Regulatory Commission (CBRC) at the time, remarked in a press conference in October 2003 that the ratio of NPLs to performing loans in state-owned banks was 24.13% at that time.

The causes of these NPLs in wholly state-owned commercial banks were quite complex. Analysis reveals that around 30% were the result of direct administrative fiats to and interference in the affairs of the banks, by all levels of government. Another 30% were the result of SOE reform. Around 10% came from administration and enforcement of justice at the regional level of government, and another 10% came from structural adjustments in manufacturing industries as led by the national government, including the closing down and merging of certain enterprises. The remaining 20% came from management problems within the banks themselves. From this analysis, it can be seen that 80% of NPLs in the system could be attributed in one way or another to the government (from Governor Zhou Xiaochuan's speech at International Financial Forum in 2004).

Looking back over the process of the first two rounds of banking reform, it should be noted that China modeled its reform on the successful experience of commercial banks in developed countries. These magic potions were not able to effect a cure for China's state-owned commercial banks, however, for the reason that developed countries existed in a completely different financial ecological factor. Earlier reforms in China emphasized copying technical models rather than innovative changes applied to the entire core system. China's underlying system was the crux. Measures taken could only treat the symptoms and not the disease, and therefore reform stagnated.

Banking Reform: the Necessity

Although China's government had already undertaken 20 years of banking reform, and various measures had actually accomplished some results, fundamental problems of state-owned commercial banks had not been resolved. In terms of reforming the system, the Chinese government now had very little choice but to go forward.

First, the banking industry in China occupies some 70% assets of the entire financial system, while the four large state-owned banks are the central supports of that system. In the course of reforms, the market share of the four large banks declined, but they still held between 45–55% of the total. This was among some more than 200 Chinese and foreign banks operating in China. Without resolving problems in the four large banks, systemic risk was a sword of Damocles hanging over the Chinese financial sector. The financial crises experienced by Japan and Asia were a wake-up call to all countries in Southeast Asia, and also to China.

Second, although capital markets had been through more than a dozen years of growth and had made certain progress, they had not achieved very much in terms of being able to allocate capital (Table 7.1). The banking industry was still the main channel for

TABLE 7.1 Capital raising from domestic stock market vs. annual increase of outstanding loans, 1993–2006 (Unit: hundred million RMB)

Year	Capital raised from domestic shares	Annual increase of outstanding loans	%
1993	314.54	6,335.40	4.96
1994	138.05	7,216.62	1.91
1995	118.86	9,339.82	1.27
1996	341.52	10,683.33	3.20
1997	933.82	10,712.47	8.72
1998	803.57	11,490.94	6.99
1999	897.39	10,846.36	8.27
2000	1,541.02	13,346.61	11.55
2001	1,182.13	12,439.41	9.50
2002	779.75	18,979.20	4.11
2003	823.10	27,702.30	2.97
2004	862.67	19,201.60	4.49
2005	338.13	16,492.60	2.05
2006	2,463.70	30,594.90	8.05

Note: investment in domestic shares is for both A- and B-shares.
Sources: People's Bank of China, State Statistical Bureau, and CSRC.

capital allocations and the four large banks occupied half of that main channel. Without resolving systemic problems in the banking industry, it was going to be hard to improve efficiency of the entire system of resource allocation. This in turn was going to affect the speed of China's development and the smooth operating of the national economy.

On March 14, 2003, newly appointed Premier Wen Jiabao made it clear that he would be paying utmost attention to the reform of state-owned commercial banks. In replying to a journalist from the *South China Morning Post*, he said, "This reform is like a battle in which we have the river at our backs and absolutely no room to pull back but to move forward. The reason we are adopting such strong measures is that this is an effort in which we cannot afford to fail." Afterwards, he also noted:

> *The government policy support is necessary for changing the state-owned banks' financial position and performance. The policies include the infusion of capital and the removal of NPLs [from the banks' balance sheets]. In the past five years, we have issued RMB270 billion special treasury bonds to supplement the banks' capital. At the same time, we have stripped away RMB1.4 trillion worth of NPLs. Resolving the problems of banks lies with fundamental reform, however. It lies with setting up modern corporate governance structures and modern financial enterprise systems; that is, with creating the underlying conditions to implement a system of share ownership, to "corporatize" the banks.*

The new round of reform was able to learn the lessons and experience from the previous reforms. The perspective of the reform had transitioned from a focus on the external operating environment to the internal system of the banks. The key to the system innovation of state-owned banks was in setting up modern enterprise systems which include that the ownership is clearly defined, the role of investors is functioning, the equities of the banks are owned by the state. The Banks, as legal entities, have full control of all their assets, they are fully responsible for operations and management, bear operating results and liable to investors for protecting and increasing their investment value. They were to become legal entities with civil rights under the law that also took on civil responsibilities. They were to set up effective corporate governance that would be the basis of proper decision-making and a necessary precondition for motivating the management with incentives and accountability. They were also seen to be a necessary precondition for carrying out effective oversight, implementing risk controls, and improving asset quality. Only through proper handling of the fiduciary relationship between bank shareholders and management could corporate governance structures be improved. Only then could the meddling and interference of interested parties be avoided, and could the control of funds by insiders be prevented.

After careful studies and discussions, it was decided eventually that the reform of state-owned commercial banks, including recapitalization by state foreign exchange reserves and ownership restructuring would be carried out in three stages. The first stage would be financial restructuring, including stripping away NPLs from balance sheets and injecting capital. Only after changing financial conditions in pilot banks that allowed them to achieve capital adequacy ratios that complied with the requirements of Basel I, and NPL ratios below 5%, would the necessary conditions be set for the second stage. This was known as "sweeping the house clean and preparing to receive the guests." The second stage, corporatization and the bringing in of strategic investors, would set up a corporate governance framework that was suited to a diversified shareholder base. This included an institutionalized decision-making process and a check and balance mechanism, with shareholders' annual meetings, Board of Directors and Supervisors, and so on. The third stage would be to list the banks publicly on the capital markets, utilizing the supervision of regulatory bodies as well as the public at large, and the effective oversight of the media to help "standardize" or "regularize" the behavior of banks and government, and thereby guarantee the interests of shareholders, depositors, and legal persons of the bank.

MEASURES UNDERTAKEN IN THIS ROUND OF REFORM

Starting in September of 2003, after much debate and careful consideration, top authority of the government decided to initiate a new round of state-owned bank reform by selecting the BOC and the CCB for corporatization pilot projects. These two banks were selected because they were relatively less burdened by the weight of historic millstones. In order to assure complete and thorough reform, the State Council set up a Leadership Group headed by executive vice premier Huang Ju in October of 2003 and the general office of the Leadership Group located at the Financial Stability Bureau of the PBC. Zhou Xiaochuan, the governor of PBC was the head of the general office. Under the direct leadership of Governor Zhou Xiaochuan, the Bureau drafted a "Proposal to Implement Corporatization" in the financial sector. It was submitted to the State Council and approved in December of 2003.

In April of 2005, a corporatization reform was then launched at the ICBC, in light of the progress at the two pilot banks. The reforms followed an understanding of "One Bank One Policy," meaning that each bank went forward under circumstances specific to itself.

Goals and Timing of the Reform

According to precepts of modern enterprise systems including "clear delineation of ownership, explicit rights and responsibilities, separation of government and enterprise, and scientific management," the general goals of this round of corporatization reform of state-owned banks were as follows:

> through financial restructuring, internal reform and strict external regulation to set up a modern financial enterprise system, establish corporate governance structures, transform business operating mechanisms, strengthen internal control and achieve sustainable growth, so that those state-owned commercial banks would have adequate capital, strict internal controls, a safe operation, excellent service and performance, and that are internationally competitive.

At the same time, the reforms were meant to guarantee that the investment made by the state in these banks was protected and would increase in value.

In terms of selecting the opportune time to undertake reform, China looked first to the lessons of Japan dealing with systemic risks in its banking sector in the 1990s. The timing had to be when China's economy was growing at a fast pace and the state had adequate financial ability to deal with the accumulated problems. Second, consideration was given to the promises China had made when it joined the WTO. By the end of 2006, foreign investment would be allowed to enter China's domestic banking market. In order to lower the risk faced by state-owned banks and to increase their ability to compete with foreign-invested banks, the main work of this round of reform had to be completed before that time. It was estimated it would take three years to complete the three reform stages from financial restructuring of bank to listing them on the market. It was imperative, therefore, that the process of bank reform be initiated no later than the end of 2003.

The Establishment of China SAFE Investments Ltd

The Leadership Group relied on the experience of mature banking industries abroad to select the format in which this round of reform would proceed, as it considered such things as system of ownership, corporate governance structures, and banking regulation. After considerable weighing and balancing of all factors, the Leadership Group decided on a holding company model other than an administrative authority such as financial SARSC. The China SAFE Investments Company Ltd was established on December 16, 2003. [SAFE stands for State Administration of Foreign Exchange. The Chinese name, and now the preferred name in English as well, is the Central Huijin Investment Company, Ltd] This entity recapitalized the pilot banks on behalf of the state, and it exercised the rights and discharge the obligation as the representative of the state ownership. Adopting this form as the way to proceed with Chinese banking reform was a courageous move. First, it meant that the provider of capital of state-owned shares could be clearly delineated or known and made accountable, and therefore that the functions of ownership could be realized. Second, it meant that the responsibilities and the functions of the provider of capital toward the safety and the returns on capital would be realized. Third, it meant that a holding company form would be convenient for capital investment and management, would make decision-making relatively more flexible, and would conform to most rules of a market economy.

China's Central Huijin Investment Company, Ltd [referred to as "Huijin"] is a solely state-owned investment company, incorporated in accordance with the Chinese Company Law and approved by the State Council. The State has provided capital to the Company for its being the investor of significant financial institutions, and as such is entitled to exercise the rights and to discharge the obligation on behalf of the Chinese government. The Company's function in equity investment authorized by the State Council and it does not engage in any other commercial activities.

The Board of Directors of Huijin is composed of nine people. Other than two Executive Board members who are from senior management, the others come from the Ministry of Finance, the PBC, and the State Foreign Exchange Bureau. The Supervisory Board is composed of three members who also come from the above government institutions. The Board of Directors makes decisions by means of voting on major matters and plays a major role in deciding on important policy of the company.

Financial Restructuring

Financial restructuring of state-owned commercial banks was a prerequisite for shareholding system reform and the subsequent introduction of strategic investors. Such restructuring included verification of and then written off asset losses, disposal of NPLs, and re-injection of capital. The purpose was to make capital adequacy ratios of pilot banks conform to the level of 8% as specified in Basel I. The percentage of NPLs had to be lowered very substantially in order to produce fundamental improvement of balance sheets of the banks, and to lay the foundations for the second stage of reform. BOC and CCB had transferred all their capital reserves as well as 2003 profits into a provision account to offset NPL losses. After verifying and canceling out the asset losses, it removed the NPL at a market-evaluated price to an AMC. On the basis of the verified asset losses and the stripping away of NPLs, on December 30, 2003, the State Council allowed Huijin to inject US$22.5 billion of capital into the BOC and the CCB each. In April 2005, Huijin injected US$15 billion into the ICBC and Huijin, together with the Ministry of Finance then each held 50% of that bank's shares. After financial restructuring, the financial conditions of these banks were greatly improved, with primary financial indicators now approaching the level of large international commercial banks.

Shareholding System Reform

After financial restructuring, the BOC, CCB, and ICBC were reconfigured from being wholly state-invested and state-owned to becoming shareholding companies. The BOC became a shareholding company on August 26, 2004, and the CCB on September 21, 2004. On October 28, 2005, the ICBC likewise became a shareholding company. The first shareholders meetings of these three banks elected their first Boards of Directors and Supervisors. Bylaws and accompanying documents were passed in accord with the Company Law and other relevant laws and regulations as legal reference. Senior management personnel were hired and initial steps were taken to establish a standard corporate governance structure. Huijin appointed six full-time Directors to the Board of the BOC and CCB each. These Directors were selected from the Ministry of Finance, CBRC, PBC, Foreign Exchange Bureau, and other governmental bodies. Huijin recommended names of candidates to the Leadership Group for approval. The Directors were to represent Huijin's function as state shareholders. The three banks also invited well-known professionals from both inside and outside China to serve as independent directors, which further improved the level of corporate governance, and therefore the standing of the banks in international circles.

The emphasis of the corporatization was on setting up and improving corporate governance. In this regard, the main work accomplished by Huijin included: first, clarifying ownership of state-owned assets in the pilot banks, and putting into effect the responsibilities of the provider of state shareholders. As the controlling shareholder, Huijin represented the state in fulfilling functions of the provider of capital. As per legal requirements, it appointed board members and supervisory board members to the pilot banks, and began to play a positive and real role in their corporate governance. This was relatively successful in resolving the longstanding problem of there being no specification of ownership representative in state-owned banks. Second, the pilot banks all formulated bylaws according to the requirements of a modern financial system, as well as a whole series of corporate governance guidelines. They set up a modern corporate governance framework in which each part had specific responsibilities including shareholders meetings, Board of Directors, Board of Supervisors, and senior management. A check and balance mechanism with concert operating system was gradually established, and the Boards of Directors with their sub-committees and Boards of Supervisors began to play a significant role. Management began to transform operating concepts of the bank, and to set up objectives that put shareholders' value in the position of highest importance. The effectiveness of corporate governance mechanisms began to take hold. The third task of Huijin was to encourage the pilot banks to speed up the improvement and reform of their internal management systems, to change operating mechanisms, strengthen internal controls and risk management, realize a responsibility system, and set up effective incentive and accountability mechanisms.

Bringing in Strategic Investors

When the State Council formulated the overall plan for corporatizing pilot banks, it made diversification of investors a key part of the process. This meant bringing in both domestic and foreign strategic investors, and changing the monolithic nature of the previous share-ownership structure. Bringing in strategic investors, especially foreign investors, was to be beneficial to improving the ownership structure of state-owned banks. This would be particularly helpful in resisting the administrative interference of government bodies and was intended to break down the "blood ties" that existed between state-owned banks and various levels of government. At the same time, it would benefit pilot banks by allowing them to absorb advanced management expertise from overseas and to carry out continuously reform and renovation of systems. Finally, it would help the banks in their goal of raising capital and listing their shares on the market, which has the practical significance of lowering the costs of reform and improving the level of corporate governance quickly.

After completing the financial restructuring and corporatization, the three banks actively set about the work of bringing in strategic investors. In line with the guiding principles laid down by regulatory authority, and according to the actual circumstances of each bank in terms of business development, they began a rigorous sifting through of potential investors. In June and July 2005, Huijin and CCB signed strategic agreements with the Bank of America and Temasek Holdings of Singapore. The Bank of America put up US$2.5 billion to purchase 9% of H-shares before their public offering; Temasek purchased 5.1% of shares from Huijin. In August of 2005, the Royal Bank of Scotland put up US$3.048 billion to purchase 9.61% of share capitalization in the BOC, and Temasek Holdings put up US$1.524 billion to purchase around 4.8% of share capitalization. In addition, the BOC brought in the Swiss Bank UBS and the Asian Development Bank as strategic investors. In April 2006, Goldman Sachs, Allianz of Germany, and American Express formed a consortium that put up US$3 billion to purchase 10% of ICBC shares.

Initial Public Offering (IPO)

The CCB was listed on the Hong Kong Stock Exchange on October 27, 2005. After exercising over-allotment options, the number of dis-tributed shares came to 30.5 billion, with issued shares constituting

13.6% of total shares. The financing derived from the share issue totaled around US$9.2 billion.

After the CCB successfully listed on the stock exchange, on June 1, 2006, the BOC also listed in Hong Kong. After exercising over-allotment options, that bank issued a total of 29.4 billion shares, with issued shares comprising 11.9% of total share capital and raising around US$11.2 billion. One month after the IPO in Hong Kong, BOC again raised money on the Shanghai Stock Exchange, issuing a total of 6.5 billion shares on the A-share market with a share price of RMB3.08, thereby raising a total of RMB19.5 billion.

On October 27, 2006, the H-shares and A-shares of the ICBC were listed respectively in Hong Kong and Shanghai at the same time. Without taking into account over-allotment options, 35.39 billion H-shares and 13 billion A-shares were issued. The price of the H-shares was HK$3.07, of the A-shares RMB3.12. After adjusting for exchange rates, the price for the two was the same. It was the highest pricing among the large state-owned commercial banks with a price to book value of 2.23. The listing of A- and H-shares by the ICBC raised a sum of US$22 billion from both inside and outside China. It thereby became the largest ever IPO in the world.

On September 25, 2007, the CCB returned to the A-shares market and listed on the Shanghai Stock Exchange. This time, the A-shares IPO issued nine billion new shares at RMB6.45 a piece, raising RMB58.05 billion. The listings of A- and H-shares on the two markets by the ICBC, the BOC, and the CCB have, in terms of market capitalization, put these three banks among the ranks of the top 10 largest banks in the world.

THE ACCOMPLISHMENTS OF THE COMPREHENSIVE REFORM OF STATE-OWNED COMMERCIAL BANKS SINCE 2003

Under the guidance of the State Council's Leadership Group working on shareholding system reform of state-owned commercial banks, reform has accomplished important progress.

IPOs Are Successful, Banks' Values Are Proved by Market

Within that one year from October 2005 to October 2006, the listing of CCB, BOC, and ICBC were immensely successful. Many new records were set in terms of the scale of financing, subscription multiples, the issue price, and other variables. The IPOs attracted global attention and were highly praised by investors both inside and outside China. The ICBC offering became the world's largest IPO as well as the world's largest offering of financial shares. It set a number of records in the capital markets. The offerings of BOC and CCB became respectively the second- and third-largest financial offerings in the world. The pricing of all three was at the top of the range; price to book value exceeded comparables listed in the Hong Kong market and those of some first-class international banks, at 1.93 (CCB), 2.18 (BOC), and 2.23 (ICBC) respectively. The PE ratio also exceeded average levels of leading international financial institutions. The price levels of all three after being listed were able to maintain excellent value; for example, the H-shares of CCB have already gone from an initial price of HK$2.35 to the current HK$7.44 (pricing at the close of trading on November 16, 2007). The stock has moreover been incorporated as a component of the Hang Seng Index in Hong Kong and the MSCI China. At present, the market capitalization of ICBC exceeds that of Citigroup and it became the world largest bank in terms of market capitalization. The corporatization of China's formerly state-owned commercial banks has been proved successful with market acceptance both inside and outside China.

Improvement in Financial Indicators

The three banks have made clear improvement on capital adequacy ratios, asset quality, and profitability after structural reform. By the end of June 2007, main financial indicators were approaching levels of respectable international banks. Financial conditions exhibited strong sustainability. Capital adequacy ratios were noticeably higher: by June 30, 2007, the capital adequacy ratios of the BOC, CCB, and ICBC respectively were 13.9%, 11.34%, and 13.67%. Asset quality had greatly improved: the percentage of NPLs for these three respectively was 3.72%, 2.95%, and 3.29%. Profitability had improved: pre-tax profits for the first half of 2007 were respectively: RMB50.932 billion, RMB50.542, and RMB58.603 billion.

Improvement in Corporate Governance

The corporatization of China's state-owned commercial banks was able to break through the old systems of state-owned financial asset control and ownership forms. The Huijin model resolved the long-term issue of there being a "vacant seat" in terms of who owned the state assets. As the controlling shareholder in the pilot banks, Huijin represented the state in fulfilling the functions of state shareholder.

After corporatization, the three banks established modern corporate governance structures including shareholders meetings, Boards of Directors, Board of Supervisors, and senior management teams. Check and balance mechanisms began to take effect among shareholders, decision-making bodies, supervisory organizations, and operational level. The company's corporate governance mechanisms began to play their proper role. In the past three years, Huijin has urged the three banks to complete a whole set of corporate governance systems, including revising the article of associations, the rules of procedure, and other such governance documents, and adjusting and improving the functions and structure of the Boards of Directors, Boards of Supervisors and their sub-committees. The rights, responsibilities, and duties of shareholders, Board of Directors, Board of Supervisors, and senior management are gradually being clarified, the new decision-making, implementations, and supervisory mechanisms with check and balance are beginning to take hold. This has broken through the old conceptual framework that concentrated all of these functions in the hands of bank insiders. A management goal that takes shareholder value as the highest objective has been put in place.

Incorporating strategic investors and listing on the capital markets not only has led to an infusion of new capital, but has also allowed the banks to bring in effective external supervision and restraining mechanisms. These have been helpful in further transforming management and operations. Respecting the laws of the market, improving information disclosure, increasing transparency, improving management practices in line with standards of other listed international banks, improving corporate governance, raising core competitiveness: all of these are being done in order to maximize shareholders' value.

By bringing in strategic investors, improving corporate governance and raising operational and management standards, the three banks have emphasized modern management experience as well as technology in the areas of corporate governance, internal controls, financial management, assets liabilities management, risk management, human resources management, and so on.

TABLE 7.2 Income to Huijin from dividends and sale of shares of three banks, 2004–07 (Unit: hundred million RMB)

Bank	2004	2005	2006	2007 (first half)	Dividend totals	Net income on sale of shares	Total income
CCB	27.93	52.98	146.14	221.93	448.98	47.21	496.19
BOC	142.00	141.12	68.53	–	351.65	21.39	373.04
ICBC	–	17.69	152.85	–	170.54	82.65	253.19
Total	169.93	211.79	367.52	221.93	971.17	151.25	1,122.42

Note: Dividend income from the CCB to Huijin included dividend to China Jianyin Investment Ltd., a 100% subsidiary of Huijin.
Source: From Huijin's statistics.

TABLE 7.3 The three banks net assets value held by Huijin as of end-June, 2007 (Unit: hundred million RMB)

Bank	Net assets (2007 to end-June)	Percentage of shares held (%)	Huijin's interest
CCB	3,257.38	61.48%	2,002.64
BOC	4,254.65	67.49%	2,871.46
ICBC	5,027.22	35.3%	1,774.61
Total	12,539.25		6,648.71

Source: From Huijin's statistics.

Preserving and Enhancing State-owned Share Values

Since its establishment, Huijin, as per the role bestowed upon it by the State Council and in fulfilling its function as controlling shareholder of key state-owned financial institutions, has done its best to accomplish the corporatization of state-owned commercial banks. It has played a key role in such aspects as bringing in strategic investors and getting the banks to list on the markets. At the same time, Huijin has consistently emphasized the performance of the banks, and, to a large degree, it has assured the maintenance and growth of the value of government shares. This, in turn, has realized the overall goals of the reform.

Since Huijin recapitalized the three banks, it has been rewarded with very good returns on its investment. Through both dividends and sale of shares, it has already realized income of RMB112.242 billion (see Tables 7.2, 7.3, and 7.4 for details).

The total capital Huijin put in the three banks came to US$60 billion. With exchange rates at the time of placing, this amount totaled some RMB496.2 billion. Up to the end of June 2007, through

TABLE 7.4 Market value of shares in the three banks held by Huijin, as of close of trading on October 31, 2007 (Unit: hundred million RMB)

Bank	Number of shares held by Huijin (in 00m)	Price at close of market on Oct. 31, 2007	Exchange rate of HK$ to RMB on that date	Market value of Huijin's bank shares (RMB00m)
CCB	1,588.42	8.81	0.96375	13,486.73
BOC	1,713.25	7.14	–	12,232.61
ICBC	1,180.01	8.74	-	10,313.47
Total				36,032.81

Source: From Huijin's statistics.

sale of shares to strategic investors and receipt of dividends, Huijin had already retrieved 22.6% of its initial investment, and the net asset value of remaining ownership in the three banks had reached RMB664.871 billion. Putting the net asset value of shares and the dividend income together, the value of Huijin's initial capital injections into the three banks of US$60 billion had already appreciated by 56.6%. On October 31, 2007, the market value of the shares held by Huijin in the three banks came up to RMB3.603281 trillion. Putting these three together—the current share value, the income from dividends and from the sale of shares—Huijin's investment has appreciated 6.5 times.

Although this round of reform in China's commercial banking system has accomplished historic breakthroughs, the banks have not yet been through a test of economic downturn. Moreover, a considerable gap remains between the top of modern international banks and China's state-controlled commercial banks. It must be recognized, therefore, that the path of reform for China's banking industry stretches far into the future.

ENDNOTE

[1] With thanks to Ge Rongrong, who contributed to this article—Ge is Deputy Director, Construction Bank Department at Central Huijin Investment Company Ltd.

CHAPTER 8

China's Restructured Commercial Banks: *Nomenklatura* Accountability Serving Corporate Governance Reform?

Nicholas Calcina Howson

Assistant Professor of Law, University of Michigan Law School[1]

Industrial and Commercial Bank of China (2003)

Nowadays, many people very mechanically think that solving [shareholders' rights] is everything and, once that happens, the bank will become successful. In reality, simultaneously with shareholder rights reform, we must also strengthen the bank's internal corporate governance ... It is simply not true that once we resolve our listing, then everything will be "OK."
—Interview with Industrial and Commercial Bank Chairman, Jiang Jianqing (*Ling Huawei and Zhao Xiaojian 2003: 74*).

China Banking Regulatory Commission (2004)

... reforms shall be centered on innovating the Banks' [China Construction Bank and Bank of China] management regime and systems, improving their corporate governance, innovating their operating mechanisms and thereby boosting their profit-earning capacity.
—Guidelines on Corporate Governance Reforms and Supervision of Bank of China and China Construction Bank (*China Banking Regulatory Commission 2004: Article 2*)

Bank of Communications Chairman Jiang Chaoliang (2006)

> *In order to fully establish a modern corporate governance system, we must consider four aspects: the lessons learned from the past decade; shareholder consciousness, which is the soul of modern corporate governance; shareholder diversification; and the function of the Party Committee within corporate governance. These are the premises that must be considered in developing a Chinese style corporate governance structure. You cannot say just because we are implementing corporate governance that we don't need the Party Committee anymore. That is not realistic... The corporate governance that we are designing has: the shareholders' meeting, the board of directors, the supervisory board, senior management, and the Party Committee, all of which work together seamlessly in corporate governance... The establishment of a Party Committee within an enterprise whose shares are controlled by the state is a reality within the Chinese corporate governance system that must be accepted.*
>
> —Interview with China Construction Bank Chairman, Jiang Chaoliang (*Hu Runfeng, Cheng Zhe, and Fu Tao 2006: 72*).

Former World Bank Beijing Mission Director Pieter Bottelier (2006)

> *...it is clear that structural reforms are moving in the right direction.... Management and regulation of the banking sector is becoming more professional and more in line with international standards. Clarity of ownership and of the responsibilities of the management and board has improved. (Bottelier 2006: 1)*

INTRODUCTION

In the wake of the Asian Financial Crisis of 1997–98, and accelerating after 2003, the People's Republic of China (PRC or China) has implemented an ambitious reform program directed at the commanding heights of what once passed for China's financial system—the large state-owned and state-managed commercial banks. Contrary to a good deal of advice offered by policy and finance specialists, China did not liquidate or fully privatize these institutions. Instead, the PRC sought to avoid the significant social (and no doubt political) costs associated with liquidation, or real privatization, by instead changing (1) the internal dynamics of, and (2) external environments applicable to, its behemoth banking institutions.

Critical among the many reform measures applied after 2003 were those directed at internal corporate governance and owner (share-holder) monitoring of these banks, including: (1) corporatization of these institutions under China's post-1994 corporate statute,[2] (2) the creation of a state investment agency to act as a real "principal" (share-holder) in the newly corporatized, yet "agent" (director)-managed, entities, (3) the introduction of minority strategic investment from abroad (and ceding of board seats to representatives of this foreign capital or execution of "technical assistance" agreements), (4) the listing of a portion of the banks' share capital on foreign and Chi-nese exchanges, and (5) the appointment of "independent directors" (*duli dongshi*) to the boards of the now public commercial banks. These substantial organizational and capital structure innovations were only part of a wide-ranging menu of reform measures applied to all aspects of bank operations. As Pieter Bottelier, the head of the first post-1949 Beijing World Bank Mission (1993–97) has written recently:[3]

> . . . *the speed of the financial sector reforms has accelerated in recent years. Most state banks have been incorporated under China's Company Law, restructured and recapitalized. Many attracted foreign strategic minority partners and the four most important state commercial banks listed successfully on the Hong Kong and . . . domestic stock exchanges. . . . Financial sector problems . . . such as the massive nonperforming loans [NPLs] overhang and the non-tradable government shares in listed companies are gradually being resolved. The legal and regulatory framework governing China's financial system is being adjusted to meet international standards and domes-tic needs . . . it is clear that structural reforms are moving in the right direction. Management and regulation of the bank-ing sector is becoming more professional and more in line with international standards. Clarity of ownership and of the responsibilities of the management and board has improved.* (Bottelier 2006: 1)

This chapter focuses on a relatively narrow aspect of the *legal* and *regulatory* sub-theme of China's commercial bank reform program: the law- and enterprise organization-based approach that has sought to change (1) how Chinese banking firms are governed *internally*, and (2) how firm managers are monitored *externally* by shareholders—the notional "owners" of the firm.[4] In doing so, this chapter strives to: illuminate how China's banks are governed even after formal and institutional reform, the effect of widely touted legal governance adjustments, and the ways in which the individuals who really control commercial banking firms are monitored and held accountable—or not—in China's truly "mixed" Socialist-market economy. Thus, this chapter is (1) a rebuttal to literally countless theoretical writings and public proclamations about the tie between "modern" or "international standard" firm governance reform on one side, and resulting bank performance on the other (Basel 1999: 3). It is (2) a rebuttal to the many regulators, officials, analysts, participants, and investors who, knowing far better, pronounce that the *internal* firm governance reform at China's state-owned banks is basically "complete" while counseling a renewed focus on firm *external* measures (tax policy, creditor protection and bankruptcy law and enforcement, interest rate policy, reserve requirements, and so on. (Xie Ping 2006: 20)). Finally, this chapter may stand as a warning as to how easily and incompletely observers and investors (Chinese and foreign) digest and credit proclaimed legal change, and overlook other perhaps more effective instruments of monitoring and corporate governance.

This chapter places some emphasis on the stock price of China's listed banks at a time when public stock valuations for Chinese listed companies do *not* yet reflect firm performance (as opposed to the overall promise of "rising China" and herd-mentality participation in "China plays"). Notwithstanding, the existence of a reported stock price will be shown to have significance in China, where the formal corporate governance mechanisms introduced here, and widely hailed in both offering prospectuses and the international financial press, may prove somewhat irrelevant. The irony of course is that the true corporate governance mechanisms shown to be effective are thoroughly rooted in a *pre*-Reform vision of state-owned enterprise (SOE) and work unit (*danwei*) governance—the *nomenklatura* system—that may now evidence a strangely benign, or at least unforeseen, entanglement with the decidedly post-Reform phenomenon of semi-efficient international and domestic capital markets.

CORPORATE GOVERNANCE REFORM — PART OF A RICHER REFORM NARRATIVE

Of the different kinds of medicine applied to China's state-dominated banking sector since the early 1990s, only some of the reforms implemented to date relate to corporate governance *per se*. However, those same corporate governance-directed reforms became relevant in the context of a number of prior or simultaneous non-corporate governance-focused changes. The other aspects of financial sector reform, described informally,[5] include: dismemberment of the "mono-bank" system that was the People's Bank of China (PBC) in the late 1970s and establishment of "specialized" financial institutions; the gradual introduction of domestic commercial banking competition with "national" scope; establishment of the "modern enterprise system" for the (non-banking) state-owned firms that made up the industrial and service economy; separation of the banks' conflicting "policy" and "commercial" functions; promulgation of substantive law and regulations authorizing and governing the financial sector (followed by the creation of an expert banking industry regulator); the application of close domestic regulation (and in some cases, domestically mandated conformity with global standards, like the 1995 PRC Commercial Bank Law's incorporation of the Basel Accords 8% floor on risk capital (achieved in 2000)); enterprise income tax reductions for commercial banks (from 55% to 33%); successive recapitalizations, including what may amount to delayed recapitalizations implemented by the disposition of nonperforming loans (NPLs) to so-called asset management companies; and the staged introduction of foreign competition—culminating in the effective opening of the Chinese commercial banking sector by December 11, 2006, promised at the time of the PRC's accession to the World Trade Organization (WTO) in late 2001.

Zhou Xiaochuan, interviewed as President of the China Construction Bank (CCB) in 2005, and later Governor of the PBC, asserted that the primary goal behind financial sector reform after 1999 and the Asian Financial Crisis was solvency, which directly counseled recapitalization of the banks by the central government, disposition of bad (uncollectible) assets, and (voluntary) conformity with international capital adequacy standards (all as revealed and confirmed by modern firm-level accounting). Notwithstanding this short-term focus, Zhou Xiaochuan also saw recapitalization and increased balance sheet strength as key bases for (1) imminent corporatization and

(2) finance-raising on the public capital markets. As Zhou said at that time:

> *In the past, we treated the state-owned commercial banks as state administrative organs and there was a good deal of administrative interference in operations, with incorrect evaluation yardsticks; we saw improvements [in addressing] these problems after the Asian Financial Crisis. From what I have observed, among the various measures several are really important: the first point is that accounting principles have been continually getting better; the second point is the implementation of a five-tier loan classification system—allowing us to set aside realistic reserves based upon the proportion of risk—the third point was the clear setting-out of the state-owned banks' reform road at the Third Plenum of the sixteenth Party Congress in 2003. As the "Resolution on Several Questions Regarding Perfection of the Socialist Market Economic System" passed at that Plenum pointed out, we must "implement share system reform [corporatization] at qualifying state-owned banks, accelerate the disposition of non-performing loans, replenish capital, and create the conditions for listing [of the reformed banks]." This road was selected only after a whole series of careful studies and analysis. (Ling Huawei 2005: 73)*

These views, and the sixteenth Party Congress policy direction cited by Zhou, were confirmation of the (far more important) internal National Finance Working Group policy aim articulated earlier in February 2002:

> *[We] should in accordance with the needs of establishing the modern enterprise system transform the wholly state owned commercial banks into modern financial enterprises with perfected governance structures, healthy operating mechanisms, clear business goals, solid finances and the relatively strong competitiveness internationally. (Hou Aiai 2002: 28)*

The formal corporatization of, and limited issuance of public share capital by, the PRC banks, and the adoption by the banks of the formal institutions of modern corporate governance, must be understood in view of these other critically important contextual, financial, institutional, policy and regulatory reforms, almost all of which are still in process. Indeed, many of the changes noted above impact directly or indirectly on corporate governance reform at the banks.[6]

THE BIG FOUR AND A HALF

This chapter focuses on the limited effects of corporatization on the Big Four state-owned commercial banks. For these purposes, the "Big Four and a Half" will be addressed to include a fifth entrant, the Bank of Communications (BoCom). This is not to ignore or diminish the sometimes very different and positive effects of corporatization and public listings at smaller or more independent national-scope commercial banks, or their regional banking cousins. In fact, corporatization and then public listing of shares was first directed at China's non-Big Four and a Half commercial banks which nonetheless enjoyed authority to do business nationally.[7] Instead, here we focus on corporate governance reform at the largest state-owned banking institutions in China, what were historically state administrative departments used to funnel capital under the planned economy. This is for reasons of space, but also because the corporate governance reform program was designed (or advertised) as a strategy that would contribute to improvement of the entire Chinese financial system, and most importantly the dominant space occupied by the Big Four and a Half.

NEW BOARDS—OLD CAPITAL STRUCTURES

The theory underlying corporatization and public listing held that the transformed enterprises would take advantage of the corporate form and provide a mechanism for interested shareholders—private, public, or foreign—to hold management (directors and senior management) accountable for operating results, and thus force them to make value-enhancing decisions. Early Chinese theorists and policymakers infatuated with "share system reform" and the "modern enterprise system" initially asserted that mere positioning of assets under the umbrella of a joint stock company legal form would magically "separate ownership and management" and force managers to be accountable in the pursuit of profits for the owners of the firm, and be subject to ongoing monitoring of any potentially opportunistic or inefficient behavior they might otherwise be tempted to engage in. In theory then, corporatization—and the establishment of a directorate/management corps responsible to shareholder-owners—was promoted as an instant panacea for the lack of operational or allocative efficiency at China's banks, not to mention a sturdy defense against manipulation of these firms by "insiders." The distribution of equity interests to a broader "public" resulting from access to the international capital markets, attendant information disclosure bounded by prospectus liability, and the phenomenon of a public market share price (and thus ongoing evaluation of the true value of the banking firm) were all thought to support the urgently desired monitoring and accountability effects.

Each of the Big Four and a Half (except the Agricultural Bank of China (ABC))[8] have undertaken slightly different programs of corporatization and subsequent establishment of "modern" corporate governance structures. All share establishment of a Board of Directors was formally atop a corporate legal person that has an absolutely dominant shareholder or group of shareholders. BoCom, the "One Half" in the Big Four and a Half, and the first Chinese bank to effect an initial public offering (IPO), is a good example. As noted in its 2005 Annual Report (and the "Corporate Governance Report" contained therein), with corporatization and a public listing allegedly came an "independent and modern corporate structure" comprised of the shareholders' meeting, the Board of Directors, and—as required under the German/Japan/Taiwan-influenced Chinese Company Law—a supervisory board, all charged with performing "check and balance functions" (Bank of Communications Annual Report 2005: 38). At the IPO, the Board of BoCom initially consisted of 19 directors, only four of which were executive directors, with the other 15 non-executive directors including the CSRC-mandated one-third five independent directors. The supervisory board had nine members, and was proclaimed to be responsible for monitoring the Bank's financial matters, and the actions of the Board of Directors and senior management. As the chairman of the board of BoCom said in 2006:

> *Now, at the board meetings, all directors have observed the utmost diligence in the process of carrying out their duties and have expressed independent opinions with respect to matters such as company strategy, audit and risk management. This is perceived most directly by the fact that at board meetings directors speak with vigor and disputes arising from the deliberation of motions have become commonplace. It is very different from the "single voice carries all" (yi yan tang) of before. (Hu Runfeng, Cheng Zhe, and Fu Tao 2006: 72)*

Yet, even after corporatization and the Bank's successful IPO, more than 40% of its shares were held by a combination of the Ministry of Finance, the National Council for Social Security Fund (NCSSF), and Huijin (a joint venture between the PRC central bank's foreign exchange bureau and the Ministry of Finance, described in more detail below). Add to those holdings the almost 20% Hong Kong Shanghai Bank (HSBC) strategic holding, and another more than 20% held principally by "legal person" shareholders (most SOEs such as the Beijing Capital Airport Group, Yunnan's Hongta, Shandong Electric Power Company, and so on), and the result was an extremely thin public float and rather badly situated group of public, collective action-challenged, shareholders. A second example, the far bigger Industrial and Commercial Bank of China (ICBC)—the last of the large banks to IPO and the true remnant of the pre-1994 PRC "monobank" retail level—presents a largely similar picture. The (new) ICBC was "established" (corporatized) by promotion (with Huijin and the Ministry of Finance acting as promoters) of a new company limited by shares in October 2005. In January 2006, the ICBC took foreign strategic investment from Goldman Sachs (5.16%), Allianz Group (2.01%), and the American Express Company (0.4%).[9] The initial, post-IPO, board structure of the ICBC was made up of thirteen directors, with four executive directors, and six non-executive directors (of which three were independent directors). The governance input by the foreign "strategic" investors in the ICBC was left to a different mechanism (at least in comparison with the other reformed PRC banks)—a "Strategic Cooperation Agreement" with pre-IPO investor Goldman Sachs.[10] Yet, even after the Bank's rather resoundingly successful dual Shanghai and Hong Kong dual-listing IPO, the capital structure remained heavily weighted in favor of China's state actors or proxies, with the Ministry of Finance, Huijin and the NCSSF holding an aggregate of 79.49% of the issued and outstanding equity (ICBC 2006: 188).

HUIJIN (CHINA SAFE INVESTMENT LIMITED)

An important player in the balance sheet amelioration and corporate restructuring implicated by reform was Huijin, formally rendered in English as the "China SAFE Investment Limited." A PRC limited liability company jointly owned by the Ministry of Finance and the State Administration of Foreign Exchange (SAFE), the entity originally acted as the vehicle for recapitalization of China's major banks using China's exploding foreign exchange reserves (the central bank recapitalizing the banks with foreign exchange funds and using the newly established Huijin as the nominal resulting shareholder/investor). As the Bank of China (BOC) stated in its IPO prospectus, the function of Huijin was "to represent the PRC government in exercising its investor rights and obligations" as a Bank shareholder, and "implement and execute PRC government policy arrangements in relation to the reform of state-owned financial institutions" (Bank of China 2006: 197). The charge was serious, or far more serious than the mission of other "state" (ministry) shareholders in China's large system of inefficient SOEs, reformed and unreformed (including the subsequently established National Commission on Management of State Assets (*guoziwei*)) As Premier Wen Jiabao said about Huijin[11] "[Huijin investment] is equity held on behalf of the state, it should have a return, it should not be used to replenish deep holes!" (Ling Huawei 2005: 74). Staffed extremely thinly, and always subject to infighting between the Ministry of Finance and the PBC (which governs SAFE), the new entity ended up as a major shareholder in China's key financial institutions by virtue of the equity investment/capitalization tasks it performed. Its narrow focus (the commercial banking sector), its relatively few "investments" (the few state-owned banks it had been asked to recapitalize), and the expertise and dynamism of its senior personnel, led to its strong participation as an interested shareholder in its investee banks—a participation that sometimes ran counter to the ideas and ambitions of its formal masters (the Ministry of Finance and the PBC/SAFE), and the expectations of the bank insiders it now "governed" (Wen Yuanhua 2006: 78). However it is seen or evaluated, Huijin stood as an early and partial resolution of China's longstanding "absent principal" quandary. For much of the Reform period, critics of both the SOE system and the succeeding corporatization program lamented the fact that there was no real "principal" to govern SOEs, leaving the SOEs prey to the insider cadres/managers closest to the enterprise (Hou Aiai 2002; Clarke 2003; Dou Hongquan 2005). Corporatization did not solve this quandary in any significant way, as the amorphous and undefined former 100% owner—"all the people" (*quanmin*)—remained the primary "owner" of the transformed firms, now "owning" through the state's reduced 70–80% equity interest. There was no specific interested shareholder, but instead an "absent principal", so that even corporatized firms were subject to continuing control and manipulation by pre-existing management and insiders, often the same people in the same roles as when the banking firm was an SOE commercial bank. Huijin, at least in the limited world of China's commercial banking institutions, altered that deficiency with panache—and in a way that initially surprised and shocked insider managers at the banks, and the prior representatives of "all the people," the Ministry of Finance![12]

FOREIGN STRATEGIC INVESTMENT

Equally important to the corporate governance reform, at least in theory, was the permitted presence of "foreign" strategic investors in China's restructured banks. In the late 1990s, the PBC and then its successor regulator the CBRC began to allow foreign minority equity investment (less than 25% in the aggregate) in certain of the non-Big Four and a Half commercial banks and even those which had domestic A-share listings—starting with the troubled Shenzhen Development Bank investment by Newbridge, an arm of the Texas Pacific Group (now TPG) private equity entity. A subsequent deal by Citigroup where it purchased a small strategic stake in Shanghai Pudong Development Bank, represented a possibly provocative innovation because it permitted foreign strategic (same industry) investment rather than merely financial (private equity or fund) investment in the commercial banking sector.[13] Finally, in 2004—and again in direct anticipation of China's large state-controlled banks launching IPOs on the international markets—the PRC began to permit foreign investment (both strategic and financial) in the newly corporatized Chinese commercial banks. These allowances were in many ways like similar pre-IPO foreign strategic investments in overseas-listing Chinese companies in other sectors, from manufacturing (Anheuser-Bush's private purchase of 5% of pre-IPO H-share listing Tsingtao Brewery Company Limited) to natural resources (BP, ExxonMobil's, and Warren Buffet's pre-IPO private purchases of equity in PetroChina and Sinopec). However, there is one important difference between such foreign investment in pre-IPO Big Four and a Half commercial banks and in other sectors. Foreign minority transactions in other sectors, pre-IPO, were meant to communicate confidence and standing to the capital markets, and rarely was there any question of such foreign minority participants—industry or not—being permitted any kind of governance input on the investee firms. Conversely, the pre-IPO minority purchases by foreign investors in China's Big Four and a Half commercial banks—much like Citigroup's involvement in Shanghai

Pudong Development Bank and HSBC's investment in the Bank of Communications—were explicitly billed as a channel through which "modern" operational techniques and better corporate governance would be communicated to the target Chinese banks. Thus, each of the PRC commercial banks that attracted foreign "strategic investors" explicitly trumpeted the purported governance effect, leaving implicit the corporate finance/capital markets vote of confidence: BoCom highlighted the involvement of HSBC and HSBC's representation on the Bank's Board of Directors (Bank of Communications 2005: 96); CCB made much of its ties with Bank of America and then Singapore's Temasek, stating that the former would provide help for CCB in "risk management, corporate governance, credit card business, consumer banking, global treasury and information technology" (Ling Huawei, Guo Jiong and Li Zhigang 2006: 49), and that both would be entitled to seats on the Bank's Board (CCB 2005: 88); the BOC made exactly the same claims regarding the Royal Bank of Scotland and Temasek's involvement, the board seat promised each, and entry into a "Master Cooperation Agreement" with the former (BOC 2006: 69), even though Royal Bank of Scotland has no obligation to buy more of the Bank in the future (contrast the Bank of America's stronger commitment (via an option agreement) to CCB)); finally, the ICBC implicitly promised benign and penetrating involvement by Goldman Sachs pursuant to the "Strategic Cooperation Agreement" it signed with that underwriting firm and the various "joint committees" and governance training immediately established.

CORPORATE GOVERNANCE REFORM, BUT UNREFORMED CORPORATE GOVERNANCE

From inception, corporatization and public listings (and the existence of a public stock price) have been recognized as, at best, a theoretical solution to the governance conundrum at China's banks. What were those "theoretical" impulses counseling corporatization and listing of China's state-owned banks as a (partial) remedy for the sector's ills? As the PBC Governor pointed out in 2005, much of the rationale directing reform of the state-owned commercial banks was equally applicable to their borrower/clients, the PRC's profoundly inefficient SOEs. In a Chinese language interview, responding to the questions, "Why did you choose corporatization and share issuance and listing as the reform direction for the state-owned commercial banks?" and "What were you thinking at the time?" Zhou responded:

> *At the time, our view was that the major reform problems encountered by commercial banks and large SOEs were the same, such as lack of separation between government and enterprise, too much administrative interference, empty governance structures, a separation between the incentive structure and cadre managers, serious bureaucratization, and lack of autonomy or pricing authority, with not enough competitive pressure... All of these issues are very similar to those faced by large SOEs that had conformed to the bureaucratic model of management and did not resemble real enterprises.... As a result, we felt that—with respect to the choice we made for state-owned commercial banks—we should refer to the successful aspects of the industrial SOE reform and implement share system reform [corporatization] and public listings. (Ling Huawei 2005: 73)*

The way to do that, Zhou opined, was to make the banks more accountable to owner/shareholders (both a broad public, and strategic investors). Thus, the first step was necessarily to transform the banks into shareholding firms. In Zhou's view, this would bring only a small cost to the state, which would agree to give up a tiny slice of equity (but no real control) for the benefit of more competitive, profit-oriented, financial institutions able to contribute to the growth of the Chinese national economy, and the PRC's national security and stability—all the while acting to curtail the terrible drain of subsidies and bailouts of insolvent banking institutions (Ling Huawei 2005: 73). Thus, the PRC's corporatization and public listing strategy had both the short-term benefit of attracting more capital into China's reforming banks to aid in the post-Asian Financial Crisis recapitalization, but also the long-term benefit of creating the mechanism and conditions for healthier, better governed, and more efficient firms.

Legal analysts said much the same thing, but focused on property rights, legal identities, and structural attributes. As one corporate governance expert at China People's University (*Renda*) Law School summarized in late 2002:

> *There are many aspects to the reasons creating the present poor situation at the state-owned commercial banks; the majority of commentators believe that the basic reason is a*

> *structural defect. Under the current structure, China's state-owned commercial banks are mere conduits for the implementation of certain government economic policies, and are unique enterprises where the property rights form is unitary (wholly state-owned), the delineation of property rights is confused, and the administrative and enterprise functions are not separated. State-owned commercial banks are not enterprises as understood under corporate law, and have never established mechanisms for risk management or that are designed to create a profit motivation. (Hou Aiai 2002: 27)*

And yet, notwithstanding these noble ambitions and even fine theoretical viewpoints, corporatization coupled with public listings of the largest state-owned Chinese commercial banks have not resulted in any real corporate governance reform. This is not the same as saying the PRC banks have not shown improved performance, which is a separate question. Instead, it expresses the lack of any connection between thoroughgoing structural legal reform and better firm governance. Some of the reasons for this are described in the following sections:

CAPITAL STRUCTURE POST-CORPORATIZATION; POWERLESS FOREIGN EQUITY INVESTORS

Notwithstanding corporatization, and even as China's banks moved from the safest corporate form (the "wholly state owned corporation" sub-*genus* of the limited liability corporation form) to formation as joint stock companies, the resulting capital structure of China's banking institutions remains overwhelmingly dominated by state or state-backed shareholders. This always was the program—to corporatize, recapitalize, and list (with the public issuance of shares acting primarily in the service of recapitalization), and yet to continue to allow state shareholders dominant ownership and absolute control in the banking firm. As Zhou Xiaochuan wrote in the *Renmin Ribao* (*People's Daily*) in May 2000:

> *. . . Commercial banking is not a sector where there is a need for 100% state ownership. Large-scale commercial banks have a major effect on the national economy, and yet the state's power to control can be embodied through [relative] equity control. . . . In order to preserve the state's full*

> *control power and preserve protection against external shocks*
> *in the period of opening to the outside world [and foreign*
> *competition] and economic system conformity [with inter-*
> *national structures], the state can maintain absolute control*
> *over a certain portion of the large-scale commercial banks;*
> *for instance, [the state] can keep a 75% equity interest. (Zhou*
> *Xiaochuan 2000: 76)*

It should be emphasized here that the problem is not that the dominating shareholder is the state or a state representative, but instead that any single shareholder (or shareholder group) holds a dominating interest in the firm and is able to elect its own personnel to the Board of Directors, with those directors in turn appointing the same personnel to the top management level. The fact that Huijin—and more importantly, the directors elected by Huijin—took an activist and unprecedented involvement in those of the Big Four and a Half to which they donated foreign exchange in exchange for equity was in many ways an unanticipated exception.

The net result of the banks' post-restructuring architecture was to create corporate vehicles where minority shareholders have almost nil governance input, and little ability to condition the behavior and strategy of the controlling shareholder, much less the insiders the controlling shareholder formally appoints. Of course, "independent directors" (*duli dongshi*) mandated for public companies in China are supposed to serve the interests of the firm's minority investors. This is a difficult task to perform, especially when such independent directors have a basic duty to act in the interests of the entire firm (surely synonymous with the interests of the 80% shareholder), no negative veto at the board level (and thus an inability to hinder decisions pressed by the majority of board directors who represent the largest state shareholder), and are often nominated from the same pool of Party insiders discussed below. Thus, while the new legal form of China's banks in theory leads to better governance of the firm (with "owners" now monitoring the way in which "their" assets are employed by their elected board and board-appointed "managers"), the lopsided and only incidentally "state"-dominated capital structure of all of China's banks effectively sets up a whole new menu of agency dilemmas—where true minority shareholders have no power to monitor or change director fiduciaries, and are completely left out of monitoring the huge majority control block that appoints the majority of the board of directors. This is now increasingly recognized as deeply problematic even in Chinese language writing on commercial bank reform (Dou Hongquan 2005: 275–314).

The chairman of the board of the ICBC made just this point in a pre-IPO interview at the inception of corporatization. Minimizing the importance of the Board of Directors as an institution, or the effect of corporatization and a public listing for some of the firm's shares, Jiang Jianqing said:

> *I must specify here that the historical problems created for state-owned banks are not due to a lack of board of directors, but are instead closely connected to multiple factors such as China's economic structure, credit structures, reorganization of state-owned enterprises and the transitional economy, etc.... [W]e recognize that we must carry out shareholder rights reform, but that is not our ultimate goal. Nowadays, many people very mechanically think that solving [shareholders' rights] is everything and, once that happens, bank reform will have succeeded. In reality, simultaneously with shareholder rights reform, we must also strengthen the bank's internal corporate governance.... It is not the case that once we resolve our listing, then everything will be "OK."* (Ling Huawei and Zhao Xiaojian 2003: 74)

In a different but equally detrimental way, the lopsided capital structure of China's state-controlled commercial banks makes any market for corporate control irrelevant to the management of the banking firms involved. It is generally accepted that if sub-standard management results in sub-par financial performance, that will be reflected in a declining share price. That declining share price would—in a deeper and more liquid capital market for the shares of a specific firm—result in an attempted takeover by a potentially more efficient or well-run concern, happy to buy the undervalued equity, replace management and/or insiders, and increase value of the underperforming firm in the future. Yet where only a limited amount of the shares are actually truly in play, and control is firmly stuck in the hands of one actor (in China, the state acting through the Ministry of Finance), such firms—and the firms' managers—are completely insulated from any such threat to control. In this context, even if a declining share price signals bad management, and leads to discomfort in management ranks, it does not carry with it the threat of takeover and restructured management (that is, loss of post).

As an alternative spur to improved corporate governance, many observers and analysts also point to the introduction of foreign minority equity investment (often accompanied by foreign governance input and "strategic" or "technical" assistance), or the competitive effects of China fulfilling its WTO commitments in the sector, as critical if not determinative factors in the reform of China's commercial banks (Berger, Hasan, and Zhou 2007).[14] This chapter rejects, or at least seeks to de-emphasize, the purported beneficial effects of foreign equity participation inside China's largest commercial banking enterprises, for much the same reasons that simple corporatization and public listing is no improvement: it does not dislodge the overwhelming power of the 70–80% shareholder and the insiders who are appointed as its (their) representatives. While such foreign strategic investors may offer business and operational insights or suggestions for new product lines, and may even have "strategic cooperation" agreements that appear to allow for significant input, the fact is that—without negotiated negative veto rights—they have no power to enforce dissenting views, block insider action, much less effectively monitor insiders or the large state equity holdings. To date, there seems to be only one working example of foreign "strategic" investor governance input at a Chinese banking firm—and that is TPG's buy-out of state (Shenzhen-level) shareholders at the widely held Shenzhen Development Bank. The degree of foreign strategic investor control in this one example is a result of unique circumstances: the "exit" of state shareholders (bought out by the foreign investors), the widely held shares (mostly public), and a central government-approved management arrangement assuring a minority shareholder extra-proportional board-level governance and executive officer appointment powers.

PARTY COMMITTEES—THE EMPEROR'S NEW CLOTHES

It is no secret that while corporatized and newly listed Chinese commercial banks have established formal "Boards of Directors" (which must now include a required proportion of independent directors), and further set up specific committees of the Boards, there is another "committee" that exercises decisive influence over governance of the bank and the directors who are—in law—the centralized management apex of the bank. This committee is widely discussed in Chinese writings and journalism about the corporatized commercial banks, but rarely referred to in foreign language writings, journalism, or offshore listing offering documents.[15] It is the Committee of the Chinese Communist Party that is established in all transformed SOEs (and even in the author's experience, township and village enterprises (TVEs) that have corporatized and sought public listings). Thus, notwithstanding the importation of the mechanism that corporate law analysts describe as a "Board of Directors", the real power in any of China's large state-owned commercial banks—and the group that largely appoints (by nomination for election by the shareholders, the shareholders dominated by the approximately 70% "state" shareholder which acts according to the instructions of the Party system) and directs the directors—is the Party Committee. The Party Committee in any bank or other SOE is in turn subject to control by the Party system (as contrasted with the state and military), with appointments to enterprise-level Party committees governed by Party personnel appointments. In the cases of all the PRC corporatized commercial banks, Big Four and a Half or not, the only evidence of this parallel Party organization in such banks' offering documents and public reports is mention of the "Discipline Committee" or sometimes even "Party Discipline Committee." This is a committee subordinate to the Party Committee in each bank that investigates and punishes bad actors in the bank *qua* Party members pursuant to Party "discipline" (distinct from "public" legal or regulatory enforcement). None of the PRC state-controlled banks that have gone public explicitly alludes to the existence of such Party committees. Instead, most public offering documents—in the section responding to mandatory disclosure on "Management"—awkwardly name a single individual who is leader of the "Discipline Committee," but without further elaboration on what exactly such Discipline Committee is or does, the way in which it is subordinate to a Party Committee, or how such Committee relates to the formal corporate governance structures.[16]

In a remarkably forthright 2006 interview, the chairman of BoCom Jiang Chaoliang describes what the Party Committee does, why it does it, and who or what it is deemed to represent. Perhaps most startling, from the standpoint of orthodox corporate governance practices, is the turned-around statement of Chairman Jiang, apparently trying to reassure his interviewer as to the real locus of control in the banks. Jiang says that "when the board of directors disagrees with the opinions of the Party Committee, the former can veto [the Committee's decision]" (Hu Runfeng, Cheng Zhe, and Fu Tao 2006: 72). This is the precise opposite of what the corporate form as it has developed since the nineteenth century, and not incidentally the PRC Company Law since 1994, promises: centralized management vested in the Board of Directors, subject to very high threshold checks on board power by (1) specialized *board* committees, or (2) the *shareholders*. Jiang conversely reveals a corporate law and governance regime that locates primary power in the hands of an undisclosed Committee—which is none of the Board of Directors, senior management, supervisory board, or shareholders' meeting—and then allows a Board of Directors—in law, the sole legal fiduciaries of the firm owners—a mere "veto" over the proposals of the same leading group. Jiang is more interesting in discussing the theoretical (and ideological) tie between the majority shareholder (the state), the Party that stands behind the state, and the interests served by the Party Committee in China's new corporate governance regime:

> *What does the Party Committee govern? First, it is in charge of overseeing strategy. The government has a [sic] 65% interest in Bank of Communications and, as the controlling shareholder, it has the power to propose strategic arrangements for the future development of the Bank. Second, [the Party Committee] oversees human resources . . . The Party Committee recommends to the Board of Directors senior management candidates with the Board of Directors making the final decision. . . . Third, [the Party Committee] oversees corporate social responsibility. Both natural and legal persons within China must undertake a certain amount of social responsibility such as lawfully paying taxes, operating business in accordance with law, and not being lawless and chaotic. If the nation implements macroeconomic measures, [the Bank] must abide by these policies. (Hu Runfeng, Cheng Zhe, and Fu Tao 2006: 72)*

There are several fascinating aspects to these comments. Most important are those which depart from an orthodox understanding of the legal or operational relationship between the roles of various actors in the corporation: (1) acknowledgement that the state is the controlling shareholder in the bank, but that the state's interest, *qua* shareholder, is communicated not through the shareholders' meeting but via the firm-level Communist Party Committee, and the Party Committee's proposals are communicated directly to the Board of Directors; (2) the Party's direct responsibility and authority for selecting and proposing senior management of the firm (albeit subject to approval by the Board of Directors);[17] and (3) the clear indication that the Party Committee (exercising authority through the Board of Directors and the Board's appointed officers) will cause the firm not to act in the direct profit-making interest of all the shareholders, but in accord with "stability," "lawfulness," and national "macroeconomic measures." Finally, Jiang reveals in the same 2006 interview how the Party Committee—at least at the Bank of Communications—in fact exercises its writ:

> *[The Bank's] Party Committee represents the interest of our largest shareholder and submits to the Board of Directors certain proposals. After the Board votes its approval, the senior management is assigned to implements [them]. When the management implements them, the supervisory board oversees whether the Board's strategic direction and senior management's implementation are lawful. (Hu Runfeng, Cheng Zhe, and Fu Tao 2006: 72)[18]*

Here, it is clear that the shareholders' interest is not represented or articulated by the shareholders' meeting, but by the Party Committee, which it should be noted has no fiduciary duty in law to the shareholders' it is said to act for.

The BOC's president, Li Lihui, was equally forthright about the function of the Party Committee at the BOC in a 2005 interview, although he shades the issue somewhat differently. After a *Caijing Magazine* reporter relayed a joke to President Li,[19] the President, BOC, responded:

> *At present, some members of the board of directors, supervisory board and senior management are Party members. The Chairman [of the board] is the Party Committee Secretary, and head of the Supervisory Board and the President are Vice-Secretaries of the Party Committee. The [Party] Committee is to monitor macro-policy, firm direction, Party structure, as well as the structure of the Party membership, and monitor coordination among different departments. In China, it is very important to employ the political power of the Communist Party. Management arrangements can solve a majority of the problems, but not all of them. For example, if asked how to develop political ideology work or how to increase employees' ethical standards, and so on—these issues must be studied by*

> *the Party Committee. So, I think there is nothing hypocritical [about this]. [Or, on the question of what to do with] 220,000 employees: lay them off, or undergo restructuring? (Zhang Xiaocai 2005)*

Similarly, ICBC President Yang Kaisheng invokes the role of the Party Committee as an undisclosed part of the governance structure, saying in 2006: "Since October 2005, Industrial and Commercial Bank has changed its system to 'Three Committees' [meaning senior management, the Board of Directors, and the supervisory board]—'Four Committees' if the Party Committee is included—operational state" (Zhang Jiwei, Yu Ning and Guo Jiong 2006: 66).

Li and Yang's comments are as revealing as Jiang's, and demonstrate both the continued existence and huge role of the undisclosed Party Committee ("macro-policy, firm direction...coordination among different departments"), its indispensable nature ("management arrangements can solve a majority of the problems, but not all of them"), and the intimate cross-relationships between *nomenklatura* posts and formal corporate posts (board chairman = Party secretary, supervisory board chairman = Party vice-secretary, president = Party vice-secretary, and so on) that mimic so closely the relationship between the Party and state organs more broadly.

This identification of the Party Committee's significant role is not meant to cast aspersions on the Chinese Communist Party, or the fact that this often undisclosed center of governance power is specifically a Communist Party committee. Instead, it only serves to highlight the true location of corporate authority in Chinese banks (and other firms), and the separation between form and function in Reform-era China. Most importantly, it indicates that incentivization of, or accountability for, directors or senior management will never be terribly relevant when such persons are not the real directing power of the firm; moreover, the real powers behind the firm are not monitored by the shareholders at all, but instead by a separate and superior Party organization.

THE *NOMENKLATURA* STAYS IN THE GAME

As BoCom Chairman of the Board (and not incidentally Communist Party Committee Secretary) Jiang Chaoliang makes clear in the interview quoted above, the Party organization (acting through the firm-level Party Committee) has the pre-eminent role in actually appointing senior management (many of whom do double duty as executive directors):

> ... *[the Party Committee] oversees human resources.... The Party Committee recommends to the Board of Directors senior management candidates with the Board of Directors making the final decision ... (Hu Runfeng, Cheng Zhe, and Fu Tao 2006: 72)*

Who are these individuals appointed to senior management posts? The great majority of them are personnel who have standing in the Communist Party hierarchy (as determined by the personnel appointments system), often in the same "system" (*xitong*) as the relevant firm, but not always. Even in Reform-era China, all SOEs and state-controlled enterprises remain a part of (or subjects for) the Party ranking system that embraces all public institutions. *Nomenklatura* appointments continue for public enterprises as they do for administrative units, only "one level down." The power to appoint individual department and enterprise leaders throughout the public sector is one of the most important vehicles for Chinese Communist Party control of all aspects of society and the political economy (Lieberthal 2004: 234–9). Thus, corporate management appointments are almost entirely informed by, and shadow, Party structure arrangements and career evaluation. Said another way, senior corporate elections (directors and supervisory board members) and appointments (management) only reflect arrangements animated entirely by the continuing PRC *nomenklatura* system.

Thus it is common to see significant firm leaders moved between corporate and government (Party) functions; for example, the chairman of China National Offshore Oil Corporation moved next to the Governorship of Hainan Province, CCB's successor to the disgraced Zhang Enzhao transferred in from the PBC (SAFE), and the new boss of Sinopec parachuted in from a senior political post in northeast China. More disorienting is the frequent interchange of senior figures in the *nomenklatura* between even competing firms in the same industry, a kind of musical chairs played not just at the very highest level, but at the operational level as well. For example, some eyebrows were raised when apparent "competitors" China Mobile and China Unicom switched highest ranking executives immediately after they had both completed international IPOs. As another example, during the summer of 2007—and in the period of a mere five days—a large-scale swap of high-level operational-level personnel (Deputy CEO level) between apparent competitors China Mobile, China Telecom, China Netcom, and China Unicom was completed.[20] Each of the companies involved issued press releases announcing the changes, and it was widely put out that the apparently distinct firms were preparing for 3G bids. Yet these executive reshuffles reveal that these four firms are subject to some other, non-firm-specific, approach. That is the *nomenklatura* system, which assigns senior government officials among Party organs and government departments—even government departments that have been corporatized as a way to raise capital on the international and domestic markets.

These apparently PRC-specific phenomena need not be cause for objection on political or organizational grounds. Who is to say that the Party (acting through the state, which is the largest shareholder in such firms) may not to assign its most competent cadres to difficult tasks at the nation's most complex political-economic organizations? Certainly, appointments of purely political personnel to manage increasingly technical tasks (such as those seen in the financial sector) are ill-advised, although the degree of intrusion by pure *nomenklatura* appointments in commercial and operational aspects of firm activities probably varies from SOE to SOE. However, it is a second reminder as to how much at variance governance arrangements are with formal appearances bestowed by enterprise reform and corporatization. Most importantly, it identifies who precisely is being monitored and held accountable in China's banks, and by whom. It is not—as the corporate form might make us think—directors and senior officers held accountable to shareholders. Instead, China's banks (and other SOEs) evidence *nomenklatura* accountable to the Party system, the same system that governs the nominal controlling shareholder of the banks: the state.

GOVERNING AN OCTOPUS

Aside from the problematic capital structure in place after corporatization, and the persistence of a powerful shadow governance system, and thus even if managers were inspired to govern Chinese banking firms in the interests of all of the shareholders, the sheer size, disparate organization, and continuing independence of branch-level actors nominally under China's banking firms act to defeat the effort. For example, at its IPO, BoCom had 92 branches, only seven of which were directly monitored by the "head office" (corporate headquarters). Twenty-seven of those branches were "provincial-level" branches, which in turn monitored 58 other branches from the provincial level (Bank of Communications Annual Report 2005: 22). At CCB, President Chang Zhenming identified the vertical governance difficulties as critical:

> *Originally, the model for operating the whole bank was by having 38 tier-1 branches, each with their own balance sheet, and then aggregation of [net] profits of each branch making up the [gross] profits [revenues] of the head office. So, the management style of the head office was to distribute all resources to the 38 tier-1 branches. (Ling Huawei, Guo Jiong, and Li Zhigang 2006: 48)*

Similarly, at its IPO, the BOC had over 11,000 branches and outlets, 580 self-service centers, and 11,600 automated service machines (BOC 2005: 120); the ICBC topped all competitors, boasting 18,038 "domestic branches, outlets, and other establishments" in June 2006, and 98 "overseas branches, subsidiaries, representative offices, and outlets"! (ICBC 2006: 102)

Chinese banking institutions are in fact very difficult to integrate vertically, as the "head office" (and now corporate center) is often akin to a rather weak and latter-day federal government with anemic command or monitoring powers over the activities of long pre-existing subsidiary departments. The reason for this is closely related to the key problem in Chinese governance generally: local (provincial or municipal level and down) identities of bank branches are closely tied to their equivalent level of government (and Party), and very often pre-date the existence of anything like a "head office." As PRC economist Wu Jinglian noted in late 2005, until the mid-1990s, branch-level actors had actually received funding direct from local-level PRC Central Bank offices, which they on-lent to local customers (*Economist* 2005: 73). Thus, for example, the Chongqing Municipal system of branches of a given state-owned bank will almost certainly be more responsive to the priorities and ambitions of the Chongqing Municipal People's Government (and Party organization) than the commands of that same bank's nominal headquarters or the "head office" of the fictional legal person that has been made the summit of its formal legal structure after corporatization. Many local level "branches" will make their own loan origination and asset creation decisions, implement their own credit standards (under pressure from the local, equivalent, level of government), and even prepare their own stand-alone, financial statements. This was recognized very early in China's financial sector reform, in November 1997, when the National Financial Working Group repeatedly issued policy commands exhorting local governments not to interfere with the operations and decision-making of their co-equal bank branches (Zhou Xiaochuan 2000: 76). Contemporary observers know that this dynamic remains in play, not simply because many "local" bank leaders respond in this way to their nominal superiors, but because so many of the significant bank scandals in the past decade have their origin in difficult to monitor local-level operations.[21] As one foreign executive who parachuted into the chairmanship of the Shenzhen Development Bank as the representative of TPG said: "Branch managers are kings in China" (*Economist* 2005: 73).

Even after restructuring, and formal imposition of mandated monitoring and enforcement procedures, it is very difficult for the senior levels of any PRC bank, spread across a huge physical and political geography, to govern technically subordinate systems. For example, after its IPO the BOC itself discovered and revealed a massive fraud at the Shenqiu branch in April 2006 (bank employees had conspired with the general manager of local company Zhoukou Wanyuan Beer to embezzle RMB146 million between 2004 and 2005). The genesis of the fraud? The importance to the local government of the enterprise conspiring with the local bank branch! As one local resident said, "the government is very supportive of Wanyuan, but bank credits alone are simply not able to satisfy its appetite [for capital]." As a BOC manager in Shenqiu admitted, "In 2005, Bank of China initiated restructuring and the Bank aggressively implemented internal controls, but the power [of the Bank head office] to implement them at the Branch level is not great. The branch manager can still control various resources within the branch and create instability due to the acts of collusion to commit fraud. In reality, the BOC's personnel restrictions and rotational system [of personnel appointments] have only been implemented recently" (Hu Runfeng, Yu Ning, and Guo Jiong 2006: 41). This institutional reality must be taken into account when analysts and reformers posit that more accountable central corporate managers will be able to affect governance at subsidiary levels of what are in fact diffuse and non-responsive institutional structures. That insight does not even question the extent to which local-level, branch actors are qualified to undertake commercial banking tasks—as CCB's newly installed chairman Guo Shuqing noted in the run-up to that bank's international IPO, "more than 90% of the CCB's risk managers are unqualified" (*Economist* 2005: 73). This difficult dynamic is only confirmed by the persistence of plainly bad, or perhaps just politicized, lending made by China's large commercial banks, whereby so-called NPLs continue apace, even as past NPLs are removed from banking firms' books by "sale" to asset management companies, or covered by recapitalizations. No doubt the new leaders of China's corporatized and public banks are making real efforts to "re-centralize" (in many cases, a misnomer, as power was originally vested in local identities of the institutions) the massive and widely disparate "branch" networks. No doubt some of the more obvious abuses—branches operating autonomously, creating their own websites, claiming independent legal person (and accounting) status, and so on—are being identified and eliminated. Yet it seems that the chances for success of "centralization" and rectification will be hampered in the same way as the Chinese central government's effort to re-centralize political and developmental control commencing in the mid-1990s.

TOO BIG TO FAIL

Finally, and notwithstanding all manner of organizational changes wrought on the Big Four and a Half banks, there is a clear recognition in the PRC and abroad that—no matter how badly run the banks may be—they will simply not be allowed to fail. This results in a classic "moral hazard" problem, at least for the individuals actually governing the commercial banks. The world-shaking consequences of any banking failure in China are not difficult to conjure. The desire not to allow China's banks to fail has been adequately signaled by China's central government and financial policymakers, and the series of recapitalizations and balance sheet restorations (effected via the likely deferred recapitalizations that are the NPL transfers to asset management companies) enjoyed by China's state banking sector. If indeed the banks are too important to fail, then management—the subject of corporate governance attention—may be permitted to escape any kind of accountability for their deeds and misdeeds, no matter the formal institutions of corporate governance applied to them. (The same of course might be said for many of the West's large financial institutions, especially in the context of the subprime mortgage loan mess and the resulting global financial crisis, or the prior Savings and

Loan scandal in the US. However, those markets maintain other, real, measures of accountability and monitoring mechanisms, such as the market for corporate control.)

MEASUREMENT DEFICIT—SOARING STOCK PRICES AND PERSISTENT NPLs

Any corporate governance scheme seeks to improve external monitoring and internal checks and balances so as to bring about better performance at the firm and increase shareholder value. With respect to China's banking institutions, there are several ways in which the specific effects of corporatization and corporate governance reform might be isolated and even measured. These include: increased profitability (fundamental change in the operations of the firm), decrease in provisions for NPLs alongside growth of high-quality bank assets (again, fundamental change in the central operations of a bank, or credit decision-making), and change in the public stock price (market evaluation of bank profitability, growth and future value). Unfortunately, in the current context of China's financial sector, each of these traditional measuring devices is problematic.

It is still too early to use basic profitability or changes in profitability, to measure the purported beneficial effects of corporate governance reform at China's banks. This is true regardless of what measure is used: return on equity (ROE), return on assets (ROA), interest rate margins, or even loan income to total revenues ratios. The reason behind this difficulty is easy to understand: China has only very recently corporatized its banks (and made into an independent legal person, much less an independent accounting unit)—thus, it is impossible to understand "change" (that is, improvement) in profitability and performance as against any even recent baseline. In addition, as with the evaluation of continuing NPLs origination or carrying, and notwithstanding the public disclosures required of four of the Big Four and a Half, there must be some continuing doubt as to the accuracy of financial reporting by the banks. While many observers hope that beneficial change will be identified using this metric, it is simply too early try to understand the relationship between corporate governance reform (not to mention regulation, public monitoring, and so on) and improved performance.

A second metric that might be useful in evaluating how managers at Chinese banks are doing in the new era, aside from profit performance or market evaluation (via price) is the continuing incidence of NPLs.

In the new age for listed Chinese banks, they are now forced to disclose (often) audited financial reports that should describe with greater
accuracy (and under the discipline of prospectus liability) NPLs, or
at least reserves against such NPLs. Without over-generalizing, and
yet taking seriously the occasional comments on this critical question
by Liu Minkang, Chairman of the CBRC, it would seem that China's
banks—and especially the Big Four and a Half—have continued to
accumulate NPLs or, said another way, have continued as firms
to make bad lending (asset creation) decisions. This worrying phenomenon has been described in the Chinese and foreign literature
(*Economist* 2005), and is the reason why at least one high profile
transaction (TPG's initial purchase of state and legal person shares
from Shenzhen Municipal shareholders in Shenzhen Development
Bank) almost collapsed.[22] One prominent report in the *New York
Times* detailed how a senior risk advisor hired by the CCB prior
to its IPO was ignored by management when he persisted in warn-
ings that "bad loans were being hidden at the bank's branches in the
"special mention" category, erroneously labeled as good loans, even
though company records showed that they were impaired" (Barboza
2006). Or, as one of the CBRC's own top officials said, explaining
why bad loan levels are not accurately revealed, "When our banks
disclose information, they don't always do so in a totally honest manner" (*Economist* 2005: 72). For present purposes, the phenomenon is
important because it places in doubt the rosy reports issued by China's
banks to the effect that—after corporatization, public listing, and corporate governance reform—the growth of NPLs has been curtailed, or
even that NPLs are decreasing. At this point, observers really have no
idea how the far-flung and difficult to govern PRC banks are faring,
and thus no way to connect the formal changes seen in governance
and any effects in operations.

Implicit in any corporate governance scheme is the idea that public stock prices, even in a mildly efficient capital markets, will reflect
some idea of the value of the firm (and most importantly the market's perception of the performance of firm managers). The prices of
public equity of Chinese state-controlled banks before the 2008 global
crash, both on overseas exchanges and as the PRC banks do follow-on
A-share offerings increasingly on domestic exchanges, probably
reflected enthusiasm for China's dizzying growth trajectory and all
"China plays" generally, rather than any evaluation of how a specific
firm is being run. After May 2006 all things "Chinese" and "securities" were hot, if not overheated. Even before the current boom

environment, economist Stephen Green pointed to one "stock market with Chinese characteristics" phenomenon: publicly listed Chinese industrial concerns that disclose negative earnings, or even insider fraud or manipulation, and see their stock prices increase! (Green 2003: 118–53) Much the same dynamic was at work with China's bank stocks, and especially in the frame of China's "bubble" stock markets and their irrational ascendance after the summer of 2006. In the commercial banking sector, a good indication of the decoupling of market price from even disclosed facts was the arrest of CCB Chairman Zhang Enzhao immediately before that bank's IPO and international listing. Zhang was replaced by a high-level state bureaucrat (Guo Shuqing) shortly before the IPO; the episode was duly disclosed in the IPO, and yet the offering went off with a resounding success and the Bank's share price has continued to climb. Much the same can be seen in the stream of horrifying disclosures about operations at the other banks and the lack of reaction in the share price of the issuers. In short, all of the four institutions with listings, domestic and foreign, in the Big Four and a Half saw their share prices rise steadily, seemingly impervious to firm-specific information, sector "fundamentals," or even broader market gyrations. Again, what was actually at work here is not difficult to see: both foreign and PRC investors were investing in banking institutions that promise to track China's startling growth, with little regard to present governance of the specific firm. (The recent massive declines are equally non-firm specific and tied to a global collapse of the equity and credit markets.) The implication of this continuing dynamic is that policymakers who advocated public listings (and allegedly reflective public share prices) for Chinese banks as part of a modern corporate governance and public markets monitoring regime were perhaps mistaken in the short term—the prices of China's bank stocks do not, generally, reflect any evaluation of firm-specific management or governance.

In sum, it is difficult—at least in the medium term—to measure precisely what effect the corporatization and corporate governance reform programs have had, or will have, on China's banking institutions in terms of making those institutions better, and more efficient and profitable. It is important to re-emphasize that the foregoing does not meant to deny that China's commercial banks have not improved performance since bank-specific reforms commenced. The problem is that it is still very difficult to determine whether or not, and to what extent, improvements in performance have occurred, and nigh impossible to specifically tie such improvements, if they exist, with changes in the corporate governance structures of the banking institutions themselves.

WHAT HAS CORPORATIZATION, PUBLIC LISTING, AND STRATEGIC FOREIGN INVESTMENT ACCOMPLISHED?

The foregoing sets forth the following propositions: (1) China has undertaken a wide-ranging reform of its state banking sector; (2) one part of that reform program involved corporatization of these banking institutions, the public listing of a portion of the banking firm's post-corporatization share capital, and the implementation of formal corporate governance mechanisms; (3) corporatization and public listings were meant to create shareholder "principals" separate from director/executive management "agents", with the former monitoring and holding accountable the latter through board elections and fiduciary duty constraints; (4) notwithstanding appearances, China's state-owned commercial banks are still governed—at least at the central level—in a relatively unchanged manner, with a Communist Party Committee acting as the paramount authority in regards to overall strategic direction and directorate/executive appointments; (5) the Communist Party and the *nomenklatura* personnel appointed to directors and executive positions are not necessarily responsive to the shareholders' interest (other than the 75% shareholder, the state, which is itself directed by the Party); and (6) corporate restructuring and public listings of China's banks may—contrary to *ex ante* theoretical formulations—have had very little effect on governance at the same firms.

Faced with these assertions, some may be forgiven for uttering the possibly heretical view that corporatization, public listings, legal change, and corporate governance reform are without any effect whatsoever in the Chinese financial sector. The reasons for this—if it is true—are as argued above: real and effective corporate governance reform has not been visited on China's large banks, precisely because the capital structure remains so unbalanced, and because the Board of Directors is the centralized management of the firm in name only, and the management (Board and senior officers) is in reality responsible to a Party Committee for the large state shareholder that was in place long before corporatization. In corporate governance terms, the powerful Party Committee is comprised of the specific group of "insiders" who control the firm in the absence of a real, autonomous, watchful, principal/shareholder: the state (or "all of the people"). (The assertive posture of Huijin, prior to its announced absorption into CIC, was the momentary exception to this negative dynamic.) Those insiders are not held accountable to either shareholders or the market (via a market for corporate control). While it remains to be seen if a system of private attorneys-general (and thus aggressive public shareholder monitoring via class action-style lawsuits) will grow in China, such a development seems doubtful given the inability of shareholders to be organized as a true cost-spreading "class," and the fact that the lawyers seeking to represent them cannot take cases on a contingency basis.[23]

One obvious long-term answer to this specific set of quandaries is increased (real) privatization of China's large, state-owned, banks—not "radical shock" privatization, or sale of control of the banks to a replacement group of (non-state) insiders, but a gradual selling down of the state's overwhelming equity interest in individual banks and to more independent and widely dispersed groups of capital: groups intimately concerned with increasing performance (and thus value) at the firms. Of course, there are huge social costs and uncertainties attendant with even gradual privatization, regardless of the sector implicated, costs that may dissuade the most aggressive reformers. Add to that the extreme sensitivity of the nation's financial sector, which still meets the overwhelming amount of capital allocation burden in China's fast-growing economy, and the chances for accelerated privatization appear dim. Given the small likelihood of real privatization or dispersal of ownership, we might then ask more intensively what real governance effects the partial program implemented to date has had, or at least promises over the medium term? Put bluntly, is there anything about the corporate and legal changes visited on China's banks that might heighten accountability of bank managers (whoever they are) and/or act as a check on opportunistic or oppressive practices? It is in this regard that the true power relationships inside China's albeit formally corporatized and publicly reporting bank firms play a perhaps unanticipated role, and one that is possibly unique in the short history of corporate governance reform.

We have noted above that in the normal course changes in the public share prices of Chinese banks will have little effect on bank firm managers, because of the absence of a market for corporate control; the inability of dissatisfied (public) shareholders to depose directors; the inability of those same shareholders to cause elected directors (or the relatively powerless "independent directors") to change management; a mostly non-existent private (shareholders') right of action; and the basic tension between (1) a Board of Directors that formally works in the interest of shareholders, and (2) a Party Committee which trumps the Board of Directors absolutely in terms of centralized management.

Yet, this analysis may take the corporate form as established in modern China too seriously, or too formally, and neglect the way in which the public share price can determine the fate (and career) of the real managers in a PRC state-controlled bank, and thereby provide incentives for better performance and loyal performance. For individuals who staff the leadership of China's state-controlled banks, whether as formal directors or officers, or most importantly as members of the Party Committee that really provides direction to the Board of Directors, are members of China's modern *nomenklatura*. They are important Party—and then state/government, and then system (*xitong*), and then firm—personnel, who gain advancement and status solely as part of the *nomenklatura* system. Therefore, the Party, which holds real power vis-à-vis China's state institutions, administrative bodies, and state-controlled enterprises is intimately concerned with how they manage the various tasks entrusted to them—from Ministerial posts to state-controlled enterprise leadership. It is in this regard that the public share price of a corporatized banking firm—whether on the NYSE, the Hong Kong Stock Exchange, or in Shanghai—will have a very significant impact upon a Party appointee's advancement within the Party political (and personnel) system. Thus, even if the market price of Chinese bank shares reflects only valuation of a tiny float (no more than 30%), it seems highly probably that the Party-appointed personnel who actually control China's banks—whether or not they are formally appointed directors, officers, or senior-level managers—will be held accountable by the Party system for the public stock price of the bank. If the bank underperforms, or is perceived to be governed badly or is subject to conflicting imperatives, the public price will fall. This in turn should lead to action or threatened action against the Party Committee members and Party appointees holding corporate positions—whether dismissal, demotion, or just frustration of career advancement. Party officials appointed to serve at bank institutions that perform and are well-perceived in the capital markets, thus conjuring a positive stock price trajectory, will be rewarded and see advancement.

Granted, these observations also lie in the realm of theory at this point, precisely because none of the Big Four and a Half which do have public listings have seen a marked decline in their share prices not related to a global failure and thus immediate action against the *nomenklatura* members assigned to manage such firms. Notwithstanding, the view provides an idea that at least one part of the corporatization and public listing reform project may be effective in governing centralized management at China's banks—something observers might have thought impossible upon a true understanding of the lopsided capital structure and Party domination of China's "reformed" banking institutions. Corporate law and governance theory tell us that the corporate form will allow "shareholders" to monitor firm "managers." The unique circumstances of China's SOEs and state-owned banks however allow shareholders to take advantage of only one of their traditional monitoring mechanisms of "vote," "sell," or "sue." Shareholders in China's banks may only sell their shares; yet those sales will cause a decline in the stock price, and thereby directly impact one very important performance metric for the real control parties at Chinese banks—the senior political cadres who have resurfaced as "directors" or "CEOs." Without doubt, this is not the optimal monitoring mechanism, and many will see this as a most attenuated and unsure imposition of accountability. While this is true at some level, there are two important responses to the objection: (1) that there is a monitoring mechanism in existence at all (responding to the widely held view that large Chinese SOEs are simply not subject to any monitoring); (2) it is as attenuated—and indirect—as any mechanism provided to widely dispersed shareholders in a Western public company. Compare the real power and leverage to monitor and effect change of the millions of shareholders in so-called "developed market" banking giants like Citigroup, Merrill Lynch, UBS, or Deutsche Bank. While in formal terms shareholders in such Western banking giants have a richer arsenal at their disposal—voting for and removing directors, the threat of takeover (market for corporate control), and class action securities fraud suits or derivative lawsuits for breach of fiduciary duties—the reality is that management in such international banking giants are as well-protected as the directors and officers of newly corporatized Chinese banks, or those who "govern behind the curtain" (*chuilian tingzheng*) from the post of Party Committee leader. Chinese state-controlled banks thus share with their developed economy peers a basic mechanism for identifying and enforcing corporate accountability—the public share price of the firm, and the financial media's attention to it. While in the West, this may result in the dismissal of a powerful CEO (witness the fate of Merrill Lynch's Stan O'Neal or Citigroup's Chuck Prince), in China, it may result in the dismissal or end of career advancement for any real power at a Chinese state-owned bank. Thus, what becomes most important for governance at Chinese state-controlled banks is much the same as that which determines the fate of Western bank executives and directors: (1) securities regulation that mandates disclosure and transparency (especially vis-à-vis financial performance); and (2) an independent media to raise, investigate, and highlight bad business decisions, shirking, incompetence, conflicted dealings, or corporate corruption. China and China's state-owned, publicly listed banks in large measure have both of those things: (1) the benefit of state-of-the-art securities regulation (as four of the banks included in the Big Four and a Half have listings outside of China and have thus subjected themselves to foreign securities and exchange regulation) and strong disclosure obligations, and (2) a significant media inquiry—from both foreign media and the incredibly independent and well-versed Chinese financial media. The unreality of Chinese share prices prior to the global meltdown in 2008—whether listed inside the PRC or abroad—could not continue forever. Once these wild over-valuations receded, and after the world moves through the global crisis of 2008 and equity markets once again reflect firm fundamentals, the public stock price of China's different state-controlled banks may well see profoundly negative movements, which will necessarily affect the careers and promotion prospects of managers of these important financial institutions.

The corporatization and public listing of China's major state-controlled banks was supposed to do several things. Important among the range of hoped-for effects was the creation of the conditions for serious monitoring and real accountability at such banks, and therefore a new world of efficiency and productivity. Notwithstanding those admirable aims, and the introduction of new legal and financial structures, the peculiarities of China's "*corporatization*-not *privatization*" (among many factors) has led to widely acknowledged and seemingly insurmountable obstacles to such monitoring of and accountability for banking firm insiders. However, that disappointment must be tempered by a recognition as to how one aspect of China's banking reform—the phenomenon of a public price for a thin, and widely dispersed, slice of ownership of the firm—does affect China's seemingly hidden and unaccountable managers, the *nomenklatura* who continue to staff the controlling heights of China's banks. This mechanism will only become more effective as China's banks return to the PRC for A-share listing on the Shanghai Stock Exchange, where the watching shareholders will be Chinese citizens (not star-struck foreign fund managers), and an ever-increasingly independent and critical Chinese financial media.

ENDNOTES

[1] The author would like to thank Ms Marianne Chow and Mr Timothy Throm, both University of Michigan J.D. law graduates for their invaluable research assistance, and professors Pieter Bottelier, Ken Lieberthal, and Zhao Minyuan for their kind and detailed comments on an earlier draft of this chapter.

[2] Amended very significantly with effect from January 1, 2006. See *Zhonghua Renmin Gongheguo Gongsifa* (The Company Law of the People's Republic of China), passed by the Eighteenth Session of the Standing Committee of the Tenth National People's Congress on October 27, 2005 (CLC 2006: 1-1).

[3] Before the People's Bank of China (PBC, China's central bank) started additional, but critical, policy reforms including interest rate liberalization and increased reserve requirements.

[4] This is properly contrasted with two related aspects: First, the *regulatory* and *externally* imposed reform strategy effected via the direct, expert, and purportedly neutral regulation of commercial banking operations in China by a government agency like the China Banking Regulatory Commission (CBRC) (to be contrasted in turn with what is so often the case in modern China: a regulatory actor which is also the owner and operator of the firms that it regulates (for example, the Ministry of Information Industry (MII) of the PRC, successor to the regulatory brief of the former Ministry of Post and Telecommunications (MPT), which maintains indirect ownership of, and operational control over, the several post-monopoly telecoms operators); second, the many aspects of China's bank reform that seek to remedy historical problems (like unrealizable assets).

[5] One analyst has written about these reforms—after 1992–93 and before 2003–04—as occurring in three distinct stages: (1) dampening the overheating of the Chinese economy in 1992–93, promulgation of the legislative bases for the financial sector (that is, a Central Bank Law and the Commercial Bank Law in 1995), and separation out of the "policy" functions from China's banks; (2) strengthening bank regulation with a five-tier classification system (commenced experimentally in 1998 and then formally adopted in 2001), recapitalization of the Big Four in 1998 (RMB270 billion), and the creation of asset management companies as the "purchasers" of bad bank debt to clear up bank balance sheets (from 1999); and (3) allowing greater foreign and domestic competition via specific approvals and accession to the WTO, establishment and empowering a new government agency tasked with expert regulation of the financial sector (the China Banking Regulatory Commission (CBRC) in 2003, the creation of a new state shareholder for the banks and as the

vehicle for further capitalizations (Huijin, established December 2003), and the implementation of new capital adequacy standards (conforming to Basel I in 2000 and Basel II from 2004) (Ito 2006). See also the basic role claimed for China's path to conformity with the Basel capital adequacy standards by PBC Governor Zhou Xiaochuan between the promulgation of the PRC Commercial Bank Law in 1995 and the following decade (Zhou Xiaochuan 2000: 74–6) and *The Economist*'s excellent summary of the complete reform program (*Economist* 2005).

6 For example, the early and basic separation out of "policy" lending functions from what became China's "commercial" banks recast the central purpose of China's banking firms, initially in name only, but increasingly in reality (especially after new "policy" banks (such as the China Development Bank) were established and became operative). Similarly, and as is discussed below, one round of bank recapitalization (in that case, using China's abundant foreign exchange reserves) enabled the birth of a dynamic and deeply engaged state shareholder (Huijin) and thus the first viable replacement of the formerly "absent principal" at China's state-"owned" banks. A final example of how divergent strains of the bank reform program impact on governance and operations would be the way in which China's new banking industry regulator—the CBRC established in March 2003—mandated asset (loan) risk classifications for far more accurate and transparent internal monitoring at China's banks.

7 The Shenzhen Development Bank was in fact the first issuer of any *type* permitted to list "A-shares" on the Shenzhen Stock Exchange, a listing that incidentally triggered off August 10, 1992 (the "8.10" incident) riots in the Shenzhen Special Economic Zone, which in turn led directly to the establishment of the China Securities Regulatory Commission (CSRC). In the years following the Shenzhen Development Bank's corporatization and then listing in 1992, all of the 12 national commercial banks have been established as, or converted into, companies limited by shares, with many gaining A-share listings.

8 Underway, at the time of this writing.

9 Importantly, as none of the foreign investors was in the commercial banking industry, each can be seen as a foreign "financial" (strategic) investor: investors who bring other business lines to ICBC (Goldman underwriting, Allianz insurance and American Express credit cards), and not a strong line in commercial bank operations or even corporate governance in the commercial banking sector.

10 At the time of its strategic investment, Goldman entered into the "Strategic Cooperation Agreement" with the Bank for a term of five (5) years, in which the Agreement promised the establishment of a "joint steering committee," "joint working groups," and a project management office residing at each of the Bank and Goldman Sachs to implement overall "strategic cooperation", deemed to include cooperation in "corporate governance" of the new Bank. (ICBC 2006: 91)

11 Repeated by PBC Governor Zhou Xiaochuan publicly in 2005.

12 As of the time of this writing, Huijin was supposed to have been folded into China's new sovereign fund investor, China Investment Corporation (CIC),

which was to take over Huijin's existing equity positions in China's banks. This makes sense, as the source of the investment capital of both Huijin and the successor CIC is the PRC's abundant foreign exchange reserves, which need to gain a better return and be directed away from China's already over-heating domestic economy. Yet, there is word in Beijing that Huijin has only been brought in as a subsidiary of CIC, and may be re-established as an independent entity once again. However, Huijin is structured and governed going forward, what remains to be seen is if the dynamism and focus seen at Huijin will be maintained once it is part of a larger investment concern. Interestingly, all of CIC's initial foreign investments were in the financial sector, including the Blackstone IPO and a helping hand extended to Morgan Stanley.

13 Interestingly, and seeming proof of the notion in some quarters of the PRC about the effect of foreign investment, some of this foreign investment bought out existing (state) shareholders in the non Big Four and a Half commercial banks involved, and thus provided no new capital for the investee banks. In this sense, the subject deals were all about PRC state and local government actors cashing out of commercial bank investments, and ceding some level of governance control to the foreign entrants (see Howson and Ross 2003).

14 As this chapter focuses on corporate governance reform, the second prong of "foreign" involvement—the introduction of foreign banking competition into the PRC—is not addressed. Suffice to say that such foreign competition has proven to be one of the most effective spurs to improved performance by China's state-owned banks.

15 See the 2007 McKinsey "alert" to its foreign clients regarding this fact, obviously something that the consultancy thought was relatively underappreciated: "...the Communist Party committee plays a pivotal role in key decisions—for example, the nomination of top executives, executive evaluation and compensation, asset acquisitions and disposals, and annual budgets. Sometimes the Party committee may even get involved in operational decisions..." (*McKinsey* 2007).

16 For instance, the BOC IPO prospectus listed, awkwardly and in complete isolation, the name "Zhang Lin" as Secretary of the "Party Discipline Committee" of the Bank in the frame of mandatory disclosure of "directors" and "officers," lists his experience (at the Import–Export Bank of China), but says not one word about what the "Party Discipline Committee" is, or how it functions. Nor is there any other mention of this Committee, or the "Secretary" of which is alluded to in the roster of senior management, in any other part of the Prospectus (BOC 2006: 208). The same is true of the ICBC in its IPO disclosure that lists, under "Management" Mr Liu Lixian, a former Vice-President of the same bank's asset management company (China Huarong), as the Secretary of the Bank's Party Discipline Committee (ICBC 2006: 179). That small squib describing Liu Lixian, and the tabular presentation of "Senior Management" (that lists "Mr. LIU Lixian, 52, Secretary of party discipline committee" (ICBC 2006: 178) is the only mention of the Party Discipline Committee, and in a section that includes "directors," "supervisors," and "senior management," and follows with fulsome disclosure on the Board's strategy, audit, risk management, nomination, and compensation committees (ICBC 2006: 171–83).

[17] How often will the Board, dominated by individuals selected as directors by the same Party Committee, refuse the Party Committee's suggestion?

[18] Jiang rather cheekily confirms that the almost 20% foreign strategic investor in this particular bank understands, and apparently approves, of this governance template "with Chinese characteristics", saying "We have discussed this with HSBC. Sir John Bond said, I know you [Jiang] are the Party Secretary and this is why you should be chairman. The guy didn't think it strange at all" (Hu Runfeng, Cheng Zhe, and Fu Tao 2006: 72). So much for foreign strategic investors changing Chinese corporate governance; it would seem that the particular conditions for entry into the Chinese market may shift the direction of influence!

[19] To the effect that "the Bank of China's independent British independent director wanted to participate in the Party Committee, but since he was not a Communist Party member, he tried to find a British Communist to participate on his behalf" (Zhang Xiaocai 2005).

[20] China Telecom's Deputy CEO Huang Wenlin moved to China Mobile, China Mobile's Deputy CEO Zhang Zhenxiang moved to China Telecom, while China Unicom's Hong Kong established "red-chip" (listed issuer's) Executive Director Li Jianguo moved to China Netcom, and China Netcom's Director Miao Jianhua went to China Unicom (Xinjing Bao 2007: B08).

[21] Witness the following disclosed examples: the BoCom's Jinzhou Branch's falsification of documents and (in cooperation with corrupt local courts) judgments to fraudulently write off RMB221 million of "bad loans" extended to 175 enterprises (and report the same to the Bank's corporate headquarters), all the while continuing to collect interest and principal payments, or exercise on collateral, on the allegedly "bad" debt, and assigning those proceeds to personal accounts; or a similar fraud practiced by the Taiyuan Branch of BoCom (using forged seals) to embezzle RMB345 million (BoCom Annual Report 2005: 155); the CCB's subsidiary branches hiding impaired loans, even before that Bank's celebrated IPO (Barboza 2006); the bribery charges leveled at the same Bank's quasi-independent sub-branches (CCB 2005: 121); the BOC's disclosure in its IPO offering document of the "Heilongjiang Incidents" (the manager of a Heilongjiang sub-branch transferred RMB939 million from customer accounts to the manager's personal accounts), fraudulent procurement of bank acceptances by the Simalu sub-branch manager, Beijing branch employees arranging RMB670 million in home mortgage loans subsequently diverted, and the notorious misappropriation of US$482 million by the managers of the Kaiping branch (BOC 2006: 161–2); and the ICBC IPO offering document (ICBC 2006: 134–6) is filled with horror stories of the malfeasance and criminal action at its enormous branch network, as was the Chinese press even at the moment of its IPO (Ling Huawei and He Xiaoxin 2006: 41). The situation at the Agricultural Bank of China, with its almost half a million employees, may be even worse when revealed in connection with its reorganization and public listing (see www.iht.com/articles/2007/01/21/business.bank.php).

[22] The valuation for selling state shareholders was tied to balance sheet valuation, and provision for NPLs, but was conditioned (or subject to purchase price adjustment arising from) an intervening investigation of the quality of bank assets. The acquirer (TPG) identified a higher volume of NPLs between signing

and closing, and thus required a negative purchase price adjustment from the exiting state shareholders (Howson and Ross 2003).

[23] No doubt, in the wider Chinese political and economic context, there are other reasons why the government and the Party are shy of the class action mechanism and contingency fee arrangements.

BIBLIOGRAPHY

Books and reports

Bank of Communications (2005), *Bank of Communications Hong Kong Offering Prospectus*, available at www.hkex.com.hk/listedco/listconews/sehk/ 2005.

Bank of Communications Annual Report (2005), available at www.bankcomm. com.

Basel Committee on Banking Supervision (1999), *Enhancing Corporate Governance for Banking Organizations*, Basel: Basel Committee on Banking Supervision.

Bank of China (2006), *Bank of China Hong Kong Offering Prospectus*, available at www.hkex.com.hk/listedco/listconews/sehk/2006.

Berger, A.N., Hasan, I., and Zhou Mingming (2007), Bank Ownership and Efficiency in China: What Will Happen in the World's Largest Nation? Bank of Finland Discussion Papers, No. 16.

Bottelier, P. (2006), Accelerating Reforms in China's Financial System, *China Brief*, 6, Issue 24, December 6, available at http://jamestown.org

China Banking Regulatory Commission (2004), Guidelines on Corporate Governance Reforms and Supervision of the Bank of China and China Construction Bank, March 11, available at www.cbrc.gov.cn/english/home/jsp/ docView.jsp?docID=560.

China Construction Bank (2005), *China Construction Bank Hong Kong Offering Prospectus*, available at www.hkex.com.hk/listedco/listconews/sehk/ 20051014/LTN20051014000.htm.

CLC (2006), *Guowuyuan Fazhibangongshi* (Legislative Affairs Office of the State Council)(ed.), *Gongsi Falu Guizhang Sifa Jieshi Quanshu (Compendium of Company Law, Regulation and Judicial Explanations)*, Beijing: *Zhongguo Fazhi Chubanshe* (China Legal System Publishing House).

Dou Hongquan (2005), *Yinhang Gongsi Zhili Fenxi* (An Analysis of Bank Corporate Governance), Beijing: *Zhongxin Chubanshe* (CITIC Publishing).

Green, S. (2003), *China's Stockmarket: A Guide to its Progress, Players and Prospects*, London: Economist Books in association with Profile Books Ltd.

Hou Aiai (2002), *Guoyou Shangye Yinhang Gaizhi Shangshi de Youguan Wenti* [Issues Concerning Structural Reform and Listing of State-owned Commercial Banks], *Zhengquan Falu Pinlu* [*Securities Law Review*], no. 2: 26–74.

Howson, N. and Ross, L. (2003) Foreign Minority Equity Investments in Chinese Commercial Banks, *China Business Review* 30, no. 4: 18–31.

Industrial and Commercial Bank of China (October 2006), *Industrial and Commercial Bank of China Hong Kong Offering Prospectus*, available at www.hkex.com.hk/listedco/listconews/sehk/20061016/LTN20061016000.htm.

Ito, S. (2006), The Acceleration of China's Financial Reforms—Pursuing More Efficient Resource Allocation, October 11, available at www.nli-research.co.jp/eng/resea/econo/eco061011.pdf.

Lieberthal, K. (2004), *Governing China: From Revolution Through Reform*, New York: W.W. Norton & Company, Inc.

McKinsey (2007)—He, Richard H. and Orr, G., "China's State-owned Enterprises: Board Governance and the Communist Party" *McKinsey Quarterly*, 2007, no. 1, available at www.mckinseyquarterly.com/article_page.aspx?ar=1929&L2=39&L3=0&rid=246.

Articles

Barboza, D. (2005), Lawsuit Involving Bribery Preceded Bank Resignation, *The New York Times*, March 22, 2005: 6.

Barboza, D. (2006), Rare Look at China's Burdened Banks—Loan Risk Advisor Warns of Cover-Up, *The New York Times*, November 15, 2006: C1 & C8.

Economist (2005), Special Report: China's Banking Industry: A Great Big Banking Gamble—Reforms of China's Banking System Have Not Gone Far Enough," *Economist*, October 29, 2005: 71–3.

Hu Runfeng, Cheng Zhe, and Fu Tao (2006), *Jiang Chaoliang: Jiaohang Po Jianzhong* [Jiang Chaoliang: Bank of Communications Breaks Out of the Cocoon], *Caijing Magazine*, no. 162 (2006, no. 13) June 26: 70–7.

Hu Runfeng, Yu Ning, and Guo Jiong (2006) *Zhonghang Shenqiu Zhihang Zai Bao Piaoju An* [Another Bank of China Shenqiu Branch Receipts Case Explodes], *Caijing Magazine*, no. 161 (2006, no. 12) June 12: 40–1.

Ling Huawei and Zhang Xiaojian (2003), *Jiang Jianqing Xijie Gonghang* [Jiang Jianqing Explains ICBC in Detail], *Caijing Magazine*, no. 75 (2003, no. 1) January 5: 70–6.

Ling Huawei (2005), *Zhou Xiaochuan Tan Jianhang Gaige* [Zhou Xiaochuan Addresses China Construction Bank's Reform], *Caijing Magazine*, no. 147 (2005, no. 24) November 28: 72–4.

Ling Huawei, Guo Jiong, and He Huafeng (2005) *Jianhang IPO Xi Li* [Construction Bank's IPO Cleansing], *Caijing Magazine*, no. 145 (2005, no. 22) October 31: 62–9.

Ling Huawei and Yu Ning (2006), *Zhonghang 112 Yi Meiyuan IPO* [BOC's US$11.2 Billion IPO], *Caijing Magazine*, no. 161 (2006, no. 12) June 12: 38–9.

Ling Huawei, Guo Jiong, and Li Zhigang (2006), *Chang Zhenming: Jianhang Xu Guodu* [Chang Zhenming: China Construction Bank Must Pass Through], *Caijing Magazine*, no. 164 (2006, no. 15) July 24: 46–50.

Ling Huawei and He Yaoxin (2006), *Gonghang IPO: Xin Gaochao Haishi Zhuanzhedian* [ICBC IPO: High Point or Turning Point], *Caijing Magazine*, no. 170 (2006, no. 21) October 16: 40–2.

Wen Yuanhua (2006), *Guoyou Yinhang Gongsi Zhili: Luoji yu Xianshi* [Corporate Governance at State-owned Banks: Logic and Reality], *Caijing Magazine*, no. 162 (2006, no. 13) June 26: 78.

Xie Ping (2006), *Yinhang Gaige Hai Xu Wanshan Waibu Huanjing* [Bank Reform Still Needs to Ameliorate the External Environment], *Caijing Magazine*, no. 166 (2006, no. 17) August 21: 20–1.

Xinjing Bao (2007), *Si Da Dianxin Yunyingshang Gaoguan Huanban* [High Level Operational Personnel Switch Posts at Four Big Telecoms Operators], *Xinjing Bao* [*New Capital News*], 2007, July 12: D08.

Zhang Jiwei, Yu Ning, and Guo Jiong (2006), *Yang Kaisheng: Gonghang Ziyou Lu* [Yang Kaisheng: The Road to Freedom for ICBC], *Caijing Magazine*, no. 159 (2006, no. 10) May 15: 64–8.

Zhang Xiaocai (2005), *Li Lihui Xishu Zhonghang Chongzu* [Li Lihui Recounts in Detail Bank of China's Re-structuring], *Caijing Magazine*, no. 160 (2005, no. 11) June 7.

Zhou Xiaochuan (2000), *Guoyou Shangye Yinhang Ruhe Chongshi Ziben* [How Can The State-owned Banks Replenish Capital], *Renmin Ribao* [*People's Daily*], May 9, 2000, reprinted in *Caijing Magazine*, no. 147 (2005, no. 24) November 28: 74–6.

CHAPTER 9

Prospects for Chinese Banks: Why Global Banks Are Drawn To China

Jamie Dimon
Chairman & CEO, JPMorgan Chase Bank

In recent years, international financial institutions have been racing to enter China's banking market. The attraction is plainly clear—exposure to rapid industrialization in the world's fastest growing major economy and a chance to seize opportunities in an under-penetrated, but fast-growing consumer banking market. By some projections, China is set to become the world's largest economy within the next few decades. The Boston Consulting Group projects that in the period between 2004 and 2010, China will generate as much as one-quarter of the increase in global banking revenues. Global financial institutions have long recognized the importance of China and with the government's encouragement, have invested in China's financial sector while also expanding the range of products and services that their own branch operations can offer.

JPMORGAN CHASE'S HISTORY IN CHINA

The history of JPMorgan Chase in China predates the modern reform era—going as far back as the 1920s when we provided wholesale banking services to a variety of foreign and domestic companies, and government agencies in China. In 1973, Chase Manhattan was the first US bank designated as a correspondent bank to the Bank of China. We opened our first representative office in Beijing in the early years of China's economic reforms and some 25 years later, received approval in 2007 to establish the first locally incorporated foreign bank in China's capital. Elsewhere in the financial sector, we have established a joint venture fund management company with the Shanghai International Trust and Investment Corporation (SITICO), which is now ranked among the top 10 asset management firms in China (by total assets under management).

Our experience has shown that in China, the only certainty is rapid change. The country is currently at a juncture where the regulatory framework governing the financial services sector as a whole could evolve in a number of directions. For domestic and foreign institutions alike, the key unknown is the pace of deregulation. Through this chapter, I hope to offer my perspective on the evolution of China's banking and financial system and how foreign financial institutions can play a constructive role in the country. As China's domestic banks join the ranks of the world's largest financial institutions, they are eager to diversify into new services and broaden their international footprint. Drawing on experience from our own evolution into one of the world's largest financial services companies, I hope to share a few lessons learned about the challenges and rewards that might be expected when an organization expands its business and extends into universal banking to cover new areas of financial services.

Ultimately, we expect the Chinese market to change for the better and believe there is room for foreign and domestic banks to learn from each other, and to mutually benefit from cooperation and healthy competition.

CHINA'S EVOLVING FINANCIAL LANDSCAPE

The most distinctive feature of China's financial landscape is the sheer dominance of banking. In 2006, bank lending accounted for 84% of the fundraising market in China—few major economies come close to this figure. As such, banking reforms have been at the very core of China's strategy to foster a more efficient financial sector. Only five years ago, the scope of products offered by Chinese banks was limited to very basic services. Regulation over the industry was tight, with interest rates firmly set by the state. The pace of reform over recent years has been remarkable, with the government demonstrating a strong commitment toward strengthening domestic banks, liberalizing interest rates, and addressing areas such as risk management and corporate governance, where there is room for further improvement.

A Market for New Services

The historical preponderance of lending in China has meant that other modes of finance are still in a developmental stage. More sophisticated services are needed to cater to the country's growing pool of middle class consumers, who are increasingly buying cars and houses, using credit cards, and planning for their families' financial futures. Economic growth and progressive privatization has also resulted in a rapid increase in the number of private small and medium-sized enterprises (SMEs) in need of banking services. Although corporate loan demand will remain strong in the future, consumer banking and the fast-growing SME sector will be important drivers of growth in China's financial sector.

The Development of China's Capital Markets

In recent years, China's capital markets have also developed rapidly in line with the overall economy. The development of a stronger and more effective capital market has been cited frequently among key targets that the Chinese government hopes to achieve. More Chinese firms are turning to the capital markets as an alternative source of fundraising and an increasing proportion of the country's savers have been channeling their money to the stock market in search of higher returns. As one of the largest investment banks and one of the largest asset managers operating in China, we see ourselves as a vested stakeholder in the development of China's capital markets and are encouraged by recent measures that expand the scope for foreign institutions both to invest in domestically listed securities and to assist Chinese institutions and residents in investing in financial products overseas.

The developments I have outlined are giving rise to new income opportunities for banks and other financial institutions—in wealth management, card services, investment banking, trade financing, and an array of non-interest-based services. All participants in China's banking sector—whether domestic or foreign—will face intense competition in providing these new services and will share common challenges in the form of changing regulations and growing customer expectations.

THE RELATIVE STRENGTHS OF FOREIGN AND DOMESTIC BANKS

Following China's 2001 entry to the World Trade Organization (WTO), foreign banks have eagerly anticipated the gradual opening of China's banking sector, which marked a December 2006 milestone when they were permitted to provide local currency services to individuals. With the country opening its retail banking sector to foreign participation, JPMorgan Chase branches in Beijing, Shanghai, and Tianjin have acquired full banking licenses to provide multi-currency services for all client types; all three branches also obtained derivatives licenses in 2004.

Domestic and multinational banks have largely targeted different segments of the market thus far. As a group, foreign banks have become competitive in foreign-currency lending and at high-end services, where they bring many years of operational experience. But market liberalizations have not led to rapid growth in their market share, as many had originally anticipated. The Chinese market has expanded significantly, but the market share for foreign banks has remained at about 1.8% over the past several years.

Chinese Banks Have Become More Competitive

China's leading domestic banks have quite simply become more competitive, having reduced their nonperforming loan (NPL) ratios to more controllable levels and instituted many improvements across the spectrum of their businesses. They have boosted management talent, and in many cases, have shifted to merit-based compensation and invested much of their recent initial public offering (IPO) proceeds toward upgrading technology to strengthen their core banking platforms. Many have also achieved improvements in organizational efficiency, risk control practices and introduced more complex financial products in partnership with overseas advisors and strategic investors.

Chinese banks are quickly assimilating into a global financial system where banking services and products must stand out against a backdrop of increased commoditization. I have no doubt that China's leading banks will rise to the level of offering similar products at standards of quality comparable to the world's leading financial institutions. They may well succeed at developing products that are better suited to the needs of their domestic customers. To a large extent, Chinese banks' local networks, home-market knowledge, and cultural affinities constitute a formidable advantage over foreign entrants.

Meanwhile, the process of becoming publicly listed institutions has diversified ownership and improved accountability at many banks. Increasingly, Chinese executives—like their global counterparts—are facing analysts and addressing investor concerns on a daily basis. Three of China's largest banks have launched overseas initial public offerings (IPOs) in recent years and joined the ranks of the top 10 global banks by market capitalization.

The Need to Diversify

The rapidly rising stature of China's leading banks is prompting observers to wonder what form these institutions may take in the years to come and how they might pursue their global ambitions.

To thrive in the new competitive order, Chinese banks will have to diversify their services to meet customer demand and possibly extend their capabilities into other areas of finance—to the extent that this is possible under China's regulatory framework. As China's economy further develops and the country's capital markets offer alternative financing channels, the traditional balance sheet-driven model will become increasingly outdated. In response to the threat of savings disintermediation, Chinese banks have naturally sought to generate higher levels of non-interest income. The progress made so far has been remarkable. As an example, mortgage loans have grown at a compound annual rate of 36% in the five-year period from 2001 to 2006—albeit from a very low base.

Although the pace of change is rapid, there is still a long way to go. Corporate lending remains the largest asset category on most Chinese banks' balance sheets, while retail banking has only become a major focus of attention in the last few years. In more developed markets, fee-based businesses typically account for at least half of banks' total incomes; in China, the proportion is just 10.8% on average for the Big Four banks. Over the next several years, the balance will shift significantly as the Chinese consumer market becomes more sophisticated and demanding. Retail asset classes such as personal loans, residential mortgages, auto loans, and credit cards will increasingly take up a larger proportion of the banking sector's asset allocation. Recent liberalizations, such as the broadening of participation in China's Qualified Domestic Institutional Investor (QDII) program will further drive demand for innovative investment products.

Wealth Management

Economic growth in China is also producing a fast-growing number of people who may be considered high net worth individuals. As a natural extension of retail banking services, wealth management will emerge as one of the major sources of retail fee growth in China's banking sector. Although specific products and distribution methods will need to be customized with the Chinese customer in mind, the service providers in this arena will be differentiated largely on the same basis as in developed markets. The successful providers of wealth management services will be those that can offer a world-class pool of talent and a broad selection of financial services, adapted to the cultural characteristics of the Chinese market. As wealth managers, international banks will be highly competitive in this arena because they bring extensive experience and professional expertise—particularly in the high-end customer niche.

Foreign Banks Face Challenges in Expanding in China

In the general retail banking market, domestic banks are likely to hold a dominant position for the foreseeable future. In practice, foreign banks currently lack the branch networks necessary to penetrate the mass market. Domestic banks have vast networks and extensive first-hand experience operating in China; the dominance of the big Chinese banks has led to their control over the supply of local currency. Although China has met its WTO commitments in the banking sector, international banks still face significant barriers to expanding their presence in China. Local incorporation requires capital of RMB1 billion to be paid up-front and requires more local administration—which in turn compels foreign banks to compete for a scarce pool of experienced talent. Due to their weaker branch networks in the country, foreign banks in China also face major funding constraints. With a lower deposit base, they must pay higher interest rates on inter-bank borrowings and are subject to higher reserve requirements and other limitations on their foreign currency business. In comparison, investment banking services carry over more readily, as the fundamentals of underwriting and advisory services are relatively universal. But here too, there is room for international investment banks to play a greater role in China's securities industry.

The competitive environment in China has prompted foreign banks to adopt differing strategies according to their resources and core advantages. Fundamentally, foreign banks that wish to participate in China have two options at their disposal: buying a minority stake of up to 20% (the ownership cap is 25% for the total foreign interest) in an existing institution, and thereby gaining access to retail customers through the domestic bank's existing network—or building a presence through gradual, organic growth. Considering the difficulties of establishing a major presence in China's retail banking market, a number of global institutions have opted to enter the market by making strategic investments in local banks, and are focusing their efforts on the development of these institutions. Some foreign banks are venturing more aggressively into the retail renminbi market, while others are targeting niche markets and the most cautious are focusing foremost on meeting the banking needs of their home clients.

Corporate Banking: Room for Cooperation

On the corporate side, China's increasingly global trade relationships have created opportunities for domestic banks to increase fee revenues by offering clearing services for the growing volume of payments flowing into and out of China, and other trade finance products and services. Meanwhile, financial reforms are setting the foundation for the development of the domestic derivatives market and lending a boost to the corporate bond market. As banks compete for new business—including from SMEs, they will need to broaden product ranges and develop their corporate derivatives business.

China's banks will need to hedge and match product offerings at a time when they may be facing increased competition for deposits—and thus potentially increased situations of mismatched maturities on loans and deposits. To manage more complex financial transactions, the mechanisms of risk management must be firmly in place. In many instances, Chinese banks may be able to enhance their banking franchise through cooperation with international banks. As an example, the Chinese partner can potentially generate fee income by offering derivative solutions to corporate clients, while drawing on the expertise and technology infrastructure of a foreign partner to provide the underlying hedge facility. In this manner, Chinese banks can gradually acquire the skills and technology needed to establish their own integrated control systems and develop best practices in middle and back-office operations.

UNIVERSAL BANKING: THE JPMORGAN CHASE EXPERIENCE

Emerging from an Era of Consolidation

Although Chinese banks are in a much stronger position today than they were just several years ago, China's banking industry remains in a nascent phase relative to more mature markets. For an indication of how the sector is likely to evolve, we may look to examples in the US and Europe, where for many leading institutions—including JPMorgan Chase—the expansion into fee-based services has progressed to the form frequently referred to as universal banking.

Under the universal banking model, a single bank offers a diversified range of financial services to retail customers, large corporations, and middle market clients alike. At JPMorgan Chase, our six business lines (retail banking, card services, commercial banking, investment banking, treasury services, and asset management) were consolidated within one global financial services firm over the course of several decades. The combination of these businesses did not occur by chance—they resulted from a confluence of environmental drivers that have created opportunities for growth in our key markets. In the 1980s, the globalization of the banking sector, changes in the US regulatory framework, and the impact of technology served to accelerate consolidation within a highly fragmented industry, initially within regional banking zones. The 1990s were a period of heightened merger activity in the US banking industry. As a result of consolidation, the number of commercial banks in the US declined from 12,343 in 1990 to 7,549 by 2005.

There are fewer players today in the US banking industry and a higher concentration of assets is held by the largest banks. Large financial institutions are better able to achieve economies of scale, diversify their product range, and maximize retention by catering to a full-range of customer needs under one roof. The largest predecessor banks of JPMorgan Chase took part in the merger movement that occurred during this period—the major transactions leading up to the formation of JPMorgan Chase included:

1991: Chemical Banking Corp. combined with Manufacturers Hanover Corp. keeping the name Chemical Banking Corp., then the second-largest banking institution in the US. Four years later, First Chicago Corp. merged with NBD Bancorp., forming First Chicago NBD, the largest banking company based in the Midwest.

1996: Chase Manhattan Corp. merged into Chemical Banking Corp., creating what was then the largest bank holding company in the US.

1998: Banc One Corp. merged with First Chicago NBD, taking the name Bank One Corp. Following a subsequent merger with Louisiana's First Commerce Corp., Bank One became the largest financial services firm in the Midwest, the fourth-largest bank in the US, and the world's largest Visa credit card issuer.

2000: J.P. Morgan & Co. merged with Chase Manhattan Corp., effectively combining four of the largest and oldest banking institutions in New York City (Morgan, Chase, Chemical, and Manufacturers Hanover) into one firm called J.P. Morgan Chase & Co.

2004: J.P. Morgan Chase & Co. and Bank One Corp. merged to form today's JPMorgan Chase & Co, a leading global financial services firm with assets of $1.5 trillion, more than 170,000 employees and operations in more than 50 countries.

Through a combination of mergers and organic growth, JPMorgan Chase has evolved into a diversified financial group with a logically related set of products that cater to both wholesale and retail clients. As of April 2007, our wholesale businesses accounted for 54% of the firm's revenues, while our retail businesses accounted for 46%. Each one of our six business lines is strong as an individual entity, but creates further value for customers through linkages with the other five. Our underlying objective is to compete against industry leaders in every niche. Toward this end, when we review performance across our business areas, the credit card division is compared to competitors such as American Express, the investment banking division to heavy-weights like Goldman Sachs and Morgan Stanley, and the commercial banking business to institutions like Bank of America.

Harnessing Synergies

The growth of our business—and especially the 2004 merger of J.P. Morgan Chase and Bank One—required a massive effort to consolidate product sets, consolidate back office functions, eliminate wasteful spending, and integrate systems. As a result of these efforts, our businesses are working in closer collaboration and enhancing JPMorgan Chase's overall relationship with the client. To offer a few examples—in 2006, we opened more than one million credit card accounts through our retail branches—an increase of 74% year-over-year. Our retail and card services teams work very closely together to optimize every aspect of the cards business, including product design, marketing, credit reporting, systems, and staffing. We are now able to offer more competitive pricing because we can underwrite credit cards using customer information from both divisions. Also in 2006, our investment bank sold 95% of the non-agency mortgages originated by our home lending business, while just two years earlier, the two businesses barely worked together.

The merger of J.P. Morgan Chase and Bank One made it possible for us to bring investment banking, treasury, and securities services to an extensive commercial banking customer base. Meanwhile, our asset management group now works closely with our commercial and investment bankers to identify clients that can benefit from private banking services. We aim to apply this collaborative approach across all of our businesses to fully leverage our organization's capabilities and relationships.

A Pivotal Point in the Development of China's Banking Sector

In China, the appetite for financial products has reached critical mass in recent years, as evidenced by the massive shift of funds out of retail bank deposits into the stock and mutual fund universe—and by Chinese companies increasingly turning to the capital markets for financing. Emerging consumer segments are already generating opportunities for cross-selling—one of the most natural acts in business. As Chinese customers demand a wider range of financial products, Chinese banks should not view universal banking as an end in itself, but rather as the outcome of rational growth in the course of meeting customer expectations.

At this juncture, banks operating in China are under considerable pressure to address the risk of disintermediation. The traditional corporate dependence on commercial banks will further diminish as new rules facilitate the issuance of corporate bonds, which will become an increasingly important source of funding for Chinese companies. In mature economies, the amount of funds raised by the corporate bond market is typically several times greater than the amount raised through the stock market. In China, corporate bond financing amounted to less than half of the capital raised from issuing shares in 2006.

As more of the Chinese banks' traditional large corporate client base switches to the capital markets for funding, so too will individual depositors increasingly disintermediate the banking sector by seeking alternatives to bank deposits. The growth of China's insurance and asset management industries will amplify pressure on some of the traditional cheap funding offered by Chinese depositors. Banks that see their deposit franchise eroded will come under pressure to develop alternative funding sources, which will help to spur the development of wholesale funding solutions.

The focus on business expansion and generating fee income will motivate Chinese banks to diversify into other financial services such as securities business, investment banking, asset management, insurance, and so on. These businesses appear to be appropriate complements that would allow Chinese banks to extend their existing lending relationships into more profitable areas. The government has already permitted banks to enter the fund market, but under the country's Commercial Bank Law, banks are not permitted to establish or take a controlling stake in non-bank financial institutions.

The exact form that China's banks take in the coming years will depend on how regulators address the question of whether financial institutions should be required to keep various financial functions separate. Commercial banking, investment banking, and insurance businesses have been largely separated in China. On a trial basis, however, the government has permitted domestic conglomerates such as the China Everbright Group and CITIC Group to establish wholly owned subsidiaries that offer banking and securities business under the same umbrella. Such moves can be seen as part of an initiative to introduce more competition into financial sectors that were previously shielded from competition under the regulatory framework.

The Walls Between Financial Industries

The question of whether different financial functions should be kept separate or allowed to consolidate is one that many countries have grappled with over the years. In the US, the stock market crash of 1929 and the Great Depression gave rise to the Glass-Steagall Act of the 1930s, after commercial banks' dealings in corporate securities were believed to have been responsible for rampant stock market speculation that eventually led to a large number of bank failures.

The wall between commercial and investment banking began crumbling in the 1980s as many banks pushed ahead with diversification to the extent that they were permitted. In 1987, Chase Manhattan Corp. became the first commercial bank to receive the Federal Reserve's approval to underwrite commercial paper, and other major banks followed suit, proceeding to underwrite not only commercial paper but also mortgage-backed securities. In 1990, J.P. Morgan & Co., which had been the last US bank to combine commercial and investment banking functions, became the first to do so again when the Federal Reserve approved J.P. Morgan's application to underwrite stocks.

Amid the reality that the Glass-Steagall barriers were wearing down, the Gramm-Leach-Bliley Act of 1999 ultimately undid much of the previous decades of law-making, opening the door to consolidation in the financial services space, while also strengthening the privacy protections of financial services customers. Several decades of reforms have brought the US financial sector back full circle to the convergence of banks, securities firms, asset managers, consumer credit companies, and other financial entities. This has only been possible as a result of giant advances in financial and risk management technology.

To reach this stage, China still has a long road ahead, but the government's embrace of reform raises the possibility that the country's leading banks may develop into financial conglomerates—whether through organic growth or by acquisitions.

Comprehensive Risk Management

Despite the inherent appeal of this "financial supermarket" scenario, the need for comprehensive risk management must not be underestimated. The task of managing the risks of different units under a single financial umbrella constitutes a major challenge once the doors are opened. At JPMorgan Chase, we have implemented a comprehensive risk management and governance framework to control our exposure to several categories of risk. Moreover, under a diversified financial conglomerate, the highest standards of ethical behavior must be instilled throughout an organization to avoid potential conflicts that might include the misuse of confidential information and hidden costs to consumers. When commercial banks attempt to enter the business of investment banking, they must resist the lure of taking on too much lending risk with a customer in order to gain advisory work.

As further relaxations in the financial sector are introduced, it is likely that financial holding companies will appear as a parent entity for a variety of financial service businesses. To improve transparency, universal banks can structure the conglomerate into legally independent subsidiaries, offering full disclosure on the profitability and financial health of each business unit.

ARE CHINESE BANKS READY FOR OFFSHORE ACQUISITIONS?

Listed Chinese banks are now massive in terms of market capitalization and assets, but their business reach is still limited in terms of functional and geographical diversification. Although the growth outlook remains very robust within China, Chinese banks may be tempted to seek offshore acquisitions to accelerate their development, especially at a time when many of their major corporate customers are increasingly making investments abroad or extending their operations overseas.

As of late-2007, we have begun to witness the first wave of overseas investments by Chinese banks. The first Chinese financial institution to buy into a US bank was China Minsheng Bank, which agreed to acquire a 9.9% stake in San Francisco-based UCBH Holdings (a bank catering to the overseas Chinese community in the US) for up to $317 million. Within weeks of this announcement, news of a considerably bigger international investment broke—the Industrial and Commercial Bank of China's (ICBC) $5.5 billion purchase of a 20% stake in South Africa's Standard Bank. Elsewhere in the financial sector, CITIC Securities has entered into a cross-investment arrangement with Wall Street investment bank Bear Stearns.

These are merely the first in what I expect to be numerous, increasingly sizable overseas deals by China's leading financial institutions, many of which are bolstered by IPO proceeds, rising profits, and surging share prices. The rationale behind these moves could include the acquisition of technology and new product capabilities, or the aim of providing a fuller range of financial services to Chinese companies operating overseas. By taking a stake in sophisticated financial institutions, Chinese banks may be able to boost human capital and import leading-edge technology and management practices back to China.

Chinese banks should, however, proceed with caution before taking on the risk of an acquisition. Much like the situation Chinese banks are in today, in the mid-1980s, the rise of Japan's financial prominence was fueled by the rapid growth of the Japanese economy, the country's relatively high savings rate, and the rise in value of the yen. In the early 1970s, seven out of the 10 largest banks in the world by assets were North American; in the mid-1980s, nine of them were Japanese. With their new-found stature, Japan's banks embarked on ambitious international expansion plans.

Today, many of the Japanese banks that made foreign acquisitions have sold these positions and are retrenching; only the Mitsubishi UFJ Financial group remains in the global top 10 by assets. Essentially, the banks were afflicted by a combination of collapsing finances and the threat of deregulation in their home market. This was later compounded by the turbulence of the Asian Financial Crisis, which severely limited their capital and made it almost impossible for many to meet the capital requirements required to operate overseas.

The experience of Japanese banks over the last 20 years can be taken as a cautionary lesson. While the climate in China differs substantially from that of Japan in the 1980s, there are certain striking resemblances: an economy rising in stature within the global economy, a ballooning trade surplus, currency appreciation, and asset price inflation fuelled by excess liquidity. In China's favor, however, the domestic operating environment for the banking sector is generally favorable. Going forward, Chinese banks must take heed of mounting risks that include credit risk as a result of macroeconomic tightening, market risk as a result of interest rate and currency adjustments, and operating risk associated with more complex product and service offerings. In addition, further interest rate deregulation may be around the corner. Thus, while China's major banks are very well-capitalized, they would be well-advised to pursue growth in measured steps.

COMPETITION AND PARTNERSHIP CAN GO HAND-IN-HAND

In summary, competition between Chinese and foreign banks will have a significant influence on the transformation of traditionally government-owned institutions into market-driven, customer-oriented commercial banks.

There is also, however, much room for cooperation—particularly in combining the local market knowledge and distribution advantage of domestic banks with the global financial resources and product innovation capabilities of their foreign counterparts. An example of mutually beneficial cooperation can be found in ICBC's launch of Oriental Pearl, China's first bank-based QDII product, in which JPMorgan Asset Management is serving as the overseas investment advisor.

With greater freedom to engage with Chinese partners, international companies can bring much-needed funding and technical expertise to their Chinese counterparts and the overall capital markets. It will take time for China to build up the infrastructure of its capital markets, and this process represents an opportunity to lay the groundwork for a sound financial industry—one that will make China even more competitive as an economic powerhouse.

We believe that as China's banking sector develops and regulations evolve, new and exciting opportunities will continue to emerge. Within 10 years, for example, we might be able to buy a controlling interest in a bank or develop a wider retail presence in the country. Continued deregulation and the development of a more robust domestic fixed income market will allow domestic and foreign banks to develop more highly differentiated product offerings to attract retail customers.

Notwithstanding our commitment and recent investments in China, we do not feel pressured to seize every immediate opportunity to participate in the market. To continue our centuries-old tradition of doing only first-class business, our responsibility is to act as a good corporate citizen in every market in which we operate. This means not only caring about business interests, but also taking responsibility for our impact on society and ensuring that the highest standard of ethical behavior is followed. Our goal is to set a course for long-term success, while building relationships and engaging with partners who share our values and a commitment toward sustainable growth.

CHAPTER 10

Agricultural Financing in China: the Difficult Transition from a Planned to a Market System

Chen Xiwen

Deputy Director, Office of the Central Leadership Group on Financial and Economic Affairs; Director, Office of the Central Leadership Group on Rural Work

Economic reforms that began in China's rural areas in 1978 stimulated the overall structural change that followed, from a planned to a socialist market economic system. Since that time, China's economy has seen 30 years of rapid growth. China has maintained over a 9% average annual growth rate in GDP; the percentage of people defined as being below poverty level in the population has declined from 30% to less than 3%. By 2006, total economic output had leapt to the fourth-largest in the world, and the volume of export–import trade to the third-largest.

Along with economic growth, industrialization, and urbanization, China's socialist economic structure has undergone tremendous change. Two aspects of this change deserve attention, from the perspective of long-term development of agriculture and rural areas.

One is that over the past 10 years, the area of cultivated land in China has decreased by close to 10%. This corresponds to accelerated urbanization. As pressures on the resources and environment have increased relentlessly, the nature of demands has changed, causing China's self-reliance in agricultural products will face further problems. Second is that nearly 200 million people from rural areas have left their homes for cities, in order to find jobs. Due to unresolved issues of social security and problems in finding housing, they are nonetheless not able to become bona fide urban residents.

How to deal with China's evolving urban–rural situation and the economic and social transformations is a tremendous and imminent challenge to China's financial system. China's financial institutions are in the process of moving from planned to market systems: they face rapid growth and hyper-rapid systemic change, complex economic structures, and asset ownership systems that are not as yet totally satisfactory. The problems must be faced and, in the new century, the new era, China's financial institutions have begun the necessary steps.

Looking back over the course of the 30 years of China's rural reform, we see that the rural financing system played an important early role in agricultural development and the economic development of rural areas. Before the mid-1990s, rural financing under the "single-function bank" system was a vital support for Chinese agriculture and rural economic development. As the banking system restructured and transitioned to being marketized and then gradually turned into a commercial banking system, this financial support for rural areas changed. Rural financial services encountered unprecedented problems. The number of entities providing financial services declined, credit went down precipitously, and funds flowed from rural areas into cities.

The question of why this happened was perplexing. Why, under the more strictly controlled system of what had been called "specialized" or "single-function banks" were agriculture and rural areas able to receive greater financial support? When banking authorities loosened controls, under a new commercial banking system that has far more complete laws and regulations, why did rural financing paradoxically undergo a severe contraction? This tightening of credit has been so severe, in fact, that it has become a huge obstacle to agricultural growth as well as to the economic well-being of rural areas. One popular view holds that with industrialization and urbanization, the return on capital invested in rural areas is far lower than it is in cities. Since it is the nature of capital to flow toward the highest return, it flows largely out of rural areas. This is a natural process, the argument goes, and can simply be attributed to the strength of the dynamics of the market.

Is this really so? Close examination shows the situation to be more complex.

AGRICULTURAL FINANCING UNDER THE "SINGLE-FUNCTION" BANK SYSTEM

China's banking system evolved through three main periods in the course of reform. First was what is called the "mono-bank period." When a planned economy prevailed, the People's Bank of China (PBC) and Rural Credit Cooperatives were the only financial institutions in the entire country. Rural Credit Cooperatives were responsible for taking in deposits from local residents and they were under the supervision of the PBC. Since enterprises under urban authorities were all owned either by the state or collective bodies, all investing activity was approved by and organized by the government. Because of this, the PBC, responsible for urban affairs, was primarily functioning to collect deposits.

Back at that time, the only part of the entire economy with any "market" significance involved credit relationships under the Rural Credit Cooperatives. In addition to being able to take in local residents' deposits, these cooperatives were allowed to extend production loans to collectives and to farming households, and they also issued small amounts of daily-living loans to farming households. It was precisely this exception that allowed Town and Village Enterprises (TVEs) later to develop at such a fast pace. Rural Credit Cooperatives were an important precondition for their growth.

The second period was what is called the "single-function or specialized bank period." The Agricultural Bank of China (ABC) was re-established in 1979; in 1984, the Industrial and Commercial Bank of China (ICBC) was formed out of a branch of the PBC. The Bank of China (BOC) became solely responsible for foreign exchange business, and the China Construction Bank (CCB) was originally given fiscal functions. A "specialized" or "single-function" banking system was thereby formed with the PBC and four banks each with its own specific role.

The third period is known as the "commercial banking system period." Commercial banks and so-called policy banks have now been separated out into two different kinds of entities. Three policy banks were set up from 1994, including the China Development Bank (CDB), the Export-Import of China Bank (China Exim Bank), and the Agricultural Development Bank (ADB). These were made specifically responsible for policy-related financing activities that had previously been undertaken by the four specialized banks. The establishment of policy banks created the conditions that allowed for banking reform of the "single-function or specialized banks." In 1995, the "Law on Commercial Banks of the People's Republic of China" was promulgated, which clarified the legal standing of the four "single-function banks" as now being "State-owned Commercial Banks."

Seen from the perspective of 30 years of change in China's banking system, China's banking authorities have gone through two great structural transitions. One was the change from a mono-bank to a single-function bank system, and the second was a change from the single-function bank system to a commercial banking system.

When the PBC was founded, it was the sole financial organization under the leadership of the Ministry of Finance. It established an operating network for deposits and loans in all rural areas throughout the country. As the process of cooperatization, or the forming of collectives began, Rural Credit Cooperatives were set up throughout China. At their peak, there were more than 100,000 such cooperatives. In the latter part of the 1950s, the PBC took more direct control over the cooperatives and put them under the jurisdiction of credit loan and deposit-taking functions of the Bank. This was the situation all the way up to the time the ABC was re-established in 1979, at which time Rural Credit Cooperatives were returned to the oversight and management of the ABC.

Since funds for "credit" were controlled by planned allocations under the mono-bank system, to a large degree, the PBC and the Rural Credit Cooperatives were merely a fund management department under the Ministry of Finance. They served fiscal and budgetary functions and operated as deposit-taking organizations. The level of financial activity was low at this time, and there were severe constraints on financing. In the early 1980s, with the transition to single-function banks, the level of financing in China rose and banks began to play the role of financial intermediaries. Nonetheless, relatively stringent financial controls remained in place. After the mid-1990s, with transition to a commercial banking system, financial activity in China increased quickly and banks began to operate with the full scope of financial intermediaries. At the same time, banking laws and a banking regulatory system were considerably improved.

As banking authorities moved China's financial system very rapidly in the direction of a market system, rural areas now discovered that funding sources were greatly diminished. Rural areas had received much greater financial support under the mono-bank and the single-function bank systems. Rural financing now saw a severe contraction under the new commercial banking system.

TABLE 10.1 1970–1995 agricultural sector and rural loans

Year	Total	TVE loans	Agricultural loans	Agricultural production	Ag/ Total%	Rural areas/ total (%)	Ag. loans/ Ag. production
1970	1,052.2	0.8	103.9	716.3	9.88	9.95	14.5
1975	1,489.4	7	99.1	1,202.4	6.65	7.12	8.24
1978	1,895.1	22	131.3	1,288.7	6.93	8.09	10.19
1980	2,495.9	56.1	226.4	1,964.5	9.07	11.32	11.52
1985	6,305.6	200	652.2	2,912.2	10.34	14.91	22.39
1990	16,579.4	1,128.3	1,680.4	7,662.1	10.14	16.94	21.93
1995	44,627.6	4,441	4,376.7	20,340.9	9.81	19.75	21.52

Notes
1. Total loans and agricultural loans are the sum of both state-owned bank loans and credit cooperative loans.
2. TVE loan statistics are for 1971 and 1976, and include statistics from credit cooperatives. Source of data: *China Financial Statistical Yearbook 1952–87*.
3. Data for TVE loans after 1978 come from "China TVE Statistics."
4. We combine collective loans from credit cooperatives and loans to agricultural households in the figures for agricultural loans.
5. Statistics for agricultural production from 1970–85 come from *China Rural Area Statistical Yearbook 1989*, the other years come from annual statistical yearbooks.
6. Agricultural production includes agriculture, fisheries, forestry, and animal husbandry. Figures for 1990 and 1995 are given at prices in those years.
Source: China Statistical Summary 2002.

Statistics in Table 10.1 made it clear that the level of loans received by the agricultural sector and rural areas during the mono-bank period, before Reform, was not in fact low. The percentage of total loans that the agricultural sector received from state banks and credit cooperatives remained at roughly 10% in the years from 1980 to 1995. If you add to the loans made to TVEs, then the percent of the total went from 9.9 in 1970 to 20% in 1995. During this same 25-year period, the production value of farming, animal husbandry, timber, and fishing rose 28 times, and the value of loans to the agricultural sector rose 42 times. Including loans to TVEs, the value of loans to rural areas rose by more than 80 times. This should be seen in the context of the total amount of all loans from state banks and credit cooperatives in the country rising by only 42 times.

After the transition from a mono-bank to a single-function bank system, the rate of increase in overall national loans and in loans to the agricultural sector was about the same. If you factor in loans made to TVEs, the credit support received by rural areas far exceeded the expansion of credit in the rest of the country.

The ABC was re-established in 1979. Using 1980 as a base year, in the period 1980 to 1993, deposits at the ABC and credit cooperatives increased by 18.7 times, with an average annual increase of 25.7%. Total loans increased 15.6 times, with an average annual increase of 24.1%. The total production value of agricultural cooperatives increased 12.3 times, with average annual increase of 22.1%. What these figures say is that rural credit services could basically respond to the growing needs of the rural economy during that period.

In the course of changing from a mono-bank system to a single-function bank system, loans to farming households increased extremely rapidly. After the country instituted the People's Commune System during the mono-bank period, the PBC did not then extend loans directly to farming households—only credit cooperatives were able to provide them with small-scale loans. In 1958, loans to farming households reached a peak of RMB1.11 billion; the total declined in the next year to RMB690 million and only in 1966 returned to a level of RMB1.14 billion. From then on, all the way up to 1980, loans to farming households stayed around the level of RMB1.1 billion.

In 1980, loans to farming households increased 57% over the previous year. For several years afterwards, such loans basically maintained an annual rate of growth that exceeded 70%. From 1979, the newly re-established ABC began to increase loans to farming households and to collective economic organizations. When the mono-bank system was shifting to a single-function bank system, the increase in availability of credit resources spurred rapid growth in agriculture and in rural areas in general, as well as a rapid increase in the income of farmers. Farmers' income doubled from 1978 to 1985; the increase from 1985 to 1990 was 72.6%, and the increase from 1990 and 1995 was 129.9%. These figures incorporate income from agriculture, animal husbandry, forestry, fishing industries, and TVEs.

RURAL FINANCING CONTRACTS

In December 1993, China's State Council promulgated a "Decision Regarding Reform of the Financing System." A structural transition ensued that changed the so-called single-function banking system into a commercial banking system. The ADB was formed to handle rural financing and to assume policy responsibilities formerly held by the

ABC. These mainly included policy-related loans for assuring adequate inventories of grain, cotton, and food oils, loans for purchasing agricultural by-products, and loans for farming expenditures. The bank served as fiscal agent in support of agriculture, both in making payments and providing oversight.

Once the policy banks were established, the CCB, the ICBC, the BOC, and the ABC became what were now called state-owned commercial banks. Innumerable joint-stock commercial banks were also established in cities and regions. As the banking system restructured, a legal and regulatory system was set in place that included such items as the "Commercial Banking Law."

One of the biggest consequences of these changes in the system had to do with collateral and the guarantees required for obtaining a loan. According to the new laws and regulations, and also according to their supervisory organizations, state-owned commercial banks could extend banking credit only on the basis of clearly defined assets. All loans required that there be sufficient guarantees and collateral. After the Asian Financial Crisis in 1997, authorities moved to a zero-tolerance stance on nonperforming assets. The performance of a loan became a personal lifelong accountability for loan officers and a much tighter credit management system was put in place.

The legal system was much improved in the course of transitioning to a commercial banking system. Restrictions on "soft-budgeting" of banks were put in place. Contrary to all expectations, however, rural financing soon experienced a severe contraction.

Agricultural production in China fell from 20% of GDP in 1996 to 11% of GDP in 2006 (see Table 10.2). The ratio of agricultural loans to all loans hardly changed between 1998 and 2006, however. It remained at about 5%, which was roughly half the level it had been during the mono-bank system. Due to the rapid industrialization of rural areas starting in the 1980s, TVEs had already become an important component of the income of so-called farming villages.

From 1995 to 2003, the production value of TVEs constituted around 45% of GDP, yet the percentage of TVE loans in the total amount of loans fell, from 8% to 4% in 2004. Table 10.3 indicates the percentage of rural area production value contributed to GDP from 1978–2004, and the percentage of rural area loans to total loans. We can see that after 1992, the percent contribution of rural area

TABLE 10.2 Agricultural production and agricultural credit loans

Year	Ag. loans	Total of all kinds of loans	% held by ag. loans	Total production of agriculture	GDP	% of ag. in total GDP
1996	1,919	61,153	3.14	13,844	67,885	20.39
1997	3,315	74,914	4.42	14,211	74,463	19.08
1998	4,444	86,524	5.14	14,552	78,345	18.57
1999	4,792	93,734	5.11	14,472	82,068	17.63
2000	4,889	99,317	4.92	14,628	89,468	16.35
2001	5,712	112,315	5.09	15,412	97,315	15.84
2002	6,885	131,294	5.24	16,117	105,172	15.32
2003	8,411	158,996	5.29	16,928	117,390	14.42
2004	9,843	177,363	5.55	20,768	136,876	15.17
2005	11,530	194,690	5.92	22,719	182,321	12.46
2006	13,208	225,285	5.86	24,700	209,417	11.79

Sources: Annual statistical yearbooks from the China Statistics Publishing House.

production value to GDP strongly increased, while after the mid-1990s, rural area loans saw a marked decline.

After the single-function banking system shifted to a commercial banking system, rural areas not only experienced a declining trend in credit and loan amounts that were inconsistent with their development potential and the scale of their economic activity, but they also experienced a diminishing of the entire rural financial system. This was manifested by a decrease in the number of financial entities, a decrease in credit loans, net outflow of funds, and management jurisdiction being withdrawn from local areas and assumed by higher authorities.

TABLE 10.3 TVE value-added and TVE loans

Year	TVE value-added	TVE loans	% of TVE value-added to GDP	% of TVE loans to total loans
1996	17,659	5,316.511	46.41	8.69
1997	18,914	5,510.74	46.94	7.36
1998	22,186	5,796.075	46.89	6.7
1999	24,883	6,288.501	47.95	6.71
2000	27,156	6,282.065	46.70	6.32
2001	29,356	6,502.575	46.00	5.79
2002	32,386	6,905.334	46.12	5.26
2003	36,686	7,661.55	45.87	4.82
2004	41,815	8,069.2	30.55	4.55

Sources: Ministry of Agriculture and TVE statistical data.

RURAL BANK BRANCHES DECLINE

When banking authorities changed the banking system from mono-bank to single-function banks, China's four specialized banks set up branch operations in virtually all of China's more than 2000 counties. The ABC even set up an operating network in every town and village.

In the next stage of banking reform, however, with the initiation of the commercial banking system reforms, each of the new state-owned commercial banks began a great withdrawal from rural areas. This withdrawal was from county- and sub-county-level branch operations. Table 10.4 shows the decrease in branches of the four large state-owned banks during the eight years from 1995 to 2003. Rarely were reductions made in urban branches—essentially all were at the county or sub-county level.

In May of 2006, the China Banking Regulatory Commission conducted a survey of financial services received by 1,946 counties (or cities), 29,140 townships, 479,817 administered villages, 100,000 farmers, and 20,000 small and medium-sized rural enterprises. By late 2005, the coverage rate of financing organizations in administered villages was only 3.28%. Of towns and villages, 65.4% had only Rural Credit Cooperatives and Postal Deposit Organizations. Rural Credit Cooperatives and Postal Deposit Organizations constituted 86.45% of the total of banking institutions, among administered towns they constituted 89.83%. On average, there are now 25.09 financial outlets in each county, 2.13 in each township, and only one in every 50 administered villages. The numbers are even lower in western rural areas, 18.96 in each county, 1.58 in each township, and one in every 80 administered villages.

TABLE 10.4 Outflow of funding due to withdrawal of state-owned banks from rural areas

	1995 No. of branches	2003 No. of branches	Decrease	% change
ICBC	38,583	24,129	14,454	−37.5
ABC	67,092	36,138	30,954	−46.1
BOC	13,637	11,609	2,028	−14.9
CCB	35,895	16,613	19,282	−53.7
Total	155,207	88,489	66,718	−42.9

Source: Website of China Banking Regulatory Commission.

During the tenth Five Year Plan (2001–05), banking outlets and employees were shown to be decreasing in 1,946 surveyed counties and sub-county locations. By end-2005, the number of outlets and employees were respectively 24.37% and 14% fewer than they had been at the time of 2001. The main reason was that the commercial banking system had reduced county and sub-county-level operations. By the end of 2005, the commercial banking system had 31,900 outlets and 431,400 employees at county and sub-county levels, a reduction of 26,200 outlets and 179,000 people.

As state-owned commercial banks withdrew on a large scale from rural areas, Rural Credit Cooperatives became the main support of those areas. As Figure 10.1 indicates, in 2004, deposit and loan balances in Rural Credit Cooperatives only amounted to around 11% of the total in the country, but they accounted for 86% of all bank loans to the agricultural sector.

RURAL FUNDS FLOW TOWARD CITIES

According to the 2007 report of the Banking Regulatory Committee, the inadequacies of the financial services network and rigidities of the credit loan management system not only led to a severe contraction in the availability of funding in rural areas, but also led directly to the increasing tendency of financial resources to be allocated to urban areas. Agricultural banks withdrew and transferred large amounts of

FIGURE 10.1   Agricultural production and loan resources

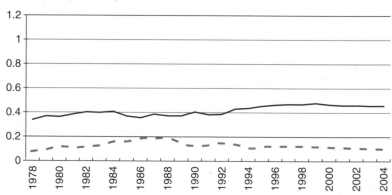

Sources: China Statistics Publishing House, China statistical yearbook for each year, China rural economy yearbook for each year, and Ministry of Agriculture's TVE Bureau's TVE statistical data for each year.

rural funds and invested them in urban areas: this can be seen in the change in percentage of rural loans to total loans. At the end of 2000, deposit balances in financial organizations at the county and sub-county level were RMB3.2787 trillion, loans were RMB2.4355 trillion, making net deposits RMB843.2 billion and a ratio of loans to deposits of 74.8%. This was 5.46% lower than the ratio of the overall national banking sector for the same period. By the end of 2005, deposits were RMB6.8953 trillion, loans were RMB3.8825 trillion, making net deposits RMB3.0128 trillion. The increase in the net deposit was 257%, but the ratio of loans to deposits was only 56.3%, 12.72% lower than the national banking sector average.

In five years, deposits in county- and sub-county banking institutions had increased at an annual average of 15.99%, approaching the level of the national banking organizations of 17.74%, but loans made by those banks had only increased at an average annual rate of 9.72%. This was far lower than the national average of 15.66%. According to records of the ABC, rural loans constituted 31.1% of total loans made by the Bank in 1997, but this had dropped to 16.9% in 2001.

At present, only around 10% of ABC loans are made to rural areas. In the mid-1980s, that figure was 98%.

RURAL AREAS TURN TO "IRREGULAR FINANCING"

According to random sampling surveys of the State Statistical Bureau's Research Team on farming households from 2000 to 2003, every farmer borrowed an annual average of RMB65 from banks and credit cooperatives, whereas they borrowed RMB190 from "private lenders," or unofficial sources. In other words, 25% was from banks, 75% was from unofficial sources.

The Ministry of Agriculture did a similar analysis, targeting 20,000 farming households. Although the sample was different, the results of the analysis were the same. Farmers were borrowing a declining amount from official or proper financing authorities: specifically, the amount declined 32.24% over the course of 15 years, from 47.76% in 1986 to 15.52% in 2000.

While China's banking industry has been undergoing rapid change, both industrialization and urbanization have been accelerating since the mid-1990s. Given these background factors, many explanations have been developed to explain the severe contraction in rural financing. The one accepted by most people relates to the difference in return on capital. Scholars who hold this point of view feel that the contraction in rural financing is necessary given the way profit is now the prime motivating factor with the establishment of a commercial banking system. They feel that the phenomenon is the result of market dynamics, and that the government should not interfere with it.

This perspective holds that the outflow of financing resources from rural to urban areas is the result of the optimum allocation of scarce financial resources. It is in accord with the goal of an efficient market.

Other scholars feel, however, that the gap in credit between urban and rural environments is too great, and is due to inadequate financial information at the farming village and household level. The information asymmetry between banks and entities administered by villages leads banks to feel that micro-loan customers have excessive costs and excessive risk.

Both these attitudes reflect only partial causes of the problem. Both points of view, if carried to logical conclusions, would require the hypothetical prerequisite that rural banking in China is fully competitive which, clearly, it is not.

There is no adequate evidence to show that the rate of return on rural investments is lower than the rate of return in cities. On the contrary, considerable research proves that the return on capital in rural areas is not only lower than that in cities, but is actually higher over an extended period of time. According to World Bank research, from 1978–2001, the marginal profit on investments in Chinese agriculture increased 16 times, and in towns and villages, it increased 15 times. During the same period, urban industry as a whole only grew 85%, while urban services industries only tripled. As Figure 10.2 on page 198 shows, the marginal profit on capital invested in TVEs was consistently higher than urban investments since the mid-1980s, and by 2001, this indicator for TVEs was five times what it was for urban industry.

OECD research also indicates the same trends. The OECD has discovered that the return on capital in China's non-state-owned sectors reached 15% in 2003 (TVEs are a key component of non-state-owned enterprises), while from 2000–05, the all-factors-of-production growth rate showed an overall annual increase of 10%.

The above data confirms the fact that the contraction of financing in rural areas was not caused by a lower return on investment. There must be other reasons for the evidence that there was not a commensurate increase in rural financing when the banking system was reformed and levels of financing increased in other areas.

In point of fact, a primary reason for the contraction in rural financing was that an excessively "modern" commercial banking credit management system could not accommodate the complex asset-ownership situation in rural areas. That is to say, the fast change of the banking system, pitted against the slow change of the rural asset ownership system, brought on a major contraction in rural financing.

"ASSET OWNERSHIP" IN RURAL AREAS MAKES IT HARD TO GET CREDIT

Financial intermediaries rely on written contracts in their operations. Risk and credit terms are determined by these contracts. In mature market economy countries, privately owned assets serve as the foundation for credit requirements. In order to lower commercial bank risk and assure that the financial intermediary can fulfill its role, a bank will often require the person receiving a loan to put up collateral of sufficient value in order to guarantee that the credit has backing. An adequate and consistent system of property rights is a prerequisite for this to work. Together with a property rights system, there has to be a set of publicly available and effective measures including asset registration, value assessment, public notarization, and so on.

Financing issues and property ownership systems are intimately related. This is particularly true when the legal system behind property that is used as collateral is the main guarantee of safeguards for the financing system. This was the basic reason a collateral guarantee system was made the operational rule of the commercial banks as China's banking system was reformed.

Property ownership and rights to assets in China's rural areas have a unique character, however. Among other things, they lack an accompanying set of adequate rules and regulations, which means that modern credit management systems of commercial banks face serious systemic obstacles in trying to apply universal rules.

Due to the lack of a social security system in China, land assets are the sole way that farmers can provide for old age, unemployment, or simple survival. Before a social security system encompasses China's entire population, it is still necessary for the government to place restrictions on certain transactions involving agricultural land assets in the country. This is to prevent the possibility of utter bankruptcy of farmers. These restrictions include buying, selling, and mortgaging the land.

Urban land belongs to the state in China, according to the current land management laws, and the legal system pertaining to mortgages and collateral reflects that. In contrast, agricultural or rural land belongs to the Collective. Agriculturally used land, farmers' homes, and the land on which they are built cannot be bought and sold and cannot be used as collateral. The Collateral Law clearly states: "buildings [owned by the person putting up collateral] and other fixed assets on land can be used as collateral," [but] "in towns and villages the usage-rights to land of towns and villages and TVEs cannot be separated and used as collateral. When factory buildings and other such buildings of TVEs and towns are used as collateral, then the usage rights of the land on which they are standing are also at the same time used as collateral." "Land usage rights of land that is owned by the Collective and used as cultivated land, land that residences are on, land used for personal use, hills for personal use, and other such collectively owned land is not allowed to be mortgaged."

China's Property Rights Law has already been promulgated, and is being implemented, but it has as yet no fundamental way to resolve the problem of ownership of assets in farming villages. To a certain degree, what we are currently facing is the problem of remaining distinctions between urban and rural areas in China. We are facing a dual property rights system that does not allow for merging the two. That is to say, the same asset in a village and in a city is associated with different property rights.

Some of these property rights are restricted by legal provisions, such as those applying to use of agricultural land and housing, but some are affected by other kinds of incomplete systems in rural areas.

Since more than 90% of mortgaged property is tied directly to financing, the lack of a clear property rights system regarding what can be used for collateral in rural areas was an important reason rural financing dropped precipitously after the commercial banking system was implemented. Many considerations compound the problem.

According to a survey of the PBC, over 16 government entities deal with registering property as collateral. These include such government offices such as the Bureau of the Administration of Industry and Commerce, the Notary Office, Housing Bureau, Land Bureau, Forestry Bureau, Mining Authorities, Education Bureau, Vehicle Registration Bureau, Agricultural-use Vehicles Bureau,

Shipping Management Bureau, Airplane Management Bureau, Identification Registration Company, Trademarks Bureau, Patent Bureau, Copyright Bureau, and so on. In certain regions, the list is even longer. The high registration expenses, the long waiting time, the ceaselessly changing regulations about asset registration, and the fact that many property rights have not yet been clarified by law often make it impossible for the person applying for a loan to know how to register collateral. Often, while one is waiting for the process of registering collateral to be completed, the business opportunity for which one wanted the loan is lost and there is no further need to press for financing with the authorities.

The special circumstances of rural asset ownership were not taken into account when the commercial banking system was set up. A set of rules that would be appropriate to rural areas, that would include appropriate credit and loan products, loan management and risk management measures, was not included in the credit and loan management revisions. This was a major factor in the great contraction in rural financing. Instead, authorities in the banking industry used international standards as their model, or the circumstances of large clients in major cities. These were the standards used to set up credit and loan products, management practices, incentive mechanisms, and so on, hence the operations of commercial banks in rural areas became totally passive.

As noted above, one key part of the design of the new system was that credit could not be extended without collateral and guarantees. In recent years, this rule has been observed ever more strictly. A great number of commercial banks can almost not accept collateralized loans even if the collateral is legal; that is, based on such things as the equipment of an enterprise, its finished goods, raw materials in inventory, and so on. In county-level bank branches, over 90% of assets used as collateral in mortgages are highly liquid real estate properties that are just in the process of appreciating.

A second problem is the system that assesses the client applying for a loan. Standards for evaluating credit rating generally are determined by the main headquarters of a bank in Beijing. The entire country implements a unified standard. Enterprises that do not reach a certain credit rating do not have the qualifications to apply for a loan, but in many cases, the standards are inappropriate for rural applicants. Third, county-level branches of state-owned commercial banks do not have the power to issue loans. Overly rigid regulations have become a key obstacle, preventing farmers from getting financial services. They are not in accord with the special considerations of rural customers who have special assets.

Take the ABC as an example. It has county-level branches throughout the country. These branches do not have the power to grant loans, however, since jurisdiction over loans is held by higher authorities. If branches don't make loans, then they have no income. In being evaluated, their most important consideration is operational income and risk management. This has put state-owned commercial banks in a very awkward predicament: if you don't make loans, you have no credit risk to worry about, but you also do not have any income. Poor performance means branches are simply presiding over losses. Due to the systemic constraints noted above, a very strange phenomenon of "having assets but no credit" has arisen in China.

According to analysis of a survey by the PBC, in 2005, all enterprises in China possessed fixed assets valued at RMB8.8567 trillion. Among this total, small and medium-sized enterprises (SMEs) had RMB4.1087 trillion, farming households had RMB4.2092 trillion. The inventories possessed by all enterprises reached RMB5.1394 trillion, among which SMEs had RMB3.0326 trillion and farming households had RMB102.4 billion. The accounts receivable of all enterprises totaled RMB5.5519 trillion, among which SMEs held RMB3.276 billion. Due to the restraints of the existing banking laws, such liquid assets as inventory and accounts receivable and agricultural assets cannot be used as collateral. Every year, roughly RMB16 trillion of assets are sitting idle in terms of generating financing: if you figure at a discount rate of 50% for loans, the asset value of these could guarantee roughly RMB800 million worth of loans.

According to statistics in the *China County Economic Yearbook*, the total economic value of production from county and sub-county levels in China is roughly 50% of the country's total GDP. China's GDP of 2006 was roughly RMB20 trillion; the contribution of counties to that was roughly RMB10 trillion. If one removes RMB2 trillion, which is derived from agriculture, the value of non-agricultural production created at county and sub-county levels should be about RMB8 trillion. Even this is a very low estimate that does not take into consideration multiple factors.

At present, loans related to agriculture total around RMB4 trillion. If you include loans to TVEs, loans obtained by county areas total around RMB5 trillion. Since we are talking about secured loans, one must deduct the following things: first, this sum may include a relatively large amount, and indeed a fair percentage that has already become nonperforming, of purchase loans in the grain system. Second, included in the RMB5 trillion are about RMB200 billion worth of small amount credit loans for farmers and linked-guarantee loans that do not require collateral. Third, a portion are credit balances that have not yet been canceled or that historically have no assets against them as collateral. According to this calculation, we presume the sum of loans *without* collateral or guarantee is around RMB1 trillion. The total of collateralized loans is therefore around RMB4 trillion. This is half the amount of county non-agricultural production. What this says is that under the existing laws and regulations, counties are indeed experiencing the very awkward and uncomfortable state of "having assets but no credit."

Because of the burgeoning need for financing in rural areas, some bank organizations have begun to adopt novel methods as market systems begin to be implemented, exploring various credit products and management ways that are in accord with the unusual features of rural clients and their financial systems. These include measures to control risk. These experimental efforts completely discard the reliance on collateral that commercial banking traditionally employs. To date, these experiments have achieved uncommon success.

In 1999, Rural Credit Cooperatives began to implement micro-credit loans that did not require collateral, and they were successful in achieving over a 98% loan-repayment ratio. Under the support of the CDB, three banks and cooperatives were allowed to implement experimental policies of extending credit loans, and the accomplishments have been striking. The three entities were the Zhejiang Taizhou Tailong Credit Cooperative, the Taizhou City Commercial Bank, and the Baotou City Commercial Bank. From November 2005 to July 2006, the Taizhou City Commercial Bank issued 611 micro-loans totaling RMB32.46 million, with an average loan amount of RMB48,200. Ninety percent of the loan recipients were farmers who had lost their land, 5% were rural inhabitants who had no jobs or were former state employees, and 5% were "farmer workers" who had come in to urban areas for work. Not a single loan was nonperforming. The CDB modified the usual commercial bank requirement of assets as collateral and instead accepted local government credit as backing for loans. Although it has issued loans that include such things as training programs for farmers, it has nonetheless earned more than RMB50 billion in profit and the non-performing loan (NPL) rate of 36% in 1988 has dropped in 2006 to 0.73%.

FIGURE 10.2   Return on capital from agriculture, urban industry, and from non-agricultural production in rural areas from 1978 to 2001

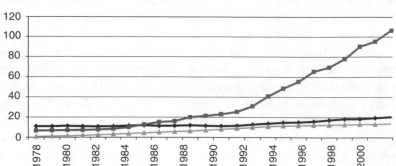

Note: Top line is non-agricultural production in rural areas, the middle line is urban industry, and the bottom line is agriculture.

One can guarantee that financial risk will be at a minimum only by conforming to regulations, by holding relatively liquid assets, and by making risk evaluation a clear and easy process. Developed countries have a private ownership system that allows the use of assets as collateral to function smoothly in this process. Because of this, costs of lending operations can be kept low. In developing countries, in a rapidly growing economic situation in which the system itself is also changing at super-fast speed, the peculiar features of a dual economy require that we proceed from the basis of our actual circumstances. It requires that we institute laws and regulations according to the system of allocated economic resources that is actually in place. If we are too rigid and dogmatic in our approach, we may not be able to include a large portion of assets as creditworthy under the new financial system. Nor will we be able to capitalize such assets by going through financial markets. This will lead to inefficiencies in the entire economy and bring on distortions in the economic structure.

REFORM IN CHINA'S RURAL FINANCE

In 1996, the State Council promulgated a "Decision Regarding Reform of the Rural Financial System." Since that time, China's rural financial reform has been through more than 10 years of difficult progress. Since the start of pilot reform of Rural Credit Cooperatives in 2003, the overall pace of reform has accelerated. In July 2003, the central government selected eight provinces to serve as test cases in Rural Credit Cooperative reform, and in 2004, test sites were extended throughout the country. From 1996–98, Rural Credit Cooperatives went through a variety of adjustments, including separating from the ABC, revising calculation of registered assets, and so on. By the end of 2002, there were 50,000 Rural Credit Cooperatives in China. The sole legal person of these was the Town and Village Credit Cooperative, overseen by the County Cooperative. In the 2003 reforms, some cooperatives that had severe negative balances (assets being unable to offset loans), and no hope of being restructured were closed down. A renewed effort was made to re-evaluate assets and restructure finances of all credit cooperatives. The ability to increase capital by issuing shares was extended to SMEs in counties, as well as unincorporated individual businesses [*ge-ti-hu*]. This basically allowed credit cooperatives to meet the capital requirements of being operating entities in the banking industry.

The reorganization of credit cooperatives adopted three different forms. First was the formation of rural commercial banks and rural cooperative banks. Second was eliminating the legal person qualification of Town and Village Credit Cooperatives, and creating Rural Credit Cooperatives with the county as the first-tier legal person. Third was to continue to preserve the legal person status system of counties and towns. At the same time, basic-level Rural Credit Cooperatives were reorganized and provincial level cooperatives were set up, responsible for managing all of the province's credit cooperatives. Central financial authorities contributed RMB200 billion of funds that, through the Central Bank, made up for or replenished the NPLs of credit cooperatives as well as their accumulated losses.

From 2004 to 2008, the central government issued a series of five documents which set out clear requirements regarding rural financial reform, specifying that the banking industry had to be opened up to allow for greater admittance of alternative organizations with different kinds of ownership structures. At the same time, the directives allowed regions with sufficient prerequisites to set up rural credit loan guarantee organizations. In 2005, the People's Bank of China initiated seven experimental loan companies in five provinces that were only allowed to take deposits, not to extend loans. In 2006, agricultural development banks that had as their main function the policy business of purchasing primary agricultural products, grain, cotton, and food oils were permitted to engage in developmental work in farming villages (including the comprehensive opening up and development of rural areas, basic infrastructure development, and so on). In 2008, the government required that rural banking organizations' entry into the system be accelerated and be granted broader admission policies.

In December 2006, the China Banking Regulatory Commission promulgated a document called "Various Opinions on Adjusting and Broadening the Admittance Policies into Rural Banking and Finance, In Order to Improve Support for the Socialist New-farming-village Construction." This permitted all kinds of capital to come into rural areas to set up Town and Village banks and loan companies, and that permitted farmers to organize Farmer's Mutual fund supporting organizations. After having been tried in test sites for half a year in 1997, this policy was extended to experimental sites throughout the country from October 2007. Although admittance was broadened in terms of investment in the rural banking industry, this policy still had fairly high barriers to entry. Twenty percent or more of control shares of a new rural bank had to be owned by a commercial bank, and loan companies could be set up solely by a commercial bank.

Since policies regarding entry into the financial services sector in China are still very restrictive and still require prior evaluation and approval, the restrictions have considerably lowered hopes that rural financial organizations will be able to resolve the severe inadequacies of financial services in farming villages.

In 2007, by decision of the Central Finance Working Committee, the ABC began to implement share system reform. Moreover, according to the principle of supporting the three "agricultures," operating on market principles, undergoing fundamental reform, and seeking opportunity for listing," the ABC is undergoing financial restructuring and process reengineering. This decision allows certain kinds of organizations to operate on market principles, undergo fundamental reform, and list on the market. In addition to this, from the beginning of the 1990s, a variety of private initiative organizations and international organizations have been allowed to experiment with all kinds of micro-credit organizations. In 2007, the Postal Savings Bank was officially established and began experimental services in rural areas. In early 2007, the central government supported test sites in six provinces for the issuing of "Policy-related Agricultural Insurance."

In the short space of a few years, authorities responsible for rural financial institutions have been through what could be called hyper-fast structural change. It has been highly unusual, whether seen from the experience of developed countries or from the experience of new economic structures. Overall, the efforts of rural financial reform over the past four years have been positive. To resolve the many inadequacies of rural financing and build a multilayered financial system that offers broad coverage, is sustainable, and meets the demands of the 'Three Agricultures' policy, will require long and hard work.

More will be needed to resolve the contradiction between the fast change of financial authorities and the slow change of what can be used as collateral due to rural asset systems and property ownership issues.

Innovative credit and loan products, a system of credit management, a system of risk control, and methods of supervision and regulation are all needed. The result must be a rural financial system that possesses unique Chinese characteristics as appropriate to the Chinese situation. It must be a system that allows rural finance to be an important force in stimulating Chinese agriculture and in allowing rural areas to join the modern world.

CHAPTER 11

Retail Banking: Mastering Wealth Management to Capture Growth Opportunities

Hans-Paul Buerkner
Global CEO, Boston Consulting Group (BCG)

Retail banking is becoming an increasingly important business for most Chinese banks, in large part because of its enormous growth potential. In many markets around the world, retail banking accounts for more than half of all banking revenues. In China, however, it represents no more than a third of the industry's revenues and this is up significantly from a few years ago. This under-penetration is at odds with the fundamental nature of this sector, and is certain to change. As a result, BCG believes that establishing a strong retail business, with a keen focus on wealth management, is both financially attractive and strategically important for many Chinese banks.

Banks in China have already begun bolstering their retail businesses with wealth management offerings. Few, however, have developed a differentiated mix of products and services that maximizes the long-term value of a client relationship. Too much emphasis is placed on perks and short-term fee generation, and too little focus is placed on tailored advice and services that are truly valued by the customer. As a result, banks tend to create expensive premium-banking models, yet still end up under-serving the large, rapidly growing segment of mass-affluent customers.

To succeed in wealth management, banks must create offerings that deliver genuine value to customers. This means, among other things, downplaying short-term-oriented, fee-based strategies in favor of building long-lasting relationships. Banks will also need to develop a deep understanding of their customers' needs, which in turn should help them shape their offerings for specific groups of clients.

ANTICIPATING THE RISE OF RETAIL BANKING AND WEALTH MANAGEMENT

Having focused on providing simple services to individuals with limited savings, China's retail banking sector has long been overshadowed by the more esteemed, complex, and large-scale corporate-banking business, which targets large state-owned enterprises. Until recently, senior bankers in Chinese banks spent most of their time serving these corporate clients. The tellers in sub-branches or outlets, which were called Savings Outlets, were responsible for serving retail customers, whose lack of personal wealth relegated them to the back pages of most banks' business plans.

The old order is being reshuffled. The relentless growth of China's economy is swelling the wealth of individuals, thereby transforming the strategic priorities for the banking sector. Although the corporate business still accounts for about two-thirds of overall banking revenues, retail banking revenues are growing twice as fast. Over time, China's banking sector will come to resemble the banking sectors in more mature markets—such as North America, Western Europe, and Asia—where leading commercial banks generate more than half of their revenues from retail activities.

The rapid accumulation of individual wealth in China will lead to the proliferation of new products that extend well beyond traditional savings accounts. As their wealth grows, retail customers will inevitably have greater demand for more complex financial products; these include mortgages, credit cards, insurance products, and investment services. The development of new retail products will provide additional revenue streams for China's commercial banks, as it has done for foreign banks overseas.

The attractiveness of retail banking comes not only from its sizable revenue and growth potential, but also from its profitability and stability. Further, retail banking can provide a stable base of funding. In mature markets, banks typically make thin margins—sometimes less than 50–100 basis points (bps)—from lending to large corporate clients, while enjoying healthy profits when serving individuals. Further, the return on equity for a wealth management business can be as high as 40 to 50% for many leading global players. In addition, the revenue streams from the retail business, especially wealth management, tend to be more stable. Prior to the financial crisis in 2007 and 2008, BCG analysis shows that the average price–earning (PE) ratios for the retail and wealth management businesses of foreign global banks typically ranged from 13 to 15, while the PE ratios for corporate and investment banks peak at about 10. This disparity indicates that investors ascribe more value to the earnings from retail banking

In China's increasingly important retail banking market, wealth management presents an exceptionally attractive opportunity. China has become the largest wealth market in Asia, excluding Japan. Total household wealth reached approximately RMB22 trillion in 2007 and is expected to top RMB38 trillion by 2010. Between 2002 and 2007, total household wealth in China is estimated to have grown by 25% annually (in real terms) and remains highly concentrated. In addition, the number of wealthy households—those that hold more than RMB0.5 million in financial assets—roughly tripled over the past five years.

Wealth management is attractive not only because of China's rapidly expanding wealth, but also because this business tends to be more lucrative than other dimensions of retail banking. In general, wealthier clients are more profitable to serve, and often subsidize mainstream offerings.

OPPORTUNITIES IN PREMIUM BANKING

Generally speaking, wealth managers serve two major client segments: high net worth individuals (HNWI), who have more than RMB10 million, and mass-affluent retail customers, who hold between RMB0.5 million and 10 million in financial assets (excluding the value of real estate, company ownerships, artwork and other physical assets). These two segments have needs and expectations that are distinct enough to warrant separate offerings.

HNWI clients are typically served by private banks or the private banking units of large commercial banks. Private banks often focus on helping their clients make appropriate investment decisions; some directly manage client assets. Their clients are sophisticated and have more complex financial needs such as structured investments, offshore investments, and estate planning. BCG estimates that China will have about 635,000 HNWI households by 2010.

Mass-affluent clients are usually served by the premium banking services within retail banks. In China, this segment is often branded as VIP Banking, Priority Banking, or Wealth Management. These customers have strong demand for less complex investment products such as mutual funds and structured deposits. Their main objective is relatively straightforward: they want higher returns on their cash holdings. In addition to investment products, premium banking also covers a wide range of services, including consumer lending, credit cards, and insurance. Most successful premium banks use broad offerings to capture the overall client relationship and ensure the highest return. According to BCG's wealth management market forecast, China will have more than eight million mass-affluent households by 2010.

Together, the households in China's private and premium banking segments own more than 70% of the country's private financial assets and represent less than 2% of all bankable households. Given this dense concentration of wealth, these households provide unparalleled opportunities for profitable growth.

This is, of course, no secret—particularly in the rarefied world of private banking. For many years, international private banks have been serving wealthy Chinese individuals through offshore centers. As the number of wealthy individuals increases and more of their financial assets stay onshore, many international banks—and a small number of local banks—are aggressively developing onshore private banking services and jockeying for market share. High profitability and growth are drawing banks to this sector, but so are practical considerations: because private banking is less transactional, a player needs only a few outlets to service its clients, making this sector more accessible to foreign competitors. Most Chinese banks, therefore, hold a relative competitive advantage in the premium banking segment, at least in the near term. This does not mean, however, that local banks will not face challengers in this space.

Since they have been allowed to offer RMB products, foreign retail banks have been targeting the mass-affluent segment because it offers higher per-customer profit and can be served by a smaller, more focused branch network relative to the mainstream segment. Moreover, compared with many local retail banks, foreign banks have well-developed, sophisticated service models that suit this segment. However, building the necessary network, staff base, product portfolio, and operations takes time. As a result, local banks still have a window of opportunity to develop appealing offerings for the mass affluent. Failing to do so will inevitably cause many of their best customers to leave, which would deal a severe blow to their overall profitability and growth.

MISCONCEPTIONS ABOUT PREMIUM BANKING

Although many Chinese banks have already realized the importance of building a strong premium banking business and have even begun offering VIP-banking or wealth management services, recent BCG research shows that more than 60% of mass-affluent customers are not fully satisfied with their banking services in China. Key areas of customer dissatisfaction include poor service in branches, especially long waiting times, the lack of tailored financial solutions, and relationship managers who do not fully understand customers' financial needs.

BCG has identified several common misconceptions about premium banking that go a long way toward explaining the widespread dissatisfaction among customers.

Myth 1: The Primary Objective Is to Maximize Fees

With gradual deregulation and disintermediation eroding their interest income, Chinese banks have diversified their revenue streams by establishing fee-based businesses. Such strategies, however, can quickly undermine a premium banking offering. A short-term focus on fees creates incentives that reward the aggressive selling of products, regardless of whether they are in a client's best interest.

Fee income is still relatively low in Chinese banks, compared to international peers. As a result, increasing fee revenue has become a priority for Chinese banks. As they work toward this objective, banks must ensure that strategies designed to maximize fees in the short term do not jeopardize client relationships. Clients are very sensitive to fees and quickly lose faith once they feel that their bank is more concerned with generating fees than it is with developing a good relationship. Once this happens, customers will become skeptical and begin second-guessing each suggested investment. In contrast, a relationship manager who establishes and safeguards a trusted relationship can be much more effective, saving substantial sales time and effort over the long term.

Myth 2: Wealth Management Is Mainly About Selling Mutual Funds

It is a common experience among premium banking clients: relationship managers are quick to recommend their latest mutual funds, even before they understand the client's investment objectives. This causes potential and existing clients to lose trust in the relationship manager and question the bank's ability to assist them in longer term financial planning. To exacerbate the situation, any walk-in customer interested in mutual funds is typically directed to the wealth management counter. This leads to a vague, undefined role for the premium banking relationship manager, who simply ends up selling mutual funds to a shapeless group of customers.

Managing wealth should extend well beyond a simplistic focus on selling investment products. BCG's market research has shown that premium banking customers value a comprehensive one-stop-shop model. A wealth manager therefore needs to provide holistic investment advice and offer the right products that fit a client's investment goals. This will only happen, of course, if the relationship manager sets out to understand the customer's background, overall financial needs and objectives, and attitude toward investment and risk.

Myth 3: The More Benefits, the Better

Banks often complement their premium offerings with special benefits that include lower fees or fee waivers on certain services, discounts at restaurants and golf courses, as well as access to VIP lounges in airports. It may come as a shock to banks, but BCG focus groups have shown that many of these perks, despite being costly to provide, hold little appeal in the eyes of the customer.

Banks should avoid offering a broad array of benefits, which tend to be both expensive and undifferentiated, and instead "cherry-pick" those benefits that are most relevant for each target segment of customers. Designing a narrower benefit scheme is far more effective and efficient, but only if the scheme, itself, is shaped by in-depth customer discovery and research.

Myth 4: Experienced Relationship Managers Bring a Ready Portfolio of Clients

Banks looking for a quick infusion of clients often try to recruit experienced relationship managers. In reality, however, relationship managers are rarely able to take a significant portion of their client portfolios with them when they move, even when they have close relationships with their customers. Moreover, BCG has found—through our extensive project experience—that cultural differences and other integration issues often complicate the assimilation of relationship managers from outside the organization.

Rather than trying to poach relationship managers, banks are likely to fare better when they cultivate talent internally. Homegrown relationship managers tend to have a better cultural fit and are able to leverage the organization's resources more effectively. As a result, they can be between 50 and 150% more productive than external hires.

Myth 5: Wealth Management Is About Luxurious Packaging

Many banks have spent a lot of time and money trying to package their wealth management businesses. China has its share of plush wealth management centers, complete with fancy brand names and images. As slick (and expensive) as these outlets are, many are simply not effective in acquiring, servicing, and selling to premium banking customers. BCG research has also revealed that most premium banking brands in China are not well-recognized by customers.

While having nicely decorated wealth management centers may seem essential, most customers do not consider this an important criterion when selecting premium banking services. Instead, they pay attention to factors such as convenience, efficiency, and the ability to get the right advice and products. If a bank cannot perfect its "software"—the core elements of a wealth management offering, like service and products—than an over-investment in superficial "hardware" will do little to develop a sustainable business. Similarly, putting a premium brand name and promise in front of the customer, without having the capability to deliver on that promise, is self-defeating.

A bank should clearly understand the value proposition it will provide to its customers, along with the experience those customers can expect to get from the bank. This understanding should help banks design channel strategies, outlet formats, and service models, as well as decide how to position and differentiate their brands.

PRIORITIZING THE CUSTOMER RELATIONSHIP TO ENSURE SUCCESS

More than any other factor, the ability to build strong client relationships will determine a wealth manager's success. To forge such bonds, wealth managers need to focus on three imperatives: first, they must develop a deep connection with their clients; second, they must provide an unparalleled value proposition; and third, they must ensure the flawless execution of their offering.

DEVELOP A DEEP CONNECTION WITH CLIENTS

Despite the importance of understanding their customers, most commercial banks—not only in China but also around the world—are not skilled at developing customer insights. Many banks underestimate the importance of knowing their customers; others are convinced there is little new to learn about their customers, or else fail to use the right approach.

Most banks can learn a lot from leading luxury goods companies, which have developed sophisticated skills in discovering what customers really want, what matters most to them, when and how customers buy, and which emotional drivers are behind their purchase decisions. These companies have recognized a simple truth: to best serve customers, you must first understand them.

To develop a comprehensive view of the customer, banks must assess three dimensions: the product dimension looks at what customers actually buy (for example, mutual funds or insurance products); the functional dimension reveals what customers need (for example, the level of investment return and degree of associated risk); the emotional dimension examines what customers feel (for example, a sense of financial security).

Luxury goods companies typically emphasize the emotional dimension and try to establish strong connections on that level. In comparison, most banks focus on the product dimension and underestimate the importance of making an emotional connection.

BCG's global research has identified seven common emotional needs of retail-banking customers (the quotes in Table 11.1 are from this research). By considering the emotional needs of their customers, banks will immediately realize that achieving true customer satisfaction requires much more than just offering competitive products and exclusive benefits. Making a customer feel understood, respected, and taken care of—at every point of interaction—is a difficult task that involves the entire banking organization.

At the same time, banks must recognize that wealth management customers are not a homogenous group. To delve deeper into the

TABLE 11.1 Retail customers are not fully satisfied with their banking services

Emotional needs	What customers are saying
Exclusivity	*"Right now, there's no aspiration to be middle class. Everyone wants to be at the top, but banks are treating me very middle class."*
Successful	*"Most of us spend a good deal of our waking hours obsessing about money. Am I saving enough? Can I retire comfortably? I need someone to tell me whether I have made and saved enough money for a comfortable retirement."*
Respected/valued	*"I was told by a customer service rep that she did not have to listen to my concerns."*
Taken care of	*"After calling two different telephone hotline numbers, I got stuck in two endless computer voice loops without ever talking to anyone."*
Trust	*"After approximately 20–30 minutes of arguing, I finally got them to admit that they had made a mistake."*
Understood	*"They don't even try to understand my situation and what is going on in my life."*
In control	*"I get the feeling I'm not in control; I'm just along for the ride."*

emotional dimension, banks should segment the customer base, perhaps by age, gender, profession, wealth level, or investment strategy (for example, wealth accumulation versus wealth preservation). Since each segment behaves differently and has distinct emotional and financial needs, banks should tailor their offerings accordingly.

PROVIDE AN UNPARALLELED VALUE PROPOSITION

Many banks in China have spent too much time trying to match their competitors' offerings, and not enough time trying to uncover what their customers actually want. As a result, most premium banking services are not adequately differentiated—they have similar ranges and types of investment products, as well as similar value-added perks. With a clear understanding of customer needs, however, a bank should be able to craft a unique value proposition that appeals to specific segments. By providing an unparalleled value proposition, a bank does not need to be the best performer across every dimension or provide expensive benefits in order to find success.

The ideal value proposition will vary as much as a bank's customer base—different customers will have different needs. The common denominator, when it comes to developing a winning value proposition, is the ability to translate customers' emotional needs into actual products and services. Customers whose emotional needs are met by

TABLE 11.2 Best practice banks fulfill their customers' emotional needs

Emotional needs	What customers are saying
Exclusivity	*"Because of my status, I get special, personalized service."*
Successful	*"I bank here because it shows that I've made it."*
	"I have the best financial resources to achieve my life goals."
Respected/valued	*"I am recognized, and treated as an important customer."*
	"My money and I are taken seriously."
	"Banking is convenient and easy; my time and lifestyle are valued."
Taken care of	*"Someone is there for me as my needs change; I have a long-term relationship with an advisor who cares."*
	"I can get expert advice and consistent high-quality service."
Trust	*"My bank is watching out for my assets even when I'm not."*
	"I get unbiased advice."
	"I can choose to use the bank's products or someone else's—whatever is best for me."
Understood	*"My bank understands my whole financial position, my lifestyle, and helps me plan for the future."*
	"Products that meet my specific needs."
In control	*"My bank helps me to be comfortable with my financial position."*
	"I can choose to manage my finances, or have someone else take care of them."

their bank will show a much higher level of satisfaction, as Table 11.2 shows.

ENSURE FLAWLESS EXECUTION

Even a great strategy will fail if it is poorly executed, while an average strategy can prosper if it is well-executed. Strategy remains important, but the key is to consistently deliver high-quality service in line with customer expectations. To achieve flawless execution in wealth management, banks must concentrate on five areas.

Establish a Proper Organizational Structure

Many world-class international banks operate their wealth management and mass-market divisions separately. An independent division enjoys more autonomy in its decision-making and is unconstrained by the operating procedures in the retail business. A best practice wealth manager is a separate and comprehensive business unit, complete with independent reporting lines. It has dedicated staff responsible for sales and servicing, and for designing premium banking products and services. All of its activities should be tailored in a way that best serves targeted customers.

Relationship managers, in particular, should be managed separately from the retail banking staff. Their performance needs to be measured against a comprehensive set of key performance indicators, which may include total AuM, net new assets, or the revenue margin of the client portfolio.

Recruit, Train, and Retain Good Client-facing Staff

As in any industry, attracting good staff is the first step toward building a successful business. When recruiting relationship managers, banks should seek out individuals who have proven interpersonal skills. Training will then make the difference between a good relationship manager and an outstanding one. Regular training in both technical and soft skills—to build product expertise and hone professional conduct, for example—will ensure well-rounded performers.

Developing a culture based on meritocracy and the recognition of good performance is critical to retaining good staff. It is far more costly for a bank to poach experienced relationship managers than it is to train and retain those they have. As mentioned earlier, we have also found that homegrown relationship managers are more productive than those hired from competitors.

Set Up Appropriate Service Tiers

Smart segmentation allows wealth managers to marshal their resources around distinct customer groups that demonstrate similar needs and behaviors, and to determine the economic potential of each group. Good segmentation also allows banks to develop a unique product offering and service model for each group. Ideally, the ultimate criterion for segmentation is customer profitability.

While there are various ways to stratify a diverse customer base, AuM and total relationship balance (which includes loan balance) are common approaches. Following segmentation, every customer should be assigned a dedicated relationship manager who handles all financial needs, queries, and transactions. Best practice banks assign the most experienced relationship managers to customers with higher AuM, and ensure that the customer-to-relationship-manager ratio is lower for higher tier customer segments.

Provide a Consistent Multi-channel Experience

Discerning customers take notice of even the smallest details, and it is not uncommon for customers who experience poor service at just one touch point to move their assets to other banks. Wealth managers therefore need to ensure that customers receive consistent, high-quality service from each channel: within the outlet, from banking machines, or over the Internet or telephone.

While managers only see the part of the business they are responsible for, customers usually interact with all channels. One channel that is frequently given less attention than it deserves is phone banking. Customers do not easily forget being ensnared in endless automated voice systems or encountering less-than-pleasant bankers on the other side of the line. Such experiences can overshadow positive experiences in other channels, and create a negative impression of the overall wealth management offering.

Develop Strong Internal Capabilities

A strong support infrastructure is critical to ensuring a successful wealth management business. Banks should maintain a comprehensive customer relationship management (CRM) database that stores all relevant customer information, including a customer's background and transaction history. In addition, they should document all non-transaction interactions.

Banks should also recognize that it costs more to serve wealth management customers than it does to serve mainstream customers in the retail bank. If the costs of a wealth management division are not managed well, large swaths of its customers can quickly become unprofitable. This underscores the need for smart segmentation, which will ensure that service levels (and costs) are commensurate with the profitability of each customer.

Internal capabilities should include a good feedback mechanism, to ensure that the business keeps up with its customers' evolving needs and demands. An institutionalized process should allow front-line staff to feed customer demands back to relevant departments. For instance, changing economic conditions may affect customers' investment requirements, which in turn may influence the pipeline of new products.

CHARTING A PATH TO SUCCEED IN PREMIUM BANKING

Banks in China are starting to recognize that a growing share of their profits will come from the retail sector, and that the country's expanding population of wealthy citizens presents a great opportunity to create successful wealth management businesses. Although banks are developing better retail and wealth management offerings, there is still a lot of work to do.

Some banks may first need to reaffirm their growth opportunities in retail banking, in general, and wealth management, specifically. A bank's leadership should make a clear commitment to succeeding in these two areas. The commitment should be reflected in the resources and talent dedicated to pursuing these opportunities.

Banks that have already embarked on premium banking strategies should ensure their organizations are capable of thriving in an increasingly competitive sector. They will need to focus on training relationship managers, for example, and building critical internal capabilities. Every player in China's rapidly evolving wealth management sector will need to revisit its offering and ask itself tough questions. Is the value proposition truly differentiated? Does it respond to customers' needs and expectations? Is it tailored to suit specific customer groups? At the heart of these questions lies a clear imperative: to succeed in premium banking, players must develop a deep understanding of the customer.

Banks have little time to waste. As wealth continues to grow rapidly, the opportunity to develop premium banking offerings becomes all the more clear and compelling—for both local and international players. Banks with underdeveloped offerings risk losing their most valuable customers, while those that field a differentiated, valued service will be in a strong position to leap ahead. For many banks in China, not winning in the retail and wealth management sectors could soon mean not winning at all.

CHAPTER 12

Growing China's Retail Banking Business

Ma Weihua

President, China Merchants Bank

China's retail banking business has grown rapidly since the 1980s. It has accompanied vigorous growth in global capital markets, innovations in financial instruments, rapid increase in numbers of Chinese consumers and greater concentration of their wealth, and it has kept pace with the fast approach of an aging society. In light of these changes, China's retail banking system has begun to be an important source of profits in the banking industry. Certain features of the business—such as that operational risk is dispersed, profit levels are stable, prices can be negotiated, and the cost of doing business is relatively low—argue decisively for pursuing a strong expansion of this sector. Such expansion also meets the internal needs of China's operational reforms in banking. Under the new situation in which banking is completely open to outside participation, it behooves us to take a look at the evolution of retail banking in China and survey the challenges that lie ahead. We must clarify our thoughts on how the industry is to grow as we move forward.

UNDERLYING CONDITIONS

For a long time, China practiced a banking system that had one "mono-bank," the People's Bank of China (PBC). In the mid-1980s, a two-tier system was set up that had both a central bank and specialized banks, and that began to explore a transition to a commercial banking system that would operate on the basis of banks as corporations. This transition created the systemic environment for the development of a retail banking industry. From a starting point of zero, China's retail banking system has now grown to a considerable size. Before the mid-1990s, China's banking system created a market structure with the core entities being the four state-owned commercial banks. The income of these banks relied almost entirely on the spread in interest rates. Each bank did its utmost to pull in deposits, so there was a kind of tug-of-war for deposits and the period became known as the "Bank deposit-book era" in Chinese banking. This period also marked the embryonic stage of China's retail banking business.

In 1995, China Merchants Bank led the way in putting out a number of new products and services. Among these were management of customer accounts, fixed demand deposits, different kinds of savings accounts, different currencies, and multi-functional services within the scope of an on-line banking service called "All-in-one-net," an electronic-currency bank card. This led to a savings deposit revolution in China's domestic banking. Other banks hastened to follow suit. The popularization of bank cards symbolized the formal initiation of China's retail banking industry.

In September 2005, a national meeting of the heads of China's joint-stock ownership commercial banks was held in the city of Tengchong in Yunnan Province. A "Tengchong Communiqué" was issued as a result, formulated by attendees at that meeting. Development of the retail banking sector was given a core strategic position in the overall process of structural change in China's commercial banks. China's retail banking industry was now officially launched. It started with a blank slate. By the end of 2006, a total of 1,175 billion bank cards were in circulation, of which 56 million were credit cards. In the year 2006, there were 1,100 products related to money management for individuals, which took in nearly RMB400 billion. As a result, the retail banking business of China leapt forward.

In recent years, China's retail banking business has exhibited the following features and trends.

Increasing Scale of Operations

First, the consumer credit business has experienced very fast growth. In March 1999, the PBC promulgated a "Guiding Opinion Regarding Developing Personal Consumer Credit." The business then developed rapidly and from residential mortgage loans for individuals it grew to include loans for durable consumer goods, loans for individual healthcare, loans for home improvement, loans for individual travel, loans for education, loans for automobiles, housing mortgages, loans for wedding ceremonies, and so on. Statistics show that, from 1997 to 2005, consumer loans in China increased from RMB17.2 billion to RMB2.2 trillion, or to a figure representing 11% of the entire amount of loans in the country. This was 120 times what loan amounts had been in 1997, with an annual average rate of increase of 182%. Among the various kinds of loans, housing loans constituted 70% of the total

Second, the bank card business has shown stable growth. In recent years, influenced by the growth of the economy, the environment for using cards has markedly improved and, with gradual public acceptance, China's credit card business has demonstrated vigorous growth. At present, China's more than 200 financial institutions are issuing bank cards, and the four state-owned commercial banks, almost all the joint stock-owned commercial banks, and a few of the large city commercial banks have issued credit cards. According to the Central Bank, by the end of 2006, the number of debit cards in circulation was 1.08 billion, or 95.6% of all bank cards in China. The number of credit cards was over 50 million, an increase of 22.7% over the previous year. In 2006, the total amount of consumer transactions paid for by credit cards came to RMB1.89 trillion, an increase of 97% over the previous year. Subtracting large wholesale-type transactions and real estate transactions, total retail transactions for consumer goods done via cards came to 17% of all retail transactions, an increase of 7% over the previous year. The percentage of total retail business transacted via cards in such large cities as Beijing, Shanghai, Guangzhou, and Shenzhen came to 30%, which approaches the 30–50% level of developed countries.

Third, intermediary business has increased quickly. China's intermediary commercial banking business began relatively late. Before the 1990s, income in commercial banking relied almost exclusively on the spread in interest rates between loans and deposits, and product innovation was limited. Only starting in the 1990s did China truly begin to develop intermediary business in banking, and gradually come up with innovative intermediary products. Over the past dozen or more years, the accomplishments of our domestic commercial banking intermediary business have been respectable. In 2006, the Industrial and Commercial Bank of China (ICBC) realized income from intermediary businesses of RMB16 billion, an increase of 55%. Intermediary business had already reached 9.14% of total revenue, an increase of 2.6% over 2005. The Bank of China's (BOC) income from net fees and commissions increased by 54.9%, that of the

China Construction Bank (CCB) by 60.5%. In 2006, the non-interest income of China Merchants Bank was RMB2.097 billion, an increase of 91.07% over the previous year. Within this figure, income from point-of-sales business, from brokerage fees on stock transactions, from agent funds, from agenting insurance, and from credit card non-interest income, increased respectively by 56.1%, 383.7%, 442%, 115%, and 80.7%. Within the overall retail banking business, the business of individual wealth management has developed at a ferocious pace. There are currently nearly 1,100 choices in the commercial banking system's suite of personal wealth management products. As noted above, these took in RMB400 billion in 2006. "Money management" has become the main thrust in retail banking operations, and "the financial supermarket," "financial advisors," "financial centers," and so on are now common terms.

Improvement in Delivery Modes

In recent years, while China has continued to improve its traditional physical network of banking locations, it has put considerable effort into broadening electronic banking services. Delivery channels for retail services have been breaking new ground, resulting in a growing number of customers every year. Since April 1997, when China Merchants Bank took the lead in issuing its online banking service called "All-in-one-net," Internet-based banking services have developed quickly. Virtually all national-level commercial banks now provide online banking services as well as some large city banks, including Beijing Bank and Shanghai Bank. In 2003, the transaction value of on-line banking in China came to RMB20 trillion, but by 2005, it had swiftly grown to 70 trillion. In June, 2007, Merchants Bank became the first bank in China to break through the barrier of RMB100 billion in cumulative transaction amount, becoming the first commercial bank in China to hit this level.

Most commercial banks in China have now also begun telephone banking services and are achieving fast growth. For example, by the end of June 2006, the telephone banking services of the ICBC were reaching 20 million people. Cell phone banking is also gaining customer acceptance quickly, since it is mobile, can be done in confidential venues, and since cell phones are so widespread. Other forms of bank services are also developing, including self-service banking, banking from home, palm banking, short-messaging services in banking, and so on. Customers for these new business lines are increasing every year.

Faster Reform

China has been pushing the pace of reforms relating to retail banking in recent years, under the guiding principles of "Get close to the market, raise efficiency, and strengthen management." The following main banking systems have been involved in the structural reform.

First, new retail banking operations have been set up at headquarters and large branches in certain municipalities, including consumer loan centers, savings deposit and money management centers, bank card centers, online banking centers, product research centers, and customer service centers. At the same time, similar money management centers have been set up in some of the smaller cities, with such centers being directly under the control of headquarters. A flattening of management has been instituted as a part of total overall reform.

Second, private finance departments have been set up in top-tier sub-branches, and supplied with professional client account managers, so that management of retail banking has been extended down the line from branches to sub-branches.

Third, in accordance with the needs of "strengthening headquarters and making branches more professional," there has been an overall increase in the extent of self-management and the quality of self-management in branches and sub-branches. Together with an integrated approach to management, credit card direct sales teams have been organized.

Fourth, Chinese-foreign cooperation has been encouraged. China's tremendous retail banking market is attractive not only to Chinese banks, but to foreign banks and financial institutions as well. It is a very tempting piece of cheese. Since entering the World Trade Organization (WTO), effective and highly fruitful cooperation has been carried forward in the areas of capital, technology, and business operations. This has been based on the principles of deepening cooperation, promoting win–win policies, and having Chinese and foreign banks cooperate through joint share-ownership. Cooperation between Chinese and foreign banks has been most outstanding in the area of credit cards. Pudong Development Bank and Citibank have jointly issued a Citibank–Pudong Card, and the ICBC, Shanghai Bank, Xingye Bank, and Bank of Communications (BoCom) have also been quick to put out credit cards in cooperation with other foreign banks. In the area of wealth management, the excellent overseas network of foreign banks, together with their back-office resources, have teamed up with the customer resources of Chinese banks, and their advantageous networks, to start a new chapter in China's wealth management.

One example is the cooperation between Communications Bank and HSBC, which have issued a bank-based Qualified Domestic Institutional Investor product (QDII). Another is the cooperation between Beijing Bank and its strategic partner ING Bank, which has forged ahead in the wealth management market. In the realm of private banking, Chinese and foreign banks are also closely cooperating. The BOC has taken a commanding height in the area of domestic personal wealth management, and with its strategic partner, the Royal Bank of Scotland, has led in the business of private banking. ING Bank will be working with the Beijing Bank also in entering the private banking market in China.

Fifth, risk management has gradually been strengthened. While the retail banking business has taken on the heavy responsibility of lowering overall levels of a bank's nonperforming loans (NPLs), retail banking operations themselves are not unblemished in this regard. People in the retail business feel that NPLs at the retail level must be kept at around 5%, since the margins between loans and deposits are decreasing and marketing costs are relatively high. This is fundamentally different from the 15% and 20% limit on NPLs for corporate loans. If banks are even a little incautious, it is hard to retrieve enough income to offset outflows.

Credit risk has attracted attention from all quarters and is being addressed with increasingly tight controls. Insurance companies are asking for a brake on car loan insurance; notices are being promulgated by the China Banking Regulatory Commission and the People's Bank of China (PBC). Two examples are the notice, in August, 2006, regarding "Further Improving the Handling of Real Estate Loans," and that on September 27, 2007, regarding "Handling Loans for Commercial Real Estate." Real estate loans are in the neighborhood of RMB4.3 trillion, and it is indeed hard to fathom the degree of risk in this large amount. The fact that many credit card companies in Korea are on the verge of bankruptcy is also sounding alarms in China about credit card risk.

One happy thing is that along with the gradual establishment and improvement of the consumer credit system, the basis for a risk management system in China has been improved. China has already established the world's largest database relating to individual credit. By the end of April 2006, the national personal credit information database had recorded a total of 488 million "natural persons," with information covering basic data on individuals, settlement account information, bank credit information, and information on housing provident funds derived from non-bank-system sources. This has basically achieved the purpose of setting up a credit file on every person who has any economic activity.

Factors Behind Retail Banking's Fast Growth

McKinsey points out that China's retail banking business will become the mainstay and an important source of revenue and profit for China's banking industry over the next 10 years. Reasons for fast growth in recent times can be summarized by the following three factors.

Sustained Increase in Personal Financial Needs

Since Reform and Opening policies began, and after 30 years of fast growth, China has become the fourth-largest economic entity in the world. Its demands on financial services are constantly becoming more diversified and more personalized. Demand for such things as personal wealth management, consumer credit loans, and SME financing have far surpassed expectations in terms of sustained fast growth, and this is providing a vast market opportunity to the retail banking sector.

First, the demand for personal wealth management is huge. In 2005, financial assets of the population reached RMB26.65 trillion, of which savings deposits totaled RMB15 trillion. In March 2007, according to the *Forbes* list of the *Global Wealthiest*, the concentration of wealth in Asia saw a clear shift with the number of wealthiest persons in China surpassing the number in Japan. The number of people in China with liquid assets greater than US$1 million now approaches 400,000, with an average net worth of US$5 million. In the next few years, asset growth is expected to continue to maintain an 8.8% increase, which is twice the expected world average. Quite apart from this wealthiest group, China has a rapidly increasing and already substantial middle class. The State Statistical Bureau defines middle class to be an annual income between RMB60,000 to RMB500,000. By this standard, in the next 10 years, the number of middle class people in China is expected to reach 350 million, as predicted by Merrill Lynch.

Accompanying the rapid rise in people's income levels is a commensurate rise in the need for professional wealth management. With concentrated wealth, more people are facing issues of high personal income tax, inheritance tax and gift taxes: people sorely need professional help in finding reasonable ways to lower taxes, and they need help in establishing financial plans for retirement and old age. For some time now, demand for personal wealth management, asset management, and so on has shown explosive growth. McKinsey's prescription for foreign-invested banks coming into China clearly indicates that personal wealth management is going to be the most profitable arena, particularly private banking services for high net-worth individuals.

Second, demand for consumer loans is huge. According to the analysis of Credit Suisse First Boston, China's consumer market is growing at a speed of 18% per year. In 10 years, the domestic consumption component of GDP will grow from the current 44% to over 50%. There is strong reason to believe that consumer loans will continue to have vast room to expand for the foreseeable future.

THE FAST GROWTH OF THE FINANCIAL MARKETS SYSTEM

The ongoing growth of China's financial markets, continuing improvement in the overall financial ecosystem, market structure, and so on have led to a critical juncture in the growth of the retail banking sector. The first important consideration is that financial institutions are getting stronger. As China's financial industry grows, we see many different kinds of organizations coexisting, with multiple functions, a complementary division of labor, and a multilayered financial structure. The system now incorporates currency, capital, gold, and foreign exchange markets. Its multilayered market structure incorporates a regulatory system that coordinates among central bank, securities, banking and insurance regulatory agencies, but that has separate regulatory jurisdictions. These improvements in the structure of the industry have created favorable conditions for retail banking.

Second, China's capital markets continue to grow. After share-ownership reform was completed, China's stock market experienced unprecedented growth and the warrants market in particular has been explosive. An index futures market will soon be implemented, and the capital markets are currently entering a favorable track. In the currency markets, Central Bank [Treasury] Notes, short-term financing notes, and other such products are coming out, and products in the currency markets are increasingly plentiful. In foreign exchange markets, with the RMB exchange rate entering a system of a managed float, foreign exchange transactions, currency swaps, and derivative product transactions are increasing in volume. The capital markets system is developing so fast that it is hard for consumers to know what to choose. Finally, integrated operations are gradually progressing. In recent years, China's banking industry has shown a trend toward integrated operation of the securities, insurance, and other financial-related industries. Fund management companies under the banks are constantly being launched and the relationship between the banking and insurance industries is growing closer by the day. Integrated operations are beneficial to creating a large platform for servicing customers. This in turn further stimulates the development of the retail banking industry.

CHANGING RULES OF THE GAME

China's banking industry is facing a tremendous change in what could be called the rules of the game, with the appearance of all kinds of new financial tools. These include such diversified direct financing methods such as short-term commercial paper, asset-backed notes, and middle- and long-term financing instruments. Changes also include the marketization of interest rates with the gradual liberalizing or relaxation of floors on deposit rates and ceilings on loan rates. They include the shift from a fixed exchange rate system to a managed float, and with it the gradual appreciation of the RMB. All of these changes present challenges to the retail banking industry. In order for commercial banks to face the challenges they must find new strategic breakthroughs and begin to implement strategic transitions.

First is the development of direct financing. Since the Central Bank authorized short-term financing paper [commercial paper] for enterprises in 2005, that market has grown very fast. By the end of March 2007, a total of 376 enterprises had issued short-term paper with a total amount of RMB488.04 billion. Medium- and long-term-maturity financing instruments will soon be authorized. From December 15, 2005, with the issuing of asset-backed securities with a total amount of RMB7 billion [called *kai-yuan* and *jian-yuan*], the asset-backed securities market has begun to flourish, and the Pudong Development Bank, the ICBC, and others have plunged in. With the gradual appearance of such diversified direct financing tools as commercial paper, medium- and long-term financing notes, and so on, the declining demand for bank loans, especially by large, high-quality customers, can be imagined. Faced with the challenges of fast growth in direct financing, the strategic choice of commercial banks should certainly be to grow their retail and intermediary businesses.

Second is the marketization reform of interest rates and exchange rates. With increasingly market-driven fluctuations in China's interest rates in recent years, domestic banks have begun to face greater risk from interest rate movements. The experience of the US, Taiwan,

Hong Kong, and similar countries proves that the marketization of interest rates generally leads to a narrowing of the spread in bank rates. This appears to be a fundamental trend. Marketizing interest rates confronts commercial banks with a variety of risks. These include contrarian risk, repricing risk, diversion of deposits risk, risk of lowering bond assets, and so on. The experience of international banks makes it clear that a strong retail banking business is important in allowing commercial banks to deal with the marketization of interest rates. The impact of a narrowing spread in interest rates is relatively less on retail banking than it is on corporate finance; many retail banking business lines, especially credit cards, consumer loans, personal wealth management, and so on, not only allow banks to receive stable interest income, but can also take in fairly respectable handling fees. In addition, the retail banking businesses create a foundation and a platform for developing intermediary banking businesses and for innovative products in modern commercial banking. Only when a bank's customer network and personal finance business have reached a certain stage can intermediary services enjoy major growth.

Third is the increasingly stringent nature of regulation of commercial banks. On March 1, 2004, the China Banking Regulatory Commission promulgated and began to implement the new management measures on "assuring adequacy ratios in commercial banks." This was done within the regulatory framework of the New Basel Capital Accord. It increased the pace of aligning with international systems with regard to capital requirements. This put great pressure on the operating systems of Chinese banks, particularly since China's bank capital raising system does not yet operate in a smooth manner. The severe capital constraints sped up the need to make strategic adjustments in banking operations. Banks face the need to adhere to a path of relatively low capital expenditures and relatively high operating efficiency. Developing ways to do this has become an urgent task. Retail banking, on the other hand, enjoys a relatively low rate of capital, its risk is more diversified, and its profit margins are larger. Because of these features, a strong growth in retail banking should be the rational choice of China's commercial banks in actively conforming to capital constraints in the regulatory environment.

CHALLENGES AND OPPORTUNITIES

Right now, China enjoys favorable conditions in developing its retail banking business and will continue to do so for a while. Given changing trends in the domestic economy and overall financial environment, however, the industry also faces severe challenges. Domestic banks will have to pay particular attention to, and deal appropriately with, the following three challenges.

International Competition

Along with the complete opening of China's banking industry, the heat is on in the war in retail banking between Chinese and foreign banks. The globalized nature of competition in China's domestic retail banking market is becoming more pronounced by the day. On the one side, Chinese banks enjoy a superior network; customer resources; high-density distribution of all kinds of credit cards; and services to this network including personal loans, wealth management, new products and services. On the other side, foreign banks have a favorable situation with regard to efficiencies in their systems and excellent management skills. Their entry into China is enabled by share participation in Chinese banks, setting up banking outlets, establishing high net worth wealth management centers, issuing new money management products, breaking into private banking business and other methods, allowing them to occupy the high-end of the retail market while gradually penetrating the middle and low end.

At the end of March 2007, the China Banking Regulatory Commission issued a "Report on Opening to the Outside of the Chinese Banking Industry." This report revealed that at present there are 312 foreign banking enterprises in China, with a foreign-currency asset value of US$103.3 billion, occupying 1.8% of the total asset value of China's banking and financial institutions. Within this total, deposit amounts came to $39.7 billion, loans came up to $61.6 billion. Up to the end of 2006, the total asset value of foreign banks in Shanghai had reached RMB590 billion, an increase of 51% over the previous year. This represented 14% of total asset value in Shanghai banks, an increase of 1.2%. On December 26, 2006, foreign banks were allowed to provide local currency services to individuals. From January to September 2007, RMB savings deposits in foreign banks increased by RMB4.2 billion, and foreign exchange deposits increased by US$447 million. In contrast, the foreign exchange deposits of Chinese financing institutions decreased by US$1.1 billion.

RMB deposits in foreign banks continue to increase at a fast pace. The strong brand names of foreign banks, their superior standards of service, and their innovative ability in creating new products make it hard for Chinese domestic banks to copy their performance in a short period of time. In addition to foreign banks, asset management companies, electronic financing organizations, and other kinds of non-banking financial institutions are rapidly penetrating the Chinese banking industry, imposing a severe test on China's domestic retail banking industry.

Increase in Operating Risk

The number of indeterminate factors influencing the functioning of China's economy and finances continues to increase. The operating environment is very complex. Operating risk, policy risk, industry-related risk, and interest- and exchange-rate risk are all on the rise. Operating in compliance with regulations means facing serious challenges. The social environment includes a daily possibility of unethical behavior on the part of employees that involves unauthorized transfer of funds. Over recent years and particularly in the last two years, tremendous increases in the personal wealth of some people brought on by stock market appreciation has had an impact on the thinking of bank employees. "Ethical risk" is at a heightened level as a result. At the same time, loan portfolios are increasing dramatically with the need for funding at all levels—if internal controls at a bank are inadequate, and funds are not available when needed, serious consequences can result.

A second major source of risk is that involved in retail loans. Collateral for those loans is based on pricing that may face a downturn in China, along with adjustments in world real estate prices, despite the hope that those prices will stabilize. This will inevitably lead to uncertainties in the retail loan business of banks. The US subprime crisis has taught us a very incisive lesson: we must operate on a stable and conservative basis and take precautions in time. We must control the personal loan risk level of our banks. In addition, even as credit card use is increasing rapidly, there is a commensurate rise in defaulting on credit card payments. We cannot slacken in efforts to improve credit card management and raise the quality of performance in that area. Another risk area lies in evaluating the accurate risk levels of different types of wealth management products. Client account managers must firmly grasp the potential problems. As products proliferate related to stock market and currency trading, their risk structure may not be easy for customers to fully understand. Under the impact of a negative financial event, poor risk management can create serious losses for the customer. The fourth risk is the problem of dealing with what is called "counter pressure" in China, or the press of people who need servicing. Along with economic development, customer demands on the quality and variety of financial services is increasing. As this counter pressure increases, it is already common to have systems whereby clients wait in line after taking a number, but these systems have incurred negative feedback. Retail banking requires accommodating customers and increasing their satisfaction, but this too brings challenges to bank management. Finally, policy-related risks are increasing. New investment management products continue to be created, requiring that banks set up ever new "firewalls" against all the kinds of risk involved. One of these involves the risk of laundering money, since investment management-type products incubate a large risk of this sort. We must be very aware that we are navigating across minefields when we try to satisfy the financial needs of high networth customers.

Internal Problems

Apart from external competition and risk factors, factors intrinsic to Chinese banks are increasingly restraining the development of commercial banking in China.

The similarity among products in China, the relative weakness in innovative capacity, and the lack of creativity is the first factor. The primary benefit of core competitiveness is often lost due to lack of innovation in types of assets and risk management business.

Second, insufficient "service consciousness" in China, and the inability to sell to the demands of the retail banking market, is another factor. All kinds of business processes and sales systems need to be reconfigured, from distribution channels to customer relations to point of sales. The entire chain needs to be addressed.

Third, the relatively backwards technology in terms of providing services in China is another issue. Computerized systems are insufficient, including all kinds of hardware and software; even the level of automation is relatively low.

Fourth, there is an outdated evaluation system for bank performance that is based on deposits as the main indicator. This restrains the overall development of retail banking in China.

Fifth, human resources are insufficiently developed in retail banking, with product and customer managers in extremely short supply. Banks lack adequate training programs for managers. Many aspects are critical, including selling methods, and professional expertise. The lack of training is serious enough that a large number of valuable individual customers lack effective management.

Raising International Competitiveness

China's retail banking business has accomplished extremely fast growth in the short space of a dozen or more years, displaying a historic leap over other stages of development, yet compared to developed countries, it still operates on a minor scale. Profits from retail banking and its percentage of business volume are still low compared to commercial banking as a whole. China's retail banking industry contains vast market potential, and at the same time faces huge challenges and fierce competition. In order to raise the international competitiveness, and realize a leap in growth, China's banks must understand and firmly grasp the principles of modern commercial banking. They must actively rely on the experience of international banks, must accelerate their reforms, and in all ways strengthen the capacity for growth.

Taking the phrase "great retail growth" as the guiding principle, China's banks must create new systems for the retail banking industry. This concept is full of implications and ramifications. In general, it means breaking through barriers between product lines, raising awareness of the value of the customer, and reorganizing the structure of resources. China's banks must stride out of the old box of "deposits, loans, and exchange business." They must make "results" the core goal. With a finer segmentation of the market, responsibilities need to be defined on the basis of the type of customers that are being targeted. Products can then be organized to address the proper management of their affairs, whether it is estate planning, tax planning, asset management, or other services. If it is beneficial to the main enterprise, then it can be rolled out as a service.

Banks need to break through the current profit structure, or the way in which groups are evaluated. The loyalty of the customer must be the key objective, so that the system can be in alignment with the goal of creating value for the customer. A retail banking system provides all different kinds of products that frequently come from different business lines and different profit centers. Since at present domestic banks in China have not yet formed a flattened structure of product or business lines, financial services can only be provided to the customer's satisfaction if different departments effectively reorganize their structures. No matter which department the product is from, the product is coming from the same bank. If the department cannot break through a fragmented profit structure, then the customer will not receive the highest degree of value. Also, banks must break through the traditional channels in the network. By making the product itself the medium, they must completely reorganize the structure of resources. Technology is useful in this regard: telephone and Internet channels are becoming more helpful by the day. A highly developed retail banking services system is inseparable from a well-functioning and advanced information network. UBS, Credit Suisse, Deutsche Bundesbank, Citibank, and HSBC, all have amply proven this in their own experience of growth. Only by breaking out of the traditional reliance on the physical network of banking locations can all the departments in a bank, all the resources, and all the channels form a legitimate service system. Only then can retail banking truly manifest fast and stable growth.

China's banks must raise retail banking to a new level of professional service. Retail banking is a service industry that provides such things to society as financing, payments, information, risk management, and so on, and therefore competition between banks is in fact competition between levels of service. The quality and efficiency of service is an important indicator in measuring the capacity of a bank to survive and grow. At present, the domestic retail banking market in China is witnessing great diversification, with ever more intense competition. Only by improving the quality of service can we participate in the development of society and the economy as a whole, and, at the same time, win greater room to operate in international competition.

Our first task is to be innovative in product development. Since the late 1980s, the international banking industry gradually transitioned to being a full-services banking system. Financial products are diversified on behalf of customer needs but integrated within a bank's overall structure. Due to the limitations of China's recent history and actual experience, its domestic banks have not yet accommodated customer needs. Only by changing this situation as fast as possible can higher quality service be provided to clients.

Our second task is to open up channels or delivery mechanisms of financial services; for example, via telephone and the Internet. Statistics show that, compared to traditional banking services, telephone banking can lower costs by 50%, while the Internet can lower costs by 88%. High-tech measures that lower costs make banks more able to provide diversified services to a wider range of customers on a broader basis. While domestic banks continue to expand their physical networks, they should be taking steps to expand their telephone, mobile telephone, and online banking services, as well as accelerating a diversification of delivery structure.

Our third task is to reform the network. This means redrawing the business model of network locations, transforming the traditional system of simply taking in deposits and handing out payments by turning the locations into profit centers and product sales centers with "consultants" rather than "tellers."

China's banks must improve the "team." Customers have ever-higher demands on banks, and financial products are ever more complex. The quality of bank employees and in particular client managers needs to be correspondingly higher. Domestic banks should strengthen training of all kinds, improve the professional quality of employees, and at the same time actively prepare a team of product managers and a professional team of investment advisors.

Management is central to the growth of a bank. Without starting from forward thinking and effective management, it is useless to talk about major advances in China's retail banking business. The experience of modern international banks demonstrates that only by emphasizing better management can the business have the kind of impetus that propels it forward to sustained growth. Domestic banks should actively plan to match the levels of international banking standards. They should focus on their own shortcomings and start with domestic aspects of organization, mechanisms, technology, and so on, then press on by advancing the bank's internationalization.

Banks must reform their organizational structure. A bank's organizational structure must be aligned with and in service to the mission of the bank. As a bank changes its market positioning, it must effect corresponding changes in its organizational structure. When a bank primarily exists to serve as a financing intermediary, its basic business is to attract deposits and issue loans and the basic demands on management are to keep assets and liabilities in balance. The bank's organizational structure depends on a secure ratio of assets and liabilities, on efficiency, and on liquidity. After a bank becomes a financial intermediary dealing in wealth management, management becomes concerned with more than merely the ratio of assets to liabilities. The change brings with it new questions of how the bank will produce, purchase, and sell investment-type products. The process is different and requires a different organizational structure from that necessary to keep assets and liabilities in balance. It requires reformulating the organizational structure. New requirements in growing a retail banking business may include VIP rooms, wealth management centers, private banking services, and so on, all of which must appear in response to new kinds of demand.

Banks must create a responsive set of management mechanisms. In assessing these mechanisms, domestic banks must adopt new asset allocation systems, integrating ideas about short term profit levels and long-term profit potentials, integrating quality control and scale of operations, integrating concepts of income and risk, gradually implementing concepts of a return on capital that allows adjustment of risk as the core assessment system. Banks should establish systems that encourage managers to make decisions on the basis of stable long-term return on investment, and not merely on short-term expansion of immediate business. They should adopt environments that are conducive to creativity, that allow for innovation in all processes, that strengthen rewards for innovation, and that in all ways promote and support the active quality of innovation.

Banks must create new customer relations systems. The growth of retail banking puts new demands on the flow of services, and creating new customer relations systems has already become an urgent task. In the past, when taking in savings deposits was the main task of a bank, disparities in wealth among customers were minor, need for investment advice was low, and levels of acceptable risk were not a major consideration. With the growth of a middle class in China, customer needs are diversifying. Customer relations systems must now be adjusted to reflect the fact that the customer is the central focus of operations. From being a monolithic system that treated all customers the same, Chinese banks now need to develop professional, multilayered systems that segment customers with a great degree of granularity and that guarantee that every client gets individualized service. The bank can no longer be a passive organization that accommodates simple needs. It must be able to provide lifelong and yet intermittent service to a variety of customers and needs, and, at each contact point, to provide customers with comprehensive services relating to all kinds of investment products.

Banks must raise the level of the technology employed by management. Modern retail banking is inseparable from advanced management tools; technology is a primary support in the business. Domestic banks must grasp the most up-to-date technological measures. Starting from a high point, they must adopt and further develop tools for managing assets and liabilities, tools for pricing the internal circulation of funds, tools for customer relations management, tools for effective accounting systems, and so on.

All of these various information systems must be integrated. Only through the strong and effective support of modern systems can banks accurately calculate the complex quantitative relationships among profit, risk, and business volume. Only then can they quantify and separate out different kinds of risk, and thereby strengthen the accuracy and scientific nature of management policies. Only then can they raise the operational level of management of the bank.

SECTION 3

CAPITAL MARKETS

CHAPTER 13

Shanghai Stock Exchange:
History and Prospects

Zhou Qinye

Executive Vice-President, Shanghai Stock Exchange

The creation of the Shanghai Stock Exchange was quite controversial. In the summer of 1985, a Nobel prize-winning economist named James Tobin declared at an international conference on China's economic policies, "China should not be setting up stock markets within the next 20 years." This opinion was shared by many experts at that time. Five years later, China formally established the Shanghai Stock Exchange on December 19, 1990, but this did not mean that people's opinions were united on the subject. For quite some time, many Chinese, as well as foreign economists, felt strongly that, "What China needs at present is not an organization like a New York Stock Exchange or a Chicago Commodities Exchange." In recent years, through actual experience, people have gradually begun to appreciate the important role that stock markets play in China's economy.

The official resumption of a securities market in China, symbolized by the establishment of the Shanghai Stock Exchange in 1990, was without doubt one of the greatest revolutions in the realm of finance since the founding of New China. In the past 17 years, the Shanghai Stock Exchange has made steady progress despite experiencing several setbacks. By September 30, 2007, the Exchange had 856 listed companies, with a market capitalization of US$3.2476 trillion, which ranked it second in Asia and sixth in the world. At the same time, the total transaction volume was as high as US$3.0198 trillion, second in Asia and seventh in the world. The Shanghai Stock Exchange has become the largest emerging market in the world and one of its most active. It has also become an indispensable component of China's socialist market economy, not only in alleviating the need for sources of funding, but also in improving the allocation of market resources, promoting systemic change in enterprises, and furthering reform of the overall financial system. It has played an extremely important role to the extent that it has been able to spur faster and better growth of the national economy.

The Exchange was born in the midst of controversy, however, and continued to grow in the midst of ongoing debate. As an entity that accompanied a wholesale transformation in the Chinese economy, it played a key role in "deepening" China's financial system. It is worthwhile to summarize what happened in the past, from today's perspective, as well as to look ahead to the future.

HISTORY OF THE SHANGHAI STOCK EXCHANGE

The Shanghai Stock Exchange was the product of reforms during a very specific period in China's history. Its development proceeded in tandem with a rise in the understanding and appreciation of the Chinese government for stock markets. A prerequisite to the birth of the Exchange was a transformation in thinking and a breakthrough in theory that mainly relied on the active leadership of the government. This came at a time when a highly centralized planned economy system was transitioning to a socialist market economy system, under very specific conditions. Looked at strategically, from an overall perspective, the many discussions of the Chinese Communist Party's National People's Congresses and the core documents passed by the government helped to dispel various concerns of society in general about starting capital markets in China. They served to unify an understanding about stock markets and they created the basic political and systemic environments in which the creation of the Shanghai Stock Exchange could go forward.

The Chinese Communist Party's thirteenth National People's Congress was held in 1987, and among other things clarified that stock and bond markets were the necessary product of marketization reforms. The Congress not only permitted, but encouraged the work of creating test sites for restructuring of certain state-owned enterprises (SOEs), and it put an end to the debate about whether or not China should have a corporate or share-holding system and whether or not a share-holding system was an important part of enterprise reform. The process laid the theoretical basis, or thought process, for the birth of stock markets in China. Given this background, off-board over-the-counter (OTC) trading received encouragement, and by December 1990, there were more than thirty different shares being traded in the OTC market in Shanghai. The traded amount exceeded US$400 million, making it the largest exchange market in China. On December 19, 1990, the Shanghai Stock Exchange was formally established. At its inception, it included a mere eight listed companies, with company size and share trading volume that was miniscule. Moreover, the location as well as investors of listed companies in the market displayed classic regional market characteristics.

The fourteenth National People's Congress of the Chinese Communist Party was held in 1992. This Congress put forth the reform goal of setting up a socialist market economy system. In 1994, the third Plenary Session of the fourteenth National People's Congress confirmed that the establishment of a stock market played an important role in setting up a socialist market economy system, and clarified that the core element in SOE reform was setting up modern enterprise systems through restructuring of assets. These assertions put an end to the debate going on in society about whether or not the stock markets should be closed down. They created a positive environment for further development of the stock markets in terms of both policy and systems. The number of listed companies at the Shanghai Stock Exchange rose swiftly after that, and the size of the market expanded as well. During this period, the Shanghai Stock Exchange began to take in listed companies from other provinces around the country, and investors were more widely distributed so that a market serving the entire country gradually began to coalesce.

The fifteenth National People's Congress of the Chinese Communist Party was held in 1997, at which it was clearly stated that developing capital markets was beneficial to nurturing and strengthening a socialist market economy system. The fourth Plenary Session of the fifteenth National People's Congress, in 1999, emphasized that the country should, "fundamentally complete strategic restructurings of Enterprises, to form a rational state-owned economic structure with a relatively complete modern enterprise system...." The reform of SOEs deepened to a stage that unified the idea of a "modern enterprise system" and a "strategic restructuring of state-owned assets."

At the same time, the main mode of strategic restructuring of state-owned assets was determined to be "using the capital markets as the stage, and using listing of companies as the core." Against this backdrop, the "Securities Law" was formally implemented on July 1, 1999, finally confirming in a legal manner the standing of the stock markets in the Chinese market economy system.

The sixteenth National People's Congress of the Chinese Communist Party was held in 2002, which called for "further pushing forward the reform and opening up of capital markets, and furthering their stable development." The Third Plenary Session of the Sixteenth National People's Congress, in 2003, raised the call to "vigorously develop capital markets and other factor markets." The State Council issued an "Opinion" in 2004, called, "Various Opinions Regarding Promoting Reform and the Opening up of Capital Markets and their Stable Development," which stated in more concrete terms the desired directions and goals. By that time, Chinese capital markets had already been elevated to the status of a strategic component of the national economy. This brought about a conceptual leap in society at large from "public knowledge" to "public plan." The Shanghai Stock Exchange was then able to mobilize a series of fundamental systemic initiatives that were best represented by the so-called "share conversion reform." It also began to implement Qualified Foreign Institutional Investors (QFII), Qualified Domestic Institutional Investor (QDII), and other systemic "Opening" measures.

The seventeenth National People's Congress of the Chinese Communist Party was held in 2007, and clearly pointed the way toward strengthening and improving financial regulation, improving the structure of the capital markets, increasing the ratio of direct funding via various channels, and improving the competitiveness of the securities industry. This Congress went further in declaring to the public that the main task of China's capital markets from this time onward was to improve market structures and to enhance the international competitiveness of the securities industry. Creativity and vigor were to be applied to this effort. In this new, current period, the tasks before the Shanghai Stock Exchange include conceptual innovation, systemic innovation, and innovation of financial instruments. The key element in terms of conceptual innovation is to create a new understanding of the position and role of the Shanghai Stock Exchange in China's economic development, of its role in China's future financial system, and of its role in international capital markets. The aim is for it to become an important component of international capital markets. A conceptual innovation must precede and then continue in concert with innovation of systems and instruments. Creating the systems and the tools are the concrete manifestation of the newly created stock markets. They are steps to achieving the marketization and the internationalization of China's stock markets.

THE SHANGHAI STOCK EXCHANGE TODAY

For the past 17 years, the Shanghai Stock Exchange has traveled a path that involved both top-down and bottom-up change. Government-directed and self-initiated marketization reforms have worked together in allowing the Exchange to focus on lowering transaction costs and raising market efficiencies. Through reform and innovation, the Exchange has been able to resolve some historical questions and negative impressions. Reforms have allowed the Exchange to construct a form of market that has the potential to be efficient, transparent, and open. They have laid an excellent foundation for further growth. The most important task of the Shanghai Stock Exchange is to set up, cultivate, and grow China's main board market. One core part of this is to form a blue-chip market that represents the main body of the Chinese economy. Before 2006, however, the market transaction volume of the entire Shanghai Stock Exchange did not reach US$100 billion. The market capitalization of just one company in the United States, General Electric, was US$377.4 billion. A small securities market was clearly not going to be able to handle the needs of a growing Chinese economy. Its capacities were even less able to compete in the international arena, to the point that such Chinese companies as China Life, Semiconductor Manufacturing International Corporation, and China Power, major companies in key national industries and companies with a certain degree of monopoly power, chose to be listed overseas.

Faced with the urgent need to strengthen competitiveness, the Shanghai Stock Exchange cooperated with relevant government authorities in actively promoting the share conversion reform, distribution system reform, market-driven merger and acquisition and restructuring; introducing management share incentives, as well as energetically courting institutional investors. Through these reforms and efforts, the Exchange substantially lowered the implicit costs of listing on the Exchange and the operating costs of post-listing.

TABLE 13.1 Partial statistical data on the Shanghai Stock Market

	1990.12.31	1992.12.31	1994.12.31	2000.12.31	2005.12.31	2007 (to 9/.30)
No. of listed companies	8	29	162	548	824	856
Total market value (US$ hundred millions)	3.70	98.61	380.80	3,625.07	3,298.93	32,476.00
Value of tradable shares (US 00m)	1.26	10.04	60.76	1,052.13	859.20	7,195.07
No. of investors (tens of thousands)	11	111	574	2,958	3,856	4,873
Total issued amount (hundred million shares)	1.76	13.5	16.6	85.2	9.63	251.8
Total financing amount, (US$ hundred millions)	0.35	31.81	4.79	80.03	3.80	362.93
Volume of trading (hundred million shares)	–	6.39	340.6	2,105	3,800	19,693
Total traded value (US$ 00m)	–	14.59	412.67	3,644.67	2,453.20	30,198.40

Source: Shanghai Stock Exchange monthly statistical reports.

After this, the Industrial and Commercial Bank of China (ICBC), China Air, China Shenhua, and other large, high-quality blue-chip enterprises approached the Shanghai Exchange to be listed. This not only expanded the size of Shanghai's market, but greatly enhanced the value of investing in the market. It made the market more vibrant for ordinary investors, and helped divert funds from savings deposits to investments. See Table 13.1 for a summary of progress from 1990 to 2007.

New Financial Products

The financial instruments available on the Shanghai Stock Exchange remain too limited. In addition to stocks and government bonds, the Exchange trades funds, convertible bonds and other new products, but the available choice of investment products has not fundamentally improved and the paucity of financial instruments indirectly increases transaction risk and transaction costs for investors. In light of the clear gap between China's and international markets, the Shanghai Stock Exchange's products right now still mainly depend on international products already existing in the international market, after they are adapted to China's national conditions. To this end, in recent years, the Exchange has successfully put out Exchange Traded Funds (ETF) and warrants.

The Shanghai Stock Exchange officially released ETF products in 2004, and by now there are already the 50 ETF, dividends ETF, and 180 ETF. Since 2007, up to September 30, the trading volume in ETF was US$10.996 billion, ranking fourteenth in the world. The Shanghai Stock Exchange started trading in warrants in 2005, and the market has taken off rapidly. In 2007 alone, up to September 30, the transaction volume totaled US$564.995 billion.

Regulatory Measures, Market Transparency

Three main problems have plagued the Shanghai market: fraudulent financial accounting of listed companies, securities companies that siphon customers' margin accounts for the purpose of trading them on their own account, and market price manipulation. Before 2006, although the nation's overall economy continually grew at around 9%, stock market indexes kept going down. One key reason was the existence of the above problems. Investors had to spend undue time and energy looking for legitimate trades, and avoiding opportunistic behavior. This greatly increased market transaction costs, and led to a large number of investors leaving the securities market.

For this reason, the Shanghai Stock Exchange has focused on the core issue of information disclosure, on how to deal with unclear, inadequately detailed or even doubtful information, and how to deal in a timely way with the unfortunate or even illegal behavior of listed companies. It successfully applied the use of expandable business report language (EBRL) to listed company information disclosure, increasing the information transparency of listed companies.

The Shanghai Stock Exchange has made use of the market to force listed companies to improve their corporate governance structures; it has improved the quality of listed companies, strengthened annual review of securities companies and their comprehensive governance, improved monthly report systems, and so on. Overall, it has improved the financial risk regulatory measures governing securities companies. The Shanghai Stock Exchange has also researched and set up real-time control systems for analytical tools and advance warning systems. It has supplied technical measures for the front-line regulators in the secondary market for discovering and dealing with insider trading, price manipulation, and other illegal behavior. It has effectively improved market order.

Opening to the Outside

Growing China's securities markets must be done with a strategic view to globalizing, in order to position the markets in the premier ranks of world activity. The "opening to the outside" of Shanghai's market is the most important component of China's financial market system. Globalizing can proceed only as the entire country's financial market system is being built, however. The principle of "prudent opening of China's capital accounts in a gradual manner" determines the fact that Shanghai too must follow a gradual process of opening.

In November of 2001, the Shanghai Stock Exchange allowed foreign-invested shareholding companies that met required conditions to apply for listing in Shanghai. In 2002, the Exchange released "Provisional Regulations on Special Membership of Overseas Members." This allowed the representative offices of overseas-invested securities organizations to become special members of the Shanghai Stock Exchange. In December 2002, the Exchange implemented a QFII system. The Exchange signed cooperative understanding memoranda with 27 overseas stock exchanges including NASDAQ, London, Hong Kong, and others. On October 16, 2006, the Shanghai Stock Exchange was selected to be a member of the Board of Directors of the World Federation of Exchanges at its forty-sixth annual meeting.

FUTURE PROSPECTS

The Chinese economy's rapid growth has relied on high investment in the 30 years since the start of Reform and Opening, but financial systems have not yet played a compelling role in that investment. As early as 1973, two economics professors at Stanford University, Ronald I. McKinnon and E. S. Shaw, advocated "financial liberalization and deepening" as growth-enhancing policies for developing countries. They pointed out that "financial repression" is a substantial barrier to successful economic development. With regard to the overall economic backdrop, China is transitioning from using a centrally planned economy model to using a market economy model. This requires that Chinese financial systems persist in this characteristic called "deepening." As McKinnon and others pointed out, the fashioning of the system is more critical to economic growth than simply putting in more investment.

China currently uses banks as the main source of funding. This relatively traditional financing mode harbors and conceals cumulative financial risk, and severely obstructs any synergistic joining of financial and industrial capital. The major task of restructuring China's industrial structure is made far more difficult as a result. In order to improve China's financial structure in a fundamental way, it will be necessary to speed up the development of the country's securities markets. Financial "deepening" has already become one of the most important questions facing the country, and the "deepening" of the securities markets is a subject of urgent concern in that process. Without deepening of markets, it will be impossible for them to mature and grow. An advanced securities market of sufficient size will become a powerful tool for propelling the sustained healthy growth of China's economy.

To this end, the Shanghai Stock Exchange intends to gradually become an international market that is able to cultivate world-class outstanding Chinese enterprises. Future reforms will start with the strategic aim of upgrading economic production and encouraging sustainable growth. The starting point will be lowering transaction costs and improving market efficiencies.

FINANCING WORLD-CLASS ENTERPRISES

The history of economic development in the world makes it clear that outstanding enterprises do not rely on slow self-accumulation of capital, but are realized through mergers and acquisitions (M&As). Securities markets are an indispensable platform in that process.

Several blue-chip shares are already traded on the Shanghai Exchange, such as the Bank of China (BOC), Sinopec Corporation, and China Life, but generally speaking, the large blue chips are rare and inadequately represent their entire industries. As a result, they do not truly reflect the trends of the national economy. We believe that within three to five years, outstanding companies and industries with relatively positive prospects will be able to source abundant funds on the Shanghai Stock Exchange. This will come with improvement in market mechanisms for restructuring companies, and merging with and acquiring existing companies. This in turn will encourage the formation of improved mechanisms for allocating resources. Transaction costs of resource allocation should fall substantially. By allowing capital to flow rationally, superior companies should be able to become world-class enterprises. This depends specifically on the outcome of the following work.

First, it depends on the creation of market-driven financing systems. Administrative controls currently interfere with too many links in the chain of financing. The application and approval process is overly complex and greatly increases transaction costs of getting funding. In the next stages, we need to go further in developing such entities as intermediary institutions and professional institutional investors. These will serve the function of screening companies that want to issue securities, and thereby contribute to greater efficiencies.

Second, it depends on improvement in delisting mechanisms. In 2001, the Shanghai Stock Exchange set up a system for delisting companies on the exchange. Under current rules and regulations, the prerequisite conditions for temporarily halting trading, resuming trading, and for complete delisting relating to whether or not a profit and loss statement shows a profit. This provides a great incentive to falsify accounts if a company is in danger of being delisted. In the next period, it will be necessary to increase the range of conditions under which a company may be delisted, and to adhere rigorously to the standards that are set.

Third, it depends on the development of the market for M&As. Setting up a standardized market for listed companies to conduct M&As should allow superior Chinese enterprises to resist the need to take in foreign ownership in order to grow. Mechanisms include lowering resource allocation transaction costs of listed companies, encouraging listed companies to restructure and merge and acquire in a way that is beneficial to long-term growth, accomplishing structural adjustments and upgrading industries. The goal is to make it easier for Chinese companies that are facing market competition and funding constraints to withstand foreign takeovers.

Fourth, it depends on improvement in the transparency of listed companies. The effectiveness and the authority of information disclosure regulations of the Shanghai Stock Exchange have already markedly improved. The next steps include improving the electronic platform for information disclosure, improving the timeliness of information disclosure, promoting an index of corporate governance, standardizing the "internal mechanisms" utilized by listed companies, and reducing "hidden information" and "hidden actions" undertaken in the course of opportunistic behavior. The goal is to reduce the time and effort investors have to put into looking for valid information, to reduce opportunistic behavior in the markets overall, and to create a better environment for market efficiencies.

THE BOND MARKET

Right now, the Shanghai Stock Exchange deals mainly in stocks. The bond market is relatively stagnant, and such bonds as are traded are dominated by government bonds. Corporate bonds are rare. This unbalanced structure is not conducive to the growth of the Shanghai Stock Exchange, and it also cannot bring along growth in other markets such as currency markets. We believe that in another five years or so, along with reforms and improvement in bond issuing systems, and with increasing awareness of the importance of bond markets by the government, bond transaction costs will substantially decline and the bond market component of the Shanghai Stock Exchange will grow tremendously. It will form an effective balance to the shares market. The Shanghai Stock Exchange intends to exert efforts to that end in the following three respects.

First, it intends to form a benchmark yield curve. A benchmark yield curve is the basic tool for analyzing interest rate trends and for setting prices in capital markets. The Chinese bond market is fragmented and liquidity is too low, however, to create a legitimate and effective yield curve in China. Prices of transactions outside the exchanges don't make a true market, and there are imbalances in supply and demand of long-term products. All of this makes it impossible for a yield curve to assist in setting market prices. The next step will be for the Shanghai Stock Exchange to promote Chinese government bonds as the standard criterion for a price-setting mechanism, and thereby to start to form a true benchmark yield curve in the country.

Second, it intends to give more weight to the development of a corporate bond market. There are only a few convertible bonds in the Shanghai Stock Exchange. Up to September 30, 2007, the total amount of financing that can be truly considered corporate bonds was US$388 million. Other bond market totals are even smaller, dramatically lower than bond-funding amounts in developed countries. Our next steps are to put time and effort into developing corporate bond markets. In doing this, the key will be to develop methods of issuing bonds that are market-driven.

Third, it intends to trade futures and other products. The Shanghai Stock Exchange has already created convertible bonds on an experimental basis. Once conditions are suitable, the next step is to put out treasury bond futures and other bond futures, and then finally to put out bond options. The emphasis will be on medium- and long-term options, and medium- and long-term bond futures. The goal in this is to improve the term structure and the varieties of derivative bond products on the Exchange, in order to hedge risk for investors and to lower transaction costs in the market.

GOING INTERNATIONAL

Although foreign-invested Chinese enterprises are already listed on the Shanghai Stock Exchange, and although there are joint venture securities companies and QFII, in general, it should be said that the Shanghai Stock Exchange is still a relatively closed market. Those foreign financial institutions that have set up subsidiaries in China are related to the "services component" of WTO stipulations, while QFII and QDII systems are methods requiring administrative application and approval, and do not go beyond the limits set by Line Eight Countries in the IMF. To date, none of the "opening up" in the market involves opening up capital accounts in international payments. Nonetheless, we believe that within five to 10 years, perhaps longer, the Shanghai Stock Exchange will undertake a greater degree of integration with international capital markets, and actively participate in competition in international capital markets. This will be in line with liberalizing Chinese interest rates, with reforms in foreign exchange management, and with the opening up of capital accounts under international payments.

At present, the Shanghai Stock Exchanges is not able to accept applications for listing from enterprises outside China's borders. This is in stark contrast to the way in which exchanges of other countries are coming to China to "snatch" the resources of the most outstanding Chinese companies to list on their markets. In the future, when capital accounts in international payments are opened, the Shanghai Securities Exchange will actively create conditions that allow it to receive applications for listing from foreign enterprises. It will gradually open up to enterprises from around the globe.

The Shanghai Stock Exchange needs not only more listed companies, but also more diverse investors and in particular overseas investors. The Tokyo Stock Exchange has a very large market capitalization, but cannot be put in the same category as New York and London due to the relative uniformity of its listed companies and its investors. Because of this, under conditions allowed for by the financial markets, the Shanghai Stock Exchange intends to adopt cost-lowering measures that allow more overseas capital to flow into the Shanghai markets, and thereby improve the breadth and depth of the overall market.

In the future, when the RMB achieves free convertibility under capital accounts and is internationalized, the Shanghai Stock Exchange will, at an appropriate time, consider issuing RMB-denominated foreign bonds. This will be done in order to open China's domestic bond market to foreign institutions that seek funding, and to promote Shanghai as a new offshore securities market.

CHAPTER 14

China's Securities Companies: Growth and Prospects

Wang Dongming

Chairman, CITIC Securities Co., Ltd

With the growth in capital markets over the past 20 years, China's securities companies have developed into entities that are now able to propel further growth. The Shenzhen Special Economic Zone Securities Company was established in 1985 as the first sign that securities companies had stepped onto the stage of the Chinese economy. By the end of 2007, there were 108 securities companies in China. At end-January 2008, the annual reports of 47 of those showed total net assets of RMB143.5 billion, and net profits of RMB80.7 billion. The industry grew from nothing to a substantial size in a very short time, along with the fast-paced development of the securities markets.

The development of the securities company industry in China can be divided into three general stages: fast initial growth, restructuring and "regularization," and finally the current period of creating effective systems.

FAST INITIAL GROWTH

The appearance of embryonic capital markets and an initial period of rapid growth lasted from 1985 to 1996. In the early 1980s, a number of financial organizations engaging in securities began to appear in China, such as trust and investment companies and securities companies. There were no stringent controls on market entry in this early period, and banks, trust companies, and other players competed head to head. The role of "securities company" was at the outset played by such entities as the China International Trust and Investment Company (CITIC) and the Bank of China (BOC). After the securities markets were formally opened in the early 1990s with the establishment of the Shanghai Stock Exchange and the Shenzhen Stock Exchange, securities companies began to proliferate.

In terms of industry structure, the business had three distinct layers at the time: nationally established securities companies, regional companies, and divisions of organizations that dealt in non-banking financial services but now also incorporated securities. The national-level companies included such large entities as Huaxia, Nanfang, Guotai, Haitong, and a few others. The regional companies included organizations directly under the provincial and municipal branches of the People's Bank of China (PBC) and the Ministry of Finance, set up specifically to deal in securities. The last category included securities departments of non-banking and finance organizations such as trust and investment companies and leasing companies.

At this stage of the industry's development, lack of an adequate legal framework and systems caused the industry to suffer from irregular practices. Since such laws as the Company Law were not suited to the rapid development of the capital markets, violations by both securities companies and listed companies could not be prosecuted due to unclear legal grounds. Securities companies and listed companies worked together to engage in price manipulation, as well as insider trading, and there was a strongly opportunistic and illicit flavor to the market.

By the end of 1996, there were more than 430 securities companies and security-dealing entities, with more than 2,600 branch offices in their networks. Their total asset value came up to RMB160 billion, with average asset value per entity of RMB372 million. Average net assets per entity were less than RMB50 million, and average capital held by each entity was a mere RMB20 million.

RESTRUCTURING

Securities markets in China were restructured and "regularized" during the period from 1997 to 2004. In 1996, with the implementation of a separation between banks and securities businesses, a specialized operation model that separated out banking and securities businesses began to take hold and the securities industry was substantially reorganized. The many "trust and investment companies" under the direct supervision of branch offices of commercial banks were closed down. Among banks, only the trust and investment companies under the jurisdiction of the headquarters of the four state-owned banks were now allowed to deal in securities. Some securities companies now were able to grow very quickly through mergers with the reorganized securities departments of former trust and investment companies. As a result, the situation now began to include securities companies operating solely in securities, and trust and investment companies, finance companies, and leasing companies operating securities as part of their business.

The Securities Law was promulgated and began to be implemented in 1999. This further impelled the large-scale restructuring and standardization of the securities industry. The Securities Law clearly stipulated regulation that differentiated between securities firms operating as brokerages and those that were part of "comprehensive" financial institutions. This led to an enthusiasm for increasing the assets of securities companies by issuing shares. Some very large securities companies were born as a result, that had initially been made up of reorganized trust and investment companies. "Yin He Securities" became the largest securities company at that time, formed by merging the securities companies formerly under the four large state-owned banks and the five trust and investment companies under the People's Insurance Company. After reorganizing, the industry began to consolidate, both regionally and as an industry.

By the end of 1999, there were 96 companies engaged exclusively in securities business, there were 243 trust and investment companies, 69 financing companies, and 16 financing and leasing companies, as well as a total of 2,440 sales outlets dealing in securities. The different kinds of organizations differed greatly in size. The registered capital of national securities companies exceeded RMB1 billion, while that of small entities was a mere RMB10 million. The scale of regional trust and investment and finance companies was generally quite small, with most having just a few sales outlets. National securities companies had subsidiaries in each large city and their network extended throughout the country. Small and medium-sized (SME) securities companies mainly had networks in their own regions, in cities under the direct jurisdiction of their headquarter location. The most densely covered areas were Shanghai and Shenzhen. The business structure of all the securities companies was similar, with the three traditional lines of business, namely brokerage, operating as a dealer, and underwriting, contributing respectively 40%, 28%, and 18% of profits. Inadequate capital and insufficient supply and demand in the system constrained the development of such new businesses as options and swaps.

After the Securities Law was put into effect, one began to see further merging and consolidating in the industry as large securities companies with real strength absorbed those that were not doing well. The success of any SME companies that were not merged could be attributed to their unique business services. Overall, a gradual consolidation began in the industry. In 1998, the top six firms held 52% of the market in underwriting business; they held 50% of the market in the brokerage business. By 2002, these percentages had gone to 76% and 56%.

Although the underpinning of a legal structure now supported the industry, the markets did not emerge from their depressed state. Because of ongoing and prevalent practices such as operating outside acceptable standards of financial accounting, which played havoc with accounts, trust and investment companies in the country were "restructured" a number of times, and a great number were unable to stay in business and had to be shut down. The management and operations of securities companies were highly "irregular" in terms of mingling funds in particular. Starting from 2001, China experienced three years of bear markets, and during this period, the illegal activities of some securities firms were exposed. Activities included, for example, transferring the money in customers' margin accounts for use of the securities companies themselves. The entire securities industry faced loss of public confidence and serious financial losses as a result.

WEEDING OUT PERIOD (FROM 2005)

A very important systemic change occurred in the Chinese financial markets in 2005. It was called share conversion reform. Before share conversion reform, state-owned shares were not tradable. The shares of listed companies were divided into two types: those that were tradable and those that were not. This led to governance problems in listed companies since the same shares did not enjoy the same rights. The successful implementation of the share conversion reform resolved a problem that had existed for years and that had obstructed the growth of the A-share market. It allowed China's securities markets to enter upon a whole new stage of development.

Reform was implemented gradually. Regulatory authorities allowed certain newly reconstituted innovation-type securities companies to start up in 2004. In 2005, authorities determined the qualifications for normalization-type securities companies and the parameters within which they would be allowed to do business. The work of differentiating among all types of securities companies and regulating appropriately then began. In July of 2005, China's Securities Regulation Commission passed "Measures on Comprehensive Governance Work Regarding Securities Companies," which set forth the basic conceptual framework for the way in which securities com panies were to operate. In the process of moderating the amount of risk in the securities industry, authorities were enabled to administer regulatory controls according to type, and to support high-quality securities companies. From the second half of 2005 until the first half of 2006, a series of new laws were passed regarding securities dealers, government repo bond buyers, underwriters, and other such important parts of the business. Rules and regulations regarding securities companies' risk control, risk management, net asset calculations, and so on were formulated at an accelerated pace.

Along with overall advances made in reviewing and examining two types of securities companies, those geared for "innovation" and those geared for "normalization," the two great problems facing the industry now became innovating and restructuring. Segmented competition among securities companies became far more fierce. "Innovation-type" securities companies vigorously promoted all kinds of innovative products. "Normalization-type" securities companies faced tremendous historical burdens; often in dire operational straits, they now focused on reorganizing. The Central Bank and the Securities Regulatory Commission set up a company called "Jian Yin Investment Company," and, together with the China Regulatory Commission Investor's Preservation Fund Company, began a restructuring of such large securities companies as Yin He Securities, CITIC Securities, and others. On completion of the restructuring, these entities re-entered the world in a wholly new incarnation. CITIC Securities, China Merchants Securities, and other innovation-type securities companies increased their size by taking relatively weak securities companies under their own jurisdiction. The restructuring led directly to a further consolidation in the industry. At the end of 2007, the market share of the brokerage business of the top 10 companies approached 60%; the market share of the underwriting business approached 90%. The top 10 securities companies basically controlled all of the market in asset management.

As a result of these actions, the entire industry saw a clear improvement in both asset quality and profitability. In 2006, the total income of 105 securities companies in the industry came up to RMB68.1 billion, with net profit of RMB25.8 billion, and a net profit ratio of 42%. Return on net assets was 4.39%. In terms of capital adequacy, the sum of net capital in 2006 saw a marked increase to RMB93.3 billion.

Brokering, underwriting, and operating as a dealer remained the primary sources of income for securities companies. The percentage of income held by brokerage services in 2007 was 60%. After the completion of the share conversion reform, the underwriting business for initial offering, secondary offering, and share allotments started up again, and underwriting short-term financing bills gradually increased; underwriting income rose to a share of 13%. The innovative-products business of securities companies was soon taking off, and such new businesses as consolidated wealth management products, asset securitization, and short-term financing bills saw quick advances. The new innovation type securities companies were able to enjoy the benefits of first-to-market status as a result. The first comprehensive asset management project was launched by a securities company in March 2005, and by 2007, there were already 26 comprehensive asset management projects, with a total of RMB47 billion of assets under management.

CHALLENGES

After more than a dozen years, China's securities industry has accomplished swift progress, but at the same time it is facing tremendous challenges, which are summarized below.

First, companies are insufficiently competitive and operate on too small a scale. Compared to international investment banks, China's domestic securities companies are relatively small in terms of assets and capital. There is a distinct gap between them and their foreign competitors. At the end of 2006, Merrill Lynch was first among the 10 largest investment banks overseas, with net assets of US$39 billion. China's average net asset value among innovation-style securities firms at the same time was just RMB15.3 billion, which is roughly 3.9% of the Merrill Lynch figure. Merrill Lynch's capital at the same time was US$112.1 billion, while China's innovative-type securities company's average net capital was a mere RMB2.1 billion. The largest securities firm in China, CITIC Securities, has capital of only RMB10.5 billion.

Second, business models are too uniform. China's securities industry uses business models that are too uniform, insufficiently differentiated. Today's international investment banks have broken away from such traditional businesses as securities distribution and under-writing, stock trading and brokering, to achieve a diversified business that includes mergers and alliances (M&As), project financing, venture investing, corporate finance, investment advisory, asset and fund management, asset securitization, financial innovations, and so on, all of which have become the core business of investment banks. Brokerage fees accounted for 74% of investment bank income in the US in the 1960s, but had declined to 11% by 2006. The income from such things as fund [sales], asset management, and capital operation has increased as a percentage of revenue from 15% to 56%. In the past 35 years, operating income in US investment banks has risen by 31 times, but the increase has not come from traditional underwriting and brokerage businesses, but rather from asset management, direct investment and securities investment, and other businesses in which the bank itself takes a position.

China's securities companies, in contrast, concentrate on traditional share underwriting and on brokering and dealer businesses. Income from the brokerage business accounts for more than 60% of total income. The profit sources of most securities companies, their business structure and their organizational structure are basically the same, and income contribution from such innovations as investment advising, and M&As is extremely low. Reliance on the conditions of the secondary market in order to survive makes Chinese companies vulnerable to market volatility. Relative to overseas companies, business models lack stability.

Third, risk management is inadequate. Securities companies are financial organizations that handle risk—handling risk is their fundamental business. Overseas securities companies have erected a framework for excellent risk management and control measures that have already become the foundation of their standard operating procedures. These are intrinsic to their operational concepts and management methods. Risk management operations of US securities companies are a matter of systems engineering. Through effective systemic restraints, most can control risk by undertaking mathematical modeling and estimation; they can predict risk, by carrying out risk forecasting, and using all kinds of derivative products to hedge against and transfer risk. At the same time, by having diversified businesses, they can distribute risk. The subprime mortgage crisis that erupted in the US in August 2007 is one example. During this crisis, the investment bank Goldman Sachs was able to maintain its expected profit, thanks to its excellent level of risk management and its excellent risk-control processes, its quantified risk management indicators. The application of these systems assured that well before the crisis had erupted, the company's internal risk control mechanisms had already started putting out warning signals, allowing the company to avoid huge losses.

In China's domestic securities companies, increasing attention is paid to risk management. There is still a tremendous gap between administrative efficiencies and controls in investment banks abroad, however, and those in China. China's securities companies lack experience in measuring modern risk, they lack electronic technology and tools to manage risk. They particularly lack professionals who are familiar with modern financial risk management, so, again, the standard of China's risk management is far below what it is in the same industry abroad.

Fourth, China's companies face increased competition from both within and outside China. Along with the growing maturation of capital markets in China, domestic securities companies are now facing the double challenge of other financial services industries and international financial behemoths.

In domestic financial markets, after CITIC Securities successfully listed on the market in 2003, many other domestic securities companies completed listing procedures by "borrowing a shell company." The net assets of the securities industry rose swiftly. At the same time, however, the competition that securities companies as a whole are facing from commercial banks and insurance companies continues to mount. At present, the banking industry accounts for over 94% of total assets in China's financial industries, insurance accounts for 4%, and securities is not even 2%. With the trend to engage in comprehensive or integrated management, commercial banks and insurance companies are using all kinds of ways, acquisitions as well as newly established entities, to enter the realm of the securities industry. China's Ping An Insurance Company long ago became a comprehensive financial services group with all the necessary licenses. Since banks and insurance companies are possessed of much greater capital power, broader networks in terms of branch offices, and a more substantial customer base, they have the absolute advantage in competition over relatively poorly capitalized securities companies.

Meanwhile, international investment banks have been increasingly taking root in China, and are already very present with regard to high-end customers and high-end businesses. This has followed the process of opening China's financial services industries to outside participation. For example, in 2007, the name "UBS" frequently appeared in large-scale financing projects for such companies as China Petroleum and Chemical Corporation and China Steel Corporation. International investment banking giants have amassed considerable experience in the areas of cross-border institutional investor services, cross-border financing and M&As, and the development of derivative products and sales. Of necessity, they are going to be pow erful opponents. Although China's securities industry has stringent licensing controls and companies can rest easy for the time being, sooner or later, the day will come when they must face a life-or-death challenge.

CHINA'S SECURITIES INDUSTRY: PROSPECTS

Complex challenges often hold limitless opportunities. In the greater picture of systemic reform and opening to the outside, China's securities companies are also facing unprecedented opportunities for growth.

With the implementation of the new Securities Law and Company Law, and the share conversion reform and other such fundamental structural changes in the market, great advances have already been made. These assure that reform of the capital markets and ongoing growth have a firm foundation. Price-discovery mechanisms of the market have gradually improved; resolving the issue of tradable and non-tradable shares in a way that benefits all shareholders is currently under way; the unfortunate legacy of historical problems has to a great degree been resolved; new risk has been checked at its source. All of these internal factors have improved the market structure, raised the quality and efficiency of the market's operations, and have made it possible for the capital markets to begin to fulfill their function. In December 2006, "Management Regulations for foreign-invested banks in the People's Republic of China" were formally inaugurated and the banking industry of China was completely opened to foreign investment, as per one of the industry's obligations upon entering the WTO. With the opening of the insurance and banking industries, we believe that the opening of China's securities industry and capital markets has already been placed upon the agenda. While the opening to international capital of China's securities industry will invite ferocious international competition, at the same time, it will bring modern management methods, the training of outstanding professionals, the ability to sift the finest of Chinese securities companies out of the pack, and the ability to accelerate the pace of their entering world capital markets.

Looking to the future, the growth of China's securities industry will mainly be seen in three areas: cross-industry mixing or the providing of "comprehensive services," marketization, and internationalization.

As the world's financial industries merge into an integral whole, and "liberalization" continues, providing comprehensive services in the industry has become a primary trend. Most countries in the world, including the US, Europe, and Japan, are operating under mixed-industry management on a global scale. China's financial industry is moving away from being segmented into discrete business lines and toward a mixed model. This is historically a necessary choice for China, and will be the final decision in China's financial industries' structural reform. Some of China's large securities companies already have first-to-market advantage in operating on a mixed-industry basis, such as CITIC Securities. While its main business is securities, CITIC is also the holding company over a fund company (Huaxia Fund) and a futures company (Jin Niu Futures Company). CITIC has also increased the scope of its business, effectively distributing risk and initiating a mixed-industry operating model.

The marketization of Chinese securities companies is mainly manifested in two aspects. One is the marketization of its operations, including the ability of a company to make decisions itself about the offering price of shares being issued and number to be issued. Second is relying on the markets to determine who should be in and out of the industry. Since China's capital markets are still operating in a very preliminary mode, with less-than-ideal laws and regulations, actions that are more policy driven than market-driven in the industry are apparent. With the gradual improvement of the regulatory environment and more standardization of operations, market-driven forces will necessarily become the core means to determining issues.

The integration of the globe's capital markets is making internationalization of securities companies a necessity. Every single outstanding financial organization in the world has made "global strategy" the focus of its highest attention. To take the four largest US investment banks as an example: while enjoying relatively stable competitive circumstances in the US, each investment bank is urgently adopting every possible method—merging, acquiring, joint-investment cooperating, direct investment, and others—to expand in Europe and in Asia. On a global scale, they are setting up business networks and have established branch organizations in all international and regional financial centers. Looking at the business with a global perspective allows a rapid increase in business scale and makes overseas business an important source of profits for investment banks. With the opening of China's domestic capital markets, China's securities companies will not be able to avoid locking horns with Merrill Lynch, Morgan Stanley, and other internationalized investment banks. This fact will force China's securities companies to pick up pace as it travels the road toward M&As and restructuring of assets. The outstanding will win and the inferior will be washed out as the market helps create a rational industry structure. In international markets, those domestic companies with real strength, such as CITIC Securities and other giants in the industry, have already set up subsidiaries and branches in Hong Kong, and have begun to test the waters of "striding out." One can foresee that the fast-growing potential of overseas markets will become a new source of profits for China's securities companies.

MEETING FUTURE CHALLENGES

The constantly improving domestic environment has created a platform to enable the growth of the Chinese securities industry. For the foreseeable future, however, that industry is still going to have to put out serious, solid efforts, to surmount the difficulties and meet the challenges head-on. These efforts include the conscious guidance of regulatory authorities, as well as self-initiated reform and the efforts of companies themselves.

In the twenty-first century, China's securities companies are facing a unique period. By recognizing the situation in a clear-minded way, facing problems with alert awareness, studying with an open mind, bravely innovating and moving into new territories, China's securities industry will be able to enjoy a promising future.

CHAPTER 15

China's Emerging Financial Markets: Challenges and Global Impact

Kevan Watts[1]

President, DSP Merrill Lynch Ltd.
Former Chairman, Merrill Lynch International Inc.

Deng Xiaoping launched a revolution when he turned China toward a market-based economy. The rate of change has been extraordinary and the benefits of change remarkable. This well-known history has played out in the capital markets as well. However, the challenges ahead are significant and the methodology of reform may need to change. In particular, the next stage may require bolder steps addressing the macro-environment as well as the continuation of the careful building of infrastructure. It is certainly the case that the faster the Chinese securities markets can mature, the more efficiently China will sustain its growth rate.

THE REVOLUTIONARY GOAL

Any discussion of the development of China's capital markets must begin with a proper understanding of the scale of the venture. The developed capital markets of the world have evolved over decades, responding to issuer and investor needs, changes in technology, and embedded in established legal regimes and broader economic and financial systems. China's policymakers set out to create securities markets in the context of wide-ranging economic reforms constrained by the practical reality of governing the most populous nation in the world across a diverse geography. In addition, they have faced impatient foreigners anxious to participate in China's growth and fuelled by an explosive growth in the global capital markets. The rapid innovation characterizing international financial flows has raised the standard, the expectations for China's capital markets, and made the implementation of each stage of reform more challenging.

The project is unprecedented in a number of respects. First, the policymakers began with no hard infrastructure, and perhaps even more significantly, little in the way of soft infrastructure. Because of China's history, issuers and investors had to be created along with the securities they can exchange, and in the context of very few experienced people and an underdeveloped legal system. Sequencing actionable reforms has been very difficult. The revolution in information technology that has been such a significant driver in financial services in the last decade has both helped and hindered the process. On the one hand, the physical infrastructure for effective markets can be built quickly. On the other, deficiencies in the partially built system can also expand quickly.

A developed capital market depends on well-managed companies, experienced investors, and prudent intermediaries seeking continuing success, all supported by an effective legal system to resolve disputes and established accounting procedures to guide the decisions of all participants. Accelerating the development of all these components simultaneously represents a Herculean challenge. Anyone commenting on the actions of China's policymakers in the face of this challenge should do so with humility.

PROGRESS TO DATE

Against this background, the progress to date has been remarkable. In a period of about 15 years, China's equity market capitalization has grown to RMB35–40 trillion or approximately US$5 trillion. There are over 1,600 companies (1,501 A-share companies, 109 B-share companies) listed on the Shanghai and Shenzhen stock exchanges. There were over 100 securities firms at the end of 2006 and 105 million individual retail accounts by the end of October 2007. In mid-November 2007, seven Chinese companies were ranked in the worldwide top 20 by market capitalization, and four in the global top 10. PetroChina became the largest company in the world by market value in 2007 with a capitalization at one stage surpassing US$1 trillion.

The average daily trading volume by value of shares in Chinese companies is now among the highest in the world (see Table 15.1).

TABLE 15.1 Average daily turnover in international markets, 1995–2007

	Average of daily turnover (US$ bn)				
	1995	2000	2005	2007 YTD	95–07 YTD
A-share	0.18	2.73	1.48	22.18	49%
HK	0.43	1.58	2.35	10.45	30%
Japan	3.01	8.99	17.28	27.54	20%
London	4.55	17.42	14.16	33.57	18%
NYSE	11.74	42.05	8.20	13.58	1%
Nasdaq	9.09	75.00	8.20	13.80	4%

Sources: Bloomberg and Merrill Lynch Research.

Parallel to this rapid development of the A-share market, China has moved ahead to create regulatory authorities. The China Securities Regulatory Commission (CSRC) has been established, and in a few short years, it has grown to employ over 1,800 officials. The CSRC is now regularly publishing exposure drafts of planned regulations on its website, and senior executives participate actively in seminars and conferences around the world on industry issues. Regulators have to compete with market participants for experienced staff worldwide; in China, the regulator had to begin from scratch.

The rapid development inside China has made an impact in Hong Kong, where market capitalization has soared, driven by the flotation of Chinese companies through the listing of H-shares. In 2006, the Hong Kong Stock Exchange led the world in initial public offerings (IPOs). More recently, as Chinese policymakers have come to emphasize raising capital onshore, the Hong Kong market has been supported more by the expectation that Beijing will relax the rules governing foreign investment. Chinese investors would then have the opportunity to purchase shares in Hong Kong that trade at a considerable discount to the A-shares for the same companies.

Of course, market conditions in the global capital markets and in those of particular countries can change very rapidly. At the time of writing, November 2007, the world's markets were adjusting to conditions of much reduced liquidity following a deterioration in the market for mortgage-backed securities and collateralized debt obligations. This deterioration has originated from emerging problems in the US market for subprime residential mortgages. It should therefore be noted that the Shanghai Composite Index lost approximately 18% of its value in November 2007, which is its biggest monthly loss since July 1994. However, this index showed a gain of over 80% in 2007.

It is difficult to judge the precise implications for the near-term performance of China's capital markets of the global liquidity difficulties. Capital controls insulate the markets in China from day-to-day flows, but China is very integrated with the global economy through trade. As the financial market affects the real economy in the US and elsewhere, we shall see just how correlated China's capital markets today are to events outside China.

PROCESS TO DATE

Looking back, it is possible to identify a number of key characteristics of the reform process that has been adopted to date.

The markets have been established by a top-down process managed by the authorities, rather than a bottom-up evolution in the face of issuer and investor needs. The authorities have focused on maintaining control of events even as they have worked to create market mechanisms. They have continuously sought to introduce change incrementally, allowing time for adjustment and reassessment.

This approach is first the product of responsible bureaucratic behavior. Second, it reflects the political imperative of managing change carefully to minimize the social pressures arising as China moves from a monolithic economy dominated by the public sector to a more pluralist, market-based system.

Inevitably, some of the partial steps have created their own problems for the future. A good example is the creation of non-traded shares. These allowed a market to develop around part of the capital structure of state-owned enterprises (SOEs) without the overhang of the government's own shareholding. More precisely, the overhang did not exist because investors assumed that the non-traded shares would always remain in government hands. This structure was seen as capitalism with Chinese characteristics. However, with the passing of time, the view developed that this class of shares would not be a permanent feature of the capital structure of SOEs. Non-traded shares came to exert significant downward pressure on the value of quoted shares as investors questioned when and how the non-funded shares would be converted. The A-share market then entered a prolonged downward cycle from 2001, and we saw the unusual combination of rapid economic growth with the correlated development of the corporate sector and yet declining share prices. Meanwhile, the Chinese authorities sanctioned the use of the offshore markets to raise capital through red chip listings in Hong Kong or H-share offerings. Progressively, as foreign investors increased their confidence of investing in the new Chinese companies, the valuation offshore improved and closed the gap with valuations of comparable non-Chinese companies.

The CSRC readjusted the balance by requiring all companies with non-traded shares to develop plans for their conversion into traded shares. This required each company to develop its own balance between the interests of the public minority holders and the various holders of the non-traded shares. Policy also shifted toward encouraging and then effectively mandating A-share offerings in preference to H-share offerings. The autumn of 2006 saw the first IPO involving the simultaneous offering of A and H-shares, the IPO of the Industrial and Commercial Bank of China (ICBC). Since then, policy has been focused on A-share offerings both for IPOs and also for follow-on offerings by already listed companies. The resolution of the non-traded share overhang combined with the significant liquidity in China has fueled an explosive growth in the valuation of the A-share market. The quick returns available have encouraged widespread speculative retail investing.

As well as introducing change incrementally, the Chinese authorities have throughout sought to maintain Chinese control of all participants in the securities markets. The non-traded shares themselves were initially a device for keeping ownership of listed companies firmly in the hands of the state. Foreign investment in the intermediaries, the securities companies, has been very tightly controlled. The leading investment bank, China International Capital Corporation (CICC), was established with foreign capital and expertise, notably that of Morgan Stanley. However, Morgan Stanley's active involvement in the operational management of CICC has declined rather than increased over the years, and the CSRC has been slow to approve new joint ventures between domestic and foreign investment banks.

Control of the listed companies has been maintained by a variety of techniques and not limited solely to the majority ownership of the big SOEs. Critically, the CSRC controls which companies can issue shares and when. This is in striking contrast to the practice in developed markets where the regulators typically review and mandate disclosure, but do not attempt to manage the timing of offerings or the identity of offerees. The challenge for regulators in making these choices are clear even without the inevitable pressure on them from interested parties when their decisions can have significant economic consequences.

Finally, the reform process has been managed through a plurality of regulatory bodies, the CSRC, the China Banking Regulatory Commission (CBRC), the China Insurance Regulatory Commission (CIRC), the National Development and Reform Commission (NDRC), and the People's Bank of China (PBC). Multiple regulators have characterized many developed markets and of course the largest capital market in the world, the US, is still regulated by a multiplicity of regulators. However, today's consensus is that this approach fails to recognize the interconnections between different markets and the multiple roles played by the individual financial services firms. In the case of China, it has also opened to question whether the incremental reform process in each segment has been fully coordinated across the markets.

A striking contrast has emerged between the approach of the CBRC and the CSRC to the question of foreign involvement. The CBRC has actively encouraged foreign banks to take significant shareholdings in advance of listing and to bring operational expertise to the management of the banks. By contrast, the CSRC has been reluctant to permit foreign securities firms to participate in the ownership and management of Chinese bankers. This variation in approach can be explained by political factors since China made only limited commitments to opening the securities industry as part of its agreement in entering the WTO. Furthermore, the CBRC arguably has much more room to maneuver in opening up the banks than does the CSRC with the securities companies. The banking system is many times larger than the securities market. Its total market capitalization today amounts to US$1.4 trillion, and several Chinese banks feature among the very largest in the world by market value. Financial flows in China remain dominated by the banking system. As a consequence, the CBRC could open up banks to foreign involvement without fear of losing Chinese control, provided that limitations were placed on the proportion of the share capital owned by foreigners.

The securities firms on the other hand are much smaller, though growing rapidly in the context of the fast-expanding domestic equity markets of the recent past. Their total market capitalization today amounts to US$85 billion. Even more significantly, until the recent rally in the A-share market, the majority of the domestic securities firms were losing money. It is extremely difficult to manage a securities business in the context of a declining market with limited available products and services, few experienced staff and shareholders who expect fast and good returns. Consequently, until recently, the CSRC must have felt constrained in its ability to permit foreign involvement without losing control. The multinational investment banks are accustomed to working across the world and move aggressively on entering new markets. In the context of the Chinese securities market, the CSRC must have feared losing Chinese control of its securities industry if it opened any meaningful proportion of the shareholding of domestic firms to foreign ownership.

Despite these plausible explanations of the variation in approach between the CSRC and the CBRC, speculation has arisen from time to time that this variation also reflected policy differences within the Chinese authorities. Any government managing change will have internal differences over the pace of change, with some arguing for faster and some slower reforms.

The multiplicity of regulators has had other consequences. It is widely argued that the development of the fixed income markets has been slowed by the division of responsibility between the PBC, the CSRC, and other bodies. Prior to 2007, the non-financial corporate bond market in China was controlled by the NDRC and the issuers have largely been limited to large SOEs with projects approved under the national development plan. The process was also cumbersome with the NDRC only approving applications once a year and requiring issues to be guaranteed by the one of the large state-owned banks.

However, at the meeting of the National Finance Working Committee held in January 2007, agreement was reached on moving some of the responsibility for corporate bond issuance from the NDRC to the CSRC. Further details of the change became clearer in August when the NDRC delegated the oversight of bond issuance by listed companies to the CSRC. Soon after, Yangtze Power became the first company to issue a bond under the CSRC's supervision and with a listing on the Shanghai Stock Exchange.

This change has been generally welcomed as a material improvement to the regulatory apparatus governing the corporate bond market. The NDRC was not established to regulate active markets in securities, but to develop and implement national economic plans. It is not surprising that it has approached its regulatory responsibilities with a quota system supplemented by case-by-case reviews of applications. The NDRC will continue to regulate "enterprise bonds," bonds issued by non-listed SOEs mostly for special projects approved by the planning agency itself.

Further reform will be needed to the regulatory apparatus governing the trading of bonds. At the moment, commercial banks are only allowed by the PBC to trade bonds on the inter-bank market and are banned from trading on the stock exchange, which is regulated by CSRC. Since commercial banks own most of the Chinese bonds outstanding, their absence from the stock exchange has starved the exchange platform of liquidity and raised uncertainty about where bonds should be traded. The PBC issued guidelines in September 2007 to allow companies to issue bonds regulated by the CSRC on the inter-bank market. This will presumably be an intermediate stage to the further rationalization of the market for corporate bonds.

The multiplicity of regulatory bodies has also impeded the development of the capital markets in derivatives and commodities. Admittedly, the authorities' enthusiasm has been tempered by a failed experiment with treasury bond futures in the mid-1990s. Beijing does appreciate the potential problems arising with multiple regulators, and it is understood that the issue was actively debated at the 2007 meeting of the National Finance Working Committee. Like the rest of the market structure, the regulatory apparatus is itself being established and developed.

So the reform process to date has involved incremental change managed tightly from the top with multiple regulatory and governmental agencies. The authorities have increasingly listened to advice from knowledgeable market practitioners and foreign regulatory agencies, but they have then taken their own decisions balancing stability and change. They have sought to build up the hard infrastructure deliberately, allowing as much time as possible for the soft infrastructure—notably the expertise and experience of the people involved—to develop in tandem. When their compromises have been followed by unintended consequences, they have been ready to change old structures to adapt to new circumstances.

The success of this approach to reform is apparent in the progress to date, not only in the capital markets, but also in the wider financial system and especially the banking system. This is not to say that China's financial system has arrived in the twenty-first century. There remain many challenges, inefficiencies, and uncompleted reforms.

FUTURE CHALLENGES

While the process of incremental change controlled from the top has broadly succeeded to date, it is less clear that this approach to reform can continue to succeed. The very success of the reform process so far has created a much more complex financial system in China than existed 10 or 20 years ago. There are many more participants and the expertise and expectations of all those involved have changed significantly.

The first consequence is that the risk of unintended consequences is probably higher than ever. Arguably, this is always the most signif icant challenge for all regulators and market authorities around the world. Look at the impact of the Sarbanes-Oxley legislation in the US. However, in the case of China, the authorities are compelled to continue to mandate change as they build the infrastructure of capital markets and financial services in general. In developed markets, in principle, change can be managed more slowly, although the rate of change in information technology has driven significant regulatory change even in well-established systems.

This heightened risk in itself is not however an adequate reason for suggesting that the key characteristics of the reform process to date need to change. It might well mandate an even more careful analysis of the probable impact of incremental changes. It might strengthen the case for merging the various regulatory bodies so they can better coordinate their actions across the various segments of the financial services industry. If anything, the increased risks of unexpected changes only serve to strengthen the process of incremental reform from above.

The possibility that the reform process must change to succeed comes rather from the key challenges ahead and the probable policy prescriptions arising. In several key areas, we appear to be approaching chasms that cannot be passed by careful steps. Giant leaps of faith will be required.

Arguably, the greatest challenge facing the development of China's capital markets today is the enormous liquidity in China. Hardly a day passes without commentary on whether a speculative bubble has developed in the A-share market in particular. During the era of Greenspan, Chinese regulators might have been tempted to argue that asset prices were none of their business, but that argument, always debatable, now looks thin in the context of the loss of confidence in liquidity following the subprime mortgage problems in the US. As it happens, the focus of China's policymakers today suggests that they do worry about asset prices. They have warned investors many times about market risk during 2007 and the PBC has progressively tightened liquidity in China.

The CSRC itself is encouraging an increase in the supply of listed companies on the A-share market, and in particular is actively encouraging the large and better established companies to list and issue new shares. Merrill Lynch's research department has estimated that the weighted average return on equity in 2006 of the companies listed in the 1990s was only 8%, compared to 13.3% for those listed between 2000 and 2005, and 18.1% for the most recent listings. This suggests the quality of the companies listed is indeed improving. Some steps have also been taken to reduce the pressure of domestic liquidity by the development of the Qualified Domestic Institutional Investor (QDII) scheme for foreign investment and more recently through discussion of a "through train" to the Hong Kong market. Both areas of policy appear in large part to be responses to strong demand from Chinese investors for Chinese stocks, demand driven by high liquidity that has limited outlets.

It is not surprising that many individuals are being attracted to invest in the equity market when their main alternative option is to place their funds on deposit with the banks at low and regulated interest rates. The quick returns that have been achieved recently by A-share market investment are bringing in very significant demand in the context of the sizable stock of financial assets relative to the supply of available A-shares. This is clearly understood from Hu Jintao down.

However, the policy measures to date and under consideration look woefully inadequate when measured against the flow of funds. This flow will only be reduced by a major realignment of the macro factors affecting liquidity. It is possible that a significant downturn in the US economy might so disrupt the current drivers of the Chinese economy—investment and exports—that GDP growth might fall sufficiently to impact confidence. Alternatively, the confidence required for liquidity could be damaged by a series of unanticipated corporate events. In China, the gearing impact might work through the corporate sector's own propensity to generate earnings from the stock market as much as operational success. In the first three quarters of 2007, approximately 22% of all A-share listed companies' pre-tax profit came from investment returns, a sizable portion of which might have come from stock market gains.

While policymakers should worry about the negative impact of a stock market collapse and realignment of valuations, there is no reason to suppose that such crises de-rail the development of securities markets. The history of developed markets is littered with major market corrections such as the Crash of 1929 or the collapse of the Internet bubble in 2000. Chinese investors themselves have endured a prolonged bear market until the reform of the non-traded shares in 2005 enabled a bull market to be re-established. However, there can be no denying that a major market correction would inflict widespread damage in the short term and, given the importance of retail investors in China, the political consequences would be significant.

While the experience in other emerging markets such as Indonesia and Mexico shows that financial market deregulation, if not managed properly, can be risky, failing to change according to circumstances can be just as painful. The Price Index of the Taiwan Stock Exchange rose from around 600 points in 1985 to about 12,000 points by January 1990. The index then dropped to 2,000 by September 1990 and the market has never truly recovered. China's current market condition has some similar characters to Taiwan's during that period—a market with significant retail presence, an appreciating currency, a closed capital account, and an environment of rising interest rates.

So what policy steps should be considered to address the risk of a future correction of today's high multiples? Even with the correction in November 2007, China's stock exchanges have increased very sharply in value this year. It is difficult to imagine similar large returns being sustained over the next year or two, and then disappointment could change attitudes and sentiment. There is no simple panacea to dealing with the challenge of continuing to build China's capital markets from where we are today; but there are a number of obvious steps, several of which will involve the authorities surrendering more control and accepting that in the future change may come from below as well as above. These are, by China's standards, the giant leaps of faith needed to cross the next hurdles.

INSTITUTIONAL INVESTORS

A priority should be the active encouragement of Chinese institutional investors. Successfully developed capital markets are dominated by institutional investors. They offer some important virtues from the perspective of efficient and robust markets. First, their investment tends to be based on analysis, not sentiment. This should help to minimize unsupported valuations, as well as encourage reinvestment earlier after market corrections. Second, many institutional investors—especially pension providers—will have a longer term perspective, again encouraging re-investment after corrections. Third, institutional investors will find it easier to create balanced portfolios across different asset classes, mitigating the dangers of over-investment in particular segments or even individual companies. Of course, this theoretical description of institutional behavior is somewhat idealized in a world where institutions themselves have to compete daily for individuals' savings. But the context in which this behavior is most apparent is the provision of long-term returns in funded corporate pension plans. Pension schemes—even defined contribution schemes—seem to be more removed from the day-to-day vacillation of the market than the direct investing habits of retail customers. Even those most skeptical of the modern asset management industry are likely to agree that pension fund providers are less likely to buy high and sell low than individual investors.

Merrill Lynch's research department has estimated that nearly one half of the A-share market's free float is owned by retail investors (see Table 15.2).

Indeed, while mutual funds are typically classified as institutional accounts, you can argue that in China today, these institutions should be classified as retail. Mutual funds are pressured by their investors for early and dramatic returns, and are susceptible to cash withdrawals. If we classify these accounts as retail, the non-institutional ownership of the free float expands nearly to three-quarters. By contrast, the more stable institutional investors—insurance companies and pension funds—account for less than 5% of the free float of the A-share

TABLE 15.2 Percent of A-share free float ownership among institutions

	A-share free float % ownership
Institutions	
Mutual fund	23
Corporate	5
QFII	3
Insurance	3
Social security fund	1
Released/unsold non-tradable shares	15
Others incl. brokers, trust companies	2
Retail	
Privately raised fund	10
Retail	38
Total	100

Source: Merrill Lynch estimates (as of October 2007).

market. In the US, corporate and public pension funds alone account for about 15% of the total US equity market.

Thus, policy should now be focused on the creation of Chinese investing institutions that are charged with providing pensions in the medium to long term. Developing a pension fund industry in China is not only important for the long-term health of the stock market, it is also important for social stability in the country as China ages, and for the long-term sustainability of China's economic growth. China's savers need to be given opportunities for efficient saving, leading to reliable safety nets in old age before we can expect the savings ratio to go down to levels more common in the rest of the world.

Similar to many developed nations such as Japan and the US, China relies on a mixture of mandatory and voluntary contributions by employers and employees to fund its pension liabilities. So far, the system has not worked very well. A decade after China's 1997 pension system reform, the mandatory pension system still only covers approximately half of China's urban workers and less than 10% of its rural population. Many employers have refused or delayed their contributions. Not surprisingly, given China's history in the second half of the twentieth century, pension assets in China are estimated by *The Economist* to have amounted only to RMB641 billion at the end of 2006, or US$85 billion. Addressing this deficiency will involve policy measures to encourage the establishment of corporate pension schemes, particularly in the areas of personal and corporate tax policy. It is likely also to require an increase in the share of salaries and benefits to corporate revenues, which currently runs at a very low level.

In the area of the capital markets themselves, the regulators should re-examine all controls on portfolio composition at pension funds and insurance companies. As corporate and personal pension funds grow, this will attract more focus from financial service firms. In principle, the providers will play an important role in the development of more rational and defensible valuations and sustainable investment habits across cycles. The stronger this segment, the more likely Chinese securities markets will recover more quickly from bear cycles and hopefully the more likely that asset values peak at lower levels, itself facilitating a more rapid recovery.

Expanding the Qualified Foreign Institutional Investor (QFII) scheme would also help to encourage the widening of the base of institutional investors in China. Regulators in China have been cautious about the size of this scheme, fearing the damaging of short-term outflows from fair weather foreign investors. In fact, foreign investors have remained very important investors in markets like Korea, India, Taiwan, and Thailand over the years. There continues to be a trend toward investing in emerging markets, and especially markets in Asia. The QFII scheme in China has not been supported by short-term foreign portfolio investors, but by a shift in portfolio allocation objectives.

The QFII program introduces new approaches to valuation and portfolio management, a perspective different to the domestic investor. If anything, foreign investors can help to stabilize or balance the market since they will review market indices against alternative investment opportunities elsewhere in the world. The practical impact in China of this counter-cyclical style is limited by the small size of the overall quota for QFIIs. A significant increase in the overall size of the quota would be highly beneficial. Indeed, it would be best to increase the quota at a time when many foreign investors are relatively uninterested in investing at today's valuations. Quotas are often best increased when no one is asking for an increase. This allows the quota increase to impact market activity over time as different intermediaries form different judgments about market timing.

SELECTION OF NEW ISSUES

A second priority should be to reduce and preferably eliminate the CSRC's role in permitting the launch of new issues. The CSRC should focus on disclosure and not selection or management of the new issue calendar. This will permit institutional investors to exercise greater influence on the new issue calendar, helping to ensure better choices are made at the outset. Provided that the development of institutional investors is encouraged, intermediaries can then use well-established pre-launch processes more accurately to gauge informal investor views on different companies and different terms of issuance. The recent history in China has been characterized by one over-subscribed offering after another, but this should be seen as essentially a reflection of the liquidity in the market. In less robust conditions, China will need to involve informed institutional investors in the decisions on which securities to issue and on what terms.

Indeed, the current sector composition of the A-share market is quite unbalanced. The oil companies and large financial companies account for over 60% of the total market capitalization. These companies are SOEs whose profitability is largely determined by the government through controls on net interest margins and domestic oil product prices. Petrochina and Sinopec contributed nearly one-fifth of the total profits earned by companies listed in China in the first nine months of 2007. When you add the large financial companies, the two sectors account for well over 50% of the total market's profitability so far in 2007.

On the other hand, by some estimates, as much as three-quarters of China's GDP is now generated by wholly private companies. This is not apparent from the composition of the stock market. Some investors therefore rather cynically regard the A-share market as more a vehicle for privatization by the Chinese authorities than a market for raising capital to fund growth in high potential companies.

Sequencing reforms is a continuing challenge and the CSRC is very unlikely to accept a reduction in its role in approving new issues in the near term. It could reasonably point to the immaturity of the investor base and its heavy dependence on individuals as two reasons why it should retrain strong controls. However, the CSRC should continuously remind itself of the practical limitations to its real ability to make good and sound choices. Well-intentioned officials can only make decisions on the basis of the information at their disposal, and this is quite often incomplete and inadequate for good decision-making in today's complex and fast-moving world. The CSRC should continually challenge itself on whether it can indeed make better selections than the Chinese investors themselves. It will not be easy to surrender this control, but in doing so, the CSRC will also put itself in a stronger position to force investors to assume the consequences of their bad decisions.

EXPANDING FOREIGN INVESTMENT CHOICES

Another priority should be to expand the ability of institutional investors in particular to invest outside China. Policymakers in Beijing have begun to experiment here, understanding the value of overseas investment in reducing excess liquidity at home and in enhancing the investing know-how of the institutions themselves. The steps to date have been quite modest and some have argued that the expectation of further appreciation of the renminbi has moderated the actual flows. But whether or not Chinese institutions want to invest abroad today, the limitations on their ability so to do should be significantly, not marginally, reduced.

The growth of institutional investors in developed markets has frequently been associated with investing outside their home markets. Experience of choices abroad has given these investors an enhanced understanding of the quality of investment choices at home. China has nothing to fear from giving its institutional investors considerable flexibility in investment abroad. Few markets can offer the long-term growth potential of China. Provided there is no major dislocation there, most sensible Chinese investors will stay at home for the foreseeable future, or perhaps more accurately will make only very selective investment abroad. This is precisely the time when policy should be relaxed to the greatest possible extent. A major relaxation in the face of pent-up demand for overseas investment could destabilize currency flows. A major relaxation in the face of limited demand does not carry this danger, and more importantly, it positions the institutional market better to develop a plurality of views over time.

EXPANDING DOMESTIC INVESTMENT CHOICES

Hand in glove should be the expansion of domestic investment choices. Again, this is already part of the Chinese policymakers' thinking, but the radical step that may be delayed too long is the deregulation of interest rates. It is no secret that the authorities have been anxious to protect the profitability of the banking system by imposing restrictions on lending and deposit rates. This protects the weaker banks and the monopolistic pricing guarantees a certain margin of profitability in a banking system still very dependent on net interest margin. No outsider can really know whether the CBRC's reforms to date have achieved enough improvement to enable this radical step to be taken. It is reasonable to assume, however, that any bureaucracy will approach such a policy change with extreme reluctance. Bureaucracies like intervening and they like control. In my experience, Chinese officials are well-educated, thoughtful, and open to reasoned arguments. They are also the product of a monolithic centralized history of government. This will not be an easy step. It would amount to a giant leap of faith, but the sooner it can be discussed, contemplated, and implemented, the better.

Two unintended consequences of a regulated interest rate regime are high property prices and underground lending institutions. Without the ability to charge differentiated interest rates based on different risk profiles, banks tend to lend more to borrowers with good asset backing such as property and other fixed assets, indirectly increasing the attractiveness of hard assets in China. In addition, bank officials are often cautious when lending to the private sectors for fear of the explanations they have to provide if such loans go bad. This has helped to create the current situation in which, while the state banking sector is generally awash with liquidity, private entrepreneurs often have to resort to underground banks for loans and pay as much as 20% a month in interest.

Another way of expanding domestic investment choices would be to permit foreign companies to list. With capital controls in place, any such listings could only be used to fund expansion in China, and so only companies with businesses there are likely to be interested in coming to the Shanghai or Shenzhen exchanges.

INTRODUCING FOREIGN EXPERTISE INTO SECURITIES FIRMS

The final more radical policy change that should be considered is a change in the CSRC's attitude to foreign securities firms' involvement in the A-share market. As discussed earlier, the CSRC has been much more reluctant than the CBRC to permit foreign firms to take stakes in domestic securities firms or to form new joint ventures. This appears to have been motivated by political considerations since China's accession to the WTO did not mandate opening its securities market. It is likely also to have been influenced by the CSRC's desire to maintain control given the much smaller size of the securities firms than the banks, and their greater vulnerability to operational control by foreign shareholders. Sometimes, the CSRC has also argued that it has been protecting foreign firms from the losses and recapitalization needs of the domestic industry.

This last argument has never been that credible. Foreign investment in financial services is a sensitive topic the world over, but the best time politically to permit investment is when the domestic firms clearly need capital and help. Thus the last 18 months or so of much-improved profitability reflecting the market trend may have made foreign investment more, not less, sensitive.

In any event, the CSRC does not appear properly to weight the technology and expertise that foreign firms can introduce. Genuinely opening the securities market to foreign participation would materially accelerate the development of the soft infrastructure needed for China's capital markets. Once the major international firms are more broadly involved in helping to manage domestic firms, the local professionals' own learning would be enhanced and accelerated. Moreover, this opening should be more transparent than the limited cases to date with all Sino-foreign joint ventures having comparable rights and obligations.

The CSRC also overestimates the foreign firms' ability to take ownership of the industry away from China. It is true that the securities industry is much smaller than the banking industry, and that its infrastructure is new and developing. But major multinationals harbor no illusions about how easy it will be to expand in China even with regulatory support. Many of the UK merchant banks and brokers were taken over by foreign firms, especially from the US in the 1980s and 1990s, and the UK industry today is dominated by non-British firms. Investment in China will be quite different. The foreigners will have to help build the infrastructure, train people, and develop the right culture, all in the context of facing a real constraint on available professionals who can speak Chinese. The firms themselves would be constrained by the same challenges as the existing brokers in terms of the character of the markets—retail orientation, high multiples, and so on. This is not an environment where progress will be very rapid. The multinationals would be helping to build the system; they would not just be buying it. Indeed, I doubt whether any of the multinationals view onshore participation in the securities market of China as a significant near-term profit opportunity. The markets are very competitive and challenging and the soft infrastructure underdeveloped. The intense interest of foreign securities firms rather reflects the future potential and the recognition that a truly global firm must have a presence in this market.

CONCLUSION

Despite the significant progress so far, there remains much to do to develop China's capital markets. The global market environment continues to develop rapidly, moving the goal posts all the time. Some of the key policy prescriptions now required, will be quite difficult for the Chinese authorities to accept. They will need to surrender more elements of control whether of the investment portfolios of domestic institutions or of the management of intermediaries. This will require an even greater readiness to change and to accept the risks of change. The prize is, however, significant. Capital markets today play a critical role in the allocation of capital globally through the pricing of risk against rapidly changing, complex, and readily available information. No one would suggest that markets are always right, but they provide a dynamic mechanism for adjustment that is more likely to allocate efficiently than centrally administered systems. The further development of China's capital markets is therefore very important to so many aspects of China's future. China must learn to grow more efficiently with less negative impact on the environment. Taking leaps of faith in capital market reform will be needed.

ENDNOTE

[1] I am indebted to several members of Merrill Lynch Research who have reviewed my comments and provided statistical material, notably David Cui and Ting Lu. However, the views expressed are mine and do not necessarily reflect the position of my employer or that of any other employee.

CHAPTER 16

China's Capital Markets

Qi Bin

Director General, Research Center,
China Securities Regulatory Commission

The reforms and liberalization starting in the late 1970s have allowed China to undergo a remarkable transformation from a centrally planned economy to a more market-oriented economy. China's capital markets began to emerge against this backdrop. The capital markets have become one of the driving forces behind a series of important economic and social reforms. In retrospect, China's capital markets have gone through three phases:

Emergence of Capital Markets, 1978–92

At the third Plenum of the eleventh Party Congress in 1978, the central government launched a long-term economic development program to revitalize the national economy. At the heart of that program were the twin strategies of reform and opening up the economy. The introduction of economic reforms meant that enterprises needed to diversify their funding channels for the first time, calling for the emergence of capital markets.

During the early stages of shareholding (or corporate ownership) reform, various stock issuance measures were developed by enterprises in the absence of regulation and supervision.

The speech made by Deng Xiaoping during his "Southern Tour" of China in early 1992 ushered in a new era of Reform and Opening to the outside world. While visiting Shenzhen, the Special Economic Zone bordering Hong Kong, Deng Xiaoping made the following remarks on the securities markets: "Securities and stock markets, are they good or evil? Are they dangerous or safe? Are they unique to capitalism or also applicable to socialism? Let's try and see. Let's try for one or two years; if it goes well, we can relax controls; if it goes badly, we can make corrections or close the markets down. Even if we have to close them, we can do it quickly, or slowly, or partially. What are we afraid of? If we maintain this attitude, then we will not make big mistakes." In that same year, China defined its key economic reform objective as the "construction of a socialist market economy." The key strategy was to transform the state-owned enterprises (SOEs) into joint stock companies and allow them to raise funds through the stock market. In the following year, the stock issuance piloted in Shanghai and Shenzhen was further extended nationwide, turning a new page for the history of China's capital markets.

Initial Development of Capital Markets, 1993–98

In October 1992, China's State Council established a Securities Committee (SCSC) and the China Securities Regulatory Commission (CSRC) under it. This marked an important milestone as China's capital markets were for the first time placed under the supervision of a single centralized regulatory framework. This propelled the capital markets into an important new stage of development. In November 1997, China's financial system was further reformed by the separation of operations and supervision functions in the banking, securities, and insurance industries. In April 1998, the CSRC became the regulator of the national securities and futures markets by consolidating the supervisory functions of the SCSC and People's Bank of China (PBC) into the CSRC. A centralized supervisory framework was established.

The CSRC has driven the formulation of a number of laws, rules, and regulations for the securities markets since its inception, facilitating the expansion of China's capital markets significantly. They also laid a foundation for further improvements in related rules and regulations.

As the market developed, there has been steady growth in the number of listed companies, total market capitalization, total capitalization of tradable equities, share issuance proceeds, number of investment accounts, and total trading volume. In addition, B-shares, denominated in RMB, but purchased with and traded in US or Hong Kong dollars by overseas investors (and later, PRC citizens were able to access foreign exchange), were issued. Chinese enterprises began to list abroad in markets such as Hong Kong, New York, and London. During this period, there were several preliminary attempts at developing the futures markets.

Regulation and Further Development, 1999–2007

The Securities Law, adopted in December 1998 and effective in July 1999, confirmed the importance of the capital markets and formalized their legal status in China for the first time. The Securities Law was subsequently amended in November 2005. These milestones had a profound impact on the development of the capital markets' legal system.

During this period, China continued reforms designed to improve its socialist market economic system to develop a more prosperous society. As economic reforms progressed, joint stock companies, both state-owned and private, increasingly raised funds in the capital markets. Financial sector reforms continued, while the capital markets grew broader and deeper. Nonetheless, some problems remained embedded even as the capital markets evolved. These problems, together with systematic and structural limitations, remained unresolved and became more serious. Starting from 2001, the market entered a four-year period of adjustment. Stock indices slumped, companies struggled to secure initial public offerings (IPOs), and listed companies also encountered difficulties in obtaining continued financing. Securities firms battled to survive, and by 2005, the securities industry had recorded losses.

In recognition of these problems, the State Council issued "Opinions of the State Council on Promoting the Reform, Opening and Steady Growth of Capital Markets" in January 2004, which triggered another round of reforms in the capital markets, including: implementing a non-tradable share reform, enhancing the quality of listed companies, restructuring securities firms, promoting the development of institutional investors, and reforming the IPO process. These reforms resulted in substantial improvement in investor confidence, and a turn-around in market sentiment and performance.

THE ROLE OF THE CAPITAL MARKETS IN THE ECONOMY

The development of China's capital markets has been made possible by China's economic and financial reforms, and also in turn facilitated

FIGURE 16.1   Number of listed companies

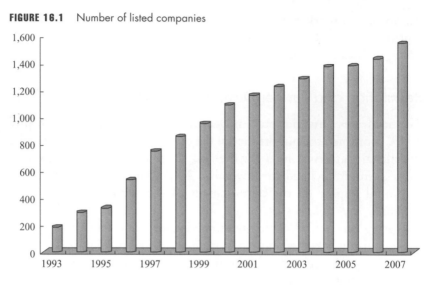

Source: CSRC.

China's economic and financial reforms. Consequently, the capital markets' impact on the evolution of the corporate sector and on the economy and society as a whole continues to grow.

The capital markets promote the development of the economy and enterprises. Early in China's reform, the capital markets began to play an important role in financing and improving the allocation of resources, facilitating the growth of the corporate sector. See Figure 16.1 for the number of listed companies. By the end of 2007, listed companies had raised a total of the US$245.9 billion from stock issues, and US$160 billion from bond issues. Listed companies have begun to represent a broader range of industries in the economy. The capital markets make it possible for Chinese companies to understand and constantly have reassessed their market value. At the same time, the capital markets have also induced fundamental changes in corporate governance and the management of SOEs and state-owned assets. The capital markets also promote the development of non-state enterprises. By the end of 2007, the market capitalization of listed companies reached US$4.5 trillion, equivalent to about 132.6% of China's GDP (see Figure 16.2). Listed companies have become an important component of China's economic system. In addition, capital markets provide new channels to attract foreign capital, facilitating integration of China into the global economic system.

FIGURE 16.2 Total market capitalization and operating income of core business of listed companies as a percentage of GDP

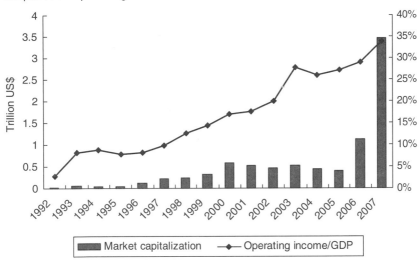

Note: 2007 data based on Q3 report of listed companies.
Sources: CSRC and *China Securities and Futures Statistical Yearbook, 2007*.

The capital markets have also provided an impetus to financial system reforms. The capital markets have reshaped the overall structure of the financial industry, and improved corporate governance at commercial banks and enhanced the profitability of financial institutions.

Meanwhile, the capital markets are demonstrating growing influence over social development. With the emergence of the capital markets, the range of investment products has expanded from just bank deposits to stocks, government bonds, enterprise bonds, convertible bonds, securities investment funds, warrants and futures, and so on, which now offer increasingly diversified investment channels to Chinese residents. As a result, Chinese individuals are becoming increasingly interested in the performance of listed companies and macroeconomic development when investing in the capital markets and sharing in the growth of the Chinese economy (see Figure 16.3). The wealth effect of the stock market has become evident through increased domestic consumption and the growth of related service industries.

The capital markets have also provided diversified investment opportunities for insurance companies and the National Social Security Fund (NSSF), and thereby indirectly supported the improvement

FIGURE 16.3   Number of investment accounts, 1993–2007

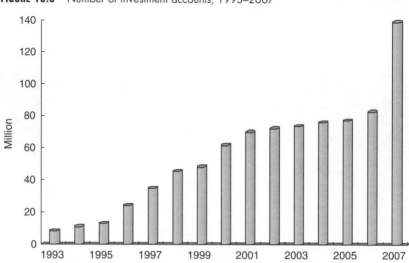

Sources: CSRC and *China Securities and Futures Statistical Yearbook, 2007*.

of the social security system. The development of China's capital markets has prompted the emergence of securities, fund management, and futures companies, which have trained a large number of financial professionals in new business fields such as investment banking, securities brokerage, and assets management.

POLICIES AND REFORMS IN RECENT YEARS

China's capital markets have developed rapidly. However, there are some deep-rooted problems and structural issues that continue to limit the effective functioning of the markets and will restrict future market expansion. China's capital markets can be best described as "emerging markets in a transitional economy." These problems and issues arose in the process of development, and have to be solved by further reforms. In recent years, the CSRC has implemented a series of reforms designed to improve market infrastructure and functionality. These measures have resulted in profound changes in China's capital markets.

State Council "Opinions"

The State Council released "Opinions of the State Council on Promoting the Reform, Opening and Steady Growth of Capital Markets

FIGURE 16.4 Main contents of opinions

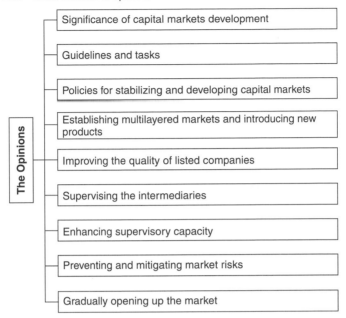

(the "Opinion)" in 2004 (see Figure 16.4). This Opinion effectively served as high-level guidance for the further reform and development of the capital markets, and elevated the development of China's capital markets to a national, strategic level.

The Opinion was the first pronouncement by the Chinese government which comprehensively described the government's understanding of the importance of developing the capital markets, the policy guidelines and key tasks to be accomplished, and the specific measures to be taken for implementation. The Opinions represented a significant elevation of the status of the capital markets to a level of national strategic importance. The State Council's move had profound historical significance, and provides guidelines for the future development of China's capital markets in the coming years.

Non-tradable Share Reform

The problematic legacy of the non-tradable shares stemmed mainly from a lack of consensus on shareholding systems in the early years; a lack of clarity over the role and functions of the securities markets; and a lack of awareness of how to manage state assets through capital markets. This inherent flaw in the system hampered the development of China's equity markets and management of state-owned assets. With the increased issuance of new shares, the impact of the so-called "overhang" of non-tradable shares on the development and growth of the capital markets generally has become increasingly obvious in recent years.

Effective resolution of the non-tradable shares problem could only be achieved through a transition to an entirely new shareholding structure. Such a system needed to eliminate differences between the various types of shares purchased and traded in renminbi, balancing the interests of shareholders owning non-tradable and tradable shares, with issues being resolved through negotiation.

In the program as finally implemented, the holders of non-tradable shares generally compensated the holders of tradable shares for the dilution suffered by making the non-tradable shares tradable by giving the holders of tradable shares a portion of the formerly untradable shares at mutually agreed prices. The final share consideration was decided by the entire shareholders' meeting of RMB shareholders based on the principles of "fair negotiation, mutual trust, and independent decision-making," and reflected the specific situation of each listed company. No government intervention or standard pricing was imposed. Any specific proposal could only be passed if at least two-thirds of the shareholders meeting voted and at least two-thirds of the holders of tradable shares (in most cases, without foreign holders of tradable shares) endorsed the proposal—the latter a measure to protect the interests of small investors in the negotiation process.

Non-tradable share reform has helped to eliminate legacy problems in China's stock market, where different liquidity rights were given to the holders of state-owned shares, legal person shares, and tradable shares, resulting in different pricing of each of these shares. After the reform, unified liquidity and pricing were established, and the secondary market started to reflect the value of the listed companies more accurately. The reform helped to a large extent to improve resource allocation efficiency in China's capital markets, while narrowing the gap with international markets in terms of fundamental market mechanisms.

Listed companies are the foundation of capital markets. In recent years, after the release of the State Council's Opinion, the CSRC initiated a series of reforms to boost the quality of listed companies, protect investors' rights and interests, and promote the sustained and robust development of the capital markets.

REGULATION OF LISTED COMPANIES

In 2004, the CSRC decentralized frontline supervision to its regional offices, a milestone in the reform of supervision of listed companies. The new supervisory structure required the CSRC's regional offices to take an active role in supervising listed companies in their respective jurisdictions, delegating the supervisory authorities and responsibilities to these regional offices, and encouraging collaboration among them. This new approach allowed the CSRC to improve the efficiency and effectiveness of supervision, maximize regulatory resources, and focus on systemic risks while giving more authority and responsibility to the regional offices. Regulatory resources have been consolidated and streamlined, and the coverage and vigor of supervision has been enhanced.

In recent years, the CSRC has released a number of regulations and rules to improve the corporate governance of public companies, which facilitated the establishment of the basic framework and principles for corporate governance of listed companies, and enabled the standardization of corporate governance practices. It has also introduced an independent directorship.

The problem of misappropriation of funds by major shareholders or related parties in many listed companies has severely hindered the healthy growth of these listed companies. To tackle these problems, a comprehensive drive for repayment of misappropriated funds was undertaken by the CSRC together with the cooperation of local governments and relevant departments. By the end of 2006, problems related to the misappropriation of company funds by controlling shareholders or de facto controlling shareholders had been mostly resolved.

The CSRC announced the "Administrative Measures on Stock Incentives by Listed Companies (Provisional) (Administrative Measures)" in January 2006. Aimed at promoting the establishment and improvement of a sound incentive and supervision mechanism for listed companies, the administrative measures prescribed that stock incentives should be mainly in the form of restricted (that is, illiquid) shares and stock options. It also set rules for implementation procedures and information disclosure of these stock incentive programs.

COMPREHENSIVE RESTRUCTURING OF SECURITIES FIRMS

By early 2004, the entire securities industry was on the brink of bankruptcy after years of risky and sometimes illegal investments and a lack of proper supervision and enforcement. In response to this situation, and with the State Council's endorsement, the CSRC launched a comprehensive restructuring program to turn around ailing securities firms. In order to address both the symptoms of the problems and the root causes, the CSRC implemented three key strategies, namely: liquidation and restructuring of failed companies, stricter supervision and industry capacity building, and the comprehensive restructuring of securities firms.

Starting in 2004, the CSRC categorized securities firms according to their risk exposure level and developed different policies and supervisory measures toward each kind of firm. The CSRC established a set of standards for assessing the operations of securities firms. Companies that were assessed as being "innovative" or "standard" were supported when expanding their business, on the condition that the potential operating risks would be measurable, controllable, and acceptable. The CSRC then conducted a survey of securities firms' risk exposure. It investigated and punished illegal or high-risk activities, such as the misappropriation of clients' deposits, bonds or discretionary funds, the misappropriation of companies' assets by shareholders or other related parties, and illegal off-balance-sheet operations. While maintaining market and social stability as a top priority, the CSRC imposed sanctions against 31 companies, whose high-risk operations could not be rectified by the companies themselves, or who had seriously violated laws or regulations based on a thorough investigation. The CSRC explored diversified models for the restructuring and merging of these companies, and punished the responsible persons according to law; mandated third-party custody of clients' assets; and revised the operating systems for government bond repurchasing, assets management, and proprietary trading. A public disclosure policy on securities firms' basic and financial information was instituted. Risk monitoring and early warning systems were developed, based on the imposition of net capital rules. Supervision of the senior management and shareholders of securities firms and their business activities was strengthened. Having learned from international experience, the Chinese Securities Investor Protection Fund Co., Ltd was established to enhance investor protection and facilitate market exit and liquidation of securities firms. At the same time, where the potential operating risk was measurable, controllable, and acceptable, the CSRC also began to allow innovation for qualified securities firms in terms of product, and business model, on a "trial and error" basis. The successful pilots established examples for

FIGURE 16.5 Net profits of securities firms, 2001–07

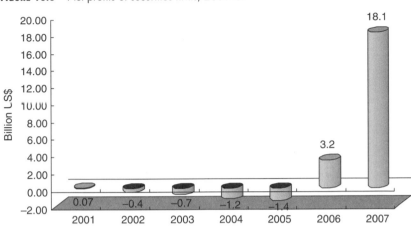

Source: CSRC.

others to follow. In July 2007, the CSRC categorized securities firms according to their risk management. By the end of August 2007, the CSRC announced that it had completed the comprehensive restructuring program for its securities firms and had achieved the desired goals (see Figure 16.5).

SECURITIES ISSUANCE SYSTEM REFORM

Between 1990 and 2000, when China's capital markets began to develop, public offerings of shares were subject to administrative approval from state authorities. In March 2001, a new *ex ante* review and approval system for public offering of stocks was introduced by the CSRC. Subsequently, more market-driven pricing gradually replaced government-driven pricing mechanisms during the offering process. As a comparison, public offerings in developed markets usually require just registration with securities regulatory authorities, and the procedures for stock issuance tend to be simple and standardized, with the issue price decided by the market. There is still room for improvement in the securities issuance system in China if only so as to continue enhancing market efficiency.

In February 2004, the "Provisional Measures on the Sponsorship System for Issuing and Listing of Securities" was put into effect by the CSRC, replacing the former lead underwriter recommendation system (with a quota for each underwriter) for issuing and listing of securities with a sponsorship system. At the end of 2004, the "Provisional Measures on the Public Offering Review Committee" were implemented. These measures abolished the secrecy rule to keep the identity of committee members confidential, and replaced anonymous voting with real-name voting by the committee members. The measures also ensured that all stakeholders under the verification and approval system for securities issuance shared legal responsibility and risks, marking the first step toward a market-oriented issuance system.

In 2006, the CSRC issued "Administrative Measures on Securities Issuance for Listed Companies," "Administrative Measures on Initial Public Offerings," "Administrative Measures on Securities Issuance and Underwriting," and other related regulations. The new systems implemented in line with these regulations improved market discipline and the efficiency of the IPO system.

With the increasing capacity of institutional investors to affect pricing, at the end of 2004, the CSRC discontinued government approval of share issuance pricing and replaced it with a book-building process, which augmented the market supervision over stock issuance. The "Measures for the Administration Securities Issuance and Underwriting," issued in September 2006, accomplished several goals. These included introducing key regulations on the book-building process, pricing, and share allotment during IPOs; improving the book-building process; and stepping up the supervision of issuers, securities firms, other intermediaries, and investors at the share issuance stage. See Figure 16.6 for a summation of the evolution of China's issuance system.

FIGURE 16.6   The evolution of the issuance system

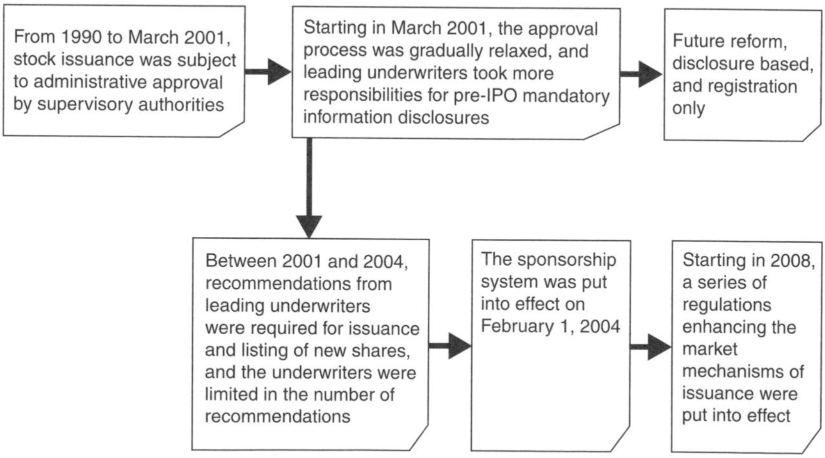

From 1990 to March 2001, stock issuance was subject to administrative approval by supervisory authorities

Starting in March 2001, the approval process was gradually relaxed, and leading underwriters took more responsibilities for pre-IPO mandatory information disclosures

Future reform, disclosure based, and registration only

Between 2001 and 2004, recommendations from leading underwriters were required for issuance and listing of new shares, and the underwriters were limited in the number of recommendations

The sponsorship system was put into effect on February 1, 2004

Starting in 2008, a series of regulations enhancing the market mechanisms of issuance were put into effect

THE FUND MANAGEMENT INDUSTRY: GROWING INSTITUTIONAL INVESTORS

Early on, China's capital markets were dominated by individual investors. This created unfavorable conditions for the long-term development of the market. Drawing upon international experience, the CSRC began to launch reforms to promote the growth of China's fund management industry in 1998 after cleaning up the so-called "old funds." During the initial stage of development, the fund industry suffered from low efficiency in operations due to lack of experience, coupled with a high degree of speculation and irregular trading. A number of "fund scandals" dealt a heavy blow to the industry. In response, the CSRC investigated the fund management industry and punished relevant parties. Starting from 2000, the CSRC put forward a strategy to aggressively develop institutional investors, seeing this as a key measure for improving the investor structure of the capital markets.

In 2002, gradual liberalization of the funds approval system was initiated by the CSRC. Approval procedures were simplified and a system of expert review was introduced, making the fund product approval process more systematic, transparent, professional, and standardized.

From the beginning of 2002 to the end of 2005, the reforms unlocked the potential of the fund industry despite an overall downturn in the market (see Figure 16.7). Total net value of funds increased

FIGURE 16.7 Total fund size and the Shanghai Composite Index, 2000–07

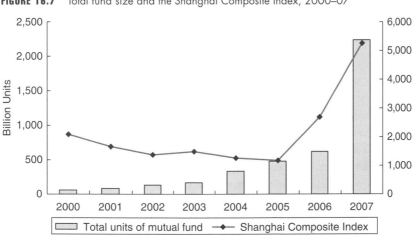

Source: CSRC.

to over US$57 billion from US$10 billion. The market value of the tradable shares held by securities investment funds also increased from 5% to nearly 20% of the total market capitalization of the tradable shares. In 2006, new funds with initial market value of US$50.5 billion were raised by the fund industry. This amount almost equals the total amount of funds raised over the previous eight years combined. By 2007, funds under management by fund management companies reached US$448.5 billion. Meanwhile, market competition introduced through this reform process sparked a sharp increase in the innovation capabilities and service quality of fund management companies. Since 2002 the Chinese fund industry has developed almost all the varieties of fund products found in mature markets, providing investors with more investment choices.

To promote market opening and competition, in July 2002 "Rules on the Establishment of Joint Venture Fund Management Companies" came into effect and, by the end of 2007, there were 28 joint venture fund management companies out of 59 fund management companies. The effective competition between domestic companies, joint ventures, and Qualified Foreign Institutional Investors (QFIIs) have not only increased product variety in the fund industry, but also helped improve the compliance and management efficiency of the industry, facilitated learning among industry participants, and improved the international competitiveness of domestic fund management firms.

In addition, with the development of the capital markets, institutional investors, such as insurance companies, enterprise pension funds, and the National Social Security Fund (NSSF) have gradually entered the capital markets. This has started to improve the overall investor structure of the capital markets and helped to correct the previously unbalanced profile of institutional investors.

LEGAL SYSTEM

The Company Law (effective in 1994) and Securities Law (effective since 1999) are two important laws aimed at regulating the capital markets. These laws were implemented to protect the rights and interests of investors, support the healthy development of China's capital markets, safeguard the economy and the public interest, and promote the growth of the socialist market economy.

The deepening of economic and financial reforms, coupled with rapid economic development, has led to many fundamental changes in the nature of the Chinese capital markets. Such changes have resulted in the emergence of new issues and challenges, in turn necessitating continued revision of the two Laws. In October 2005 the Standing Committee of the National People's Congress of the People's Republic of China amended the Company Law and Securities Law. The amended Laws took effect on January 1, 2006.

Since 2006, many legal issues in the Chinese capital markets have been resolved, and the legal system has been gradually refined, leading to a series of profound changes. The markets expanded rapidly in 2006 and 2007. By the end of 2007, the Shanghai and Shenzhen Stock Exchanges had hosted 1,550 listed companies, with total market capitalization of US$4.5 trillion, ranking the highest among emerging markets, equivalent to 132.6% of the GDP of China. The total funds raised through IPOs in 2007 reached US$62.9 billion, ranking the first in the world. Daily trading volume averaged US$26.1 billion, and China's capital markets were among the most active markets in the world. The clearing and settlement systems as well as the supervisory system were tested at the time of exponential increase of trading volume and market expansion, and proved to be stable.

CAPITAL MARKETS: PROBLEMS THAT NEED TO BE ADDRESSED

China's buoyant economic outlook, together with its need to further modernize, provides China's capital markets with a historic opportunity to develop further. Yet, compared with the future demands generated from China's economic growth, and the developmental status of other emerging and mature markets, China's capital markets still have many areas for further improvement.

The size of the market needs to be much larger. At the end of 2006, the total value of securities assets constituted only 22% of China's total financial assets. Although this had increased to 37% by the end of September 2007, the ratio remained relatively low and the overall scale of China's capital markets is still small. Between 2001 and 2007, the ratio of funds raised from domestic capital markets to the annual incremental amount of bank loans was 9.5%, 4.1%, 3.0%, 4.5%, 2.1%, 8.4%, and 22.0% respectively. Even though the ratio has increased over the years, it has remained relatively low. By the end of 2007, the total amount outstanding on the bond market in China accounted for only 26.7% of the total market capitalization of the stock market. This contrasts sharply with more mature markets

FIGURE 16.8   Composition of financial assets in China and other countries

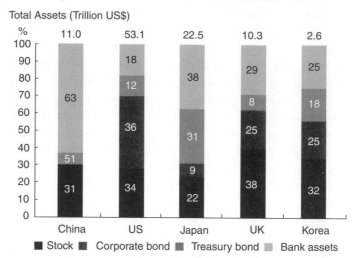

Note: For China, the data are as of the end of September 2007, and for other countries the data are as of the end of 2006.

Sources: CSRC, CBRC, www.chinabond.com.cn, and World Bank.

such as the US, and other emerging markets such as Korea and India (see Figure 16.8).

The amount of listed shares in the equity market is limited. This percentage is even lower for some listed companies with large capitalizations. Meanwhile, the Main Boards of the Shanghai and Shenzhen Stock Exchanges are still relatively small. The SME Board (Small and Medium-sized Enterprises Board) established at the Shenzhen Stock Exchange is still at an early development stage with limited scale and industry coverage. The share transfer system also needs improvement.

The core competency of stock exchanges needs to be enhanced. Currently, a very limited range of products is traded on stock exchanges in China. Trading systems need further optimization. The revenue structure of the stock exchange is undiversified.

The bond market, especially the corporate bond market, is lagging behind. By the end of 2007 the total outstanding value of the bond market was US$1.2 trillion, accounting for only 35.3% of that year's GDP. This amount is far below that of overseas mature markets. Meanwhile, the structure of the bond market is sub-optimal. The corporate bonds market lags far behind. In China's domestic market, only short-term commercial paper, convertible bonds, and corporate bonds issued by already listed companies are considered true corporate bonds. By the end of 2007, they amounted to only 4.2% of the total bond market. In addition, the bond markets are fragmented with an unbalanced investor base.

Further reform of the share issuance and the listing process is greatly needed. First, the current system is still prone to too much administrative control and complex approval procedures. On one hand, the current system is still a merit based approval system with considerable administrative influence during the process. Issues such as listing companies' creditworthiness, securities issuance size, and time for listing are still largely controlled by the regulator. Yet most overseas mature markets use registration-based systems for stock issuance. These are more convenient and efficient for issuers, since the price-determination process is totally market-driven. On the other hand, the current system does not leave enough room for intermediaries and professional institutional investors to play a meaningful role during the pricing process. Second, the bond issuance system is fragmented. Specific approval rules and regulations by different regulatory authorities vary widely, and this creates different issuance standards for different types of bonds. Also, the enterprise bond issuance process is still based on quotas, which are prone to administrative influence. All these problems have impeded the bond market's healthy development.

What's more, due to the lack of liquidity of treasury bonds, the yield curve on all debt instruments is far from complete. This results in a lack of benchmark interest rates during bond issuance and secondary trading, in turn reducing the market's price-determining efficiency.

The absence of short-selling has long prevented the development of an effective arbitrage mechanism in the equity market. This has impeded the pricing process from functioning fully, reducing overall operational efficiency. Currently, China's stock transaction cost (50 basis points on average) is higher than that of more mature markets.

China's stock market currently comprises of the domestic A-share and B-share markets, along with red-chip and H-share markets in Hong Kong. The bond market comprises the inter-bank market, exchanges, and bank OTC markets. The segregation of the market, coupled with the absence of an arbitrage mechanism, undermines the market efficiency of China's capital markets.

Corporate governance must be greatly improved. Although notable progress has been made in enhancing the corporate governance of listed companies in China, problems remain, due to some historical and systemic constraints. Controlling shareholders of some listed companies directly intervene in the listed subsidiary's daily business.

Governance in some listed companies only exists on paper, but not in reality; shareholder general meetings, board meetings, and supervisory board meetings all become a mere formality. In some state-controlled listed companies, ownership structures are unclear and management insiders take control. The integrity of senior management in some listed companies is unsatisfactory.

Market-driven screening mechanisms need to be improved. First, the delisting process needs further improvement. On one hand, the existing process does not have enough flexibility. On the other, current delisting criteria are too simplistic, lacking in different criteria for different Boards. This is not helpful in promoting a multilayered market system in China. Second, market-driven merger and acquisition (M&A) mechanisms need to be improved. Some M&A transactions involving state-controlled listed companies are still affected by administrative factors, and in some cases transaction prices are heavily influenced by administrative direction. The level of compliance and integrity remains relatively low among market participants, and illegality and irregularities still sometimes occur. The lack of a well-functioning market-based M&A mechanism or market for corporate control has weakened corporate governance in listed companies, and hampered the capital markets' resource allocation capability. Meanwhile, foreign participation in the M&A market has been increasing rapidly with the gradual opening of the capital markets to foreign participants. Under these conditions, it is becoming a major challenge for the market regulator to promote an "open, fair, and equal" environment for the M&A market, to crack down on insider trading and market manipulation effectively, to optimize the market-based M&A mechanism continuously, and to deal with the legal and policy issues which arise in cross-border transactions.

Competitiveness

International comparisons show that China's securities firms are still relatively small, and thus their core competitiveness needs to be further enhanced. Compared with major international players, except for shareholders' equity, China's securities firms are still relatively small in total assets and assets under management.

China's firms show little differentiation in business models. At present, China's securities firms generate most of their profits from the brokerage business. High value-added services such as direct investments and M&A advisory services only represent a small proportion of net income. Most firms' business models are simple and very similar.

China's firms have weak corporate governance and internal controls. First, current ownership structures in the securities industry are sub-optimal, hampering efforts to further improve corporate governance. There are two extreme situations. In some securities firms, shareholding structures are highly concentrated with one dominating shareholder. In such cases, the management team is usually controlled by the dominant shareholder. In some other firms, the shareholders' structures are very diffuse with a large number of small shareholders, weakening the supervisory function of the shareholders' meetings and of the Board of Directors over management, making the company vulnerable to insider control and managerial entrenchment.

Current corporate governance at securities firms still needs improving. In some cases, institutions such as the shareholders' general meeting, the Board of Directors, and the Board of Supervisors do not fulfill their mandates as required by law and regulation, which makes it easier for senior management to take control. Internal control in some securities firms is only a formality and implementation is very weak. Consequently, in some securities firms, there are few internal checks and balances among business units and between headquarters and branches. Furthermore, most securities firms have not set up effective incentive and disciplinary mechanisms. Because of this, management of some securities firms tends to focus on short-term results. This makes it very hard to enhance overall competitiveness of the securities industry, which is centered on the deployment of human capital.

Innovation capability needs further enhancement. Currently, there are many constraints acting on securities firms with respect to the development of new products, new business, or new forms of organization, and the overall industry innovation capability is limited.

According to the statistics from the Shanghai Stock Exchange and the Shenzhen Stock Exchange, China's stock market is still largely characterized by short-term investment and a shortage of long-term investors (see Figure 16.9 which shows the dominance of individual investors). Compared with investors in more mature markets, the average turnover ratio in China's stock market is high. From an investment behavior perspective, individual investors, especially SME individual investors, tend to hold and trade in small-cap, low-priced, poorly managed, and high-PE stocks. Also, in contrast to institutional investors, they hold shares only for a short time and trade relatively frequently.

FIGURE 16.9   Market shares of different types of investors in China's stock market at the end of 2007

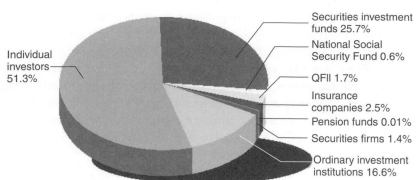

Individual investors 51.3%

Securities investment funds 25.7%

National Social Security Fund 0.6%

QFII 1.7%

Insurance companies 2.5%

Pension funds 0.01%

Securities firms 1.4%

Ordinary investment institutions 16.6%

Source: CSRC.

China's institutional investors tend to hold shares for shorter periods of time, trade more frequently, and exhibit a stronger desire for short-term investment gain, at least when compared to their international counterparts. In addition, existing institutional investors are too homogeneous in their investment strategies and investment pools, which could be detrimental for the long-term development of China's stock markets.

Fund management companies' business models are simple and undifferentiated, while the range of fund products is limited. Despite their rapid development, China's fund management companies tend to have an uneven structure of assets and products. The absence of a well-balanced shareholder structure and a long-term incentive mechanism for fund management companies has become a significant stumbling block in the fund management industry's future development. In addition, the substantial expansion of China's fund management industry has generated an urgent need for qualified fund managers. The absence of this talent has slowed the industry's growth.

Compared to securities investment funds, the participation of other institutional investors in the capital markets is still low and their market influence is limited. First, China's social security system lags behind the nation's overall economic development. Second, insurance company investment in the capital markets remains small both in absolute terms and in the ratio to total assets of the insurance industry. The relative underdevelopment of these institutions, as well as their low participation in the capital markets, has contributed to the shortage of long-term investors in China's capital markets.

China has an underdeveloped private placement fund management business. In overseas markets, privately placed funds are well-developed with a large number of participants. In contrast, domestic private equity funds are comparatively insignificant and their development is slow due to poor management and a lack of exit strategies; accordingly, their market influence is limited. Consequently, it is overseas venture capital and private equity funds that have been played a dominant role in China.

Legal Environment

As with any emerging market in a transitional economy, the development of China's capital markets is still constrained by some structural and institutional problems, which can only be solved along with the gradual improvement of the legal system. Also, with the fast development of the capital markets in recent years, adjustments, revisions, and improvement of the existing laws, rules and regulations will be an ongoing task.

The evolution of a regulatory and supervisory framework lags behind market development, and supervisory capacity needs to be further enhanced. In addition, due to constraints from bureaucratic systems and related factors, the overall qualification of the regulatory professionals is less than satisfactory and the overall efficiency of regulation and supervision is still suboptimal.

Enforcement efficiency needs further improvement. More efficient cross-agency regulatory and supervisory coordination is needed. What's more, self-regulatory organizations have not functioned fully, and still lack the ability to work independently from regulatory agencies. Building up a strong equity culture is still an ongoing process.

STRATEGIES AND PROSPECTS

First, China's capital markets are expected to provide a full range of financial support to the sustained development of the economy. Second, the need to transform China's industrial structure and improve the economic development pattern in the future will require better resource allocation through the capital markets. Third, the diversification of financial risks from the banking sector can only be achieved if the capital markets are dynamic and viable. Fourth, capital markets are expected to provide financial services and products to facilitate the reform and management of the pension system, the healthcare system and the rural economy, contributing to the building of the "harmonious society." Fifth, with the globalization of the financial markets, competition among capital markets and financial centers around the world is becoming more intensive. The competitiveness of the capital markets has become an important component of national strength.

With all of these opportunities and challenges, it is important for us to review and learn from the history of China's capital markets development, understand the trend of market development, formulate appropriate strategies and tactics, and ensure sustainable development of China's capital markets. China is facing tremendous opportunities as well as challenges in the future development of its capital markets.

The strategic objective of China's capital markets is to become fair, transparent, and efficient, thereby achieving higher efficiency of resource allocation. In addition, China hopes to become more open and influential in the world financial system. To achieve these objectives, China follows the "Opinion of the State Council on Promoting the Reform, Opening and Steady Growth of Capital Markets," and applies the following five fundamental principles:

- promoting capital markets as part of a national development strategy and increasing public awareness of their importance
- incorporating capital markets into the national economy, while coordinating development with economic and social goals
- engaging in further liberalization by providing incentives to market participants
- enforcing the rule of law and strengthening market regulation
- gradually opening up the market to improve China's global competitiveness.

Prospects for China's Capital Markets (2020)

The past two decades have seen China's capital markets develop in a way that few would have anticipated in 1990. Building on such experiences, while borrowing international best practices, I feel sure that China will in the future map out a capital markets development strategy to fully realize its market potential. In this way, China's capital markets will grow and prosper while making significant contributions to the economy.

By 2020, China's legal and regulatory framework will be more sophisticated and complete, supporting a market system that is more fair, transparent, and efficient. China will also have significantly extended the depth and width of its bond, stock, commodities, and financial derivatives markets, bringing a rich collection of product offerings and a variety of trading platforms to help Chinese enterprises gain financial strength.

By the time China's capital markets reach maturity in 2020, securities, fund management, and futures companies will have achieved higher standards of management, sounder governance, more effective incentive schemes, and more sophisticated risk management structures. A large number of financial professionals with both global and local knowledge will join the workforce to serve in China.

By 2020, China's capital markets will have developed from an emerging market in a transitional economy to a more mature market. These fully operating markets will meet the needs of China's growing economy, functioning as a key element in a harmonious society.

CHAPTER 17

Opening, Reforming, and Growing China's Bond Markets

Lin Yixiang

President, Tianxiang Investment Consulting Company

A Chinese bond market existed for a brief period in the early 1950s after the founding of the People's Republic of China (PRC) in 1949. However, because of policies in place between 1969 and 1980 that called for "no internal or external debt," the bond market ceased to exist. In 1981, China again issued government bonds, initiating a new era for China's bond markets.

GOVERNMENT BONDS

The development of China's government bond market can be divided into three stages: 1981–87, initial stage; 1988–94, funding the national deficit; and after 1994, the growth of a government bond market.

The years 1981–87 marked the beginning of the process. China's adoption of "Reform and Opening to the Outside World" policies required a reallocation of national income by the government, which in turn meant that the government ran deficits in 1979 and 1980. In order to supplement the treasury, the State Council promulgated "Regulations on State Treasury Securities of the People's Republic of China," and the Ministry of Finance began to issue government bonds. This formally marked the start of China's bond market. Issues were small, however, with annual issuance face amounts totaling less than RMB10 billion.

FIGURE 17.1 Comparison of balances of liquid treasury bonds and amount of issued bonds as percent of GDP

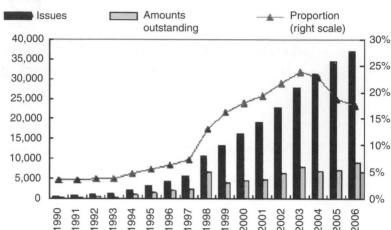

Source: TX Investment Consulting Co. Ltd.

From 1988 to 1994, although issues increased somewhat in size, state treasury bonds were primarily used to make up shortfalls resulting from Ministry of Finance overdrafts held by the Central Bank when the Ministry borrowed from it to finance government operations. As a result, the internal forces at play in the government bond market remained rudimentary. After 1994, the State Council formally ruled that the Ministry of Finance was no longer allowed to create overdrafts at the Central Bank. The issuance of government bonds thereby became the only measure by which the state treasury could make up deficits and pay interest on its debt. The government bond market expanded briskly as a result. See Figure 17.1 for a visual representation of issues and amounts outstanding from 1990 to 2006. In 1995, for the first time China's government bond issues exceeded the benchmark of RMB100 billion.

After 1997, China implemented proactive financial reform policies in order to deal with the Asian Financial Crisis, as well as to expand domestic demand. Government bond issues increased quickly until they had reached a level of RMB650 billion in 2006. In recent years, in order to establish a more ideal yield curve for government bonds, the Ministry of Finance has issued a balanced number of key term bonds on a fixed-maturity and rolling basis with one-, two-, five-, seven-, and 10-year maturities (see Figure 17.2). At the same time, it has improved management of government bond balances, with a

FIGURE 17.2 Term structure of treasury bond issues since the year 2000 (Unit: hundred million RMB)

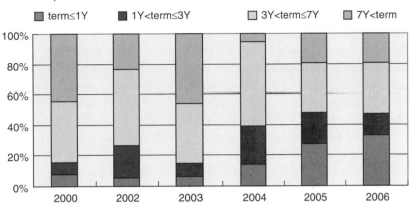

Source: TX Investment Consulting Co. Ltd.

relatively greater increase in the issuance of short-term bonds so that the term structure of the national debt is gradually moving toward a more rational structure.

CORPORATE BONDS

The development of corporate bonds in China saw important milestones in the three critical years of 1987, 1993, and 2007. Before 1987, the market was populated by financial products that resembled bonds and were issued by corporate borrowers without supervision or any real legal or regulatory basis. The assertion of unified control over the corporate bond market began in 1987. After 1993, corporate bonds issued in conformity with the law enjoyed substantial growth. Since 2007, government and market regulatory authorities have drafted and implemented a number of measures to promote the further development of a corporate bond market in China.

Before 1987, Chinese enterprises raised money through methods which included the issuance of corporate bond-like instruments. Borrowers issued these instruments either to the public at large or through internal channels. It is estimated that by the end of 1986, a total of RMB10 billion worth of such paper had been issued. Since there was no central control or regulatory oversight of this activity, the market was basically in a stage of "spontaneous generation." In 1987, the State Council promulgated "Provisional Regulations on Management of Corporate Bonds," and began to impose unified controls over the bond issuing process. In the same year, it drafted a corporate bond issuance plan.

In August 1993, the State Council promulgated "Measures for the Administration of Corporate Bonds," and at the end of that same year, the National People's Congress passed the "PRC Company Law." China's corporate bond market began to enjoy a period of stable growth with year-by-year increases in the amount of issued bonds. In 1997, the State Council promulgated "Trial Methods on Managing Convertible Bonds," which opened up a new financing channel for enterprises able to make use of this important vehicle. In May 2005, the People's Bank of China (PBC) drafted and promulgated "Measures for Management of Short-term Financing Bills," providing a legal basis for commercial paper instruments.' These went into effect on May 25, 2005, and again offered a new channel to enterprises for short-term and working capital finance (see Figure 17.3).

China's corporate bond growth entered a new stage in early 2007, when Premier Wen Jiabao noted in a National Finance Working Committee meeting that the government would encourage development of the bond market, expanding the size of corporate bond issues, and in general expanding the use of corporate bonds in direct financing. On June 1, 2007, the "Enterprise Bankruptcy Law of the PRC" came into effect. The new Enterprise Bankruptcy Law strengthened protection for, and confirmed priority rights to, creditors, as well as greatly improving the legal framework for corporate bonds as an identity

FIGURE 17.3 Issue amount of China's corporate bonds, convertible bonds, and commercial paper by year (1992–2006) (Units: hundred million RMB)

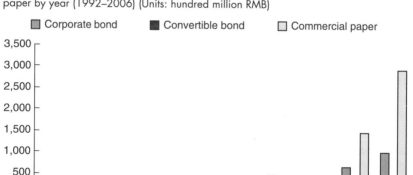

Source: TX Investment Consulting Co. Ltd.

of debt. On August 14, 2007, the China Securities Regulatory Commission (CSRC) officially promulgated and put into effect the "Pilot Measures for Corporate Bond Issuance," which, compared to the original "Measures for the Administration of Corporate Bonds," greatly broadened the scope of who could become an issuer, simplified procedures for and improved the efficiency of issuance, eliminated a review system that was heavily influenced by administrative and planning procedures, implemented an auditing system, and permitted a system of one-time approval for multiple issues by the same corporate debtor. The interest rate of issues was gradually marketized in accordance with these new measures. The system of mandatory guarantors was eliminated. The uses to which issuance proceed could be put were broadened. The oversight and regulatory authority of the CSRC over corporate bonds was clarified and confirmed. Multiple and redundant layers of regulation were streamlined. Responsibilities of intermediary institutions were strengthened, a fiduciary duties responsibility system was instituted, rights of bondholders were strengthened, and so on. At present, China's corporate bond markets are in the process of accelerative development.

FINANCIAL BONDS

PRC commercial banks were authorized to start issuing financial bonds in 1985; in 1988, non-bank financial organizations were permitted to issue financial bonds; in 1994, policy banks (that is, non-commercial banks, and non-bank financial institutions) were established and became the main financial institutions issuing financial bonds.

In 1985, in order to encourage diversification of financial assets and expand the sources of capital for financial institutions, the Industrial and Commercial Bank of China (ICBC) and the China Agricultural Bank began to issue financial bonds. After this, other financial institutions gradually followed suit, so that by 1987 some RMB9.5 billion worth of bonds had been issued. In 1988, certain non-bank financial institutions were allowed to openly issue bonds. In 1994, after policy banks were established and made separate from commercial banks, policy-type financial bonds began to be issued. Since policy-type financial bonds were in fact backed by the credit of the national government, the issuing of these instruments went relatively smoothly. The scale of these policy-type issues expanded year by year so that by

FIGURE 17.4   Amount of financial bond issues by year, 1998–2007 (Unit: hundred million RMB)

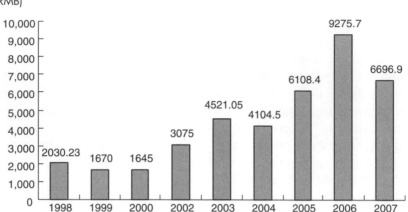

Source: TX Investment Consulting Co. Ltd.

2006, they had reached the aggregate face amount of almost RMB1 trillion (see Figure 17.4).

ASSET-BACKED SECURITIES

Asset securitization was tested for the first time in China in 1992; in 2005, the China Development Bank (CDB) and China Construction Bank (CCB) served as pilot institutions permitted to issue asset backed securities (ABS) and mortgage-backed securities (MBS). These issuances mark the formal start of asset securitization in China.

China started asset securitization relatively late. However, with the active participation of financial organizations and the strong encouragement of regulatory authorities, from a starting point of zero, the country made a number of breakthroughs in this area and the sector began to achieve rapid growth. In 1992 a project in Hainan was the first to issue "real estate investment securities," which started China on the learning curve in asset securitization. From 1996 to 2002, China issuers issued a series of offshore securitized products, and in 2003 and 2004, a few domestic-issuer securitized products were authorized. In March 2005, the CDB and CCB were authorized to serve as pilot institutions for the issuance of securitized credit assets and MBS, indicating the formal start of domestic ABS in China. At the end of 2005, the CDB successfully issued RMB4.177 billion of ABS and the CCB issued RMB3.019 billion worth of residential MBS on the inter-bank market. These were the first large groups of ABS issued under the aegis of official policy authorization. The results of these two pilot cases formed a milestone accomplishment in the asset securitization industry in China. In addition, two other ABS products were released in 2005. China had taken the important step of moving from a theoretical position on asset securitization to a practicing and implementing position, so that 2005 was described as the "founding year" for asset securitization in China.

China's securitized assets then went from RMB17.134 billion yuan in 2005 to RMB47.151 billion in 2006, an increase of 175.20% in one year. In 2006, the volume of securitized products issued in the Shanghai and Shenzhen exchanges by listed companies was RMB16.405 billion, an increase of 65.04% over the RMB9.94 billion yuan in the industry's "founding year." In the inter-bank market, the total value of asset securitization products traded was RMB12.380 billion, an increase of 72.49% over the RMB7.177 billion of 2005. By the end of December 2006, China's securitized products aggregate to a face value of RMB47.151 billion.

However, the market for China's ABS products is limited at present, and the insufficient number of investing participants constrain real market liquidity. Relative to the active order-taking seen for initial offerings, the secondary market has continued to be subdued. Laws and regulations with regard to securitized assets continue to lack teeth and credit-rating organizations lack public credibility. The underlying asset market that can be used in securitization is not yet fully developed, also influencing the pace at which securitized products can develop in China.

MARKET SYSTEMS

A secondary market for bonds in China began in 1987 with an over-the-counter (OTC) trading system. The establishment of the Shanghai Stock Exchange in 1990 allowed the bond market to proceed on both OTC and Exchange systems at the same time. In 1997, all banks withdrew from the Exchange market and set up an inter-bank market. Since that time, this inter-bank market has become the main market for China's bonds.

Before 1987, government bonds could be sold only on the primary market—there was no secondary market. On January 5, 1987, the Shanghai Branch of the PBC announced "Provisional Regulations on OTC Trading of Securities," which confirmed that government bonds, financial bonds, and approved enterprise bonds could be traded OTC at approved financial institutions. In early 1988, China implemented a government bond "trading program" at seven municipal pilot sites, marking the birth of China's government bond market. From 1990 to 1991, the Shanghai Stock Exchange and the Shenzhen Stock Exchange began to allow trading of government bonds. The market proceeded both OTC and at the Exchanges. The Exchange market employed a trading system driven by "declaration forms." In 1997, in order to prevent commercial bank credit from being diverted into the stock market, the Central Bank required that all commercial banks completely withdraw from the stock markets. At the same time, it established a market specifically for commercial banks to carry out bond trading; namely, the National Interbank Bond Market. The inter-bank market uses a trading system that is driven by timely price quotations. After this, the Central Bank successively permitted insurance companies, securities companies, mutual funds, finance companies, and trust companies to enter the inter-bank bond market and carry out transactions, thereby basically incorporating the entire Chinese financial system.

Within the last few years, the inter-bank bond market has grown to become the largest bond market in terms of depository amounts. At present, China's bond markets include the internal market (Shanghai Stock Exchange and Shenzhen Stock Exchange), and external market (inter-bank market and OTC market). Transactions on the internal Exchange markets are mainly concentrated at the Shanghai Stock Exchange, and participants, other than banks, include all kinds of investors from the public at large. The Exchange serves as a retail market, and is based on an aggregate auction or call auction with the Exchange acting as the market-maker, implementing clean price transactions, with settlement done on the basis of net amounts. The largest part of the external market outside the Exchanges is concentrated in the inter-bank market, whose participants include all kinds of institutional investors. This market is as a wholesale market. It conducts negotiations between both sides in coming to a deal, and settlement is done amount by amount. This inter-bank market represents the main body of the bond market, accounting for approximately 90% of total bond holdings and transactions (see Figure 17.5).

EVOLUTION OF BOND-TRADING METHODS

In addition to spot transaction methods, China's bond markets have gradually incorporated a repo market, a forward market, interest-rate swaps, government bond futures, and two-way quotation systems.

FIGURE 17.5 Comparison of volume on Exchanges and inter-bank bond markets (Unit: one hundred million RMB)

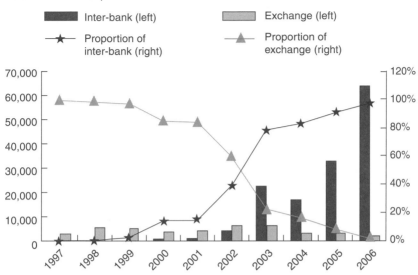

Notes: 1 The volume of the inter-bank bond market does not include the volume associated with open market operations. 2 The Exchange bond trading includes treasury bonds, corporate bonds and convertible bonds that are traded in exchange bond market.
Source: TX Investment Consulting Co. Ltd.

Development of the Repo Market

China's government bond repurchase, or "repo" transactions began in 1991. Not long after the Securities Trading Automated Quotation (STAQ) system was set up in July 1991, at the Shanghai Stock Exchange, it was announced that a government bond repo business had commenced. In the second half of 1993, the Shanghai Stock Exchange set up national bond repo products. Given the constant growth in government bond issues and the daily increase in spot transactions on the bond market, together with the fast growth of China's stock markets, a tremendous demand for capital developed. Repo financing, using government bonds as the main tool, expanded swiftly. Without rigorous market controls or regulations, and without a unified bond custodial and clearing system, the market soon became highly irregular. It suffered from the widespread practice of fake orders or sham repurchases, which harbored and incubated a tremendous amount of risk.

In 1995 the PBC, the Ministry of Finance, and the China Securities Regulatory Commission jointly implemented a plan to clean up the repo market. In 2004, the inter-bank bond market set up a securities management system for clearance and guarantee of outright purchase, or what in China is called "buyout repo." In 2006, the China Securities Industry Association published a guide to collateralized bond repo authorization agreements and on May 8, 2006, began to implement its terms. This document specified the rights and obligations of investors and securities companies in the course of carrying out a collateralized bond repo business, and clarified the legal relationships of both sides. It standardized the business conduct of both sides, which gradually helped put China's repo market on the right course. Soon, the business grew fast in the inter-bank market. The volume of repo business is now far greater than the volume of spot transactions.

Development of Bond Forward Transactions

In order to promote the marketization of interest rates, and improve the liquidity of the spot markets, after initiating the "buyout repo" business, in May 2005, the PBC published "Regulations on the Administration of Bond Forward Transactions on the National Interbank Bond Market." These regulations were implemented from June 15, 2005. Not long after, the PBC published an accompanying set of relevant documentation. On June 13, 2005, the Central Clearance Company published "Regulations on the National Interbank Bond Market Bond Forward Transactions Clearance Business" and "Detailed Regulations on Custodial Measures Relating to Margins in Bond Transaction Clearing." On June 15, 2005, the national inter-bank bond market bond forward transaction clearance business was formally opened. However, according to the Regulations, the period of forward transactions could not exceed 365 days, so it was hard to fully utilize the benefits of forward transactions in terms of hedging and price determination. At the same time, there was an imbalance in the participation structure of forward markets: commercial banks led the way. After being initiated, therefore, the forward market was not in fact very active (see Table 17.1).

Development of Interest-rate Swaps

On January 24, 2006, the PBC put out a "Notice on Matters Concerning Pilot Projects for the Development of RMB Interest Rate Swaps." This allowed for the establishment of institutions at which RMB interest rate swap transactions could be tested. At present, the floating

TABLE 17.1 Bond forward transactions by number and amount transacted, 2005–07

Year	Transactions	Traded value (100 million RMB)
2005	108	177.99
2006	398	664.46
Q1 2007	253	357.19
Q2 2007	291	648.95
Total	1,050	1,848.59

Source: China Monetary Policy Report Quarter Two, 2007.

rate reference in interest-rate swap transactions is divided into two types: market rates and controlled rates. Market interest rates mainly use the seven-day buy-back interest rate (R007) as their standard. The controlled reference interest rate is mainly the one-year fixed-term deposit rate that is publicly announced by the PBC; in addition, there are half-year fixed-term deposit rates, and three-year loan interest rates.

In order to establish a market interest-rate system that uses money market-based rates as its core, that can guide in the setting of market prices for money market products, further cultivate the Shanghai inter-bank offering rate (SHIBOR), encourage the development of money markets and the market for derivatives, the National Interbank Offering Center was authorized to develop an Internet-based network (www.shibor.org) for the publication of a window on interest rate swap pricing information based on SHIBOR. This was formally put up on the Internet on July 4, 2007. However, since R007 is at present the most important short-term interest rate on the market, and fairly strong in representational value, and at the same time since it is a real, transaction-based, interest rate, more than 90% of interest-rate swaps still use R007 as their reference interest rate. Only a small portion of institutions use the various maturities of SHIBOR.

Regulatory restrictions currently limit participation in the market for interest rate swaps to those who meet certain requirements. Most financial institutions are not allowed to participate in the RMB interest rate swap market as a result. These include non-bank financial institutions outside of the scope of designated pilot institutions and a portion of high-quality asset small and medium enterprise (SME) commercial banks. This greatly limits the depth of the interest-rate swap market, and liquidity of the market is influenced as a result. Even though transactions on the swap market have increased rapidly

TABLE 17.2 Interest rate swap transactions, 2006–07, by number of transactions and nominal value

Year	Transactions	Notional principal amount (100 million RMB)
2006	103	355.7
Q1 2007	276	393.64
Q2 2007	636	639.02
Total	1,015	1,388.36

Source: China Monetary Policy Report Quarter Two, 2007.

since 2007, in terms of number and scale of transactions, the market overall is still at an early stage (see Table 17.2).

Development of the Government Bond Futures Market

The China Government Bond Futures transactions started on December 28, 1992. At the time, Shanghai's Stock Exchange offered the same business only to dealers for their own accounts, but the trading was very slow. On October 25, 1993, the Shanghai Stock Exchange opened up trading in government bond futures to the public at large. At the same time, the Beijing Commodities Exchange, in its Futures Exchange, took the lead in starting a government bond futures exchange function. From 1994 until before the Spring Festival [Chinese New Year] of 1995, the government bond futures trade grew very quickly.

Many regulatory aspects of the market had not been completed; however, product offerings were inadequate, and risk management was largely neglected, so that excessive opportunism and reckless behavior appeared in the market. This led to deeply negative consequences. In May 1995 the China Securities Regulatory Commission (CSRC) shut the business down. It issued an "Emergency Notice Regarding Temporary Cessation of All Government Bond Futures Trading Pilot Projects Throughout the Nation," which stopped trading in government bond futures. To this day, the market for government bond futures has not been restarted.

Instituting a Two-way Quotation System

After the inter-bank bond market was formally commenced in 1997, trade was insufficiently active and liquidity in the market was

FIGURE 17.6 Comparison of bond annual turnover rate in Inter-bank bond market

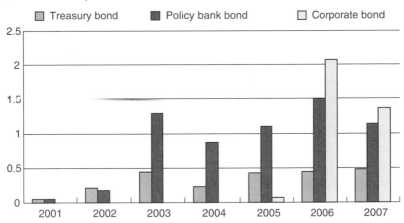

Note: Turnover ratio = annual volume/[(amount outstanding at the end of last year + amount outstanding at the end of this year)/2].

Source: TX Investment Consulting Co. Ltd.

inadequate. In order to improve market liquidity, in April of 2000, the Central Bank issued "Control Measures on Transactions in the National Interbank Bond Market." This allowed financial institutions that passed an approval process to carry on bond transactions on the basis of a two-way quotation system. In 2001, the PBC issued "Notice by the People's Bank of China Regarding Issues Relating to the Scope and Support of the Interbank Bond Market Two-way Quotation Business," which sets forth regulations governing conditions that dealers engaging in the business had to follow, as well as their rights and obligations. It confirmed the basic framework for the two-way quotation system among dealers. In July 2001, the Central Bank approved nine commercial banks as inter-bank bond market-makers in the two-way quotation market. After the two-way quotation market was implemented, liquidity in the bond market improved to a degree (see Figure 17.6).

DEPOSITORY AND CLEARING SYSTEMS

At the very beginning, China's bond market traded physical pieces of paper. Trading now is paperless with trading records maintained electronically. In 1996, a clearing organization was established in the form of a central securities depository (known by the acronym CSD).

The bond clearing organization was called the "China Government Securities Depository Trust & Clearing Co. Ltd", or CDC for short. This was a major event in the development of China's bond market depository and clearing systems.

Before 1996, when government securities used physical paper that had no record name, there was no unified depository or custodial organization. After being issued, bonds were held by agent organizations acting as custodians. Due to the lack of a central custodial organization some of these agents used "proxy depository slips," which caused the over-issuance or sale of "empty" or nonexistent government bonds. This led to tremendous market risk.

At the end of 1996, after approval by the State Council, China's central securities depository, namely the CDC, was formally established. In the same year, the CDC independently developed bond record-keeping systems. In addition, under the guidance of the PBC, a bond distribution system and an open market operating system were also established. In 1997, the national inter-bank bond market began to form and the PBC designated CDC as the organization responsible for recording, depository, and clearing systems. In 1999, CDC's central bond business system began to operate and the foundation for operation of an inter-bank bond market was thereby greatly improved. In 2004, CDC put into effect a redemption process for bond transactions. In October 2005, CDC implemented the initial steps for an inter-bank bond transaction clearing system called "straight-through processing" (STP). At present, straight-through processing (STP) in the trading and bookkeeping system and delivery versus payment (DVP) in the settlement and payment system provides a secure and efficient platform for the transaction and settlement on the inter-bank bond market.

The CDC is the overall depository for China's bond markets, taking direct custodianship of bond assets traded by participants on the inter-bank bond market. The equivalent for China's securities markets serves as a branch depository, holding the securities from transactions at the Exchange including bond assets of participants. The four large state-owned commercial banks serve as depositories for the secondary market, and for OTC participants in the bond market.

OPENING OF CHINA'S BOND MARKET

An important component of the policy of "Going Out" for China's bond markets—that is, expanding the bond markets beyond China's borders—has been the issuance of bonds in the international markets. In the 1980s, China successfully raised funds by issuing bonds in Japan, Germany, and Hong Kong. In 1996, China's government successfully issued 100-year Yankee bonds in the US market. In June 2007, the PBC and China's National Development and Reform Commission (NDRC) jointly issued a Notice called "Provisional Methods for Issuing RMB-denominated Bonds by Domestic Financial Organizations to the Hong Kong Special Administrative Region." This allowed financial organizations within China but outside of China's Hong Kong Special Administrative Region to issue RMB-denominated bonds in Hong Kong. Nonetheless, the sums raised by China are relatively low compared to other countries and regions, far lower than in developed countries, and also lower than the amounts raised by developing countries in the international capital markets generally (see Table 17.3).

In recent years, given the increase in China's foreign exchange reserves, another important part of the "Going Out" policy has been to encourage Chinese institutional investors to make overseas investments. On April 14, 2006, the PBC promulgated "Notice No. 5 (2006)," which loosened restrictions on the banking, funds, and insurance industries in making investments in overseas markets. In July 2007, China also began to implement a policy of Qualified Domestic Institutional Investors (QDII). This marked a new era in the "Going Out" of China's financial industry, although in the initial period, institutions that actually "Go Out" invest primarily in the area of fixed-income products.

In terms of allowing institutional investors from outside China's borders to invest in China markets, in 2005, the "Fanya" (PAIF) and Yazhai China Fund (ETF) received permission to enter the China interbank bond market. In September of 2006, China formally began to implement a Qualified Foreign Institutional Investor (QFII) system to a

TABLE 17.3 The comparison of international bond amounts outstanding in 2006 (US$10 billion)

	Treasury bond	Policy bank bond	Corporate bond
Average of developed country	51.97	640.50	75.69
Average of developing country	16.61	15.12	6.08
China	5.60	23.00	2.30

Source: BIS.

limited degree, allowing foreign investors to invest in domestic (equity) securities markets. By the end of June 2007, 52 foreign institutions had received QFII status, and the quota amount approved for their investments had reached US$9.995 billion. At present, however, QFIIs are allowed to invest only in Exchange-traded bonds, and are not permitted to enter the inter-bank bond market.

With regard to admitting foreign bond issues into China, in 2005, the Asian Development Bank and the International Finance Corporation were authorized for the first time to issue RMB-denominated bonds in the China inter-bank bond market. By June 2007, these two organizations had together issued RMB-denominated bonds totaling RMB3 billion.

Finally, domestic financial organizations have received permission to issue US dollar-denominated bonds within the borders of China. In 2003, the CDB issued solely US dollar-denominated financial bonds for the first time in the PRC inter-bank bond market. By the end of 2006, the accumulated amount of US dollar-denominated bonds issued by the CDB and the Export-Import Bank of China (China Exim Bank) amounted to around US$2.63 billion.

THE UNBALANCED STRUCTURE OF CHINA'S BOND MARKETS

Given that RMB-denominated assets are not yet fully convertible (whether with regard to bond issuers, or bond investors, or the currency in which assets are issued), we would still have to say that China's bond markets are still relatively closed.

By the end of 2006, China's domestic government bond depository amount was US$1.18 trillion, or 46.34% of the value of China's GDP. If you subtract from that amount the Central Bank notes used by the Bank to remove excess liquidity from the market, this percentage drops to around 30%. This is far below the level of developed countries such as the US, Japan, and Germany, and it is also lower than a developing country such as India, indicating that China's bond markets have not yet lived up to the role they should play in the national economy. Relatively speaking, China's government bond markets are underdeveloped. The immature state of the corporate bond market is even more striking. In 2006, corporate bond financing in China amounted to only 2.76% of the GDP, far below the percentage of

TABLE 17.4 The amounts outstanding of domestic bonds in proportion to GDP among different countries in 2006

Country	GDP (US$ bn)	Domestic bond (US$ bn)	Proportion
Germany	2,860.47	2,247.7	78.58%
United Kingdom	2,357.58	1,237.6	52.49%
Japan	4,463.59	8,401.2	188.22%
United States	13,262.074	22,315.5	168.27%
Canada	1,273.144	983.9	77.28%
France	2,227.33	2,244.5	100.77%
Italy	1,841.042	2,576.8	139.96%
China	2,554.2	1,183.6	46.34%
India	854.482	325.7	38.12%

Sources: BIS, Bloomberg, and TX Investment Consulting Co. Ltd.

GDP in countries with mature markets such as the US (see Tables 17.4 and 17.5).

Every year, the amount of financing that China's corporations procure from only issuances comes up to only around 74% of total financing derived from the stock markets. This shows a clear bias in favor of equity capital markets financing. In developed countries, the sequenced of use of different corporate finance mechanisms is implemented in accord with the theory of "optimal financing." For example, in the US, corporate finance derived from the bond markets is 4.46 times what it is from equity capital markets. In England, the same figure is 4.9 times the amount of funding from stock markets (see Table 17.6 on page 324).

TABLE 17.5 International comparison of corporate bond amounts outstanding for various countries in 2006

Country	Corporate debt issuance	The proportion of GDP
China	70.416	2.76%
Germany	143.238	5.01%
Canada	117.859	9.26%
France	265.222	11.91%
Japan	672.614	15.07%
Italy	296.392	16.10%
United States	2,790.63	21.04%

Sources: BIS and Bloomberg database, and TX Investment Consulting Co. Ltd.

TABLE 17.6 International comparison of the ratio between debt financing and equity financing of listed companies

Country	2001	2002	2003	2004	2005	Average
China	0.19	0.46	0.55	0.50	1.97	0.74
US	6.11	5.06	7.27	3.62	3.65	4.46
UK	3.93	3.63	6.28	6.94	4.98	4.90
Japan	5.14	5.67	2.61	2.54	N/A	4.14

Sources: China Statistical Yearbook Summary 2006, NYSE website, and other sources for calculations.

The reasons for sluggish growth in China's corporate bond issuing market can be attributed primarily to significant governmental interference. First, corporate bond issuers face an arduous approval process before being allowed to issue debt; this includes not only a determination as to whether or not the corporation will be allowed to issue bonds, but in what quantity, at what level of interest rates, and whether or not the use of the proceeds is acceptable. Second, multiple layers of control assure that both the approval and the issuing process are extremely complex, and therefore the efficiency of the bond issuance as a mechanism of corporate finance is low. Third, mandatory guarantees of corporate bonds actually prove counterproductive, in terms of the credit rating that the market attributes to the issuer and to any objective appraisal of the issuer's ability to repay the obligation. Fourth, restrictions determine which entities can issue bonds: basically issuers are limited to state-owned enterprises (SOEs), since privately operated enterprises still face many difficulties in issuing corporate bonds. Finally, the market lacks credible and marketized credit rating agencies.

Nonetheless, with the appearance recently of "pilot projects for testing methods of corporate bond issuance," there is some hope that all of these phenomena will begin to change. Before the current company system and credit system are improved, however, China's use of corporate bonds for financing still faces large challenges.

In terms of the structure of available products in the bond markets, China's debt-financing tools are still relatively meager in comparison to developed markets (see Figure 17.7). Virtually all bonds are issued either by government entities or entities that enjoy government backing. The structure of bond products is also not rational—other than Central Bank debt instruments, China's bond products are dominated by government bonds and financial bonds.

FIGURE 17.7 Structure of China's bond market by amounts outstanding (2006)

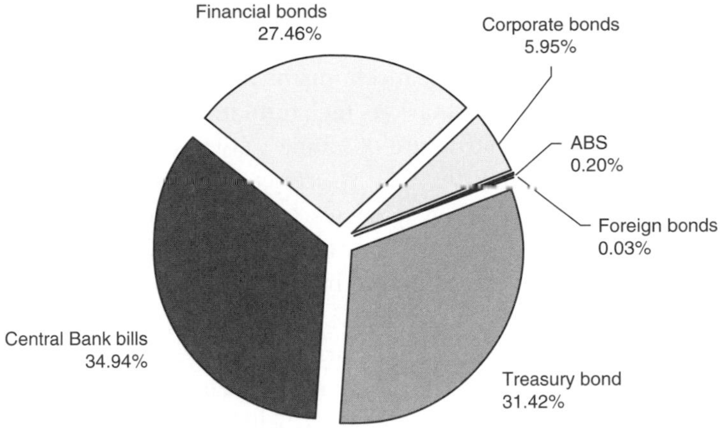

Financial bonds
27.46%

Corporate bonds
5.95%

ABS
0.20%

Foreign bonds
0.03%

Central Bank bills
34.94%

Treasury bond
31.42%

Source: www.chinabond.com.cn

UNBALANCED INVESTOR MIX IN CHINA'S BOND MARKETS

In terms of investment in bonds, commercial banks hold an absolute dominant position by the volume of bonds in their portfolios, followed by insurance organizations and funds (see Figure 17.8). National-level commercial banks hold 70% of all bond inventories, and 81% of all bond are held by all commercial banks. The uniformity of this body of investors contributes to the lack of liquidity in the market. Other

FIGURE 17.8 Structure of investor participation in China's bond markets (2007)

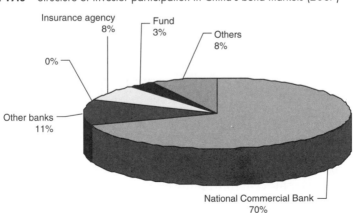

Insurance agency
8%

Fund
3%

Others
8%

0%

Other banks
11%

National Commercial Bank
70%

Source: www.chinabond.com.cn

institutional investors such as pension funds, mutual funds, foreign institutional investors, and so on, are relatively minor players in the market, leading not only to a lack of liquidity, but also constraining the normative price discovery mechanisms of bond prices.

China's corporate bond markets face fundamentally the same problems. In July 2007, the structure of China's corporate bonds holdings was: individual investors 0.03%, insurance companies 51.2%, commercial banks 19.2%, credit agencies 6%, and funds 6.6%. Insurance companies held by far the dominant position. The US's weighting of investors is quite different. In the first quarter of 2007, US statistics indicate that household owners of corporate bonds held 11.4%, among institutional investors, US life insurance companies held 18.5%, foreign institutional investors held 28.3%, commercial banks held 8%, private pension funds held 3%, mutual funds held 8.5%, government-supported institutions held 4.93%, and so on. Relatively speaking, the holdings of US institutional investors are more evenly balanced.

OTHER FACTORS CONSTRAINING THE GROWTH OF CHINA'S BOND MARKETS

Other factors constraining bond markets relate to the issuers, the investors, the intermediary institutions, and the basic market infrastructure including the regulatory environment.

In China, an ideal system of modern corporate governance has yet to be achieved; that is, one that includes an independent Board of Directors, and that respects the roles they should play in supervising and motivating managers. If the great bulk of enterprises in China want to issue corporate bonds, they must improve their creditworthiness and ability to honor repayment obligations—but with the exception of large state-owned groups and large financial institutions. With regard to the investors, institutional investors still need to become stronger, market liquidity needs to be improved, and there are still restrictions on certain investments. For example, life insurance companies may not purchase un-guaranteed bonds. Looking at the intermediary institutions, credit rating organizations still lack authority, the public credibility of accounting firms has to be improved, law firm opinions still have to be allowed to play a role, market-making dealers still have to improve their operations, and so on.

In terms of the basic market infrastructure, current laws and regulations are inadequate. The bond markets are fragmented and lack a unified, interactive, depository, and settlement system. In terms of regulatory oversight, mechanisms for information disclosure and protection of bond investors' rights are still in great need of strengthening. In addition, there are multiple regulatory bodies with duplicate efforts, while self-regulatory mechanisms in the industry have yet to play an important role.

China is still changing its economic structure. The country's financial systems are incomplete: interest rates have not been fully marketized; that is, they are not fully market-driven, while financial derivative products are in their infancy. Those products related to the bond spot market include only simple bond forward and interest-rate swaps. Options, contract swaps, and other such derivatives are still lacking. This incomplete financial system makes it difficult to satisfy investors' need for risk management. The situation is not conducive to guarding against and ameliorating financial risk in general, and is another key factor constraining China's spot market for bonds.

PROSPECTS

Based on an optimistic appraisal of China's economy and the ongoing process of Reform and Opening over the next 20 years, we believe that the bond market in China will have tremendous growth and will, indeed, become an international fixed income market.

China's bond market is still tiny at present and far below the level of advanced countries, but that is precisely why the market has such enormous potential to grow. In July 2007, the inventory of China's bonds was around 50% of China's total GDP and stock market capitalization added together. If you subtract the Central Bank notes that the Bank uses to remove excess liquidity, this percentage drops to around 30%. The experience of advanced countries over the past 16 years has shown that bond markets as a percentage of GDP have at least doubled in that space of time. For example, in the first quarter of 2007, US bonds were roughly 207% the value of the US's GDP; in 1991, the figure was 102%. In the same year, the ratio for Japan was 71%, while at present, it is around 150%. In the same period, the percentage in England went from 27% to more than 170%!

Given the important recognition by both the Chinese government and scholars that China needs to speed up the growth of direct financing and lessen reliance on commercial banks, the prospects for the Chinese bond market are enormous. The author feels that as China's corporate governance structures improve, as social credit systems are established and a foundation of appropriate laws and regulations is put in place, in another 10 to 20 years, the ratio between China's bond market and GDP (not including Central Bank notes) has the promise of exceeding 100%. At the same time, within the next 20 years, Chinese corporate bonds have the hope of seeing tremendous growth, occupying something like 40% to 50% of GDP.

Bond varieties will diversify, and even high-risk junk bonds may serve the investment needs of specific investors. In addition, the potential for asset securitization markets in China is huge and will increasingly be realized.

More Internationalized Bond Markets

We forecast that the degree of internationalization in China's domestic bond market will increase significantly by the year 2020. First, foreign investors will become important participants in China's domestic bond markets, China's government bonds will become a part of foreign exchange reserves of central banks in other countries, and China's government bonds and corporate bonds will enter the global asset portfolios of large-scale international financial institutions.

Second, RMB "foreign bond" markets will become an important market; that is, foreign governments and international corporate groups will issue RMB-denominated bonds inside the PRC. Third, due to the internationalization of the RMB, by 2020 a sizable RMB "Eurobond" market will appear overseas. We feel that Hong Kong may become the most important RMB "Eurobond" market, while Shanghai will be able to provide offshore market services for RMB "Eurobond" transactions.

Looking further into the future, although China's bond markets have a long way to go, we believe that they will become an important component of both global and domestic capital markets. China's bond markets will definitely serve an important function in improving and growing domestic and foreign capital markets.

CHAPTER 18

China's Asset Management Industry

Fan Yonghong
Chairman of the Board, Huaxia Fund Management Company

Sustained rapid economic growth has characterized the Chinese economy since the start of the country's Reform and Opening policies. China's GDP reached RMB21.09 trillion by 2006, making it the fourth-largest economic entity in the world. As China's economy merges with the global economic system, it is increasingly playing a role in influencing that system.

China's capital markets began operating relatively late in the global scheme, but given the tremendous impetus of the country's economic growth, they have quickly traversed a course that took some decades in more developed countries. Share reallocation reform has been quite successful since 2006, taking capital markets to a whole new level. By the end of September 2007, total market capitalization in China broke through RMB23 trillion and the securitization ratio exceeded 100% (the ratio of capital market capitalization to the total GDP of a country), making China the world's largest new market.

As a stabilizing and central force, an asset management industry signals a degree of maturity in capital markets. China's asset management industry has displayed very noticeable achievements in going from an irregular to a regular industry that is based on rational investing as opposed to opportunistic trading. Whether judged in terms of the size of assets, types of products, number of investors, or establishment of laws and regulations, the industry has experienced incredibly fast growth. The appearance of stock investment funds has had a particularly positive effect on the development of the capital markets. The size of China's asset management industry currently comes up to more than RMB3 trillion, which covers nearly 40% of China's

A-share market. There are more than 90 million investors, making the asset management industry the most important institutional investor in China.

THE START OF FUNDS IN CHINA

The development of an asset management industry in the West can be traced back over 100 years. The growth of the industry accompanied the appearance of a tremendous amount of idle capital in society. Although it originated in the traditional business of private banking, asset management as an independent industry is a fairly new development even in the West, and Chinese people are just now becoming familiar with it.

Conceptually, asset management means using effective management operations to conserve and create more value for both monetary and non-monetary assets. A narrower definition of asset management generally addresses the process of pooling assets by institutional investors and actually investing in capital markets. In still more concrete terms, asset management can be understood as having an investor (individual or institutional) authorize an asset manager to represent him or her in managing, buying, and selling monetary funds or other securities assets as a kind of financial business. The essence of the business is fiduciary responsibility over investing.

Since asset management is a new concept to China, the country went through a long period of unstructured and irregular behavior as the industry emerged. This was in part due to the fact that China's market environment is far from perfect.

A fund called "China Eastern" initiated the asset management business in China in 1985. The China Eastern Investment Company set up the fund in Hong Kong and it became the start of the great flow of China's eventual investment fund business.

Soon, a number of government-originated funds were being organized that targeted overseas investors and that invested in China-related activities such as China trade, China-region economic development projects, and high-tech Town and Village Enterprises (TVEs). More than 20 such Chinese government-initiated funds had been set up in Hong Kong by the end of 1992. Operating inside China, these funds transmitted investment concepts into the country, as well as international management and industry knowledge. To a degree, this hastened the birth and the rapid growth of China's own investment funds.

With the acceleration of enterprise reform and share allocation reform in China, as well as fast economic growth and the opening of the Shenzhen and Shanghai Stock Exchanges, financing needs of microeconomic entities increased rapidly after 1991. Shackled by restrictions on extending credit and other regulatory and policy constraints, commercial banks were unable to respond to the growing demand. Certain provinces and municipalities were therefore allowed to begin pilot projects in "securities funds" or similar financing methods, after meeting procedures for approval that were administered by branch offices of the People's Bank of China (PBC). The first fund inside China was successfully set up in July 1991. It was called the "Pearl Trust Fund," and was capitalized with RMB69.3 billion. The Wuhan Securities Investment Fund and the Nanshan Venture Investment Fund were established in October of the same year. By September 1993, a total of 78 other investment funds had been set up, again after review and authorization by the PBC, with total value of funds under management coming to RMB7.6 billion. It is customary in the sector to call these funds that were set up before the promulgation of the "Provisional Measures on the Administration of Securities Investment Funds" the "Old Funds."

With the proliferation of these Old Funds came the increased presence in the Chinese capital markets of securities companies. Against this backdrop, securities companies began an effort to test the waters by serving as agents in an asset management business. A modern and significant asset management industry grew out of these initial efforts of both the Old Funds and the securities companies serving as "agents" for them.

Unfortunately, a regulatory system necessary for building trust in the entire wealth management system was lacking. Investors were leery and their distrust expanded not only to investment advisory services of securities companies, but also to the entire financial system. What happened with the Old Funds is a good example. Owing to the absence of a unified set of laws and regulations, governance structures of the Old Funds were not in line with the basic principles of fiduciary responsibility. Managers, custodians, and fund promoters were often indistinguishable from one another. Funds were mainly started by investment and securities companies under the aegis of large banks, insurance companies, and large enterprise groups. Clearly demarcated lines of responsibility did not exist. The size of the funds was generally small, and the distribution channels were not standardized. The portfolio composition of investments was extremely unscientific, investment efficiency was low, and there was little built-in capacity for risk-avoidance. A number of Old Funds invested heavily in real estate projects or other physical plant projects which deprived the funds of any liquidity. In the mid-1990s, when the real estate sector cooled, the asset values of these funds contracted leading to huge losses for fund investors.

Despite this, the appearance of these Old Funds seemed to stir a long-slumbering consciousness about asset management in people's minds. The funds served as a harbinger of the asset management industry that was soon to come. People experimented with all kinds of reckless behavior in the course of investing, but in the process they accumulated valuable lessons that were to become the foundation for a more regular set of laws and regulations governing the new fund-management system.

STANDARDIZING CHINA'S ASSET-MANAGEMENT INDUSTRY

In the mid- and late 1990s, the asset management industry overseas started booming. By the end of 1998, assets invested in funds globally had surpassed US$7 trillion. This surpassed the asset size of commercial banks to become the largest component in the financial industry. In China, after 20 years of economic growth and savings accumulation, savings of urban and rural residents combined had reached a sum of RMB5.34 trillion by roughly the same year. Balances in insurance funds and all kinds of retirement and social security funds amounted to several hundred billion RMB. With an urgent need for wealth management, common people looked more and more to the newly born fund industry.

Closed-end Funds

Capital markets in the late 1990s were still grappling with the burden of state-owned enterprise (SOE) reform and restructuring. Although the environment was not ideal, the capital markets still managed to grow at a rate of 30% per year, providing a good foundation for the growth of China's fund industry. After several years of feeling their way forward, of experimenting with the Old Funds, people began to be aware that the real value of a funds industry was not just to give a "blood transfusion" to the stock market, but also to generate rational investing concepts so that the market as a whole could follow a path of stable growth. Under the strong support of government policies, pilot projects in closed-end funds were initiated, imbued with great hopes and expectations.

The formal implementation of these pilot projects was marked by the "Provisional Measures for Securities Investment Fund Management," promulgated by the State Council in November of 1997. The Provisional Measures provided detailed regulations regarding the establishment of funds, fund raising of and trading, custodian and management responsibilities, rights and duties of those who held them and so on, meaning that from henceforth, China's funds had rules they could follow and had therefore entered upon a path of more regularized growth. In the second half of 1998, the CSRC gave approval for five new funds: Jintai, Kaiyuan, Xinghua, Anxin, and Yuyang. It approved five commercial banks as qualified custodians, and it approved the establishment of five fund management companies.

The closed-end funds were able to absorb the lessons learned by the Old Funds. Starting out with bylaws, and under a legal structure and regulatory framework, they were able to achieve breakthroughs with respect to fund operation, product innovation, and internal controls. Their size and number grew rapidly, standards of management improved quickly, and they succeeded in laying a good foundation for the growth of the funds industry. From 1998 to 2002, assets in China's closed-end funds increased from RMB10.742 billion to RMB71.708 billion, an annual growth rate of 60.74%.

Open-ended Funds

In October of 2000, the CSRC formally promulgated "Pilot Measures for Open-ended Securities Investment Funds." These then became the rules and regulations governing the open-ended funds industry. International experience demonstrates that open-end funds are the mainstay of any investment funds sector: in the US, UK, and the Hong Kong and Taiwan Regions of China, over 90% of all funds are open-end funds. In 1998, however, since the market climate in China was less than ideal, and asset markets were in a very preliminary stage, it was necessary to start with closed-end funds. As the market developed and became more open and transparent, people could begin to focus on an open-ended system in which shares could be redeemed at any time.

In 2001, three companies were authorized to issue open-ended funds, and with this China's fund industry entered a whole new era. The three were the Hua An Fund Management Company, the Nan

Fang Fund Management Company, and the Huaxia Fund Management Company. In contrast to the closed-end funds, the degree of "marketization" of open-ended funds was much higher. Shares could be purchased or redeemed at any time, which contributed both to motivating and to restraining fund managers—it gave them the incentive to improve their management and to provide higher returns for investors. Moreover, open-end funds carry out trades on the basis of net asset value of fund shares, which eliminates the common discounting problem seen at closed-end funds. At the same time, open-ended funds won the trust of average investors by operating in more transparent mode with greater information disclosure. In 2001, assets under management in open-ended funds reached RMB11.8 billion.

While many were pleased with the way open-ended funds shielded them from greater risk, they were to find that the funds industry as a whole "encountered a bear market on a narrow path" for the next five years. China's A-share market was highly subdued from 2001 to 2005 as the market index fell nearly 50%. Severely challenged, China's fund industry began to borrow from modern international practices as it accelerated new product innovations, putting out a variety of such low-risk products as bond funds, capital-preservation funds, currency funds, exchange traded funds (ETF), and so on. To meet the needs of investors, it actively developed social security funds, enterprise annuities and others. At the same time, the industry improved its customer servicing and marketing and sales. In 2003, the "Law on Securities Investment Funds" was passed, replacing the old "Provisional Measures," and the legal environment for fund management advanced to a new level, now propelling a rapid growth in open-ended funds. From 2001 to 2006, open-ended fund assets grew from RMB11.801 billion to RMB694.519 billion, an average annual growth rate of 125.92%. As a percentage of total fund assets, open-end funds reached 81.05%, becoming the most important financial tool in China's asset management industry.

Asset Management as the Largest Institutional Investor in China

With the significant amendment of the "Company Law" and the "Securities Law," together with the smooth implementation of share allocation reform, in 2006, China's capital markets reached a turning point. By September 2007, the Shanghai Share Index showed a historic gain to 5552, a rise of 456% over two years earlier, when the Index stood at 998 in June of 2005. Total capitalization value of the two Exchanges in Shanghai and Shenzhen now exceeded RMB23 trillion. China's capital markets had completed their long counter-economic cycle, and become a true barometer of China's economic conditions.

The beneficial market environment brought with it a historic opportunity for the funds industry. Asset values leapt upward and the number of customers expanded tremendously. By September 2007, assets under management broke through RMB3 trillion, or a 250% growth over the level at the end of 2006 when the total was 856.5 billion. The percentage of fund-managed assets in China's A-share market exceeded 36%, and the number of investors exceeded 90 million. All the standard international market fund products appeared, including stock funds, bond funds, mixed funds, currency funds, ETF, and others. In order to meet the many different investment styles and needs—that is, growth, value, income, and indexation to the market—and to gain the broad acceptance of investors, funds covered various investment goals, and incorporated various investment concepts. Successful in these regards, funds have now grown to become the largest institutional investor category in China's capital markets.

LESSONS

Looking back over the course of the development of China's asset management industry, we can see that it was the necessary consequence of a market economy's growth to a certain level. Growth of the industry occurred against the backdrop of an increasing need for wealth management among people, and a gradual strengthening of capital markets. Still, the speed of its development has surprised people. It has by now developed into a diversified industry that includes various institutional-investor funds, insurance funds, social security funds, dealers, and Qualified Foreign Institutional Investors (QFII). Funds have become the most representative institutional investors in China's capital markets, and their experience to a large degree reflects the course of China's asset management industry. Summing up the successful experience of these funds, we can discern the following main aspects.

Government Guidance and Marketization Reform

Unlike the way in which many mature markets grew by following a long "self-evolutionary" path, China's asset management industry has consistently been promoted and guided by the government. The government guidance has been done in harmony with the course of self-evolution, however, and with marketization reform.

China's fund industry started in the midst of highly unfavorable market conditions. Initially holding only 5% of domestically issued shares, it nonetheless quickly advanced to the current holdings of 36%. As a reference point, the US fund industry took 25 years to reach the same percentage. In Taiwan, the process took 20 years. The reason China's fund industry was able to accomplish such fast growth can, to a large degree, be attributed to the appropriate handling of the relationship between governmental controls and market "self-evolution" or pure market forces. As regulator, the government passed laws and regulations that both guided and encouraged the industry in its growth and product innovations. At the same time, the government led a marketization reform that intended to allow the market to act, to release the potential of the market by providing it with incentives. This second aspect of the government's role is particularly noticeable in developing the market for open-ended funds from 2001 to 2006.

The first group of open-ended funds was issued in 2001. This brought greater competition into the fund industry and started the process of marketization reform. From 2002, under the guidance of the CSRC, authorities simplified and standardized the review and approval procedures, turning them into a more transparent and professional system. After 2003, the system was opened up to broader participation, and the government went a step further in devolving authority down the line. Authorities worked to make Chinese registration procedures more in line with overseas practices. By now, the Chinese fund industry has become fairly competitive with regard to the companies themselves, their selling channels, and their custodial organizations. It has become the most dynamic and most marketized of any sector in China's capital markets.

Setting up a Fiduciary System

Since ancient times, China's financial industry has operated on the basis of trustworthiness, taking the activities of "Jin merchants" in Shanxi (then "Jin") Province as its model. [Early banks or *piao-hao* were centered in Shanxi in the Qing dynasty in China.] Financial industries abroad have also made "fiduciary responsibility" the foundation of their culture and their spirit. Yet, relatively speaking, China's wealth management industry has faced certain problems, and the fundamental reason can be traced to a lack of trust in the financial services industry by most investors. This can be seen in the slow failure of the Old Funds and in the brief duration when securities' companies acted as "agents" in asset management.

Starting with the closed-end funds, China's financial industry has been built on the foundation of modern international practices as adopted from abroad, and on fiduciary responsibility. China passed legislation clarifying the rights and obligations of fund holders, fund managers, and fund custodians, which assured that these three are all mutually independent as well as mutually regulating. The legislation formed a scientific basis for governance structures so that the operating environment of the industry could rely on established systems. According to stipulations in the "Fund Law," the holders of fund participations are the actual owners of the fund's assets, the custodian of the fund is the actual legal and economic entity responsible for protecting the fund's assets, and thus is the "owner in name only" of the assets. Importantly, the fund's assets are independent both of the fund manager and of the custodians. At the same time, regulations stipulate that every fund management company must strictly abide by its obligations of information disclosure. Each must appoint a compliance officer, and an independent Board of Directors that is responsible for oversight of the funds operations and that, to the greatest possible degree, safeguards the interests of investors.

Experience has shown that setting up third-party custodial systems, requiring detailed information disclosure at regular intervals, and making operations transparent has not only strengthened investors' confidence, but has also allowed the fund industry as a whole to avoid any large scandals over the past 10 years. Indeed, the wealth management industry has been praised as being the most "sunny" or "open to scrutiny" of any financial sector.

Stimulating Growth with Innovations

The growth of China's fund industry has been led by product innovation. As a whole, the industry enjoys a clear advantage in being late to the market. Building on an established foundation of international experience, China's fund industry has progressed rapidly from closed-end funds to open-ended funds, to innovations in ETFs, to stock funds, bond funds, capital-conservancy funds, and currency funds—in other words, to having a diversified product base, and all in the space of less than eight years. Among all of these products, the issuing of currency funds and ETFs can be taken as representative of the process.

From 2001 to 2005, China's stock markets entered a slump, and investors focused far more on capital preservation than on capital appreciation. Low-risk funds were therefore required by the investor market. At the same time, along with the rise in incomes and savings of citizens, the need for a low-risk alternative to savings deposits became more and more apparent. A money-market fund was born in December 2003. As a good substitute for simple bank deposits, the fund was in line with the demand for low-risk products, it had low entry costs and was easy to enter and exit, and so satisfied the relatively high liquidity needs of investors. From this initial offering, money-market funds grew rapidly and became an important factor sustaining China's financial industry at a time when the stock market was depressed.

ETFs constitute one of the newer innovations in recent years in the international financial industry and one that has grown tremendously since being initiated. There is still a substantial gap between capital markets abroad and various aspects of China's capital markets framework, however, including China's trading system and legal and regulatory structure. Therefore, it remains to be seen whether or not China can put out ETF products that are suited to China's circumstances. Some developments have shone a positive light on the entry of ETFs into China, though, including technological changes implemented by the Shanghai Stock Exchange under the guidance of the CSRC. The Shanghai Exchange's "50 ETF" was successfully promoted in December of 2004, and the functioning of the fund has lived up to and even surpassed its hoped-for goals. It has won the approval of investors, and the size and market influence of the fund has grown. The successful presentation of this ETF is a signal that China's fund industry innovation has stepped up to a new level, and greatly diminished the gap between it and international competition.

China's fund industry has emphasized the creation of products that satisfy a range of investor needs, including different risk, income, and diversification requirements. Each innovation in the industry has spurred its further development, so the industry as a whole has quickly traversed a path that more developed markets took dozens of years to achieve. Innovations have become the strongest motivating force. Putting appropriate products out at the appropriate moment has become a core factor in the success of China's fund industry.

The Future of China's Asset Management Industry

China's asset management industry continues to display tremendous vitality. Investment funds are the largest institutional investor type in the country. Insurance funds entering the capital markets doubled as limits on investing were loosened. QFII approvals were expanded and investor enthusiasm rose daily. After administrative or "governance" restructuring, the expansion of securities companies is apparent. Private placements became ever more transparent. Looking to the future, China's asset management industry is moving into the best period it has enjoyed to date.

WEALTH MANAGEMENT

Sustained economic growth and accompanying growth in capital markets have provided a solid foundation for the asset management industry. China's GDP reached RMB21.09 trillion in 2006, making China the fourth-largest economic entity on the globe. Foreign exchange reserves reached RMB1.3 trillion, highest in the world. Savings of citizens reached a sum of RMB16.16 trillion, which was three times the amount in 1998. A constantly increasing need of ordinary people for wealth management is providing vast room to grow for the asset management industry. Using asset management as an effective way to turn savings into investment is, at the same time, helping the capital markets move from a volatile "boom" to a safer "maturity," thereby giving impetus to the overall growth of China's economy.

INTERNATIONALIZATION

Asset management is a kind of "overseas invention." Beginning with pilot open-ended funds, China's asset management industry has invited foreign partners to join in technical cooperation, and has studied and absorbed the lessons of overseas funds. Once China joined the WTO in 2001, the pace of opening by China's capital markets picked up, further propelling internationalization. More and more QFIIs have entered China's domestic market since 2003. While bringing in more competition, they have also given tremendous impetus to the growth of China's own asset management industry.

Currently, three fund companies are officially approved by the CSRC as Qualified Domestic Institutional Investors (QDIIs). These are Huaxia, Nanfang, and Jiashi, and they are permitted to engage in overseas securities investment management. The fund system's QDII products will soon be competing with international competitors in the global securities markets. Looking to the future, China's fund management personnel will be setting up branch organizations overseas and carrying out sales activities in other markets. The strategic thinking is transitioning from "Import into China" to "China Going Out." Opportunities and challenges exist together, but China's asset management industry is more and more coming onto the "same track" as international markets.

NEW FINANCIAL TOOLS

As the degree of China's openness to the outside world continues to grow, it is absolutely necessary for China to establish and develop its markets for financial derivatives. The further development of such financing methods as stock futures, financing bills, options, and interest rate swaps is also a way to improve the price efficiency ratios of the entire financial market. With regard to the asset management industry, a series of products with different risk and income characteristics can be created on the foundation of these tools that satisfy the needs of more investors. Improving already existing products (such as ETFs, indexed funds, capital preservation funds, and so on) will have a positive influence as well. We expect the asset management industry to have a relatively broad degree of participation in the Stock Index Futures that is soon to be opened.

EDUCATING INVESTORS

Although Chinese investors are increasingly moving away from blind opportunistic trading and in the direction of rational investing, and although their general level of sophistication has improved, they are still immature in terms of investment behavior compared to investors abroad. Many investors lack basic knowledge about investing; they understand little about risk, product differences, capital allocation, and other such fundamental concepts. This tells us that efforts so far to educate Chinese investors as to risk awareness have been insufficient. It also reveals that there are great differences in domestic investors' understanding of different products. As seen from the international experience, it is clear that a well-educated base of investors is the foundation and guarantee of healthy growth in the asset management industry. As the degree of complexity of financial instruments increases, and as overseas investments bring investors in touch with completely new markets, there is an ever-greater need for training. Cultivating a population of investors who operate rationally is going to become a major issue in attempts to grow China's asset management industry.

China has made great progress in erecting concepts of value-based investing, guiding stock markets to rational pricing, improving the corporate governance structures of listed companies, expanding wealth management products for investors, and so on. This is merely a beginning. We hope that in the not-too-distant future, China's asset management business will indeed go from "boom" to "maturity," and will become an important component of international capital markets. We hope that it will play an ever more important and more active role in global capital markets.

CHAPTER 19

Venture Capital/Private Equity in China[1]

John S. Wadsworth, Jr and Wu Shangzhi

Chairman, Ceyuan Ventures; Chairman, CDH Investments

EARLY DAYS 1990 TO 1998—LESSONS LEARNED[2]

By the 1990s, China had already become a popular destination for foreign direct investment (FDI). From a level of $57 million in 1980, FDI had expanded to $4 billion per year in 1991, but almost all of this investment was made by foreign multinationals and other strategic investors who were looking to take advantage of China's abundance of low cost labor, newly established free trade zones (known as Special Economic Zones) that provided low cost land and minimal taxes, and the future opening to China's 1.3 billion consumers. In spite of the challenges and failures, the general optimism of the strategic investors combined with steady and gradual changes in China's shift in protecting the property rights of foreigners eventually led to a growing interest by foreign financial investors and the first significant wave of investment by private equity/venture capital (PE/VC) funds in the early 1990s.

Technically, though, the Chinese PE/VC industry started in the mid-1980s when the central government decided to sponsor local venture capital funds as part of the overall reforms in China's lagging science and technology sector. These initiatives led to the creation of numerous government-funded VC firms, often staffed with former officials from the local government and former managers in state-owned enterprises (SOEs). These government-funded firms were thrust into a Chinese market environment without previous VC/investment experience, often hampered with bureaucracy and a

343

government agenda. VC, as then promoted by the Chinese government, was not a meant to be a tool for properly allocating capital to finance change, but rather a mechanism for the government to try to drive macroeconomic growth by encouraging technology innovation and commercialization. Therefore, the government-funded VC firms pursued investments from a policy driven point of view and not based on the basic principles of investing that underpin the success of venture investing in Silicon Valley or other developed markets. Due to the lack of experience, most of these investments failed and by the mid-1990s most of these firms were in financial difficulty or closed—most notably the collapse of China New Technology Venture Investment Co. founded in 1985.

The first real wave of commercially driven PE/VC funds came in the early 1990s when foreign firms raised funds specifically to make investments in China. Most observers point to International Data Group (IDG)'s formation of the first foreign venture fund to operate in China. Foreign funds accounted for 95% of total funds raised

TABLE 19.1 Funds raised (US$ millions) and number of new funds

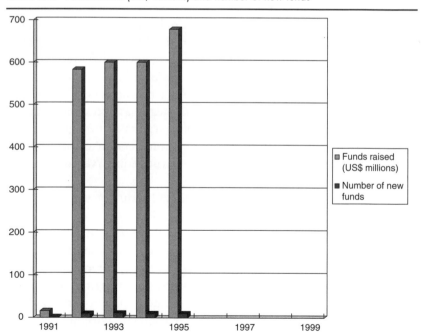

during this period. Although the increase in fundraising was impressive during this period, China's venture capital industry remained relatively obscure compared to Western and Hong Kong VC/PE markets.

Why did the first wave of international VC investment begin in the early 1990s? By then, many of China's economic reforms had begun to generate fundamental changes in China's overall economy. China's market-oriented reform began in 1978 with the privatization of agriculture, gradual SOE autonomy, and legal acceptance of small private enterprises. The Shanghai Stock Exchange and Shenzhen Stock Exchange were officially opened in December 1990 and April 1991, respectively. In 1992, Deng Xiaoping formally broke the traditional ideological backlash against the market economy when he famously declared: "black cat or white cat, it is a good cat as long as it catches the mouse." A few months later, the fourteenth Congress of the Chinese Communist Party officially endorsed the establishment of a "socialist market economy," spurring greater SOE autonomy, price reforms and the process of opening up China's economy to the world. Various tax exemptions and tax reduction plans were also granted to foreign investors, including venture capitalists. All these reforms laid a solid foundation for China's financial market boom in the 1990s and stimulated the economy to grow at approximately 11% per year from 1991 to 1994.

The reforms and robust economic growth ignited the imaginations of international investors. Although foreign investors generally knew little about investing in China, many were optimistic they could use their knowledge of the capital markets to profit from China's shift from a planned economy to a market economy. Moreover, China's firms had started to list on overseas stock exchanges. In October 1992, Brilliance Automotive (an SOE) became the first Chinese firm to be listed on the New York Stock Exchange, followed by nine initial public offerings (IPOs) listed on the Hong Kong Stock Exchange in the following year.

One of the most telling takes of investors' enthusiasm in China was the story of Asian Strategic Investment Management Company (ASIMCO), a VC firm founded by Jack Perkowski, a veteran investment banker in the US. The story goes that Perkowski started fundraising after Thanksgiving in 1993 and raised $75 million by Christmas. In six weeks, he had raised a total of $150 million. The demand to "get into China" was so overwhelming that he raised another $160 million in 1995 without any tangible results and only the dream of consolidating China's automotive parts and beer industries.[3] ASIMCO was not alone in chasing the China dream. A number of other funds were raised at that time on big-picture enthusiasm, but with a lack of practical understanding of the challenges of investing in China's domestic markets.

In hindsight, most of these funds under-performed due to the lack of an essential understanding of China's business environment. Particularly, these inexperienced fund managers seem to have underestimated the difficulties of:

- aligning interests with SOEs, both in setting up investment funds, as well as executing a "turnaround strategy"
- creating an exit in the domestic capital markets due to "legal person share" illiquidity issues
- judging the quality of Chinese business managers and evaluating the sustainability of business models in face of the rapid changes that were occurring in China's overall economy.

According to the *Asian Venture Capital Journal* (AVCJ) the majority (67%) of PE/venture funds in the early 1990s were joint venture funds.[4] These early investors believed that by creating joint ventures with SOEs, they would have allies to overcome the myriad challenges of investing in China, including the challenge of generating deal flow and overcoming regulatory issues.

For new investors in China, the challenge of generating deal flow was a real obstacle to creating profitable investments. In developed capital markets, PE and VC investors rely on their reputation, proprietary deal sourcing networks, and market intermediaries such as investment banks, accounting firms, and law firms to attract potential deals. However, this infrastructure had only begun to develop in China in the early 1990s, and foreign investors had no existing deal flow structure to rely upon to source transactions. Although there is no shortcut for PE/venture firms building their own reputations and developing proprietary deal sourcing networks, these early entrants tried to speed up the process by leveraging SOE relationships.

The new foreign-backed funds also had no experience dealing with China's regulatory bureaucracy. This lack of experience combined with a dearth of experienced Chinese investment professionals resulted in most investors employing a myriad of ineffective strategies for dealing with these regulatory risks. These risks included a weak legal and regulatory environment that was radically and erratically shifting from a centrally planned economy with heavy government influence to a market-driven economy. Some foreign investors also believed that there was a real risk that the Chinese government might expropriate international VC investments. Therefore, international investors often sought SOE partners to create joint ventures because they hoped that these SOE connections would act as political buffers against arbitrary bureaucrats with their state connections. In the context of a transitory economic and legal framework, these foreign investors hoped that powerful domestic partners would bring them into China's decision-making circle so that they could influence government actions related to their portfolio companies. Unfortunately, the goals of the SOE partners were not in line with those of the foreign investors and, in most instances, these partnerships failed to produce positive results.

In terms of target deals, early foreign investors invested almost exclusively in China's SOEs, despite their well-known weak corporate governance and little incentive to pursue enterprise growth. In the early 1990s approximately 90% of all venture-backed firms were SOEs.[5] This could not be explained by the lack of private firms in China. Private enterprises had been allowed to exist since the late 1980s and there were more than six million private firms by 1992.

Several reasons may explain foreign investors focus on investing with SOEs in the early 1990s. First, SOEs appeared to enjoy the most favorable access to resources in China. SOEs could obtain capital, human resources, and raw materials from the government at low or no cost. Second, SOEs had monopoly or better market positions in many important sectors. Third, all IPOs of domestic Chinese companies listed on either domestic or overseas stock exchanges had to be approved by government regulators and there was a favorable quota for SOEs. These favorable conditions seemed to make investments in under-performing SOEs look attractive to inexperienced China investors.

Based on PE firms' success in developed capital markets, investors misjudged the difficulty of executing similar "turnaround" strategies of under-performing industrial SOEs in China. Since these investors had no experience working with Chinese management teams, they were unable to create investment structures that properly aligned their interests with Chinese managers. For PE investors backing growth and or "turnaround" opportunities, they believed that, as in developed markets, the financial investors required majority ownership positions to "control" their portfolio companies, which was difficult to obtain in China. These early investors also relied heavily on legal contracts to gain "control," which highlighted the mismatch in goals and expectations of the investors' with their SOE shareholders and portfolio companies' management teams. Without a robust and functioning "Anglo-Saxon" based legal system, the standard investing strategies that were effective in developed capital markets failed to produce similar successful results in China. More fundamentally, though, these strategies failed because the investors did not fully understand the complexity and difficulty of changing the corporate cultures of the SOEs from a planned economy mentality to a market-driven, profit mentality. The issue of ownership percentage and board representation was overwhelmed by more practical challenges of motivating managers to run their businesses to generate shareholder value rather than other entrenched goals, such as, employment, size, and political objectives.

In addition to legal structural issues, early investors in China faced a significant challenge to exit their investments. During this period, many international investors expected that the exit obstacles imposed by Chinese securities law were "short-term" problems. However, the long-anticipated policy change to allow joint venture enterprises (such as foreign VC-backed SOEs) to be listed on China's domestic stock exchanges did not materialize until the turn of the century after 2000.

The "exit" problem was, probably, the most critical issue that investors needed to solve to generate profitable investments in China. Given the sensitivity of transforming the country from a planned economy to a market-driven economy and questions of public versus private ownership, China's early security regulations limited the trading of shares on the public markets to newly issued shares. The shares held by existing shareholders prior to an initial public offering (IPO) were divided into various categories but were all treated as "legal person shares." These "legal person shares" of domestic Chinese companies, regardless of who owned these shares, were prohibited from being traded on any public market. Although a Chinese company listed on the Hong Kong Stock Exchange as a H-share or on the Singapore Stock Exchange as an S-share, or on the New York Stock Exchange as an N-share, such companies continued to be regulated by China's regulatory regime, which meant that "legal person shares" could not be traded on the public markets. Since investors were holding "legal person shares" in the SOEs that they had invested, they were not able to use the public markets to exit their investments even if they successfully engineered an IPO on a foreign market.

During this early period, most investors failed to fully understand the issue and tried a number of ineffective strategies, such as:

- Many investors expected that these arcane rules regarding "legal person shares" would be changed within the holding period of their investment. So, they simply invested directly into China-based companies as a joint-venture partner. Since the rules did not change until after 2004 to allow these "legal person shares" to be freely tradable, many investors were quickly disappointed and the strain of not being able to exit their investments caused problems at the operating level even in well-managed, profitable companies.

- Others attempted to resolve this issue by structuring their investment through an offshore holding company, which would own majority control of the domestic China-based operating company. Typically, the financial investors held their ownership offshore while the Chinese management teams, if they had any share ownership, held shares in the onshore operating company. In this simple structure, the offshore holding company would become the listed vehicle, which seemingly solved the exit problem. However, investors and managers quickly discovered that this structure provided no incentive for the Chinese management teams to profitably manage their companies. With a weak legal system and lack of experience and understanding of the functioning of companies in a market-driven economy, many of these companies either failed to reach their exits or disappointed investors when they did achieve an exit.

- A few other creative structures were used, such as co-investing with multinational companies (MNC) with the expectation that the financial investor's stake could be sold to the MNC. These structures "solved" the immediate "exit" challenge, but they failed to create a business structure in which the financial investor was adding much value and, as a result, was typically left in a weak negotiating position. These creative structures rarely generated attractive returns for the financial investors.

In addition to difficulties creating proper structures that would allow financial investors predictable exits, there were also very few skilled and trained Chinese investors active in the market at that time. The basic skills of private equity investing—such as analyzing business models, performing in-depth due diligence, and judging the quality of the management teams—that are taken for granted in developed markets did not exist. China's opaque markets and unconventional business environment prevented most foreign investors from being able to accurately research and evaluate the investment opportunities. Given the fact that China had only recently begun to change its economy to be market-driven, the standard measures of quality for management teams were substantially different from those in developed markets. All of these "soft" aspects of evaluating investment opportunities made investing in China challenging.

While it is difficult to find accurate evidence on the performance of VC firms in the early and mid-1990s, several proxies indicate that results were likely to have been poor. The first proxy of performance is whether firms that raised their first China investment fund were able to raise a second fund. Failure to satisfy previous investors usually leads to failure in raising new funds. Of the 33 international funds raised between 1991 and 1997, only one venture firm was able to raise a follow-on fund to invest in China after 1997.[6]

The second proxy for performance is the performance of listed VC firms. Due to the difficulty of obtaining IPO approval from the Chinese government, some VC firms listed themselves (for example, the venture firm itself was taken public) to provide liquidity for investors. Most of the firms were listed between 1992 and 1994. *Asian Venture Capital Journal (AVCJ)* tracked these funds' performance and showed that on average, in 1998, the share prices of these funds were only 48% of their IPO prices.

The third proxy is performance of PE/venture-backed IPOs of portfolio companies (mostly SOEs). According to the *AVCJ*, foreign VC firms invested in 18 venture-backed IPOs from 1991 to 2001. All but one firm had lost value compared with their IPO price.

In 1997, China International Capital Corporation (CICC)'s direct investment department structured and led a US$40 million investment in Eagle Brand Holdings, which was one of the largest ceramic tile and sanitary ware manufacturers in China at that time. While other foreign investors were more comfortable investing in SOEs because of their political connections, or co-investing with a multinational, such as American Standard, to expand their business in China, this investment in a local, Chinese entrepreneur would prove that a PE investor could work with a local management team and profit from the organic growth of the company. In order to avoid the shortcomings of the exit strategies listed above, the investors restructured the company in a similar fashion as other "red-chip" listed companies, such as China Telecom and China Mobile. The other critical difference with previous failed exit strategies is that the investment in Eagle was structured so that the Chinese management team held ownership in the offshore holding company alongside of the financial investors, effectively aligning the interests of all shareholders toward building shareholder value. Eagle Brand listed on the Singapore Stock Exchange in February 1999 and, based on the IPO price, generated significant returns for all stakeholders, including management, the government, and the financial investors. This transaction is recognized by many observers of China's PE/venture market as one of the first "red-chip restructurings" used to structure a PE investment, which ultimately transformed private equity investing in China.

1998–2003: TURNING POINT

The Internet boom and the exuberance of the US public equity markets in the late 1990s played a critical role in the development of venture capital in China. With the successful listing of a handful of Internet and Internet-related companies, financial investors were finally able to generate returns that their limited partners expected for the risk of investing in China. This was the beginning of a dramatic change that would take place in China's PE/VC industry.

In the late 1990s, US investors were highly enthusiastic about China, in general, and, more specifically the growth prospects for China's Internet market. Based on statistics collected by the China Internet Network Information Center (CNNIC), the Chinese government's authoritative source for information regarding the Internet, Internet users in China grew from only 250 in 1992 to about six million by end 1999. Most foreign analysts believed that the CNNIC reports underestimated the actual number of Chinese Internet users, and Internet luminaries, such as Nicholas Negroponte, were predicting ten million users by 2000. In hindsight, these forecasts were not too far off. China had become the second-largest Internet market in the world, with approximately 50 million users by end 2002.

Based on these statistics and other attractive demographics, foreign advertising executives were also optimistic for future growth in Internet advertising revenues on Chinese websites, which further fueled investors' imaginations and provided the incentive for both the experienced and inexperienced to seek venture capital investments in China's nascent Internet industry.

One example of the complexities surrounding this wave of investing in China is the story of SINA.com. In hindsight, SINA represented a real-life test of one investment strategy that was being pursued at the time. One of the key drivers for foreign venture capitalists to enter the China market was the belief that they could "add value" by bringing together (x) new technologies and breakthrough business models that were being developed in Silicon Valley, with (y) Chinese entrepreneurs who could adapt these business models to create successful businesses in China's developing market economy.

SINA.com was created in December 1998 by merging two of the largest Chinese websites: Sinanet.com of Sunnyvale, California, US, and Stone Rich Sight Information Technology Company Ltd (SRS) of Beijing, PRC. SRS was a software company established by Stone Group in 1993. It was best known for Richwin, which launched in April 1994, and was a proprietary software product that allowed users to view Chinese-language content and switch between Chinese and English languages without regard to the underlying operating system. SRS launched its first website in 1996. Sinanet.com was founded in 1995 and was the leading website targeting overseas Chinese with proprietary software that allowed Chinese users to view Sinanet's website without installing Chinese enabling software.

This merger was financed with the original round of investment being led by Walden International Investment Group ("Walden"). Making this merger work was not easy or a foregone conclusion. From May 1999 until its IPO in 2001, SINA.com raised approximately US$85 million from a "who's who" list of investors that were active in China at the time, including: Goldman Sachs's proprietary venture group, Robertson Stephens, Chase Capital Partners, Crosslink Technology Partners, Crystal Internet Venture Fund, Economic Development Board of Singapore, Dell Computer Corporation, Creative Technology Ltd, Pacific Century CyberWorks Limited, Softbank Corp., IDG, Warburg Pincus, Sumitomo Corporation, Trend Micro, United Overseas Bank of Singapore, and CICC's private equity group.

While some of these investors had experience investing in China, many were new to China's VC environment. In addition to risks regarding the merging of Silicon Valley ideas with the business realities of China highlighted above, the Chinese government had enacted an extensive regulatory scheme governing the operation of SINA's business. To comply with Chinese regulations, SINA used a complex legal structure that is referred to as a "Chinese-Chinese-Foreign" (or "*zhong-zhong-wai*," or "CCF") investment structure. This legal structure was developed by foreign lawyers for limited partner foreign investors to invest in the build-up of China's telecommunications industry. Fortunately for financial investors and China's VC/PE industry, SINA became one of the first CCF-structured investments backed by institutional financial investors to successfully go public on an offshore stock exchange.

At the time of the IPO, SINA was one of the leading online media companies and value-added information service providers for China and the global Chinese communities. It had revenues of less than US$15 million in 2000 with projected revenues of about $25 million for 2001. The company was not profitable, but the combination of the "China Dream" and exuberance for all things related to the Internet generated a successful IPO. After the IPO the company successfully transformed itself from a pure Internet portal relying almost exclusively on online advertising to a company with multiple and sustainable revenue streams, and it remains one of the leading Internet companies in China today.

Other successful investments made by PE and VC investors during this period included the following companies:

Sohu.com (Nasdaq: SOHU), one of China's leading Internet companies, was founded by Mr Charles Zhang in August 1996 as a Delaware-registered US holding company, with an initial seed capital investment of $225,000 from a group of MIT professors; namely, Edward Roberts, Nicholas Negroponte and Brant Binder.

- In February 1997, the company launched its original content site and in early 1998, changed its business model to create the first popular Chinese search directory with a similar business model as Yahoo.com's search directory. During the same period, Sohu completed its first round of financing from Intel Semiconductor Ltd (Intel), Dow Jones & Company (Dow Jones), Morningside, and Pacific Technology Venture Fund (IDG).
- At the time of the IPO, Sohu was one of China's most popular Internet portals.
- After the IPO, the company successfully transformed itself from a pure Internet portal relying almost exclusively on online advertising to a company with multiple and sustainable revenue streams, and it remains one of the leading Internet companies in China today.

AsiaInfo Holdings, Inc. (Nasdaq: ASIA) is a leading provider of telecommunications network integration and management solutions in China. Its software products and network services enable its customers to build, maintain, operate, manage, and improve their Internet and telecommunications infrastructure.

- AsiaInfo was founded by Edward Tian and James Ding in Texas in 1993. AsiaInfo began with the dream to build China's national telecommunication backbone. Based on this dream, they received angel financing from Vantone Industry Group, a domestic real estate company. The investment was led by Mr Gongquan Wang, who was a founding partner of Vantone and had moved to Silicon Valley to learn about venture investing. With the newly raised capital and support from Wang, AsiaInfo moved its operations from Texas to China in 1995.
- AsiaInfo began generating significant network solutions revenues in 1996 and software solutions revenues in 1998. At this stage of development, Edward and James sought additional capital to fund its growth from established venture capital firms. Mr Chang Sun of Warburg-Pincus Ventures led this round of investment and provided active support at the board level to assist the founders manage the rapid growth of their company.
- Prior to its IPO in 2000, AsiaInfo had not only built China's national backbone, but it had also built the provincial access networks for all of China's major national telecom carriers, including China Telecom, China Mobile, China Unicom, and China Netcom.
- After the IPO, the company shifted its focus from Internet infrastructure construction to the provision of telecom software solutions, and continues to be a leading company in this industry.

However, the US economic recession from 2001 to early 2003 led to a sharp decrease in the exit opportunities for venture capitalists. Consequently, many VC firms scaled back investment activity in China—and the amount of investments decreased from US$518 million in 2001 to US$419 million in 2002.

THE GROWTH PHASE: 2004–2007

The year 2004 was the turning point for PE in China. The following years were marked by impressive growth throughout the industry.

The pace and scale certainly exceeded most PE professionals who were active in China at the time.

In 2004, a few high-profile PE and VC-backed IPOs achieved listings on international stock exchanges with substantial gains for their PE investors. They included not only the venture successes like Shanda, Baidu, Focus Media, but also companies in traditional industries such as, Mengniu, Li Ning, Gome, and Yurun. Successful exits of PE/venture-backed companies have continued since that date. As a result, VC and PE investments in China were finally recognized as a profitable investment asset class. This has resulted in the few leading funds that were raised in the period from the late 1990s to 2003 to generate very attractive returns. Not only were a few, isolated deals successful, but this time around the whole fund produced returns that outpaced investors expectations.

Obviously, institutional investors took notice. Before 2004, most institutional investors seemed to come to China to study and only a few actually invested. For example, it took CDH, which now has more than US$3 billion of assets under management, almost a year to raise US$100 million in 2002. The fund was backed by early and visionary limited partners, GIC Special Investments, AlpInvest Partners Limited and development institutions such as International Finance Corporation.

After 2004, the investment climate changed dramatically. In 2005, CDH was able to raise its second fund after a few months of active fundraising, which was over-subscribed with commitments from mainstream limited partners, including major US endowments, fund of funds, large family offices, and insurance companies. By the time CDH raised its third PE fund at the end of 2006, they had committed capital of US$1.6 billion from more than 60 limited partners from throughout the world.

Along with a substantial increase in interest by international limited partners, the period also saw the growth of Chinese PE and VC and fund managers. In 2005, a number of "homegrown" private equity funds were raised, most notably CDH raised its second fund at US$300 million and SAIF raised its second fund at US$600 million. At the time, these funds were considered to be very large single-country funds.

During this period, a number of other local Chinese teams raised significant amounts of money, especially venture funds, such as IDG Venture who teamed up with Accel to raise US$250 million. In 2004, Ceyuan Venture raised its first fund with $120 million of commitments from international limited partners. Other funds that were raised at this time include Sequoia Capital, Capital Today, Softbank China, and TDF.

By 2007, SAIF and CDH had raised funds that had committed capital in excess of US$1 billion. While these funds seemed large when they were raised, many new funds have entered the market at similar or even larger sizes, such as Hopu, a fund managed by Fenglei Fang with Temasek and Goldman Sachs as anchor investors, which is reported to have raised its first fund at US$2.5 billion. Hony Capital, Blue Ridge Capital, and CITIC Capital all have raised their latest funds at above US$1 billion. Looking at the growth of the Chinese economy and the companies and investment pace of these leading players, continued growth of China's private equity market is likely.

At the same time as these "homegrown" funds were being formed and thus expanded, the global firms also increased their presence in China. Before 2004, only a few global buyout firms were active in China, including Warburg Pincus, Morgan Stanley, Goldman Sachs, Carlyle, GIC, and Temasek. Now, many more have joined the market, with KKR, Blackstone Group, Bain Capital, APAX, and 3i all having set up dedicated China teams since 2004. Still more are busy recruiting and setting up their China offices.

Although the total commitment amount of all these new entrants into the China market is a dramatic increase from the pre-2004 period, it is still small in comparison to capital commitments in developed markets and the overall size and growth rates of China's economy. That said, the competition to secure the most attractive deals and to recruit professional talent has intensified greatly.

The global firms have brought substantial experience, particularly in their value-added approach and their global network, to the China PE market. As a result, the competition among firms has increased and all firms are struggling to find the best strategies that are suited for their competitive strengths as well as China's evolving business environment. The global buyout firms have discovered that there may be fewer control deals, particularly in size and profile, than they expected, which has forced some of them to adjust their investment strategies to pursue minority investments at smaller transaction sizes. Armed with larger funds, China's "homegrown" PE managers, such as CDH and Hony, have begun to invest in larger deals, which are both buyout as well as growth capital deals.

Overall, the China market probably has close to 100 VC firms with fund sizes of greater than US$100 million. Some continue to focus on pure venture deals. However, leading players, such as Sequoia and IDG, have also raised growth capital funds while maintaining their core venture business. CDH and CITIC Capital have begun their initial efforts in building multi-product alternative asset management businesses, adding on real estate and hedge funds under the same institutional structure. Legend is building a similar platform with Hony Capital, Legend Venture, and its real estate investment company being managed under the same group structure.

With the growth of China's PE and VC market, international investors now have a choice between "homegrown" firms, such as CDH and Ceyuan that are managed by local investment professionals and local investment committees, vs. internationally sponsored funds, such as KKR and Sequoia Capital that are local affiliates of global funds. Given that both VC and PE are very local businesses in which people are critical to all aspects of the investment process, the jury is still out on which of these business models will generate the best returns for investors in China's PE and VC markets.

LOOKING FORWARD: 2008 AND BEYOND

Recently, there have been a number of important developments and changes in China's private equity industry; namely, regulatory changes affecting exit structures and growth of renminbi-denominated funds.

Change of exit structure. Due to regulations issued in September 2007, foreign PE investors will not be able to rely on "red-chip" structures to facilitate exits on international stock exchanges as they have in the past. In the meantime, China's domestic A-share market completed the reform, which will allow full tradability of legal person shares over time. As a result of these changes, foreign PE investors must now look to exit their investments primarily through listings in China's domestic A-share market. This has important implications for foreign PE investors in its competitive position against local currency-based investors, as well as tax and legal changes. However, the high valuations and liquidity of the A-share market seem to provide sufficient advantages to provide an attractive exit for PE investors. Although the exit channel has changed, on balance, the exit routes available to PE investors remain open and feasible.

Renminbi-denominated PE. There is an increasing interest in PE both by the government and related industry participants in China. In June 2007, China's regulators amended the partnership law to allow the formation of domestic limited partnerships. Since then, the State Council has instructed the National Development and Reform Commission to develop a regulatory framework to develop a local currency-based PE industry. The government has approved a few state-sponsored industrial funds, such as Bohai Industrial Investment Fund, which is the first fund to be approved and is already operational. Although it is too early to predict the eventual success or failure of such a venture, a few more funds have already been approved.

It is also reported that the State Council has approved the State Social Security Fund, which is the country's pension fund, to invest up to 10% of its assets into PE-related assets. This could amount to RMB50 billion. Based on this development, one can reasonably assume that insurance companies and other financial institutions will also be allowed to invest in this asset class in the near future.

With China's trade surplus and increasing amounts of foreign direct investment continuing to expand its foreign exchange reserves, China's government has shifted its focus to improve the quality of foreign investment and restrict the overall amount of future foreign direct investment (FDI). As a result, more industry sectors are expected to be restricted and/or prohibited for foreign investment. Private equity investors will have to work hard to overcome these new challenges and do more to change their image with government officials and the general public to ensure access to investment opportunities in China's leading companies. In spite of these obstacles, foreign PE investment amounts have increased significantly and are expected to continue to play an important role in merger and alliance activities, as well as financing venture and growth companies.

Some predictions for the future include:

1. Foreign currency-based PE investment will continue to increase in all areas of buyout, growth capital, venture, as well as real estate. While their amount will continue to increase, their market share is likely to decline from the current 80–90% to 50%–60% over the next few years. With the strong support of international limited partners, foreign currency-based PE firms, including both global and "homegrown" players, will continue to play an important role in PE and VC financing of China-based companies.

2. More RMB PE funds will be set up. In addition to state-approved industrial funds, there will be market-orientated funds with participation of both institutional investors, as well as high net worth individuals. Local insurance companies and

trust companies will also become important sources of capital. These RMB funds will take significant market share from the foreign currency-based PE firms that currently dominate the market. However, this will be a gradual process and it will take time for these new domestic investor groups to understand and enjoy the benefits of investing in this asset class.

3   Competition will introduce positive developments. More value-added service will be provided by PE firms to their invested companies. Firms will become more differentiated by their investment strategy, focus, and specialization as the "low hanging fruit" will disappear. We can anticipate the emergence of leading players in all asset classes, covering the range from buyout to growth capital, to venture and real estate. Concurrently, though, some managers, both foreign and local, will disappoint investors, and there will be the natural segmentation of the market, with the top-quartile performers generating a disproportionate amount of the value and the rest providing market average returns. China's alternative investment sector will not be an exception to the experiences of the developed markets.

4. The government will support the development of the PE industry. However, there is still a lack of understanding of exactly what value PE investors provide to the market. In many cases, the industry suffers a poor image. Significant work needs to be done to assist the government to develop a supportive environment, as well as to educate regulators and the general public about the contribution that PE and VC investors bring to their portfolio companies, specifically, and to society in general.

5. Venture capital (VC) in particular creates new jobs in old and new economies. It is now well-established that the job market growth in the US in the last 20 years has been largely fueled by the creation of new companies. As larger and older companies cut costs and trim employment, new companies fill the gaps. Venture backed companies play a prominent role in this activity.

6. It is well-established that Venture backed IPOs are better received in the market than IPOs that are not sponsored by venture firms. While it is still in its early days in China to make the same observation, no doubt, in the years to come, this will establish the preeminence and importance of venture firms in the IPO market.

ENDNOTES

[1] The editors would like to extend their appreciation to Stuart Schonberger for his support of this project and for seeing this chapter through to completion.

[2] Certain information in this chapter was adapted from a dissertation written by Wendy Wei Xu submitted to Princeton University Department of Economics in partial fulfillment of the requirements for the A.B. Degree on April 28, 2006 entitled "China Venture Capital: Analysis of the Market and Investment Process."

[3] Studwell, Joseph. 2002. "The China Dream: The Quest for the Last Great Untapped Market on Earth, *Atlantic Monthly Press*.

[4] *Asian Venture Capital Journal*, January 1995, Hong Kong. For more details see www.avcj.com.

[5] *Asian Venture Capital Journal*, January 2002, Hong Kong.

[6] January 2002, *AVCJ* (www.avcj.com).

SECTION 4

INSURANCE

CHAPTER 20

China's Insurance Markets: Reform, Growth, and Prospects

Yuan Li

Assistant Chairman, China Insurance Regulatory Commission

The insurance industry is one of the three great pillars of the financial system. China's insurance industry has traveled an unusual path of development, as has the economy in general, and has become an important part of the national economy. After New China was established in 1949, the country began managing its own insurance business and the People's Insurance Company of China was established as a state-owned enterprise, engaged in all forms of insurance. From 1959 to 1979, the guiding line of economic thought at the time felt that insurance was unnecessary. The insurance business in China therefore ceased to exist for 20 years. In 1980, a domestic insurance business was revived and the industry began to grow along with the entire national economy. Since Reform and Opening, the industry has gone through three major stages: from 1980–85, when it was newly restored as an industry; from 1986–91, when it grew in stable manner; and after 1992, when it experienced very rapid growth.

Since the sixteenth Party Congress, held in 2002, the insurance industry has worked particularly hard to realize major national policy goals by taking steps that are described in this chapter.

Since that year, China's insurance industry has maintained a growth rate of 18.2% per year. In 2007, insurance premium income came to RMB703.58 billion, which was 2.3 times the income in 2002. By the end of 2007 the industry included 110 companies, 68 more than in 2002. Their gross assets totaled RMB2.9 trillion, which was 4.5 times the amount in 2002. In terms of total insurance premium, China ranks ninth in the world, up from sixteenth in the year 2002. The years since 2002 have seen reforms progressing, growth rate increasing, quality of growth improving, and areas of service and influence on society expanding. The industry has improved in efficiency, scientific approach, and risk avoidance; it has grown both within and outside China; and built a stable base for future growth.

"Marketization"

Before restructuring, more than 70% of insurance companies in China were facing difficulties. They were under-capitalized, their ability to pay back on claims was inadequate, it was hard to get rid of non-performing assets, historical burdens were heavy, basic management was poor. Such bottlenecks held back the entire industry. In line with the needs of setting up a socialist market economy system, and with the State Council's encouragement, restructuring became insurance companies' primary responsibility. The China Insurance Regulatory Commission guided the process. The transformation of state-owned companies into share-holding corporations helped transform management, bring about new business mechanisms, and introduce new vitality into the industry.

Systemic reform and the listing of insurance companies on the market were successfully and smoothly carried out. In November 2003, the People's Insurance Company of China was listed in Hong Kong and became the first domestic financial enterprise to list outside the borders of China. In December 2003, China Life Insurance listed in both New York and Hong Kong, recording the highest amount for a public listing in the international capital markets. In June 2004, Ping An Insurance (Group) Company of China was listed in Hong Kong, to become the first financial insurance enterprise to list as a group company outside of China. In 2007, both China Life and Ping An successfully returned to the A-share market, while China Pacific Insurance Group successfully listed on the A-share market to become an important emblematic company for the industry. At present, there are six Chinese insurance companies listed on markets inside and outside of China. Most of these have set up relatively standard corporate governance structures, and created the underlying conditions for modern insurance enterprise systems.

Listing and market reforms have resolved the problem of insurance companies' appearing to be what they were not; that is, having the form but not the substance. Continuing to improve corporate governance structures, bringing in strategic investors; improving share-holding structures; strengthening restraints on shareholders; making the shareholders pay more attention to company growth; making Boards of Directors and management levels more professional; creating effective balancing mechanisms through establishing proper governance structure among shareholders, decision-makers, supervisors and the management. All of these systemic changes, including strengthening the role of internal auditors in the companies, should enable regulators to help listed companies abide by domestic laws and listed company laws of markets where the companies were listed, by industry standards, and management innovation.

The reforms have raised the competitiveness of insurance companies. Listed insurance companies have been rewarded by the approval of both domestic and foreign investors, as reflected in their share price. China Life, on the domestic A-share market on the first day of its listing, exceeded RMB1 trillion in value to become the biggest listed insurance company in the world in terms of capitalized market value.

The international influence of Chinese insurance companies has been rising. China Life of China was ranked 192 in *Fortune 500* in 2006, up 98 places from 2003. China Life was also ranked as number 309 among the world's top 500 brands. Ping An was listed as first place in management among Asian insurance companies, as well as among China-region companies. At the same time, it was number five overall among all companies in the Asia region. In April 2007, the prestigious Asian finance journal *Wealth* named Ping An as the company with best corporate governance, based on its internationalization, openness and transparency, and its stringent regulations.

"Internationalization"

By the promises made upon China's entering the World Trade Organization (WTO), the Chinese insurance market was opened to foreign participation somewhat earlier than other markets in the financial industry, and the transition period to full opening was also shorter. The three-year transition period for entering the WTO ended on December 11, 2004, after which China's insurance market entered an era of being totally open to the outside. China's insurance industry then began to display the effects of "internationalization."

First, insurance companies in China were opened to international participation. With economic globalization and financial integration, the ties between China's insurance market and international markets grow closer by the day. The major multinational insurance groups and insurance companies in countries whose insurance business is well-developed have all entered China. By the end of 2007, 43 foreign-invested insurance companies from 15 countries and regions had set up 134 operating entities in the country. At the same time, given the stimulus of China's "Going Out" strategy, insurance companies have voluntarily learned from the experience of international financial markets and some have already become internationalized public companies by listing on exchanges outside of China and developing overseas businesses.

Second, various segments of the business in China were opened to international participation. By now, the realm in which foreign-invested insurance companies can operate has basically been opened. Foreign-invested life insurance companies can provide health insurance to Chinese citizens and foreign citizens, as well as group insurance and pension insurance services. The scope of their business has become exactly the same as Chinese life insurance companies operating in China. Foreign-invested non-life insurance companies can provide all businesses except statutory insurance. In addition, the reinsurance business of China has always emphasized distributing and transferring risk in international markets and the internationalization of that business has always been high. When China entered the WTO, it promised to permit foreign reinsurance companies to provide life insurance and non-life insurance reinsurance business into China through wholly owned subsidiaries of foreign entities or joint ventures.

Third, insurance markets in different parts of China were opened to international participation. The opening to the outside of insurance markets continues to expand. Regional restrictions have already been eliminated for foreign-invested insurance companies operating in Chinese markets. Before entering the WTO, five cities in China were open to foreign insurance business. After entering, and during the transition period, this was sequentially expanded to 15. As of December 11, 2004, foreign-invested insurance companies can provide insurance services in any region of China. In terms of business the business of foreign-invested insurance companies has grown constantly and its market influence has gradually expanded, lending new vitality to the growth of China's own insurance industry. By the end of 2007, foreign-invested insurance companies occupied around 5.97% market share of the insurance market in China.

Fourth, China's regulatory bodies were linked to the global system. The China Insurance Regulatory Commission has entered both the International Association of Insurance Supervisors and the International Organization of Pension Supervisors. In 2006, it hosted the thirteenth annual conference of the former with close to 700 representatives coming from 94 countries around the world. This was the largest such annual conference ever held, with the most people from the most countries. The voice of China's insurance industry is appearing in more and more international insurance forums, in order to strengthen Sino–US and Sino–European bilateral and multilateral insurance regulatory cooperation, set up cooperative mechanisms with Asian insurance regulators, and actively participate in international insurance regulatory regimes.

"Standardization"

A modern regulatory framework with respect to the "three pillars" has now been achieved to a preliminary degree in recent years. China's insurance regulation did not exist before and now it does. It has made constant improvement over the course of what can be divided into three main stages. The first focused on regulating market behavior. In the initial stages of China's insurance industry, there were few market entities and the wholly state-owned insurance companies enjoyed absolute reign, while any insurance regulation was mainly with regard to market behavior. At that time, although the concept of regulating solvency was considered, it was not yet put into effect. The second stage emphasized both market behavior and solvency. As entities in the market continued to increase and market competition heated up, risk-avoidance and assuring the stability of the markets became the main task of insurance regulation. In early 2003, China's Insurance Regulatory Commission promulgated "Regulations Concerning Solvency Lines and Supervision Index of Insurance Companies (the Regulations)." This was a substantive step with regard to regulating debt payment capacity. The third stage was to set up the regulatory framework for the three pillars. Relying on the core regulatory principles of the International Association of Insurance Supervisors, China promulgated a "Directive Regarding Standardizing Corporate Governance Structures of Insurance Companies" in 2006. It incorporated into this the regulatory systems for insurance companies' governance structures, their solvency requirements, and market behavior—which thereby formed in preliminary fashion the three pillars of a modern insurance regulatory framework.

The regulatory system for the insurance industry is constantly being improved. In order to realize a foundation for regulatory work, and gradually institute a standard, systematic legal system under which regulation can take place, we must now address the following actions.

First, we continue to strengthen our operating and regulatory practice according to insurance laws. We revised Insurance Law, and formulated provisions that relate to policy-type agricultural insurance. We actively promote reform of administrative approval procedures. Since 2002, the Insurance Regulatory Commission drafted and passed 36 Regulations relating to department-level entities, as well as a series of documents specifying procedures, but far more needs to be done.

Second, we have encouraged business innovation in conjunction with improving business regulatory systems. On product supervision, progress has been made to institutionalize insurance policies by using standard and familiar terms. As an effect, products are designed to closely meet the market and customer needs. On sales and distribution, we encourage close cooperation of banks and insurance companies in order to develop standardized insurance products, and enhance sales management of new life insurance products.

Third, in line with the needs of human resource development, we have enhanced the review of qualification standards and supervision of senior management staff in insurance companies.

Fourth, in line with the needs of modernizing regulation, we have strengthened the establishment of information and statistical systems. An insurance statistics information system has been built, and more insurance information systems are being built in order to centralize data and consolidate operating systems.

Finally, we have improved risk management by setting up "five main lines of defense" in regulating the industry. This includes internal corporate controls serving as the base; supervision of solvency adequacy as the core; on-site inspections as the main means to compliance; supervision of fund management as a key link in the process; and insurance security funds serving as a final protective screen. The risk prevention, control, and recovery process ensures risk is dealt with through a long-term systematic approach, so even if facing losses, the insurance security funds will carry out necessary payment to the insured person. To the greatest possible degree, we must protect the interests of the insured person and ameliorate any negative effects of nonpayment on society at large.

A NEW STARTING POINT

The insurance industry stands at a new starting point in its development. During this period, it faces unprecedented growth opportunities, but also unprecedented challenges. In general, the opportunities are greater than the challenges.

New Opportunities

China's economy has maintained fast growth for a relatively long time, and wealth has been accumulating for both individuals and the society at large. This has greatly increased the insurable assets of the society, as well as injected a long-term source of fuel into the insurance industry. The per capita GDP of China has already broken through US$2,000 per year. According to international experience, premium income rises faster than economic growth at this level, which means that China's insurance industry will continue to grow at a fast pace. As economic development raises people's standards of living, consumption in the areas of healthcare, caring for the elderly, education, housing, cars, and so on increases. Insurance needs increase correspondingly. The percentage of middle-income people is rising and people's demand for safety and securities has shown a marked increase: insurance consumption has become the most important component of modern consumer demand.

Improving modern financial systems in China will require speeding up the growth of the insurance industry. China's insurance assets are roughly 4% of financial assets right now, while in developed countries that percentage is generally over 20%. The latent potential of the insurance industry in China is tremendous. The savings of Chinese residents now totals some RMB17.3 trillion. A large portion of this is set aside to provide for individuals' future needs in terms of aging and medical needs. Along with the rise in standards of the insurance industry, that latent potential will gradually be transformed into reality. Comprehensive management of finance and globalization of finance will also expand the field of vision of the insurance industry. On the one hand, it will benefit cooperation with the banking industry and other financial institutions, at a deeper and broader level, it will allow the concentration and reformulation of resources. On the other hand, comprehensive management will also benefit the insurance industry as it adopts the experience of other financial organizations as well as international financial and insurance industries. China's industry is now in a position to "gain mastery by coming late to market."

China is rapidly becoming an aging society. Around 150 million people are currently over the age of 60, which is 11% of the total population. It is estimated that by 2014, this elderly population will exceed 200 million, and by 2026, it will reach 300 million. The need for social security increases as a society ages, and the pressure on governments to create social security systems is ever greater. The insurance industry will be the beneficiary of this process. However, the total amount of social risk is also increasing with the changes in China, including industrialization, "informatization," urbanization, marketization, and internationalization. All of these bring profound change to the economic structure, the social structure, and the structure of benefits. They require a profound transformation in ways of thinking. The structure of risk is becoming ever more complex. Improving risk management systems for society is an urgent need as the insurance industry develops. Insurance is the basic measure of risk management under a market economy. It is imperative that insurance companies accept this responsibility as a way to ameliorate social risk.

Insurance is a kind of marketized way to transfer risk, a way to enable mutual-assistance mechanisms and social management mechanisms in society. As the functions of government in our socialist market economy system undergo change, the government is using more market mechanisms to improve resource allocation efficiencies and to resolve social problems. As government functions are transformed, the insurance industry will play an ever-larger role in the workings of the market economy. Second, there is an ever-wider awareness of social risk and the role of insurance. In the future, more and more people will come to understand insurance and purchase it as an important way to manage personal risk as well as personal wealth.

New Challenges

China's insurance industry has made striking accomplishments, but significant obstacles impede future progress. China's insurance industry started up rather late. It rests on a fairly fragile foundation and is not yet suited to the development of an "economic society." In terms of insurance penetration, which is insurance premiums as a percentage of GDP, the world average is 8%, whereas China's is 2.85%. In terms of insurance density, which is based on per capita premiums, the world average is US$512, whereas China's is US$73. China's insurance penetration rate and density are not only backwards with respect to developed countries, but they are backwards with respect to many developing countries. The coverage rate of insurance in China is relatively low, so that the industry is yet to have larger influence in terms of social structure and social harmonization. The ratio of compensation to catastrophic loss is not even 5%, whereas the world average in general exceeds 30%.

The external environment in which the insurance industry operates in China is ever more complex and the industry is ever more tightly tied to the overall economy. Macroeconomic fluctuations, monetary policy adjustments, changes in interest rates, exchange rates, and capital markets all have a direct or indirect impact on insurance industry. As the sphere in which the industry operates expands and channels for investing expand, the symbiosis between insurance and the capital, currency, and foreign exchange markets only deepens. Risk factors faced by the industry grow constantly and the potential for transferring cross-market risk and cross-industry risk is ever greater.

Current systems and mechanisms that encourage a scientific approach to the growth of the industry are not ideal. Some behavior is not in line with scientific perspectives and cannot, in terms of the system, be effectively restrained. Enforcement of regulatory systems and internal corporate governing systems is inadequate. Innovative mechanisms and protective systems are stagnating; the scientific development of the industry needs improvement.

FUTURE PROGRESS

In the coming period, the overall goals of industry reform are to form large insurance (financial) groups and professional insurance companies that have high international competitiveness and self-innovative capacity. They are also to set up a modern insurance industry that has effective market systems, a broad range of services, standardized operating trustworthiness, sufficient solvency adequacy, strong overall competitiveness, and quality and operating results that do not compromise each other.

Before the end of 2010, our goal is to double the country's income from insurance premiums over what it was in 2005. We want to break through RMB1 trillion in premium income, and achieve gross assets under management by the insurance industry that exceed RMB5 trillion. By the time the national goal of establishing a "middling-prosperous society" is accomplished, we want to make China's insurance market overall rank among the leading market in the world, with insurance premium income and per capita premium income reaching a level comparable to those of medium-developed countries in the world.

This will require a broad range of services, and fully enabled insurance functions. Insurance should be extended to all industries, to all areas of society, and to all aspects of people's lives. The percentage of insured amounts to the total national wealth, and the percentage of insurance compensation to total social disaster and "catastrophic losses" should reflect a marked increase as an indicator of the contribution that insurance is making to society. In setting up a national disaster management system, the insurance industry should play an important role in improving social security systems and strengthening the management of social risk.

To do this, we need to make sure that insurance is included in all development plans and that policies which contribute to the national economy and people's livelihood are supported. We want to strengthen and enable all policies supporting the growth of the insurance industry. Education regarding insurance must be included in grade-school and middle-school curriculums, in order to improve public awareness of its merits.

CHAPTER 21

Strategy of China's Largest Life Insurance Company, China Life

Yang Chao

Chairman, China Life Insurance (Group) Company

China's financial reforms are currently entering a new era. The financial industry is at a critical juncture and experiencing tremendous new growth. As a key component of the financial system, the insurance industry will be facing challenges and opportunities in this process of change. China Life is the largest comprehensive services insurance company in China. It therefore shoulders considerable responsibility as the industry leader. It must stand up to the oncoming wave of change, meet the challenges, and lead the way forward.

STRUCTURAL CHANGE TO FINANCIAL SYSTEMS

China's financial industries have grown at a ferocious pace in recent years. The results of reform are clear, as the financial arena increasingly opens to the outside, as overall functions of the financial system are brought into play, as regulatory and legal structures are strengthened. The entire financial industry has undergone historic change and is now playing an increasing role in supporting and stimulating China's economic growth. In line with ongoing reforms, China's financial system is in the midst of structural change.

First, it is transitioning from dealing with regional markets to dealing with international markets. It is already open to the outside, and foreign financial institutions are entering or preparing to enter China's markets, penetrating all of the various links in the financial system. The country's fast-paced growth has attracted tremendous international capital and the implementation of the Qualified Foreign Institutional Investor (QFII) system has opened a channel for foreign investment capital to pour into Chinese markets. China's financial markets have already become an important component of global financial markets, and indeed are exerting more and more of a direct influence on them. The impact of fluctuations in China's interest rates, exchange rates, and stock markets can be seen to varying degrees around the globe.

Second, the system is transitioning from operating in a fragmented nature with discrete industry structures to operating under an integrated unified comprehensive model. The degree of merging and the overlapping interests of businesses have been hastened by growth of the financial markets. Innovative measures with regard to products and services and comprehensive operating methods are becoming the rule at most financial institutions. This has received active support from state policies, which have vigorously promoted comprehensive operations in the overall industry. The eleventh Five Year Plan of 2006 specified that the financial industry would be serving as a pilot example in undertaking comprehensive integrated operations. This was an important signal. It meant that the comprehensive operations of the industry had been given the blessing of state policies and that remaining obstructions would now gradually be eliminated.

Third, the market system is transitioning in structure from being fledgling to becoming more mature. The development of financial products, price determination, sales, and trading are already moving toward marketization. Financial policies, measures, and systems are also becoming marketized, while financial regulation is moving away from administrative controls and in the direction of market guidance. All of the three main pillars of the financial system—banking, securities, and insurance—are seeing intensive change as the transformation of the entire system goes forward.

The insurance industry is a case in point. Its size and power has notably increased. In 2006, income from insurance premiums was RMB564.1 billion, 1.8 times the figure in 2002; total capital exceeded RMB200 billion, which was 5.6 times the figure in 2002. Gross assets exceeded RMB2 trillion, which was six times the figure in 2000. It took 24 years for the insurance industry to accumulate its first one trillion in assets after it was restored in 1980. Since then, it has taken a mere three years to accumulate its second one trillion. Operational efficiency of the insurance industry has steadily risen, while profit levels have gone up year-by-year and the nonperforming asset rate has fallen to below 1%. Under the influence of international insurance markets, the entire insurance industry in China has shown constant improvement.

Systemic reforms in the insurance industry are making steady progress. China Life Insurance Company, People's Insurance Company of China, and China Ping An Insurance Company have already successfully listed on the stock market. China Reinsurance, China Pacific, and others are also actively seeking to list on the market. Instituting modern enterprise systems in insurance companies has laid the foundation for healthy growth in the industry.

Insurance products are growing more diversified by the day. With new needs for wealth management, new products have been offered to the public that build on the foundation of traditional guarantee-type products and that are in line with the rapid growth of China's capital markets. These include investments and wealth management products such as dividend insurance, investment-linked insurance, universal insurance, and so on. In less than 10 years, China's insurance industry has traversed a path that took many years in more developed economies.

More efficient use of capital is now apparent. The insurance industry responded briskly to the policy memorandum known as the State Council's Document #23, and increased its share ownership in banking, securities, and other important fields. China Life is a shareholder in the Guangdong Development Bank and in CITIC Securities; China Ping An has purchased the Shenzhen Commercial Bank, and many insurance companies have participated in the listing of the main state-owned commercial banks as strategic financial investors. Among these, insurance companies invested in the Bank of China (BOC) and the Industrial and Commercial Bank of China (ICBC) with RMB18.89 billion of A-shares and HKD12.51 billion of H-shares respectively. They now hold 23.2% of the BOC's A-shares and 5.8% of its H-shares, and 30.5% of the ICBC's A-shares, and 6.8% of its H-shares.

Structural changes in the financial industry have brought about tremendous changes in the situation with regard to financing in China. In the past five years, gross assets in China's insurance industry have been growing at 34.8% per year. The average growth rate far outpaces that of bank-type financial institutions. The insurance industry's percentage of assets in the industry as a whole has risen from 2% in

2001 to 3.8% in 2005. The insurance industry has now become an indispensable part of how financial resources are allocated in China.

CHALLENGES AND OPPORTUNITIES: LIFE INSURANCE

This period of structural transition in China's financial system is also a period of strategic opportunity. It is therefore a critical moment in the national policy goal of establishing an economy in which all in China enjoy a modicum of prosperity. The insurance industry has an important role to play in that policy.

Through mergers and acquisitions (M&As), the industry can now achieve multiples in growth. International experience has shown that M&As are an important way to catapult growth, and indeed many of the premier international financial insurance groups were formed via this method. Chinese state policies currently encourage insurance companies that meet certain standards to become internationally competitive financial insurance groups. After restructuring, methods of growth include M&As.

Through capital injections, the insurance industry has the ability to infiltrate the securities, funds, and banking industries. At the end of 2006, the insurance industry in China broke through RMB2 trillion in total assets. Insurance institutions had already become the most important institutional investors in China's domestic capital markets. In 2006, a number of insurance companies served as strategic financial investors in the market listings of commercial banks and securities firms. They invested in the Guangdong Development Bank, CITIC Securities, and the Shenzhen Municipal Commercial Bank through purchase of shares.

Through expanded investments, insurance companies can greatly increase their sources of profits. With changes in financial regulatory policies in China, channels through which insurance funds can make investments have greatly expanded and the investment environment continues to improve. Insurance companies now have many avenues by which they can increase their return on investment. They can strengthen capital allocations, increase their return on capital, improve investment structure, and so on. In addition to the original investment channels, a further opening in the areas of stock investing, investments in basic infrastructure, use of foreign exchange funds, the expansion of Qualified Domestic Institutional Investor (QDII) channels all create beneficial conditions by which insurance companies can raise their return on investment (ROI). Among these, in terms of basic infrastructure investments, the insurance industry is actively participating in such regional and municipal projects as railroads, highways, and new urban high-rise developments. The industry is taking a further step in expanding its financial participation in state-supported key industries and regional economic construction. This is allowing the industry to make thorough use of the function that pooling large amounts of funds can play. For example, projects include investing in the Bohai Industrial Investment Fund, the acquisition of the China Southern Power Grid Co. Limited, participating in the construction of the Beijing–Shanghai high speed rail system, and participating in basic infrastructure projects in such places as Hubei, Shanxi, and Xinjiang. All of these are important contributions to the country's infrastructure, and at the same time, they allow the insurance industry to receive stable income from its investments.

The pension funds market will be providing a new channel for sustained growth of the life insurance industry. The industry is uniquely suited to developing that market. Not only is China's population large, but the country also has more elderly people than any other country in the world. China has already entered the stage of enduring a rapidly aging population. As this trend increases, and there are more and more retirees, the social requirement of caring for them will mean that the resulting need for corporate pensions will be tremendous. Professionals in the field estimate that, by 2010, the market for corporate pensions will be on the order of RMB1 trillion. By 2030, the total amount of China's pension fund assets will reach US$1.8 trillion, making China the world's third-largest market in pension funds. Insurance companies have a first-to-market advantage in this arena, which should become a primary driver of the sustained growth of the life insurance industry.

While looking at the opportunities for growth, we must clearly recognize the challenges as well. Challenges attending the transformation in financial systems in China can mainly be seen in the following two ways.

First, reforms with respect to marketizing interest rates will strongly impact the operations and management of the life insurance industry. China's economic growth has exhibited sustained growth, but at the same time, inflationary pressures have been building. A robust monetary policy is one of the country's most important instruments in terms of macroeconomic measures; China has already entered a period of rising interest rates. Allowing supply and demand to determine the price of money will be an important step in further improving the socialist market economic system. As the market system gradually adjusts and as we learn to deal with these macroeconomic measures, the marketization of interest rates in China will accelerate. Interest rates are the most important basis for price determination for other financial products. Along with the marketization of interest rates, reform in the area of marketizing insurance premium rates is unavoidable. This will raise new demands on the ability of insurance companies to determine prices, to make investments, and to manage risk.

The second challenge we face is that market competition grows fiercer by the day. China's insurance industry currently encompasses over 100 companies. Both domestic and foreign operations are surging into the market. The entry of premier international financial insurance groups into China raises demands on the competitiveness of local companies and on the structure of the insurance markets. At the same time, the blurring of business lines among different financial institutions in China continues to increase, bringing competition to the life insurance industry from such financial institutions as banks, securities companies, and funds. The establishment of banking system fund management companies fundamentally changed the competitive situation and the business models of China's funds industry. The growth of the corporate pension fund business meant that banks, insurance, and funds have all begun to compete in the area of pensions. Meanwhile, large commercial banks are actively preparing to enter into the life insurance business, and will soon become competitors in what had been the insurance market. Along with this increased competition, competitive measures have also begun to shift from traditional price competition to competition based on comprehensive service capability.

LIFE INSURANCE: STRATEGIC OPPORTUNITIES

Taking advantage of the opportunities to grow our industry is not only good for us, but serves the national policy of "building a socialist harmonious society." The challenge is to formulate realistic and feasible growth strategies.

First, we must accurately position ourselves with respect to the direction of future growth. The greatest distinction between the insurance industry and the securities and banking industries is that insurance deals in risk, it is a risk management industry and risk management is at the core of life insurance operations. We must thoroughly grasp the functions of economic compensation, capital raising and financing, and social management. We must expand insurance coverage, uncover latent market potential, and preserve the fast, healthy growth of our core business on behalf of people's various needs.

Second, we must explore and set up mechanisms that transform savings resources into insurance resources. At present, the savings rate of citizens in China continues to stay at a long-term and relatively high level. By the end of 2006, the sum of Chinese savings reached RMB16.2 trillion, an increase of 1.5 times over 2000. This amount can be thought of as the foundation of sustainable growth of the insurance industry. In transforming that resource into insurance resources, we must start with the concept of "mechanisms." We need the support of overall government policy. Next, we need the support of government tax policies in particular. Then, we must speed up innovations in insurance products; and finally, we must increase the penetration of insurance into the banking sphere.

Third, we must speed up the building of a financial insurance group by reconfiguring resources. The establishment of a financial insurance group in which each part is able to supplement the other, with shared resources, is the desired end result of comprehensive management of the insurance industry. At present, China has nine insurance groups, and the merging of insurance companies with other financial institutions is ongoing. With the transformation of the overall model of the financial system, the way to improve the international competitiveness of our industry is to speed up the establishment of a financial insurance group.

Fourth, we must establish a life insurance market that is rational, trustworthy, and open. A rational market requires that entities avoid disorderly and vicious price competition. A trustworthy market requires that each entity operates honestly, grows under standard rules, and respects obligations. An open market requires that market barriers and monopolies be broken down in order to implement fair competition and raise market efficiency.

Fifth, we must strengthen the stamina of the life insurance industry by utilizing the leveraging functions of capital. The life insurance industry has the benefit of long-term stable sources of funding. Through mobilizing and properly using capital, we can employ M&As within the industry to speed up growth. Through investment in the securities, funds, and banking industries, we can improve our own profitability. Through strategic cooperation with certain industries and regions and participation in key projects, we can expand our overall resources. The foundation on which the growth of life insurance depends is not only providing risk guarantee, but also greater return on investment to customers. We do this by raising yields on investments and by improving the leveraging functions of capital.

CHINA LIFE PLANS

Against the backdrop of a financial system that is undergoing transition to a new model, China Life has instituted plans for strategic growth in line with the following mission:

- [to] lead by a scientific attitude toward growth;
- to make all efforts to establish a large modern financial insurance Group that employs rational utilization of resources;
- to have clear comprehensive strengths and a strong core business that applies an appropriate degree of diversification;
- to create a company that is respected by society and by the world, that incorporates high internal value, has strong core competitiveness and sufficient stamina to carry on sustained growth, that intends to be large, strong, and excellent.

According to the needs of "managing internationalization, marketizing operations, standardizing systems, making policy-making more scientific, and human resources more professional," it is time for us to go a step further in reaching the goal of creating a premier, international, financial insurance group that "has deep and real strength, progressive governance, healthy systems, tight internal controls, advanced technology, first-class management, excellent service, outstanding brand, and harmonious growth."

Under this strategic mission, the forming of a "Group" by China Life must proceed in a stable fashion and achieve clear results. In the first half of 2007, China Life's total revenue from insurance premiums was RMB133.1 billion, total assets were RMB1.0731 trillion. The company held 42% of the entire assets of the insurance industry in China, and it had become the only insurance group in China with assets that exceeded RMB1 trillion. Among the global *Fortune 500*, China Life for the first time entered the ranks of the top 200, to stand at number 192. Together with 11 other famous brands in

China, moreover, it is now listed among the top 500 brands in the world. The value of its brand is set at RMB58.8 billion. At the same time, the listed share company under its banner is number one in market capitalization among life insurance companies worldwide that are publicly listed on exchanges. Its asset management company has already become one of the largest institutional investors in China's capital markets. Its financial assets insurance company showed an excellent start, its pension insurance company has solid capital, and the prospects for market growth are very considerable.

The core of China Life's strategy is, "Super-strong core business, with appropriate diversification." At present, the core business includes personal insurance, property insurance, pension insurance, and asset management. The foundation on which the group rests cannot be shaken at any time, it must focus the strength and increase the intensity of growth, assure the ability of the company's core business to expand in the market, assure its profitability, its sustainability, its management capacity, its ability to be an industry leader, its ability to serve an "economic culture," and so on. In all these ways, it must lead the rest of the industry in creating core competitiveness within China Life. "Appropriate diversification" means adhering to a working tenet of supporting and promoting the growth of the core business. Such support must contribute to raising the company's investment yields; second, it must serve the growth of the core business; and third, it must be backed up with corresponding human resources and technology. In strategic implementation, as conditions mature, the banking and securities industries will also become core businesses of China Life.

In line with its overall strategic goals, China Life has formulated the following feasible and effective measures to achieve growth:

- We are reconfiguring resources to improve competitiveness. One primary goal is to aid and enhance the strength of the Group.
- We are restructuring to enhance sustainable growth.
- We are addressing the imbalance in insurance that currently exists between cities and rural areas; we are strengthening our work in rural areas and at the same time strengthening our lead in the cities.
- We are innovating, in order to satisfy customer needs through product diversification.
- We are leveraging capital in order to grow as fast as possible.

The two important wheels that propel a company forward are business development and the leveraging of capital. In 2006, China Life initiated a whole series of major investments. These had relatively good returns, strengthened our leading position in the insurance as well as the capital markets. They allowed us to gain favor among both domestic and overseas investors. Strategic share investments were made to help harmonize the company's insurance and capital businesses.

China's Life's development strategy of "super-strong core business, appropriate diversification" meets the needs of the changing model of China's financial system, as well as the growth of the insurance industry. It is in accord with existing conditions in China's insurance industry and has enabled China Life to display powerful leadership. In the course of transforming the way China's financial system works, China Life will continue to bear responsibility for both its own industry and for society by actively promoting reform, speeding up development, strengthening management, and continuing to pursue the strategic goal of forming a Group.

CHAPTER 22

The Emergence of China's Insurance Industry

Wu Yan
Chairman, People's Insurance Company (Group) of China

EXPLORING THE WAY FORWARD

Over the two decades from 1980 to 2000, an insurance industry gradually formed in China through a process that included marketization of insurance entities and the establishment of regulatory structures. After 1990, China took a number of steps to further the end result. The country established an insurance regulatory system with the promulgation of the Insurance Law, and the establishment of the China Insurance Regulatory Commission. It established an insurance market system by allowing the establishment of shareholding insurance companies such as Ping An and China Life, and by bringing in such foreign insurance institutions as AIG and Manulife. It also adopted an insurance agency practice, encouraged specialized lines of property and life insurance, and generally created the systemic foundations for the industry.

Since 2000, recognizing that the industry was still not developing at a pace fast enough to meet the needs of the economy or of people's demand for insurance, the government determined that the primary task in this early period was to speed up the transition from an industry that functioned on the basis of economic compensation and financing facilities to one that also functioned for social administration. A concurrent goal was to speed up opening to the outside. By the end of 2007, 43 companies from 15 countries and regions had entered China's insurance markets, and foreign-invested entities held a 5.97% market share of the business. In Shanghai, which opened earliest to outside participation, foreign-invested insurance companies held a 26% market share by the third quarter of 2007. China's own domestic industry continued to strengthen as well, and by the end of 2007 there were 110 Chinese insurance companies, 68 more than there had been in 2002. Capital from private sector served as the primary source of funding for these newly established companies.

One major first step in this whole process was to corporatize the state-owned companies by restructuring them. In November 2003, the China People's Property and Casualty Insurance Share Company Ltd, under the China People's Insurance Group, successfully listed on the Hong Kong Stock Exchange to become the first Chinese financial enterprise to list overseas. The restructuring and subsequent listing of other Chinese insurance companies could now follow suit. China Life soon listed sequentially in Hong Kong, New York, and Shanghai, to become one of the largest insurance companies in the world in terms of market capitalization. The China Reinsurance Group then also completed its corporatization in October 2007, becoming the largest insurance company in Asia in terms of registered capital and the fifth-largest in the world.

During this period of transition, China's insurance industry has also sustained ongoing reform of asset management models. In so doing, it has effectively improved the yields on utilization of capital (see Figure 22.1). It has promoted the specialization of and concentration of insurance funds. In July 2003, the China People's Asset Management Shareholding Company Ltd was established, becoming the first asset management company for insurance funds in China.

FIGURE 22.1   Return on insurance capital, 2001–07

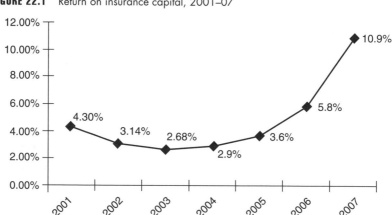

After this, all major domestic insurance companies in the country set up specialized asset management companies that were authorized to handle insurance funds. China currently has nine insurance asset management companies, and one asset management center. These are authorized to handle the internal insurance funds of each Group or entity as well as third-party insurance assets.

The industry has also broadened the channels through which insurance funds or capital in general can be invested. Since the year 2000, the government has authorized investment in corporate bonds, subordinated bonds, corporate convertible bonds, commercial banks' financial bonds, short-term financing instruments, international development agency bonds, stocks, and also investments in infrastructure, as well as overseas investments. This has greatly enhanced the flexibility of investment vehicles and improved the industry's return on capital. Capital invested by insurance institutions has basically been diversified (see Figure 22.2), and the structure of assets in these institutions is constantly being improved.

Since 2000 the various links in the chain of the insurance industry have been improved by the creation of different kinds of entities in the business. These include insurance groups, specialized insurance companies, and various intermediaries. One task has been to assure

FIGURE 22.2 Comparison of investment categories of insurance funds Nov. 2000 and Oct. 2007, showing % in bank deposits going down from 49% to 27.9%, and that in shares and investments going up from 5% to 26%

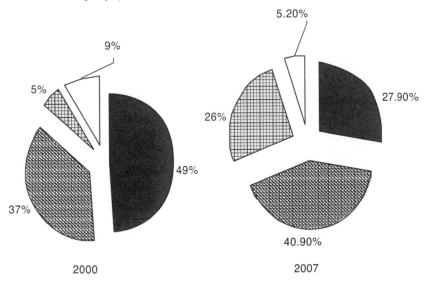

2000

2007

a comprehensive mix of businesses in the large insurance group companies. In 2000, in line with specialization principles of property and life-insurance businesses, the Ping An and China Pacific insurance companies set up operating structures that were now in the form of "Groups." In line with the trend to form group companies, since 2003, the China People's Insurance, China Life, and China Reinsurance companies have established group companies and completed redeployment of assets in all aspects of their business. At present, China has eight insurance group companies. Some of these, such as China People's Insurance, China Life, and Ping An, are actively setting up financial entities in which they hold controlling shares. These then have specialized subsidiaries dealing in finance and in insurance; the aim is to have an outstanding core business that is enhanced by mutually supportive lines of business.

A second task has been to develop specialized insurance companies, handling specific types of business. China has established a number of such companies since 2003. Among these are five health insurance companies including China People's Health Insurance, an automobile insurance company, Tian Ping Auto Insurance, a property and liability insurance, Chang An, four agricultural insurance companies including the Shanghai An Xin Company, and five pension insurance companies including the Tai Ping pension insurance. Both agricultural and pension insurance have been greatly improved by the establishment of these specialized companies (see Figure 22.3).

A third task has been to grow the intermediary markets. In 2000, China authorized the establishment of the country's first insurance

FIGURE 22.3   Agricultural insurance premium income, 2004–07, in hundred million RMB

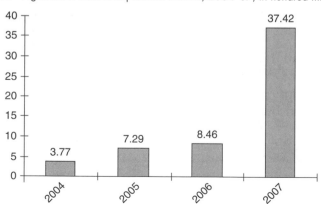

FIGURE 22.4 Percentage of personal insurance premiums going through banks, 2001 to 2007

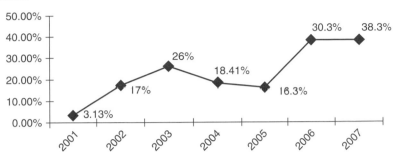

agency, the Jiang Tai Insurance Agency. By the end of 2007, there were 322 authorized firms dealing in insurance brokering or agenting. In 2007 they realized premium income of RMB16.688 billion, which represented 2.37% of national insurance premium income. Property insurance premiums constituted RMB13.551 billion of this total, which was 6.78% of all national property insurance premiums. Cross-business intermediaries in the industry have grown swiftly, especially in the area of banking insurance channels, which has become one of the main channels for China's insurance industry (see Figure 22.4).

Guided by the mission of promoting growth in the industry and providing services in support of growth, a modern regulatory system governing China's insurance industry has developed over these years. China's Insurance Regulatory Commission has set up a structure composed of the three main components of a modern system. These oversee solvency adequacy, market behavior, and corporate governance. The Commission has greatly improved the effectiveness of regulatory legislation by setting up five main lines of defense in regulating the industry. Internal corporate controls serve as the base; supervision of solvency adequacy is core. On-site inspections are the main means to compliance; supervision of fund management is a key link in the process. Insurance security funds serve as a final protective screen.

While taking a path that has unique Chinese characteristics, China's insurance industry has accomplished remarkable achievements. Since 2000, growth in the industry has propelled it to a position of number nine worldwide in terms of premium income (see Figure 22.5 on page 388). In 2001, premium income was RMB211.23 billion; in 2006, it had reached RMB564.1 billion, and in 2007 it was RMB703.58 billion, or roughly US$96 billion. Insurance industry assets are growing at an average annual rate of 16%. In end-2004, gross assets of the

FIGURE 22.5   Insurance premium income 1980–2007 (hundred million RMB)

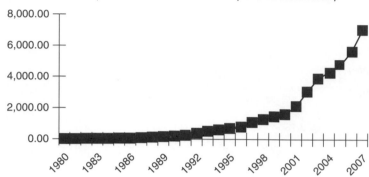

industry were RMB1.1854 trillion (see Figure 22.6). By the end of 2007, they had reached RMB2.9 trillion.

China's insurance market had for years been operated on a monopolistic basis. It is now diversified to the extent that it has a variety of coexisting organizational structures, a variety of coexisting forms of capital, and a variety of coexisting institutions. This enables market structures with a high degree of competition and fairer competition, with more complete functions and with a more rational division of labor. The market structure is more able to move the industry forward.

Penetration rates for insurance in China have been increasing. In 1980, the figure was 0.1%; in 2000 it was 1.79%; and in 2006 it had reached 2.8%, as per Figure 22.7. Per capita insured amounts [density]

FIGURE 22.6   Total assets in the insurance industry, 2002–07 (trillion RMB)

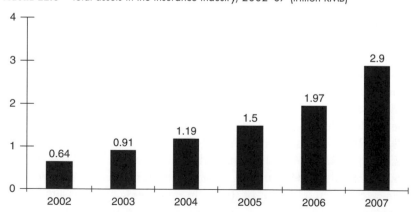

FIGURE 22.7 Insurance penetration or "depth," 1980–2006

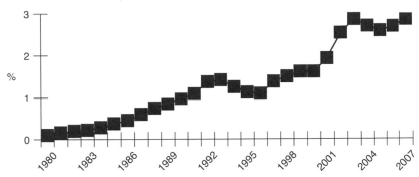

were RMB0.47 in 1980, RMB126.85 in 2000, and RMB431.3 in 2006, as per Figure 22.8.

In terms of assuming responsibility for risk, in 2006 China's largest non-life insurance company, the China People's Property and Casualty Insurance Company, took on RMB31.5 trillion in liability reserves, which was 1.5 times the GDP for that year. In terms of compensation amounts, in 2006, the entire insurance industry paid out RMB143.85 billion, three times the amount paid out in the year 2000. In the five years from 2003 to 2007, accumulated compensation in the insurance industry came to over RMB680 billion. The industry has effectively been able to provide guarantees and meliorate risk.

A NEW GOLDEN AGE OF GROWTH

China's insurance industry currently stands at a point of strategic opportunity. Overall economic growth in the country continues to

FIGURE 22.8 Per capita insured amounts [density] 1980–2006, in RMB along the left axis

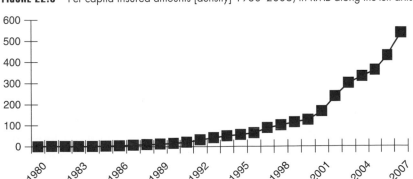

provide an excellent foundation for its future prospects. As the economy grows, people's financial assets will continue to restructure and improve in terms of distribution. One excellent expression of this is the percentage of insurance assets held by people and the way financial markets are handling them with greater diversification of asset management products. In 2001, 83% of individual financial assets in China were held in the form of cash and savings deposits. Just 13.5% were in stocks, and 1.7% was in insurance. By end-2005, these percentages had changed to 81.8% in cash and savings deposits, 8.7% in stocks, 8.9% in insurance, and 1% in other financial assets. Fast economic growth and the rise in people's incomes have contributed to increasing resources for insurance companies as expenditures on consumption of insurance products grows. The percentage of consumption spent on service industries is known to increase rapidly when GDP per capita breaks through US$2,000. In China, the insurance industry is facing a "golden age" in terms of the composition of consumption expenditures. There is already a marked increase in the need for information on insurance products among urban residents. In 2002, less than one-third of urban households paid any attention to information on insurance. In 2006, that figure had risen to 60%.

China's population is changing structurally in terms of its age distribution. The rapidly aging population is also going to lead to huge increases in the demand for certain types of insurance. In 2005, there were already 144 million people over the age of 60 in China. This figure is growing quickly: due to demographic changes in the mid-twentieth century, China's population is not only aging, but the steepness of the curve at which it is aging is increasing. The year 2030 will see the peak in China's elderly population. The demographics of the country create a tremendous opportunity for the insurance industry to participate in social security systems.

Looking at the investment climate for utilizing insurance funds, at present, the scope of investment opportunities is broadened to encompass direct investment in industries and indirect investment via financial investments. This includes investment in bonds and other debt instruments, investment in equity shares, from domestic to international. Channels through which investments may be made are also continuing to broaden and asset management functions of insurance companies will continue to improve.

In brief, China's insurance industry is being encouraged to seize the opportunities that lie ahead. It is being asked to continue to reform and to open to the outside by realizing the following strategic measures.

First, the industry must continue to improve regulatory systems. This includes regulation over solvency adequacy, improvement of solvency assessment, and strengthening of enforcement. It includes improving effective governance in financial groups that have insurance as their core business. Emphasis should be placed on supervising related transactions and capital adequacy ratios, centralized risk controls, corporate information disclosure, and qualifications for serving in senior management positions. It includes expanding services in commercial insurance, on top of the base of existing corporate pension funds, and improving cooperation with health insurance, liability insurance, and what is known as the "three-agricultures" insurance, which means insurance applied to the various components of the rural population.

Second, mandatory insurance systems should be implemented in such fields as coal mining. Insurance companies must continue to search for effective means to cooperate with rural areas that are transitioning to urban centers, particularly in health insurance, and they must gradually increase coverage in all geographic areas in commercial insurance. They must strengthen and improve regulation over market behavior, severely discipline illegal behavior as well as unfair competition, and strengthen concepts of trustworthiness and prudent operations, in order to make market competition more standardized and orderly.

Third, companies must open up new realms in asset management, and increase the asset size of insurance (financial) groups. By 2015, industry analysts are predicting that China's financial asset management business will have grown by over six times, from US$300 billion today to US$2 trillion. China will become the world's second-largest wealth management market in the world, second only to the US. Insurance companies must hasten their ability to manage third-party assets, such as corporate pension funds, and the wealth management of individuals. Through strengthening asset management, they must form new growth areas as fast as possible, further improve the structure of their investments, and improve investment returns.

Fourth, companies and the industry as a whole must improve market penetration in both urban and rural areas, but must especially move into new geographic regions that are currently under-served. On the one hand, companies should focus on more in-depth development of urban business. Their emphasis should be on exploring how to work together with the administrative units in cities centered around neighborhoods or residential communities, how to work with their property management companies, and how to explore the best operating models under the transition of different forms of communities. Insurance companies should preserve their leading position in urban business, even as they put greater efforts into expanding business in rural areas. They should focus on enhancing good relations with rural administrative entities. They should actively participate in policy-type agricultural insurance, in new cooperative health insurance initiatives, and provide the necessary insurance to both the unemployed and to inhabitants of rural areas that travel elsewhere for jobs. They should focus on providing comprehensive services to people in rural areas in all aspects of the business: production, distribution, and services.

Fifth, through all possible means and channels, insurance companies should develop a sales and service network in rural areas, explore operating models that are appropriate to local circumstances. They should analyze changes in consumption in rural areas and develop lower-end business models targeted at local consumption patterns and that can be effective in introducing new insurance concepts into rural areas.

Finally, the industry should develop into new product areas as it sets up social security services for the population at large. It should promote growth of liability insurance, it should actively participate in establishing social security systems, grow the market for pension funds, and develop the growth potential for corporate pensions. It should take full advantage of the opportunity provided by the reform of the healthcare system to develop authorized management services in health insurance, and it should actively participate in social insurance services such as basic health insurance in both rural and urban areas.

PROSPECTS

Rapid but stable economic growth is the foundation on which China's insurance industry can maintain fast growth. According to the latest economic growth plans of the Chinese government, by 2020, per capita GDP is to reach US$3,500 at unchanged year-2000 exchange rates, which at market exchange rates would translate into around US$7,200. When that happens, China's GDP will enter the ranks of mid- to mid-upper income countries in the world. By 2010, premium income from China's insurance industry is forecast

TABLE 22.1 Forecast size of China's insurance markets in the years 2010 and 2020

Year	GDP (RMB)	Exchange rate (US$/RMB)	Depth income	Insurance (RMB)	Premium income (US$)	World ranking
2010	30.7 trillion	1:6	4%	1.288 trillion	204,700 million	6
2020	66.28 trillion	1:4	7.5%	4.971 trillion	1.243 trillion	3

to surpass RMB1 trillion; penetration will reach 4%, and per capita insurance or density will reach RMB750, as seen in Table 22.1. By 2020, the penetration rate may well reach the current world level of 7.5%. Gross income from insurance premiums will surpass US$1 trillion at that time, and China will then be one of the three largest insurance markets in the world.

Looking at income elasticity with regard to increases in insurance premiums, since 2001, the income elasticity to insurance premium increases was consistently doubling. According to this calculation, premium income in 2010 and 2020 will reach, respectively, RMB1.2 trillion and RMB5 trillion. By 2010 and 2020, total assets of the insurance industry should be on the order of RMB5 trillion and RMB20 trillion, respectively.

China's insurance markets in the future will allow different kinds of markets to supplement one another. Large, medium-sized, and small insurance companies should be able to grow in tandem. With advantages of scale, in terms of comprehensive operations, large companies will be operating in a stable manner in China's markets and will then be able to explore overseas expansion opportunities. Small and medium-sized companies, in turn, should use their advantage of specialized operations to focus on certain regions for niche growth. In terms of business structure, China's insurance industry is expected to transition quickly from providing mostly individual insurance and property insurance to also providing liability and credit-risk insurance.

Between 2010 and 2020, the total income from non-life insurance business in China is expected to increase in a stable manner and possibly reach the world level of 42% of total insurance income. In terms of product structure, due to the high savings rate of Chinese people, investment products similar in nature to savings deposits have the highest potential for growth and may become a new force in growing non-life insurance businesses. In addition, with the development of "new agriculture" throughout China's rural areas, reform of social

FIGURE 22.9 Average growth rate of major economies in the world 1999–2004 (as measured in GDP), and average growth rates in insurance income

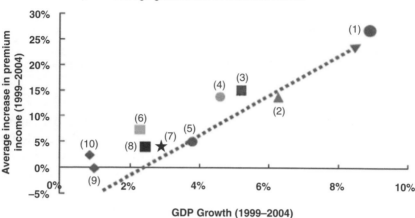

1. China; 2. Russia; 3. Thailand; 4. India; 5. Turkey; 6. Brazil; 7. Poland; 8. USA; 9. Japan; 10. Germany.

Source: Sigma.

security systems, and the establishment of a multi-tiered social security system, liability insurance, health insurance, pension insurance, and agricultural insurance will be seeing great historic opportunities. The percentage of liability insurance in non-life insurance should be approaching world levels by 2020 (see Table 22.2).

China's insurance companies will be taking a more active posture in the whole process of internationalization. First, within the country, the domestic market will be further opened. Emphasis will be placed on bringing in specialized insurance companies in the various fields of pension, health, liability, and agricultural insurance, and especially in guiding foreign investment into the hinterland of China. Second, more

TABLE 22.2 Forecast of figures comparing non-life insurance and life insurance businesses, 1995–2020 (units: 00 million RMB)

	1995	2000	2005	2006	2007	2010E	2020E
Non-life insurance (1)	292	598	1,281.11	1,580.35	2,086.48	4,500.00	20,000
Life insurance (2)	161	998	3,646.23	4,061.09	4,948.97	8,400.00	30,000
(1) : (2)		6.4:3.6	3.7:6.3	2.6:7.4	2.8:7.2	3.0:7.0	3.5:6.5 4.0:6.0

Sources: China Insurance Regulatory Commission website and China statistical yearbooks of 1996 and 2001.

and more Chinese companies will be developing business outside of China, emphasizing mutual benefit and win–win strategies, opening markets by participating in share ownership, mergers and acquisitions (M&As), as well as newly established entities. The unequal status of "bringing in" and "going out" should be changed as insurance operations truly globalize. International business will become a large piece of the business of Chinese insurance companies. Third, asset allocations will be ever more internationalized; with rapid accumulation of domestic insurance assets, domestic insurance companies will necessarily utilize international markets and global resources.

In the course of further reform, China's insurance industry is raising its own international competitiveness. The share structure of major companies, or group companies, will become ever more effective, accountability and corporate governance will be improved, product innovative capability will strengthen, risk management will be enhanced, and capital and financial strength will be more solid. Both solvency adequacy and profitability will be more pronounced, forming greater ability to control resources and ensure sustainability. The large companies, which include China People's Insurance Group, China Life Group, Ping An Group, and China Pacific Group, will, depending on their market positioning and developmental needs, restructure internally, set up specialized subsidiaries, and become comprehensive international financial groups with strong core businesses and mutually supportive subsidiaries. More world-class insurance giants are expected to form in China between 2010 and 2020 and, following on the example of China Life, to enter the ranks of *Fortune 500*.

As diversification continues in China's insurance markets and business continues to grow, M&As and reorganizations will characterize the business for some time. Within the insurance industry, there is bound to be consolidation of smaller firms that have inadequate management skills or an insufficient capital base, a low market share, or an inability to achieve economies of scale. M&As will also allow large financial groups to build strength outside the insurance industry. Mutual interpenetration and M&As among insurance, banking, and asset companies will become more common to the extent that even very large institutions may merge or restructure their ownership. Large M&As and restructuring will spur the overall restructuring of insurance capital and market resources in general, going a step further in improving the international competitiveness and sustainability of the Chinese insurance industry.

Looking over recent history, China's insurance industry has accomplished notable achievements and accumulated considerable experience. The first 20 years of the twenty-first century presents an important strategic opportunity to China's social and economic development, and similarly a strategic opportunity to China's insurance industry. Standing at a new starting point in history, China's insurance industry is expected to stride into an even more promising future.

CHAPTER 23

China's Insurance Market

Jacques Kemp
CEO, Asia & Pacific, ING

China's vast and still largely untapped insurance market has been one of the main focal points of expansion for multinational insurance companies in the past 15 years. Its attraction for global insurers is obvious: with a combination of sheer size, low service penetration and strong economic impetus, the market promises to deliver lucrative new growth to companies able to carve out a market position.

With China's gradual reintegration into the global market place and ascension to the World Trade Organization (WTO), the procession of foreign insurance companies entering China grows longer by the year. Currently, of the 100 licensed insurers in the country, more than 40 are foreign-funded joint ventures or wholly owned foreign companies.

These foreign insurers have achieved strong growth over recent years as market access has increased. But without the nationwide reach of their Chinese peers, the market share of foreign joint ventures has remained small and success has come from focusing on building a presence in the major coastal markets, such as Shanghai and Guangzhou.

As the market has become increasingly saturated, however, some foreign insurers arriving late to the China market have preferred to gain exposure to the China market through strategic investments into Chinese insurers. In addition, with the major coastal markets reaching a saturation point, more foreign insurer ventures are marking out their territory in the hinterlands.

This chapter will examine the strengths and weaknesses of different approaches to entry into the China market, and assess the performance and challenges experienced by foreign insurers in recent years. It will also look at how regulators and market participants can work together, based on common objectives to drive the development of the industry and discuss the importance of free market principles to creating a competitive and efficient market. Finally, the chapter will discuss the future path of development for China's insurance industry, and the role foreign insurers can play as a catalyst for the industry's continued evolution.

A 200-YEAR HISTORY

Amid the scramble to enter China's insurance market over the past decade and the challenges of operating in an unfamiliar environment and culture, it is easy to forget that foreign insurers have a history of business with China dating back more than two centuries.

Indeed, the first insurers in China were established by European businessmen in the early nineteenth century to serve maritime traders during the Qing Dynasty, and over the next century steadily amassed a strong presence in the country. This dominance did not end until the middle of the twentieth century, when foreign insurance companies withdrew from China against the backdrop of first the Japanese occupation during the Second World War, and later, the rise of the centrally planned economy, under which the need for insurance was obviated.

Following a 40-year hiatus, a carefully regulated trickle of foreign insurers was allowed back into China in the early 1990s against the backdrop of China's gradual re-engagement with the global marketplace.

AIG was the first foreign insurer to be allowed to do business in China, winning a license to operate a wholly owned life and non-life insurance business in Shanghai through a branch office in 1992. Following AIG, Tokio Marine & Nichido Fire became in 1994 the second foreign insurer to receive authorization to operate a branch in Shanghai, providing services mainly to Japanese companies in China.

Winterthur Swiss Insurance became the third foreign insurer to open an office in Shanghai in 1996, and was the first foreign company in China to offer property insurance. In the same year, Manulife Insurance became the first foreign insurer to establish a Sino–foreign insurance joint venture in partnership with the China Foreign Economic and Trade Trust Investment Company, a subsidiary of the Sinochem group.

Two years later, in 1998, China allowed two more foreign insurers to establish joint ventures. Allianz teamed up with Dazhong to launch its joint venture in January 1998, while Aetna partnered with China Pacific Insurance (CPIC) 10 months later. Through ING's acquisition of the Aetna's US financial services and international life insurance operations in July 2000, Aetna's stake in the joint venture, Pacific Antai Life Insurance, was subsequently transferred to ING, who became the first foreign insurer to own two insurance joint ventures in China.

Subsequent to those initial moves, foreign insurers have been beating a path into the Chinese market as fast as the China Insurance Regulatory Commission has allowed them. As at the end of June 2007, a total of 45 foreign insurers from 15 countries were licensed to operate in China, and these companies have set up a combined total of 128 operational institutions.[1]

CHINA'S WTO COMMITMENTS

In order to understand the business environment for foreign insurers in China today, it is instructive to review the blueprint for market opening that China committed to in the course of its ascension to the WTO.

The strategic importance of the insurance industry to economic development and its enormous untapped growth potential made it one of the most hotly contested areas of China's WTO negotiations, and was reported to be the final hurdle as China entered the final phase of its trade negotiations with WTO member countries.

In the event, the agreement covering the opening of China's insurance market focused on four areas: the clarification of the licensing process, the elimination of geographical restrictions, the expansion of product scope, and the determination of ownership parameters.[2]

China agreed to adopt an objective and transparent licensing process for foreign insurance partners without limiting the number of licenses that would be issued to each country. Basic license application requirements included a total asset base of US$5 billion or more, 30 years of experience operating in a WTO member country, and two consecutive years of operating a representative office in China.

On geographical restrictions, China agreed to extend the list of cities in which foreign insurers and insurance brokers were permitted to provide services from Shanghai, Guangzhou, Dalian, Shenzhen, and Foshan, to Beijing, Chengdu, Chongqing, Fuzhou, Suzhou, Xiamen,

Ningbo, Shenyang, Wuhan, and Tianjin by the end of 2003, eliminating all remaining geographical restrictions at the end of 2004.

On the scope of activities, China agreed to permit foreign life insurers to underwrite individual but not group policies once it joined the WTO, and extend their activities to health insurance, group insurance, and pension/annuities insurance by 2004. Meanwhile, foreign non-life insurers were to be permitted to underwrite master policies and large-scale commercial insurance, as well as underwrite policies for Chinese enterprises abroad, and provide property insurance, related liability insurance, and credit insurance for foreign-funded enterprises upon China's entry to the WTO, and allowed to engage in the full range of non-life business by 2003.

In terms of ownership restrictions, China agreed to allow foreign non-life insurers to set up branches or joint ventures, and own no more than 51% in those operations when it acceded to the WTO, and set up wholly owned ventures by 2003. Foreign life insurers were to own up to 50% stakes in joint ventures in China, and choose their partners independently upon China's WTO accession.

China also allows foreign insurers and financial services companies to take strategic stakes in domestic insurers. Since 1999, China has allowed foreign companies to take up to a 25% stake in certain Chinese insurance companies, with each individual foreign investor owning no more than 5%.

These rules have recently been revised to allow a single foreign investor to hold up to 20% of a domestic insurer, although total permitted foreign ownership remains capped at 25%. For the transaction to be approved, the investors must have more than US$2 billion in assets, a record of profits for three straight accounting years, and a credit rating higher than "A."

ENTRY STRATEGY: SINO–FOREIGN JOINT VENTURES

The majority of foreign insurers have chosen to enter China through joint ventures and many in alliance with domestic companies from non-insurance sectors. This model has appealed to foreign insurers because non-insurance companies are generally passive partners, allowing the foreign insurers to exert almost complete management control over their joint ventures. In this way, foreign insurers have had greater freedom to shape the business and determine its overall strategy.

Foreign insurers, which have teamed up with a non-insurance Chinese partner, are also theoretically in a stronger position to negotiate the buyout of its partner's stake if or when regulations eventually allow foreign enterprises to wholly own Chinese insurance companies. In addition, non-insurance partners have allowed foreign insurers to work with a clean slate in building their joint ventures, training the sales force from the ground up, rather than trying to re-train an existing group of insurance agents, which has already been operating in a vastly different corporate culture and practices. That said, the acute shortage of skilled labor in China's rapidly expanding insurance industry has made the task of constructing a sales force from scratch an increasingly difficult challenge.

Joint ventures can prove fragile especially so for the ones involving cross-cultural alliances, as countless examples through the modern history of business show. In order to succeed over the long run, the Sino–foreign insurance joint venture needs to be built upon a shared vision, which combines the experience, technical expertise, and management practices of the foreign partner with the local market knowledge, connections, and distribution strength of the local partner.

However, building the consensus and understanding needed to allow a joint venture partnership to thrive is invariably easier to discuss than it is to achieve. As participants in Sino–foreign joint ventures in any industry can attest to, cultural differences can pose serious obstacles to effective communication and conflict resolution.

According to the consensus of academic studies, the main obstacle to effective communication between Chinese and foreign business partners originates from differences in the value system. Chinese people are believed to place a stronger emphasis on collectivist values, which lead them to value harmony in relationships and protect the social face of their peers. As a result, Chinese people tend to avoid aggressive ways of dealing with differences. By contrast, people from Western cultures tend to be guided more by individualistic values, which lead them to confront their differences more directly.[3]

To bridge this cultural divide, many foreign insurers have followed the well-worn path of drafting in experienced senior executives of Chinese ethnicity from Hong Kong and Taiwan, who have the prerequisite understanding of Western management practices allied to a Chinese cultural background, to help manage their joint ventures.

As China's exposure to the international business community grows, it can be expected that Chinese and foreign joint ventures will improve their understanding and appreciation of cultural differences, paving the way for closer cooperation, and more culturally sensitive systems of goal setting and reward structuring. Communication is important not only to guide the workforce, but also at the executive level in order to avoid a mismatch of ambitions between joint venture partners.

Depending on its rate of expansion, a life insurance start-up enterprise may take as many as seven years to break even. At some insurance joint ventures, this wait for profit has become a source of tension, with the domestic partner running low on patience. This is particularly prone to happen when the domestic partner's expertise lies in another industry, such as manufacturing, where investments yield returns over a much shorter time scale. Expectations clearly need to be understood and managed on both sides.

Because joint venture insurance companies in China will take years to become profitable and in the meantime drain capital as they expand, foreign insurers have sought cash-rich domestic partners. This is a critical issue, given the high prudential requirements set by the regulators for opening new branches. While the minimum registered capital for the establishment of a joint venture insurance company is RMB200 million, the enterprise must subsequently add RMB20 million to its registered capital for each new branch it opens unless its total registered capital has reached RMB500 million. This financial burden of expansion is only likely to get heavier as regulations change and more capital-intensive products are launched.

As such, foreign insurers have favored partnerships with well-capitalized companies for which the insurance joint venture would represent only a minor investment. In addition, some foreign insurers have pre-empted future capital requirements by establishing a venture with enough financial clout at the outset to open as many as 10 branches.

However well-capitalized the joint venture is, it is clearly important for foreign insurers that have elected to team up with non-insurance companies to ensure their partners have a detailed understanding of the capital commitment and time required to build a successful insurance joint venture. For those foreign insurers that have failed to adequately prepare their domestic partners for the journey, there have been frequent and disruptive disputes.

Aside from capital, foreign insurers have also placed a strong emphasis on brand strength in selecting a Chinese joint venture partner. This is because most of today's best known global insurance companies have yet to build up any significant brand awareness in China, and must therefore rely on the names of their domestic partners to build up brand trust.

Not all joint venture insurance companies are interested in building awareness in the mass market, however. Some have opted to approach the market using the boutique model, providing bespoke financial services to the growing ranks of the super-affluent in China.

ENTRY STRATEGY:
STRATEGIC INVESTMENTS

As an alternative to establishing a joint venture, some foreign insurers and financial institutions have opted to enter the Chinese insurance market through strategic investments into domestic insurers.

In 1994, Ping An Insurance, China's second-largest life insurer, became the first Chinese insurer to sell a stake to foreign strategic investors in a US$70 million deal for a 15% stake with Goldman Sachs and Morgan Stanley. In 2002, the company sold another 10% stake to HSBC for US$600 million.

In 2000, New China Insurance, China's fourth-largest national insurance company, sold 24.9% of its equity for US$116.9 million to five foreign investors, including Zurich Insurance Company, the International Financial Corporation (a member of the World Bank), Meiji Life Insurance Company, and Holland Financial Services Company.

In the same year, China's fifth-largest life insurance company, Taikang Insurance, was granted approval to sell a 24.9% stake for US$145 million to a foreign consortium, including Winterthur Life and Pensions, the Government of Singapore Investment Corporation, and Softbank.

In December 2005, an investor group comprising of private equity firm Carlyle Group and Prudential Financial took a combined 24.98% stake in China Pacific Life Insurance Co. by injecting US$410 million into the third-largest life insurer in China. In May this year, CIRC approved Carlyle and Prudential to transfer that stake for a 19.9% stake in China Pacific Insurance (Group) Co., the parent company of China Pacific Life Insurance Co.

Strategic investment generally requires a greater initial capital commitment than a joint venture, but provides the foreign insurer with a quicker path into the China market. While a joint venture may need 15 years to establish a nationwide presence, the strategic investment allows the foreign insurer to gain wide market exposure instantly.

This has appealed, in particular, to foreign insurers that have arrived late to China. The competitive landscape has changed dramatically in recent years, with the market becoming increasingly overcrowded. This has made it more difficult than ever for a newcomer to succeed through a fledgling joint venture in China.

But strategic investments are also attracting foreign insurers that have already made substantial inroads into the China market through joint ventures, as they open the door to synergistic relationships. For example, AIG purchased a 9.9% stake in PICC Property and Casualty Company in 2003, and leveraged the strategic relationship to underwrite personal accident and health insurance business in China through the domestic insurer's extensive nationwide distribution network.[4]

On the downside, strategic investments cannot provide the level of operational and boardroom control most foreign insurers would like. Regulations effectively restrict the shareholding that a foreign insurance company can own in a domestic insurer to 25%. If foreign ownership in a Chinese insurer increases to more than 25%, the enterprise is reclassified by the authorities as a foreign-funded enterprise. Thus, the foreign insurer making a strategic investment must console itself with a role in which it serves more as consultant than decision-maker in the Chinese insurance company, although this is not to say that the foreign insurer cannot provide certain level of business leadership from this position.

For domestic insurers, the strategic investment brings two main benefits; namely, a capital infusion and the opportunity to tap into international management experience and risk management expertise. The sale of a strategic stake to a foreign insurer often represents a commitment by the domestic insurer to embrace organizational change. This may include the restructuring of operations, a new business direction, or the adoption of international best management practices, improved corporate governance, and advanced risk management techniques. Foreign strategic shareholders help facilitate such transformation by making their global resources available to Chinese insurers, which may include drafting in experienced senior executives from overseas.

MARKET SHARE GAINS

As market access has been gradually raised following China's entry into the WTO, foreign insurers have enjoyed significant business growth, even though their premium income remains relatively small. As at the end of June 2007, foreign funded insurance ventures generated a combined RMB16.28 billion in premiums, representing a 4.38% market national share.

Foreign life insurers contributed the bulk of this business, generating RMB14.99 billion in premiums, which represented a 5.9% market share (compared with 1.85% in 2000). Foreign non-life insurers generated RMB1.28 billion in premiums for a 1.13% market share (compared with 0.54% in 2000).[5]

These market share figures reflect the vastly greater reach enjoyed by domestic insurers across the entire China market. With the sales network to compete with domestic insurers on these terms, foreign insurers have chosen instead to focus on the major coastal cities such as Beijing, Dalian, Guangzhou, Shanghai, Shenzen, Suzhou, and Tianjin, which generate the bulk of economic activity.

Foreign insurers have achieved a much greater degree of success with this narrow geographical focus. In Shanghai, foreign insurers have grown their market share aggressively from 14% in 2003 to 22% as at the middle of 2007, and 26% as of September 2007.[6] With these urban markets now reaching saturation point a total of 81 insurance companies were licensed to operate in Shanghai at the time writing, later entrants to China are opting to develop hinterland markets.

When Groupama, France's largest insurance company, launched its non-life operations in 2004, it chose Chengdu, the capital city of Sichuan, as its headquarters. More recently, Great Eastern Life Assurance of Singapore also set up its joint venture life insurance company within Sichuan, in the municipality of Chongqing.

Meanwhile, the national insurance market continues to grow at an astounding pace. From 2001 to the end of 2006, insurance premium income in China's has surged at a compound annual rate of more than 25%, reaching RMB564.14 billion at the end of 2006, compared with RMB143.03 billion at the beginning of 2001 (see Figure 23.1 on page 406 for premium growth through 2005). In the first half of 2007, premium income rose by more than 20% from the year earlier to RMB371.8 billion.

The total assets of the insurance industry have witnessed even stronger growth, expanding at a compound annual growth rate of 35.6% to RMB1.97 trillion in 2000 from RMB317.41 billion in 2006.[7]

FIGURE 23.1   Insurance premium growth

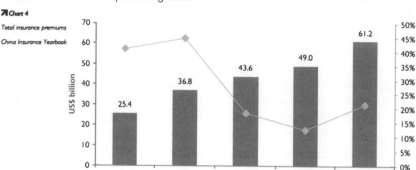

With the market continuing to expand along an upward if moderating trajectory, the CIRC has predicted that insurance premiums in China will double to RMB1 trillion—around the same size as the Singapore economy—by the year 2010. This will be driven by the growth of affluence, which will see consumers spend more on items such as cars, houses and travel, as well as the aging population, which will increase demand for medical insurance and savings plans.

TACKLING THE HUMAN RESOURCES CHALLENGE

The rapid growth of the economy in China is leading the country down the path of a labor shortage according to economists. In a report released in 2005, the McKinsey Global Institute predicted that Chinese universities would produce around 1.2 million graduates qualified to work for world-class companies from 2003 to 2008, but demand from foreign companies and foreign-funded joint ventures alone could absorb 60% of that pool of talent. The same report predicted that by 2015, China would need 75,000 internationally experienced managers to drive its worldwide business aspirations, but had only 3,000 to 5,000 managers with such capabilities as of 2005 (see Figure 23.2).[8]

One of the pain points in the supply of skilled labor identified by analysts is the quality of education. While China is churning out gradates at a remarkable rate, the proportion of graduates that have enjoyed the standard and relevance of education needed to function in a world-class company remains relatively small. Observers believe

FIGURE 23.2 China's talent shortage

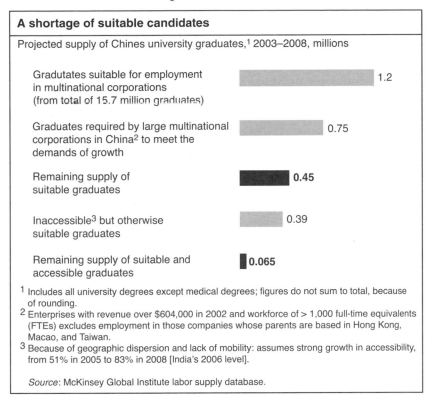

A shortage of suitable candidates

Projected supply of Chines university graduates,[1] 2003–2008, millions

Gradutates suitable for employment in multinational corporations (from total of 15.7 million graduates) — 1.2

Graduates required by large multinational corporations in China[2] to meet the demands of growth — 0.75

Remaining supply of suitable graduates — 0.45

Inaccessible[3] but otherwise suitable graduates — 0.39

Remaining supply of suitable and accessible graduates — 0.065

[1] Includes all university degrees except medical degrees; figures do not sum to total, because of rounding.

[2] Enterprises with revenue over $604,000 in 2002 and workforce of > 1,000 full-time equivalents (FTEs) excludes employment in those companies whose parents are based in Hong Kong, Macao, and Taiwan.

[3] Because of geographic dispersion and lack of mobility: assumes strong growth in accessibility, from 51% in 2005 to 83% in 2008 [India's 2006 level].

Source: McKinsey Global Institute labor supply database.

China must look to overhaul its educational system to ensure the quality of university graduates improves over the long term. This includes revising the funding structure for higher education, revamping curriculums to meet the needs of commerce and industry, and improving the quality of English-language instruction.

According to the Chinese Academy of Social Sciences, China will start to feel the talent crunch in 2010[9] even though for insurance companies, the shortage of skilled labor has already hit home in the wake of the industry's breakneck growth. Recruitment and training have become the single biggest challenge for all market participants. In market studies and reports, foreign joint ventures have voiced concerns over the lack of suitable personnel to fill positions across the entire spectrum of careers in the insurance industry, from sales agents and executive directors, to actuaries and underwriters, to internal auditors, compliance officers, and other back office staff. The problem is likely to persist, given many foreign insurers estimate they need to expand the headcount by as much a 133% in the next three years to maintain the targeted pace of expansion.

In a recent survey of senior executives at foreign-funded insurance ventures, recruiting and training competent staff, and recruiting and training in the distribution channels were ranked as the two most pressing challenges by senior executives of foreign insurance companies in China.[10]

The quality of staff has a strong bearing on the effectiveness of distribution channels. Without the necessary training, sales personnel have the knowledge to sell only a limited range of products. For example, through the bancassurance channel, which is estimated to generate some 20% of premiums in the life market, insurers have been confined to underwriting mostly low margin and single premium products, because the sales staff at banks do not have sufficient training to sell more sophisticated offerings. Single premium products generate only one-tenth the value of regular premium products.

Additionally, staff turnover rates have increased to alarming levels amid the shortage of experienced, qualified industry professionals. It has been reported that in some organizations, staff turnover is as high as 40%[11] Unsurprisingly, pay checks are expanding. In the past five years, salaries in the insurance sector have grown by an average of around 25% per annum.

To ensure experienced staff stay on board, insurers have to steadily raise salaries, yet surveys of employees suggest the Chinese worker is as motivated by other factors such as career opportunities and work environment, as they are by attractive compensation. Companies with high staff retention are often found to focus on providing more career development and training opportunities to their employees, and then linking these training opportunities back to compensation.

The ability to offer a clearly defined merit-based career development path and job rotation within an organization is a classic strategy for enhancing staff retention. Employees also respond to companies that have gone the extra distance to build community spirit in the organization through social gatherings, company trips, and a strong platform for human resources communication and dialogue. Continued professional development is another critical area in the battle to retain employees, given the high value placed on education, career development, and training in Chinese culture.

Many foreign joint venture insurance companies are providing the funding for their employees to study for new professional qualifications. Companies can offer to subsidize an employee's MBA program in return for an agreed number of years of service after graduation. Some foreign-funded insurance joint ventures have also established in-house business schools to facilitate regular staff training and educational programs aimed at raising employees' competence and knowledge levels.

Foreign funded ventures and domestic insurers with strategic links to foreign insurers have the advantage of being able to draw upon the global resources available to them to enhance staff retention. With access to a global network of insurance operations, these enterprises can provide local employees with the opportunity to work overseas on year-long assignments to attain a deeper understanding of business practices and approaches in developed markets, or bring overseas experts to China to conduct specialized training for local employees on-site.

Lastly, compensation can be structured to enhance staff retention. Transparent, performance-based incentive structures, such as bonuses or retirement savings plans, can be introduced. In addition, pay packages and raises can be linked to both performance and skill development, and employees made to understand clearly how compensation is linked to opportunities for skill development.

A COMMON AGENDA

Aside from the talent crunch, one of the chief concerns expressed by foreign insurers has been China's progress in increasing market access to foreign-funded insurance ventures. According to surveys and reports, there is a wide consensus among foreign insurers that market liberalization has not been implemented at a pace consistent with China's trade agreements in the wake of its accession to the World Trade Organization.

One of the main points of contention is the regulatory procedures for new branch openings. Foreign insurers contend the approval process for opening new branches is discriminatory, with domestic insurers able to apply for multiple branch openings concurrently while foreign applications are processed sequentially. In addition, investment management regulations appear to be skewed in favor of the big domestic insurers. Prudential requirements for opening an insurance asset management company, for example, are set at a level that makes internal investment management prohibitive to all but the largest Chinese insurers.

Tackling such issues should be seen as part of a broader challenge faced by China in creating an efficient and effective regulatory environment for the insurance and financial services industry, which both the regulator and market participants need to work together to overcome.

According to the Institute of International Finance, a worldwide association established to promote risk management and the development of best practices and standards in the global financial services industry, the development of a sound financial regulatory system should be based on shared objectives that the financial services firms and regulators can work together to achieve. These shared goals are economic growth and competition, stability and security in the financial system, and consumer protection and customer services. Based on these shared fundamental aspirations, a broad consensus on guiding principles can be developed to provide a framework for China's insurance industry and broader financial services sector to increase the efficiency of regulatory processes.

International cooperation is required to ensure the regulatory environment in China addresses issues raised by the global expansion of financial services companies and the increasingly integrated nature of financial markets. Regulators can reduce differences and duplication in the regulation of institutions operating across multiple jurisdictions through solutions such as standardization and mutual recognition.

Regular open dialogue between market participants and regulators promotes the identification of regulatory needs and improves the quality and effectiveness of public policy. A disciplined and methodical process of consultation, which engages the industry and other stakeholders at the earliest possible stage in the formulation of rule changes, is the backbone of this dialogue and has proven to significantly increase the effectiveness of regulation.

It is also for the mutual benefit of the regulators and the industry when legislation is not reactive but based on proactive policy goals. Regulation should also be expressed in terms of principle, clearly articulated to the public, and involve the minimum rules needed to achieve its aim. Regulators also need to guard against over-regulation. Legislative change should be used only when the industry itself cannot reasonably be expected to find a path to achieve a policy goal or solve a problem. An approach that encourages industry self-supervision has historically proven to lead to more efficient regulation.

In a similar spirit, market participants should be given maximum flexibility to interpret a principle or rule, so long as they can demonstrate that the objectives of the principle or rule are met in the market participant's actions. This principle is critical to fostering innovation and efficiency in the market, which ultimately benefits the consumer.

As part of the process of checks and balances, impact assessments are needed to ensure that the burden of regulatory change to the industry is commensurate to the problem it aims to rectify. Additionally, periodic reviews help to ensure that the original objective of a regulatory adjustment is being achieved, and determine whether there are ways to accomplish the same goals, which are more effective and efficient.

Finally, regulators need to provide fair notice of regulatory requirements before taking enforcement action against any market participants, and they should impose penalties that are appropriate to the gravity of the violation.

THE CASE FOR MARKET LIBERALIZATION

According to a guidance report on insurance regulation in emerging markets by the International Association of Insurance Supervisor (IAIS), stability in an emerging insurance market can only be achieved "when prudential standards are met and when markets operate competitively, professionally and transparently in an international environment."[12]

By allowing competition, foreign market participants have proven in other emerging markets that they can raise the bar on service quality, bring product innovation, and transfer technological knowledge and best management practices. Increased competition also leads to the specialization of services by insurance companies looking to develop competitive advantages. The results are improved services and higher market efficiency.

To the extent that liberalization will strengthen an emerging insurance industry, it will theoretically have a wide spectrum of benefits for the whole economy.[13] For China, this means the mobilization of the massive national savings that lie dormant in domestic bank accounts to help fund economic development, such as national infrastructure and education projects. With the advantage of decades of international investment experience, foreign insurers could help allocate this capital more efficiently and set a benchmark for domestic insurers.

Second, a stronger insurance market will encourage international trade and foreign direct investment. For foreign companies looking to set up shop in China, the availability of reliable insurance services is a key consideration. Third, a liberalized insurance industry in which foreign market participants bring their greater financial strength and risk management capabilities, would enhance the financial security of policyholders. And possibly most important for China, a strong, efficient insurance market will facilitate the transformation of the social security system from a state-funded pension to a multifaceted welfare system, which can more capably shoulder the financial burden of its rapidly aging population.

ADDRESSING CONCERNS ABOUT FOREIGN PARTICIPATION

With some justification, many governments in emerging economies view the development of strong domestic insurance institutions as an essential element of their country's economic and political independence, but it is questionable whether such strong local enterprises can be forged in an environment of protectionism. As history shows, domestic industries can often stagnate rather than grow without the free flow of ideas and innovation that comes from an open market with foreign participation.

Regardless of whether protectionism does or does not work to the advantage of an infant industry, some observers believe that if the domestic insurers of an emerging market have not been able to build the economies of scale to survive in a competitive environment in two or three decades of operating within a vacuum, the likelihood is they never will.[14] On the other hand, arguments that an over-reliance on foreign insurers can compromise national security have some historical basis. A rival nation in conflict could sanction the withdrawal of its domestically controlled insurers to cripple trade, although it is also true that exposure to foreign insurers could be diversified through the regulatory process to minimize such risks.

Another pitfall of liberalization is the potential outflow of funds through the repatriation of profits. But the outflow of funds could be offset by the inflow of foreign direct investment triggered by the development of a strong insurance industry through liberalization. On balance, there is more to gain from opening up the insurance market to foreign participation than there is to lose, so long as liberalization is accompanied by a sound regulatory framework.

EDUCATING THE MARKET

Education has a significant role to play in the development of the insurance market in China. As the need for insurance was obviated by the two decades in which the Chinese economy governed by centrally planned socialism, the Chinese consumer's awareness and understanding of insurance and its value remains relatively underdeveloped. The majority of consumers continue to view insurance as unnecessary. The mass media could prove an effective channel for changing attitudes toward insurance, but China's size and the vastly different needs of various consumer segments mean that education must also be tailored to specific groups.[15]

In urban areas, educational efforts should focus on the mass-affluent segment of consumers who can afford life insurance products. The government could target this group by sending out an annual statement, summarizing their social security benefits, and pointing out the possible shortfalls in protection and how insurance could help address the issue.

In rural areas, where the basic functions of life insurance are still poorly understood, the problems of communication are much greater. Efforts should start with the consumers most likely to purchase life insurance, such as villagers in thriving areas and people who work for township enterprises. Various observers and industry participants have suggested that education on the basics of life insurance should start as early as the primary school level to drive the point home.

DRIVING MARKET EVOLUTION

As China's life insurance industry matures, it is expected to follow a similar path of development to developed markets in its product offerings. This means a process of evolution from straightforward life insurance and savings vehicles, to mutual funds and sophisticated retirement solutions, to bespoke wealth management solutions providing a holistic blend of financial advice, information, products, and services.

At the same time, distribution channels will become more diverse. Life insurance companies currently rely on their own branch network and agency sales force in China, but will gradually shift to distribution through independent intermediaries, such as financial planners, banks, and independent financial advisors, before adding

Internet-based distribution channels when consumers become more sophisticated.

Foreign insurers are likely to be among the chief market participants bringing product innovation and new business approaches to China's insurance industry. By bringing innovative new products, marketing approaches, and distribution methods, which have already been tested in more developed markets, to the table, foreign insurers can drive the evolution of China's insurance industry and accelerate the adoption of more efficient business models by domestic insurers.

Domestic and foreign insurance companies have basically five strategic options to grow their business by expanding their existing core, as shown in Figure 23.3.

Meanwhile, as foreign insurers become more entrenched in China, domestic insurers are expected to begin to extend their reach, first to have enough presence in those provinces and cities where Chinese wealth is reaching a certain minimum level. In the meantime, some large insurers will go international. This is already happening elsewhere in the financial services sector, with the Industrial & Commercial Bank of China (ICBC) lately setting up branches in New York and Moscow. China's biggest bank is also making strategic

FIGURE 23.3   The strategic growth options to expand the core

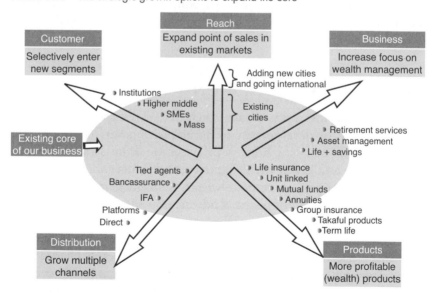

Source: ING's strategic framework to grow the core

overseas investments, including the purchase of a stake in a South African bank.

CONCLUSION

China's insurance market has come a long way in a short time, establishing a fully fledged framework for market supervision, nurturing a sizable homegrown insurance sector, and taking significant steps to opening up to foreign participation in just two decades. In order to take the industry further forward, the regulator and the industry need to work in unison to affect change based on the common goals of driving economic growth, upholding financial sector stability, and ensuring consumer protection. Guiding principles for the way insurance companies and the regulator can work together include regular, open dialogue between the regulator and market participants and other stakeholders to improve the quality and effectiveness of regulation, the clear articulation of policy objectives, and the adoption of the least rules possible to achieve them. In addition, policy objectives should encompass a greater focus on driving awareness of the need for insurance among the public through education in schools and other channels.

Going forward, the insurance industry has a critical role in helping China achieve important economic and social objectives. Insurance providers serve as an important channel through which public savings can be channeled into and allocated efficiently around capital markets to help drive sustainable economic growth. The insurance industry also has a critical role to play in the creation of a new pension system to safeguard the financial security of the country's aging population.

Foreign insurers can help accelerate the changes needed to help the industry achieve these objectives. By providing leadership in product innovation, governance, and business practices, foreign insurers can be the catalyst for the development of greater efficiency, better customer service and consumer protection in the industry.

ENDNOTES

[1] Xinhua, July 2007.
[2] Insurance and China's Entry into the WTO, Stephen P. D'Arcy and Hui Xia, University of Illinois at Urbana-Champaign, 2002.
[3] Collectivist Values and Chinese Employees' Trust of their Japanese Leaders, Dean Tjosvold and May Wong, Lingnan University, and Chunhong Liu, Helen, Dong Hua University.

[4] Foreign Investment in Chinese Banks presentation, Nick Hope, Stanford University, and Fred Hu, Goldman Sachs and Tsinghua University, October 2005.

[5] Xinhua, May 2007.

[6] Xinhua, October 2007.

[7] China Insurance Market 2007, *China Knowledge Press*.

[8] China's Looming Talent Shortage, Diana Farrell and Andrew J. Grant, *McKinsey Quarterly*, 2005.

[9] Xinhua, May 2007.

[10] Foreign Insurance Companies in China, PricewaterhouseCoopers, September 2007.

[11] Foreign Insurance Companies in China, PricewaterhouseCoopers, September 2007.

[12] Guidance on Insurance Regulation and Supervision for Emerging Market Economies Report, IAIS Emerging Market Issues Committee, September 1997.

[13] Foreign Insurers in Emerging Markets: Issues and Concerns, Harold D. Skipper, Jr, PhD 1997.

[14] Foreign Insurers in Emerging Markets: Issues and Concerns, Harold D. Skipper, Jr, PhD 1997.

[15] A Life Insurance Policy for China, Stephan H. Binder, Heidi Z. Hu, and Peter B. Walker, March 2006.

CHAPTER 24

China's Social Security System: Issues and Prospects

Gao Xiqing

*Former Vice Chairman, National Council for
Social Security Fund Council;
President and Chief Investment Officer,
China Investment Corporation*

All countries face the challenge of meeting the social security needs of their populations. As the world's most populous nation and one that is in the midst of switching tracks toward a market economy, China is facing challenges that are perhaps particularly severe. In the early 1990s, China initiated reform of its social security system in the process of setting up a socialist market economy structure through reform of state-owned enterprises (SOEs). China began this effort while faced with a rapidly aging population. After 15 years of hard work, feeling our way forward, we are pleased to see the beginnings of a uniquely Chinese system. At the same time, we are quite aware that we cannot disregard ongoing problems and very serious challenges.

HISTORY OF CHINA'S SOCIAL SECURITY REFORMS

Before Reform and Opening policies began, China's rural residents continued the tradition of having families bear the burden of caring for their elderly. Residents in cities and towns, who were state employees, made use of the planned economy system and relied on SOEs for lifelong security. After Reform and Opening, changes in the economic system meant that social security issues became more pronounced. Professionals in the field were well aware of the necessity of such

417

reform and put forward all kinds of proposals to the government. The third Plenary Session of the fourteenth Communist Party Congress passed a "Decision" in 1993, as an important component of governmental decisions on overall economic reforms. This was entitled, "Decision on Various Issues Regarding the Establishment of a Socialist Market Economy Structure," abbreviated to "Decision" below. For the first time, clear goals and principles with regard to social security reform were articulated. The 15 years since 1993 can be divided into three main periods as social security reform proceeded.

The first stage was initiated by the 1993 Decision. The Decision stipulated that an old-age insurance system be set up that had national coverage; that is, was a unified national system, and that emphasized the integration of pooled national funds and individual accounts. The Decision confirmed three principles in social security reform with regard to setting up a system. First was that it had to be national in character, a system that incorporated all administrative levels of the country. Second, that individual "pension insurance" accounts of employees in cities had to be funded, and that both employers and employees should be required to pay in to the system. The third principle was that the regulation, and the actual management, of social security funds should be separate functions. In 1995, the State Council began reforms of a nationally based social security system. To that end, it proposed two methods of implementing these reforms and suggested that regional governments could voluntarily select which they wished to follow. They could, moreover, be creative in their methods of implementation, depending on local circumstances. The second stage was initiated by a decision promulgated by the State Council in 1997 that is abbreviated to "Document 26" below. It was titled, "Decision Regarding the Establishment of a Unified Old-age Insurance System for Employees of Enterprises." The emphasis of this decision was placed on the standardization of a basic old-age insurance system for employees of enterprises.

In terms of setting up systems, Document 26 first summed up the previous four years of lessons and experience in the phrase, "integrate all accounts, manage mixed accounts." It noted that, "Many problems must be resolved since this program is still in 'pilot' stage: basic old-age insurance systems are not standardized, the burden on enterprises is severe, the level of general funding is low, management systems are incomplete." As a result, it recommended a plan whereby all employees of enterprises throughout the country implement a standardized plan with regard to basic old-age insurance. This included the "five standardizations;" namely, standardizing the percentage of payments contributed by the enterprise, standardizing the percentage paid by individuals, standardizing the size of individual accounts, standardizing pension payments, and standardizing transitional methods of paying pensions through intermediaries.

The third stage was initiated by a document issued in 2001 by the State Council as a policy statement regarding implementing a pilot social security system in Liaoning Province. It was entitled, "Measures on Pilot Implementation of a Social Security System in the Cities and Villages of Liaoning Province" (abbreviated as the "Liaoning Policy" below). The emphasis of this was that individual accounts must "be realized" or funded. This indicated that China's social security system had, in institutional terms, "moved forward to a semi-funded system in its implementation." Previously, the government had not required that individual accounts be managed separately from socially pooled funds. As a result, mismanaged funds soon ran up losses and faced a total inability to meet payout obligations. Since there was no external funding support such as from the Treasury, receipts could not offset expenditures in a pay-as-you-go system. The misuse or siphoning out of individual account funds was unavoidable. The result of managing "mixed accounts" for many years was that by the end of 2005, there were more than RMB80 billion worth of empty accounts.

The challenge was to achieve a gradual "realization" or funding of individual accounts, without putting undue burdens on enterprises, employees themselves, and the Treasury. The objective was to have individual accounts gradually begin to perform their necessary functions. The government adopted measures that would allow individual accounts to receive supplemental Treasury funding under a distributed burden system. In terms of the percentage of contributions, enterprise contributions were no longer entered into individual accounts, but were put totally into the socially pooled funds. Employee contributions were set at 8% of the employee's wages, which was all put into the individual account. In 2001, Liaoning served as the first pilot province to put this into effect, with individual accounts starting at a funding rate of 8%. In 2004, the pilot provinces were expanded to include Jilin and Heilongjiang provinces, and the individual account funding percentage was lowered to 5%. In 2005, pilot provinces were further expanded to include eight other provinces, municipalities, and regions, with the funding percentage further lowered to 3%. When provincial finances had difficulty supplying the provincial portion, the Central Treasury shared the cost with the regional government on the basis of 75%/25%.

This third phase in the evolution of China's social security system was a period of the most rapid rise in coverage rates. On the one hand, this was due to the mutual efforts of tax collectors and social security authorities, which caused the participation rate in social security as well as payout rates to increase tremendously. On the other hand, it was due to rapid increases in the income of both regional and central governments. The system saw constant improvement in cities and villages. In provinces, municipalities, and farming villages where conditions permitted, a social security system was gradually established that greatly expanded the coverage of the social security network.

CHALLENGES

China's social security reform has gone from zero to respectable results in the space of 15 years. At the same time, challenges facing the system are increasingly severe. These are due in part to the following factors.

China's society is aging very rapidly. The country instituted a planned parenthood system from the 1970s and promoted the policy of one couple, one child. As a result, the birth rate of the population went through a period of substantial decline, then came into equilibrium at a relatively low level (see Figure 24.1).

The left-hand axis shows "population birthrate." One can see a spike in the rate in 1964, then a basic decline to 1.8 in the mid-1990s and maintenance at that level.

FIGURE 24.1 China's birthrate (1949–2002)

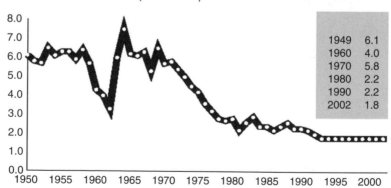

Source: State Population and Planned Parenthood Commission (2004).

FIGURE 24.2　Accelerating increase in elderly population over next 30 years

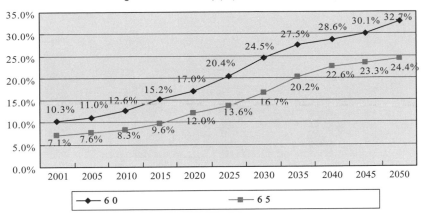

Note: Top line is percentage of the total population over 60. Bottom line is the percentage of the population over 65.

Source: China Population Research Center, 2003.

At the same time, life expectancy rose swiftly, given a general rise in the standard of living and improvements in public health. The percentage of older people in the population rose dramatically as a result. In 2000, the percentage of people who were over 60 and over 65 were, respectively, 10% and 7%. China had already begun to be an "aging society." In 2003, China's Population Research Center predicted that before 2050 China's aging rate and percentage of older people would be as in Figure 24.2.

According to research at the Center, from now until 2035, the percentage of people over 60 and over 65 will grow at 3.53% and 3.73% respectively, much higher than the rates of 2.18% and 2.64% for the period from 2000 to 2005. After 2035, although the increase in the aging rate will ease slightly, the percentage and absolute numbers of older people in the entire population will continue to increase. By 2050, the number of people over 60 and 65 in China will reach 450 million and 336 million, respectively. They will constitute 32.7% and 24.4% of the entire population. By 2050, therefore, one in every three people in China will be over 60 years old, and one in every four will be over 65 years old. The number of people over 65 will total some 336 million, roughly equal to the current population of the 15 countries in Europe.

The rate at which the Chinese population is aging greatly exceeds the global average (see Figure 24.3 on page 422). In 2000, the

FIGURE 24.3 Comparison of people over 60 years old in China and in the world at large as a percentage of total opulations (2000–30).

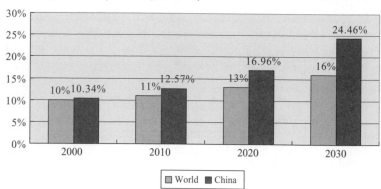

Source: World Bank (2004).

percentage of people over 60 years old in both China and the world at large was about 10%. The two were roughly the same. By 2030, however, this percentage will go to 16% for the world at large, whereas in China it will reach 24.5%. This is indicates the speed at which China's population is aging. It means that from today onward, for a long time, not only will there be many more elderly in need of being cared for, but their percentage will grow relative to young people. The ratio between the elderly and people who are still employed and have to fund the care of the elderly will grow at an ever-faster rate. The oncoming force of the bulge is going to be a huge challenge to a social security system that is only now beginning to take shape.

A second challenge is providing equal coverage. The social security system is de facto segmented for a number of systemic reasons. The first form of segmentation is between those who are and are not covered. Current employment–related pooled-funding pensions for old age merely cover urban employees in cities and towns. Three major groups are not fully or even reasonably covered. One is the entire population of people living in rural areas, who represent the largest segment of people in the country. The second group is people who have come in from the countryside and who currently live and work in cities. The third is workers in state organizations and institutions.

The second form of segmentation shows up in discrepancies in how much is contributed to individual accounts. Only certain regions have undertaken funded pilot programs. Most provinces have not undertaken them at all. Those who are undertaking such pilot projects utilize different percentage rates. Moreover, current policies clearly state that when participating individuals travel across provincial lines in their employment, their individual accounts and the amount accumulated can move together with them. When someone really does cross a regional border, or change to a different enterprise, however, as a practical matter, it is very questionable whether or not his account moves with him or her. Since it is not in fact possible to maintain one's pooled funding in many areas, and since individual accounts cannot in fact be transferred, this results in leaving the "security" of the group.

That the current social security system exhibits excessive "segmentation" and differences in application is undeniable. This not only discourages workers from moving from one region to another, but since the distribution of allocated funds is unfair, it negatively impacts social security reform. To use Chongqing as an example: in Chongqing, the rate at which farmers can get benefits from social security is not even 2%, while in some districts, it is not even 1%.

A third challenge is that rapid increase in revenues of both provincial and the national government will be hard to sustain over an extended period of time. From the past 15 years of reform, we can see that levels of government revenue influence, to a large degree, the direction of social security reform. At the outset, the Decision recommended setting up a combination of pooled funding and individual accounts. Since revenues of the government were limited at the time, and the costs of overall reform were onerous, the treasury's investments in social security were rather slender. This meant that enterprises and individuals shouldered most of the burden. The intent was to set up a partially funded system, but in fact the system continued to be the old "pay-as-you-go." In recent years, government revenues have been growing in excess of 30% per year. The government's investment in social security has greatly increased, the government has provided great support for "realized" or "funded" individual accounts, and it has made the establishment of a partially funded social security system possible. Government support has played a crucial role, whether it has been in municipal or rural areas.

Whether or not such support will be sustainable over a longer period is questionable. If it is not possible to sustain current levels, how will that influence reforms that are currently underway? Most importantly, who will bear the costs of transitioning from a pay-as-you-go to a funded system? Until the transition is complete, there will be a gap in individual accounts when people who are currently working become retired and eligible for payments. Between 1995 and

2000, many institutions both inside and outside China calculated the costs of switching from one system to another, and their differing results derive from different hypothetical situations. Even at the most conservative estimate, however, the cost of changing the system will be in the order of RMB2 trillion. The party ultimately bearing the burden of changing the system will be the government.

These are all factors that must be considered when policymakers formulate policy about future reform of the social security system.

Management of the System

The success of social security system reform depends on factors in two key areas. One is systems design. This includes whether or not the system incorporates forward-thinking considerations, whether it has considered all aspects in the plan, whether or not it can activate positive participation by all administrative levels, and so on. Another key area is the quality of management of the system. Improving management not only can raise efficiency of and lower costs at all the links in the system, including taking in contributions, investing funds, and so on, but even more importantly, it can increase levels of trust in the system by those who are contributing. This enables the system as a whole to function and generate the ultimate benefits, across the social network as well as across ongoing periods.

Under a system of pay-as-you-go, since there is in fact no real accumulation, demands on management levels of the system are not in fact too high. When individual accounts are funded, however, how to manage those funds and best utilize them in an accumulated fund is a very important factor influencing the next step of social security reform.

Over the past 15 years, reform of China's social security system has been able to amass a certain body of positive experience, but the process has also run up against many new questions. Faced with the growing challenges of an aging society, we believe that, from today onward, China's social security reform should focus on four key issues.

Developing the Partially Funded Social Security System

Professionals in the field continue to debate the issue of what kind of social security system is ideal. The four alternatives are: a pay-as-you-go system, a completely funded system, a system that is "layered" and that has individual accounts as the main focus, or a nominal individual account system. Which alternative should be selected depends upon specific circumstances of the country and the overall balance of the situation. Given China's population structure and the rate at which it is aging, and considering the current economic growth of the country, a partially funded system is the correct answer, one that integrates pooled national funds and individual accounts. Many experts are concerned about China having a partially funded social security system. Their concerns focus on two aspects. One is that investment of a partially funded system will harbor a considerable degree of risk. Second is that it will be difficult to realize satisfactory returns on investments of a partially funded system.

Some scholars point out that a mandatory pension system has the chance of becoming a risky experiment in a country with fledgling financial markets such as China, and that this puts the retirement income of a huge pool of people at risk. Any mistakes could lead not only to the loss of the funds, but also to a reversal of financial market reforms. We agree that there is a degree of risk in investing accumulated funds, but we should analyze this investment risk from a more dynamic perspective.

First, we should recognize, objectively, that market risk already exists. At the same time, we should be coldly aware that even without a mandatory funds-accumulation system, in order to satisfy their own future old-age needs, people are already putting a portion of their savings into the capital markets. The objective reality of the need to provide for old age and the current reality of the capital markets is already harboring what scholars feel is the "potential for high risk." Therefore, only if the government first views the existing risk in a proper light can it give guidance through effective norms.

Second, political risk is of even more concern than market risk. In fact, the social security system is facing all kinds of risk. Market-type risk is engendered in the course of investing, but there is also the political question of whether or not the entire system can continue to operate. The latter kind of risk is without doubt the greater. Many countries that practice a system of pay-as-you-go find themselves modifying their social security systems in mid-stream, because they cannot afford the heavy cost of pensions. They raise the percentage of required contributions, lower the level of resulting social security benefits, or extend the age at which people can retire and begin to earn benefits, all of which are a shock to those currently paying into the system and anticipating benefits. This ultimately contributes to political imbalance and social unrest. Having a partially funded system makes government and individuals each bear a portion of the responsibility as well as the risk, and thereby reduces the political risk of the social security system.

As for different levels of investment income, it is best to compare investment income that has been adjusted for risk. Whether in terms of theory or of actual historical experience, it is clear that higher risk investment vehicles have the possibility of higher returns than low-risk vehicles, but low-risk vehicles by definition involve less risk. Through long-term investment models, it is possible to iron out income fluctuations by using profits in good times to make up for losses in bad times, and using higher and lower income instruments to achieve a balance.

Broadening the Coverage of Social Security System

One of government's most important responsibilities is providing fair social security benefits to the public. In a country that is in the process of changing its economic structure and that is in fast-growth mode, the significance of setting up a fair and broadly based social security system is even greater. China is in the process of economic transformation. Certain overall economic reforms necessarily have a greater impact on certain segments of the population, and therefore influence their income or the benefits they receive in an unequal way. A broadly based social security system can cushion the impact of other economic reforms on people, and can play a role in ensuring the security of the system as a whole. While China's economy undertakes structural transformation, it is also, currently, experiencing a period of high economic growth. Such fast economic growth often widens the gap between different levels of society. A broadly based coverage of social security can, to a degree, ameliorate their differences in income.

A broadly based social security system with adequate coverage will mainly be able to carry out reforms for the following three key groups of people. First, it will bring the huge population in rural areas into the system. Considering that farmers also have the land as a certain security net when they are older, social security coverage for villages should attempt to be as wide as possible, but at a fairly low level. It should aim to break through regionalism, and should attempt to advance in an orderly, sequential manner. Second, it will bring in those people who previously were farmers, but are now living off wages. Understanding that mobility is very high in regions with "peasant workers," and that the seasonal nature of their work is very high, we need to set up flexible systems of contributions and payouts that can be trans-regional, trans-industry, and trans-time based. We must actively encourage peasant workers to participate in the system.

Third is to bring in people working in government and institutions. The number of people working in the government and in state institutions is considerable, and it is urgent that we incorporate them in a social security system. Funding for the social security of this group currently comes out of the pocket of the Ministry of Finance. A number of inherent problems exist in this situation. Not only have current receipts not formed an effective accumulation, but the level of obstacles to getting benefits after retiring are also substantial, to the degree that this kind of system is unsustainable. As the government budget is made more transparent and with the formation of accountability mechanisms, and the increasingly large gap between incomes of retired people from enterprises and institutions, this has already attracted considerable social concern. Calls for reforming the social security system between the government and institutions are increasing. After reforms in housing and healthcare for people who work in institutions are completed, reforms in social security should be promoted at the earliest possible time, and the financial mechanisms related to shouldering the burden should be confirmed and at the earliest possible time.

Resolving the Transition Cost of the Social Security System

Relative to the system of paying out with current income, or "pay-as-you-go," it is easy to see that a system of accumulated funds is more sustainable. The key factor is not in the benefits of the funded system, but in how to resolve the very practical problem of who is going to pay the costs of transition.

We feel that we must handle the subject with a cautiously optimistic attitude. The government should be cautious about the size of these costs and its own responsibilities, but it must not adopt an attitude of avoiding the issue. Coming to grips with the costs of transition is a responsibility that any government accepts in transitioning its social security system. Estimates of costs vary, depending on the organization making the estimate. We should use population aging models and estimate the costs very carefully, incorporating such factors as future social security needs. We must not allow expectations to be set too high with regard to future benefits.

While costs of changing the system are going to be high, at the same time, we should recognize that, right now, China is in an ideal situation to handle them. For the next few years, government revenues are going to maintain high growth rates, on top of the current firm foundation. In addition, the Chinese government has tremendous state-owned assets in its hands. These include working state-owned assets and their profits, as well as state-owned public resources such as wireless frequencies, 3G licenses, natural resource taxes, land transfer taxes, and so on. If we do not grab the opportunity, and at the earliest time, pay into a funded social security system, then these resources will naturally be frittered away on current expenditures.

Improving the Management of the Social Security System

The Decision of 1993 set up the basic system of social security, and the experimental "individual accounts" led on to the partially funded system. The framework for China's social security system has been achieved. Improving on it incrementally will be the task for the next period, but in addition, the emphasis should shift to the more concrete matters of improving management. In principle, the management practices of social security should have the effect of mobilizing the active participation of all concerned in order to accomplish a secure and highly effective system.

To do this, the government should further separate the responsibilities and functions of organizations involved in social security management, and at the appropriate stage, separate the functions of overall supervision from professional management. For example, at the end of 2000, we set up a State Social Security Fund Council. After operating for seven years, this has become a pension fund manager with considerable professional experience. Even though it has taken on the mission of social security, in terms of operations, it is an institution that manages funds.

With regard to administrative institutions, more publicly accountable organizations should be brought in, to make policies more transparent and to assure that social security, which is of tremendous concern to everyone, is given the greatest degree of public scrutiny. As for professional management, we should draw in marketized institutions to guarantee the safe functioning of the funds, and utilize all kinds of marketized instruments to improve the efficient use of capital. Through raising current yields, we will be able to lessen our burden in the future.

We should set up a unified, transparent system for managing social security, one that is better able to encourage people to join in and make social security contributions. At present, there is still some debate as to whether or not to go a step further in raising the level of general funding. We feel that ascertaining the level of funding should be linked to confirming responsibilities at all levels of government with regard to social security. Put simply, the funding responsibility should be assigned to whichever government level is the ultimate holder of responsibility for the social security. Social security is a mechanism that requires long-term sustained management, so it is suited to management methods that match responsibilities with rights or powers.

No matter at what level social security is funded, when participants move to other regions, the management of social security funds should not be allowed to serve as an obstacle to the free flow of labor. Moreover, the investment of funds should not adopt prejudiced management or investment that is essentially "taken" or "owned" by the local place of origination, but should follow general investment principles, in achieving balanced allocations with manageable risk

China is facing the need to resolve the social security of 1.3 billion people, which is a monumental task. In order to meet the burden of covering a rapidly aging population, we must firmly adhere to the principles enunciated in 1993 of "an integrated system of pooled national funds and individual accounts," and resist any segmentation of the system or narrow coverage. We must gradually fund individual accounts and continue to improve quality of management in order to establish a safe, efficient, unified, transparent, and sustainable social security system.

SECTION 5

MONETARY POLICY

CHAPTER 25

China's Monetary Policy: Facing the Challenges of Financial Globalization

Wu Xiaoling
Former Deputy Governor, People's Bank of China

On February 23, 2005, the Managing Director of the International Monetary Fund (IMF), Rodrigo de Rato, used the term "global imbalances" in remarks entitled "Correcting Global Economic Imbalances—Avoiding the Blame Game." He urged everyone to take responsibility for implementing an orderly adjustment to economic imbalances. What can China do to participate in this effort? Both theory and practice tell us that managing our own affairs wisely, adhering to principles of equality and mutual benefit in trade and to sound principles of international economic relations will be beneficial to world stability and stable growth. This chapter will address some of the challenges that China is facing in implementing monetary policy, given the backdrop of globalizing economics and finance.

SELECTING MONETARY POLICY TOOLS

Since the start of Reform and Opening, China's monetary policy has gradually formed a systemic framework that incorporates long-term and intermediate goals, and both operational measures and guidance mechanisms. In theory, the most important thing a Central Bank considers in deciding what policy measures to adopt is whether or not there is an inflationary or deflationary trend in the economy. Since 2002, the challenge facing the People's Bank of China (PBC),

FIGURE 25.1   Foreign exchange holdings and base money supply increase, 2000 to 2007 in six-month intervals

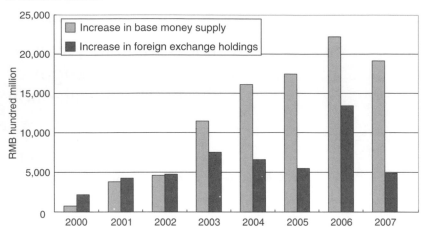

Source: China financial statistics yearbook.

however, has been to maintain exchange rate stability under inflationary circumstances that are not so evident, and to decide what hedging operations to adopt to achieve that stability (see Figure 25.1). The choice of tools and the timing and degree of response have become important issues, therefore, in the implementation of China's monetary policy in recent years.

Central Bank Bills as a Tool of Open Market Operations

An array of monetary policy tools such as the rediscount rate, provisional funds rate, open market operations and window guidance are commonly recognized by central banks. Open market operations are widely used in market economy countries in particular, because of their transparent nature. The PBC began to carry out open market operations in 1996. These were used many times between 1998 and 1999, but were basically stopped from 2000 to 2002, due to the putting in circulation of large amounts of foreign exchange holdings and the reduction in government bonds held by the PBC. In April 2003, because of a need to reduce liquidity in commercial banks, the PBC began to issue Central Bank bills (also called Central Bank notes, with maturities ranging from three months to three years.) By September 2007, the total amount issued came to RMB3.9 trillion.

Issuing Central Bank bills was not something the PBC invented. In its economic adjustments of 1997, the Bank borrowed on the experience of the Central Bank of Korea, which had in the past issued Central Bank financing securities. In 2003, the PBC issued notes as a hedge against the excessive growth in foreign exchange holdings as an action determined by the unique foreign exchange reserves system of China.

A country's foreign exchange reserves can be held by the Ministry of Finance or can be held by the Central Bank. When the Ministry of Finance holds foreign exchange reserves, it can use surplus funds in the treasury to acquire foreign exchange, which then become reserves. At this point, the increase in foreign exchange reserves can only influence banks and monetary policy operations by increasing or decreasing financial deposits in the Central Bank.

If there is no surplus of funds in the treasury with which to purchase foreign exchange, then the entity responsible in the country, whether that be the Finance Ministry or the Treasury, must issue government bonds for the purchase. This influences the structure of funds in society, and consequently also bank credit and monetary policies. In general, at such time as the Ministry of Finance decides to issue bonds in order to purchase foreign exchange, specific actions or operations are undertaken by the Central Bank. The Central Bank can adjust liquidity in the commercial banking system (excess reserves or money supply), by going through public finance agencies to issue or to purchase bonds on the open market. By going through open market operations, it can also influence money market rates.

When foreign exchange reserves are held by the Central Bank, then the increase in foreign exchange reserves must see an equivalent paying out of "base money." When the money supply being let into the system exceeds the normal rate of money supply that is needed by the economy, the Central Bank must undertake hedging operations to take in excess liquidity. If there are no priced securities on the balance sheet of the Central Bank that can be sold, then it simply has to write a note to a lender, or raise the provisional funds rate, or issue its own debt instruments, that is to say, Central Bank bills. Since the Finance Ministry's public funds are mainly kept in the Central Bank, whether it is issuing government bonds or issuing Central Bank bills, the amount of money in public circulation will decrease. Both actions will serve the purpose of decreasing commercial bank's liquidity, and so will have an influence on money market rates.

From the above analysis, we can see that when foreign exchange reserves increase, the result in macroeconomic terms is the same whether government bonds or Central Bank bills are issued. Which method to choose depends on the foreign exchange reserves system.

In guiding money market rates, the PBC can choose two different methods to issue Central Bank bills. One is called a "price tender" and the other a "quantitative tender." Under most circumstances, the issue of Central Bank bills will be by price tender method, but when market rates stray from the goal of the PBC's targeted adjustments, the PBC will choose the quantitative tender type in order to guide market rates. From November of 2003 until August of 2006, the PBC employed quantitative tenders to guide money market rates downwards.

Central Bank bills are generally issued with maturities of three months, six months, one year, and three years. When the Ministry of Finance issues government bonds, it first confers with the PBC in order not to conflict in terms of maturity dates. The aim is to have mutually supportive maturies [and pricing] in order to form a risk-free yield curve.

The "Provisional Reserve Funds Rate"

The statutory provisional reserve funds rate is one of the Central Bank's traditional policy tools. In 1984, when the PBC was operating solely as the Central Bank, it set the rate depending on the type of deposits. The rate for deposits made by enterprises was 20%, for agricultural communities it was 25%, for savings it was 40%. In 1985, all of these were unified into the single rate of 10%. From 1987 to 1988, China experienced severe inflation, and in 1987 and 1988, the PBC adjusted the rate to 12% and then 13% respectively, and it asked all banks to maintain no less than 5% in provisional reserve funds. In order to standardize the management of provisional reserves, the PBC did away with different rates and allowed commercial banks to use the statutory provisional reserve funds rate in their accounting. It also decreased the rate from 13% to 8%, and in 1999, further lowered the rate to 6% in order to halt deflation and encourage commercial banks to make loans.

On August 23, 2003, the PBC announced that on September 21, it would be adjusting the rate one percentage point upward from 6% to 7%, in an attempt to rein in an overly fast increase in commercial bank credit. The rate for agricultural credit associations was maintained at 6%, however, in order to support reform in agriculture and in agricultural credit systems.

From April 2004 until October 2007, the PBC adjusted the rate another 12 times, each time by one half of a percentage point until the rate was 13%. At the same time, starting in April 2004, it implemented a differential rate for those institutions whose capital adequacy ratios were less than 8%, whose asset quality was not high, or whose credit was growing too fast. It applied a rate that was higher than the ordinary increase of half a percentage point.

There are differing views on the frequent use of this rate as a policy tool by the PBC. Some question the purpose of utilizing the tool, others the severity or strength of it, and still others wonder whether there is much room left for the tool to be effective.

We believe that while the central bank operates base money supply passively, it can deploy the deposit reserves requirement as a tool to control excessive deposits and restrict rapid expansion of credit and loans of commercial banks. This has only a supplementary effect on the base money supply, and its effect on society is neutral and moderate. Every year, the PBC provides its money supply plan to "society," [the country] depending on the growth in the economy and adjustments needed in prices of goods. So long as the money supply growth is not lower than the expected range, then the operations of the PBC can be neutral. Whether it uses the provisional funds tool to absorb excess money supply in commercial banks, or utilizes open market operations to retrieve money supply in commercial banks, both may be regarded as "neutral" measures. The PBC is simply aiming to guide money market rates. When the PBC utilizes open market operations to pull liquidity out of commercial banks, it is put in a passive position. Whether banks subscribe to Central Bank bills or not, and at what rates, depends on their loan intentions and on the interest rate spread in their loan portfolio. It is always possible that these considerations will force the rate of the Central Bank bills upwards. When the PBC utilizes the tool of the "provisional funds rate" to soak up liquidity, the Central Bank is in an active position or acting on its own initiative, and is able to maintain the interest rate level. These operations by the Bank do not have profit as their goal, so costs are not a consideration. The underlying rationale is to adjust the level of money market rates.

China's provisional reserve funds are interest bearing, and a 1.89% interest rate covers the cost of holding deposits in commercial banks.

In terms of financing, using the provisional funds tool to hedge is also a moderate policy with regard to commercial banks. Seen in this light, China still has room to maneuver in using the provisional funds tool.

Utilizing Interest Rate Tools

The PBC has consistently promoted the marketizing of interest rates, that is, making interest rates market-driven, in its goal of transitioning to indirect macroeconomic financial measures. The overall line of thinking in marketizing China's interest rates follows a sequence: marketize the money markets and bond rates before the rates of loan portfolios, marketize foreign currency rates before the rates of China's own currency; marketize large-sum deposit rates before small amount rates. Four main tasks remain to be completed in the marketization of China's interest rates. First, the PBC is just in the process of making the Shanghai inter-bank offered rate (SHIBOR) into the base rate for money markets. Second, the money markets still do not have a smooth and complete risk-free yield curve. Third, the PBC is still setting the benchmark rates for different maturities of loans. Fourth, among the depository and loan rates of financial institutions at the PBC, the rediscount rate and the discount rate of financial organizations to customers have not yet formed a mechanism that is mutually beneficial. Since the PBC still controls the ceiling or upper limit of commercial bank's deposit rates and the floor or lower limit of loan rates, it is hard for money market rates to guide the rates passed along to customers. The intent of the PBC in guiding money market rates through open market operations is not effectively transmitted to society at large; that is, to credit channels. At present, therefore, this is a "weak muscle" in the monetary policy measures of the Bank. Improving this situation is the next step in the main direction of marketizing money market rates.

When the Federal Reserve of the United States implements monetary policy, it mainly sets a target rate for federal funds and goes through open market operations to guide money markets in achieving that rate. The federal funds rate indirectly influences financial market rates by going through changes in the yield curve on Treasuries, and thereby guides market expectations. In China, since money market rates and the rates for customers of banks are separate from each other, when the PBC wants to affect interest rates, it needs to consider the application of tools in two different layers of the system. One is

FIGURE 25.2 Comparison of savings deposit rates in China and the US, 1996–2005

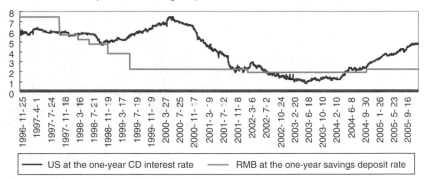

in guiding money market rates; the other relates to the interest rate levels of banks with respect to their customers.

Since 2003, China's economy has had a tendency to overheat. To restrain it from excessive overheating, the PBC has guided money market rates upwards, while at the same time raising deposit and loan rates of banks. It has attempted to restrain demand in guiding expectations. However, from July 2002 until November 2004, the one-year CD rate in the US was below the one-year deposit rate in China (see Figure 25.2), which has limited the ability of the PBC to employ interest rate tools. When the general expectation is of an appreciation of the value of the RMB, there is a tremendous attraction for international capital to flow into the RMB. Precisely because of worries about international flow of funds, the PBC is extremely careful when it uses interest rate tools. During 2003–06, the Bank only adjusted bank loan rates three times, and deposit rates twice, and moreover each time the adjustment was a mere 0.27 of one percentage point, far lower than the interest rate adjustments made between 1988 and 1989, and in 1993.

China's asset prices have been rising swiftly since 2007. The PBC has recognized that the temptation for international capital to flow into the country has not just been due to the disparity in interest rates between China and the US, but also due to the tremendous benefit of China's reappraised assets. Therefore, it has raised its willingness to tolerate a lesser disparity between Chinese and US rates. At the same time, since 2007, inflationary trends in China have become more and more pronounced. Under these circumstances, the PBC has adjusted deposit and loan rates upwards five times, raising the benchmark deposit and loan rate from 6.12% to 7.29%.

EXCHANGE RATE ADJUSTMENTS

On June 15, 2007, the Executive Board of the IMF adopted a "Decision on Bilateral Surveillance Over Members' Policies." The core provision of this was that the IMF does not need to prove that a country has acted intentionally in "manipulating" exchange rates, but only needs to show that the country's policies have "resulted in" the creation of "fundamental exchange rate misalignment." It need not show intention, but only the results of "a long-term, large-scale surplus or deficit in current accounts." If that is the case, the IMF can determine that the country is "manipulating" its exchange rate and can act accordingly. From 2005, the US Congress has repeatedly put forward resolutions with regard to the RMB exchange rate, asking that it be appreciated in order to ameliorate the negative trade balance of the United States with China.

We feel that the negative trade balance between China and the US does partly relate to exchange rates, but more fundamentally to the economic structures of each country. As with all countries in the world, trade gaps are determined by the economic conditions in each country. A flexible exchange rate can help reduce, but cannot fundamentally resolve the problems. The Japanese yen and the German mark appreciated greatly against the US dollar in the 1980s and 1960s respectively, but the trade gap between the US and those two countries did not diminish (see Figures 25.3 and 25.4).

FIGURE 25.3 Comparison of 7-day Inter-bank rate of RMB and 7-day LIBOR rate of USD

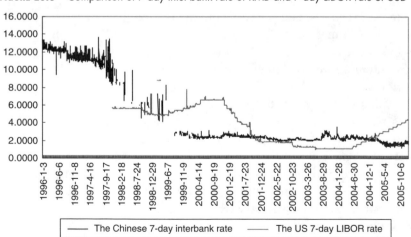

Sources: China financial statistics yearbook and IFS.

FIGURE 25.4 Exchange rate of the German mark against the US dollar (line) and Germany's balance of trade (columns), 1971–2006

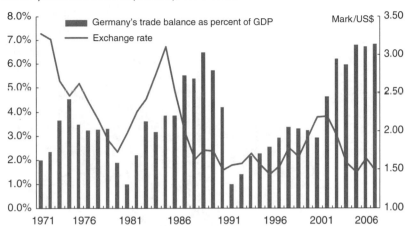

Sources: CEIC and Datastream.

Factors forcing the US into a trade deficit include the large-scale shift of US manufacturing overseas, the low US savings rate, and the fact that the US dollar is the global currency for accounting purposes. The absolute amount of the deficit and the annual increase in the percentage of the US GDP that it occupies is indeed cause for concern (see Figure 25.5). In addition to being a difference in calibration or measures of accounting for the US trade deficit with China, the deficit is also the result of previous US deficits with other Asian countries that are now shifting in the direction of a greater deficit with China (see Figures 25.6 and 25.7 on pages 442 and 443).

China's high savings rate, low consumption rate, and unsustainably high rate of investing have determined the fact that China's economy relies on exports. The fast pace of economic growth in China has attracted investment from many countries. China's foreign trade policies since Reform and Opening, specifically the Chinese practice of "rewarding exporting and restraining from importing," have resulted in the piling up foreign exchange. China's policies of "import substitution," and "filling up the gaps" in manufacturing, and its policies with regard to foreign exchange that mandate "being relaxed [about forex] coming in, but strict about its going out," have had a braking effect on outflow of foreign exchange. These policies have allowed China to maintain consistent increases in a favorable balance of trade. Adjusting interest rates alone without a fundamental reversal of these

FIGURE 25.5   Exchange rate of the Japanese yen against the US dollar (line), and Japan's balance of trade as a percent of GDP (columns), 1977–2005.

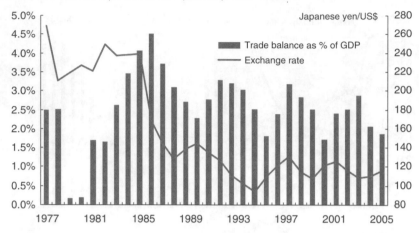

Sources: CEIC and Datastream.

FIGURE 25.6   China's deficits in trade accounts and current accounts against east-Asian countries (right-hand columns) and surplus in trade and current accounts against the US (right-hand columns), 1990–2006.

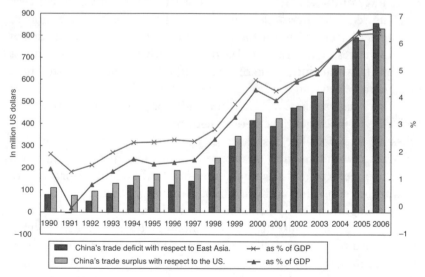

FIGURE 25.7   Comparison of US trade imbalances with other countries (as per US statistical measures) 1998 and 2005

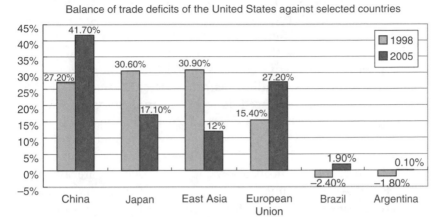

Balance of trade deficits of the United States against selected countries

Note: US balance of trade deficits in 1998 and 2005 against selected countries

Sources: CEIC and IFC.

economic policies and without adjusting China's economic structure would only do harm to China as an economic entity.

China has already become an important propelling force in world economic growth—hurting China's economy will impact world economic development. It is precisely because of this fact that China's government is undertaking RMB exchange rate reforms that are based on principles of voluntary action, gradual advance, and controllable actions. This is not a matter of "manipulating exchange rates," but is rather the responsible attitude of a major country that is conscientious about the effect of its policies.

The hedging operations undertaken by the PBC with regard to the ongoing increase in foreign currency reserves are done in order to gain time for economic structure adjustments. The hedging is limited, but we must maintain a sense of urgency. Since 2007, this sense of urgency about structural adjustment of China's economy has grown stronger, and has created favorable conditions for strengthening the voluntary nature of China's monetary policies. The stable and consistent policy determination of the Chinese government is to accelerate economic structural adjustments while supplementing them with an increase in the flexibility of exchange rates.

GLOBAL INFLUENCE OF POLICIES

Over the past 30 years of Reform and Opening, China's economy has gradually been transformed from a planned to a market economy system. China's use of macroeconomic measures has been maturing in concert with this transformation. From relying primarily on planning and administrative controls in the 1980s, the role of "economic" [or market-based] adjustments has increased since the 1990s. In 1993–94, China experienced its worst inflation since Reform and Opening. The CPI reached 14.7% and 24.1% in those two years, factory prices of industrial products rose by 24% and 25.1%, and M_2 increased by 31.3% and 37.3% (M_2 is one measure of money supply in an economy and is a key indicator used to forecast inflation). Faced with the runaway situation, the Chinese government adopted measures to deepen reform and carried out a series of economic adjustments. It implemented comprehensive reforms in pricing, taxes, and public finance, and in the financial and foreign exchange systems under former Premier Zhu Rongji's leadership. These set the foundation for a public finance system that now separately administers local and national taxes. Standardizing the relationship between the central government and regional or local governments enabled the strengthening of a financial system that allowed macroeconomic oversight by the Central Bank and that put market restraints on commercial banks. A pricing system was gradually instituted that is based on market supply and demand as opposed to the two-track system of fixed prices for some commodities and some customers and market prices for others. China reformed its system of managing foreign exchange, first implementing a mandatory controlled foreign exchange system, next a two-track official- and market-pricing system, and then a managed float that uses supply and demand as the basis. The passing these reforms enabled a reorganization of the market structure, strengthened market regulation, restrained excessive growth in investment and consumption, and allowed China's economy to achieve a "soft landing" in 1997. From a rate of 14.1% in 1992, GDP growth fell to 8.8% in 1997; from a CPI of 24.1% in 1994, it fell to 2.8% in 1997. This reform and the macroeconomic measures allowed China to withstand the Asian currency crisis of 1997. Since the reforms of 1993, both monetary policy and policy implementation of the PBC have been "marketized," and fluctuations in China's economy have been far less than they were in the 1980s (see Table 25.1).

TABLE 25.1 Macroeconomic indicators since 1980 including rate of increase of GDP, CPI, loans, and M$_2$, with actual and variance from the "standard" for the three periods.

	GDP rate of increase (%)	CPI rate of increase (%)	Loans rate of increase (%)	M$_2$ rate of increase (%)
Actual	9.75	7.45	21.43	24.54
Variance from standard	3.47	6.32	7.87	6.83
Actual	9.99	1.77	22.06	26.15
Variance from standard	3.24	8.35	6.65	7.74
Actual	9.54	1.24	14.94	16.48
Variance from standard	0.94	1.45	3.04	2.36

Macroeconomic indicators in China since 1980, including rate of increase of GDP, CPI, loans, and M$_2$, with actual and variance from the "standard" for the three periods.

Moving into 2007, China's economy faced relatively strong inflationary pressure, which was the result of years of accumulating "contradictions" or unresolved problems. One problem has been that since 2003, China's economy has maintained a high growth rate, and the demand has sparked:

- increases in the prices of energy and raw materials. Pressures that built up over the years began to be felt in end-user products.
- an increase in the income gap between people in the countryside and people in the cities. Farmer's wages had not moved for years while, with the upgrading of manufacturing, higher quality labor meant higher labor wages.
- an escalation in the costs of production and prices of by-products, which further increased the costs of some industrial goods.
- an increasing degree of internationalization of the Chinese economy, which meant that prices of international energy, raw materials, and agricultural products put latent pressure on the prices of Chinese products.
- broad growth of the Chinese economy, which to a large extent was based on the artificially controlled overly low pricing of energy and resources. It stood to reason that resource-based pricing should bring along the pressures of price inflation.
- a reappraisal of China's assets. Pricing of assets in RMB meant that the pricing was kept relatively low. But against the backdrop of a globalizing economy, the financial response to asset reappraisal was to increase domestic demand, and with an increase in prices came inflationary pressures.

As it was hard to get consensus on macroeconomic measures in policy circles, monetary policy measures were not put into action in a timely manner.

At the same time, there was a need for general reconsideration of bank reform and the workings of the capital markets, and this was a lot to consider. The results of the measures undertaken by the PBC with regard to currency supply were not ideal. Money supply exceeded the targeted goal, and this too increased the likelihood of price inflation.

From the above analysis, one can see that China's current inflationary pressures are being propelled by cost pressures. Keeping inflation within an acceptable range is one of the most important duties of the Chinese government. Monetary policy in the future has to be ready to help meet this goal.

Although the relative importance of China's economy has risen and its influence is increasing, China's massive population still means that per capita GDP ranks sixty-ninth in the world. At a poverty level of US$1 per day per person, China still has 135 million people living under the poverty line. China's economic policies must therefore first resolve the problem of bringing people to a moderate standard of living. Increasing domestic demand and raising the standard of living is the country's primary duty. The Chinese government cannot, therefore, seek to go further in increasing its foreign exchange reserves. The true level of the RMB exchange rate is the level of supply and demand after a domestic market has fully developed. A relatively stable and yet flexible RMB exchange rate mechanism is beneficial to adjusting China's economic structure, and it is also conducive to economic harmony with the rest of the world.

Since the RMB is still not a fully convertible currency, China's monetary policies lack highly effective mechanisms for influencing world financial imbalances. Since 2003, China's exchange rate policies have been the target of international attention. China's monetary policies have achieved a certain response in international financial markets when they are announced, but the influence mostly stops at the level of expectations about China's economy. Whether they go further in actually influencing international financial flows or not requires further research.

China's monetary policies will necessarily have greater global influence as China's economic and financial systems merge with those of the rest of the world. The influence of international factors on Chinese monetary policies will also increase. This linkage necessarily raises a tough challenge for the formulation and implementation of monetary policy by the PBC. Raising the professionalism of people in the Monetary Policy Commission, and improving the quality of employees in the Bank in general are urgent and important tasks. As appropriate, it is also urgently important to enhance the Commission's role in the monetary policy system.

CHAPTER 26

Convertibility of RMB-denominated Capital Accounts: Process and Experience

Hu Xiaolian

Deputy Governor, People's Bank of China; Administrator, the State Administration of Foreign Exchange

Accomplishing convertibility of the RMB is key to China's ongoing Reform and Opening policies and to the reforms of its financial system. The policy direction was made clear back in December 1993, when authorities stated, "The long-term goal of China's foreign exchange reforms is to realize convertibility of the RMB. In order to reach this goal, we must move gradually and in the proper sequence of events, and we must proceed in accordance with the country's conditions and abilities. At the current stage, we must first accomplish convertibility of RMB-denominated current account transactions." In December 1996, China successfully realized this initial goal. In 2003, China went a step further in loosening restrictions on cross-border capital transactions, in discrete stages and under conditions of effective risk management. In 2007, China yet again reaffirmed the goal of "improving the formation of an RMB exchange rate system by gradually accomplishing convertibility of capital accounts."

China has carried out reforms in its foreign-exchange system in three distinct stages since the start of Reform and Opening. The process has been one of gradual and prudent "opening" or "releasing" of capital accounts.

The first stage was from 1978 to 1993. The main goal at the time was to attract long-term stable direct investment, and at the same time, take advantage of favorable rate loans from foreign governments and international financial institutions. Investment in securities was severely restricted. In 1978, the first foreign-invested enterprise was established; in 1979, the first Representative Office of a foreign bank was set up; in 1982, yen-denominated bonds in a Chinese enterprise were issued overseas for the first time; in 1991, the first RMB-denominated special class of stock—B-shares—were issued; in 1993, a Chinese enterprise issued H-shares abroad for the first time.

The second stage was from 1994 to the early twenty-first century. During this period, China unified the two-track exchange rate system and began to implement a managed float that was unified and based on market supply and demand. China also established a nationally based unified inter-bank foreign-exchange market and, at the end of 1996, accomplished convertibility of RMB-denominated current accounts. Scarcity of foreign exchange was still a restraining factor in China's economic development at the time. Because of this, China made active use of foreign investment as the main element in opening capital accounts. Government policies made it easy for foreign capital to invest in China, borrowing offshore debt, and allowing profits to be exchanged and taken out of the country. At the same time, large- and medium-sized state-owned enterprises (SOEs) that were of sufficient quality were selected for listing on international capital markets. To an appropriate degree, China raised funds abroad and utilized foreign loans.

In order to guard against financial risk and foreign-debt risk, the country regulated the size and structure of foreign debts, while strengthening and improving its statistical monitoring of foreign debt. It is worth pointing out that during the Asian Financial Crisis of 1997, an abrupt disaster that challenged all neighboring countries, the Chinese government announced that it would not devalue the RMB. China's emphasis was on strengthening controls over capital outflows, on avoiding a spread of the crisis, and on supporting the stability of China's and other country's economies and financial systems.

The third stage lasted from the start of the twenty-first century up to now. During this time, China entered the World Trade Organization (WTO), and continued to implement structural reforms of the economy. The country's market economy system was further improved as Reform and Opening entered a new stage, and China's foreign-exchange structure gradually began to achieve fundamental change. The extreme lack of foreign exchange now transitioned to an overly fast increase in foreign exchange reserves and to an overly favorable balance of trade. Policies to do with capital accounts began to encourage ways to allow currency to flow outwards, and thereby contribute to a new two-way "Opening." China began to focus on implementing a "Go out" strategy that encouraged and supported those Chinese enterprises with requisite conditions to set up branch organizations abroad and to invest there. Certain domestic organizations were encouraged to grow their investments in overseas securities, in orderly fashion. At the same time, China promoted the "Opening to the Outside" of its own financial system and capital markets. In measured steps, it enlarged the scope of where and what kinds of financial services business could be done, and aimed to bring in investment in securities, overseas strategic investors, and so on. All of this contributed to a healthy development of China's financial markets.

In recent years, we have made clear progress in promoting the convertibility of capital accounts in the following ways. First, we have given strong foreign-exchange policy support to enterprises that are "Going out"; that is, taking their operations abroad. From 2002, certain provinces and cities in China served as pilots for reform in overseas-investment foreign-exchange controls. In these areas, enterprises could purchase foreign exchange for investment overseas, within a certain limit, and in accord with certain conditions. We eliminated the requirement for investigation and survey of foreign-exchange overseas investment risk, and for guaranteeing a certain return on the exchange. We simplified relevant auditing procedures. In May 2005, we expanded the number of pilots to cover the entire country, and expanded the amount of foreign exchange that could be purchased for overseas investment. We lowered the restrictions on authorization of the foreign exchange source. In 2006, we eliminated the restrictions on the amount of currency that could be purchased for overseas investment, and made it more convenient for banks to provide funding for overseas investing. In five years, overseas direct investment has led to an exchanged amount of US$21.6 billion. Of this, US$10.8 billion was exchanged in 2007, a 32% increase over the previous year.

Second, we have expanded the channels through which investments can be made overseas. In April 2006, China implemented a Qualified Domestic Institutional Investor (QDII) system. Domestic commercial banks, insurance organizations, and institutions managing overseas securities investments and money management for customers were mobilized to participate. In 2007, China took a further step in permitting commercial banks to invest in overseas stocks, stock funds, and other such products. Qualified trust companies were allowed to operate fiduciary overseas money management businesses. We loosened restrictions on insurance companies investing overseas. We permitted qualified fund management companies and other institutions to consolidate funds from institutions and individuals within China and invested them in stocks outside. By the end of March 2008, 53 domestic commercial banks, fund management companies, and insurance companies had met the requirements and received authorization, and the total capital outflow was US$40.09 billion. The QDII system has enriched the investment choices of China's citizens, and expanded the ability of domestic financial institutions to invest overseas.

Third, we have expanded the opening of China's domestic securities markets in a stable manner. In November 2002, we adopted a Qualified Foreign Institutional Investor (QFII) system for those overseas institutions that met the requirements. We lowered the barriers to entry in the QFII program, and we shortened the lock-up period in which investors had to keep their funds in China. At the end of 2007, the total QFII quota was raised from US$10 billion to US$30 billion. By the end of April 2008, 52 foreign institutional investors had invested US$10.395 billion, and the total capital inflow was US$10.03 billion. The QFII system has played a very positive function in China, in terms of importing advanced investment concepts and spurring the healthy development of domestic capital markets. In October 2005, we gave permission for the Asian Development Bank and the International Finance Corporation to issue RMB-denominated bonds within China, which was the beginning of the orderly opening of the bond market within China.

With the expansion of China's Reform and Opening to the outside, and the RMB convertibility related to items under capital accounts, the following changes have been brought about in capital accounts.

The size and influence of capital and financial transactions has constantly increased. At present, business activity is still the main factor influencing China's international balance of trade, and the favorable balance of trade is mainly the result of current account transactions, but capital and financial transactions are increasing very fast. From 2002 to 2007, the capital and finance items of China's international balance of trade increased at an average annual rate of 51.9%. Current account transactions over the same period increased at a rate of 24%. In 2007, the sum of capital and financial item transactions reached US$1.77 trillion, eight times the amount in 2002, which was

US$220 billion. Capital and financial items constituted 40.8% of the international balance of trade, an increase of 17.5% since 2002.

Capital inflows are mainly in direct investments, but the percentage in stock and debt financing has been increasing. In the early period of Reform and Opening, capital inflows into China were mainly in the form of direct investments by foreign companies. With the deepening of financial reforms, and the expansion in capital accounts, stocks, bonds, and so on, the capital inflows have increased in these non-direct investment types. According to International Investment Position statistics, the percentage of China's foreign debt attributable to direct investment in China has stayed at around 56%, while investment in stocks and bonds has increased from 8.9% in 2004 to 12.5% in 2006.

The channels for capital outflow are constantly being improved, which is beginning to create a more rational two-way flow. In the past, under conditions of foreign-exchange scarcity, China adopted various restrictive measures to prevent the outflow of capital, and was for a long time a country with net capital inflows. In recent years, with sustained economic development, foreign exchange reserves have continued to accumulate, and conditions for investing overseas have improved, so both citizen and government investment overseas has continued to expand. Starting in 2003, China turned a net foreign liability into a net foreign asset. By the end of 2006, the net foreign asset totaled US$662.1 billion, an increase of 57% over the previous year. Clearly, China is developing ever-closer ties with the world's economy and with international financial markets.

CONVERTIBILITY OF RMB-DENOMINATED CAPITAL ACCOUNTS

It is generally believed that the free flow of capital is beneficial to such things as productivity, savings, and technology. It enables an efficient allocation of resources around the globe, speeds up the transfer of technology and professional management skills, and helps disperse investment risk in global markets. This brings with it economic growth and the development of financial markets. The strategic goal of developing countries is generally, therefore, to achieve capital account convertibility of their currencies.

However, developing countries generally have financial systems that are inadequately developed—their ability to withstand risk is poor, their exchange rates are insufficiently flexible, and so on. There tends to be a large gap between the economic development level and status of financial systems of developed and developing countries. If the orderly opening in developing countries is infelicitous, if sets of reforms are not aligned with measures to guard against risk, it is very easy for underlying structural deficiencies of the country's financial system to come to the fore. This can increase the risk of banking and currency crises, and can lead to swift economic decline and loss of social welfare. IMF research shows that, after opening up capital accounts, more than two-thirds of the International Monetary Fund's members exhibited problems of one kind or another, some of them on the level of crises. A country must be conscientious in how it opens up capital accounts; it must guard against the risks that a free flow of capital can bring upon a country.

In line with international experience and China's own circumstances, we have the following understanding of China's convertibility of RMB-denominated capital accounts. First, Reform and Opening is the powerful engine behind developing "socialism with Chinese characteristics." For China's economy to merge into the global economy and for China's economy to develop on a wider stage, it is necessary to accomplish convertibility. The process of Reform and Opening includes gradual realization of this goal. Institutional mechanisms that are not adapted or suited to this development trend must be changed; policies, rules, and obstructions that are not beneficial to this development must be eliminated. In promoting capital account convertibility, we must continue to liberate our thinking, open up the way ahead, and deepen reform. Through convertibility, we will be able to go further in Reform and in Opening to the outside.

Second, gradual realization of convertibility must be firmly rooted in the circumstances of China's conditions and must accommodate China's unique characteristics. The forms that the process will take and the environment in which it proceeds are complex. Our basic national condition is that we are in the early stages of socialism. Setting up the initial stages of a socialist market economy requires constant opening to the outside, strengthening China's comprehensive national power, and improving the competitiveness and the market tenacity of her enterprises. However, China's population is enormous, and the pressure to maintain employment during the process of industrialization and urbanization is intense. China's domestic financial markets are not well-developed, macroeconomic tools are lacking, and the capacity of the financial system as a whole to withstand foreign shocks is yet to be strengthened. Globally, the scale of financial markets and capital flows are increasing by the day, and their diversification and complexity are reaching new heights.

Although many countries in the world have already realized currency convertibility, and can offer their own experience to China as a model, it has to be recognized that China is not just a developing country and a very large one, but is also a country in the process of disengaging from a planned economy system. There is no ready-made model that China can simply put on. We need to match awareness of our own national conditions with a global point of view; that is, we must study international experience for what is useful, and at the same time, proceed from actual conditions.

Third, accomplishing convertibility requires overall planning, and sequential implementation of the incremental steps. "We do the easiest first, and then the harder, dividing the process into manageable steps." We promote convertibility according to the needs of changing circumstances as we proceed with Reform and Opening. In terms of sequence, in general, we proceed according to "first inflows and later outflows; first long-term and later short-term; first institutions and later individuals." "First inflows" refers to the former scarcity of foreign exchange, which required attracting capital inflows while restricting capital outflows. As foreign exchange resources have increased, currency outflows are being encouraged in an orderly manner. "First long-term and later short-term" refers to encouraging long-term and stable capital movements in order to lower the risk of abrupt and large short-term inflows and outflows. As China's financial markets develop and investors gain in experience, and as our capacity to handle investment risk improves, we gradually allow investment flows in such high-liquidity areas as securities. "First institutional, and then individual" refers to encouraging enterprises, financial institutions, and so on to develop their investments first in order to keep investment risk at a minimum. Relatively speaking, the investments of institutional investors are concentrated, their ability to withstand risk is stronger, and they can be more easily regulated as a group. With the increase in personal wealth and the need and ability to invest, as well as improved awareness of risk, we will gradually expand investment to individuals.

In terms of methodology, we mainly adopt the "first test, then promote" approach. We first undertake pilot cases or tests, and after accumulating experience, gradually promote a given measure. Examples are direct investments abroad and investments in the securities arena. In terms of pace and speed, we evaluate such factors as need, conditions, capability, and situation, and proceed in orderly fashion and stable manner, while being able to grasp opportunities and break through at the appropriate time.

Fourth, accomplishing RMB convertibility requires incorporating all the various parts into a comprehensive whole, which means careful harmonization in the course of policy implementation. Implementing RMB convertibility is a form of systems engineering. Constituent parts are systems in themselves. To succeed, we must develop financial markets, improve financial regulatory systems, speed up reform of financial enterprises, strengthen and advance financial policy measures, and in the process harmonize all of the links and chains in the financial system. From start to finish, China must strengthen measures relating to risk containment as the country reforms all components of the system.

Much has been done. In terms of developing *financial markets*, in recent years, China has rapidly built an infrastructure for capital markets, the share conversion reform is basically completed and stock markets are growing briskly. In 2007, 120 enterprises undertook initial public offerings (IPOs) in China's stock markets, raising a total of RMB447 billion in capital. As opposed to financing from bank loans, the direct-financing proportion of enterprise funding is clearly increasing. In currency markets, foreign exchange markets, gold markets, derivatives markets, and so on, China has taken large strides forward with improved functionality. In terms of improving *financial regulation*, in recent years, China has strengthened and advanced financial regulation and made initial steps in setting up a legal framework for prudent regulation. It has strengthened overall regulation of financial institution credit risk, market risk, and operations risk. It has strengthened protections for investors in equities. The ability of the financial system to withstand risk has been greatly improved. With regard to reform of *financial enterprises*, since 2003, China has undertaken to synthesize a number of measures. It has brought in strategic investors, injected capital, restructured the system for listing on the market, and undertaken other such measures to speed the reform of state-owned commercial banks. At the same time, it has sped up and improved corporate governance structures within banks and strengthened comprehensive governance at securities companies with the result that their market competitiveness and ability to withstand risk has markedly improved.

By the end of 2007, the nonperforming loan (NPL) ratio of the main commercial banks had fallen to 6.72%, there were more than 161 banks reaching capital adequacy ratios of 8% or more, and 79% met asset quality standards. With regard to *financial measures*, the marketization of interest rates has been promoted more vigorously since 2003. A money market rate has been initially established that serves as the underlying basis for this; market supply and demand is playing a fundamental role; and the Central Bank applies market-driven policy tools as a way of managing the interest rate system. In July 2005, we improved the reform of RMB exchange rate mechanisms, and as a result, the flexibility of the RMB exchange rate has clearly improved. Faced with a situation of over liquidity, the Central Bank has implemented a variety of comprehensive monetary policy measures to preserve the basic stability of the macroeconomic financial environment, such as increasing deposit reserve ratio, exchange rate, open market operation, interest rate, and adopting window guidance, and so on.

Fifth, convertibility requires improving regulatory mechanisms and risk-control measures. In an economy that is globalizing and financial markets that are being integrated into an organic whole, the risk contained in cross-border capital flows can be abrupt and contagious. Since the 1990s, the Asian Financial Crisis, the Latin American currency crisis, the American subprime mortgage crisis, and other such financial perturbations have followed one after another. This shows that, given financial globalization, financial risk has a strong propensity for swift and infectious results. International capital flows are complex and ever-changing, and the "opening" of one country increases the possibility of external shocks. In the process of making capital account convertible, risk avoidance must be paramount. In the overall deployment of reform, China must take into account its stage of economic development, the degree of maturity of its markets, the degree of resilience of its enterprises, and the adaptability of its financial regulatory agencies. It must strengthen and improve regulatory measures that are realistic, that are prudent, and that are effective. We must guard against shocks related to international capital flows through adjusting capital entry conditions, control the capital amount, monitoring and analyzing cross-border capital flow for alarming movements. We must increase the ability to withstand and to dissipate risk, including having a more elastic economy and more adaptable entities, a broader and deeper market, more effective macroeconomic measures, and so on. This is one area in which we need to do more work.

Looking to the future, the trend to global integration of economies is irreversible. Financial markets will only become more interwoven. The ties between China and the world can only become more tightly integrated. We intend, firmly and resolutely, to pursue the path of Reform and Opening. In this process, we seek to further the goal of capital account convertibility, always proceeding in accord with Chinese national conditions and the needs of the country's development.

CHAPTER 27

China's Money, Bond, and FX Markets

Xie Duo
President, China Foreign Exchange Trade System

The reform of the money, bond, and FX markets has always been an important part of China's financial reforms; and the progress of these reforms is of great significance for financial institutions' operational mode transformation, marketization of exchange and interest rates, capital account openness, and the implementation of fiscal and monetary policy. Since 1994, the rapid development of China's money, bond, and FX markets has created vital and fundamental market conditions for the implementation of the country's macroeconomic policy. With China's economy and finance opening up further, the development of its money, bond, and FX markets is exerting an increasing influence on not only the domestic economy and finance, but also on financial markets around the globe.

This chapter makes a brief review of the establishment, reform, openness, and development of China's money, bond, and FX market, with a focus on the framework of individual markets, as well as the relationship between these markets. Due to space limitations, this chapter will elaborate on the inter-bank market, the main part of China's money, bond, and FX markets. A discussion is also presented on the new challenges for the current money, bond, and FX markets in terms of money management and macro-adjustment.

MONEY MARKET

Money market refers to the market where financial institutions make transactions of short-term financial instruments for short-term financing and liquidity management. The money market serves as a link between various financial markets in any financial system. At present, China's money market is mainly made up of the inter-bank funding market and the bond repo market.

Inter-bank Funding Market

The inter-bank funding market is the core component of China's money market. Funding is the short-term financing transaction made by financial institutions, such as commercial banks, in a guarantee-free manner in the inter-bank market. In the modern banking system, deposit-taking institutions must set aside legal reserves;[1] provisional payment of large amount may lead to inadequate reserves, thus creating demand for short-term funding among financial institutions. As no guarantee is required for this transaction, funds are often transferred between the reserve accounts of the two trading parties in the People's Bank of China (PBC). Therefore, funding is the most efficient mode of short-term financing.[2]

China's funding market was set up in the 1980s. Since the inception of the country's financial markets, the PBC has imposed strict control on loan scale for financial institutions, due to the lack of instruments available in the money and capital markets. At that time, many institutions used the funding market as the means to counter financial control and obtain medium- and long-term funds. In the coastal areas that were first opened to the outside world, large amounts of funds flew in to fill the inadequacy of local funds. Such a form of funding was always long term and lost the original significance of funding. Around 1993, financial institutions made frequent funding among each other. The major form was non-financial institutions, such as trust investment companies, borrowing funds from commercial banks, and investing these short-term funds in securities and in the long-term real estate industry. In this way, funding became a major monetary source for the then inflation and asset bubbles, and, therefore, a key area for the central government's macro-adjustment and financial regulation around 1993.

Since January 1996 the PBC has unveiled reforms in the funding market, starting a national unified market for inter-bank funding. As compared with the funding market before the reforms, the new market framework has two major features. First, definition is set for financial institutions eligible to trade in the funding market. With the new system, financial institution participants in the market can be classified into two types: members of the inter-bank funding market and general participants. Members of the national inter-bank funding market include headquarters and authorized branches of commercial banks, urban commercial banks, financial firms, and some securities companies. Other financial institutions are general participants. Members of the funding market have to make funding transactions via the e-trading system offered by the National Interbank Funding Center (NIFC). Other financial institutions can make transactions on their own, and put their records in local branches of the PBC. Second, the PBC sets limits on funding maturity and quota for all types of financial institutions. For commercial banks, the funding term should be no more than four months,[3] and the funding quota is set according to the proportion of the deposit balance. For non-banking financial institutions, the term must be within seven days, and the funding ceiling is decided in light of their capital. The management on maturity and quota is to prevent financial institutions from excessive funding or changing short-term borrowed funds into sources of long-term funds. Similar control is also carried out in some other developing countries.

It is worth noting that the arrangement of all the funding market members trading through the NIFC trading system is of great significance for macro-management. First, market members conclude trading contracts through the trading system; this has raised trading efficiency and benefited the forming of a national unified market. Second, via the trading system, the PBC can effectively manage funding maturity and quota, thus preventing financial institutions' excessive funding and using short-term funds in a long-term way. Third, such an arrangement helps the PBC to get an insight into the fluctuation of liquidity in the financial system. As China gradually opens its capital account, such a function of the trading system will be increasingly important. When the financial markets see money speculation, this system will help the PBC to quickly decide the source and scale of funds in money speculation and, based on that, to take timely monetary policy steps to counter the speculation.[4] With China deepening its reforms on financial institutions and financial institutions strengthening their capability of internal risk management, the PBC modified the "Administrative Measures for Interbank Funding" in August 2007, which has promoted the development of the funding market by further loosening the control on market access, funding maturity and quota. However, the basic spirit of management is the same.

The funding market is also an important reason for China's decision to leave interest rates to market forces. In June 1996, the PBC allowed financial institutions to decide the funding rate according to

supply and demand in the market, and started periodic announcement of interest rates on the inter-bank funding market. In developed
economies, inter-bank funding rates are often one of the benchmarks
to set the rates of other financial products. Since 2003, the PBC has
accelerated the reforms on interest rates and gradually lifted the control on the ceiling of loan rates as well as the lower threshold of
deposit rates. To promote interest rate marketization and strengthen
the function of money markets as a benchmark interest rate indicator in a marketized system, the PBC in January 2007 introduced the
Shanghai Interbank Offered Rate (SHIBOR), which is the calculated
average of daily rates for inter-bank funding offered by 16 quotation
banks. The SHIBOR is a wholesale and guarantee-free rate of single
interest. Currently, the SHIBOR, issued by the NIFC, includes maturities of overnight, one week, two weeks, one month, three months,
six months, nine months, and one year. Many financial institutions
have adopted SHIBOR as the benchmark rate for the trading of many
financial instruments. With the PBC likely to further lift controls on
deposit and loan rates in the future, the SHIBOR will play an increasing role as the benchmark rate for various types of financial products.

Figure 27.1 shows the consistent tendency between the one-year
interest rate and monetary policy. The seven-day funding rate reflects
the movement of market positions recently. In recent years, transactions are more and more active in the funding market in terms of

FIGURE 27.1   Seven-day and one-year SHIBOR in Jan–Oct 2007

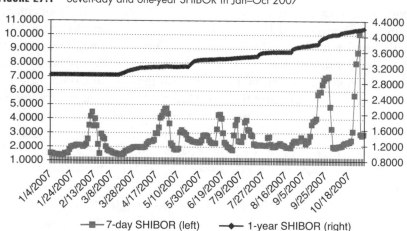

Source: www.chinamoney.com.cn

TABLE 27.1 Turnover in the inter-bank funding market

Year	(billion RMB) Credit lending
1996	587.2
1997	409.8
1998	99.0
1999	329.2
2000	672.8
2001	808.2
2002	1,210.7
2003	2,411.3
2004	1,455.6
2005	1,278.3
2006	2,150.3
2007/01–2007/10	7,426.7

Source: www.chinamoney.com.cn

turnover (see Table 27.1). In 2006, the inter-bank funding market witnessed a turnover of 2,150.3 billion yuan, up 68% year-on-year. From January to October 2007, the growth rate kept accelerating. However, such a funding volume is still small when compared to the scale of China's financial system.

At present the inter-bank funding market faces two challenges. First, China's funding market is not influential due to its small turnover. The development of the funding market calls for further reforms of China's financial system, a stronger credit system, and higher efficiency in the payment system of the PBC. The second problem is how to define the funding of non-banking financial institutions; in particular, whether securities companies' short-term borrowing from commercial banks belong to the funding business. In light of the development of the securities market, the demand by securities companies for short-term funds is an objective existence. However, when such a demand is channeled into the funding business, interest rates of funding will reflect not only the supply and demand of reserves of deposit-taking institutions, but also the fluctuations in the capital market. This will limit the possibility for the PBC to take the funding rate as its target of operation, thus impairing the effectiveness of monetary policy operation. As a result, a rational option is that securities companies, as clients of commercial banks, can ask for short-term loans from commercial banks in line with the conditions for loans. The lack of a credit system among financial institutions has dragged the development of the funding market, leaving financial institutions' demand for liquidity management unsatisfied. Therefore, the PBC has spared no effort in advancing the inter-bank bond repo market since 1997.

Bond Repo Market

Bond Repo is a transaction in which Party A sells a bond to Party B and agrees to repurchase it at a specific date in the future and at a pre-agreed price. In a repo transaction, trading parties trade not for buying or selling bonds, but for short-term financing.[5] As for credit risks, bond repo is safer and more effective than funding.

Before 1990, China's money market was dominated by inter-bank funding. In 1991, bond repo was introduced. At first, repo transactions were mainly made in securities exchanges; namely, Wuhan Securities Trading Center, Tianjin Securities Trading Center, and the Securities Trading Automatic Quotation (STAQ) system. Unfortunately, all these trading markets had serious flaws in custody and trading, underwent severe risks of credit and payment, and were closed by the authorities one by one. Before June 1997, bond repo focused on the Shanghai Stock Exchange, and banks were able to participate in the transactions of bond and bond repo here. In the process of these transactions, exchange repo became a major means by which non-banking financial institutions obtained funds from commercial banks. The trading was closely related to the stock market. In early 1997, to prevent bank funds from entering the stock market, the State Council decided to ban commercial banks from trading in the exchange repo market and said that the inter-bank bond market would introduce repo transactions. After that, the inter-bank market unveiled a series of infrastructure arrangements of custody, trading, and settlement to suit the over-the-counter (OTC) market mode. Such arrangements have ensured a safe operation of bond repo and successfully prevented commercial bank funds from entering the stock market via repo. In the meantime, the development of the inter-bank bond repo market has provided the PBC with a market foundation for open market operation.

Currently, the inter-bank repo market[6] has more than 1,400 financial institutional members, including domestic commercial banks and their authorized branches, branches of foreign-funded banks in China, domestic and foreign insurance firms, securities and fund companies, and rural credit cooperatives. Besides, thousands of enterprises participate in the bond repo market, helped by the system arrangement

TABLE 27.2 Bond repo transactions in the inter-bank market (billion RMB)

Year	Pledged repo	Outright repo	Total
1996	–	–	–
1997	31.0	–	31.0
1998	102.2	–	102.2
1999	395.6	–	395.6
2000	1,578.2	–	1,578.2
2001	4,013.3	–	4,013.3
2002	10,188.5	–	10,188.5
2003	11,720.3	–	11,720.3
2004	9,310.5	126.3	9,436.8
2005	15,678.4	222.3	15,900.7
2006	26,302.1	289.2	26,591.3
2007/01–2007/10	35,142.4	595.0	35,737.4

Source: www.chinamoney.com.cn

of agent settlement business. Therefore, the inter-bank market has become a typical institutional investors market. As the repo market has more diversified members than the funding market and the repo risk is lower than credit lending, repo transactions are more active than funding and repo interest rates are more stable, showing a picture closer to the real situation of financial market liquidity. Table 27.2 shows that the turnover in the inter-bank repo market has witnessed explosive growth since 1997. Bond repo market is now the financial market that sees most active transactions in China. Bond repo transaction has satisfied financial institutions' demands for liquidity management. As set in the transaction rules, the longest maturity for bond repo is one year, though most transactions focus on maturities within seven days. In October 2007, pledged repo within seven days accounted for 89% of all the pledged repo in terms of turnover, which indicates that financial institutions are managing their short-term funds mainly by bond repo.

Despite great progress, China's repo market still has huge scope for further development, especially when compared with developed countries. First, inter-bank repo transactions are made by financial institutions, primarily to adjust positions. The demand for repo is far weaker than that in developed markets. Second, participants in inter-bank repo are mainly financial institutions at present. Effective measures should be taken to attract non-financial institutions to participate in repo trading, so as to activate the money market and strengthen the transmission effect of monetary policy. Third, the forms of repo are too limited. In the future, the inter-bank market based on the current operation of outright repo, bond lending, and bond forward needs to introduce more new businesses so as to further boost the bond repo market.

BOND MARKET

Over the past decade, China's bond market has witnessed big strides. However, in general, direct finance has lagged behind its indirect counterpart. In direct finance, the bond market development is behind the stock market. In the bond market itself, the corporate bond market lags behind the T-bond and financial bond market. In the next stage of financial reforms, the bond market will be the focus of China's financial markets.

The Inter-bank Bond Market: Establishment and Progress

Currently, China's bond market consists of the inter-bank market, exchange market, and bank-customer (retail) market. Until 1997, the exchange market and the bank–customer market dominated the bond market. In June 1997, the inter-bank bond market was established.[7] After 10 years' development, great changes have occurred in this market in terms of both depth and width. It has become the most important part of China's bond market. As shown in Table 27.3, bonds of different types are now issued and traded mainly in the inter-bank market.

Since 1997, a series of reforms on bond issuance has been launched in the inter-bank bond market. To begin with, PBC promoted the marketization of bond issuance. Before 1998, policy financial bonds,

TABLE 27.3 Bond market structure (billion RMB)

	National total	Inter-bank	Pct. of inter-bank	Exchange	Retail	Others
Bonds issued (2007/01–10)	5,643.3	5,626.2	99.7%	13.4	3.7	–
Bonds outstanding (end-2007/10)	10,984.6	9,753.6	88.8%	351.0	43.6	836.6

Sources: www.chinamoney.com.cn and www.chinabond.com.cn

with their amounts and rates decided by the PBC, were issued to designated commercial banks according to the PBC's calculation of the proportion of new deposits in these banks. In 1998, the PBC introduced a reform on the issuing mechanism of these bonds. Since then, the China Development Bank (CDB) has been issuing policy financial bonds in the market-based manners like public bidding. In August 1998, the CDB offered its first bonds in the inter-bank bond market in the new mode. Later, the Export–Import Bank of China and the Agricultural Development Bank of China (ADB) issued, by means of bidding, all their domestic policy financial bonds in the inter-bank bond market. In October 1999, the Ministry of Finance started issuing T-bonds in the inter-bank bond market, also by bidding. In 2000, all the treasury bonds were issued in the inter-bank market by bidding. Within a mere three years, the inter-bank bond market had smoothly realized market-based issuance, marking a great transformation in China's bond market.

As China deepens its banking reforms, the inter-bank market has introduced new bond varieties, as shown in Tables 27.4 and 27.5. These new types of bonds launched one by one as part of the reforms include: bank subordinated bonds to add banks' supplementary capital; housing loan securities and loan assets-backed securities in line with asset securitization; and corporate short-term financing bills designed to improve the structure of corporate financing. In recent years, the PBC has issued a large amount of central bank papers, so as to address the rise of RMB input for the inward flow of forex and thus

TABLE 27.4 Structure of outstanding bonds in the inter-bank market (billion RMB)

Variety	Balance (end-2007/10)	Pct.
T-bonds	3,088.7	31.668%
Central bank papers	3,171.1	32.512%
Policy financial bonds	2,595.1	26.607%
Subordinated bonds	191.9	1.967%
Short-term financing bills	316.6	3.246%
General financial bonds	96.6	0.991%
Corporate bonds	266.4	2.731%
Bonds of International Development Institutions	3.0	0.031%
Hybrid bonds	12.3	0.126%
Asset-backed securities	11.9	0.122%
Total	9,753.6	100.000%

Source: www.chinamoney.com.cn

TABLE 27.5 Cash bond transactions in the inter-bank market (billion RMB)

	T-bonds	Policy financial bonds	Corporate bonds	Central bank papers	Others	Total
1997	1.0	–	–	–	–	1.0
1998	3.3	–	–	–	–	3.3
1999	3.5	4.2	–	–	–	7.7
2000	46.8	21.5	–	–	–	68.3
2001	50.5	33.4	–	–	–	84.0
2002	279.2	157.1	4.8	–	–	441.2
2003	812.3	1,349.7	16.8	906.0	–	3,084.8
2004	474.0	1,008.1	6.5	1,012.0	3.6	2,504.1
2005	1,034.5	1,561.0	22.6	2,892.8	502.5	6,013.3
2006	1,207.6	2,574.5	429.1	4,239.6	1,805.7	10,256.4
2007/01–2007/10	1,364.8	2,048.0	346.3	6,902.5	1,128.8	11,790.4
Total	5,277.5	8,757.4	826.0	15,952.9	3,440.6	34,254.4
Pct.	15.4%	25.6%	2.4%	46.6%	10.0%	100.0%

Source: www.chinamoney.com.cn

stabilize money supply. Now the central bank papers have grabbed the biggest share in the inter-bank bond market.

In the inter-bank bond market, the issuing rate and trading price are now decided by the market. The reform of the primary bond market has created conditions for the development of the secondary bond market. In the inter-bank market, 52 primary dealers of the PBC open market form the core of bond underwriters; 16 financial institutions are authorized bond market-makers, raising bond-market liquidity with their two-way quotations. The inter-bank bond market has embraced paperless bonds and unified custody and trading platforms. Through the aforementioned infrastructure, the inter-bank bond market has set up the framework of a modern OTC market, and the liquidity of bonds has been improved considerably in the inter-bank market.

The development of the inter-bank bond market has started to influence the operation of financial institutions as well as the central bank's monetary policy implementation. First, the development of the inter-bank bond market has offered space for commercial banks to adjust asset composition and lower the excess reserves in the PBC. In 1997, bond assets accounted for 5% of the total assets of commercial banks. At the end of 2006, the ratio was up to 29%. As the proportion of bond assets has gone up, commercial banks have improved their asset quality by lowering the deposit/loan ratios. Also, the rising ratio

FIGURE 27.2 Yield curves in the inter-bank bond market

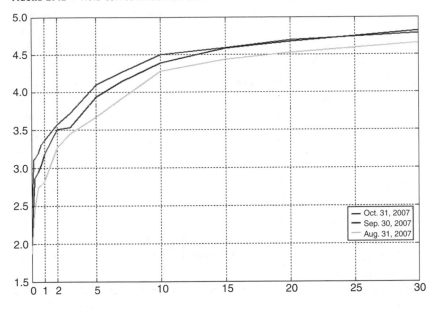

Source: www.chinamoney.com.cn

of bond assets enables commercial banks to cut their excess reserves and manage their liquidity by bond repo when market changes.

Second, as the market plays an increasing role in the issuing and circulation of bonds, the inter-bank bond market has started to form a comprehensive term structure of bond yields decided by the market (see Figure 27.2). This is a positive drive for China's reforms to leave interest rates to market forces. The term structure of bond yields in the inter-bank market serves as a significant reference for the PBC to judge the inflationary trends in the future; it is also a major basis for the pricing of other financial products.

Third, with the higher ratio of bond assets and money market development, commercial banks and other financial institutions are more sensitive to the PBC's policy operation, thus creating conditions for the PBC to go in for stronger efforts for open market operations.

China's Bond Market: Challenges and Outlook

First, the scale of investors should be enlarged in the inter-bank bond market. At present, members of the inter-bank bond market are not closely linked to other non-financial institutions and individual investors, undermining the improvement of market efficiency and liquidity. The inter-bank market is gradually opening itself to all types of non-financial institutions, and through bank–customer transactions, the wholesale bond market has been connected with the retail market in which individual investors and non-financial institutions participate. However, non-financial institutions remain inactive players; the wholesale and retail markets are loosely linked; and the improvement of market efficiency is not obvious. The link between the inter-bank market and the exchange market is an important issue that needs to be addressed in the development of China's bond market in the coming years. It is also a necessity for raising market efficiency and liquidity. How to link the inter-bank market and the exchange market, in essence, means how to address the relationship between the institutional investor market and the retail investor market.

Second, bond varieties are still inadequate and the demand for bonds is yet to be balanced with the supply. On one hand, the comprehensive development of China's financial markets provides residents with increasing investment options of financial instruments, and raises the proportion of short-dated deposits in commercial banks. On the other, commercial banks also expand their long-term assets, such as individual housing mortgages. Under such circumstances, commercial banks are facing an increasingly serious problem of term mismatch in their asset–liability structure. Therefore, they need bond assets for liquidity management. In the meantime, commercial banks need to securitize their assets, such as housing mortgages, in order to cut the duration of their assets and put interest rate risks under control. Currently, China's bond market has made initial attempts at housing mortgage securitization and loan asset securitization. Nevertheless, the promotion of these two types of securitization necessitates the addressing of many legal and financial issues.

Third, greater efforts should be made to advance the corporate bond market. The question of how to develop corporate bonds has always been a key issue and a difficult problem in China's financial market. The financial reforms in the next stage will make great efforts to develop corporate bonds, according to the spirit of the financial working conference of the CPC central committee. In issuing corporate bonds, the key point is how to handle the credit risks of these bonds. In general, three options are available: (1) to limit the issuing scale; (2) the system of bank guarantees lowers the risks of corporate payment; and (3) to actively promote the institutional investors' market and to strengthen corporate governance structure, information disclosure, and institutional investors' ability to identify and endure risks. The first two options, the dominant mode over the past decade, cannot meet the requirements of the current economic and financial development in the country. The inter-bank bond market should explore the third method.

MONEY MARKET, BOND MARKET, AND OPEN MARKET OPERATION

In 1998, the PBC stopped its direct adjustment dominated by loan scale management. Instead, the PBC, in more cases, has adopted a mode of indirect adjustment based on the market. With the rising trading scale of the money market, the PBC has strengthened its open market operation in the money market since 1998. Now, the PBC has set up a system of open market primary dealers.[8] According to requirements of monetary policy goals, the PBC will trade with the primary dealers after it has decided the operational strategies for that week. Trading forms include: cash bond transaction and repo of T-bond and policy financial bonds, and issuing central bank papers. Through open market operation, the PBC adjusts the growth of base money, realizes the target of the money supply, and strives to stabilize the short-term interest rates of the money market. In the policy framework that takes money supply as the intermediate target, base money is a major operational target for the PBC. With China's unbalanced economic structure and RMB exchange-rate regime, as well as the excessive RMB input by the PBC for the inward flow of forex, open market business is now an important tool for sterilization operations to stabilize the growth of base money, and to ensure the fulfillment of the money supply target. Since 2003, China's FX market has shown an increasing tendency of supply–demand imbalance. Therefore, the PBC has issued large amounts of central bank papers in the inter-bank bond market, in order to sterilize the liquidity that has grown too fast. The monetary policy operation by the PBC in 2007 is the practice of "realizing monetary policy target mainly through money market operations," which is a meaningful experience for the PBC.

Through its intensifying correlation with the interest rate of the PBC's open market operation (see Figure 27.3), the money market interest rate has emerged as one of the key policy targets of the PBC's adjustment through open market operations. However, as interest rates of deposits and loans of commercial banks are still controlled by the PBC, and money market tools account for a low ratio in

FIGURE 27.3   SHIBOR and the interest rate of one-year central bank paper in 2007

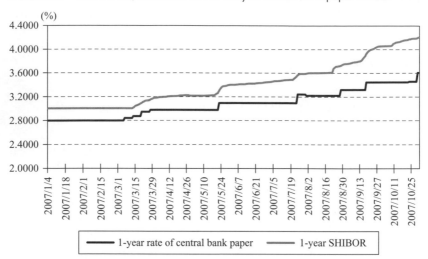

Source: www.chinamoney.com.cn

commercial banks' assets, variations of short-term interest rates in the money market exert no direct impact on either commercial banks' deposit and loan interest rates, or the yield rates of other financial assets. Therefore, the PBC cannot make effective adjustment to such goals as money supply through operations in the money market.

The funding rates among financial institutions vary vastly according to their credit levels. Well-established institutions, such as state-owned commercial banks and joint stock commercial banks, enjoy a relatively stable inter-bank funding rate, while the rates of smaller institutions with poor asset quality are often above the market average with obvious fluctuations. Comparatively, the disparity is less distinct when it comes to the bond repo rates among different types of institutions, because bond repo, a way of bond-pledged funding, bears far lower risks than inter-bank funding.

FX MARKET

To reform the financial and foreign trade system and check inflation, China launched a significant reform of its FX administration system in 1994. With this reform, China introduced a system of FX sale and purchase, set up a unified inter-bank FX market, and realized a managed floating of the RMB exchange rate. The launch of the inter-bank FX

FIGURE 27.4 Forming and covering of positions in FX sale and purchase

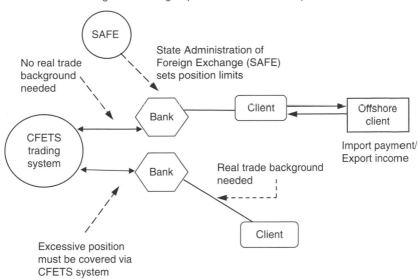

market and the managed floating exchange rate regime has effectively promoted a sustained and rapid development of China's economy. In July 2005, with major changes in the economic and financial environment at both home and abroad, China carried out another important reform in its FX market. The reform was designed to increase RMB flexibility and give the market a larger role in adjusting the supply and demand of foreign exchanges. Also, the reform was expected to create conditions for RMB convertibility under capital and financial accounts.

At present, China's FX market is made up of the retail market and the inter-bank market (see Figure 27.4). In the retail market, enterprises and individuals can buy or sell FX in designated FX banks[9] in compliance with the FX Administrative Rules and policies on FX sale and purchase. The inter-bank FX market consists of designated FX banks, eligible non-banking financial institutions, and non-financial firms. Designated FX banks are major institutions that link the retail market with the inter-bank market. The China Foreign Exchange Trade System (CFETS) is in charge of offering trading platform, clearing, and information services for the inter-bank market.

With changes in China's balance of payments (BOP) and macro economy, deregulation of individuals and enterprises' holding of FX is accelerating. Exporters can keep a rising ratio of FX income in their accounts; restrictions on enterprises' retaining incomes under the current account have been lifted in 2007. As for individuals, the quota of buying FX has risen to US$50,000 in 2007; Qualified Domestic Institutional Investor (QDII) offers people a channel to buy FX for offshore investment. Convertibility under capital and financial accounts has also sped up considerably.

The position management system of FX-designated banks is one of the core systems in China's management of its FX market (see Figure 27.4). Before the July 2005 reform of the exchange rate forming mechanism, members of the inter-bank FX market made FX transactions only by automatic price matching. When there was a mismatch between supply and demand in the market, commercial banks were not able to address the mismatch automatically, due to the position quota. The mismatch had to be balanced by the PBC. Therefore, the market was weak in self-adjustment. Under the new arrangement, commercial banks can choose between the two trading modes: automatic price matching and OTC.[10] The monetary authority has raised the position quota of FX market-makers, and the PBC has stopped direct participation in daily transactions in the FX market. Instead, the PBC now makes indirect adjustment through primary FX dealers. In this way, commercial banks are exerting a growing influence on market supply and demand, and market forces are playing a larger role in deciding the RMB exchange rate. In the meantime, commercial banks cannot hold negative positions and FX transactions must be made in the unified trading platform, according to relevant stipulations. Therefore, a single commercial bank cannot influence the spot or forward exchange rate of RMB by manipulating the market. This has ensured smooth operation of the RMB exchange-rate mechanism.

Market factors decide the central parity of the RMB exchange rate (see Figure 27.5), and the floating band of RMB is obviously widening. In the current market framework, the CFETS asks all inter-bank FX market-makers for quotations for RMB/US$ before the market opens every day. With these quoted prices as samples for calculating the central parity of RMB/US$, the CFETS calculates the central parity of the day by averaging these prices in a weighted manner after deleting the highest price and the lowest one. This calculated central parity of the RMB against the US$ is then issued immediately in www.chinamoney.com.cn, as well as other media on a daily basis. The weight is decided by the CFETS according to the quoting institution turnover and quotation in the inter-bank FX market. At present, the FX market has 22 market-making banks, including nine

FIGURE 27.5 Trading modes in the inter-bank FX market

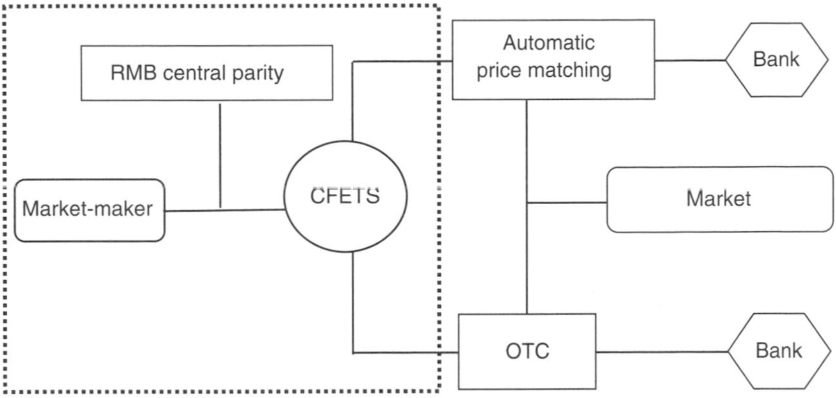

Market-maker:

(1) Trade under the two modes: adjusting supply–demand and offering liquidity.

(2) Participate in the forming of RMB central parity.

foreign-funded banks. In the inter-bank market, the daily floating band of the spot RMB/US$ rate is 5% around the central parity. The daily floating band for the spot prices of RMB against other currencies is 3% around their central parities. It is worth noting that there is no limit on the spread between a central parity and the central parity the day before. Furthermore, no administrative control is set for the RMB/FX forward rate or the RMB/FX swap rate. This shows that market factors are playing an increasingly important role in deciding the RMB exchange rate. Under the new arrangement of the exchange-rate regime, the floating band of RMB exchange rate has expanded remarkably (see Table 27.6).

TABLE 27.6 Floating band of RMB/US$ exchange rate (basis points).[1]

Year	Q1	Q2	Q3	Q4
2005	38	67	1,905[2]	229
2006	548	405	1,115	1,170
2007	945	1,248	1,100	680[3]

Source: www.chinamoney.com.cn

[1] Floating band is the spread between the highest and lowest transaction prices in a quarter.

[2] RMB appreciated by 2% on July 21, 2005.

[3] As of end-October 2007.

FIGURE 27.6 RMB/FX forward and swap transactions

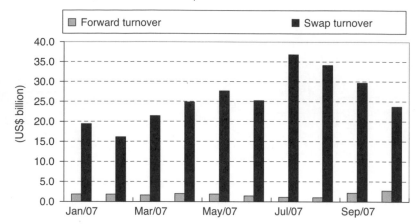

Source: www.chinamoney.com.cn

Against the backdrop of increased band of RMB exchange rate floating, the inter-bank FX market has introduced RMB exchange rate derivative products, so as to meet the demands of enterprises and financial institutions to hedge RMB exchange rate risks. In August 2005, the RMB forward was launched. In April 2006, the RMB/FX swap was introduced. In August 2007, the market began to trade RMB/FX currency swaps. With its dual functions of managing exchange rate risks and liquidity, FX swaps are more popular among financial institutions, as manifested in its mounting turnover (see Figure 27.6).

In light of the situation in the two-odd years after the reform, the current RMB exchange rate forming mechanism shows the following features. First, the RMB exchange rate has seen a wider floating band and two-way fluctuations, but remains relatively stable. Second, OTC is becoming the prevailing mode of trading. Third, commercial banks, as FX market-makers, are playing a more important role; the PBC is shrinking its direct intervention; and market forces in deciding the RMB exchange rate are increasingly obvious. These new changes after the reform increasingly exhibit the features of managed floating RMB exchange rate regime.

Currently, the major challenge for China's FX market is the expectation for one-way movement of the RMB exchange rate, due to the long-term imbalance in BOP. Such an expectation has prevented the market from playing its function of adjustment smoothly. With the gradual opening of China's capital and financial accounts, capital flow will exert a larger impact on supply and demand of the FX market, and the RMB exchange rate will be more flexible. Under a situation of larger changes in market supply and demand as well as more flexibility of the RMB exchange rate, the question of how to develop derivatives to avoid RMB exchange rate risks and construct an FX market of more depth and width has become an important pre-condition for further increasing the flexibility of the RMB exchange rate. Therefore, it is imperative to hasten the construction of the FX market.

CONCLUSION

China's money, bond, and FX markets have witnessed rapid development over the past 10 years or more. With the diversification of trading varieties in the markets, most mainstream cash products in the global markets are now available in China's inter-bank market, which has satisfied the demands of market players and contributed to the rapid rise of the trading scale. In the meantime, the number and range of market participants are constantly expanding, the market structure keeps getting better, and market depth and width are improving.

The money market has become the link between various financial markets in China. The scale of fund trading has grown swiftly. Money market instruments, such as repo and lending, have emerged as major means for financial institutions to adjust fund position and manage liquidity. Money market interest rate is now the benchmark rate for various types of financial products and one of the major goals of the Central Bank's open market operation. In the bond market, all the bonds are now issued in a marketized manner, thus making the bond market an important source for governments and enterprises to raise funds and a major arena for the central bank to sterilize liquidity. Reasonable bond market yield curves acceptable in the market are now forming in the bond market, offering the basis for pricing financial instruments and enhancing interest rate marketization. China's FX market is undergoing fundamental changes after the reform on exchange rate forming mechanism in 2005. The trading mechanism in the FX market is increasingly reasonable, market factors' influence on RMB exchange rate has been strengthening steadily, and the flexibility of the RMB exchange rate has notably risen. Based on the development of China's money, bond, and FX markets, the indirect adjustment of PBC's monetary policy is becoming more and more effective.

Still in their early development phase, China's financial markets are separated to some extent, with limited market instruments available for trading and a low level of trading scale. With the interest rates of deposits and loans still under control in China, changes in money market interest rates can exert only a limited impact on other financial markets, such as the credit market. The RMB exchange rate's function to adjust BOP is yet to take full effect. Therefore, conditions should be actively created to advance the development of China's money, bond, and FX markets, so as to meet the requirements of financial market development and, based on that, raise the efficiency of macro policy operation, including monetary policy.

ENDNOTES

1. As of November 26, 2007, the rate of legal reserves was 13.5% in China, far higher than the level in developed countries. The ratio of legal reserves in some developed countries, such as Canada, Switzerland, Belgium, and Australia, is zero (Kevin Clinton 1997). Scholars against zero-reserves in developed countries hold that the system of zero-reserves cannot maintain an effective funding market, and may deprive central banks of the benchmark short-term interest rates in the money market.

2. US federal funds market is the most typical funding market and the federal funds rate is now the most important target interest rate of the FED. However, the development of e-trading technology and paperless book-entry bonds has made repo safer than and nearly as efficient as funding. Repo is now also an important mode of short-term financing (Moorad Choudhry 2006). This chapter will discuss the advancement of repo in China's money market in the next section on the repo market.

3. In August 2007 the PBC issued "Administrative Measures for Interbank Funding," which stipulates that the funding of some institutions can be as long term as one year.

4. When international money speculators borrowed the Thai baht from Thai commercial banks in 1997 the Thai central bank failed to gauge accurately the trends and scale of funds, which caused its fatal wrong judgment in intervening in the FX market. Therefore, the Central Bank's knowledge about the trends of funding is a prerequisite for opening up the capital and financial accounts. For more on the Thai central bank's money operation during the crisis, see Xie Duo (1997).

5. Repo can be classified into outright repo and pledged repo. China's bond market traded outright repo at first, and then turned to pledged repo for the reason of trading tax.

6. In international financial markets, the inter-bank market often refers to market among financial institutions. The market participants are not limited to commercial banks.

7 It was a controversial issue for commercial banks to hold T-bonds. In early 1997, relevant authorities required commercial banks not to purchase T-bonds with credit funds. But since 1998 when China turned to a proactive fiscal policy, commercial banks have expanded their investment in T-bonds.

8 The primary dealers of the open market include 52 financial institutions, including domestic and foreign commercial banks, securities companies, insurance firms, and fund companies.

9 Banks need to obtain approval from the State Administration of Foreign Exchanges to become designated FX banks. FX-designated banks make specific transactions with other banks in the trading platform offered by the CFETS. According to current stipulations, FX position of a designated FX bank should not be negative.

10 From Jan 2006, OTC trading has been the main mode in China's inter-bank foreign exchange market.

BIBLIOGRAPHY

Choudhry, M. *The Repo Handbook*, Elsevier, 2006.

Clinton, K. *Implementation of Monetary Policy in a Regime with Zero Reserve Requirement*, Bank of Canada Working Paper, 1997.

Cook, T.Q. and R.K. LaRoche, *Instruments of the Money Market, 7th Edition*, Federal Reserve Bank of Richmond, 1993.

European Central Bank, *Euro Money Market Study 2006*, 2007.

Fabozzi, F. *The Handbook of Mortgage-backed Securities*, McGraw-Hill, 2006.

Garbuck, F.D. *The Evolution of Repo Contracting Conventions in the 1980*, FRBY Economic Policy Review, 2006.

Kuroda, I. *Towards More Effective Monetary Policy*, Palgrave MacMillan, 1997.

Martellini, L., P. Priaulet, and S. Priaulet, *Fixed-Income Securities*, John Wiley & Sons, 2003.

Michie, R.C. *The Global Securities Market: A History*, Oxford University Press, 2006.

Mundell, R.A. *Monetary Stability and Economic Growth*, Edward Elgar, 2003.

People's Bank of China (PBC), *China Monetary Policy Report*, All series.

People's Bank of China (PBC) *Measures for the Administration on Interbank Lending*, 2007.

People's Bank of China (PBC) *Provisions Governing the Forward Transactions of Bonds in the National Inter-bank Bond Market*, 2000.

State Administration of Foreign Exchange, *Circular of the State Administration of Foreign Exchange on Further Improving the Administration of Foreign Exchange Collection and Settlement in Trade*, November 1, 2006.

State Administration of Foreign Exchange. *Detailed Rules for Implementing the Measures for the Administration on Individual Foreign Exchange*, February 1, 2007.

Wu Xiaoling, *Liquidity Surplus and Risk in Financial Market*, speech at the Finance: China's New Finance Pattern Forum, September 13, 2007.

Xiang Junbo, *Harmonious Finance: Global Economics and Financial Expectation*, speech at the International Financial Forum in Lujiazui, September 1, 2006.

Xie Duo, Thailand's Maladjustment of Macroeconomic Policy and Monetary Crisis, *International Economic Review*, 1997.

Zhou Xiaochuan, *Financing Support for the Enterprises to "Step Abroad,"* speech at the International Investment Forum 2007, September 8, 2007.

Zhou Xiaochuan, *Learn Lessons for the Next Battle*, speech at the Summit of Chinese Bond Market's Development, October 20, 2005.

CHAPTER 28

Financial Futures Markets in China

Zhu Yuchen

President, China Financial Futures Exchange

Constant innovation is the source of vitality in all financial markets. New concepts are the inexhaustible force behind sustained growth of financial markets around the globe. In the 1970s, the most important concept was financial derivatives. In the 20 years from 1986 to 2005, the nominal value of financial derivative products globally enjoyed explosive growth, increasing by 183 times. According to the BIS (Bank for International Settlements), the nominal value of derivative products worldwide was US$600 trillion in 2006. This is roughly equal to 12 times the GDP of the entire globe, and to 13 times the value of shares traded throughout the world. A vigorous approach to developing derivative-product markets has become a strategic goal in most countries, as a way to improve the structure of their own financial markets, and as a way to approach the globalization of finance. On September 8, 2006, China formally began to explore and to put in place a financial futures market. The "hanging out of a shingle" of the China Financial Futures Exchange marked this beginning.

BACKGROUND: FINANCIAL FUTURES IN CHINA

China's capital markets were blessed with an important opportunity for growth when the Chinese economy sustained strong, stable, growth after years of reform measures and of "Opening" to the outside. The capital markets reached a major turning point when the State Council put out an "Opinion" in 2004 called "Various Opinions Regarding Promoting Reform and Opening of Capital Markets and Their Stable Development," and began to implement the resulting reforms. The basic infrastructure of the markets continued to improve as volume increased, trading became more active, and the number of investors' accounts rose briskly. By the beginning of November 2007, China's two markets in Shanghai and Shenzhen included 1,610 listed companies and had a total market capitalization of RMB33 trillion, roughly 120% of China's GDP. The two markets combined were already the fourth-largest in the world. They were gradually becoming a barometer of the Chinese economy. The rapid expansion in volume, and the clear "marketization" of the process established a firm foundation for creative growth. The exchanges began to serve as a stimulus for the healthy functioning of the national economy in China.

Nonetheless, China's capital markets continued to exhibit some features that were quite pronounced, and that related to the fact that China has been in transition mode from one kind of economic system to another. The building of fundamental market systems was still relatively weak, the structure of the market was not ideal, and internal balancing mechanisms were inadequate. Stock market risk has accelerated in recent times due to an increase in the range at which shares are trading, and to the very rapid expansion in volume. Price volatility shows a clear increase, and market operations harbor latent crises. Episodes of relatively high volatility have appeared since 2007 in particular, influencing the normal operation of the market. The rate at which shares trade hands is quite high; participants' speculative psychology is severe.

For capital markets to enjoy long-term stable growth, they need quantitative and, even more importantly, qualitative improvement. They require fast operations and improved mechanisms. They need volume and improvement in structure. As market size increases and market-driven forces continue to improve, conditions for instituting a financial futures market in China are gradually maturing. Starting a futures market in shares and other financial instruments at the earliest possible time has become an objective necessity in order to deepen capital markets. It has become an urgent need for all kinds of investors in order to deal with market risk. Setting up a China Financial Futures Exchange and growing the market is an important strategic "deployment" in the development of finance in China. It is highly significant in terms of actively growing futures markets in a stable manner, improving market functions, enabling better resource allocation, expanding the size of the spot market, enriching the diversity of traded products, improving market structure, speeding up reform of the system, and improving the ability of the national economy to withstand risk.

STOCK FUTURES: GROWING CHINA'S CAPITAL MARKETS

Stock futures have become one of the most important tools for managing risk in stock market systems around the world. They hold the most important position in the entire spectrum of financial derivatives. According to the US's Futures Industry Association, the trading volume in global share futures, options, and individual-share futures/options totals some 68% of the total trade in derivative products worldwide. The positive role that stock futures play in avoiding systemic risk, enhancing resource allocation, and spurring new product development has gradually been accepted by markets. Promoting stock futures will have a profound influence on the creative growth of China's capital markets in the future. Reasons are as follows.

First, from the global experience, we can see that one outstanding role of stock futures is diminution of risk. Through purchase and sale of futures contracts, systemic risk in the stock markets can be effectively divided, transferred, and re-absorbed. Stock futures provide a tool for the market to preserve value and avoid risk; they provide an exit route for risk and dissipate market risk in daily price fluctuations. They allow a dynamic state to preserve overall financial balance, by increasing the elasticity and flexibility of the market overall, thereby promoting market health, stability, and sustainability.

Second, at present, China's stock markets lack mechanisms for short selling. Only when the price goes up is an investor able to profit. When the market falls, all investors have to bear the loss. The establishment of stock futures will provide measures for short-selling, forming a two-way balancing mechanism that gets away from the constraints of a one-way system, and effectively avoids the phenomenon of stratospheric prices. This can be likened to driving a car: not only do you have forward drive, but you have a braking capability, and the ability to reverse, which provides a degree of safety.

Third, once stock futures are incorporated into the market, they will serve as a model in stimulating the creation of a series of financial innovations, leading to an era of self-propelled advances in the financial markets. After their birth in the US in the 1970s, financial futures led to a wave of financial innovations that have continued for more than 20 years. They have been described by the 1990 Nobel prize-winning economist, Harry M. Markowitz, as, "the most important financial innovation in the twentieth century." The reason is that stock futures organically link the futures market with the stock market. They use the margin system, two-way trades, T+O methods, cash settlement, and a whole series of mechanisms that are an innovation in themselves. As a very basic kind of financial derivative, stock futures are the cornerstone of other derivative markets. They provide convenient models for other products to follow.

Fourth, implementing a stock futures market in China will enhance the growth of stronger institutional investors. By forming a more diversified and differentiated structure, a futures market provides greater margins for financial institutions. Business models can improve; overall competitiveness will gradually rise. A financial ecosystem that encompasses diversified products and a multiplicity of investment strategies will allow for a multilayered, legitimate, financial industry.

Fifth, implementing a stock futures market will bring greater prosperity to both commodity futures markets and financial futures markets. In order to guarantee the smooth promotion of financial futures products, including stock futures, authorities have drafted and approved laws and regulations pertaining to market framework, businesses models, standards for market entry, institutional regulations, investor protection, and so on. An entire system of regulations has been drawn up, among which many systemic innovations can be applied to commodity futures markets. For example, in order to increase ability to withstand risk, a stratified clearing system with different classes of members, a collateral system for underwriting clearance problems, a system of co-guarantors in clearing, and so on have been set up. These allow risk to be dispersed through multiple layers, they also strengthen awareness of market risk, and they guarantee overall safety in the market. At the same time, by stiffening the qualifications needed to enter the financial futures business, rules greatly increase the overall actual strength of companies involved in futures.

SYSTEMIC FRAMEWORK: THE PATH AHEAD

Economically mature countries have a wealth of experience in operating financial futures markets. There is a large gap between that experience and the situation in China. China's legal and credit environment has a long way to go in developing intermediary institutions and regulatory measures, so developing a futures market will require a long period of cautious exploration. The establishment of financial futures markets in China must proceed on the basis of certain key principles: "maintain high standards, move forward at a deliberate pace," "have an overall plan and divide it into implemented stages," and "finish each task before starting the next as we proceed, in order to guarantee the stable and safe operations of a financial futures market."

Financial futures markets have over 30 years of history in other countries, but in China, they are a new concept. China's national conditions dictate that we adopt a gradual approach that abides by the basic principle of "plenty of preparation, stable implementation, risk avoidance, strengthened regulation, and gradual growth." Relationships among potentially contending factors must be handled with care. One is the relationship between growth and regulation: the pace of innovations has to be in line with the ability of the market to absorb risk. Second is the relationship between financial futures and commodity futures markets. We must harmonize the implementation of reform measures in inside- and outside-the-market products, and standardize procedures. Different governmental departments handle various aspects of various markets—effective communications among these must lead to cooperative regulatory measures. The third relationship that must be handled with care is that between individual and institutional investors: we must assure adequate risk awareness among all participants. Mature financial futures markets are dominated by institutional investors. We must vigorously publicize the professional nature and high-risk nature of this market, and actively encourage and cultivate institutional investors. Finally, we need to recognize our own limitations as we attempt to bring in international experience. We must be fully aware of the unique nature of risk in futures markets, and while we derive lessons from abroad, we must keep in mind China's actual situation.

As China develops markets in financial derivatives, it will adopt a method referred to in Chinese as "Moving forward gradually, with measured steps, in proper sequence." We must grasp the principle of "from slow to fast." We must have a spirit of "feeling for the stones with our feet as we cross the river." This includes controlling the pace of the initial growth period, focusing on gathering practical experience, and scoping out a path that is suited to China's national conditions in developing a financial derivatives market.

Second, we must grasp the principle of "from few to many." We must prudently consider the size of the underlying market, its liquidity, and other such basic conditions for launching a futures market. We absolutely must not move before our underlying base is ready, before conditions are sufficient to carry the additional load. We must not be rash in promoting derivatives prematurely.

Third, we must grasp the principle of "coordinated growth of inside-the-market and outside-the-market." The subprime crisis in the US makes it clear that the demands on participants in the two are different. China must strengthen risk-control systems of market institutions. In the early period, the focus should be on developing internal markets, and promoting the coordinated development of "inside" and "outside" markets.

Fourth, we must grasp the principle of following a gradual and sequenced approach to opening the market to the outside. International experience indicates that bringing in foreign investors to an appropriate degree and in a controlled and gradual manner is beneficial to the healthy development of a local derivatives market. Opening too precipitously without adequate regulation can lead to a tremendous inflow of foreign investment that can have negative effects on the local market.

Fifth, we must strengthen the coordination of regulatory agencies with jurisdictions that move across both markets and governmental departments. The financial derivatives market is linked to all financial markets. The moment it encounters an incident, the shock will transmit to other markets, so there must be cross-departmental and cross-market comprehensive handling of regulation. Only then can risk effectively be contained. Other countries have cross-departmental regulatory coordination institutions that are set up in advance, such as the US's President's Working Group, and India's High Level Clearance Committee (HLCC). Their effectiveness is apparent when sudden incidents occur. At present, there is a cooperative regulatory system within the China Securities Regulatory Commission (CSRC), but there is a need to go further in improving cross-departmental coordinating regulatory agencies.

Innovations in Developing the Financial Futures Market

The financial futures market contributes to managing risk, but it is also a market in which risk is relatively high. In order to guarantee that risk is containable, China's Financial Futures Exchange has set up four important arrangements in terms of systems design. These borrow from the wealth of experience in China's commodities futures market, and take the general practices of international markets into consideration.

The first arrangement is risk containment systems. Their primary purpose is to separate the spot market and the futures market

The second arrangement is a clearance membership system. China's Financial Futures Exchange is at present the only place undertaking financial futures trading. Membership in the Exchange will be divided into four categories: Trading members, Trading and Clearing members, Clearing members, and Special Clearing members. Clearance proceeds in the following order: from the Exchange to Clearing members, from Clearing members to Trading members, from Trading members to Customers. By stiffening the qualification requirements of Clearing members, we assure that only institutions with very solid credentials become Clearing members. Those members with insufficient qualifications must go through Clearing members for clearance. This then forms a multilayered, risk dispersed pyramidal form of risk management system, which is beneficial to helping the market withstand risk.

The third arrangement is a Clearing Co-guarantor system. The Clearing members of the Futures Exchange must provide collateral funds or security, which serves as a common guarantee of funds against any clearing members' transgressions. The Clearing Co-guarantor system assures that in the early period of functioning, the financial futures market will already have a common security or collateral fund of a very considerable size, which increases the financial ability of the Exchange to withstand risk. It sets up a buffer zone in dissipating risk.

The fourth arrangement is a regulatory control system managing margin funds. The CSRC operates according to the overall principle of safety first, then consideration of results. It has set up a new custodial system for handling margin funds and has established a China Futures Margin Regulatory Center to handle operations. Once the business of financial futures is professionally managed by futures companies, the margin funds will be transferred into safe custodianship of the regulatory system. Under the custodial system of handling margin funds, the possibility of futures companies siphoning off customers' margin funds will be greatly reduced.

CHOOSING PRODUCTS

After considerable analysis and debate, China has selected 300 listed companies for an index that forms the country's first listed "futures" product. The index includes 300 shares on the Shanghai and Shenzhen exchanges. The 300 were selected after consideration of the following factors: (1) at present, the 300 Futures Index of Shanghai and Shenzhen Exchanges is the only cross-market index that is cooperatively put out by the two Exchanges; (2) the composition of the index encompasses the great majority of shares invested in by institutional investors, which is beneficial in countering risk; (3) the rate of market coverage is high, the percentage of tradable market value is over 60%, so there is a strong ability to withstand market manipulation; (4) liquidity of shares that are included is relatively good, the percentage of trades that are consummated is high, the daily rate of shares trading hands is high; (5) there is an appropriate relationship between risk and return, there is a fairly good market representation; and (6) management of the index conforms to international precedents, and shares have a fair degree of name recognition.

The Shanghai–Shenzhen 300 Futures Index reflects the guiding principle of controlling risk as a core concern. The "contract multiplier" of the 300 Futures Index is 300. Averaging out present share prices, the face value of the index is roughly around RMB1.8 million. Even though this face value is relatively high, even in international terms, the positioning of the product is primarily aimed at servicing institutional investors. In designing the product, we determined that the main customers would be institutional investors, given limitations of other types of investors. We then adopted relatively high margin levels, to assure that the market would be stable in its early stages. We set limits on the range in which daily prices are allowed to fluctuate. We adopted "fusing" mechanisms, so that once the index trades to a limit, these bring "market cooling"functions into play. We took great care in designing the system, incorporating aspects that could prevent any kind of market manipulation.

After the Futures Index is listed on the market, China will continue to develop and list other financial derivative products. The basic thinking is: first inside-the-market derivative products, then outside; first stock-type futures, then later interest-rate and currency futures; first stock futures and later stock options. In the end, we will create a full range of products that includes share futures and options, bond futures and options, and foreign exchange futures and options.

China's financial futures markets are situated at what could be described as the "beginning point." China is the only one of the top 20 large economies on the globe that does not have a financial futures market. It therefore has vast future potential and should be able to participate substantially in global markets. However, the road ahead may not be easy. If we are confident, and stick to a scientific attitude in analyzing developments, if we combine the experience of overseas mature economies with local experience, if we are willing to innovate and deal with problems, if we move forward actively but in a sequenced and gradual way, we will carve out a path for the financial futures markets that is in accord with international standards, and that also accommodates the unique circumstances of China.

CHAPTER 29

China's New Currency Regime and Onshore FX Markets

Stephen Green

Senior Economist, Standard Chartered Bank

China's renminbi will one day soon be a major global currency, quoted on markets around the world. It will be the currency in which much of Asian trade is denominated and a reserve asset of central banks around the world. At present, however, it is still in the midst of making several transitions, from a fixed peg to a free float; from no real foreign exchange (FX) market to one where banks and others actively trade and take positions in the CNY [the ISO 4217 currency code abbreviation for the currency of China] with forwards, swaps, and other derivative products; and from a closed to an open capital account. A lot is going on—and the pace of change is often dizzying. The challenges for the regulators are formidable. New products and changing rules inevitably affect other parts of the FX system, financial sector, and macro-economy. Multiple agencies are involved, creating coordination challenges, and, unfortunately, if ever there were a currency that was politicized, it is the renminbi, adding further complications. This chapter aims to provide a comprehensive analysis of China's currency reforms thus far, insights into the new CNY markets, both spot and forwards, and details of the concurrent reforms to China's capital account framework.

THE CNY EXCHANGE RATE REGIME

From 1994 to July 2005, the CNY was officially managed on the basis of a "managed floating exchange rate based on supply and demand."

491

FIGURE 29.1   The Standard Chartered Bank CNY Barometer. A higher reading indicates more appreciation pressure

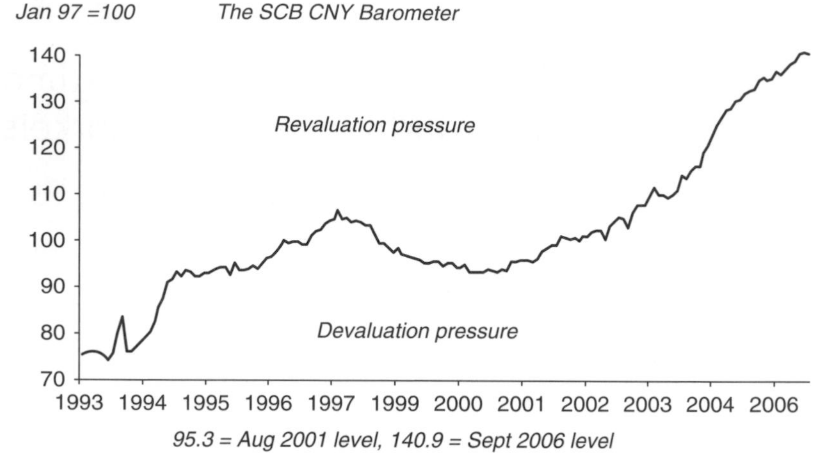

Jan 97 =100   *The SCB CNY Barometer*

95.3 = Aug 2001 level, 140.9 = Sept 2006 level

Sources: SCB Global Research and CEIC.

However, in practice, particularly after the Asian Financial Crisis in 1997–98, China's currency was pegged rigidly to the US$ at CNY8.276/US$. Trading took place only within a very narrow band, some 0.007%, around this point. Despite intense pressure from the US, China's leadership refused calls for a large CNY revaluation and backed a policy of "basic stability" for the CNY against the US$ from 2003. Domestic debate intensified in 2005, with many onshore economists calling for more flexibility in the exchange rate rather than a significant appreciation. We backed these calls, believing that in the long run, China could not run an independent monetary policy without a freer CNY and that, given the steady productivity growth, the CNY should indeed gradually appreciate against most of its trading partners' currencies. We created a Standard Chartered Bank CNY Barometer to measure the pressure on the currency—shown in Figure 29.1. Our call was that China would first move to a trading band, +/–3% against the US$, but that the authorities would only gradually test these new limits of volatility. Our call was for a move in Q2–3 2005. We did not believe that a currency basket was likely since a basket is operationally complex, and the main issue in the short term seemed to us to be the US$–CNY rate.

On July 21, 2005, China revalued the CNY 2.1% against the US$, and introduced a "new" currency regime, officially defined as "a

FIGURE 29.2 The US$–CNY and nominal effective exchange rate

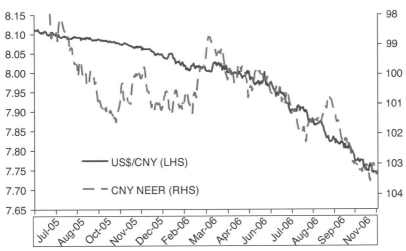

Note: The basket to which the CNY is referenced has not been released, though the main constituent currencies have been. Our CNY NEER is based on a basket of three currencies—US$, JPY, and EUR—in the ratios of 60:20:20.

Sources: Bloomberg and SCB Global Research.

managed floating exchange rate based on market supply and demand with reference to a basket of currencies." Note the similarity in the description with the previous regime. However, in practice, this one is more flexible. Overall, the CNY has appreciated moderately, by an additional 4.9% against the US$ by the end of March 2007. However, the pace of appreciation has gradually picked up, although there are still months of slow movement like March 2007. Figure 29.2 shows the path of US$–CNY, as well as that of the nominal effective exchange rate.

Officially, a basket of other currencies is used as a "reference" for the CNY. Major trading partner currencies (US$, EUR, JPY, and Won) are reportedly included, and we suspect that the basket is structured as a nominal effective exchange rate, as in Singapore. The weightings have not been disclosed, but we would imagine that the majors account for over 70%. According to People's Bank of China (PBC) governor Zhou Xiaochuan, the US$ accounts for "much less than 50%." Current practice appears to be to allow the CNY to appreciate gradually against the US$, rather than reflect the movements of the EUR, JPY or other basket constituents. We think the basket regime will probably only begin to play a significant role as firms start using

FIGURE 29.3   Intra-day trading volatility in US$–CNY, % movement from opening fixing

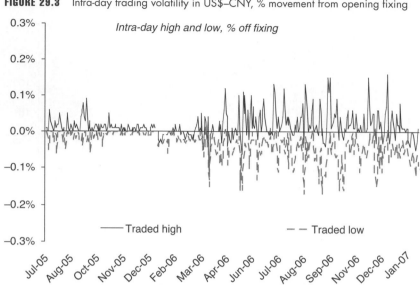

Sources: Bloomberg and SCB Global Research.

other currencies apart from the US$ for their invoicing. But we do not see the practice of invoicing using US$ getting any less common.

On any day, the CNY can move +/–0.3% against the US$, +/–3.0% against other major currencies (an initial band of +/–1.5% turned out to be unworkable because it conflicted with the US$–CNY limits). However, since that reform, inter-day US$–CNY volatility has actually been constrained to within +/–0.15% intra-day movement. This is shown in Figure 29.3. This is actually a large band—since in theory, the CNY could appreciate against US$ by 0.3% a day for weeks on end. In practice, movement is two-way, with the Central Bank intervening indirectly to manage appreciation pressure.

Much criticism has been leveled at China's exchange rate, including charges from some that it is vastly undervalued and is being "manipulated." These criticisms are partly rooted in the US–China trade deficit, which we show in Figure 29.4. In 2006, it totaled US$232 billion, according to US figures (which exaggerate the scale of the surplus since they include all exports from Hong Kong). The figure also tracks the proportion of the total US trade deficit accounted for by China—it is volatile but it has grown in recent months, and China now accounts for about one-third. This is of course politically risky.

FIGURE 29.4 The US–China goods trade deficit, US$ million and % of total US deficit

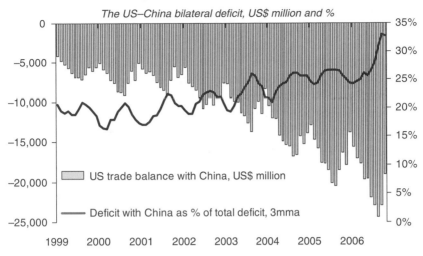

Sources: CEIC, SCB Global Research, Ahearne, BEA, IMF, and OECD.

The debate about the CNY is complex. Our views are the following. First, we do not believe the CNY is being manipulated—it was a fixed nominal peg from 1994 to July 2005, and is now making a gradual (albeit too gradual) transition toward a free float. This is being taken slowly because of the risks involved to the economy of quicker change. Gradual moves allow China's exporters to adjust, as their costs relative to their revenues rise. We agree that change could happen a little faster without catastrophic results, but we also believe that gradualism is the default position of conservative government policy, not a duplicitous strategy for manipulating export prices.

The manipulation charge is important since it has legal significance. The US Treasury is mandated by the 1988 Omnibus Trade and Competitiveness Act to report annually on the exchange rates of other countries and, in consultation with the International Monetary Fund (IMF), to consider whether countries manipulate their exchange rate for "the purposes of preventing effective balance of payments (BOP) adjustments or gaining unfair competitive advantage in international trade." (The IMF has worked hard behind the scenes to educate and encourage Beijing into moving toward a more flexible exchange rate regime, but it resists using the word manipulation or calling for a big one-off revaluation. From the IMF's perspective, it is CNY flexibility that is key, not revaluation.) Moreover, the Omnibus Act makes clear that "motivation" is the key for a manipulation finding to be made—in order to be deemed a "manipulator," China has to be judged to be trying to prevent effective balance of payments adjustments or trying to gain an unfair trade advantage. So far, the US Treasury has argued that the current framework is a necessary transitional step before greater flexibility in the near future (with which we agree). However, there is still political pressure on the US Treasury to make it determine "manipulation" on the part of China. If it were to find manipulation, the consequences are unclear. The Treasury is mandated by the 1988 Omnibus Act to initiate negotiations, in consultation with the IMF or bilaterally, to ensure that China adjusts its exchange rate to allow efficient BOP adjustment and to eliminate the unfair advantage. But that is what the Treasury has been doing for the past three years. The Act does not give the Treasury any legal means of enforcing such a change.

Second, the renminbi is not the cause of the US–China trade imbalance. Rather, this is caused by China's comparative advantage in labor-intensive manufacturing (a factory worker earns approximately US$2,000 (including benefits) a year in China and US$30,000 in the US), China's good infrastructure and attractive tax regime (where would you open a factory?), as well as the predisposition of the US consumer and government to dis-saving, and the restructuring of global supply chains. Firms that previously manufactured and exported from Taiwan, South Korea, Japan, the EU, the US, and so on are now doing so from China, meaning that others' exports to US are now being channeled through China. To understand this supply chain restructuring argument, take a look at Figure 29.5. It shows China's share of imports into the US from Asia steadily rising, to about 55%. But at the same time, Asia's share of all US imports has remained steady at about 35%. In other words, China is absorbing manufacturing capacity from Asia, the result of China acting as a low value-add assembly point for others' goods. If China is "stealing" anyone's jobs, it is Asia's, rather than the US's—and protectionist legislation against China on textiles, for example, would just forces jobs to be created in third markets like Vietnam, India, or Bangladesh.

The concentration of final assembly and other processing-related industry is critical to the overall trade surplus. China is a huge trading nation; trade accounted for US$1,763 billion, 68% of GDP in 2006. However, despite its prodigious advantages and openness, its trade surplus is relatively new. In 2006, the overall goods trade surplus was US$168.9 billion, 6.5% of GDP, while we estimate the C/A surplus at US$230 billion, 8% of GDP. These are shown in Figure 29.6. But

FIGURE 29.5 Imports into the US from Asia and China. Total imports from Asia as a % of total US imports, and China imports into the US as % of total imports from Asia

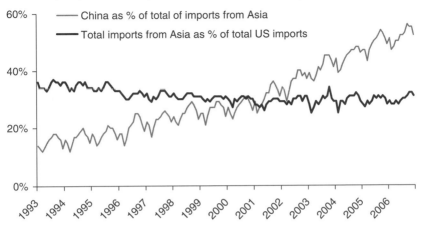

Sources: CEIC and SCB Global Research.

now take a look at Figure 29.7 on page 498, which shows China's overall trade surplus, as well as the balances in the processing and non-processing trade sectors. Processing has accounted for all of the last few years' surpluses; in 2006 the processing surplus was US$187.5 billion, 7.2% of GDP. China's own trade account was in deficit to the tune of US$18 billion in 2006, –0.7% of GDP. Processing trade is

FIGURE 29.6 China's trade surplus (US$ million and % of GDP)

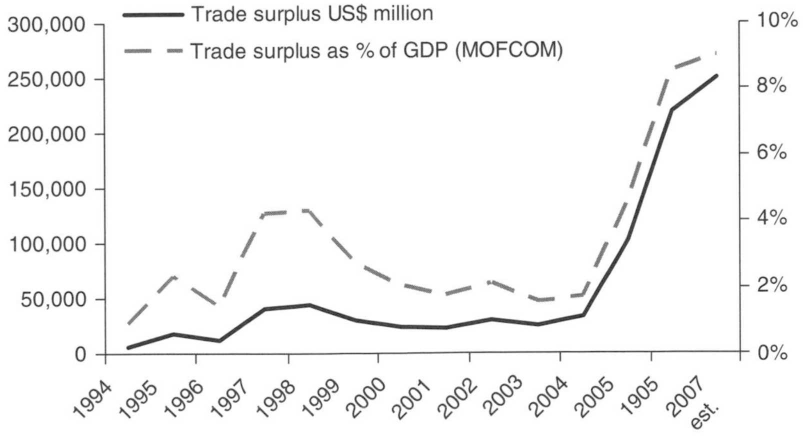

Sources: SCB Global Research and CEIC.

FIGURE 29.7   China's overall trade account, as well as processing and non-processing balances (% of GDP)

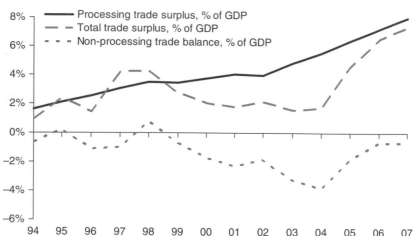

Note: Includes SBC 2007 forecasts.

Sources: SCB Global Research and CEIC.

naturally surplus generating, and as more capacity is transferred from Asia and so on, China's overall surplus will get bigger.

CNY appreciation will not do much to solve this surplus—since not only will it make China's exports more expensive, but it will also increase the buying power of the CNY in Asia, thus making the inputs, whether it is raw materials or computer components, cheaper. Our research suggests that a 20% appreciation of the CNY would only add less than 3% to the price of the average PRC-processed good. As a result, many in Beijing now believe that CNY appreciation has to be part of a portfolio approach to solving the trade surpluses, with higher taxes and other measures also used to start discouraging low value-added processing industries from concentrating in China. These measures also include opening up the capital/financial account on the outflow side, and closing it down further on the inflow side, changes that we will deal with in the final section of this chapter. However, these measures are currently being implemented too slowly to make much of a difference—and we expect the trade surplus to continue to climb in both dollar and percentage of GDP terms until at least 2009.

These arguments are well-known, and yet some US politicians continue to push for legislative action against China. One bill that was finally shelved in 2006 was the Schumer–Graham tariff bill. This bill, sponsored by two senators, to implement tariffs of 27.5% against Chinese imports would have, (1) primarily hurt US consumers and US corporates as their costs were hiked; and (2) be judged illegal. International trade law dictates that World Trade Organization (WTO) members are not allowed to implement tariffs that are not notified at the time of entry into the WTO. However, given the pent-up concern over China in Washington, DC, other more workable legislative proposals are being drawn up. One idea is to increase the ease with which anti-dumping tariffs could be applied against Chinese imports. Our third belief is that from a strategic political perspective, the CNY is a red herring for the US. There is little means, apart from crude protectionist (and likely illegal in terms of international trade law) legislation to force Beijing to move faster. Besides, given our analysis of the basic reasons for the US deficit with China, CNY appreciation—even by 20%—is not likely to help. For this reason, we believe that focus on issues such as subsidies, intellectual property rights protection as well as market access, where the US not only has the moral high-ground but also legal WTO-compliant tools for action, would be a more fruitful course for policy.

Fourth, no one really knows by how much the CNY is undervalued: various economic models provide different answers, depending on various assumptions about what the capital account should be, trade elasticities, and so on. Recent studies conclude that any single estimate of undervaluation is suspect, and we might add that all these studies are based on historical data—foreign currency markets move daily on new economic data, sentiment, as well as political news. Given the uncertainty surrounding the equilibrium rate, and the fate of the US$ in the near future, it is only prudent for Beijing to move gradually. One obstacle to faster movement was FX market infrastructure—and tools to allow corporate China to hedge their exposures to a newly flexible currency. Much of this infrastructure is now in place, a subject to which we now turn. Much of the needed infrastructure was created in 2006, providing one of the planks for slightly faster appreciation since Q3 2006.

TRADING: CNY AND FX SPOT ONSHORE

The China Foreign Exchange Trade System (CFETS), otherwise known as the National Interbank Funding Centre (NIFC), hosts China's market for FX trading and clearing. It was established in April 1994 as a subsidiary of the PBC and works closely with the State

Administration of Foreign Exchange (SAFE, which reports directly to the PBC, as well as to the State Council) on FX matters. The CFETS FX platform replaced a nationwide system of "swap" centers where trading firms and others in need of FX conversion could trade spot. There are currently two distinct spot trading platforms supported by CFETS. One hosts CNY currency pairs, US$–CNY, JPY/CNY, EUR/CNY, HKD/CNY, and GBP/CNY, while the other supports eight FX currency pairs (on which more below). These two markets may be merged using the FX pairs' platform late in 2007. The FX inter-bank market operates alongside the other three inter-bank markets: those for bonds, inter-bank borrowing (the CHIBOR market), and one nascent platform for commercial drafts, all also managed by the CFETS/NIBFC (the two organizations appear to be co-terminus). The CFETS FX system operates as a membership exchange with a nation-wide real-time trading system. The majority of CFETS members are banks, but since August 2005, NBFIs and other companies with large FX conversion needs have been allowed to apply for membership, allowing them to bypass banks for their FX needs. Members make back-to-back (that is, anonymous) quotes on the platform, and there is real-time order matching. The clearing function is integrated, so members get a centralized, two-way, netting and clearing system.

In addition to the CFETS platform for the CNY spot, an OTC market was established on January 4, 2006, and now operates for the five CNY pairs. Both markets now trade from 9:30 am, to 5:30 pm. CFETS offers members centralized order matching, while the over-the-counter (OTC) market involves members agreeing to prices and volumes on a bilateral basis via the phone, Reuters, and so on, although the final deal confirmation has to be also made on the CFETS platform. The centralized CFETS market is more efficient, but it is also more expensive. The CFETS trading system collects a 0.03% and 0.01% fee (from non-market-makers and market-makers respectively), based on the net daily traded volume from all members. However, the CFETS OTC market fee is only 0.001% per deal on both sides, a significant saving. High fees reduce the incentives for speculation, but also serve to restrict liquidity in the spot market. As a result, the large majority of trading—perhaps 90%—currently takes place on the OTC market.

The sole purpose of the previous CFETS FX platform was designed to suck up excess FX to ensure the US$–CNY fixed exchange rate was protected. Under the old system, an importer was required to surrender all his FX revenues to a bank, and the bank was then required to surrender most of its FX to the CFETS market (only being allowed to maintain a small in-house FX position authorized by the SAFE). The CFETS was the main counter-party. Traders did not know who they were dealing with, even if everyone knew it was indirectly the PBC. In sum, CFETS was not a trading platform at all. It began its transition to a market in the 1990s, but still has some way to go. From January 2006, the PBC no longer acts as the sole market-maker on CFETS. Instead, licensed commercial banks make markets in CNY spot. Twenty-three bank market-makers are willing to provide two-way prices and liquidity for the market. The Bank of China (BOC), since it is the predominant foreign trade bank, probably still accounts for the majority of trading. Officially, the PBC is not active in the CFETS market, but given that its FX reserves continue to grow it evidently must be using market-makers as its agents for its own operations.

CFETS trading volume has grown rapidly. In 2004, according to official figures, US$209 billion was traded, some US$829 million a day. CFETS ceased publicly releasing trading volume in July 2005, since the daily trading volume was recognized as a decent proxy for net FX inflows into China, and this information was determined to be too sensitive to release. Volumes are now a closely guarded secret. The vast majority of transactions are US$–CNY (some 98% in 2004) since the dollar is (1) the currency in which most of China's trade and investment is denominated; and (2) domestic banks have traditionally booked non-US$–CNY trades offshore and then executed the US$–CNY leg onshore because of the lack of onshore liquidity in non-US$–CNY pairs.

Each day's US$–CNY "fixing" (the opening price) is calculated by CFETS and announced at 9.15 am each trading day. The fixing price is officially calculated as the weighted average of bids submitted by the market-makers during 9.00–9.15 am. Our trader makes his or her bids on the basis of the previous day's trading, as well as global market developments. The weighting method has not been disclosed. However, the bid by the BOC is likely to be the most influential, given its dominance of the onshore FX market. Trading currently usually takes place in a band on either side of the fixing, although in early 2007, trading began taking place only below fixing. Clearly then, the fixing is a crucial aspect of this regime and the pace of CNY appreciation, but the method behind it is not quite transparent.

The CNY spot settlement convention is now T+2, although we can offer clients T+0 and T+1 if required. The PBC limits the bid–offer spread that market-makers can offer to 1% of the market price. Market practice varies within this bound. As long as the bank has a limit for CFETS' counter-parties we can trade, otherwise banks have to sign separate counter-party agreements. For the centralized CFETS CNY market (and the CFETS FX pairs market), the PBC assumes all counter-party risk, meaning such documents are not required.

CFETS is the favored platform, but it has its issues. Much debate has taken place over the relative merits of the CFETS platform, other platforms, and OTC trading. The CFETS system is at present the only centralized platform upon which FX transactions can be made in China—whereas in other FX markets, banks and firms have a choice of other systems like Electronic Broking Service (EBS) or Reuters, and so on, which offer lower transaction costs, tighter dealer spreads, and greater transparency. At present, the PBC appears ambitious to ensure that China's FX market operates on just one platform where trades can be monitored, rather than allowing them to become dispersed. The current upside to the PBC of its management—the ability to regulate trading and pricing—evidently outweighs the problem of the PBC taking on counter-party risk and the administrative impediments to efficiency. Advisors to the China Foreign Exchange Trade System (CFETS), as well as domestic banks, have lobbied for greater independence for CFETS, as well as greater member involvement, and lower fees.

CNY/Yen trading began in 1995, and in April 2002 CNY/Euro trading began in China. On May 18, 2005, eight new "FX currency pairs" (EUR/US$, AUD/US$, GBP/US$, US$/JPY, US$/CAD, US$/CHF, US$/HKD, and EUR/JPY) were introduced on a new, distinct Reuters-designed CFETS platform. Banks trade with a minimum volume of US$100,000 per trade. The system offers two methods for dealing: (1) a one-click and deal method (in which one clicks on an anonymous quote, and then confirms and deals); and (2) where an order can be placed on the system, which is then automatically matched. Bid–offer spreads are considerably narrower compared to the larger margins that could be theoretically offered on an OTC basis. Many banks, however, tend to square their positions internally and offshore where liquidity is better. In the CNY market, each market-maker faces counter-party risk on OTC trading. However, in the FX pairs market (as in the centralized CFETS market), the PBC assumes all counter-party risk and trading is anonymous. One reason for this was to allow all banks access to the market: many large banks do not have credit lines for many of China's city commercial banks and cooperatives because of their relatively high levels of risk. Those banks that do agree to deal with them charge large margins to cope with the risk. The CFETS FX pairs market allows these small banks to trade FX and to get the same price as everyone else. This system does create counter-party risk for the PBC.

THE CNY ONSHORE AND OFFSHORE FORWARDS MARKETS

If the renminbi is to become a flexible currency, then corporates need the ability to hedge it. Forwards and swaps are among the simplest means of doing this. Beginning in 1997, the PBC allowed forwards trading to take place onshore and ultimately, seven local banks were able to transact forward contracts on an OTC basis though there was little demand. The PBC provided guidance on pricing and bank clients required proof that they needed to hedge for trade purposes. Foreign banks were also allowed to offer these products in theory, but the annual FX trading volume requirement (US$20 billion) for a license was much larger than any of them could meet. After the AFC, the US$–CNY exchange rate rigidified, and there was little point of hedging in such an environment, so the volume of forwards trading fell even further.

On August 9, 2005, the PBC allowed the trading of CNY forwards contracts in the inter-bank market by banks with CNY spot and derivative licenses. Qualified banks may also apply for a license to offer forward agreements to their clients. After six months trading of forwards, the same regulations allowed the same banks to trade FX swaps (see below). Trading of forwards is permitted on the inter-bank market between license holders, and between licensed banks and their customers, as long as the latter have an underlying trade or investment need for the position.

Readers familiar with how a forward contract works should skip the following paragraph, which explains how a forward contract works. The reason why a forward outright transaction works to eliminate FX risk is that its price is determined by the interest rate differential between the two currencies. Consider doing all of the following transactions simultaneously.

(a) Borrow US$100 for one year, starting from spot value date, at an interest of, say, 5%.
(b) Sell those dollars and buy yen for value spot, which is, say, US$/JP¥100.

(c) Deposit the yen for one year, starting from the spot value date, at a rate of, say, 3%.

(d) Sell forward now the yen principal and interest that mature in one year's time into dollars.

The market will usually ensure that the forward (that is, step "d") is priced so that these simultaneous transactions neither generate a profit nor a loss. In a normal transaction in the international markets, a "forward outright" is comprised of two separate trades—a spot trade and a "forward swap," put together to produce a net future FX sale or purchase. Say a customer wants to buy €10 million in 12 months from its bank, using US$. In order to limit the bank's risk, the bank's side of the transaction is structured in two parts. The bank's spot desk sells the €10 million today at the spot rate. At the same time, the bank's forward desk engages in a forward swap contract, buying €10 million today in the money market and agreeing to sell it back at the forward date. The net result of the transaction is a €10 million sale to the customer at T+12 months and the bank's only exposure is the interest differential between US$ and EUR—it does not care what happens to US$/EUR. This is because the bank has borrowed US$ to sell EUR on the spot desk, and so must pay US$ interest, but at the same time, it has bought EUR on the forward desk and thus receives interest on the EUR deposit. The forward price covers this differential and also includes a margin. The result of the combination of the two trades is a net sale of €10 million to the customer in 12 months.

Onshore forwards in China are deliverable or non-deliverable. Onshore CNY forwards are mostly traded with clients on a deliverable basis; but non-deliverable ones can be traded too, and are more popular on the inter-bank market. Onshore forward tenor is not limited as long as the underlying transaction extends to this period and there is market liquidity (for which there is for up to one year). The onshore forwards market is legally based on CEFTS documentation, though many foreign banks, including Standard Chartered, also use international agreement materials to supplement these legal terms. At present, CNY forwards are booked on CFETS on a system similar to that used for booking OTC spot deals. All transactions are charged 0.001% on the volume on each side.

Trading has been dominated by a small number of banks, including the foreign banks such as Standard Chartered. But the forward is not as liquid as was previously expected/hoped. One onshore trader's estimate is that combined forward and swap turnover was around US$1 billion a day in Q1 2007, and most of the quotations are on the right-hand side. The lack of liquidity is explained by three factors. First, if a corporate wants to buy US$ forward the trade is cheaper offshore in the non-deliverable forwards (NDF) market, which was pricing in a 4–5% per annum appreciation for much of 2006. In contrast, the onshore forwards market is priced off interest rate differentials, which for much of 2006 and up to the time of writing in March 2007 were in effect pricing in a 2.5% appreciation. Second, given the government's keenness to manage expectations, most exporters expect CNY appreciation of 4%, maybe 5%, and since few expect more volatility than this given the governments commitment to ensure stability, there are few incentives for buying forwards. After all, forwards and swaps, and so on, are for coping with risk—and to a large extent, the authorities are still managing this for corporates. Third, documentation can also be an administrative challenge, given the need to provide proof of trade or investment transactions for each and every transaction.

An offshore NDF market can be traded freely by offshore entities. However, domestic entities are not allowed to transact there, and as a result it is primarily a market for speculation on CNY appreciation and/or hedging for offshore corporate entities. Onshore banks may not market or broker NDFs. Domestic firms with offshore entities can of course transact NDFs offshore through those subsidiaries. The spread between the offshore CNY NDF and onshore CNY forward narrowed and disappeared after the opening of the onshore forward market in Q4 2005, as Figure 29.8 shows. While the January 2006 rules banned banks and corporates from hedging offshore, market-makers were allowed to do a spot transaction to hedge a forward transaction onshore—something that was not previously allowed. This move allowed banks to effectively hedge their exposures by structuring "real" forwards (that is, a spot and a forward swap). All banks on the CFETS system must operate a long US$ position on their combined book (both spot and forwards), which has meant that interest rate parity sets prices in the onshore forwards market. In contrast, prices in the offshore NDF market are set based on appreciation expectations.

Liquidity in the onshore forwards and swap markets has grown steadily. However, there are still limits to its growth. We look for a number of rule changes that would serve to boost trading and liquidity. For one, banks were, as of the time of writing, not yet

FIGURE 29.8   Prices of onshore and offshore 12-month CNY forwards

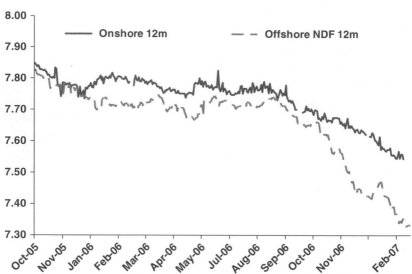

Sources: Bloomberg and SCB Global Research.

permitted to offer FX swaps to their corporate clients—although they were free to transact among themselves. At least one FX swap between the Central Bank and large commercial banks took place in November 2005, and more after are suspected. In mid-2006, local banks started FX swaps among themselves, primarily involving international banks swapping FX they had borrowed from offshore with domestic banks who have surplus onshore CNY. Second, borrowing limits—there are limits to a foreign bank's ability to borrow from (1) offshore (through the foreign debt quota) and (2) the inter-bank market (1.5 times the banks' registered branch capital). Once this position is maxed out, the spot/forward desk has no more access to funds to finance its position. Relaxation of this would aid forward and swap liquidity.

RE-REGULATING THE CAPITAL ACCOUNT

China's capital account is gradually being opened up and restricted at the same time. Since the early 1990s, the process has followed a number of general principles: first open up inflows, then outflows; first relax restrictions on long-term capital movements, then restrictions on short-term ones; first loosen controls on overseas fundraising, then allow non-residents to raise funds in China; first relax restrictions on financial institutions, then on non-financial institutions; and so on. However, in recent years, with CNY appreciation pressures, a whole swathe of new rules has also closed down routes for inward capital movement. As anyone who has attempted to do business across the border knows, capital account regulations change regularly and sometimes get very complicated. Here we provide a short history of capital account liberalization and outline the situation at the time of writing. We divide the section into two parts: the first looking at foreign currency into renminbi transactions; the second the other way.

Foreign Currency into CNY

Retail—until February 1, 2007, a non-resident could exchange FX into CNY up to US$50,000 a month (so US$600,000 a year), and a resident could do US$10,000 a (working) day (so US$2.6 million a year). You could do this over the bank counter. After this date, everyone could only exchange US$50,000 each year. The new rule will be enforced since each bank has been connected to the SAFE's real-time FX monitoring system, which records each transaction against one's identity card or passport. The only obvious hole in these rules is the one that allows non-residents to exchange FX funds into CNY for the purposes of buying a property. This allows one to convert up to 100% of the sale price, and the CNY funds must be remitted direct to the seller. There are lots of document requirements, so it will not be easy to get around.

Why did the SAFE and the China Banking Regulatory Commission (CSRC) make such a big change? They believed that "hot" money was coming in via this route—and they wanted it to stop. The statistics bear this fear out. Figure 29.9 shows growth of all household savings deposits at PRC financial institutions—which has held steady at about 15–20% for the last five years. The other line is growth in household FX savings, which shows a precipitous deceleration of growth. Holding FX has become costly. In addition, remittances from offshore—often we suspect PRC money sent abroad in the 1980 to 1990s for safe-keeping—have been large.

Corporate—in 1994, foreign-invested firms were allowed to open foreign exchange accounts, and in 1997 qualified domestic firms were allowed to follow. Thanks to the seven major adjustments that have occurred since 1994, the current rules stand as follows. FX receipts derived from trade or non-trade business can be converted into CNY without any restrictions—no pre-approval from the State

FIGURE 29.9   Growth in all households deposits and FX deposits (y/y%)

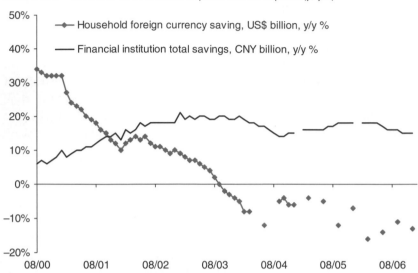

Sources: SCB Global Research and CEIC.

Administration of Foreign Exchange (SAFE) is required. For firms with FX spending less than 80% of their FX revenues, they may now keep up to 50% of their FX revenues in FX. Firms with more than 80% may keep 80%. New firms can keep US$200,000 worth of FX revenues for their first year's business. The SAFE also regulates the time period in which "excess" FX can be kept: it was recently extended to 90 days. The hope here is obviously to encourage firms to keep more of their FX, thus releasing pressure on the SAFE and the build-up of China's FX reserves.

In April 2005, SAFE required that export receipts in excess of US$200,000 (or any remittances for unclear purposes) go first into a special settling account in order to be properly examined before being released to the exporter. This appeared to be an effort to check that exporters were not exaggerating their export revenues as a means of importing extra FX into China. Funds from this account can be remitted out of the country freely, but if they are to be converted into CNY, the SAFE requires more supporting evidence than normal to approve the conversion.

If a corporate wishes to convert FX for a capital account purpose (for example, an investment project) the conversion is subject to the bank's approval, a power granted the banks by SAFE in 2002. If the conversion is over US$200,000 in value, the applicant has to explain the purpose of the payment. Case-by-case SAFE approval is not required.

Starting in 2003, with CNY revaluation expectations on the rise, many corporates increased their foreign currency borrowing and then converted into CNY. As a result, SAFE reintroduced controls on FX conversion. In June 2004, SAFE banned firms from converting domestic FX loans into CNY without an underlying export transaction.

Portfolio—in 2002, China introduced the Qualified Foreign Institutional Investor (QFII) framework that allows international banks and fund management firms to bring in capital to invest in Chinese equities, bonds, and money market instruments. Applications must be made to both the SAFE and CSRC for a QFII quota. There are restrictions on qualification requirements, operational procedures, and outbound remittance of funds. Curbs on early repatriation are particularly tight. For instance, a closed-end fund manager has to wait three years before beginning to remit funds out of China, and each remittance must be less than 20% of the total. The total QFII quota was recently enlarged from US$4 billion to US$10 billion as of end March 2007. However, the expansion of the QFII quota has been affected by concerns about increasing the FX reserves. SAFE director Hu Xiaolian said in February 2006 that SAFE would like to shorten the lock-up period for keeping funds onshore from one year for funds—we understand that could probably be shortened to three months. QFIIs have other complaints with restrictions, but liquidity is a big one, so this is undoubtedly positive.

Banks—the authorities have moved to restrict China's foreign currency debt build-up. In June 2004, the SAFE introduced regulations that set a quota on how much FX funds each foreign retail bank could borrow from offshore to lend to customers. Such borrowing is defined as short-term foreign debt. (There is also a medium- and long-term quota, and this is governed by the National Development and Reform Commission. However, the banks have difficulties in using this for reasons we won't go into here.) Foreign banks have had an incentive to bring funds in from their branches offshore for a number of reasons, including mismatches between large demand for US$ loans and limited onshore US$ deposits and costs. Loans are not the only problem. The banks' foreign debt quota also includes FX deposits made by non-resident individuals and firms (that is, firms without legal status on the Mainland). SAFE has made some efforts to ease the foreign banks' discomfort. For instance, in early 2005, SAFE allowed foreign banks to apply for a single country-wide quota (rather than individual branch quotas), which could be allocated around the country as and when needed. Second, it appears possible that SAFE may decide that non-resident firms' FX deposits should no longer be counted as part of the quota, but come under a separate regime. This would be positive, opening up more space for FX loans. However, in practice, the situation has got tougher for foreign banks. In March 2007, SAFE ruled that the short-term quota for all banks was to be reduced by some 40%.

CNY into Foreign Currency

Corporate—in 2005, the CNY borrowing of Foreign Investment Enterprises (FIEs) in China came under tighter control, also as a consequence of SAFE's efforts to constrain the growth of foreign debt. SAFE has used FIEs' investment "gap" as a means of achieving this. This is the gap between a firm's "total investment amount" (an aspirational amount for all its investment in China recorded at the company's formation) and its registered capital. On average, the former tends to be two to three times the later, but some companies have no "gap" at all. Under the regime instituted in April 2005, borrowers were under a duty to register any onshore borrowing with SAFE, who would then check if the firm still had enough "gap" to accommodate it. The lending bank then had a duty to check the firm had approval. After new regulations were released in December 2005, this framework changed. The client is not under obligation to get approval from the local SAFE, and the lending bank is only required to report in a timely fashion the loan to SAFE. The "gap" is not an issue now at the time of the loan. However, if the borrower defaults, the "gap" becomes an issue. The lending bank would call upon the offshore parent to deliver on its guarantee. The borrower would then have to go to SAFE to register the foreign debt, at which point the firm may be fined by it. The challenge then arises for the bank, in that it receives foreign currency from the offshore parent that it needs to convert and SAFE may not permit the conversion. This means that the lending bank faces a nonperforming loan (NPL) on its CNY book (not good) and repayment in a foreign currency that it cannot convert (also not good). Thus, the lending bank has to bear this in mind when doing the initial credit assessment of the borrower.

Portfolio—at present, Chinese citizens and firms may not freely convert CNY for the purposes of investing in overseas investments.

However, a number of holes have been opened up in this restriction. A few large Chinese insurers (including China Ping An) have permission to invest US$2 billion overseas, but so far these are placements and insurers are not permitted to trade. They are reportedly waiting for new regulations to expand their investment ambit out of US Treasuries and H-shares. In March 2006, the National Social Security Fund (NSSF) opened an official account with the Hong Kong Stock Exchange and was reported to have started buying equities in 2006.

Retail—Chinese citizens can now hold FX in cash, sell FX to banks, and buy and sell between foreign currencies onshore. Restrictions on them converting CNY into FX have been relaxed, allowing US$50,000 a year to be freely converted. The bank and securities regulators have also authorized the retail Qualified Domestic Institutional Investor (QDII) scheme, in which some 20 institutions have been authorized to raise some US$19 billion through retail fund offerings, which can then be taken offshore and invested in fixed and equity-linked instruments. Popular response to these offerings was initially poor, with one concern being that with the CNY appreciating, any non-CNY investment could be costly, and the second being the domestic stock market that tripled in size over June 2003–February 2007. However, a number of banks, led by Standard Chartered Bank, have offered QDII products with CNY-appreciation protection, linked to structured notes that are themselves linked to equity instruments, and these have proved popular.

Table 29.1 shows our estimates of the potential outflows that could come out of China over 2007–08 as efforts to support outflows are accelerated. We expect some US$75 billion to leave China over 2006–07.

Investment—in previous years, SAFE has used a national quota to limit the amount of outward Foreign Direct Investment (FDI).

TABLE 29.1 SCB estimates of potential outflows from China over 2007–08 (US$ billion)

Potential official outflows—SCB est., 2006–08, US$ billion		
	Current funds	Potential for outflow (starting date)
Insurance companies	220	44 (2006)
NSSF	32	5 to 10 (2006-07)
Provincial pensions	55	12 (2008)
QDII	12	12 (2007)
Total	319	73–78 (2006-08)

Sources: SCB Global Research and CEIC.

However, this system has been steadily reformed, beginning in 2001. From October 2001, enterprises in Zhejiang province could freely purchase FX for outward investments, and to freely use any profits generated by these investments. This policy was gradually extended to other provinces. SAFE scrapped the quota for outward FDI in 2006 and said it would establish a "Going-Out Fund" to support enterprises investing overseas. There has been no hint as to scale or scope of business of this fund though. A delayed registration system (as opposed to pre-deal approval) is being instituted nationwide as of year-end 2006. Official FX flows are US$10–15 billion a year, but some analysts suspect that more funds exit informally.

Profit remittance—from 2004, SAFE has allowed qualified multi-nationals to conduct more flexible FX funding management within the group across borders. In particular, approved domestic units of the multinational corporations (MNCs) can lend FX loans to their overseas units, a major breakthrough. In October 2005, SAFE began an experiment for MNCs headquartered in Pudong, Shanghai. If successful, these reforms could be nationalized. Qualified MNCs were allowed to use after-tax profits to make FX loans to overseas entities, permitted to open offshore accounts, and the procedures for remittances for non-trade items were simplified.

SECTION 6

SERVICES

CHAPTER 30

China's Legal System and the Financial Industry: The Past 30 Years

Wu Zhipan

Vice-President, Peking University,
Director, Financial Law Institute, Peking University

A full 30 years have passed since the start of China's economic reforms in 1978. While China has learned from the experience of other countries and entered the general flow of international systems, it has also pursued a uniquely Chinese path. The process, one of exploration and creativity, has been something our forefathers could scarcely have imagined. China's legal system has made tremendous advances in line with the speed with which China's financial markets have developed. Looking back over these 30 years with regard to the financial industry, it is useful to summarize the experience in China, not only for the international community in understanding our systems, but for ourselves in order to encourage ongoing improvements in our legal system.

HOW CHINA'S FINANCIAL LEGAL SYSTEM DEVELOPED

China's legal system with regard to the financial industry has developed in step with Reform and Opening to the Outside World, and can be divided into three major stages. The first was from 1978 to 1992. Reform and Opening policies began in 1978 with the process being likened to "feeling for the stones with your feet as you cross the river." This earthy description was further clarified by the phrase, "taking a planned economy as primary and market adjustments as supplementary." As for those issues that could not be determined through debate, we simply carried forward with the understanding that the path was going to be tough. "We should not question whether the cat is white or black—it's a good cat so long as it catches mice" said Deng Xiaoping. We broke through old restraints by emphasizing actual results, and by encouraging the idea of moving forward and growing.

During this period, we promulgated such laws as the "Law on Wholly Foreign-invested Enterprises," the "Law on Chinese–Foreign Equity Joint Ventures," and "the Civil Procedure Law (Provisional)." These provided a certain legal backing with regard to the establishment of branches of foreign financial institutions in China, as well as litigation involving financial institutions.

The drafting of the Constitution in 1982 was a momentous event in China. The Constitution stipulated that a planned economy would be carried out on the basis of a system of socialist public ownership, but clarified that the national economy could be safeguarded by using "overall balancing" that employed a planned economy but was "supplemented by market adjustments" in appropriate proportion. The Constitution allowed foreign enterprises and other economic entities or individuals to invest in China, and allowed them to engage in a variety of "economic cooperation" activities with Chinese enterprises or other economic entities. At the same time, the government raised "socialist legal principles" that included "having laws that could be followed and requiring that laws be followed, enforcing them with severity and assuring that infringement be corrected." It was understood that in order to develop "socialist democracy," it was necessary to strengthen the socialist *legal* system, and make democracy "systematized" and "legalized."

Not long after this, China's government raised the concept that a socialist economy was a "planned *product* economy," established on the foundation of a system of public ownership, but consciously based on and employing the rules of "value." In response to this, China promulgated the "General Principles of the Civil Law" in 1986. These Principles revised regulations regarding "enterprise legal persons" and regarding "rights and duties." In 1988, the Constitution itself was amended, and the revisions clearly stipulated that "privately managed economic activities" could be considered supplementary to a system of socialist public ownership. They also stipulated that "usage rights to land could be transferred, in accordance with laws and regulations." New provisions now provided legal backing for the ability of commercial banks to expand their offerings: from offering only credit loans they could offer mortgage loans as well. The new laws and regulations provided the legal backing to protect and properly adjust civil relations and legal rights between citizens and legal persons.

The second stage of China's legal reform was from 1992 to 2001. After 1989, China experienced a period of economic stagnation including decreased international investment and trade. In 1992, however, Deng Xiaoping went on his "Tour to the South," which included public declarations on national policy. He emphasized that "a planned economy is not equivalent to socialism, for capitalism also has planning. A market economy is not equivalent to capitalism, for socialism also has markets. Both planning and markets are simply economic measures." This line of reasoning pointed in the direction of a socialist *market* economy. We were able to break through the conceptual restraints that had plagued us for so long, and to establish the goal of setting up a "socialist market economy" system.

During this period, at the third Plenum of the fourteenth National Congress of the Communist Party, the Central Committee of the Chinese Communist Party, passed a "Decision Regarding Issues Concerning the Establishment of a Socialist Market Economic System," which raised China's actual experience to the level of theory or policy. China formally entered the World Trade Organization (WTO) in 1999, which indicated that the development of the country's socialist market economy had reached a new stage. China's government now brought forth the precepts "Govern the Country According to Law," and "Establish a Socialist Country Ruled by Law." These precepts were to be the underlying principles for governing the country and assuring the growth and development of its socialist market economic system. Laws promulgated over the next few years were drafted in accord with this thinking. They included the "Company Law" in 1993, the revised (and unified) "Contract Law" in 1998, the "Law Against Unfair Competition" of 1998, the "People's Bank of China Law," "Commercial Banking Law," "Financial Instruments Law," and "Guarantee Law," all in 1995. In 1988, China promulgated the "Securities Law," and revised those parts of the Criminal Code that dealt with economic crimes, as well as revising the "Criminal Procedure Law."

It is worth noting in particular that a 1993 revision to the Constitution specified that, "China is in the initial stages of socialism," and, "the country is implementing a socialist market economy." Then, 1999 revisions to the Constitution went a step further in clarifying that under the conditions of a socialist market economy, the country's basic economic system and system of allocation of resources required that, "at the initial stages of socialism, the country must adhere to a basic policy of public ownership, but supplemented by a diversified ownership system. Both develop the basic economic system together. [We must] adhere to [the principle of] distribution to each according to his labor, but allow diversified distribution systems to coexist at the same time."

These provisions in the Constitution clarified the road ahead for the establishment and growth of China's socialist market economic structure, by providing a firm constitutional foundation and firm legal guarantees.

The third stage in China's evolving legal system dated from 2002 to the present. In October of 2003, at the third Plenum of the National Party Congress, the Party passed a "Decision by the Central Committee of the Communist Party on Certain Questions Concerning Improvement of the Socialist Market Economic Structure." This then became a new indicator of economic structural reform in China. With yet another revision of the Constitution at the second meeting of the tenth National People's Congress held in March 2004, it was clear that China's legal system under a socialist market economy had entered a new, third, stage in development. In this stage, with ongoing Reform and Opening and with constant improvements in China's socialist market economic structure, China's legal system also moved forward, as described below.

From 2002 to 2004, the National People's Congress and its Standing Committee promulgated laws that had to do either directly or indirectly with the financial industry. These included: an explanation of regulations regarding credit cards contained in the "Criminal Law" of 2004, and (all as revised in 2004) an "Electronic Signature Law," "Auction Law," "Foreign Trade Law," "Treasury Bonds Law," "Land Management Law," "Securities Law" (minor 2004 amendment), "Company Law" (minor 2004 amendment), and so on.

In 2005, the National People's Congress again revised the "Individual Income Tax Law," the "Company Law," and the "Securities Law." In 2006 it promulgated the "Anti-Money Laundering Law," the "Notarization Law," "Auditing Law" (2006 revision), the "Bank Regulatory Administration Law" (2006 revision), the "Partnership Enterprise Law" (2006 revision), the "Enterprise Bankruptcy Law" (2006 revision), and so on. In 2007 it promulgated the "Property Law," the "Labor Contract Law," and another revision of the

"Individual Income Tax Law." The above noted that major laws relating to the financial industry played a major role in guiding and guaranteeing the reform and growth of the financial system.

CHINA'S FINANCIAL LEGAL SYSTEM

Several aspects should be noted as preface to understanding China's financial system reforms. First is the tremendous change underway in China's entire economic system, especially the changes in economic management systems. These include, for example, the devolution of previously held centralized powers to subordinate entities, the ability of the market to affect more economic activities, the increasingly liberal policies with regard to opening to the outside world, and the attracting of overseas capital—including that from Hong Kong, Macao, and Taiwan—into Chinese markets. Second is the speed with which the economy has been growing, which has required the support of large amounts of capital while at the same time requiring risk management and guarantees should risk ever materialize. Third is that the goal of reform has been not merely to raise efficiency, but to give consideration to fairness, to realize an economy in which people are moderately well-off and content, and one that results in sustainable growth that benefits society.

The underlying background to China's reforms has meant that the approach our legal system takes with respect to the financial industry is different from those of other countries. China has been accumulating its own successful experience as it moves ahead on its distinct path of legal system development.

Financial management, in particular, has gone from centralization to devolution of authority. One of the important components of financial system reform in China has been a transition from excessively concentrated powers to an appropriate "devolution." This can be seen in the laws and regulations that have been passed. For example, in 1987, the "Provisional Measures on Bank Administration" did not allow regional governments to set up commercial banks. This gradually changed as the Merchants Bank and the Shenzhen Development Bank were authorized in Shekou and Shenzhen. The experimental start of regional commercial banks had begun. By 1995, when the "Commercial Bank Law" was promulgated, there was already no question about setting up regional or local commercial banks—the only question was how much registered capital they were required to have. A national commercial bank required registered capital of RMB1 billion and its branches' operating capital could not exceed 60% of the bank's capital. To establish a regional municipal commercial bank required registered capital of RMB100 million, while in farming villages, the registered capital required was RMB5 million. Regional commercial banks could set up branches and operate only within their own region, and were not allowed to cross over jurisdictions to engage in business.

The devolution of powers relating to management of the financial system was also demonstrated by the fact that jurisdiction over the financial, securities, and insurance industries that had been concentrated in the People's Bank of China (PBC), was gradually separated into three different departments. In 1987, when China promulgated the "Regulations on Administration of the Banking Industry in the PRC," regulation of the banking, securities, trust, and investment industries was addressed in one body of law. The many provisions regarding the securities industry drafted in the early 1990s by the PBC, and its Shanghai and Shenzhen branches maintained the PBC as the primary entity in charge. The PBC and its branches remained in charge of securities as well as currency, and the situation was still described as "combining two into one," as opposed to splitting out one into two. Only with the drafting of the "Commercial Bank Law" of 1995 and the "Securities Law" of 1998 were the two regulatory regimes separated out in terms of legislation.

China then established three separate institutions—the China Securities Regulatory Commission (CSRC), the China Insurance Regulatory Commission, and the China Bank Regulatory Commission—for specific and separate oversight and regulation of the securities, insurance, and the money and credit markets industries. Pursuant to the authority granted in the Securities Law, Insurance Law, and Commercial Banking Law, the three regulatory bodies then drafted all kinds of regulations and rules with specific provisions governing administration and management in their respective industries. These rules and regulations became the concrete expression of the Laws noted above as they were applied, and played an extremely important and helpful role in the enforcement of financial legislation. The division of regulatory powers increased the vitality of the financial industry. It allowed an industry that had been concentrated in the hands of the four state-owned banks to be transformed into an industry with hundreds of large, medium, and small banks throughout China, each vigorously displaying its own abilities, competing for business. The quality of services and operations in general improved dramatically.

Property Rights Reform

"Ownership" of financial institutions has gone from a state-owned system toward diversification. Another attribute of China's financial system reform was the diversification of property rights or ownership systems. This was formalized in financial legislation. Before the Shenzhen Development Bank was listed on the Shenzhen Stock Exchange in 1990, all of China's commercial banks were entirely state-owned. There were as yet no commercial banks of a joint stock or "corporatized" form. By 2007, three of the four largest state-owned commercial banks of China had shares listed on the domestic and international stock exchanges, having first completed reforms in share ownership and becoming corporations.

Chinese–foreign joint-venture commercial banks, as well as the branches of solely foreign-owned commercial banks, have now appeared in China's large cities. Municipal credit cooperatives have been merged to form municipal "commercial cooperative banks." For example, 99 municipal credit cooperatives in Beijing were merged to form the Beijing Municipal Cooperative Bank, which later changed its name to the Beijing Commercial Bank. Still later, after receiving investment from foreign financial institution shareholders, it has been transformed into a joint stock company called the Beijing Bank. The transition of three of China's large state-owned commercial banks to joint stock corporations has been effected pursuant to the stipulations of China's "Commercial Banking Law," "Company Law," and "Securities Law." The three, the Industrial and Commercial Bank of China (ICBC), the Bank of China (BOC), and the China Construction Bank (CCB), have accomplished systemic reform, listed on markets both inside China and abroad, and now entered the ranks of the world's 10 largest banks by capitalization.

Before 2000, few securities companies in China were directly listed, and most therefore found it hard to get financing. For some time, their operations were in grave danger. In 1994, a trust company was listed on the Shanghai Stock Exchange and only then changed into a securities company; all the rest had to endure hard times throughout the bear market period. Chinese securities firms gradually began to be listed only in 2006. After China joined the WTO, jointly invested securities companies began to appear in the country from the year 2000. Because of this, the original state-owned securities companies in China that were of a unitary nature in terms of ownership now began to diversify. Insurance companies and trust companies also began to shift from being monolithic state-owned entities to becoming diversified entities.

The diversification of the ownership of financial institutions has been one method of increasing their vitality. It has improved professionalism and raised efficiency.

China's financial industry is increasingly operating on the basis of legal foundations. All of China's financial industries have begun to recognize that "there is now law on which to rely." The operations of commercial banks must comply with the Commercial Bank Law, as well as all kinds of laws and regulations promulgated by the PBC and the China Banking Regulatory Commission (CBRC). The securities industry must comply with the Securities Law, and relevant laws promulgated by the CSRC. The insurance industry must comply with the Insurance Law. Trust companies and investment funds must comply with laws relating to trust companies and the administration of funds.

In Chinese, the character for "law"—*fa*—has both a narrow and a broad meaning. The limited interpretation of "law" is more in line with the idea of basic "principles"—this is a perception of law that has long been true in China. Revisions to narrowly defined laws can occur every 10 years or so. The broader meaning of *fa* includes a large number of administrative directives, plus the bylaws and precedents of any given unit or economic entity. Broadly defined law incorporates more concrete or specific items, and is adjusted relatively frequently. When the narrow or "principles" meaning of the term *fa* had not yet been framed into laws, the broader meaning had the function of regulating and assuring the smooth functioning of the markets. After the principles have been formulated into laws, the broader category of directives and rules takes on the burden for concrete explanations, regulatory supervision over technical measures, guidance on daily internal controls, and so on. China's securities exchanges commenced trading in 1990, for example, yet the Securities Law was promulgated only in 1998, and effective in 1999. For eight years, oversight of the securities markets relied on regulations issued by the central office of the PBC and the PBC's Shanghai and Shenzhen branches. The markets were regulated by the CSRC only after the CSRC itself was established in 1993. When the Securities Law was promulgated, administrative regulations of the CSRC continued to supplement it with interpretation and enforcement.

The standardization and legalization of the operations of financial institutions has brought their operations more into the light, made daily operations more transparent, improved the assurance of consumer benefits, and made the markets far safer.

Macroeconomic Measures in the Financial Markets

Since financial markets have a great influence on peoples' livelihoods, and since the markets are also characterized by risk, there is not a country in the world that does not intervene in the functioning of such markets. Macroeconomic measures taken by the US government after the market crash in 1929 and during the Great Depression, measures taken by Europe after the war in 1945, and macroeconomic intervention in the financial industry by the Japanese government in 1990 are evidence of this fact. When the Asian Financial Crisis erupted in 1997, measures taken by the governments of Korea, Singapore, and China's Hong Kong Special Administrative Region were just a present-day iteration of earlier actions by other nations and necessary in the increasingly globalized world economy. During the eruption of the subprime mortgage crisis in the US in 2007, the US federal government also used fiscal means to stimulate the economy, frequently lowering interest rates, reducing taxes, and so on, in order to stimulate the economy and avoid further economic decline.

It is patently obvious but bears reiterating that China is a large country in the midst of rapid change and economic development. China's population is so large that per capita resources are, relatively speaking, inadequate. The financial markets are at a fairly early stage of development, so it is absolutely necessary for the central government to apply forceful macroeconomic measures to aid their functioning. For example, when the "Commercial Bank Law" was drafted, the PBC was given the responsibility to assure the stability of the value of the RMB. The term "stability" implies neither appreciating nor depreciating the currency too quickly, and also implies not allowing large rises or falls in price vis-à-vis other currencies. At present, China's RMB exchange rate mechanism, as China's spokesmen have said, is "a managed float that responds to changes in the market." This foreign exchange policy is backed by legal provisions in China's "Foreign Exchange Management Regulations."

China's macroeconomic measures with regard to the financial industry are also in accord with laws and regulations. The "Government Working Report" and the "Financial Budget" passed by the National People's Congress set goals for all kinds of economic indicators, such as GNP growth rate, price levels, employment rate indicators, relative energy use, and so on. When the government sets budgets, it carries out market interventions within a certain range, as prescribed by law, according to these budgetary goals and indicators. When any indicator exceeds the prescribed range, giving a sign that the economy is over-heating or slowing down too much, the government may use indirect macroeconomic measures to deal with the problem. The measures with regard to the financial industry are specified in the "Law of the People's Bank of China." These include, for example, the ability to adjust the reserves rate on deposits, the interest rates on loans, the discount rate, open market operations, and the issuance of short-term notes or paper. The government can also adopt fiscal measures to undertake adjustments, such as adjusting the income tax of enterprises, the tax on interest from deposits, the stamp tax, individual income tax, and so on.

Macroeconomic adjustments of the financial markets by the central government preserve stability in the national economy and in society at large, and assure economic well-being and sustainability. Particularly when a market loses vitality, central government interventions become imperative.

FINANCIAL AND LEGAL SYSTEM REFORM

China has created a fairly complete legal framework over the past 30 years with respect to the financial industry. Enforcement of the law is currently being improved. As a result, China has amassed a considerable wealth of experience in this regard. In particular, China continues to be very alert regarding inflation. In terms of monetary policy and fiscal policy, it has not espoused inflationary or deficit policies for a long time. This domestic experience has been reflected in the provisions of the "Law of the People's Bank of China" with regard to monetary policy. In the "Securities Law" and "Insurance Law," a number of stipulations manifest the same degree of caution and conservatism. All of this has to do with China's experience of hyperinflation in its recent past.

It has been said that "law is a kind of local knowledge." Another aspect of the way that China focuses on local experience and conditions is the way China does not blindly copy models from abroad. China has been very good at carrying out reforms that are appropriate, and making sure that foreign experience is adapted to the social and cultural environment of China. One example relates to the question of "combining the operations of different industries" with regard to the commercial banking, securities, and insurance and trust industries. China has indeed adopted appropriate reform measures: each of the "Commercial Bank Law," the "Insurance Law," and the "Securities Law" adopted a cautious attitude toward the prospect of "mixed-industry" or comprehensive operations. Only nearly 10 years after the effectiveness of the first statutes regulating these aspects of the financial industry, when the above Laws were revised in 2005, were regulations that strictly prohibited mixed operations of any kind modified to allow the "conditional relaxation of restrictions."

Local experience is also manifested in the use of so-called compatibility provisions in Chinese law. The US and some other countries use a system of legal precedent whereby under the same facts of a case and the same evidence, different lawyers can raise different case principles to support different points of view. When courts release opinions, they have majority opinions and minority opinions, as well as different principles supporting different rationales. In China, local experience has meant that we adopt something called "compatibility provisions" to help determine the outcome in a legal dispute. For example, under China's "Securities Law," the stock exchanges have adopted a membership system, yet the ownership of the exchange still belongs to the state, and the Chairman of the exchange is appointed by the securities industry regulator, the CSRC. Another example: the Commercial Bank Law stipulates that banks are not allowed to offer credit loans to "friends." The Law does not define this, and there is indeed no need to further explain or define the scope of "friends," since in actual bank operations and in actual court experience, the Chinese have an unspoken understanding of all who might be considered "friends." Legal provisions that may appear to be vague are in fact adopting this idea of compatibility. It simplifies complex issues and makes the drafting and enforcement of law far easier. This is another reflection of the principle that was reflected in Deng Xiaoping's advice to the effect of, "No further debate—the road ahead is going to be tough."

China's methods of drafting legislation and administering the law have specific features. Summing up, they can be described as follows.

Legislative powers relating to the financial industry are concentrated in the central authority. In some countries, legislative authority relating to banking, insurance, and securities industries is granted to different levels of central and local government. In China, all legislation with regard to financial industries concentrates rights and powers in the hands of the central government. Regional authorities generally do not have legislative authority in this area. This guarantees that a large country in which regional economies are uneven and the population is vast will have financial legislation that is uniform. This has been China's way for 2,000 years, ever since the Qin dynasty unified such things as currency, the axle width of vehicles, and weights and measures. The same is true today.

A second aspect of China's legislative and judicial systems is that the costs of enforcement are distributed. A legal system costs money and requires funding from society. If nobody supports or pays for the costs of enforcement, then the law is reduced to mere words on paper and ceases to have any real effect on social life. Since the economies of developing countries are not always well-organized, and tax revenues are limited, enforcement costs generally are not borne solely by the national government, but are distributed over regional and local units of society, and even dispersed to the level of communities, households, or even individuals. For example, the judicial system of China is divided into four layers, each of which has the fiscal responsibility to pay for its own level. In financial cases in China, parties to a lawsuit must bear a certain portion of the costs of litigation. This portion of costs represents litigation fees, and the method of determining the sum is to apportion it by "levels" as a percentage of the total cost. In the process of reforming our financial system, in order not to increase the burden of corporate and citizens' taxes, we have used this method of distributing the costs. It has enabled us to carry out enforcement of law in the financial sector.

A third aspect of the way China legislates and administers its legal and regulatory system is the way in which cultural factors are taken into full account, especially in terms of financial management and regulation. All large countries must of necessity have a large and centralized government. China has had a strong central government over the course of many centuries. The supervisory oversight by financial regulatory agencies demonstrates this central control. China undertakes thorough investigations of financial regulatory institutions every year. From confirming that operating measures conform to laws and regulations, from labor market liquidity to jobs, financial accounts to the worksite, management to employees, political study sessions to business training, all must be guided by law and regulation. Even though China is regarded as a country whose financial legal system is less than perfect, and not up to the rigorous standards and perfection of developed countries, no Enron-like case has yet appeared in China. There also has not been anything like the subprime mortgage crisis in financial credit that erupted last year in the US and is continuing to influence global markets.

In countries with a so-called perfect legal system, the appearance of notorious cases has to make one wonder if legal perfection is sufficient to keep this kind of thing from happening. We often do not see the same kind of thing happening in countries in which legal restraints are imperfect. The answer may have to do with the financial culture of a country.

In a culture in which excessive credit, excessive opportunism, and excessive profit-seeking stimulate excessive behavior, "people will cut off other people's heads to make money," as the Chinese saying goes. A perfect legal system becomes all form and no substance, and practical measures are futile in dealing with egregious behavior.

China's traditional culture has always emphasized the maintenance of a surplus. A common wish at New Year's is that you have slightly more than you need every year. The Chinese revere sayings like "repair the house before it rains." Chinese financial culture reflects this behavior, and the tradition has influenced the ways in which the current Chinese government is exercising prudence in handling financial legislation and enforcement.

FUTURE DEVELOPMENTS

The future of China's financial legal system can be summarized by the words: study, absorb, and improve. After China entered the WTO, domestic financial markets were further opened to the outside, and the domestic financial system moved further in line with international practices. In the next period, between now and 2020, China's systems need to learn from advanced foreign countries, to absorb their best attributes and extensive experience. At the same time, we must merge our own experience with that from overseas, make sure the better attributes of our own systems can accommodate those from overseas, and explore what can be introduced from outside as well as what should be maintained of China's unique features as the country develops its financial legal system.

We must improve deficiencies in our own system, both the gaps and the aspects which no longer accord with practicality, and we must revise provisions and regulations accordingly. We must continue to improve the quality of the drafting of our laws, get a better handle on the market cost of legislation, and understand and accurately forecast the consequences of having society bear the costs of enforcement.

Ultimately, we must assure that the laws which are promulgated are a positive incentive to the financial markets rather than an obstacle to their development.

Since 1978, China's experience in developing a legal framework for the financial industry has shown that we should adhere to our own unique path in building a socialist financial legal system. We should be fully vigilant as we move forward, using what has been successful and rejecting what has not, so that we can provide ever stronger guarantees for the healthy and sustainable growth of China's financial sector.

CHAPTER 31

Legal Services in the Field of Banking and Finance

Xiao Wei

Managing Partner, Junhe Law Offices

CHINA'S LEGAL PROFESSION AFTER REFORM AND OPENING

The legal profession in China has needed the fortitude to endure setbacks as it grew under the conditions of a changing New China. A legal system, in the true sense of the word, and a legal profession, could only begin to exist in China after Reform and Opening, when China began democratic processes, began to strengthen its legal system, and began to develop a market economy.

On August 26, 1980, the National People's Congress (NPC) formulated the first legislation to do with lawyers since the establishment of New China; namely, "Provisional Regulations on PRC Lawyers." On May 15, 1996, the NPC passed the first law on lawyers since the start of New China, called "Law on PRC Lawyers." On October 28, 2007, the NPC revised and passed a new version of this law, which went into effect on June 1, 2008. The legal professional in China has grown rapidly over this period and there are now over 130,000 professional lawyers in the country.

In the early period of the resumption of the legal profession, lawyers' functions remained limited. A legal framework was still in its infancy, the centrally planned component of the economy was still pronounced, and the government still relied mainly on administrative fiat to run the economy. Law office activities related mostly to civil cases and litigation. Services soon began to expand into legal services for foreign direct investment, foreign trade, real estate mortgages, and so on, but seldom were lawyers involved in financial affairs. As securities markets began to develop in China, as well as insurance, as banks were restructured and listed on the market, and with the further development of bond markets, stock funds, and industry-related funds, Chinese lawyers began to offer legal services on a more comprehensive basis in the realm of finance.

PROVIDING LEGAL SERVICES TO THE SECURITIES INDUSTRY

Lawyers began to enter the financial arena more frequently as they started participating in the securities business in particular. In 1993, capital markets with a national scope began to form in China and the government began to issue documents relating to standardized procedures. Lawyers became an indispensable part of the legislative process and were soon involved in the securities business as well.

Their initial role related mainly to share issuing and company listing on the markets. This included the issuing of RMB common shares (A-shares), of foreign-invested shares that were listed within China (B-shares), of foreign-invested shares that were listed outside of China (H-shares), as well as red-chip shares.

The China Securities Regulatory Commission (CSRC) was established in October of 1992. It soon began issuing a series of laws, regulations, and bylaws. On June 3, 1993, the CSRC issued a "Notification Regarding Information Required of Companies That Are Publicly Issuing Shares." On April 22, 1993, its "Provisional Regulations on Share Issuing and Trading" began to be implemented. On December 25, 1995, the government passed regulations regarding "Foreign-invested shares that are listed inside China as shareholding companies." All these regulations required that a company that was applying for authorization to issue shares to obtain a legal opinion, issued by a law office. This made lawyers an indispensable participant in the securities markets, and lawyers began to join in the business of A-shares.

According to "Provisional Regulations of the Ministry of Justice and the China Securities Regulatory Commission Regarding Confirmation of Qualifications of Law Firms and Lawyers," only lawyers selected and confirmed by the Ministry of Justice and the CSRC could participate in certain activities. These included restructuring and reform of state-owned enterprises (SOEs), setting up share-ownership companies, and work related to the issuing and distributing of securities. Only selected and approved companies could provide legal opinions and legal working reports as per regulations of the CSRC.[1]

As securities markets developed, the cohort of lawyers associated with the business expanded and their quality improved. According to statistics of the Ministry of Justice and the Legal Association, 409 law firms were qualified to engage in securities business by 1999. These became a major force behind the ability of the securities markets to move forward in China. At the same time, however, seriously inadequate awareness of risk considerations among typical law firms at the time created problems. Professional qualifications were not high, work habits were rather rough and ready, and most lawyers were unfamiliar with overall management aspects. In addition to their being insufficiently risk-aware, many lawyers were unduly influenced by the previous system of government recommendations and government review and approval. Lawyers did not rigorously apply industry standards and business rules in diligently fulfilling their responsibilities. Investigations were more form than substance, so the legal risk of the issuer was often not adequately brought to light. Some lawyers even evaded responsibility and intentionally covered up problems associated with an issuer and the potential risk involved. Such failure to issue clear legal opinions meant these lawyers were not fulfilling their intended role in preventing and dispersing liability.

In 1999, through the "Securities Law," the CSRC undertook a major overhaul of stock issuing systems. It eliminated the previous system of quotas, the limited number of licenses that were granted to chosen entities, allowing them to list. It eliminated the former process of administrative recommendations and review and approval, and began to implement a system of recommendation by primary underwriters, together with a ratification system that vetted issuers of shares. The ratification system was one in which "each attends to his own duties," so that those granting licenses or approving and those seeking approval could not be the same person. The recommendation and ratification systems were meant to distinguish clearly the responsibilities and risk features of all entities involved, the Board of Directors of the entity issuing shares, the regulatory agencies, the primary underwriters, the lawyers, accountants and other intermediaries, the investors, regulatory personnel, and so on. The aim was to have market participants and regulators exert mutual restraints on each other, each "attending to his own duties and interests," in order to form a securities-issuing system that is in accord with "marketized" or market-driven principles.

Under the ratification system, lawyers are key in intermediary organizations. Together with primary underwriters, professional accountants, evaluators, and so on, they contribute to guaranteeing the quality of the securities and the quality of the information that the issuer is providing to investors.

The legal opinion and legal working report provided by lawyers are necessary documents as part of any application for issuing securities. In addition, however, they form the baseline from which regulators work when they confirm compliance with regulations, and they form the underlying basis for legal guarantees justifying investors' confidence.

On September 16, 1999, the CSRC issued, "Rules Regarding the Audit Committee of the CSRC." By these rules, the new audit committees must include lawyers. From this point on, lawyers were involved in the process of auditing, which further elevated their standing in the securities arena.

In 2006, together with the revision of the "Company Law," a "Securities Law" was issued and the CSRC passed a series of regulations on first-time public issuing of securities and refinancing. The scope and method of legal opinions in the process was adjusted accordingly. In practice, lawyers can serve as legal advisors both to issuers of securities and to primary underwriters. In terms of the underwriters, lawyers generally write at least part of the prospectus.

In 1994, the State Council issued, "Special Regulations on Corporations' raising of funds by listing overseas," and the former Securities Commission of the State Council and State Council Office for Restructuring the Economic System released "Rules on Preparatory Steps to Listing Companies Abroad." In 1999, the Securities Commission released "Application and Authorization Procedures and Regulatory Guide to Domestic Enterprises Applying to List on the Growth Enterprise Market [GEM] of the Stock Exchange of Hong Kong." Some large- and medium-sized SOEs restructured into the form of shareholding companies and then listed on overseas exchanges by issuing H-shares (including but not limited to the Main Board in Hong Kong, New York, Singapore, Tokyo, and London.) Some small- and medium-sized shareholding companies listed on the GEM in Hong Kong by issuing H-shares. These restructurings and listings involved a number of governmental departments and organizations, including but not limited to approval agencies, state asset-management departments, the CSRC, the Stock Exchange on which the entity intended to list, and so on. In this process, lawyers coordinated the work among intermediary organizations and the company being listed, and provided legal opinions both to the intended stock exchange and to relevant Chinese authorities, including the CSRC. In the course of this process, some companies issued A-shares first, then H-shares, and others H-shares first, then A-shares, and some simultaneously. Lawyers coordinated the regulatory requirements among intermediaries, both inside and outside China and with listing companies.

In 1995, the State Council promulgated "Regulations on Foreign-invested Corporations Listing inside China." In 1996, the former Securities Commission of the State Council issued, "Implementing Procedures for the Regulations on Foreign-invested Companies Listing in China," and in line with these regulations, lawyers participated in the work of listing and issuing B-shares.

In 1997, the State Council promulgated "Notice Regarding Further Strengthening of the Management of Listing and Issuing Shares on Overseas Markets." During the period, a group of large SOEs set up overseas companies and then undertook listing and public issuing of shares. This included but was not limited to China Telecom, COFCO, China National Offshore Oil Corporation, and China Unicom. These listing activities generally required special authorization from the State Council, and Chinese lawyers again coordinated the work of organizations both inside and outside China, so that listed companies complied with relevant laws and regulations. At present, some red-chip companies intend to issue A-shares on the Shanghai Stock Exchange, and since relevant laws and regulations are not yet clearly defined, lawyers are assisting issuers and relevant authorities in providing legal opinions.

In 2000, CSRC issued, "Notice Regarding Issues to Do with Overseas Companies with Domestic [Chinese] Rights and Interests That Are Listing and Issuing Shares Overseas." Around this time, a group of privately owned enterprises—that is, not state-owned—began to set up companies outside of China and undertake public offerings of shares, on exchanges including but not limited to the GEM in Hong Kong, and NASDAQ. In this process, lawyers submitted legal opinions to the CSRC as according to the above regulations, in order to obtain "no comment letter" from CSRC to list on the part of the issuers. The 2000 "Notice" was annulled in 2003, and at present similar listing proposals mainly use the Securities Law and "Regulations" issued by the Ministry of Commerce in 2006 called, "Provisional Regulations on Foreign Investors Merging with and Acquiring Domestic Enterprises," as well as a Notice put out by the State Foreign Exchange Management

Bureau called, "Notice on Issues to Do with Domestic Chinese Citizens Going Through Special-purpose Overseas Companies to Raise Finance and Bring Back Invested Foreign Exchange into China." In this process, based on their experience and their connections with relevant authorities, lawyers are providing opinions on whether or not such listings have to go through a CSRC-approval process.

After companies issuing A-shares are listed, they come under the regulatory jurisdiction of the CSRC and either the Shanghai or the Shenzhen Stock Exchange. Lawyers then provide legal services to them regarding compliance with the regulations. This includes, but is not limited to providing testimony at shareholders' meetings, reviewing and approving a company's information disclosure documents, and so on. With regard to A+H-share companies, lawyers coordinate domestic and overseas intermediary organizations in fulfilling the different requirements of each. As per relevant provisions of the CSRC,[2] some lawyers are to be nominated as independent directors on the Boards of listed companies in order to use their professional knowledge to assist listed companies in improving legal-person corporate governance structures and in strengthening policy understanding of the capital markets. From 2005 to 2007, the CSRC and other governmental bodies issued a series of regulations to do with share distributions of listed companies, the purpose being to resolve the remaining historical problems of a portion of shares that are not fully tradable on the market. In this process, lawyers fully coordinated the work of carrying out share conversion among shareholders, in order to achieve a significant contribution to the Chinese securities markets.

PROVIDING LEGAL SERVICES TO COMMERCIAL BANKS

The share system reform (or corporatizating reform) and public listing of China's banking industry began with medium-sized banks, such as the Shenzhen Development Bank, the Shanghai Pudong Development Bank, and the China Merchants Bank. It was only after this that large state-owned banks began restructuring and then listing on markets, including the Bank of China (BOC), the China Construction Bank (CCB), and the Industrial and Commercial Bank of China (ICBC). Before the reform of the commercial banks, the legal services that lawyers provided were generally limited to the drafting of business contracts, and to assisting with agented and commercial loans, individual mortgage loans, and so on. In 2003, the State Council decided to undertake share system reform or "corporatizing" of the BOC and the CCB, and in the process of restructuring and bringing in strategic investors, then completing a public offering and listing on an exchange, lawyers began to provide a broader range of more in-depth legal services to banks.

These services included participating in the design of the restructuring proposal; for example, whether to use partial restructuring or wholesale restructuring, and helping with issues of how to transfer existing creditors' rights and debt liabilities over to a shareholding company.

Due diligence were an important part of lawyers' services in the process. Their main function was to provide a realistic foundation for the feasibility of restructuring proposals, and to help draft them. They had to help determine whether or not banking operations were in accordance with laws and regulations, whether or not certain problems required adjusting and resolving; they had to provide a foundation for public disclosure in the process of listing, which also served as the basis of information when lawyers provided legal opinions.

The process of doing due diligence under domestic laws and regulations had not previously existed in China. It progressed gradually from a starting point of zero in terms of the necessary requirements and standards.

At present, there are still unclearly defined areas with regard to due diligence and the various stages of restructuring. In terms of listing stages, lawyers must provide legal opinions and legal working reports as per the Regulation of the CSRC called "Information Disclosure Requirements of Publicly Listed Share Companies Regulation #12: Legal Opinions and Legal Working Reports on Public Offerings of Securities." The scope of and standards applied to due diligence must at the very least comply with demands of the legal opinions and lawyers' working reports noted in this regulation.

As a result, the scope of due diligence with regard to banks covers numerous aspects. For example, it includes registrations and authorizations for doing any kind of financing business; conformity to regulations of all types of operations; large debt liabilities and creditor responsibilities; external investments and how they are handled; important financial information; transformation and improvement of internal control systems; labor and social securities to employees; consolidated tax reporting and other tax considerations; any litigation, arbitration or administrative fines and punishments that are pending; and so on.

Large state-owned commercial banks frequently have many thousands of branch organizations. Undertaking sufficient due diligence on their operations requires the reading and review of tons of documentation, which is another unprecedented challenge facing lawyers as they undertake due diligence with regard to commercial banks.

Lawyers have played a key role and provided a tremendous amount of legal services with regard to the handling of nonperforming loans (NPLs) in particular. This has come in the course of commercial banks' restructuring and listing, with regard to bringing in strategic investors and clarifying the business relationship between strategic investors and investee banks, as well as focusing on internal corporate governance issues before and after listings.

LEGAL SERVICES AND THE INSURANCE INDUSTRY

Legal services provided to the insurance industry in recent years have been mainly in the following four areas: share reform restructuring or "corporatizing" of insurance entities, bringing in foreign strategic investors, utilization of insurance funds, and corporate governance structures of insurance companies.

In 1999, the "Decision by the Central Committee of the Chinese Communist Party on Major Issues to Do with State-owned Enterprise Reform and Development" listed requirements for share system reform of large and medium-sized SOEs undertaking standard listing as well as those Sino–foreign joint ventures becoming shareholding companies. The implementation of share system reform of state-owned insurance companies began at the end of 2002. It entered a critical stage in 2003. By 2004, the share system reform or "corporatization" of state-owned insurance companies had basically been completed. In the process, many legal issues required the close participation of lawyers, including which reform model to follow, division of assets and transfer proposals, as well as setting up the corporation itself. Lawyers were fully engaged in the process of resolving these issues, giving opinions, and providing professional legal services. They prepared documentation regarding relevant transactions and assistance on completing approval procedures, as well as exploring the possibility of bringing public investment into the process of system reform.

China formally entered the WTO on December 11, 2001. In the course of entering, China made commitments regarding opening its insurance industry with specific timetables for designated parts of the market. Starting end-2003, China authorized non-life-insurance companies to establish wholly foreign-owned companies in China, and eliminated all business restrictions on their activities. Starting at the end of 2004, China lifted restrictions on foreign-invested insurance companies operating in China, and also opened up all business lines to foreign-invested insurance companies with the exception of business relating to statutory insurance. At the end of 2005, China eliminated this restriction to statutory insurance as well. With the honoring of WTO commitments, more and more overseas investors came into the Chinese insurance market, through setting up offices, buying shares in Chinese insurance companies, and setting up their own wholly owned and joint-venture companies. In this process, lawyers were allowed to serve as legal advisors to China-invested insurance companies, as well as to overseas investors in the drawing up of investment proposals, in investigating the qualifications of both domestic and overseas shareholders, in drafting transaction documents, in negotiating, and in the process of authorization and final closing services. They provided relevant legal services for all the various links along the way. By helping foreign investors understand the Chinese legal environment for the insurance business, as well as helping Chinese insurance companies understand international regulations, lawyers effectively were able to draw upon advanced management experience and to apply it in China. They were highly effective in promoting communications and understanding between China's insurance companies and foreign investors when it came to the application and approval process with relevant Chinese authorities.

On June 15, 2006, the State Council issued "Various Opinions on Reform and Development of the Insurance Industry." These opinions expanded the channels through which insurance funds could be invested—they established principles regarding a measured expansion of investment in securitized products, infrastructure, overseas assets, and investment in commercial banks. Previously, insurance funds were highly restricted in their application. Although these Opinions relaxed the restrictions, insurance companies still encountered numerous legal problems in actual implementation due to the inadequate legal framework in which the new principles could be applied. The professional skills of lawyers were very helpful in assisting insurance companies in resolving many legal aspects, including helping insurance companies with due diligence in the areas in which they intended to invest, in drafting risk-control legal measures, in demonstrating compliance with regulations of the parties receiving investment, as well as helping insurance companies complete verification and approval procedures regarding the existing legal system.

In recent years, under China's overall requirements with respect to deepening systemic reform of insurance companies, the China Insurance Regulatory Commission (CIRC) has put forth ever higher demands on internal controls of those companies. These include, "Guiding Opinion (Initial Form) on Standardizing Internal Corporate Governance Structures of Insurance Companies," issued on January 5, 2006; "Regulations on Required Qualifications of Board Members and Senior Management Personnel in Insurance Companies," set out on June 12, 2006; and "Management Procedures for Independent Board Members," issued on April 6, 2007. In order to comply with these regulations, lawyers are closely involved in helping insurance companies adjust their internal corporate governance procedures, including revising documents on corporate governance. They make recommendations to insurance companies on structural changes, revise corporate bylaws as required by certain regulations, and help insurance companies set up legal training as required of employees by regulatory commissions, in the areas of internal controls and risk-avoidance methods.

In the future, in order to continue promoting the healthy development of the insurance industry, lawyers will be expanding their services to include professional skills in the following areas:

- participating in legislation relating to the insurance industry as well as relevant policy formulation
- borrowing on the experience of the securities industry, in which lawyers serve as an extension of the regulatory agencies, responsible for investigating whether or not insurance companies are in compliance with corporate governance structures, utilization of financing funds and insurance-premium funds, and providing professional evaluations to these regulatory agencies
- providing professional evaluations on compliance of insurance contracts with regulations.

LEGAL SERVICES AND OVERSEAS PRIVATE-PLACEMENT FUNDS

Private placement only really started up as a part of Chinese investment in the year 2000. From US$800 million in that year, it now totals over US$10 billion. Private placements for China's three state-owned commercial banks, before listing, came up to US$5.5 billion.[3]

The size of China's private placement financing has exceeded that of Japan since 2005, making China the country absorbing the largest amount of private placement investment funds in Asia. These funds total more than 30% of all financing in Asia.

Overseas private placement funds have brought about a tremendous change in the way in which foreign companies invest in China, and have brought a commensurate challenge to the legal system. The greatest difference in the way foreign funds now carry out investments, as opposed to the traditional fashion, is that the investing is done via purchase of equity rather than new issuing. This difference is naturally reflected in the different demands made on lawyers that are being hired to assist the entities involved.

As soon as funds began to come into China, the Chinese legal profession started providing relevant legal services. In the early period, however, these were limited to due diligence services to overseas funds; that is, to satisfying demands of investors that any entities being invested in were meeting legal operating procedures. The work was often undertaken as reference material for the legal requirements of taking a company public.

The increase in private placement has greatly expanded the number of mergers and acquisitions (M&As) taking place in China, and China's lawyers are now transitioning from undertaking routine due diligence services to providing investment structure plans for investors, and to drafting core legal documents. The structural plans and legal opinions of China's lawyers become an important factor influencing the policy of private placement investors. In recent years, China's lawyers have tried hard to accommodate the reasonable legal demands of overseas private placement funds, to allow those demands to be realized within the Chinese legal framework. In order to guarantee the investment needs of the investor, and allow Chinese enterprises to benefit from this rapidly developing channel of funding, Chinese lawyers have made many excellent contributions in the design and operations of private placement funds in China. In putting innovations into practice in actual cases, Chinese lawyers have spurred further advances in the development of China's financial legislation.

LEGAL SERVICES AND THE BOND INDUSTRY

The participation of lawyers in the bond industry in China can mainly be seen in the issuance and listing on the market of various kinds of bonds, including but not limited to, enterprise bonds, corporate bonds, convertible corporate bonds, financing bonds, short-term commercial paper, and so on. In 1993, the State Council promulgated "Regulations on Enterprise Bond Management"; in 2004, the National Development and Reform Commission promulgated a "Notice Regarding Further Strengthening and Improving the Management of Corporate Bonds." These were mainly to provide legal precedents to enable large- and medium-sized SOEs to issue bonds to the public. Such issuing required review and authorization by the National Development and Reform Commission and other authorities; included in the reports sent to these authorities were legal opinions provided by lawyers. According to "Regulations on Bond Issuing" put out by the Shanghai Stock Exchange, those corporate bonds already issued could be traded on the Shanghai Stock Exchange, but lawyers first had to provide a legal opinion on them.

According to "Issuing Methods of Listing Companies" put out in 2006 by the CSRC, as well as earlier relevant regulations, A-share listed companies could now issue convertible corporate bonds. Such issuing came within the scope of "refinancing" of such listed companies, and required the submission of legal opinions by lawyers, as well as reporting to the CSRC for evaluation and authorization.

In 2005, the PBC issued "Management Methods on Short-term Financing Instruments and Other Standardizing Documents," to provide legal backing for companies to issue short-term (not over one year) debt instruments. Such financing has to be approved by the PBC, and legal opinions have to be included in documentation that is submitted for review and approval.

In 2005, the PBC also issued, "Methods of Financial Bond Issuing in the Nationwide Inter-bank Bond Market." Those entities allowed to issue financial bonds include policy-type banks, commercial banks, finance companies of enterprise groups, and other legal person financial institutions. Such issuance requires authorization from the PBC, and application materials sent to it must include legal opinions.

In 2005, the PBC, the Ministry of Finance, the National Development and Reform Commission, and the China Securities Regulatory Commission issued, "Provisional Measures for RMB-denominated Bond Issuing by International Development Agencies." Issuing entities were those international development finance institutions undertaking development-related loans and investments. After being evaluated and approved by four ministries as well as the State Council, these were authorized to issue RMB-denominated bonds. The twelfth provision of these provisional measures stated, "International development agencies that are issuing RMB-denominated bonds must have China-certified lawyers undertake legal services as according to the 'Law on Lawyers of the People's Republic of China'." In practice, lawyers were already providing legal services on special projects for the Asian Development Bank and other overseas financial institutions in issuing RMB-denominated bonds.

In 2007, the CSRC issued "Experimental Measures on Corporate Bond Issuing." These regulations are to be applied to corporations that have been established under the "Company Law," which in practice mainly refers to listed companies. Issuing corporate bonds requires approval from the CSRC, and application materials require legal opinion documentation.

In 2007, the China Banking Regulatory Commission issued, "Opinion on Effective Risk-avoidance with Regard to Corporate Bond Guarantees." The regulations discontinued or ceased to allow bank guarantees for corporate debt that related mainly to project financing, and, in principle, bank guarantees would no longer be provided for enterprise bonds or corporate bonds. This and other regulations increased the difficulty of issuing corporate bonds so that in practice lawyers now need to assist in resolving guarantee problems relating to issued bonds.

LEGAL SERVICES AND THE FINANCIAL INDUSTRY

China has already formulated a legal framework for the financial system as it relates to banking, insurance, trust companies, and securities. Financial law forms the core, with various regulations, rules, and other documents serving as an accompanying system that is multi-tiered and multifaceted. Nonetheless, law general lags behind economic activity. Due to the phenomenal speed of financial developments in China, China's financial legislation is still lacking in certain respects. On the one hand, the legal system for the financial sector is simply incomplete; for example, stock index futures have to date not yet been instituted, and a civil responsibility system in stocks has not yet been effectively set up. This, to a large extent, influences legal services and the role that lawyers can play in these areas. On the other hand, there are still differences of opinion and also lacunae with regard to specific financial laws and regulations. This means that administrative entities have to make either official or unofficial explanations and supplement the law in the course of implementation. This not only affects the precision of the law, but it also creates problems for lawyers when they try to provide legal services. The situation creates the need for lawyers to have excellent relations with administrative institutions, in order to resolve specific problems in the course of business.

Over the course of the past 20 years, the legal profession in China has built up a considerable body of lawyers and law firms that are expert in financial law. At the same time the level of expertise of all lawyers in this field in China is not uniform, and less experienced lawyers sometimes negatively influence the understanding of the public about the state of financial law in general. Due to the pace of developments in the financial sector, and the constant appearance of new financial products, lawyers need to keep improving not only their professionalism with respect to the law, but with respect to new financial developments, in order to improve the quality of their services.

China's law firms have grown rapidly over the past 20 years. Quite a few started out with just a few lawyers and have now grown to include several hundred. Nonetheless, China's law firms are still quite young and indeed immature in terms of their own business management. They lack necessary governance institutions to the extent that the management and efficiency of some offices have definite problems. Some of China's larger law firms have made efforts in recent years to improve management systems and have made quite notable progress.

Due to the opening of China's legal services market, international law firms, as well as some foreign-national and regional law firms, have now set up more than 100 representative organizations in China. Although these organizations are not allowed to hire Chinese lawyers or provide Chinese legal services, by laws and regulations, in point of fact many do so. Moreover, their business volume has increased extremely quickly. Demands for Chinese lawyers are increasing as a result. International law firms generally hire headhunters, companies to look for outstanding talent among Chinese law firms. It has long since been an indisputable fact that legal talent in the field of financial services draws the highest pay. China's law firms are therefore faced with the challenge of a brain drain, of talent flowing out their doors. In the past two years, law firms have been adjusting pay scales and benefits upwards in an effort to deal with this. They have improved internal training and the cultural environment of the workplace, and there has been some improvement in the ability to retain talented personnel.

CONCLUSION

The pace at which financial businesses are growing poses intense challenges to Chinese law firms. Under new economic conditions, the strengthening and improving of financial legal services will require the common efforts of many social sectors. Speaking more specifically, governmental organizations need to go further in strengthening legislation and enforcement work, in order to provide a better professional environment in which lawyers can provide financial legal services. Lawyers themselves need to improve the quality of their work and their knowledge of the financial industry, as well as improving their professional ethics. Overall, they need to become more professional and more specialized. Law firms need to set up standard management models in order to provide a reliable platform upon which their lawyers can provide higher quality legal services.

Only through the efforts of all sides will Chinese legal services in the financial sector move forward. Only then will China's lawyers be able to make a contribution to the opening and the growth of China's financial industry.

ENDNOTES

[1] See October 28, 1994, "Regarding Legal Opinions and Legal Working Reports' Form and Content" in the #6 Provision of information disclosure requirements of publicly issued shares.

[2] August 16, 2001, "Opinion" of the China SRC entitled, "Guiding Opinion on Having Listed Companies Establish Independent Directors on their Boards."

[3] Among which, the ICBC completed US$2.6 billion in private placement; the BOC US$1.5 billion; the CCB US$1.4 billion.

CHAPTER 32

The Accounting Profession in China: Review and Outlook

James Turley
Global Chairman and CEO, Ernst & Young

REVIEW OF THE ACCOUNTING PROFESSION IN CHINA: A HISTORICAL PERSPECTIVE

The earliest signs of Western accounting methods used in China can be traced back to the nineteenth century with the introduction of double-entry bookkeeping. Up until then, single-entry bookkeeping was the norm for businesses. The establishment of the Treaty Ports along the eastern coastal belt of China brought with it foreign businesses and practices, the emergence of Chinese enterprises, and the development of Chinese financial institutions. Yet it was not until the Republican era (1912–49) that the economy had modernized sufficiently to pave the way for the accounting industry to evolve into a profession that was different from simple bookkeeping both in terms of sophistication and rigor. Up until that point, however, the development of commerce alone was not enough for accountancy to evolve into an established profession. The state needed to play a pivotal role, which duly took place when the Ministry of Agriculture and Commerce regulated, and therefore recognized, accountants as a profession for the first time, in 1918. Another important development was the establishment of a professional body, in Shanghai a few years later, which would seek to uphold standards of knowledge and learning, and encourage the adoption of codes of behavior. (See the article "Becoming Professional: Chinese Accountants in Early Twentieth century Shanghai," in *Accounting Historians Journal*, June 2003.)

Much has changed from then to now, not least of which the phenomenal growth in the number of professional accountants in China. Still, from a broad historical perspective, the healthy and proper development of China's accounting profession today relies on much the same factors now as then. Rapid economic development alone is insufficient to ensure the proper growth of the profession. Economic growth merely ensures that demand for accountants is high. The associated needs for quality, knowledge, and standards require human efforts that go beyond what economic growth can deliver. The combination of supportive government policy and the promotion of professionalism within the industry itself are therefore crucial for the proper development of the accounting profession in China.

Evolution of the Accounting Profession

With the founding of the People's Republic of China (PRC) in 1949, the development of the accounting profession took an alternative course from the preceding decades, particularly in the early years of the PRC, as the state embarked upon a thorough program to create a centrally planned economy based on the model of the former Soviet Union. The new government inherited a profession that had grown steadily through the years, from roughly 200 registered accountants in the mid-1920s to around 3,000 by 1949. Many of these registered accountants were based in Shanghai, which had prospered as a commercial center before the founding of the PRC. As economic structures were centralized with the state as the sole arbiter of power, ministries were established along industry lines as organs through which enterprises, and therefore industries, were directly controlled. As a result, the accounting profession directly served the interests of the state. By the 1950s, the Ministry of Finance issued national accounting rules in an effort to standardize basic principles and methods for the accounting industry, a reflection of the maturation of state planning after the initial years of accelerated economic reconstruction. This was a critical step for the development of the socialist economy, as the Ministry of Finance instructed each of the industrial ministries to issue separate accounting systems for enterprises within those respective industries. Accounting systems were also devised based on the mode of ownership. Based on these principles the accounting profession developed in such a way that the relevance of performing audits faded under the centrally planned economy during the period between 1949 and 1978.

The economic reform policies that began in earnest in 1979 had deep implications for the accounting industry. The economic reforms saw the introduction of "Socialism with Chinese characteristics." This saw China move toward a socialist market economy, whereby market forces would be introduced in favor of state planning in terms of price determination within the economy. In essence, the state switched its mode of control over enterprises from direct to indirect mechanisms, which would give enterprises greater freedom to reduce economic inefficiencies through better allocation of resources. The consequent accounting reforms were necessary, because the accounting systems developed for a planned economy were no longer appropriate for the new economic structures that started to evolve in the reform era. New forms of ownership began to emerge as reforms took root, undermining the hegemony of state ownership in traditional industries as new businesses flourished. Suddenly, the existing accounting systems, which were either industry-specific or ownership-specific, seemed out of date.

Once again, policymakers sought ways to make the accounting profession relevant for the changing economic circumstances. The Law on Chinese–Foreign Equity Joint Ventures, which was promulgated in July 1979, meant laws had to be drawn up in relation to how these enterprises would be taxed. Crucially for the profession, the new tax rules required foreign-owned enterprises, both wholly owned and joint venture, to have their annual financial statements audited by certified practicing accountants (CPAs). The demand for accounting services directly contributed to the establishment of new accounting firms in China, the first of which was established in Shanghai on January 1, 1981. However, these accounting firms provided their services mainly to foreign-owned enterprises. For the majority of businesses in China, which at the time were state-owned enterprises (SOEs) or collective enterprises, an independent audit was not required. Instead, the state performed audits and tax examinations on its enterprises. As with other sectors of the economy, the government decided to open the accounting industry to competition, permitting accounting firms belonging to global networks, including the Big Four (Ernst & Young, Deloitte Touche Tohmahsu, PricewaterhouseCoopers and KPMG), to open representative offices on mainland China in 1981. These were mainly for liaison and consulting purposes rather than provide audit and other professional services, with the global networks' member firms using Hong Kong as a base for more significant operations.

In 1983, the Ministry of Finance issued the Experimental Accounting System for Chinese–Foreign Joint Ventures, which was revised and formally promulgated in 1985 as the "Accounting Regulations of the People's Republic of China for the Joint Ventures using Chinese and Foreign Investment." The system dealt with the accounting equation, financial statements, accounting terminology, and accounting rules. In 1985 the National People's Congress approved the "Accounting Law," which was a milestone for China's accounting profession, and would prove important for China to move toward international accounting conventions. Indeed, a year later, in July 1986, the State Council announced the "CPA Regulations." These laws and regulations clearly set out the functions of accounting and the duties of accounting personnel. As in the past, the industry itself had to take a central role in promoting its professional interests, and so the Chinese Institute of Certified Public Accountants (CICPA) was established on November 15, 1988, under the supervision of the Ministry of Finance. Like other accounting associations, the CICPA's charter focuses on professional standards, self-regulation and examinations.

A Step Toward International Standards

The decade that followed the adoption of economic reforms and the Open Door Policy, the latter of which encouraged foreign investment and trade, had helped to change the face of the profession altogether, as accounting needs evolved. These economic reforms introduced new user groups to China, such as foreign and domestic investors and banks. New user groups maintained their own financial information based upon their own requirements, which were not the same as those of the government. Consequently, the emphasis on users' needs began to shift from a single domestic government to a range of stakeholders, which included foreign investors, creating the existence of different reporting methods within China. This was because Chinese financial statements, apart from those of Sino–foreign joint ventures, were fundamentally different from their international counterparts. Moreover, foreign stakeholders often found Chinese financial statements difficult to understand. Instead of using the internationally adopted accounting equation (assets = liabilities + owners' equity), the Chinese "balance sheet," more appropriately referred to as the "balancing of funds statement," used the equation (sources of funds = applications of funds).

In 1992, the Ministry of Finance took decisive action to respond to the new accounting needs of foreign-invested enterprises and the newly established category of joint stock companies. This resulted in China issuing new regulations, the "Accounting System for Experimental Joint Stock Enterprises," and the "Accounting System for Foreign Investment Enterprises," in May and June of that year, respectively. These accounting reforms marked another step in developing standards based on internationally recognized norms, and marked a small yet decisive shift away from the existing accounting systems developed for a planned economy. Although the two new accounting systems adopted international accounting conventions in general, the main drawback was that their application was limited to enterprises with specific modes of ownership, viz. foreign-invested enterprises and joint stock companies. However, a new development was just around the corner, which would mark 1992 as arguably the most important year for the modernization of the accounting profession in China. In November, China promulgated the "General Accounting Standard for Enterprises" (known as the "General Standard"), which put China's accounting system firmly on course toward international accounting conventions. This was similar to an accounting framework on which specific accounting standards were based. The General Standard, which comprised 10 chapters, divided into 66 paragraphs, was a hybrid between a conceptual framework and accounting standards. At a relatively general level, the General Standard prescribed the format of financial statements and the treatment of various captions in financial statements. This laid the foundation for the issuance of a series of specific accounting standards, which were similar to, but not the same as, the International Accounting Standards. A year later, on October 31, 1993, the National People's Congress approved the CPA Law. While the "General Accounting Standard for Enterprises" laid the foundation for the development of China's accounting standards, the formation of the CICPA and the promulgation of the CPA Law laid the foundation for the development of the accounting profession in China. With the Big Four established on the mainland a decade earlier, the Ministry of Finance granted special approval to Big Four member firms to form joint venture accounting firms with local firms set up by the Ministry for that purpose. This move enabled the member firms of the Big Four global accounting networks to provide auditing, advisory, tax, and other professional services in China, including serving multinational corporations through inbound investment services. Except for the foreign invested enterprises, there was no requirement for annual audit for Chinese enterprises in general.

The Impact of the Securities Markets on the Accounting Profession

The establishment of the Shanghai Stock Exchange and the Shenzhen Stock Exchange in December 1990 also had implications for the accounting profession. Companies were subject to different accounting rules depending on if they were issuing so-called A-shares, which are RMB-denominated stocks restricted to investment by Chinese nationals; or B-shares, which are denominated in foreign currency and were restricted to investment by foreign investors. A-share listed companies were required to issue annual financial statements prepared in accordance with the Accounting System for Experimental Joint Stock Enterprises, and audited by locally qualified CPAs. B-share listed companies had to issue annual financial statements prepared in accordance with International Accounting Standards and audited by international accounting firms. The domestic experience with securities markets in Shanghai and Shenzhen emboldened China to test the waters in Hong Kong, as an initial batch of nine SOEs were restructured before being listed on the Stock Exchange of Hong Kong in 1993. The specific class of shares were dubbed "H-shares" and represented the first time Chinese enterprises raised funds outside mainland China. H-share issuance in Hong Kong has become one of the most popular routes for raising capital for Chinese enterprises. By opening a channel to attract foreign funds, China was also opening another way in which China would be subject to new accounting ideas. H-share companies are regulated by the Stock Exchange of Hong Kong, which requires companies to prepare financial statements under either Hong Kong or International Accounting Standards, and are audited under either Hong Kong or International Standards of Auditing. Professional services are provided to H-share listed companies mainly by member firms of the Big Four and other global networks. The flourishing of H-share listings has been a principal driving force for the growth of the member firms of the Big Four and other global professional services networks in recent years.

After issuing the General Standard and the two accounting systems, the Ministry of Finance in 1994 started a work program to develop a set of "Specific Accounting Standards." These standards were similar in nature, format, and content to the International Accounting Standards. By 2001, the Ministry of Finance had promulgated, 16 specific standards for accounting. The Ministry also promulgated the "Accounting System for Business Enterprises" in 2000, which codified the accounting practices introduced by the specific standards. All listed companies, joint stock companies, and foreign invested enterprises had to adopt the "Accounting System for Business Enterprises."

In 1994, the CICPA embarked on a project to establish a comprehensive system of auditing standards. These standards were eventually issued by the CICPA, with the approval of the Ministry of Finance, between 1995 and 2003. The standards were issued in batches, with a total of forty-three "General and Specific Independent Auditing Standards," "Auditing Practice Pronouncements," and "Auditing Practice Guidelines," which were modeled on International Standards on Auditing, with some slight differences. The issuance of these auditing standards was a milestone in the development of China's accounting profession. These standards set out clearly the responsibilities of CPAs, provided work standards for them, and protected their professional interests. The setting of the accounting and auditing standards in the 1990s was a demonstration of China's commitment to improving the quality and standards of the accounting profession with a view to harmonizing China's professional practice with international practice.

By the time the Ministry of Finance and CICPA issued the accounting and auditing standards, there had been significant changes to the International Accounting Standards (and renamed as International Financial Reporting Standards) and International Standards on Auditing. Following the adoption of International Financial Reporting Standards for companies listed in stock exchanges in the European Community starting 2005, countries worldwide were increasingly adopting International Financial Reporting Standards, or encouraged their national accounting standards to converge with International Financial Reporting Standards (IFRS). Similarly, International Standards on Auditing had gained a wider application worldwide.

In early 2005, both the Ministry of Finance and CICPA embarked on projects that aimed at overhauling the two sets of Chinese standards. These were completed in early 2006, with the new sets of Chinese accounting and auditing standards getting closer to their international counterparts than ever before. The China Accounting Standards Committee and the International Accounting Standards Board held a successful convergence meeting on accounting standards in Beijing in late 2005. Both parties agreed that establishing and improving a single set of high-quality global accounting standards would be the logical response to the growing trend of economic globalization. China stated that convergence was among the fundamental goals of their standard-setting program, with the intention that an enterprise applying Chinese accounting standards should produce financial statements that are the same as those of an enterprise that applies IFRS. At around the same time, the Chinese Auditing Standards Board (CASB) and the International Auditing and Assurance Standards Board (IAASB) held a meeting to discuss convergence of auditing standards. Similar to accounting standards, both parties agreed that establishing and improving a single set of high-quality global auditing standards would be the appropriate way to meet the challenges posed by the trend of economic globalization. CASB stated that the fundamental principle of drafting the Chinese auditing standards would be to improve the Chinese auditing standards system and ensure it converges with the International Standards on Auditing as soon as practicably possible, consistent with the pace of development of China's market-based economy and globalization and international convergence trends.

The China Securities Regulatory Commission (CSRC) also played an important role in the regulation and development of the accounting profession. Though the CSRC did not set accounting standards and auditing standards, it, together with the Ministry of Finance, licensed those accounting firms that provided securities market-related professional services, such as acting as auditors for Chinese-listed companies and companies seeking to list. The CSRC set disclosure requirements for various reports of listed and to be listed companies, such as their annual reports, interim statements, and prospectuses.

Progressively minded policies have also allowed the accounting profession to prosper in China. These have included the commitment to improve accounting and auditing standards and the establishment and the activities of CICPA to support professional growth. Economic factors, such as soaring inbound investment and the robust growth of the stock markets have contributed as well. The accounting profession has grown from about 7,000 CPAs in 1992 to over 72,000 CPAs (plus another 70,000 non-practicing accountants) at the end of September 2007, with some 6,500 accounting firms in mainland China alone.

While there has been significant growth in the profession overall, most of the accounting firms focus on providing audit services, with the result that, until recently, the member firms of global networks have been the main providers of non-audit services. Demand for non-audit services has grown more modestly in the past compared with audit services, mainly due to corporate culture and fee considerations.

Those that require non-audit services are typically foreign invested enterprises and companies that have issued H-shares. Both groups are clients of the member firms of global accounting networks. However, with government support, this is changing. As discussed later in this chapter, China is proactively responding to globalization by supporting convergence with international accounting and auditing standards, and encouraging its enterprises to grow bigger and stronger, and to expand overseas. Supporting internationally recognized standards and enterprise growth are not mutually exclusive, but complementary, since overseas expansion by Chinese enterprises will fuel demand for non-audit services, while more and more international businesses will require international standards to meet the requirements of international investors and capital markets. The adoption of global best practices therefore should not be limited to audit services, but also include non-audit services in areas such as internal control system, risk management, information technology, tax, actuarial services, valuation, internal audit, and securitization. These areas are currently mainly served by the China member firms of global networks. However, in time, local firms are likely to develop in these areas to provide more comprehensive services to clients as demand increases.

THE PROFESSION TODAY AND THE CHALLENGES AHEAD

China's accounting profession has enjoyed unparalleled growth since 1992, in part because the government recognized the central role the profession plays in the development of a competitive and modern economy, and therefore created the appropriate legal framework in which it could flourish. Of course, this period of phenomenal growth of CPAs has coincided with spectacular economic expansion, with double-digit growth for a number of years. The profession in China is dominated by local firms, although most are relatively small in size. At the end of 2006, the vast majority of the 6,500 accounting firms in China were local firms. The largest local firm by revenue reported income of some RMB220 million in 2006, employing about 850 people, of whom 360 were CPAs. The second-largest firm recorded revenue of RMB210 million in 2006, employing some 1,120 people, of whom 440 were CPAs. As a snapshot as to the size of the larger local firms, the top 12 local firms each earned revenue in excess of RMB100 million in 2006, while those clustered around the hundredth place typically reported revenue of between RMB20 million and

RMB30 million, and employ 100 to 200 people each, of which 50 to 60 were CPAs. In recent years, local firms as a group have experienced strong revenue growth, mirroring the strong performance of the economy, on average growing at 20% per annum, with revenue for the group in the region of RMB20 billion in 2006.

The number of joint venture firms has increased from four in the early 1990s to seven in 2006, with another 27 local firms joined as members, and seven as affiliates, of the other global accounting networks. There are also 17 representative offices of foreign accounting firms in China. The China member firms of the Big Four networks had annual revenue of between RMB1.2 billion and RMB2 billion in 2006, with a headcount ranging from about 3,000 to 4,500 people on the mainland, of which 300 to 500 were CPAs, at the end of 2006.

The services on offer, while broadly similar, do differ. For example, around 70 firms, including local firms and members of global networks, have special licenses to provide securities-related professional services. The number licensed to undertake securities-related services has been stable over the past 10 years. However, the number is expected to decrease owing to new licensing rules announced in 2007.

RECENT MARKET DEVELOPMENTS

Most mainland China-listed companies are audited by large local firms. For the 2006 annual audit, of the total 1,457 companies listed in Shanghai or Shenzhen, 1,356 were audited by local firms, representing 93% of the market. On the mainland, the largest local accounting firm by client audits some 90 China-listed companies, while the top 12 local accounting firms together audit 560 China-listed companies, equivalent to 38% of the total number of China-listed companies. Most of the initial public offerings (IPOs) in the mainland market have been assisted by large local accounting firms. There were about 70 IPOs on the two mainland China stock exchanges in 2006, about 80% of them hired local firms as reporting accountants.

On the other hand, the China member firms of the global networks audit only a fraction of China-listed companies—about 100 (7%) in total at the end of 2006. However, in terms of market capitalization on the mainland, China member firms of the global networks audit nearly 60% of the total as of the end of 2006. The China member firms of the global networks have an added advantage of having the knowledge and resources to help clients with matters outside of mainland

China. Most commonly, this involves providing audit and accounting support for companies seeking access to capital markets outside mainland China such as by listing H-shares in Hong Kong, Rule 144A transactions, and IPOs in the US. Most of the 148 H-share companies listed in Hong Kong, with a combined market capitalization of about HK$5,500 billion as of November 2007, are audited by the global network member firms. They also acted as the reporting accountants of all the 24 H-share IPOs in 2006 and all the six H-share IPOs in the first 11 months of 2007, which has raised about HK$300 billion and HK$60 billion in total.

In the mainland, the China member firms of the global networks only have a relatively small number of the A-share IPO engagements, acting as reporting accountants for only about 20% of the IPOs in 2006. However, in terms of funds raised, China member firms of the global networks acted as reporting accountants for about 80% of the total in 2006. The situation was the same for the first 11 months of 2007. China member firms of the global accounting networks, although acting as reporting accountants for less than 15% of the 110 A-shares IPO in the first 11 months of 2007, assisted in raising funds of about RMB320 billion, which accounted for about 80% of the total funds raised on the A-share IPO market. This is because, as a result of a policy shift by the government that began in late 2006, the very large companies that have already issued H-shares in Hong Kong "returning" to mainland China capital markets by issuing A-shares, and companies that had planned H-shares have either decided to issue A-shares first, or drop H-share plans altogether in favor of A-shares. These very large companies usually engage China member firms of the global accounting networks to act as their reporting accountants.

Geographically speaking, member firms of the global accounting networks have a broader reach within China owing to their nationwide networks. China is well-served when it comes to qualified accounting professionals, with the member firms of global accounting networks focusing on the major commercial cities such as Beijing, Shanghai, Guangzhou, and Shenzhen, while the 6,500 local firms virtually blanket China in small and large cities in every province with their relatively smaller practices. The China member firms of global accounting networks mainly serve larger listed companies, many of which maintain Hong Kong listings, and foreign invested businesses. The largest 70 local firms serve the majority of mainland China-listed companies and unlisted large SOEs. Meanwhile, the audit and accounting needs of the local small and medium-sized enterprises are met by the large pool of the relatively smaller local accounting firms. It has become common practice that nearly all of the large SOEs engage the services of local accounting firms, and only choose to switch to the China member firms of global networks when an IPO (especially an IPO outside mainland China) is planned.

In general, local accounting firms provide audit, accounting, and business support for rapidly growing small businesses, both public and private. They assist these businesses in obtaining funding through bank lending or access to capital markets. The local firms also provide other attestation work such as capital verification, special purpose audits, and non-attestation work such as valuation and tax services. The China member firms of the global accounting networks, because of their network client base, provide inbound investment related services and annual audits for multinational clients, many of which are referrals from member firms in other countries and territories. China member firms of global networks utilize their international knowledge to assist large companies regarding the adoption of global best practices in critical business areas, such as risk management, information technology, accounting processes and controls, actuarial product pricing, and risk analysis. The China member firms of global networks also assist large mainland China companies to expand domestically and internationally, often through transaction assistance provided by the China member firms themselves or by other member firms in different countries in the global network. The China member firms of global networks also provide suggestions to regulatory authorities regarding effective oversight approaches, standards and regulations development, as well as helping address local and emerging global issues that have a bearing on the profession in China. Both the local firms and the China member firms of global networks provide a constant stream of well-trained CPAs for the accounting industry and commerce. The exposure to sophisticated clients and the availability of structured training and coaching programs tends to mean that CPAs from the China member firms of global networks are more likely to go on to new employment opportunities at large listed companies or foreign-invested enterprises.

Professional Services: Outlook and Implications

Based on current trends in the accounting profession, the local firms, particularly the smaller ones, are likely to continue to focus on the accounting, auditing, and bookkeeping needs of small and emerging companies. The smaller firms will likely continue to offer a relatively narrower range of services, mainly audit and other attestation work. Undoubtedly, the vast majority of local firms will continue to cater to the basic accounting and auditing needs of most of the companies in China. Indeed, they have an important role to play, as the main providers of professional services to companies outside the major cities, particularly those in the remote and less developed areas of China. By contrast, some of the larger local firms are differentiating themselves from the smaller accounting firms, especially those that are licensed to audit mainland China-listed companies. Indeed, larger local firms are growing in ambition, with some expanding through mergers, resulting in the emergence of several very large local firms. Others are acquiring small and medium-sized firms, not only in mainland China, but also in Hong Kong, to provide them with a means by which they can offer capital markets-related professional services outside mainland China. Another route is for large local firms to sign up as member firms and affiliates of middle-tier global accounting networks. Local accounting firms are expected to continue using these routes to expand domestically, and in some cases, as a means to gain access to business that has traditionally been the strength of members of the Big Four, such as outbound services.

Apart from serving their multinational clients, the China member firms of global networks have strategically positioned themselves to focus on the large, public, or going-public companies, helping them prepare for capital market access and provide the financial information required by investors. Such services will no longer mainly be for China companies listed or seeking listing in Hong Kong or overseas, but also for those that have already issued H-shares and are looking to raise funds domestically on the A-share market, those that are solely pursuing an A-share strategy, or those contemplating dual A- and H-share fundraising strategies. In any event, the China member firms of global networks will continue to help these companies adopt global best practices in key operating areas, including, but not limited to internal control, risk management, and corporate governance.

The China member firms of global networks also provide market knowledge to assist Chinese companies in expanding globally. The China member firms of global networks can draw upon the knowledge and resources of fellow member firms within the network to advise their clients more effectively in implementing overseas expansion strategies, including through M&As. These services include carrying out the due diligence work on overseas targets, followed by assisting in the preparation of reports for the purpose of meeting M&A rules, and other stock exchange and regulatory requirements, as well as for raising funds for the acquisition. The process also involves completion audits and fair value adjustments, tax planning and tax compliance, annual audits for the acquired overseas company, and other professional assistance services that are needed to bring the acquired company's operations and management in line with the acquirer.

The China member firms of global networks also contribute to the strengthening of the Chinese financial system in various ways, such as their promotion of sophisticated financial and performance management methods and approaches that can help clients become stronger competitors in the global market. Moreover, the China member firms help raise confidence in Chinese capital markets, not only through their audit work, but also by providing the professional services supporting financial disintermediation, which helps raise the appeal of financial instruments other than stocks, such as corporate bonds and mortgage instruments. Another important development occurring among the China member firms of global networks is the process of localization. New accountants typically require 10 years or more to become a partner at a Big Four member firm. Since establishing joint venture firms in China over a decade ago, the global networks are now in a position to promote more of their experienced local staff to partner status. It is anticipated that these newly promoted partners may well become the future leaders within the China member firms of global networks.

The complexity of the Chinese economy means there is a wide variety of groups to be served, and so, over time, having a broad mix of accounting firms does help to serve these varying client needs, making it entirely possible for firms to develop their own niches. At the same time, strong prospects for the Chinese economy means the accounting profession will continue to find it a major challenge to keep pace with the ever-increasing demands of the market. Both local firms, large and small, and the China member firms of global networks, will remain crucial to the broad and deep development of the Chinese economy.

Regulating the Accounting Profession

The accounting professional in China is regulated by a number of authorities: the Ministry of Finance, CSRC, and CICPA. Firms are licensed by the Ministry of Finance. For those firms that provide securities-related professional services, an additional license issued jointly by the Ministry of Finance and CSRC is required. As a professional body, CICPA has oversight authority over the firms and the individual CPAs. Accounting firms have to file annual returns to these authorities for license renewal purposes. The Ministry of Finance, CICPA, and CSRC carry out an inspection of accounting firms from time to time. The authorities also have powers to discipline the accounting firms and individual CPAs.

In the US and Europe, independent oversight authorities, such as the Public Company Accounting Oversight Board (PCAOB) in the US and the Financial Reporting Council in the UK, have been set up in the past few years to regulate the auditors of listed companies. This is consistent with a global trend for the establishment of such organizations, the goal of which is to assure a high level of integrity, independence, and quality. Furthermore, there is a global trend toward the convergence of regulatory requirements, in the same way as accounting and auditing standards are converging. These new global developments may well influence China as it formulates future policies and regulations for the accounting profession.

Setting Accounting, Reporting, and Auditing Standards

In China, accounting standards are set by the Accounting Regulatory Division of the Ministry of Finance. The China Accounting Standards Committee is a consultative organization that provides suggestions and recommendations to the standard setters. For specialized industries such as banking and insurance, additional detailed requirements are set by the relevant regulators such as the China Banking Regulatory Commission (CBRC) and the China Insurance Regulatory Commission (CIRC). Auditing standards, on the other hand, are set by the Professional Standards Department of the CICPA, which are then approved by the Ministry of Finance.

The setting of accounting and auditing standards in China goes through a due process that is similar to those in other countries. Exposure drafts are prepared and then issued for comments from various interested parties, such as local CPA institutes, accounting firms, and academics, as well as from the general public. The Ministry of Finance and CICPA are also supported by pools of experts, who they consult on a regular basis on the setting of standards. These pools include not only experts from local accounting firms, regulators, and universities, but also experts from the member firms of global networks. The Ministry of Finance has organized a number of international symposiums in the past on the development of accounting standards, where experts from various countries have participated. In addition, in 1994, the CICPA formed two expert consultation committees for the development of auditing standards. One committee comprised mainland China experts, while the other was drawn from those from the Hong Kong, Macao, and Taiwan regions, and countries outside China.

Both local accounting firms and the China member firms of global networks have contributed to the setting of the accounting and auditing standards, by providing comments in general and also by having experts taking part in the relevant committees. The China member firms of global networks draw upon their global resources and knowledge to share with the standard-setters their experience of standard setting in other countries, and their knowledge of international accounting and auditing principles and practices. The local firms on the other hand provide feedback on the potential issues that could arise upon the implementation of the standards.

Latest Developments in China's Accounting Standards

Following the promulgation of the latest series of Chinese Accounting Standards for Business Enterprises (CAS) in February 2006, Chinese accounting standards are now much closer to IFRS than before. Similar to experiences in other countries that have adopted IFRS, or have their national Generally Accepted Accounting Principles (GAAP) closely based on IFRS, there are implementation and interpretation issues that are caused by being principle-based rather than rules-based. As noted earlier, the Secretary General of the China Accounting Standards Committee and the Chairman of the International Accounting Standards Board (IASB) signed a joint statement in November 2005, in which the IASB noted that some countries had added provisions and included implementation guidance to reflect the specific circumstances pertaining to those countries, and that this was a pragmatic and advisable approach with which China agreed. Since the issuance of CAS in 2006, the Ministry of Finance has been issuing Implementation Guidelines on CAS. Most recently, the Ministry of Finance issued CAS Interpretation No. 1, which provides further clarification of treatments in various areas in the form of 10 questions and answers. CAS is only just being implemented by listed Chinese companies for the first time in 2007. Many of the Chinese companies listed in Hong Kong have also issued A-shares on the mainland, and so are required to also publish financial statements that are prepared in accordance with CAS. Since CAS is principle based, it is imperative that Chinese companies avoid adopting one interpretation of CAS in one listing location, such as Shanghai, and another interpretation in another listing location, such as Hong Kong. A level playing field and full comparability are needed to ensure capital markets operate efficiently and accounting standards and highly credible.

In addition to refining its interpretation of CAS, China should continue to participate in the global dialogue aimed at ensuring consistent interpretation of standards. It is equally important that the China Accounting Standards Committee and the IASB work together to eliminate any remaining differences in these standards in principle and in practice, and for China to maintain and update its accounting standards on an ongoing basis to ensure it is in step with the constantly evolving IFRS requirements. As a result of the success of the November 2005 joint meeting, the China Accounting Standards Committee and the IASB have agreed to meet periodically and strengthen the exchange and cooperation of the two parties so as to achieve convergence of CAS and IFRS.

China should work closely with other countries and regions toward eliminating the multiple reporting systems; for example, China GAAP for Shanghai-listed companies, Hong Kong GAAP for Hong Kong-listed companies, and US GAAP for New York-listed companies. This might occur with the global adoption of IFRS, but it should be monitored closely and aimed for as soon as reasonably practicable. Following the recent announcement by the PCAOB that foreign private issuers filing IFRS financial statements are no longer required to provide reconciliation statements to US GAAP, global capital markets are getting one step closer to the convergence goal. Support from China toward such a goal would also naturally aid this process, and indeed, the Ministry of Finance has been working closely with the Hong Kong Institute of Certified Public Accountants (HKICPA) with a view to enabling companies with both A-shares and H-shares to prepare one set of financial statements that meets the reporting requirements for both A- and H-share markets.

Instead of a unilateral convergence toward IFRS, China should take a more active role in helping to shape and interpret IFRS. Dr Zhang Weiguo, who was the Chief Accountant of the CSRC, joined the IASB in 2007 as a full-time board member. The appointment of a Chinese board member to the IASB will no doubt help facilitate the convergence and promote consistent interpretations of IFRS and CAS.

Latest Developments in China's Auditing Standards

Following the promulgation of the latest series of Chinese Auditing Standards in February 2006, auditing standards in China are now closer than ever to International Standards on Auditing (ISA). CICPA has also issued detailed explanatory and implementation guidelines to help auditors adopt the new auditing standards for their 2006 annual audits. Continual training and monitoring by the CICPA would help ensure that all CPAs implement and comply with the new auditing standards. Indeed, during the summer of 2007, CICPA inspected more than thirty audit firms that are licensed to provide securities-related audit services, with a primary inspection focus on compliance with the new auditing standards. It is worth stressing the need for China to avoid using two sets of auditing standards, one for IFRS, US GAAP, and Hong Kong GAAP, and another for China GAAP audits. It is a fair statement to say that strong capital markets and investor confidence depend on high-quality audits no matter which market the company trades on, and what accounting standards its financial statements are based on. The goal of eliminating multiple reporting systems applies not only to accounting standards, but is also relevant to auditing standards. It goes without saying that China would stand to gain from participating in the process to help achieve a global set of reporting standards. Currently, CICPA and HKICPA have been working toward a common goal of enabling auditors of companies with both A- and H-shares to issue a single audit report on the financial statements that meets the reporting requirements for both mainland China and Hong Kong markets.

Reporting to Investors

While accounting standards set out the general disclosure requirements for financial statements, CSRC has issued a number of standards on the form and content of securities-related reports. CSRC standards set out additional disclosure requirements for financial statements of listed companies, as well as the form and content of annual, interim, and quarterly reports. CSRC standards also stipulate the form and content of IPO prospectuses, and special disclosure requirements for annual reports and prospectuses of companies in specialized industries, such as banks, insurance companies, securities companies, and property development companies. CSRC standards require highly detailed disclosures that are comparable with the disclosures made by companies listed on other overseas exchanges. In addition, CSRC has issued standards on corporate governance. Listed companies are required to disclose in their annual reports corporate governance matters, as well as any departures from the requirements of the CSRC corporate governance standards.

The Shanghai Stock Exchange and the Shenzhen Stock Exchange have issued a set of guidelines for listed companies to report on their internal control. The internal control guidelines are highly comprehensive, and require listed companies to have internal control systems that cover financial reporting, operational effectiveness, and legal compliance. The guidelines call for an internal control framework that has eight elements, including risk identification and risk management. The guidelines also require listed companies to include in their annual reports a self-assessment report of the internal control systems, and for their auditors to report on the self-assessment report. Currently, the requirements are not mandatory, but listed companies are encouraged to include such a report in their annual reports.

The Ministry of Finance has undertaken a project that aims to establish a system of internal control standards, which includes a framework standard, detailed internal control standards, and standards on the assessment of internal control. Various task forces and sub-projects have been set up and a number of exposure drafts have been issued. This is a major project, the completion and implementation of which will greatly enhance both the internal control systems of Chinese companies and the transparency of reporting on internal control systems.

In summary, the Chinese authorities have been continuously improving the disclosures and transparency of China-listed companies, and positive progress has been made on both fronts. One of the new emerging global trends is for companies to provide more non-financial information and financial information that is more forward looking in nature, as opposed to being purely historical. Investors are also asking for more timely information to facilitate decision-making, and also information in such a form that users can easily rearrange and analyze according to their personal preferences. Progressive and forward-thinking policymakers should take note and consider ways in which these new investor demands could be taken into account when formulating new rules to improve the transparency in reporting.

Non-audit Services

With rapid economic growth and globalization, the demand for non-audit services is increasing significantly, not only from Chinese companies expanding overseas, but also from local companies faced with competitive pressures. In addition, the convergence efforts of the regulators in accounting, auditing, and regulatory matters also have implications for non-audit services, such as internal control. Chinese accountants need to be adequately trained to provide these non-audit services. As discussed in the next section, Chinese universities have a critical role to play as a primary provider of training for these areas. However, the surge of demand has been so quick and the demand so strong that importation of such skills is inevitable in the near term. Here is where the China member firms of global networks can contribute, by developing and providing the relevant skills, and drawing upon the resources of their global networks. The imported knowledge can be grown exponentially through on-the-job training and knowledge transfer to local professionals within these firms. The training and nurturing of local professionals in non-audit services can be enhanced by the China member firms of the global networks participating in program design and teaching at universities, and by the placement of graduates to these firms to turn their classroom learning into practical experience.

Human Capital and the Role of Universities

The growing demand for professional services in China is creating an unprecedented demand for accounting professionals, underscoring the role of universities as the single most important source of supply of new recruits. While the number of university students studying accounting and related subjects has evidently increased in recent years, it has not been nearly enough to match demand, particularly when there are increasing opportunities for accounting and finance majors in other areas of industry and commerce. Finding effective strategies to boost the numbers of accounting majors is a prerequisite for the proper growth of the profession, which in turn will help foster economic growth and corporate expansion overseas. Of course, that is not all. Growing inbound investment by multinationals and the expansion of Chinese companies overseas is generating demand for audit, tax, and transaction professionals who have international experience and who can understand the complexities of reporting financial transactions across national borders. Related to this, universities should promote greater use of foreign languages in education; for example, by using English to supplement Chinese in the teaching of certain subjects. Information technology skills, and effective communication skills, both verbal and written, are also useful for the development of young accounting professionals. Conventional accounting and auditing training is needed, but the profession is also short of subject expertise in many areas, such as management accounting and performance reporting, planning and budgeting processes, M&As processes (valuation, integration), control system design and management, corporate finance, as well as knowledge in law and economics. As for accounting and auditing, teaching should not be confined to current Chinese practices, but be extended to cover international practices and be forward looking in nature. Problem-solving is a skill that needs to be developed too, which could be nurtured through developing case studies that integrate a number of subject areas to mimic real commercial situations, acting as a useful supplement to single-subject lectures. Greater academic cooperation by Chinese universities with overseas universities could be a useful way in which Chinese universities can tap into overseas teaching resources, either by bringing in teachers from overseas or by sending students abroad. Perhaps one of the most important lessons is professional ethics, which universities need to teach in a holistic manner to ensure such principles are inextricably tied to the proper conduct of the accounting profession.

In summary, the Chinese accounting profession is looking to universities to provide many more quality- and international-orientated accounting majors. This will help satiate some of the immediate demand in the profession, but over the longer term, high caliber graduates are needed to become tomorrow's leaders—top managers of listed companies, of large financial institutions, of regulatory bodies, as well as partners of large accounting firms. To achieve that, the higher education system requires sufficient resources to enable them to meet the demands of the profession.

CONCLUSION

Currently, large local accounting firms have the depth and reach to handle all but the largest Chinese companies, particularly those with an overseas or H-share listing. In fact, most China-listed companies are audited by local accounting firms. As the large local accounting firms get even bigger and stronger, more listed companies, including some with overseas or H-share listings, will migrate to audit firms other than the China member firms of global networks. In the long run, well-conceived, market-based measures that help to distinguish the stronger local accounting firms from the rest, will enable the larger local accounting firms to increase their penetration into the large company market.

In the US and Europe, a significant barrier to entry in the large company audit market is enormous liability exposure and the inability to obtain adequate insurance coverage. Addressing liability risk is essential, not just for increasing competition, but also to ensure that the audit function is sustainable. Many countries have already recognized the need to reform audit liability regimes. Liability risk is not yet a major threat to the Chinese accounting profession, but it could be argued that recent events and changes in the legal climate could make the environment more litigious. Steps should be taken to ensure that liability risk will not become a significant barrier to entry in the large company audit market in China.

A key consideration in this regard involves questions of when and how to appropriately respect judgments of management and auditors. This becomes critical when the Chinese accounting standards and auditing standards have both moved from a more rule-based approach to a principle-based approach. Regulators and the legal system must be able to respect professional judgments made in good faith, and which are rational, well-considered, and properly documented.

Regulatory complexity and the lack of convergence among both local and overseas regulators can also act as a barrier to entry because of the significant investment in the compliance-oriented infrastructure required to operate in such a regulatory environment. A coordinated and consistent local regulatory environment, together with an effort to converge with international regulatory requirements, will facilitate large local firms to further penetrate into the local and overseas-listed large company market.

Overall, measures to increase auditor choice, especially at the top end of the market, may take time to develop and work their way into the market. Any proposal for increasing competition must be considered for its impact, not just on choice, but on audit quality and independence. Also, a careful assessment should be made of unintended detrimental consequences that could result from any intervention in the market place, particularly actions that impact the fundraising in markets outside mainland China and the effect on inbound investment of multinationals, both of which currently rely on a single network of firms to provide seamless, consistent, high-quality professional service to client investments worldwide, including those in China.

While nobody likes to be inspected by their regulator, the entire profession will improve as a result of it and investors' confidence in the profession will improve, too. In order to have a more positive impact on audit quality and foster greater confidence in regulatory oversight, the inspection process could be increasingly focused on evaluating the quality control systems of audit firms and in requiring firms to take corrective measures rather than imposing punishment.

Finally, the accounting profession plays a critical role not only in the Chinese capital markets, but also in the Chinese economy and in supporting the government's policy to encourage Chinese enterprises to expand overseas. In order to fulfill that role, the Chinese accounting profession as a whole has to attract the best people to the profession, to develop highly skilled personnel with a broad range of skill sets, not just in accounting and auditing. Well-trained quality professionals form an essential pillar supporting the development of China's capital markets, which in turn contribute to the long-term economic success of China. As in other parts of the world, prudential enforcement and avoidance of disproportionate regulatory action, auditors' liability reform and regulatory convergence are some of the key issues that need to be addressed to ensure the sustainability and growth of the profession in China. Meaningful and tangible progress around these priorities will allow the profession to naturally evolve to expand choice, and to continue to attract world-class talent.

CHAPTER 33

China's Taxation and the Financial Industries

Xu Shanda
Former Deputy Commissioner, State Administration of Taxation

B anking, insurance, and securities are the relevant industries included in China's "financial taxation system." Financial taxation is an important component of China's tax revenues and has a profound influence on the development of these industries as well.

China's modern taxation system began in the early part of the "Minguo" or Republic of China period (1912–49). At that time, its main components were business tax, income tax, stamp tax, and tax on securities exchange. After the founding of New China (1949), the "financial taxation system" mainly referred to the three categories of industrial and commercial taxes (including business tax and income tax), tax on interest income, and the stamp tax.

In 1950, industrial and commercial taxes began to be levied on enterprises and on interest income, as well as stamp duties. Regulations to do with the industrial and commercial tax stipulated that such industries as banks and insurance would pay a business tax as calculated on their gross earnings, at a rate of 4%. Later, this was changed in the case of banks to be levied on the spread between interest rates on deposits and loans. The income tax rate on the industries noted above was the same as for other industries, a graduated or progressive rate of 5% to 30%. Publicly managed enterprises did not pay income tax, however, but rather employed a system of handing over their profits to the government. The regulations on taxation of interest income stated that the taxpayer was defined as the one actually earning the interest; the basis for calculating the tax was the total amount of earned interest, and the tax rate was 5%. Starting in 1959, the tax on interest income was stopped. Regulations on the stamp tax stated that the basis for calculating tax would be the sum noted on the relevant commercial document and the rate would be relative (0.1% to 3%) or fixed, depending on specific circumstances.

In 1958, industrial and commercial taxation was consolidated and specific banking and insurance tax provisions were eliminated. It was decreed that income of the state's banks and its insurance business would be exempt from the consolidated industrial and commercial tax. The stamp tax was incorporated into the consolidated industrial and commercial tax. In 1972, a new industrial and commercial tax was passed that did not have separate provisions for taxation of banking or insurance. Instead, it ruled that business income from the state's banks, credit cooperatives, and insurance companies was exempt from industrial and commercial tax.

After Reform and Opening, considerable changes were made in China's financial taxation system. The individual income tax law put into effect in 1980 specified that personal income in the form of interest, dividends, and bonuses would be taxed at 20%, but interest on savings deposits in state banks and credit cooperatives were exempted. In 1982, regulations were passed with regard to the industrial and commercial tax on banks making the basis on which tax was calculated the income after deducting the amount paid out in interest on deposits. The tax rate was set at 10%. For ease of collection, this later was changed to a tax basis of total business income, and the tax rate was adjusted downward to 5%. Income of foreign banks was set at a consolidated industrial and commercial tax rate of 5%. Operating income of foreign enterprises was defined as according to foreign enterprise income tax law. In 1984, regulations were passed stating that foreign companies undertaking banking or insurance business in Special Economic Zones would be taxed at a consolidated industrial and commercial tax rate of 3% of income. Tax benefits allowed them to enjoy lowered taxes or to be exempt from tax altogether.

In 1984, China began to implement a policy of "changing profit to tax," for state-owned enterprises (SOEs); that is, changing the paying of profits to the paying of tax on the basis of income. Overall reform with regard to the industrial and commercial tax was also undertaken. With regard to the financial and insurance industries, operating income now became the basis for calculating tax, at a tax rate of 5%. At the same time, there was a tax of 55% on enterprise income.

The "Foreign-invested Enterprises and Foreign Enterprise Income Tax Law of 1991" stipulated that the tax rate on income of both foreign-invested Chinese enterprises and foreign enterprises was now 30%. It was up to local government to decide whether or not to levy an additional "regional or local" income tax of 3%. In Special Economic Zones and other regions as permitted by the State Council, foreign-invested banks, Sino-foreign joint-venture banks and certain other financial institutions could, if they complied with regulations, reduce that rate to a 15% enterprise income tax.

In 1992, a stamp duty on stock trading was instituted. Both sides to a transaction used the actual price of a trade as the basis for calculating tax and each paid a stamp duty according to a stipulated rate. The rate was modified quite a few times, and at present is 0.3%. However, if investors buy or sell units in securities investment funds, then they are exempt from the stamp tax.

The individual income tax law was revised in 1993, but continued a policy of exempting interest income from tax. The tax on income from transferring property was increased to 20%, but income from stock transfers was not taxed. In 1999, the individual income tax law was revised again, and the exemption on interest income on savings accounts was eliminated. Income from interest on savings in either RMB or foreign currency accounts in institutions within the borders of China was now taxed at a rate of 20%. On August 15, 2007, this was revised down to 5%.

After the 1994 tax system reform, a business tax continued to be levied on the financial and insurance industries with the basis for calculating tax the "business amount" or turnover of the enterprise. The tax rate was set at 5%. "Business amount" was defined as the total money received, as well as any income derived from business activities. Only reloaning, foreign exchange, priced securities, non-commodity futures trading, insurance businesses, and so on were allowed to calculate business turnover after subtracting certain expenditures. Although the income tax of most enterprises was set at 33%, tax on financial and insurance industries' income remained at 55%. Later, while most state-owned banks and state-owned insurance companies continued to be levied at the 55% rate, other financial and insurance enterprise tax rates were revised downwards to 33%.

Financial taxation revisions of 1997 unified the income tax rates of all financial and insurance enterprises, which were lowered to 33%, but at the same time, the business tax on these industries was raised to 8%. From 2001 to 2003, the business tax rate was lowered one percentage point per year, so that from 8% the rate was gradually restored to 5%.

On January 1, 2008, the new enterprise income tax law was applied in uniform fashion to Chinese and foreign-invested enterprises, including financial and insurance industries, and the rate was adjusted to 25%.

CHINA'S FINANCIAL TAXATION SYSTEM: MAIN COMPONENTS

At present, the main taxes imposed on financial industries in China are: business tax, stamp tax, enterprise income tax, individual income tax, housing tax, municipal real estate tax, land-use tax in cities and towns, contract or title-deed tax, municipal maintenance and construction tax, vehicles and vessels tax, and an educational fees surtax.

Business Tax

Business entities or individuals undertaking financial or insurance business are considered the "taxpayer" of this tax. Such entities include banks, credit cooperatives, securities companies, securities exchanges, financial leasing companies, securities fund management companies, financial affairs companies, trust investment companies, securities investment funds, insurance companies, and other institutions that have obtained permission to be established by the People's Bank of China (PBC), China Banking Regulatory Commission (CBRC), or China Insurance Regulatory Commission (CIRC).

Companies engaging in financial and insurance industries must apply the provisions of this tax. "Financial" means businesses engaged in currency, capital, and financing activities, including making loans, raising capital, leasing, selling or trading financial products, and so on. "Insurance" means the business of concentrating funds through contractual obligations and applying them to the economic benefit of an insured party.

The basis for calculating tax for banks includes interest income, fee income, buying and selling securities, income from margin on foreign exchange, and so on. Usually, tax is levied on the full amount of interest income from loan business. Tax levied on foreign exchange reloaning uses the basis of loan interest income less the interest on the borrowed amount. The full amount of insurance premiums is used as the tax basis in the insurance industry. The trading of stocks, bonds, and other priced securities or non-commodity futures uses the difference of the sales price and the buying price as a tax basis. Licensed financial leasing enterprises' tax basis is calculated as the difference between the entire amount received from the party leasing and the actual costs of the leasing.

Tax rates—the business tax rate levied on financial and insurance industries—is 5%.

Stamp Tax

The taxpayer is defined as being both business units and individuals who transfer property based on written documents that include contracts entered into within China, documents concerning transfer of ownership, business accounts, any rights or benefits received, licenses, and so on. Stamp tax on these forms of evidence of transfer must be paid.

The main items requiring stamp tax in the financial industry are purchase and sales agreements, loan contracts, property insurance agreements, transfer of assets agreements, transfer of business accounts, rights, licenses, stock transactions, and so on.

Purchase and sales agreements pay stamp tax figured at the rate of 0.03% applied to the transaction amount. Loan contracts are affixed at 0.005%. Property insurance contracts are figured at 0.1% of the insurance fee, but "liability insurance," "guaranteed insurance," and "credit insurance" contracts are taxed at a fixed price of RMB5. Documents relating to the transfer of property are affixed at 0.05% of the amount carried on the document. Stock trading is figured at the price at which the transaction closed, and at a tax rate of 0.3%. Capital book accounts are affixed at 0.05% of total paid-in capital and additional paid-in capital. Other rights transfers, licenses, and so on are affixed at a per-transaction fee of RMB5.

Enterprise Income Tax

The taxpayers are defined as being enterprises and or other organizations inside China that receive income within the borders of China. This includes resident enterprises and non-resident enterprises.

The basis for calculating enterprise income tax for enterprises is the taxable income amount of those enterprises. The taxable income amount means the gross income for a fiscal year less non-taxable income, exempt income, and less amounts from previous years' losses and other items that are allowed to be deducted.

The income tax rate for enterprises is 25%.

Individual Income Tax

The taxpayer of "individual income tax" is defined to be those individuals who have a residence inside China, or who do not have a residence, but abide one full year inside China. They must pay individual income tax on all income received from both within and outside the borders of China. Those persons who do not have a residence in China and also do not live in China, or who have no residence but stay less than one year, must pay individual income tax on all income received within the borders of China.

China implements an individual income tax that regulates according to income category, with regard to taxable items and the income basis for calculating the tax. The primary categories with regard to the financial industry are interest, dividends, bonus income, property transfer income, and so on. The full amount of interest, dividends, and bonuses is taxable as income. The taxable amount on transferred property is calculated at the price sold less the original price at which the property was bought, less fees (for example, on shares). At present, individual income tax is not levied on income from buying and selling units in managed funds.

Income from dividends and bonuses and from transferred property is taxed at 20%. The tax rate on income interest has dropped from 20% to the current 5%.

Other Taxes

Housing Property Tax and Municipal Real Estate Tax

China at present still adheres to a different housing tax system for Chinese and non-Chinese taxpayers. For units funded from inside China and for Chinese citizens, the tax used is the "housing tax." For foreign-invested Chinese enterprises, foreign enterprises, and foreign citizens, the tax used is the municipal real estate tax. The owner of the property in either case is the one who pays the housing tax or the municipal real estate tax. The housing tax is calculated on the original price of the housing less a one-time deduction of from 10% to 30%. The tax rate is 1.2%. If the housing is rented out, the rental income is the basis of taxation and the rate is 12%. The municipal real estate tax uses a standard housing rate to calculate the tax or a standard renting rate as the basis of taxation. When the standard housing rate is used, the tax is 1.2%. When the standard rent is used, the tax rate is 12%.

Land-use Tax in Cities and Towns

The land-use tax is applied to land in cities and towns, and is levied on the unit or the individual who is using the land. The basis for calculating the tax is the number of square meters the taxpayer is actually using. Each square meter is taxed at between RMB0.6 and RMB30, the specific amount being determined by the provincial-level local government, and depending on whether the city is large, medium-sized, or small.

Contract or Title-deed Tax

The deed tax is applied to the transfer of ownership when land that is being used is transferred or housing that is owned is transferred. The person to whom ownership is being conferred is the taxpayer. In the case of land or housing, the transfer price at which the land or housing is being transferred is the basis on which tax is calculated. The rate is between 3% and 5%, with the specific taxation rate being determined by the provincial-level local government.

Municipal Maintenance and Construction Tax, and Educational Fees Surtax

The value-added tax, consumption taxes, and business tax involved in the municipal maintenance and construction tax and the educational surtax are all levied on units and individuals, but are only applied to domestically invested enterprises and units and to Chinese citizens. The basis of taxation is the actual value-added, consumption, and business tax amount paid by the taxpayer. Depending on the region and the city, county, or town of the taxpayer, municipal maintenance and construction tax rates can be 7%, 5%, and 1%. The educational fees surtax is standardized at 3% of the surtax rate.

Vehicles and Vessels Tax

This is a tax levied on vehicles and vessels, and the taxpayer is the person or "managing entity" who owns the vehicle. Passenger cars and motorcycles are taxed by unit; freight trucks are taxed by weight. Boats are taxed by net tonnage.

FURTHER ISSUES

First, the collection of taxes in the financial arena does not extend to all those who should pay tax. Coverage is incomplete. Second, certain types of taxes are too high. Third, a portion of the taxation system is unreasonable and should be changed.

Tax Collection Is Incomplete

At present, some financial enterprises and some kinds of financial income have not been included in the scope of the taxpaying system. Tax collection policies have not yet adapted to the way financial innovations have developed, for example. One main problem is in the field of financial derivatives, which have yet to be clarified.

All kinds of derivative instruments have begun to appear in China as the socialist market economy moves forward. The currently administered tax system is unable to cope with the new circumstances.

Tax collection with respect to financial leasing companies is also not ideal. Leasing businesses are in fact of an investment nature, but they are not able to enjoy the preferential tax policies of normal investment, such as the exemption policies. A second problem comes in determining the tax basis of their business tax. Foreign-exchange interest costs incurred by leasing companies are allowed to be deducted from leasing income, but RMB interest costs are not allowed to be deducted. Third is the problem of double taxation of the business tax when re-leasing immovable assets.

Since the implementation of the Trust Law of 2001, the Trust markets have grown constantly, but taxation policies with regard to their businesses and organizations have not yet been clarified.

Certain Items Are Taxed at Too High a Rate

The main taxes impacting financial industries are the enterprise income tax and the business tax, as judged by their percentage of total tax revenue. In 2006, total tax revenue from China's financial industries was RMB202.51 billion, of which enterprise income tax totaled RMB108.1 billion, or 53.4%, and business tax totaled RMB70.34 billion, or 34.7%.

After the enterprise income tax underwent reform by having "two laws merged into one," foreign-invested and Chinese companies applied a standardized income tax rate that dropped to 25%. The previously unequal treatment of Chinese and foreign-invested financial institutions was then basically resolved, together with the issue of some statutory rates being too high. Items that can be deducted from income before applying tax have also been standardized and the wage standard for calculating tax has been eliminated. Wages and salaries paid out by enterprises now can all be deducted, and standards for the amounts that can be included in charitable contributions, advertising fees, cost of business receptions, have been broadened. However, the overly strict standards for reserves against bad debts have not yet been resolved.

Problems with overly high tax rates now mainly show up in what are called "circulation taxes," which include the business tax, stamp tax, municipal maintenance and construction tax, and tax-like educational fees surtax. Insurance businesses are taxed the "business tax" according to the insurance industry rates, and then are taxed the municipal maintenance and construction tax, and the educational fees surtax based on that business tax amount. The business tax rate is 5%. Taxpayers of the municipal tax vary depending on location, but since most financial industries are based in cities or county-level towns, the rate generally applied is either 5% or 7%. The educational surtax is standardized at 3%. Although the stamp tax rate is low, it is generally applied to the overall amount of a given transaction (such as a loan contract), so the resulting tax can be substantial.

Looking at the overall impact of the business tax components and adding them up, we can see that financial enterprises generally pay more than 5.5%.

In comparison with most countries in the world, which either do not levy circulation taxes or make financial industries exempt from them, the nominal tax rate of China's business tax and stamp tax on securities business is clearly on the high side. The 0.3% stamp tax on stock transactions clearly is high, although this is related to the fact that for the time being individual income tax on these transactions is not levied. In comparison with such industries as communications, transport, construction, posts and telecommunications, and so on, the financial industries business tax rate is 2% higher. Not including the stamp tax, the circulation tax rate of financial industries is at least 3.3%. This is 66.7% higher than the 2.2% of the other industries.

Moreover, due to the following reasons, the actual tax burden on financial industries' circulation tax can be even higher. Under most business tax circumstances, the entire amount of business volume is considered in figuring the tax, not the net amount (such as margin). This is unlike the value-added tax in which one is allowed to deduct the value-added tax amount that was included in the purchase price. The tax base for the business tax includes fees earned outside the price, some commission fees that do not in fact constitute enterprise income, such as the "fee for transferring ownership" paid on behalf of the securities exchange, the "account opening fee," and so on. These are included in the tax base for the business tax.

Some Tax Collection Methods Are Unreasonable

There are discrepancies in the circulation-type taxes of the financial industry with regard to Chinese and foreign companies. China-invested financial enterprises are required to pay more in terms of these taxes than foreign-invested financial enterprises. In addition to having to pay the business tax, Chinese financial enterprises also have to pay the municipal maintenance and construction tax and educational fees surtax, while foreign companies do not need to pay these. Moreover, while interest income is taxed on the full amount for normal loans, for foreign-exchange transfer loans only the margin is taxed. Superficially, the policy looks similar for Chinese and foreign-invested banks, but since Chinese banks mainly deal in RMB loans, while foreign-invested banks deal in foreign exchange loans, foreign-invested banks carry a lower actual tax burden than Chinese banks.

As for income realized by individual investors in financial instruments, at present interest on deposits is taxed at 5%, while dividend income from share investments, including government bonds and also bonuses, is taxed at 20%. Income derived from investments in fund units is exempted from individual income tax at the present. To have some income taxed, and some not taxed, leads to inequities in tax levies, but also contorts the flow of funds and negatively impacts the efficient allocation of capital.

Regarding the taxation of some new insurance products, there is as yet no clear policy opinion. These include such things as dividend income. At present, these have not been included in the scope of what is defined as taxable personal income. This seems unreasonable, compared to the way in which interest on bank savings deposits is taxed.

REFORM OF THE FINANCIAL TAX SYSTEM

Reforms and improvements in the system will affect the sustainability, stability, and health of the financial industries. Below are initial thoughts on steps that might be taken.

Establish a Policy on Financial Derivatives

We should learn from the experience of foreign market economy countries and, within the framework of China's existing tax system, draft and improve the tax collection policy on derivatives. The most important thing in this regard is the basis for calculating the business tax, which should be defined as the net amount (or the margin) and not the entire revenue.

As for dividends on investments in the insurance industry, we can begin to consider including this kind of income in the scope of taxable individual income.

We must adjust the tax collection policy on financial leasing companies, and provide a fair tax collection environment. In collecting business tax on the leasing industry, we should eliminate the discrimination against RMB financing, and allow leasing companies to enjoy the same treatment as enjoyed by foreign currency interest income. As for re-leasing business, we should eliminate double taxation problems and adjust the collection policies accordingly.

Adjust the Business Tax Levied on the Banking Industry

In order to lower the tax burden of the banking industry and increase the international competitiveness of Chinese banks, we must adjust policies to do with the business tax on banks. One view supports increasing the scope of the value-added tax, and switching the business tax to value added on banks, or adopting measures currently in effect in most OECD countries of levying value-added tax on non-primary business activities and not on primary business activities. Another opinion feels that at present it is not feasible to switch the business tax to value-added tax under the current system. Instead, we might consider lowering the business tax on banks. Still others feel that for the time being we should not change the business tax rate, but instead should tax only marginal interest that banks derive from loans. Still others feel that since restructuring and corporatization of state-owned commercial banks has just been completed, it is unwise at this time to lower the business tax rate. Instead, in order to increase the competitiveness of these banks, we can consider having the state and local governments refund their business taxes, in order to raise their capital adequacy ratios, and support their growth. All of these opinions deserve further research.

Individual Income Taxes with Respect to Income from Sale of Shares

It is unreasonable for a system to be organized in a way that levies tax on some of the benefits from capital and not on others. The exemption from individual income tax of trading fund units on the securities exchange is a policy that resulted from special historical conditions. It was done in order to stimulate growth of the securities markets. The tax law specified that it was a "temporary exemption of one kind of individual income tax." At the appropriate moment, this policy should be changed. It can be announced well ahead of time; for example, five years. Within those years, the tax rate can gradually be raised to 20%. At the same time, share transfer income should be made to correspond to the basic regulations of income tax, especially the provision of offset of income against losses over a period of years. In order to encourage long-term investment and discourage or restrain speculation, we might consider implementing a lower tax on long-term investors, and tax short-term investors at the normal asset income rates. Such a differential tax rate will restrain undue speculation, and reduce risks in the share markets. Finally, with regard to restoring personal income tax on income from the stock transactions, we should reconsider all the various kinds of taxes with regard to stock transactions, particularly the stamp tax.

Enterprise Income Tax: Standard Deductions

After the new enterprise income tax law was implemented, standard deductions were made more reasonable than before, but should be taken a step further. In principle, any fees or payments with regard to enterprise operations should be allowed to be deducted before calculating tax. As for deducting such things as bad debts and other items that have a relatively large impact on financial enterprises, appropriate adjustments should be made. The "standards" at which the writing off of bad loans can be made should be broadened and the relevant timeframe should be shortened.

583